THE
PLAYBOY INTERVIEW

The PLAYBOY INTERVIEW

Edited by G. Barry Golson

PLAYBOY PRESS

New York

Manufactured in the United States of America.

FIRST EDITION

Library of Congress Cataloging in Publication Data

Main entry under title:

The Playboy interview.

     1. Biography—20th century. 2. Interviews.
3. Interviewing (Journalism) I. Golson, G. Barry.
II. Playboy.
CT120.P55   081   80–52441
ISBN 0–87223–668–4
     0–87223–644–7 (pbk.)

Designed by Tere LoPrete

CONTENTS

FOREWORD   *vii*

Miles Davis   *3*

Bertrand Russell   *13*

Helen Gurley Brown   *24*

Malcolm X   *37*

Albert Schweitzer   *54*

Vladimir Nabokov   *61*

Cassius Clay/Muhammad Ali (two interviews)   *76*

Martin Luther King, Jr.   *112*

Madalyn Murray   *136*

George Lincoln Rockwell   *153*

Timothy Leary   *179*

Mel Brooks (two interviews)   *202*

Fidel Castro   *235*

John Wayne   *261*

Albert Speer   *282*

Germaine Greer   *326*

Tennessee Williams   *352*

Walter Cronkite   *370*

Joseph Heller   *393*

Jimmy Hoffa   *418*

Jerry Brown   *435*

Jimmy Carter   *456*

Pat Moynihan   *489*

James Earl Ray   *520*

Anita Bryant   *550*

Dolly Parton   *578*

Marlon Brando   *608*

Edward Teller   *644*

John Lennon and Yoko Ono   *675*

AFTERWORD   *722*

FOREWORD

On a hot summer day in 1976 in Plains, Georgia, Jimmy Carter arose from the armchair in his living room. Because the two journalists from PLAYBOY had deliberately ignored several hints that their time was up, Carter apparently felt it was the only way he could bring the interview to a close. It was a week after his nomination at the Democratic convention, and just a few minutes before he would answer one last question at his front door. He was moving across the living room, stepping over the tape-recording equiment. He shook his head and said in a bantering tone, "You guys must have some kind of blackmail leverage on Jody Powell. I've ended up spending more time with you than with *Newsweek*, *Time*, and all the others combined." He paused. "Of course, you have an advantage the way you do your interviews, coming back again and again with follow-up questions. I don't object, but it sure is exhausting."

As presidents and poets, artists and athletes, saints and scoundrels have found, PLAYBOY interviews *are* usually exhausting. From the feature's earliest days, the idea has been to push harder, to probe more deeply, to ask and ask questions again until the interviewer, the editor, and the subject himself agree, with tired sighs of relief, that, whatever else has happened, something like the definitive interview has taken place.

Through the years this single department, by no means the most prominent feature in a prominent men's magazine, has been consistent enough to be called "the command performance of American journalism" in *The Washington Star* and "the best Q-and-A in journalism today" by the *Writer's Digest*.

This book is primarily an anthology of thirty-one of the most memorable interviews published in the past eighteen years. But because they are pieces of magazine journalism, meant to be read at particular moments in time, I have provided a brief commentary to put the interviews into context, namely, the background that existed as each interview was published. And because they are known as "candid conversations," I have sketched in some candid details, as recalled by the participants, on how each interview came to be—including occasional tensions behind the scenes, telling incidents, and the impact some interviews had upon publication.

Readers of the magazine who remember their favorites may dispute the choices in this collection, but the sheer volume of nearly two hundred published interviews makes some kind of selectivity necessary. Similarly, space requirements would have meant only a small, unrepresentative sample could have been published if the text and introductions were to be reprinted at their original length. To make space for a fuller range and variety of interviews, the biographical summaries in each original introduction have been substantially reduced and the text has been lightly edited—but never to spare either the interviewer or the subject the embarrassment of hindsight. Much of the delight of the older interviews comes from the discovery—or the reminder—of what seemed important at the time. What has been distilled are some of the overlong elaborations on a theme—a factual recap of an event that was new then but is familiar now, for example—or remarks that were relevant only in the month they appeared—such as plugs for forthcoming books or movies. No interview has been shortened by more than fifteen percent.

A capsule history of the Playboy Interview would begin with editor-publisher Hugh M. Hefner striding into the magazine's editorial offices in Chicago one afternoon in 1962. He wanted, he said, to launch an interview feature in PLAYBOY that would treat a subject in unusual depth. At the time, he had just folded the glossy but unsuccessful *Show Business Illustrated*, and he mentioned to Editorial Director A. C. Spectorsky that *SBI* had in its inventory some interviews with performers and musicians—perhaps one of the pieces could provide the basis for a Playboy Interview. Spectorsky instructed a young associate editor, Murray Fisher, to rummage through the inventory and see what he came up with.

The most promising material Fisher found was an incomplete interview with jazz musician Miles Davis, conducted by a writer named Alex Haley. What interested Fisher about Davis's remarks was less the obligatory talk about music than the rage expressed about being a black man in white America. Fisher assigned Haley to complete the interview, and the writer returned to Chicago several weeks later with many hours of tape—more than could be transcribed and published under prevailing standards.

The dynamics that were to shape the interview started then: Fisher pushing for more space, more frankness, more controversy—sometimes abrasively—and Spectorsky, the gentlemanly editor who had fought hard for the magazine's respectability, restraining Fisher, opting for caution and brevity and taste. At the time, interviews in other publications were often embedded selectively in an article, with the writer's opinions and interpretations as the focal point of the piece. Hetner insisted that the Davis conversation run as a straight Q-and-A, with the journalist serving as the magazine's voice—tough and probing, but neutral. Art Paul, the magazine's art director, who had been with Hefner since 1954 and created the Rabbit Head symbol, laid out the distinctive design of the feature: the three pictures at the bottom of the page with provocative quotes beneath them, and the use of boldface type to identify each speaker. And so the first Playboy Interview appeared, dated September 1962.

The philosophy that Hefner, Spectorsky, and Fisher evolved for the Interview was to range widely for a mix of prominent people of accomplishment—and occasionally of notoriety. Not all celebrated, interesting people were good interview candidates; it was the ability of a subject to express himself or herself verbally and with candor that Fisher researched before suggesting a name to Hefner. An obvious point, perhaps, but one that Fisher learned by trial and error after assigning a few interviews with celebrated, colorful people who answered questions monosyllabically.

Since in the early Sixties PLAYBOY's reputation was that of an adventurous publication, at least by contrast to the more established press, it was natural for the editors to seek out interview subjects who hadn't received extensive, or objective, coverage in the mainstream media. So it was in the pages of PLAYBOY in those early years that many Americans first read in depth the views of such people as Malcolm X, Jimmy Hoffa, George Wallace, Madalyn Murray, and George Lincoln Rockwell. (In this retrospective summary, we'll be referring to some interviews that are not reprinted here, for reasons already discussed.)

Because of the nudity in the magazine, it was not always easy to persuade prominent people—at least prominent Americans—to grant interviews, so Fisher occasionally cast his net in foreign waters. European notables were either more worldly or more removed from the furor that still surrounded Hefner's magazine in America, so at least a few PLAYBOY readers must have been surprised in 1963 and 1964 to find substantial interviews with Bertrand Russell, Albert Schweitzer, Vladimir Nabokov, Jean Genet, and Jean Paul Sartre.

As time went on, it was not merely the roster of prestigious names that established the Playboy Interview as an increasingly respected journalistic forum. In an era when the press traditionally shied away from discussing the private behavior of public figures, and largely protected its readers' sensibilities from colloquial or vulgar language, the Interview presented people's language as it was actually spoken. Fisher

routinely instructed his interviewers to raise topics not normally discussed for publication—childhood traumas, failed marriages, moments
of rage, and, yes, when it was appropriate, sexual experiences.

Although the question of just how much the magazine should dissociate itself from a controversial subject was a hotly debated topic
(and continues to be so among PLAYBOY's present editors), it quickly
became apparent that the Interview was a forum for strongly divergent
views. If Fidel Castro, Joan Baez, and Ralph Nader were to speak out,
so would H. L. Hunt, John Wayne, and William Buckley. Well before it
was fashionable, Interview subjects were arguing against racial discrimination, the war in Southeast Asia, monopolistic practices, unjust drug
laws, environmental pollution, and blind patriotism. Not surprisingly,
there were also a fair number of Interview subjects who *defended* most
of the above.

During the years when Fisher edited the interviews, from 1962 to
1974, he imposed rigorous standards on the work done by the interviewers. As John Brady put it in *The Craft of Interviewing,* "Preparations
for a Playboy Interview are legendary." The journalist to whom he gave
an assignment was required to submit several hundred written questions, which Fisher would discuss and edit. At least a month would be
spent researching the subject's life and interviewing his friends and
enemies. Once the interviews started, the writer was instructed to spend
as much time as the subject would give him—and then to ask for more.
A writer rarely came back with less than five or six hours on tape, and,
in recent years, twenty hours of recorded conversations have not been
uncommon. Thomas Weyr, who has studied the magazine's origins and
development in *Reaching for Paradise* (New York Times Books), said of
Fisher: "He made the Playboy Interview a form of literary expression
that neither the looser models—from the *Paris Review* to *Redbook*—
nor the television version ever matched."

The technique originated by Fisher was to sift and refine the raw
verbiage of a tape transcript into a linear, continuous conversation. The
emphasis was placed on what the eye could read rather than on what
the ear could comprehend. This meant there was always a process of
distillation and condensation, of reshuffling and rearranging, but with
sufficient faithfulness to the original that the material had the verisimilitude of natural, spoken conversation. It was never a matter of "improv-
ing" a person's language, but of squeezing out the repetitions and
meanderings, the pauses and false starts, which are mentally edited out
by listeners but not by readers. That the technique is successful is supported by the fact that many of the interviewees have volunteered
publicly that the published interviews reported *exactly* what they said—
even though no interview has been published verbatim.

When Spectorsky died in 1972, Arthur Kretchmer was named to succeed him. And in 1974, Fisher left the magazine and I began to supervise the interviews. While Hefner had approved the selection of interview subjects in the past, he began to delegate more editorial authority in the early Seventies, so it was I who proposed and Kretchmer who disposed.

One procedural change we made was in the area of editorial control. Through the Sixties, many interviewees were shown edited versions of their interviews and given virtual copy approval. This was consistent with the practice of most publications—even today—of checking quotes with the speaker before publication. But as Kretchmer and I sought out interview candidates more attuned to breaking news, we also became aware of occasional attempts to sanitize a printed conversation—in effect, to censor it. So after 1974, I instructed our interviewers to make it clear to each subject that the magazine retains editorial control of what it publishes. If the editors feel it is necessary, galleys will be shown to an interviewee for an accuracy check—to make sure that dates and figures and names are correct. Even this has produced its share of rewriting efforts, but the magazine's string of newsmaking interviews in the past six years is due in part to having drawn the line at a time when many celebrities attempt to control all that is published or broadcast about them.

The Interview's more recent tradition—timeliness—is an interesting one, considering that PLAYBOY is a magazine with a three-month lead time. Since extensive preparations for an interview are required, a subject must often be selected six months before the magazine will be on the newsstands. Nevertheless, while PLAYBOY's interviewers cannot compete with electronic journalists, or even the peerless reporter Oriana Fallaci, whose work most often appears in weekly publications, the Plaboy Interview has had an uncanny history of immediacy.

Jerry Brown's interview, for example, happened to appear on the week he declared for the presidency in 1976. Jimmy Hoffa granted his last interview only a month before his disappearance. James Earl Ray escaped from prison while the interview was in progress. Religious deprogrammer Ted Patrick's interview on cult abuses was halfway done when the Jonestown massacre occurred. Edward Teller was defending the safety of nuclear reactors as the accident at Three-Mile Island took place. William Shockley announced his involvement with a sperm bank as he was being questioned about his genetic theories. John Anderson's interview appeared the week he announced his independent candidacy. And, most tragically of all for a generation of readers brought up on Beatles music, John Lennon's interview with his wife, Yoko Ono, was his longest ever and one of the last before his death on December 8, 1980. Whether it has been a sixth sense or just coincidence, the appearance of many of the magazine's interviews has not lacked in drama.

Although the feature has always had the PLAYBOY imprint, in the end it has been the work of individual journalists whose demanding craft is not always understood by the public. Some of PLAYBOY's interviewers went on to become celebrated themselves: Alex Haley, of course, who wrote *Roots*; Alvin Toffler, author of *Future Shock*; Kenneth Tynan, the late author and critic; even Mike Wallace gave it a try, before deciding to conduct interviews elsewhere. Conducting and putting together a print interview such as this one is unlike most other journalistic or literary endeavors. While a talented writer may not necessarily be a good interviewer, a successful print interviewer is always an effective writer—and a good deal more: persistent, diplomatic, curious, infinitely patient, aggressive . . . and just a little compulsive. Among the many men and women who have conducted PLAYBOY interviews, a few stalwarts should be singled out: Larry Dubois, Larry Grobel, Ken Kelley, Richard Warren Lewis, Larry Linderman, Eric Norden, Samantha Stevenson and Robert Scheer. PLAYBOY senior editor Gretchen McNeese has also been a key figure, both as interviewer and editor.

Finally, a personal note. I joined PLAYBOY's editorial staff in 1972, but before that I had been an avid reader of the magazine's interviews. In my commentaries on the early interviews, I have relied on the recollections of the participants and on my own research, and have attempted to be objective about events surrounding the interviews. Where the interviews under my supervision are concerned (between 1975 and 1981), if I cannot be objective, I can at least share with the reader some of the enjoyment and a few of the behind-the-scenes stories that have been part of a fascinating job. Where I have participated in some incidental way, I have referred to myself in the third person to remain consistent with accounts involving other editors and interviewers. (Besides, it's part of the PLAYBOY tradition that the questions are never asked in the first person, but in the form of the editorial "we." Which led Mel Brooks to respond to the first question in his Playboy Interview: "Who's *we?* I see only one person in this room. . . . Are you asking questions for the entire sexually liberated Playboy organization?")

As to occasionally assessing the significance or impact of a specific interview from an outsider's viewpoint, I have relied mainly on Weyr's unauthorized and often critical history of the magazine. *Reaching for Paradise* is one of only a few outside sources available, possibly because of the difficulty much of the press and the publishing world has had in assessing the magazine's serious work dispassionately. (PLAYBOY is still not listed in the *Reader's Guide to Periodical Literature* in the nation's libraries.)

Not all of the PLAYBOY interviews published through the years will endure. Some have been superficial, and a few merely trendy. But not many other published features—or broadcast programs, or newspaper columns—have had an eighteen-year run with the prospect of more to come. The idea has always been to get a good conversation going, and pass it on. These conversations are good, and they have resonance.

G. BARRY GOLSON
Executive Editor
PLAYBOY
New York, 1980

THE
PLAYBOY INTERVIEW

MILES DAVIS

September 1962

Interviewer: Alex Haley

In the summer of 1962, the word "integration" had a noble, fresh-sounding ring. Although it was the year the first "Negro" (as blacks are referred to in these early interviews) entered the University of Mississippi, the year black churches were bombed, Klan rallies were held, and blacks and whites marched together through the South, the struggle for civil rights was often given superficial and patronizing coverage by much of the American press. Certainly Martin Luther King, Jr., and James Meredith were afforded sympathetic treatment, but the voice of black rage—direct, bitter, unaccommodating—was not often heard.

So the publication in September of an interview with jazz musician Miles Davis must have been a departure for PLAYBOY's readers. Davis had a reputation for blowing a fine trumpet, but it may have been surprising to find that he was such a passionately forthright critic of white oppression—when he would talk to whites at all.

Alex Haley was a veteran of twenty years in the Coast Guard when he began a writing career in his middle forties. Assigned to interview Davis for Hefner's unsuccessful *Show Business Illustrated,* he completed it on assignment to PLAYBOY. The original intention, of course, was that Davis might open up to Haley because both were black men, but in fact Davis was against the entire white establishment, and that included a black writer on assignment.

Haley began by spending evenings at New York's Village Vanguard, where Davis and his group were performing. From time to time, Haley would sidle up to Davis during breaks in the music, ask him a few questions, and tape his perfunctory and often hostile answers. Haley dogged the musician, attending every performance, and followed him around during the day.

One afternoon he followed him up to a gym in Harlem, where Davis would box. That day Davis was in the ring, looking around for a sparring partner. He spotted Haley, recognizing him as the persistent writer who hung around him at the Vanguard. He waved Haley into the ring and gave him a pair of boxing gloves. Haley, a gentle man, did his best as Davis peppered him with punches. In a clinch, Haley agreed with Davis that writers and reporters were a hateful, untrustworthy breed. Davis laughed and agreed to start talking straight with him—for publication in a white man's magazine.

On his return to PLAYBOY's offices in Chicago, Haley and editor Murray Fisher had the tapes transcribed, and then began the process that would be the model for all subsequent interviews: assembling a jigsaw puzzle of bits and pieces of conversation into a smooth flow, retaining the flavor and style of the spoken words. Hefner and Spectorsky had decided that the interview should be published anonymously. And so that first month (and for several years after that) the introduction made no mention of the writer who had conducted the interview.

Thomas Weyr characterized the Davis interview this way in 1978: "The Davis interview would prove a PLAYBOY benchmark, and not only because of the searing discussion of race it presented. It marked the beginning of the Playboy Interview, which, in the last sixteen years, has become one of the most vibrant and important public-opinion forums in the United States." Weyr added: "The Uncle Tom shuffle many whites expected from black entertainers was not for Davis. Much of what infuriated him in 1962 has since been corrected or at least eased, but then it had bite, and, in the pages of PLAYBOY, a pungent novelty."

PLAYBOY: Linked with your musical renown is your reputation for bad temper and rudeness to your audiences. Would you comment?

DAVIS: Why is it that people just have to have so much to say about me? It bugs me because I'm not that important. Some critic that didn't have nothing else to do started this crap about I don't announce numbers, I don't look at the audience, I don't bow or talk to people, I walk off the stage, and all that.

Look, man, all I am is a trumpet player. I only can do one thing—play my horn—and that's what's at the bottom of the whole mess. I ain't no entertainer, and ain't trying to be one. I am one thing, a musician. Most of what's said about me is lies in the first place. Everything I do, I got a reason.

PLAYBOY: What types of people do you find especially irritating?

DAVIS: Well, these people that's always coming up bugging me until they get me to act like this crap they heard. They ask you things, you say what you think, and if it ain't what they want to hear, then something's wrong with you and they go away mad and think you don't like them. I bet I have had that happen 500 times. In this last club I played, this newspaper reporter kept after me when I told him I didn't have no more to say. He wasn't satisfied with that. After the next set, he come up again, either drunk or playing drunk, and shoved into me. I told him to get the hell out of my way, and then he was fine—he went right out and wrote that. But he didn't tell how it happened.

And I'm mad every time I run into the Jim Crow scene. I don't care what form it takes. You can't hardly play anywhere you don't run into some of these cats full of prejudice. I don't know how many I've told, "Look, you want me to talk to you and you're prejudiced against me and all that. Why'n't you go on back where you're sitting and be prejudiced by yourself and leave me alone?" I have enough problems without trying to make them feel better. Then they go off and join the rest saying I'm such a big bastard.

I've got no plans of changing what I think. I don't dig people in clubs who don't pay the musicians respect. The average jazz musician today, if he's making it, is just as trained as classical musicians. You ever see anybody go up bugging the classical musicians when they are on the job and trying to work?

Even in jazz—you look at the white bandleaders—if they don't want anybody messing with them when they are working, you don't hear anybody squawking. It's just if a Negro is involved that there's something wrong with him. My troubles started when I learned to play the trumpet and hadn't learned to dance.

PLAYBOY: You feel that the complaints about you are because of your race?

DAVIS: I know damn well a lot of it is race. White people have certain things they expect from Negro musicians—just like they've got labels for the whole Negro race. It goes clear back to the slavery days. That was when Uncle Tomming got started because white people demanded it. Every little black child grew up seeing that getting along with white people meant grinning and acting clowns. It helped white people to feel easy about what they had done, and were doing, to Negroes, and that's carried right on over to now. You bring it down to musicians, they want you to not only play your instrument, but to entertain them, too, with grinning and dancing.

PLAYBOY: Generally speaking, what are your feelings with regard to race?

DAVIS: I hate to talk about what I think of the mess because my friends are all colors. When I say that some of my best friends are white, I sure ain't lying. The only white people I don't like are the prejudiced white people. Those the shoe don't fit, well, they don't wear it. I don't like the white people that show me they can't understand that not just the Negroes, but the Chinese and Puerto Ricans and any other races that ain't white, should be given dignity and respect like everybody else.

But let me straighten you—I ain't saying I think all Negroes are the salt of the earth. It's plenty of Negroes I can't stand, too. Especially those that act like they think white people want them to. They bug me worse than Uncle Toms.

But prejudiced white people can't see any of the other races as just individual people. If a white man robs a bank, it's just a man robbed a bank. But if a Negro or a Puerto Rican does it, it's them awful Negroes or Puerto Ricans. Hardly anybody not white hasn't suffered from some of white people's labels. It used to be said that all Negroes were shiftless and happy-go-lucky and lazy. But that's been proved a lie so much that now the label is that what Negroes want integration for is so they can sleep in the bed with white people. It's another damn lie. All Negroes want is to be free to do in this country just like anybody else. Prejudiced white people ask one another, "Would you want your sister to marry a Negro?" It's a jive question to ask in the first place—as if white women stand around helpless if some Negro wants to drag one off to a preacher. It makes me sick to hear that. A Negro just might not want your sister. The Negro is always to blame if some white woman decides she wants him. But it's all right that ever since slavery, white men been having Negro women. Every Negro you see that ain't black, that's what's happened somewhere in his background. The slaves they brought here were all black.

What makes me mad about these labels for Negroes is that very few white people really know what Negroes really feel like. A lot of white people have never been in the company of an intelligent Negro. But you can hardly meet a white person, especially a white man, that don't think he's qualified to tell you all about Negroes.

You know the story the minute you meet some white cat and he comes off with a big show that he's with you. It's 10,000 things you can talk about, but the only thing he can think of is some other Negro he's such close friends with. Intelligent Negroes are sick of hearing this. I don't know how many times different whites have started talking, telling me they was raised up with a Negro boy. But I ain't found one yet that knows whatever happened to that boy after they grew up.

PLAYBOY: Did you grow up with any white boys?

DAVIS: I didn't grow up with any, not as friends, to speak of. But I went to school with some. In high school, I was the best in the music class on the trumpet. I knew it and all the rest knew it—but all the contest first prizes went to the boys with blue eyes. It made me so mad I made up my mind to outdo anybody white on my horn. If I hadn't met that prejudice,

I probably wouldn't have had as much drive in my work. I have thought about that a lot. I have thought that prejudice and curiosity have been responsible for what I have done in music.

PLAYBOY: What was the role of the curiosity?

DAVIS: I mean I always had a curiosity about trying new things in music. A new sound, another way to do something—things like that. But man, look, you know one of the biggest things that needs straightening up? The whole communication system of this country! Take the movies and TV. How many times do you see anybody in the films but white people? You don't dig? Look, the next movie or TV you see, you count how many Negroes or any other race but white that you can see. But you walk around in any city, you see the other races—I mean, in life they are part of the scene. But in the films supposed to represent this country, they ain't there. You won't hardly even see any in the street crowd scenes—because the studios didn't bother to hire any as extras.

Negroes used to be servants and Uncle Toms in the movies. But so much stink was raised until they quit that. Now you do have some Negroes playing feature parts—maybe four or five a year. Most of the time, they have a role that's special so it won't *offend* nobody—then it's a big production made like that picture is going to prove our democracy. Look, I ain't saying that people making films are prejudiced. I can't say what I don't know. But I see the films they make, and I know they don't think about the trouble a lot of colored people find with the movies and TV.

A big TV network wanted to do a show featuring me. I said no, and they asked me to just look at a show featuring a big-name Negro singer. No, I ain't calling no names. Well, just like I knew, they had 18 girls dancing for the background—and every one of them was white. Later on, when I pointed this out to the TV people, they were shocked. They said they just hadn't *thought* about that. I said I knew they hadn't. Nobody seems to think much about the colored people and the Chinese and Puerto Ricans and Japanese that watch TV and buy the things they advertise. All these races want to see some of their own people represented in the shows—I mean, besides the big stars. I know I'd feel better to see some kids of all races dancing and acting on shows than I would feel about myself up there playing a horn. The only thing that makes me any different from them is I was lucky.

This black-white business is ticklish to try to explain. You don't want to see Negroes every time you click on your set. That would be just as bad as now when you don't see nobody but white people. But if movies and TV are supposed to reflect this country, and this country's supposed to be democratic, then why don't they do it? Let's see all kinds of people dancing and acting. I see all kinds of kids downtown at the schools of dancing and acting, but from what I see in the movies and TV, it's just the white ones that are getting any work.

Look, man, right in music you got the same thing happening. I got this album, *Someday My Prince Will Come,* and you know who's on the jacket cover? My wife—Frances. I just got to thinking that as many record albums as Negroes buy, I hadn't ever seen a Negro girl on a major album cover unless she was the artist. There wasn't any harm meant—they just automatically thought about a white model and ordered one. It was my album and I'm Frances' prince, so I suggested they use her for a model, and they did it.

But it ain't all cases where white people just didn't think about the other races. It's a lot of intended discrimination, right in music. You got plenty of places that either won't hire Negroes, or they hire just one that they point out. The network studios, the Broadway pit bands, the classical orchestras, the film studios, they all have color discrimination in hiring.

I tell you why I feel so strong about the communication system. I never have forgotten one time in Europe this nice old man told me how in World War II, the Europeans didn't know what to make of Negro troops. They had their picture of this country from our magazines and movies, and with a very few exceptions like Pops Armstrong and Joe Louis and Jesse Owens, they didn't know about any Negroes except servants and laborers.

PLAYBOY: Do you feel that your views are shared by most Negroes? And Puerto Ricans? And Orientals?

DAVIS: I can't speak for them last two. I'm in no position, I just know what I personally feel *for* them. But I know that pretty nearly *all* Negroes hardly have any other choice about how they feel. They ain't blind. They got to *see* what's happening. It's a thousand big and little ways that you run into the prejudices of white people. Just one thing—how long have Negroes been looking at immigrants coming into this country and can't even speak the language, and in the second generations, they are in places the Negroes haven't got to yet.

Look, not long ago this big magazine had this Southern truck driver saying he'd carry sandwiches if they let Negroes eat in them Maryland highway restaurants. But where he wants to eat ain't my point—I'm talking about what he said. He said, "You give them a finger, they take an arm" and a lot more. You dig? When it comes to human rights, these prejudiced white people keep on acting like they own the damn franchise! And, man, with the world in the mess it's in now, we trying to influence on our side all them Africans and Arabs and Indians and Chinese . . . You know two thirds of the people in the world ain't white? They see all this crap with Negroes and supposed to feel white people really think any different about them? Man, somebody better get straight!

Another thing—there was no upset about them restaurants not serving Negroes, until it was an African they turned away. You think every Negro in the country don't see what it says? It says that we been here

400 years, but it wasn't no mess until they put out an African that just flew over here on a jet.

PLAYBOY: Do you, in your position as a famous Negro, meet prejudice?

DAVIS: I told you, someway or other, *every* Negro meets it, I don't care who he is! Look, man, I sent for an electrician to fix something in the house. When he rang the bell, I answered and he looked at me like I was dirt, and said, "I want to see the owner, Mr. Davis." When I said, "You looking at him," the cat turned beet red. He had me figured as the porter. Now he's mad and embarrassed. What had I done to him but called to give him work?

That same week, I had seen a lot of them West Point cadets, and in a bar I asked why there was so many of them in town. Man, I just asked the cat a question and he moved up the bar and didn't speak! But then somebody recognized me and he got red as that electrician. He came trying to apologize and saying he had my records. I told him I had just paid enough taxes to cover his free ride at West Point, and I walked out. I guess he's somewhere now with the others saying I'm such a bastard. It bugged me so, man, I wasn't worth a damn for two or three days. It wasn't just him ignoring me I was thinking about, but in two or three years, Gregory, my oldest boy, may be doing some Army time. How am I supposed to feel about him maybe serving under this cat?

PLAYBOY: In your field, music, don't some Negro jazzmen discriminate against white musicians?

DAVIS: Crow Jim is what they call that. Yeah. It's a lot of the Negro musicians mad because most of the best-paying jobs go to the white musicians playing what the Negroes created. But I don't go for this, because I think prejudice one way is just as bad as the other way. I wouldn't have no other arranger but Gil Evans—we couldn't be much closer if he was my brother. And I remember one time when I hired Lee Konitz, some colored cats bitched a lot about me hiring an ofay in my band when Negroes didn't have work. I said if a cat could play like Lee, I would hire him. I didn't give a damn if he was green and had red breath.

PLAYBOY: Do you find that being the head of your band adds to your problems?

DAVIS: Fronting a band ain't no fun. A lot of people don't understand that music is business, it's hard work and a big responsibility. I hate to even think what all I've been through to play my horn, and still go through. I put everything I've got into it. Even after a good rehearsal, I feel empty. And you add to playing your instrument the running of a band and you got plenty of problems. I got my own family, and the guys that work for me, and their families to think about. On one tour, I had this white woman in Kansas City meet me when I came off the stand and wanted me to come to her table with her and her husband for a drink. I told her I didn't like to do that, and she hollered, "They said you're like that!" I felt like throwing down my horn and kicking it. But I said to myself I was going to try and educate at least that one couple. So I went over and talked to them.

I told them an artist's first responsibility was to himself. I said if he kept getting upset with what other people think he ought to do, he never would get too far, or he sure wouldn't last. I tried to make them see how I had worked all my life to play myself and then to get a band worth people paying to hear. I said that a lot of times when people in a club wanted to talk to me, I needed to be worrying about something about my band. They said they understood. I hope they did.

PLAYBOY: You've won all the trumpet polls. After yourself, how would you rank others?

DAVIS: *After* me! Hell, it's plenty great trumpet players don't come *after* me, or *after* nobody else! That's what I hate so about critics—how they are always *comparing* artists . . . always writing that one's better than another one. Ten men can have spent all their lives learning technical expertness on their instruments, but just like in any art, one will play one style and the rest nine other ways. And if some critics just don't happen to like a man's style, they will knock the artist. That bugs the hell out of musicians. It's made some damn near mad enough to want to hang up their horns.

Trumpet players, like anybody else, are individualized by their different ideas and styles. The thing to judge in any jazz artist is does the man project, and does he have ideas. You take Dizzy—he does, all the time, every time he picks up his horn. Some more cats—Clark Terry, Ray Nance, Kenny Dorham, Roy Eldridge, Harold Baker, Freddie Hubbard, Lee Morgan, Bobby Hackett—a lot of them. Hell, that cat down in New Orleans, Al Hirt, he blows his ass off, too!

PLAYBOY: Is there any special reason you didn't mention Louis Armstrong?

DAVIS: Oh, Pops? No, why I didn't mention him is because I was talking just about modern-jazz players. I love Pops, I love the way he sings, the way he plays—everything he does, except when he says something against modern-jazz music. He ought to realize that he was a pioneer, too. No, he wasn't an influence of mine, and I've had very little direct contact with Pops. A long time ago, I was at Bop City, and he came in and told me he liked my playing. I don't know if he would even remember it, but I remember how good I felt to have him say it. People really dig Pops like I do myself. He does a good job overseas with his personality. But they ought to send him down South for goodwill. They need goodwill worse in Georgia and Alabama and Mississippi than they do in Europe.

PLAYBOY: Are there any particular places or clubs that you don't like to play?

DAVIS: There are plenty I *won't* play! I won't take a booking nowhere in the South. I told you I just can't stand Jim Crow, so I ain't going down there in it. There's enough of it here in the North, but at least you have the support of some laws.

I won't play nowhere I know has the kind of audiences that you waste your breath to play for. I'm talking about them expense-account ofays that use music as a background for getting high and trying to show off to the women they brought. They ain't come to hear good music. They don't even know how to enjoy themselves. They drink too much, they get loud, they got to be seen and heard. They'll jump up and dance jigs and sing. They ain't got no manners—don't pay their women no respect. What they really want is some Uncle Tom entertainment if it's a Negro group on the stand. These are the kind will holler, "Hey, boy, play *Sweet Georgia Brown!*" You supposed to grin and play that. I hate to play in a place full of those kind of squares so bad that if there wasn't nobody else to play to, I'd invest in some more property and just stay home and collect rents. I can't stand dumb-ass people not respecting the other customers that have come to hear the music. Sometimes one table like that has bugged me so that when I get home or to my hotel, I walk the floor because I can't sleep.

I told you I ain't going to play nowhere in the South that Negroes *can't* come. But I ain't going to play nowhere in the North that Negroes *don't* come. It's one of two reasons they won't, either because they know they ain't wanted, or because they don't like the joint's regular run of music. Negroes ain't got as much money to throw away in night clubs as white people. So a club that Negroes patronize, you can figure that everybody that goes there comes expecting to hear good music.

PLAYBOY: What is your opinion of the jazz audiences in Europe?

DAVIS: European audiences are generally more hip about the background of jazz than most of the fans here. Some cats hardly heard of here are big record sellers in Europe. In this country, it's more following of personalities. You want to hear something funny? One club-owner friend of mine said a lot of people pay their money to come where I'm playing just because they want to *see* me—they heard I'm so bad. Ain't that a bitch?

But this country has a lot of great fans. You know, they appreciate what you're trying to do, and that inspires a musician to give his best. I know some Americans that don't stop with just knowing jazz, but that even *think* just like musicians.

PLAYBOY: Would it please you if the image of you changed, that people quit regarding you as a tough guy?

DAVIS: Well, nobody wants to be always accused of something he ain't done. But people that want to think that, it's their worry, it ain't mine. I'm like I am, and I ain't planning to change. I ain't scared of nothing or nobody, I already been through too much. I ought to be dead from just what I went through when I was on dope. I ain't going around anywhere trying to be tough and a racist. I just say what I think, and that bugs people, especially a lot of white people. When they look in my eyes and don't see no fear, they know it's a draw.

PLAYBOY: Have you always been so sensitive about being a Negro?

DAVIS: About the first thing I can remember as a little boy was a white man running me down a street hollering "Nigger! Nigger!" My father went hunting him with a shotgun. Being sensitive and having race pride has been in my family since slave days. The slave Davises played classical string music on the plantations. My father, Miles the first, was born six years after the Emancipation. He wanted to play music, but my grandfather wanted him to be more than an entertainer for white folks. He made him go to Northwestern to be a dental surgeon. My father is worth more than I am. He's a high-priced dental surgeon with more practice than he can handle—because he's good at his business—and he raises hogs with pedigrees. It's a special breed of hogs with some funny name I would tell you, but I never can remember it.

PLAYBOY: You're said to be one of the financially best-off popular musicians. Is this correct?

DAVIS: Well, I don't have any access to other musicians' bankbooks. But I never have been what you would call poor. I grew up with an allowance, and I had a big newspaper route. I saved most of what I made except for buying records. But when I first left home as a musician, I used to spend all I made, and when I went on dope, I got in debt. But after I got enough sense to kick the habit, I started to make more than I needed to spend unless I was crazy or something.

Now I got a pretty good portfolio of stock investments, and I got this house—it's worth into six figures, including everything in it. My four kids are coming up fine. When the boys get in from school, I want you to see them working out on the bags in our gym downstairs. I keep myself in shape and teach the kids how to box. They can handle themselves. Ain't nothing better that a father can pass along.

Then I got my music, I got Frances, and my Ferrari—and our friends. I got everything a man could want—if it just wasn't for this prejudice crap. It ain't that I'm mad at white people, I just see what I see and I know what's happening. I am going to speak my mind about anything that drags me about this Jim Crow scene. This whole prejudice mess is something you would feel so good if it could just be got rid of, like a big sore eating inside of your belly.

BERTRAND RUSSELL

March 1963
Interviewer: Norman MacKenzie

In mid-Camelot, even Kennedy "liberals" did not question the need for a strong military. The New Left had not yet formed, *Catch-22* was still a cult book, and pacifism was something odd and just a bit unsavory. Which seemed to be good enough reasons for Fisher to assign journalist Norman MacKenzie to interview Lord Bertrand Russell, the renowned mathematician, philosopher, and pacifist.

It was supposed to be a "theme" interview: Lord Russell's passionate call for disarmament and his castigation of both superpowers would certainly provide enough substance for an extended conversation, Fisher thought. But as it turned out, Lord Russell had some unconventional views on other matters, too, calling for a new outlook on sexuality, for a revamping of sexual education, for a new and open morality—topics congenial to PLAYBOY, but not often articulated by such a respectable spokesman. It was Fisher's—and PLAYBOY's—first real coup.

If the long and stormy life of Bertrand Arthur Russell can be said to possess any unifying thread, it is an enduring attitude of passionate skepticism, a lifelong refusal to accept any truth as immutable, any law as infallible or any faith as sacred. During the nine decades of his dedication to dissent, the erudite Earl Russell, a member of the House of Lords, has been awarded the Nobel Prize for literature in recognition of his pioneering research in mathematical philosophy and symbolic logic, and honored with Britain's distinguished Order of Merit for service to his country. But he has also been reviled as an enemy of religion and the flag; jailed for his ringleadership of passively nonviolent demonstrations against nuclear armament; and variously extolled and execrated for his contentious convictions on free love, women's suffrage, sex education, pacifism and preventive war.

As the London Times wrote last May on the occasion of Lord Russell's 90th birthday, "for every one who grasps even the outline of his contribution to mathematical logic, 10,000 wear the little button that he wears." The button is the badge of the Campaign for Nuclear Disarmament, a militantly antimilitary movement of which he is the combative champion. As spiritual leader of the famed Committee of 100, a ban-the-bomb group that commands widespread popular support in Britain, he has also earned international eminence—and a brief prison term for civil disobedience—as the most articulate agitator for the controversial cause of unilateral disarmament.

In October 1961—after a decade of mounting personal outcry against the unabating arms race—Russell warned his uneasy listeners at a ban-the-bomb rally in London's Trafalgar Square that they would be lucky if any of them were alive in a year's time. That year has passed, and nuclear holocaust has not yet overtaken us. We began our interview by reminding Lord Russell of this prophetic miscalculation.

PLAYBOY: Inasmuch as the world has successfully survived the year since your Trafalgar Square address, Lord Russell, would you care to revise your estimate of the likelihood of an atomic war?

RUSSELL: I said at Trafalgar Square that we would need luck as things were, and we have been extremely lucky so far. But I don't see any reason to be optimistic. I still feel that the human race may well become extinct before the end of the present century. Speaking as a mathematician, I should say that the odds are about three to one against survival. The risk of war by accident—an unintended war triggered by an explosive situation such as that in Cuba—remains and indeed grows greater all the time. For every day we continue to live, remain able to act, we must be profoundly grateful.

PLAYBOY: In a scathing reference to President Kennedy, Premier Khrushchev and Prime Minister Macmillan, you said in 1961 that "they are the wickedest people who have ever lived in the history of man, and it is our duty to do what we can against them." Did you actually mean to say that Kennedy, Khrushchev and Macmillan are the worst of a gallery of villains which includes Hitler and Attila?

RUSSELL: That was an arithmetical statement. Just as it is a wicked thing for one man to murder another, it is 10 times as wicked to murder 10 others, and 1,000,000 times more wicked to be responsible for the death of 1,000,000 men. No man in history has ever had the chance to murder on such a scale. In the past there have been long and bitter wars that caused appalling destruction, but at the end there were still people who could build again. Today we face the prospect of total obliteration in a single day. If mankind is to survive at all, intelligent people must learn to think and act in a less provocative manner than in former times.

PLAYBOY: Did not the avoidance of nuclear war over Cuba last October reassure you about the prudence and restraint of both Kennedy and Khrushchev?

RUSSELL: There *are* signs that the politicians are beginning to realize the implications of the power they wield. But they have not fully assimilated them. So much seems to depend on very personal factors with politicians— even on what they have had for breakfast and whether they have indigestion when they have to make some important decision. What I am saying is this: When two great powers disagree about anything—it doesn't matter what—they must find a way to settle it somehow by arbitration or by ne- gotiation, not by war or threat of war. We know only too well that if you threaten someone with war and he doesn't give way, then you may find yourself committed either to war or to backing down—and *that* choice has almost always been resolved by war. The Berlin crisis is a case in point. Here the Russians have been somewhat aggressive; they are trying to secure a change in the status of West Berlin by what amounts to threats of war. In the case of the Cuban crisis, on the other hand, Khrushchev has shown himself to be less belligerent than Kennedy, and in effect, at a crucial moment last October, was responsible for avoiding a war of nuclear devasta- tion. Full credit must be given to him for this. He acted with great restraint in a crisis of the first magnitude. I hope it may presage similar responses should the Berlin question reach a comparable peak of crisis. The essential thing to understand is that no conceivable solution to any problem is worse than a nuclear war. It is necessary to realize before it is too late that any act—whatever its motive or rationale—is to be considered wicked if the consequence is an atomic holocaust.

PLAYBOY: What do you believe was the effect of your own personal inter- vention with Khrushchev—via your much publicized cable appealing for Russian prudence in responding to the American blockade of Cuba?

RUSSELL: He carried out the promise he made in the letter replying to my cable—the promise to do nothing rash that would risk conflict. Within hours of my communication, 12 Soviet ships had turned back from their Cuban destination and Khrushchev had stopped further shipment. This left Cuba illegally blockaded in violation of international law. I believe that if a blockade is defensible when applied to Cuba, then the precedent can be applied also to Berlin and even to Britain, which is an advanced American nuclear base. America should remember the War of 1812 when the United States would not tolerate a British blockade. This is the very heart of what

I have been saying for years: If nuclear bases are intolerable in Cuba, then they are intolerable anywhere in the world. Nuclear bases threaten the survival of mankind and the Cuban crisis has shown us how very close we are to annihilation.

PLAYBOY: Do you think the Russian position on Berlin may bring us closer still?

RUSSELL: I can't tell. There are all these different possibilities. There is *intended* war, resorted to when one side really thinks it can win. That is the least likely cause in this case. Then there is escalation—a little war growing into a big one. There is also threat and counter-threat, where each side hopes the other will give way—a course inevitably bringing such dangerous factors as prestige and national pride into play. But what is most likely in Berlin or elsewhere is simply war by misinterpretation. You may get a meteor or something like that showing up on a radar screen, and someone will press the button. There is no time to consider. It could so easily happen, in a day, in a moment . . .

PLAYBOY: Can you make any estimate of the destructive consequences of such a disastrous "misinterpretation"?

RUSSELL: This is a question for experts, though all experts are biased. For an uninformed person such as me, it is very difficult to make any precise forecast. But I could give you a *minimum* estimate. I believe you must generally estimate that, at the very least, the price of nuclear war would be that half the population of both America and Russia, plus the whole of the population of Western Europe and Britain, would be wiped out.

Fear is very much a part of the incentive for armaments. If the fear were removed, each side would be more reasonable. I think that if the West were to voluntarily divest itself of nuclear weapons as a token of its peaceful intentions—this would greatly impress the Russians. They would then feel that they had nothing to fear and that they could enormously reduce their own expenditure on armaments. They would spend their money on consumer goods instead.

PLAYBOY: Does your disarmament plan involve also the abandonment of conventional weapons?

RUSSELL: We should not interfere with conventional weapons unless there is general nuclear disarmament. We would then discard all but a very small number of conventional weapons.

PLAYBOY: It has been said by some political observers that this eventuality will remain entirely academic as long as the U.S. continues to insist on inspection without disarmament, and the U.S.S.R. on disarmament without inspection. Would you agree or disagree with this appraisal?

RUSSELL: It does rather look that way. One side says that America is to blame for the stalemate and the other says Russia is responsible. You get the same sort of explanation in both countries. That, roughly speaking, has been the excuse for not reaching agreement. But I think the true explanation lies deeper than that. Neither side *wants* agreement, and they have to have something plausible to disagree about. You must realize that in both countries there are political and military factions—lobbies, if you like— which exert powerful pressure for extremist policies. On both sides they consist of people with interests in armaments and all the apparatus of preparation for war. There are military commanders in power on both sides, and their vested interest is in exercising that power. In fact, military people carry much more weight in the making of policy than does public opinion.

PLAYBOY: Would you say, then, considering this climate of opinion within as well as between Russia and America, that there is any realistic hope of drafting a global disarmament plan which would be acceptable to both sides?

RUSSELL: No, not at present. There is no possibility of attaining or sustaining general disarmament until East-West tension has lessened.

PLAYBOY: In 1957 you wrote in *The New Statesman*, the liberal British journal, an appeal to Premier Khrushchev and then-President Eisenhower for just such a lessening of world tension, to which both the Russian leader and John Foster Dulles responded with public reassurances. Six years have elapsed since then without a noticeable decline in global strife and division. At this critical moment in the cold war, would you care to make another such appeal—perhaps suggesting specific ways in which relations can be improved—to Khrushchev and President Kennedy?

RUSSELL: If I were to make another such appeal, I would have to begin by repeating what I said in 1957. I should say simply to both men: "You seem anxious to destroy the world, to create vast misery and total destruction. All this preparation for war is childish—and suicidal. If you could only begin to tolerate each other, you would be perfectly happy." I would go on to suggest that the overridingly urgent necessity is to come to an agreement; this is far more important than the precise form the agreement takes. Last summer I sent a message to Moscow in which I expressed the wish that in all negotiations between East and West, the negotiator for the Communists should begin by saying that the universal victory of capitalism would be less disastrous than nuclear war. At the same time, the Western spokesman should start by admitting that the universal victory of communism would be preferable to the destruction of mankind. In a speech last July, Khrushchev singled out this suggestion and said that he entirely agreed. I was rather pleased. I would suggest further that the likelihood of war could be lessened immeasurably if both sides would place a great deal more emphasis on the ghastly destructiveness of war. At present the major organs of publicity in both East and West are inclined to make the public believe that nuclear war wouldn't really be so terrible after all. That is why I am opposed to Civil Defense preparations. They are diabolical inventions calculated to tell lies and to deceive. Everyone who knows anything knows that.

People may think themselves safe in their deep shelters—but they will roast. Governments must be made to give up the habit of lying in order to persuade people to die quietly. Thirdly, I would strongly recommend an agreement on both sides not to teach that the other side is wicked. For Americans, communism is the Devil; for the Russians, capitalism is the Devil. The truth is that neither is wickeder than the other. They are both wicked.

PLAYBOY: Do you see *no* difference between the moral positions of America and Russia?

RUSSELL: No. They *both* have abominable systems. I am inclined to prefer the American system, but only because it is more allied with what I am used to. If I had been born a Russian, probably I should prefer the Russian system.

PLAYBOY: Have your views changed since you returned from a trip to Russia in 1920 to write one of the earliest and sharpest criticisms of the Soviet regime?

RUSSELL: I still take exactly the same view. Up to the time of Stalin's death, it was really quite horrible. Since then, I think, things have not been quite so bad—though I still don't care for the Soviet system at all. I just don't happen to like the American system either. The Americans tell you they stand for freedom: What they mean is that you must be quite willing to perish in order to be free in hell. In Russia they punish you if you espouse capitalism; in America they punish you if you espouse communism. What is the difference? But it is not worthwhile for us to go into the question of whether Russia or America has the better system. There are merits and demerits on both sides. The only important matter is to find some way of compromise between them which will avoid war. At present each has an entirely melodramatic conception of the other, and I think that the Russian Government in particular encourages this view by not allowing Russian tourists to visit other countries except in small organized groups. The same applies to Western visitors in Russia. This is a great pity. But there also seems to be some kind of fear in the West that if you get to know Communists, you will begin to admire them and finally be won over by them. Not a bit of it. There is simply no other way to achieve on each side an understanding of the real nature of the other.

PLAYBOY: Do you consider it possible to strive for these same aims *without* waiting a century—by relying on the UN?

RUSSELL: It can't be done through the UN as it is now, because the UN does not embrace China. Its exclusion is a colossal stupidity. The veto also is an absurdity. Some nations, moreover, are very much more powerful and populous than others, and you cannot invest a little nation with the same weight as a big nation. What you will have to do is divide the world into regions. You might, for example, have North America as one group, Europe as another, Russia as a third, China as a fourth, and so on. You would have to work it out with a view to making it more or less equally balanced in population. And the various regions ought to be so constituted that their internal relations would be foremost in importance and their relations to the outer world secondary in importance. I would leave each region complete autonomy for its own affairs. The world government would become involved only when there were contests or disputes with other regions. We shall not long survive without some such system.

PLAYBOY: On a personal level, why have you chosen to adopt a policy of civil disobedience as a means of promoting the cause of peace?

RUSSELL: Purely to get attention. All the major organs of publicity are against us. It was extremely difficult to get any attention at all until we resorted to it. I have no views in principle either for or against civil disobedience. It has always been practiced at different times and places. With me it is purely a practical question of whether to do it or not, a method of propaganda.

PLAYBOY: Do you feel that the authorities have the moral right to prosecute and imprison those involved in such nonviolent demonstrations for peace—as they have done to you?

RUSSELL: I have no right to complain about being punished for breaking the law. I complain only if I am not permitted to break it. I recognize that if you go outside the law you cannot complain if it is made a little awkward for you, but it ought to be possible to do so. If I suddenly took it into my head that I wanted to assassinate the Queen, then I should expect to be punished. You do that sort of thing with full foreknowledge of the consequences.

PLAYBOY: You were recently threatened with expulsion from the Labor Party for urging Western representatives to attend a Moscow "peace" conference and state their views. Aren't such occasions always turned to their own advantage by the Communists?

RUSSELL: On the contrary. Members of the Committee of 100 went to Moscow last summer and presented their point of view very effectively indeed. They got publicity both inside and outside of Russia. Many Americans have asked me why I don't preach my ideas to the Russians as well as to the West, and the answer is that I *do*. Certainly the Russians disagree with much of what I say, but I have found it just as easy—or as difficult—to get publicity for my views in the Soviet press as in the English press. The question I wondered about was whether they had bowdlerized what I said. I have taken the trouble to get translations of what they printed and found that they have been completely faithful. They have not altered a scrap.

PLAYBOY: In addition to disseminating your views personally on both sides of the Iron Curtain, you were the initiator of a series of peace conferences, of which the first was held in Pugwash, Nova Scotia, between groups of scientists from East and West. What positive results do you feel have emerged from these symposia?

RUSSELL: They have made a contribution toward informed opinion. For one thing, as a result, the test-ban negotiations came very much closer to success than they would otherwise have done. But the Pugwash meetings have not accomplished as much as one might have hoped. There was a lack of effective publicity. The public won't listen to informed opinion. They want uninformed opinion.

PLAYBOY: In 1916, you were fined £100 by the Lord Mayor of London for circulating a pacifist leaflet which the law deemed "likely to prejudice the recruiting and discipline of His Majesty's Forces." Your intention, you said then, "was to procure, if possible, a change in the law, or failing that, to secure a change in administration." Does the same intention motivate your current antiwar activities?

RUSSELL: Yes. Then, of course, I was defending the rights of conscientious objectors in World War I. I do not wholly share their views, but I felt, and still feel, that one should respect their convictions. They believe what I do not believe: that it is wicked to take part in *any* war, however righteous the cause. I supported the war against Hitler, and have become a pacifist today largely because of the destructiveness of nuclear warfare.

PLAYBOY: Even if a nuclear conflict is avoided, either through disarmament or a continuing balance of power, Khrushchev has made it clear that future "peaceful co-existence" will entail a continuing nonviolent struggle on the ideological front and an intensified campaign of economic competition which he predicts will eventually "bury" us. What posture do you feel the West should adopt in combating this threat?

RUSSELL: Neither of these conflicting interests will be arbitrated equitably and amicably until we have a truly representative and authoritative world government. In the absence of one, it will be a tug-of-war, a question of who is stronger. A continued program of economic and educational aid to underdeveloped countries, meanwhile, would be a significant means of strengthening the Western position. It would be better, of course, if such aid were given cooperatively by both sides, but I don't think that this is practical politics at the moment. In either case, it should be given not on cold war grounds, but simply because these people need help.

PLAYBOY: Do you share the apprehension of leading sociologists and economists concerning the implications of unchecked population growth in such overcrowded and underproductive areas as Africa, China, India and parts of Latin America?

RUSSELL: The population problem has, in my opinion, been rather exaggerated. It can be solved by adequate birth control, and I don't think that Catholic objections will prevent the increasingly widespread use and acceptance of contraceptives. After all, Roman Catholics represent only a small segment of the world's population. India and China are the really big problem areas, and both are inclined to favor birth control.

PLAYBOY: Do you agree with many historians and social scientists who foresee that the next century will witness "an inexorable economic and social evolution," as one commentator has expressed it, "from the tradition of individual enterprise to the psychology of mass man"?

RUSSELL: Societies comprised of small farmers, merchants and artisans will soon be anachronistic. Almost everybody is already part of something big. If we are to preserve individual liberty in this new world of huge firms and institutions, we must begin thinking in different terms from the tenets of classical liberalism. We will be able to deal with the "curse of bigness," as Justice Brandeis called it, only by democratizing industry. I would like, for example, to see rules providing for the popular election of directors and managers in each industry. The important thing is to ensure the limitation and equitable division of power. At present economic power is too much concentrated in the hands of a few big men who control the lives of others to an undesirable degree. The Russians—in fact, socialists of all countries—make the cardinal error of believing that if you have a democratic state running industry, then it automatically follows that the industries themselves will be democratic. But to put state officials in place of capitalist officials changes nothing; they are still men, still wielding the same power. Unless state officials are made responsible to all us underlings, nothing will ever be achieved by nationalization.

PLAYBOY: So far we have been talking mainly of the issues which have preoccupied you during the last half-dozen years. But your life's work has encompassed a multitude of causes. Which of them has mattered most to you?

RUSSELL: Though they have mattered differently at different times, the question of international peace certainly transcends any I have ever been concerned with or any issue that previously excited me. But I have derived great satisfaction from many of my interests—matters of the mind more than anything else. Mathematical logic has been the source of perhaps my deepest intellectual gratification. It has given me very great pleasure to feel, in an important field of human knowledge, that I may have made some lasting contribution to man's understanding of things which were once beyond his grasp, but which can now be comprehended and manipulated. I am also pleased with the aftermath of my campaign for women's suffrage and my efforts to secure a more enlightened sexual morality and behavior. They have gone almost as well as I would have liked them to go. When I was young, one talked to a woman in a different language than when talking to a man. There was a cultivated unreality in intercourse between men and women which I thought was very bad indeed. Today things are utterly different. Young people don't realize how much change there has been. But we still need much more freedom and frankness in sexual instruction. Another matter to which I have always attached great importance in education is that schools ought not to teach nationalism. Every school, with hardly any exception, has as one of its objects the deception of children. They teach them patriotism, to salute the flag. But the flag is a murder symbol, and the state is a pirate ship, a gang of murderers come together. When they salute the flag, they salute the symbol of bloody murder. All this is perfectly clear, valid psychology.

PLAYBOY: On the occasion of your 90th birthday, Lord Russell, you said, "In old age, one becomes aware of what has, and of what has *not* been achieved." Did you mean this observation to apply to the fruits of your own efforts in behalf of the various causes you've espoused?

RUSSELL: Let me reply this way. Contrary to the customary pattern, I have gradually become more and more of a rebel as I have grown older. Since boyhood, my life has been devoted to two different objectives which for a long time remained separate. It's only in comparatively recent years that they have come together. One has been to discover whether anything could actually be *known*; this was a matter of philosophical inquiry. The other has been to do whatever I could to help create a happier world. I cannot claim that what I have written, said and done about social and political problems has had any great importance. It is easy to have an immense effect if you dogmatically preach a precise gospel such as communism. But I do not believe that mankind needs anything dogmatic. I think it essential to teach a certain hesitancy about dogma. Whatever you believe, you must have reservations. You must envisage the possibility that you may be wrong. I want to see individuals retain the kind of personal flexibility and initiative that they ought to have. This means that they cannot and must not be forced ino a rigid mold. In my lifetime, freedom—which once seemed to be gaining ground—has come to be regarded as weakness. When I was young, I thought the battle for tolerance had been won. But more recently we have reverted back to the intolerance of the great religious wars. And when I was young, I set out with the belief that love—free and courageous love—could conquer the world. I perhaps thought that the road to a free and happy world would be shorter than it has turned out to be.

PLAYBOY: Do you feel now that this dream of a free and happy world was perhaps little more than the kind of utopian vision which has always inspired man in youth—and so often disenchanted him in maturity?

RUSSELL: It is something more. There is not anything to stop it from coming to pass except our own silliness—a silliness forced upon us by an education which teaches us that *our* country is vastly better than any other, and that in all respects it is always in the right. It would not be difficult to build a peaceful world if people really wanted it. It is certainly worthwhile to live and act and do what one can to bring it about. I haven't changed my earlier views in that respect. I still believe exactly what I said when I was 80, when people were asking me much the same question. I have lived in the pursuit of a vision, both personal and social: personal, to care for what is noble, for what is beautiful, for what is gentle, to allow moments of insight to impart wisdom in mundane times; social, to envision in imagination an attainable society in which the individual can grow freely, in which hate and greed and envy will die because there is nothing to nourish them. These things I still believe. So you can see that the world, for all its horrors, has left me unshaken.

HELEN GURLEY BROWN

April 1963

Interviewer: Richard Warren Lewis

By the time the Playboy Interview was six months old, the mix of political, artistic, and entertainment figures the magazine would hope to feature as interview subjects was already apparent. The choice of Helen Gurley Brown could be explained as a change of pace, of course—but still, what was the author of *Sex and the Single Girl* doing in a forum already regarded as serious and thoughtful?

The fact is, Brown's views were downright revolutionary for her time—never mind that she was already accenting her words and using teeth-gritting phrases like "pippy-poo." At a time when Mamie Eisenhower was still on the most-admired list, when the women's magazines were printing recipes and family homilies, when men's sexual behavior was barely discussed in major publications and women's wasn't even acknowledged, Helen Gurley Brown was saying some unsettling things.

Richard Warren Lewis, a free-lance writer living in California, had an easy time interviewing the voluble author, but ran into a patch of publishing irony when he submitted his manuscript to Fisher in Chicago. In her interview, Brown explained how her book publishers had forced her to change the phrase "fuck you" to "drop dead." But PLAYBOY, which had pioneered the use of explicit photography, was not about to pioneer the use of explicit language—at least not *that* word. Fisher wanted to break the taboo at once; Spectorsky felt it was a question of taste and wanted to omit the reference altogether; Hefner mediated and instructed the editors to publish it as "f--- you," which in itself was considered by many an overly suggestive departure. It took several more years for the barriers to fall and the dashes to disappear.

More important, in an era that restricted contraceptives to the safely married, and that dismissed abortions as the stuff of back alleys and coat hangers, here is Helen Gurley Brown discussing her diaphragms, snapping that "girls who get pregnant are jerks," and calling for the overhaul of American abortion laws. Though she would be no heroine to feminists a decade later, her ideas, such as they were, must have been thought-provoking to readers in 1963.

The reader will also note that although many of Brown's ideas now sound familiar, no mention is made of *Cosmopolitan* magazine in the interview. That, of course, is because it wasn't until two years later that Brown took over the floundering consumer magazine and transformed it into the successful publication for single women that it has become. This interview is in effect a first run-through of the style and breathless language that were to characterize the future *Cosmo.*

Within the past year, a Los Angeles advertising woman who used to spend most of her time tub-thumping bras and pancake make-up has metamorphosed into a pundit for millions of lonely and bewildered American women. With the publication of Sex and the Single Girl, *Helen Gurley Brown became the first in a new school of lovelorn literati to parlay sexually candid advice into a hefty bank account.*

In a series of interviews conducted in her Hollywood-and-Vine office and her expansive Pacific Palisades home, PLAYBOY *captured Mrs. Brown's more outspoken personal views on pregnancy, abortion, affairs, fame and matrimony.*

PLAYBOY: How did you happen to write *Sex and the Single Girl?*
BROWN: My husband, David Brown, thought up the idea. I was out of town visiting my mother and sister and David found some old letters of mine, letters I wrote to an old boyfriend. I always kept carbon copies of those letters. He sat down and read them from beginning to end. And when I got home he said: "You really have a delightful writing style. I'd like to think of something for you to write." This was the spring of 1960. We were talking again about something I might be able to write a few months later and he said: "I had an idea the other day about how a single girl goes about having an affair, how she clears the decks for action. What does she do with the guy she's already seeing? What's the best place for her to consummate this affair? What's her life like? What kind of person is she?" I said: "My God, that's my book, that's my book!" When I got into writing the book, it became much more serious and sincere than we ever thought it

would be. It got to be not tongue in cheek, but quite sincere—with a little light touch.

PLAYBOY: What was the thinking behind the book's sincere little title?

BROWN: Originally it was called *Sex for the Single Girl,* which I liked better. It was my husband's title. The publishers felt that it was too racy, that it sounded like we were advocating sex for all single girls. So they changed *for* to *and.* I suppose it's faintly misleading; however I think if we said *Sex and the Single Woman,* without justifying it, it might indicate it was a sex tome dealing with the sex life of the unmarried female in America. The fact that we called a girl a girl was one justification for the title. Another, every single chapter always refers to sex. In the chapter on money, it says that being solvent is sexy and there's nothing less sexy than a girl who has the shorts. And it's sexy to be able to balance a checkbook and not to spend a boy blind. We made sure that all the chapters did tie back in. I don't think of sex as the act of sex exclusively. I don't think sex appeal exists only between two people who are lovers. Therefore, I would consider part of a single girl's arsenal of sex appeal her apartment and her clothes and the fact that she can give an intimate little dinner.

PLAYBOY: Have you received much mail from readers of the book?

BROWN: Yes, and the preponderance of mail is very happy stuff. The large proportion of it comes from single women who say: "Thank you, Helen Gurley Brown" or "You're what we've needed" or "You've changed my life and now I can hold my head up" or "I've stopped seeing my psychiatrist."

I get a lot of mail about how to keep from having a baby. I wrote a whole section on that and felt very strongly that it should be in the book. My publisher felt we were taking a pretty bold stand about all this stuff anyway without going so far as to tell people how not to have babies. So he took it out. And I fought for it, but it came out anyway. This mail I get is from girls who are quite sincerely interested in knowing. For some reason they feel they can't talk it over with their doctor. My inclination is to tell people exactly what I think they should do: They should get fitted for a diaphragm. What else would you do? I was never pregnant. Nobody has to get pregnant, it's so very silly. I was just as silly a little girl as everybody else was. I was no great brain, I'm still not. Except I always did have the good sense to try not to have a baby. It shouldn't be that much of a problem. As married girls who are trying to have babies know, it's quite difficult. You can only conceive 12–18 hours during a month. Therefore it's not all that simple, although I've had many pregnant girlfriends.

PLAYBOY: How do you feel about abortions for these pregnant friends?

BROWN: Having an abortion isn't that difficult either. It's really not that dangerous anymore, since penicillin. Now they shoot you full of 95,000 volts of penicillin and you can go back to work on Monday. It was once a very dangerous thing because of infection, because these operations had to be done in the backs of garages or somebody's office. If a girl were able to go to a hospital now, there would be practically no danger to her. There is some chance of becoming barren, but if the operation isn't performed by an idiot, it's quite simple. The only problem with an abortion is finding someone who can perform it. And also, it's hideously expensive. It's like dope. I understand the going rate now in Los Angeles is $500, and it has to be cash and right then. Well, kids don't have that kind of money. Career girls don't, either.

PLAYBOY: Did your pregnant friends follow your abortion advice?

BROWN: I had a roommate who was pregnant and who wouldn't admit she was. It was an immaculate conception. It hadn't happened to her, boy. She was throwing up every morning before she went to work. She was getting as fat as Patty's pig. She said she had a virus. My other roommate and I finally said: "Barbara, don't you think you ought to see a doctor, maybe?" Finally she went to a doctor and wouldn't admit to him that she'd had intercourse. After she was getting fatter and fatter and sicker and sicker, he said: "You're pregnant, aren't you?" And she said: "I guess I am." Then she started doing things at home to try to unload this baby. It really was quite touching. Of course, nothing did any good. She was young and healthy. She had an abortion—the rates were $300 then. The boyfriend got the money and a few months after that they were married. They now have two children.

PLAYBOY: Well, that's a happy ending. What about American abortion laws?

BROWN: The whole thing needs overhauling It's a shame girls have to go to Mexico or Europe to be operated on. It's outrageous that girls can't be aborted here. I guess the rule as of the moment is that it must endanger the mother's life. But never mind that this little child doesn't have a father. And never mind that its mother is a flibbertigibbet who has no business having a baby. Abortion is just surrounded with all this hush-hush and horror, like insanity used to be. The whole country is going to be over-run by people. Charles Darwin's nephew, who writes on anthropology, says that by the year 2000, we're going to be stacked up on top of each other. So from that anthropological viewpoint alone, it's silly to prevent abortions. One of my good friends was pregnant a couple of years ago, and her own doctor gave her the usual party line: "Marry the guy." I think that's hysterical. It's wrong for a chap to get married when he's not ready to get married, when it's going to louse up everything. I always felt it was my responsibility as a girl having an affair. And I didn't have a diaphragm until I was 33 years old. If you like someone, and he likes you, he's really not interested in getting you pregnant. My God, it's the last thing in the world he wants to do. The few times when somebody just can't wait, you just put your foot down. I'm as highly sexed as the next girl. But it doesn't matter how much of a hurry you're in. You say: "This isn't going to happen until . . ." No problem. Girls who get pregnant are careless little jerks.

PLAYBOY: Your publisher deleted all this from the book?

BROWN: Yes, he felt it might hurt sales, that I was going pretty far, anyway, in talking about the sexual life of unmarried women. And if I went so far as to tell a girl how not to have a baby, we would be thrown out of the Authors League or something. It was a commercial consideration. The publisher didn't want to kibosh the whole thing by making people furious.

PLAYBOY: Did you run into any additional censorship problems with your publisher?

BROWN: There was one line that they cut out in the first chapter. It was exhorting the single girl to be proud of herself and I said: "I think you should have a quietly 'F _ _ _ You' attitude about the whole thing." In the galleys, my publisher changed it to "Frig You" attitude and I got up as fast as I could and said: "Are you mad? A lady would say 'F _ _ _ You' but she would never say that other thing." So he said: "Well, I don't think you ought to say that. It just doesn't sound right." We changed it to "a quietly 'Drop Dead' attitude." We also had a little go-round about the word *pushover*. In the chapter describing why a girl has affairs, I said there are girls who only feel secure when they're in bed with a man. This is the greatest gift that a man can give them. And they feel uneasy unless they're getting this from a man. And then I said this may not be the clinical definition, but this is my definition of a nymphomaniac. My publisher corrected this and said: "Look, you're not a doctor, you don't know what a nymphomaniac is, so why don't we say this girl obviously is a pushover?" I just hit the roof. I hate that word. I don't think a pushover is a pushover. It's as though she was saying: "No, please don't do it to me, please don't, I wish you wouldn't do it, please don't. Oh well, I'm too weak and I'll just give in." *Au contraire*. She's asking for it. She needs it. She needs the reassurance. When a man is making love to you, the United Nations building could fall down and if he's really a man, he won't stop for a minute. Therefore it's pretty exhilarating. It does give you a feeling of power. Men, in most cases, would be more like wild, uncaged beasts if they were stopped in the middle of a sex act, more than a woman would. I understand a nymphomaniac in that respect. Any girl who goes to bed with a man has a reason. I don't think one of them is that she just doesn't know how to say no. A few, maybe, are so socially inept that they don't want to hurt anybody's feelings so they go through with it. But very few. I absolutely insisted on getting that word *pushover* out of there.

PLAYBOY: There are other critics who object to your language as well as the book's content. Norm Porter, a columnist for an Olympia, Washington, newspaper, says: "The book never quite attains the high level of smut by innuendo accomplished in the Springmaid Sheet ads. There's more polish and tone than most of the deodorant or laxative copy." What do you think he means by that?

BROWN: He hates the book. It's not his book. And there probably is some sly reference to the fact that it sounds like advertising copy. If it sounds like ad copy, I'm delighted. That's good writing.

PLAYBOY: Are phrases like little bitty, teeny-weeny and pippy-poo examples of good writing?

BROWN: Those phrases seem to have annoyed some people, especially the word "pippy-poo"—they just climb walls. I can't blame it on my copywriting background. I write letters that way. Let's just say I've made a thing out of writing very girlishly. I just didn't pick out 20 ridiculous, silly, girlish words and say: "OK. I'll drop them in like eggs into an Easter basket and see what comes out." I don't think these words offended anybody but men.

PLAYBOY: A female reviewer, writing for the *Miami News,* said: "The style is over-breezy. If Mrs. Brown never italicizes another word or uses another exclamation point, she'll still have used both devices more than one woman should in a lifetime."

BROWN: If this woman doesn't like my style, she shouldn't read my book. That's just her interpretation of it, that it's breezy and too girlish and it just babbles on and on. Most people feel it's a very easy book to read.

PLAYBOY: Some readers have accused you of regarding males as little more than setups for exploitation and manipulation. In the book, you speak of us variously as pawns, slaves, toys, pets and seven-year-olds. You use terms like "bagging a man." Your own courtship is described as "a year's battle with trident and net." You say: "Let your friends help you rope him, you tie him." Is this a posture you've adopted to appeal to the popular female conception of men, just to sell books, or do you actually regard men as inferior beings?

BROWN: I've been through analysis and as far as I know, I do like men. And I don't like them as something to exploit. I've never exploited a man. I'm all for equality, a single standard of wages. Women should pull their own weight. In fact, I don't even blame men for not getting married. My gosh, if I were a man, before I married I would have to be so sure, because I know what can happen. I testified for a good friend in a divorce case and I'd always liked his wife, but it grinds me. She got all the community property. It's just as though he hadn't done a thing for the last 13 years, as though he just didn't exist. She gets unbelievable alimony and child support. I go absolutely ape when I think about what happens in these situations. This business of competing with men, also, is so asinine. People should be judged on what they are, what they have to contribute, not on how they're constructed.

PLAYBOY: But you have deprecated men, haven't you?

BROWN: I don't think so. If a man were writing such a book, he would probably pick on the foibles of girls. I think if a girl did all the things that are recommended in this book, a man would be very happy with her.

PLAYBOY: You say in the book that female man-haters may be suffering from what is known as penis envy. Will you elaborate on that?

BROWN: Well, I'm treading in an area that I'm not competent to talk about or probably even to mention in my book. It's quite presumptuous. However, in a study of Lesbianism, among the reasons given for this condition is the fact that a woman wants to be a man. Her father probably hoped that he'd have a son and he had a girl so all her life she has been taught to envy and to wish that she were a man. And I think this penis envy is a very commonplace thing. It comes up in most analyses. It's supposed to exist with all little girls even if they don't become Lesbians, because a man is built differently than they and you can see what he has. It's very showy and she doesn't have anything like that.

PLAYBOY: Why did you deal with this subject when you admit you are unqualified to talk about it?

BROWN: Well, it's in the chapter called "How to Be Sexy." And I indicate you can't be sexy if you don't like men. You may be jealous of them. You may be jealous of a job they hold or of their so-called superior advantages. In psychiatry they find that little girls like this thing a man has. It's fun. Penis envy usually is eradicated when a girl finds out how wonderful it is to be used in its proper respect to her.

PLAYBOY: Have you found its proper use?

BROWN: Yes, I really like sex. But I feel people who go around yapping about it too much or those who are absolutely preoccupied with sex and talk about nothing else may have a bit of a problem. There are thousands of people who are happily mated who don't talk about it, either to each other or to anyone else.

PLAYBOY: Is it fair to say that women use sex as a potent instrument in manipulating men?

BROWN: It's a very strong weapon. It's been used since antiquity. If all things were equal, if we really did have a single standard, if men and women held the same jobs and got the same things out of being married, then I think it would be very wrong. As things stand, there aren't enough men. It is desirable to get married in most people's view. A husband is a priceless commodity. Whatever means you use to get a husband, outside of blackmail and things that are illegal, I think are all right. Practically every gal that I know has slept with the man she married before she married him. Most of those people have had to take a stand someplace along the line, like the girl who'll say: "C'mon now, either we're gonna get married or I'm gonna stop coming over here and being your little geisha girl every night." A woman desperately needs to get married more than a man does. She wants and needs the baby. So to get what she wants, she uses every available weapon. Sex is one of them. I talked about this to my favorite psychiatrist, who thinks it's just outrageous that I say that women *do* use sex as a means of getting what they want. He says people should never use sex for anything except the sheer enjoyment of it. I agree with him theoretically. It's such a marvelous thing, you shouldn't kick it around. It's terrible when you tamper with it. If you sleep with somebody you don't like you get everything out of kilter. But this is what happens. Some women use sex to get material things. That's a little wrong. It's so much more fun if you get those things other ways, the legitimate ways.

PLAYBOY: Some of your readers have said you encourage the tease, the flirt and the charmer to nail their man with scientific exactitude by staring raptly into his eyes, flirting openly across the room with perfect strangers, flattering him, telling him lies. You advise girls to "belt below the belt." Are these some of the "legitimate" ways you have in mind?

BROWN: Well, that's the silliest thing I ever heard. I would defy anybody to say that I'm for the cheat. I'm definitely against cheats. And if I've ever said, "Be a liar," I would argue about that. I said sometimes you have to use a tactful lie to get out of something you absolutely can't do. You have to say: "Look, you're attractive" and you may think he's a toad. I definitely am for the compassionate lie. I defy you to say that mature men are against women who flirt. The kind of person you're talking about is somebody I didn't describe at all. As for looking into a man's eyes, I don't think that's anything to go climb up the ceiling about. Or that if I look at you that way I'm a tease. There is a kind of girl who does that sort of thing. She absolutely drives a man to the jumping-off point by squirming all over him in the front seat of an automobile, and then she says: "Well, so long, Hank." Now, does that have anything whatsoever to do with what I discussed in my book? I don't think so. I adore a woman to be feminine, to be female and to attract a man so that he wants to see her again. That's the sole purpose of my book, not to exploit men, but to be companions to them.

PLAYBOY: Your book has been described as lacking a sense of sensual joy, of romance, in its approach to sex. If this is so, yours would appear to be a cold-blooded, clinical attitude about one of the warmest and most joyful of human experiences. Do you, yourself, view the act of love with this clinical detachment, this coldly predatory attitude?

BROWN: I don't think I ever talked about the act of copulation in my book. I say many times that getting there is half the fun for a female, that she likes the letter writing and the romantic build-up. I say that there's a kind of cliff-hanging romance between people who are having an affair which doesn't exist in marriage. I'm not the great expert on how wonderful it is to go to bed with a man. I'm not selling bedmanship. I'm trying to get men into a girl's life. When she gets the men, she'll fall in love. I never say just go to bed for bed's sake. However, I do think there's too much of this falling hopelessly, hideously, horribly in love because you've been to bed with a man. Because of our mores in this country and our con-science-stricken girls, they feel that any man they sleep with must be the man to end all men and presumably must be the one that they marry, and the sooner the better.

PLAYBOY: Have you personally used the various snares and practiced the assorted wiles you've preached in your book?

BROWN: Yes, many of them.

PLAYBOY: Do they work?

BROWN: Of course they work, or I wouldn't be recommending them. The entire book is based upon personal experiences or experiences of close friends.

PLAYBOY: Do some of your ground rules for luring men—"mad" beach towels, "crazy" ski caps, "shocking pink" cars, big-name matchbooks scattered around the apartment—strike you as trivial or superficial?

BROWN: Oh, heavens no. I think anything you can do to attract a man is absolutely OK. If we were talking about a mink-lined bathtub, a zebra-striped, er, I was going to say nightgown, but that sounds very interesting to me—if we were in some area where there was some question about taste—I can't imagine why anybody can find fault with crazy ski caps. Every time I talk to a bunch of girls they say: "How do we meet men? What can we do to meet men?" These are fairly off-beat ways of meeting a man, but there are 4,000,000 too few men around. If a girl just stands there with her mortal soul ready to be probed and sweet and smiling, nothing may happen.

PLAYBOY: Which techniques did you use to bag your own husband?

BROWN: I cooked dinner for him two or three nights a week. However, I don't think you can or should bag a husband that way. All these lures, attractions, baits that I have suggested are perfectly legitimate ways for a girl to have men in her life. Getting married is something else. A marriage should be predicated on other things, of course, than lures or bait. It should be predicated on whether people have a lot in common.

PLAYBOY: In your book you say, "If a man, married for years, wants to take a single girl to dinner, it can hardly break up his marriage. He may even arrive home a happier, more contented man." Also you speak ap-provingly of "The many husbands and wives who have an understanding that he may frisk about a bit without recriminations." Suppose your hus-band, David, pulled this frisky bit. Would you handle it with the same lighthearted insouciance?

BROWN: Answering the first part, I was talking about men in other cities on business trips. I would stand by that. It does not break up his marriage and it was not anyplace where it would have humiliated his wife. I can't imagine my husband being in New York City and not being with somebody. I wouldn't want him sitting alone in his hotel room. If it were a girl, it wouldn't be the end of the world. I don't think he would tell me, probably, and I don't think I would want him to. Civilized people don't go around hurting their partners by going into lascivious detail about their every death wish for the partner and their every love wish for another girl.

Further, I don't think I condoned husbands and wives who have an understanding. I just said that some husbands and wives have an understanding, a tacit understanding that the husband may frisk about a bit. There are such situations, and I did not say it's good, it's bad, it's horrible, it's right or wrong or anything else. Now suppose the same thing happened to my husband. I can't imagine it happening to my husband, frankly, because my husband did most of his frisking during the years that he was married twice, and during the years between marriages. David is now 46. I'm his third wife. I don't think he's feeling a great need to be frisky. He married a sexy, sophisticated, worldly, uninhibited, man's kind of woman. We're not going to have children. We have a grown-up sort of hedonistic life. On the other hand, I did most of my frisking by the time I married him. I had been dating for 23 years, so I had a great deal of the play out of my system. Probably most of it. Now, if my husband were frisking about like a spring lamb, there would be something quite wrong with our particular marriage. How I would handle it I don't know. I'd say we were in trouble. The subject just wouldn't come up unless—I'm blind. Of course I've had much experience observing unhappily married men, so I think I'd be able to spot one. What might happen five or ten years from now, I can't think. Most women who allow their husbands to frisk a bit—I think those girls are the ones who are kind of relieved not to be going to bed with their husbands. The thing is never discussed, but some of the married men that I know have that kind of arrangement. And their wives are really quite pleased to get rid of them. Their wives are fond of them but they've just really had it in the bed department. That's how most frisking arrangements are arrived at. If a woman is really nutty about the guy in bed, I don't think there is too much frisking.

PLAYBOY: Do you feel it's true that most women are less eager to go to bed than men?

BROWN: That may not be true in all cases. I keep hearing about the raging nymphomaniacs that are beating down doors. There are also married girls who need the physical relationship very much and aren't getting it at home and they aren't interested in too much except the act of sex itself. You keep reading about attractive 34-year-old married girls who go after the mail boy or the paper boy. In my own experience, the act of love per se is not something that you go out grabbing for, you don't need to. Maybe it has something to do with the kind of background you come from. If you're taught that going to bed is horrible until you get married, that it will ruin your life, there's this built-in reluctance to go to bed too quickly. I was the kind of girl who always seemed to be reluctant. I've never been involved with a man that I was pursuing actively physically. My experience was always in being the pursued one. Now this doesn't mean that I wasn't pursuing in my own way, the way that I mentioned in the book, such as hanging on every word and wearing low-cut dresses and all the rest of it. I was being aggressive in my way, but as far as actually being taken to bed, I was presumably resisting and someone was trying to talk me into it.

PLAYBOY: Apropos bed, in your book you say: "Not having slept with the man you're going to marry I consider lunacy." Does this advice apply to all women?

BROWN: I'd make one amendment if I were rewriting the book. That would be right there. I might add: "if you're over 20." I don't think teenagers should go around sleeping with each other even if they are going to be married. Maybe I should have said if you're over 25 I consider it complete lunacy. But I stand on the rest. We must always remember that these are my biased, personal, opinionated, unqualified remarks about everything. I am brave and I do take a stand. I don't pussyfoot too much. A marriage should be for life if you can possibly get it to be, and I do not see how you can know someone in every way without participating.

PLAYBOY: What physical types of men have appealed to you most?

BROWN: I think there's kind of a physical thrill of being with someone who's physically stronger than you. And I don't mean that diminutive men can't be absolutely fabulous lovers, and just wonderful and gentle and sensual and sexy as all get out. However, I do think there's a certain amount of pleasure in being with someone who's quite strong. This was something that happened to me several times. I'm small boned. I wasn't overpowered, I don't mean it that way, that if it was a gorilla or a King Kong I'd say: "Hooray." It's just a very nice feeling to be with someone very firmly so you can't get loose.

PLAYBOY: Is there a dividing line between sleeping around before marriage and out-and-out promiscuity?

BROWN: Sleeping around is a very derogatory term and promiscuity is obviously something bad. If you say where does the demarcation come between a girl being a decently sexed, healthy person and sleeping around—OK. There is no specific demarcation. I can't judge anything quantitatively. I would have to know how old she is, how long she was tied up with one person. For example, I was involved with one particular Don Juan for five years. I was very faithful to him, so nothing went on during that period. Who's to say that's a better relationship than if I'd had an affair with a different man every year? It seems unlikely that you would have as many as two or three or ten bed relationships a year without something being kind of skitterish, because the most delightful thing in the world is to have one real lover. It's more fun to have one man at a time. When there is multiple bedding down, and by that I mean you sleep with more than one man at a time, that's not being true.

PLAYBOY: Your five-year relationship with a Don Juan seems to have left its mark. In the book, in commenting on Don Juans, you criticize their calculating ways, saying their "drive and attention to detail are awe inspiring," that "their ruthlessness is to be pitied." What is the difference between those manipulating men you put down and the manipulating bachelor girls you praise and advise?

BROWN: A Don Juan's sole aim, if I understand the term, is to prove his masculinity, about which there may be a great deal of doubt in his mind. Most literature on the subject indicates that he really doesn't love women at all. He really loves himself. Far from really loving, as we know it, he exploits. He's a sick character. In my book, I never at any time said it wasn't wonderful to have a man to be with, to love, to marry if you want to, or if not, to have at least for a loving friendship. Life without men is a very barren, arid, unhappy situation. However, there are not enough men to go around. The girl is the underdog. The first thing I hoped to do was to convince her she was not the underdog. She mustn't think of herself that way. Inasmuch as society has put her in that position— i.e., if you don't have a husband you're some kind of schmuck—to be able to get out of that position and show society that you really aren't a creep, here are some of the things you can do. I didn't present men as something to be exploited. Her goal is to surround herself with loving friends. At no time does the book ever say love 'em and leave 'em, beat the hell out of 'em, take their money away from them, make them unhappy. Always it suggests that the relationship be a loving one. However, this girl is the underdog. She *does* have to watch out.

PLAYBOY: Are the two that dissimilar in their methods?

BROWN: The technical method is not that dissimilar. The means have a similarity. However, you could compare the pursuit of a confidence man who is trying to con a millionaire out of his money to the methods of a Washington hostess who's trying to snare the most important ambassador in the city to come to her dinner party. No one has the corner on charm. I don't know of anything more ruthless, more deadly or more dedicated than any normal, healthy American girl in search of a husband.

PLAYBOY: In your book you say: "Crass and callous though it may make her seem, the desirable woman is usually more favorably disposed toward a man who is solvent and successful than someone without status." Do you equate sex appeal with money?

BROWN: I love money. I don't mean it to be a crucial thing, although I've never known a really loaded, wealthy guy who didn't have all the girls he wanted. Maybe it's mean and horrible. But it's definitely a nice accessory. Of course there are more important things than money, but I get bored with people who are constantly deprecating it all the time. They really like it as much as I do. And I don't think it can be denied that a man who has a little money can attract more girls whether it's to take them to bed or whatever he wants to do with them.

PLAYBOY: You now have considerable affluence of your own as a result of one "pippy-poo" book. Can you sum up the reasons for your success?

BROWN: This whole thing that's happened to me is so ridiculous. It's a fluke. It's crazy. But one thing that has become most apparent to me is the ridiculousness of saying that we aren't like we really are. PLAYBOY says we're like we really are and it's OK to be like that. My favorite psychologist, Albert Ellis, is always harping on this subject. He decries that nobody ever writes about the fact that sex is fun. Why do we have to pretend that we love people that we hate and that marriage isn't a horrible bore much of the time? The reason my book is successful is that there's none of this crappiness about it. I said as well as I could what it was really like. Any time anyone can say of your book: "Yes, this is how it really is," you're apt to have a hit on your hands, if it isn't too grisly. You can have verisimilitude and be commercially successful if it's a subject about which people don't mind listening or looking. And what could fit the bill better than sex?

MALCOLM X

May 1963

Interviewer: Alex Haley

Haley's next assignment would embroil him not only in the racial politics of the nation that tumultuous year, but, more personally, in the internal affairs of PLAYBOY magazine. Spectorsky did not want politics, especially touchy racial politics, in the magazine. When Murray Fisher proposed an interview with the fiery Black Muslim Malcom X, it was too much for Spectorsky. "Why should we give him a podium?" he asked. "It's not a podium," Fisher insisted, "it's a witness box, and we get to cross-examine him."

It was a refrain that would be repeated many times through the years, even among succeeding editors in the Seventies: What was and was not "responsible" when it came to presenting someone's unpopular views, and to what extent should the magazine dissociate itself from them?

Hefner decided on the names suggested for the interview, and in this case sided with Fisher. But when Haley brought the tapes in, Spectorsky came up with a way of detoxifying the interview: The introductions to the interviews, which had been expanding to become biographical sketches of the subjects, were written in the magazine's voice. So Spectorsky insisted that it be laced with apologies for the ideas Malcolm X represented: ". . . a damning self-indictment of one noxious facet of rampant racism." The readers had to know that the magazine disapproved.

Haley recalled years later that Malcolm X was an even greater challenge to talk to than Miles Davis. The man hated everyone—whites, Jews, middle-class blacks, liberals, and Abraham Lincoln. He refused at first to speak of anything except the Black Muslims, and repeatedly baited Haley, telling him he did not believe the "white devils" at

PLAYBOY would publish the interview. A breakthrough occurred the afternoon that Haley brought up an unlikely topic: Malcolm's mother. Malcolm paused in one of his diatribes, looked curiously at Haley, and said, in a soft voice: "It's funny you should ask; I can remember *everything* about her. . . ."

The publication of the interview produced an avalanche of mail. Weyr writes in *Reaching for Paradise*: "The facts that Haley brought out in the interview were familiar enough to readers of the press and the news magazines. But never before had they been explored in such depth and at such length in a national publication. Some of what Malcolm told Haley seems quaint, as does so much unachieved 1960s rhetoric. But Malcolm's arguments for black separatism retain their force of logic."

A Doubleday editor was sufficiently impressed with the interview to propose to Haley that it might be the basis of a book about Malcolm. Although Doubleday later withdrew, and Grove Press became the publisher, Haley's collaboration with Malcolm was an immense success under the title *The Autobiography of Malcolm X*.

Fisher also played a role in the *Autobiography,* helping Haley edit the material (as he would later help in editing *Roots*), and recalls in meeting Malcolm that the firebrand was beginning to cool down toward the end of their collaboration. "I guess it takes someone like me to make Martin Luther King seem reasonable," he told Fisher one day with a rare smile. In the coming months, Malcolm would stay in contact with both Fisher and Haley, sending them postcards in a childlike scrawl and hinting that he was beginning to think that "coexistence between the races" might be possible.

In February 1965, a week before the book galleys from Grove Press were due on Haley's desk, Malcolm X was assassinated.

Within the past five years, the militant American Negro has become an increasingly active combatant in the struggle for civil rights. Espousing the goals of unqualified equality and integration, many of these outspoken insurgents have participated in freedom rides and protest marches against their segregationist foes. Today, they face opposition from not one, but two inimical exponents of racism and segregation: the white supremacists and the Black Muslims. A relatively unknown and insignificant radical religious Negro cult until a few years ago, the Muslims have grown into a dedicated, disciplined nationwide movement which runs its own school, publishes its own newspaper, owns stores and restaurants in four major cities, buys broadcast time on 50 radio stations throughout the country, stages mass rallies attended by partisan crowds of 10,000 and more, and maintains its own police force of judo-trained athletes called the Fruit of Islam.

Predicated on the proposition that the black man is morally, spiritually and intellectually superior to the white man, who is called a "devil," Muslim doctrine dooms him to extermination in an imminent Armageddon—along with Christianity itself, which is denounced as an opiate designed to lull Negroes—with the promise of heaven—into passive acceptance of inferior social status. Amalgamating elements of Christianity and Mohammedanism (both of which officially and unequivocally disown it) and spiked with a black-supremacy version of Hitler's Aryan racial theories, Muslimism was founded in 1931 by Elijah Poole, a Georgia-born ex-factory worker who today commands unquestioning obedience from thousands of followers as the Honorable Elijah Muhammad, Messenger of Allah. At the right hand of God's Messenger stands 36-year-old Malcolm Little, a lanky onetime dining-car steward, bootlegger, pimp and dope pusher who left prison in 1952 to heed Muhammad's message, abandoned his "slave name," Little, for the symbolic "X" (meaning identity unknown), and took an oath to abstain thereafter from smoking, drinking, gambling, cursing, dancing and sexual promiscuity—as required of every Muslim. The ambitious young man rose swiftly to become the Messenger's most ardent and erudite disciple, and today wields all but absolute authority over the movement and its membership as Muhammad's business manager, trouble shooter, prime minister and heir apparent.

In the belief that knowledge and awareness are necessary and effective antitoxins against the venom of hate, PLAYBOY asked Malcolm X to submit to a cross-examination on the means and ends of his organization. The ensuing interview was conducted at a secluded table in a Harlem restaurant owned by the Muslims. Interrupting his replies occasionally with a sip of black African coffee and whispered asides to deferential aides, the dark-suited minister of Harlem's Muslim Temple Number Seven spoke with candor and—except for moments of impassioned execration of all whites— the impersonal tone of a self-assured corporation executive.

Many will be shocked by what he has to say; others will be outraged. Our own view is that this interview is both an eloquent statement and a damning self-indictment of one noxious facet of rampant racism. As such, we believe it merits publication—and reading.

PLAYBOY: What is the ambition of the Black Muslims?
MALCOLM X: Freedom, justice and equality are our principal ambitions. And to faithfully serve and follow the Honorable Elijah Muhammad is the guiding goal of every Muslim. Mr. Muhammad teaches us the knowledge

of our own selves, and of our own people. He cleans us up—morally, mentally and spiritually—and he reforms us of the vices that have blinded us here in the Western society. He stops black men from getting drunk, stops their dope addiction if they had it, stops nicotine, gambling, stealing, lying, cheating, fornication, adultery, prostitution, juvenile delinquency. I think of this whenever somebody talks about someone investigating us. Why investigate the Honorable Elijah Muhammad? They should subsidize him. He's cleaning up the mess that white men have made. He's saving the Government millions of dollars, taking black men off of welfare, showing them how to do something for themselves. And Mr. Muhammad teaches us love for our own kind. The white man has taught the black people in this country to hate themselves as inferior, to hate each other, to be divided against each other. Messenger Muhammad restores our love for our own kind, which enables us to work together in unity and harmony. He shows us how to pool our financial resources and our talents, then to work together toward a common objective. Among other things, we have small businesses in most major cities in this country, and we want to create many more. We are taught by Mr. Muhammad that it is very important to improve the black man's economy, and his thrift. But to do this, we must have land of our own. The brainwashed black man can never learn to stand on his own two feet until he is on his own. We must learn to become our own producers, manufacturers and traders: we must have industry of our own, to employ our own. The white man resists this because he wants to keep the black man under his thumb and jurisdiction in white society. He wants to keep the black man always dependent and begging—for jobs, food, clothes, shelter, education. The white man doesn't want to lose somebody to be supreme over. He wants to keep the black man where he can be watched and retarded. Mr. Muhammad teaches that as soon as we separate from the white man, we will learn that we can do without the white man just as he can do without us. The white man knows that once black men get off to themselves and learn they can do for themselves, the black man's full potential will explode and he will *surpass* the white man.

PLAYBOY: Do you feel that the Black Muslims' goal of obtaining "several states" is a practical vision?

MALCOLM X: Well, *you* might consider some things practical that are really impractical. Wasn't it impractical that the Supreme Court could issue a desegregation order nine years ago and there's still only eight percent compliance? Is it practical that a hundred years after the Civil War there's not freedom for black men yet? On the record for integration you've got the President, the Congress, the Supreme Court—but show me your integration, where is it? That's practical? Mr. Muhammad teaches us to be for what's *really* practical—that's separation. It's more natural than integration.

PLAYBOY: In the view of many, that is highly debatable. However: In a recent interview, Negro author-lecturer Louis Lomax said, "Eighty percent, if not more, of America's 20,000,000 Negroes vibrate sympathetically with the Muslims' indictment of the white power structure. But this does not mean we agree with them in their doctrines of estrangement or with their proposed resolutions of the race problem." Does this view represent a consensus of opinion among Negroes? And if so, is it possible that your separationist and anti-Christian doctrine have the effect of alienating many of your race?

MALCOLM X: Sir, you make a mistake listening to people who tell you how much our stand alienates black men in this country. I'd guess actually we have the sympathy of 90 percent of the black people. There are 20,000,000 dormant Muslims in America. A Muslim to us is somebody who is for the black man; I don't care if he goes to the Baptist Church seven days a week. The Honorable Elijah Muhammad says that a black man is born a Muslim by nature. There are millions of Muslims not aware of it now. All of them will be Muslims when they wake up; that's what's meant by the Resurrection.

Sir, I'm going to tell you a secret: the black man is a whole lot smarter than white people think he is. The black man has survived in this country by fooling the white man. He's been dancing and grinning and white men never guessed what he was thinking. Now you'll hear the bourgeois Negroes pretending to be alienated, but they're just making the white man *think* they don't go for what Mr. Muhammad is saying. This Negro that will tell you he's so against us, he's just protecting the crumbs he gets from the white man's table. This kind of Negro is so busy trying to be *like* the white man that he doesn't know what the real masses of his own people are thinking. A fine car and house and clothes and liquor have made a lot think themselves different from their poor black brothers. But Mr. Muhammad says that Allah is going to wake up all black men to see the white man as he really is, and see what Christianity has done to them.

You must understand that the Honorable Elijah Muhammad represents the fulfillment of Biblical prophecy to us. In the Old Testament, Moses lived to see his enemy, Pharaoh, drowned in the Red Sea—which in essence means that Mr. Muhammad will see the completion of his work in his lifetime, that he will live to see victory gained over his enemy.

PLAYBOY: The Old Testament connection seems tenuous. Are you referring to the Muslim judgment day which your organization's newspaper, *Muhammad Speaks*, calls "Armageddon" and prophesies as imminent?

MALCOLM X: Armageddon deals with the final battle between God and the Devil. The Third World War is referred to as Armageddon by many white statesmen. There won't be any more war after then because there won't be any more warmongers. I don't know when Armageddon, whatever form it takes, is supposed to be. But I know the time is near when the white man will be finished. The signs are all around us. Ten years ago you couldn't have *paid* a Southern Negro to defy local customs. The British Lion's tail has been snatched off in black Africa. The Indonesians have booted out such would-be imperialists as the Dutch. The French, who felt for a century that Algeria was theirs, have had to run for their lives back to France. Sir, the point I make is that all over the world, the old day of standing in fear and trembling before the almighty white man is *gone*!

PLAYBOY: You refer to whites as the guilty and the enemy; you predict divine retribution against them; and you preach absolute separation from the white community. Do not these views substantiate that your movement is predicated on race hatred?

MALCOLM X: Sir, it's from Mr. Muhammad that the black masses are learning for the first time in 400 years the real truth of how the white man brainwashed the black man, kept him ignorant of his true history, robbed him of his self-confidence. The black masses for the first time are understanding that it's not a case of being anti-white or anti-Christian, but it's a case of seeing the true nature of the white man. We're anti-evil, anti-oppression, anti-lynching. You can't be anti- those things unless you're also anti- the oppressor and the lyncher. You can't be anti-slavery and pro-slavemaster; you can't be anti-crime and pro-criminal. In fact, Mr. Muhammad teaches that if the present generation of *whites* would study their own race in the light of their true history, they would be anti-white themselves.

PLAYBOY: Are you?

MALCOLM X: As soon as the white man hears a black man say he's through loving white people, then the white man accuses the black man of hating him. The Honorable Elijah Muhammad doesn't teach hate. The white man isn't *important* enough for the Honorable Elijah Muhammad and his followers to spend any time hating him. The white man has brainwashed himself into believing that all the black people in the world want to be cuddled up next to him. When he meets what we're talking about, he can't believe it, it takes all the wind out of him. When we tell him we don't want to be around him, we don't want to be like he is, he's staggered. It makes him re-evaluate his 300-year myth about the black man. What I want to know is how the white man, with the blood of black people dripping off his fingers, can have the audacity to be asking black people do they hate him. That takes a lot of nerve.

PLAYBOY: Do you admire and respect any other American Negro leaders— Martin Luther King, for example?

MALCOLM X: I am a Muslim, sir. Muslims can see only one leader who has the qualifications necessary to unite all elements of black people in America. This is the Honorable Elijah Muhammad.

PLAYBOY: Many white religious leaders have also gone on record against the Black Muslims. Writing in the official NAACP magazine, a Catholic priest described you as "a fascist-minded hate group," and B'nai B'rith has accused you of being not only anti-Christian but anti-Semitic. Do you consider this true?

MALCOLM X: Insofar as the Christian world is concerned, dictatorships have existed only in areas or countries where you have Roman Catholicism. Catholicism conditions your mind for dictators. Can you think of a single Protestant country that has ever produced a dictator?

PLAYBOY: Germany was predominantly Protestant when Hitler—

MALCOLM X: Another thing to think of—in the 20th Century, the Christian Church has given us two heresies: fascism and communism.

PLAYBOY: On what grounds do you attribute these "isms" to the Christian Church?

MALCOLM X: Where did fascism start? Where's the second-largest Communist party outside of Russia? The answer to both is Italy. Where is the Vatican? But let's not forget the Jew. Anybody that gives even a just criticism of the Jew is instantly labeled anti-Semite. The Jew cries louder than anybody else if anybody criticizes him. You can tell the truth about any minority in America, but make a true observation about the Jew, and if it doesn't pat him on the back, then he uses his grip on the news media to label you anti-Semite. Let me say just a word about the Jew and the black man. The Jew is always anxious to *advise* the black man. But they never advise him how to solve his problem the way the Jews solved their problem. The Jew never went sitting-in and crawling-in and sliding-in and freedom-riding, like he teaches and helps Negroes to do. The Jews stood up, and stood together, and they used their ultimate power, the economic weapon. That's exactly what the Honorable Elijah Muhammad is trying to teach black men to do. The Jews pooled their money and *bought* the hotels that barred them. They bought Atlantic City and Miami Beach and anything else they wanted. Who owns Hollywood? Who runs the garment industry, the largest industry in New York City? But the Jew that's advising the Negro joins the NAACP, CORE, the Urban League, and others. With money donations, the Jew gains control, then he sends the black man doing all this wading-in, boring-in, even burying-in—everything but buying-in. Never shows him how to set up factories and hotels. Never advises him how to own what he wants. No, when there's something worth owning, the Jew's got it.

PLAYBOY: Isn't it true that many Gentiles have also labored with dedication to advance integration and economic improvement for the Negro, as volunteer workers for the NAACP, CORE and many other interracial agencies?

MALCOLM X: A man who tosses worms in the river isn't necessarily a friend of the fish. All the fish who take him for a friend, who think the worm's got no hook in it, usually end up in the frying pan. All these things dangled before us by the white liberal posing as a friend and benefactor have turned out to be nothing but bait to make us think we're making progress. The Supreme Court decision has never been enforced. Desegregation has never taken place. The promises have never been fulfilled. We have received only tokens, substitutes, trickery and deceit.

PLAYBOY: What motives do you impute to PLAYBOY for providing you with this opportunity for the free discussion of your views?

MALCOLM X: I think you want to sell magazines. I've never seen a sincere white man, not when it comes to helping black people. Usually things like this are done by white people to benefit themselves. The white man's primary interest is not to elevate the thinking of black people, or to waken black people, or white people either. The white man is interested in the black man only to the extent that the black man is of use to him. The white man's interest is to make money, to exploit.

PLAYBOY: Is there any white man on earth whom you would concede to have the Negro's welfare genuinely at heart?

MALCOLM X: I say, sir, that you can never make an intelligent judgment without evidence. If any man will study the entire history of the relationship between the white man and the black man, no evidence will be found that justifies any confidence or faith that the black man might have in the white man today.

PLAYBOY: Then you consider it impossible for the white man to be anything but an exploiter and a hypocrite in his relations with the Negro?

MALCOLM X: Is it wrong to attribute a predisposition to wheat before it comes up out of the ground? Wheat's characteristics and nature make it wheat. It differs from barley because of its nature. Wheat perpetuates its own characteristics just as the white race does. White people are born devils by nature. They don't become so by deeds. If you never put popcorn in a skillet, it would still be popcorn. Put the heat to it, it will pop.

PLAYBOY: You say that white men are devils by nature. Was Christ a devil?

MALCOLM X: Christ wasn't white. Christ was a black man.

PLAYBOY: On what Scripture do you base this assertion?

MALCOLM X: Sir, Billy Graham has made the same statement in public. Why not ask *him* what Scripture he found it in? When Pope Pius XII died, *Life* magazine carried a picture of him in his private study kneeling before a black Christ.

PLAYBOY: Those are hardly quotations from Scripture. Was He not reviled as "King of the Jews"—a people the Black Muslims attack?

MALCOLM X: Only the poor, brainwashed American Negro has been made to believe that Christ was white, to maneuver him into worshiping the white man. After becoming a Muslim in prison, I read almost everything I could put my hands on in the prison library. I began to think back on everything I had read and especially with the histories, I realized that nearly all of them read by the general public have been made into white histories. I found out that the history-whitening process either had left out great things that black men had done, or some of the great black men had gotten whitened.

PLAYBOY: Would you list a few of these men?

MALCOLM X: Well, Hannibal, the most successful general that ever lived, was a black man. So was Beethoven; Beethoven's father was one of the blackamoors that hired themselves out in Europe as professional soldiers. Haydn, Beethoven's teacher, was of African descent. Columbus, the discoverer of America, was a half-black man.

PLAYBOY: According to biographies considered definitive, Beethoven's father, Johann, was a court tenor in Cologne; Haydn's parents were Croatian; Columbus' parents were Italian—

MALCOLM X: Whole black empires, like the Moorish, have been whitened to hide the fact that a great black empire had conquered a white empire even before America was discovered. The Moorish civilization—black Africans—conquered and ruled Spain; they kept the light burning in Southern Europe. The word "Moor" means "black," by the way. Egyptian civilization is a classic example of how the white man stole great African cultures and makes them appear today as white European. The black nation of Egypt is the only country that has a science named after its culture: Egyptology. The ancient Sumerians, a black-skinned people, occupied the Middle Eastern areas and were contemporary with the Egyptian civilization. The Incas, the Aztecs, the Mayans, all dark-skinned Indian people, had a highly developed culture here in America, in what is now Mexico and northern South America. These people had mastered agriculture at the time when European white people were still living in mud huts and eating weeds. But white children, or black children, or grownups here today in America don't get to read this in the average books they are exposed to.

PLAYBOY: Can you cite any authoritative historical documents for these observations?

MALCOLM X: I can cite a great many, sir. You could start with Herodotus, the Greek historian. He outright described the Egyptians as "black, with woolly hair." And the American archaeologist and Egyptologist James Henry Breasted did the same thing.

PLAYBOY: You seem to have based your thesis on the premise that all nonwhite races are necessarily black.

MALCOLM X: Mr. Muhammad says that the red, the brown and the yellow are indeed all part of the black nation. Which means that black, brown, red, yellow, all are brothers, all are one family. The white one is a stranger. He's the odd fellow.

PLAYBOY: Since your classification of black peoples apparently includes the light-skinned Oriental, Middle Eastern and possibly even Latin races as well as the darker Indian and Negroid strains, just how do you decide how light-skinned it's permissible to be before being condemned as white? And if Caucasian whites are devils by nature, do you classify people by degrees of devilishness according to the lightness of their skin?

MALCOLM X: I don't worry about these little technicalities. But I know that white society has always considered that one drop of black blood makes you black. To me, if one drop can do this, it only shows the power of one drop of black blood. And I know another thing—that Negroes who used to be light enough to pass for white have seen the handwriting on the wall and are beginning to come back and identify with their own kind. And white people who also are seeing the pendulum of time catching up with them are now trying to join with blacks, or even find traces of black blood in their own veins, hoping that it will save them from the catastrophe they see ahead. But no devil can fool God. Muslims have a little poem about them. It goes, "One drop will make you black, and will also in days to come save your soul."

PLAYBOY: As one of this vast elite, do you hold the familiar majority attitude toward minority groups—regarding the white race, in this case, as inferior in quality as well as quantity to what you call the "black nation"?

MALCOLM X: Thoughtful white people *know* they are inferior to black people. Even Eastland knows it. Anyone who has studied the genetic phase of biology knows that white is considered recessive and black is considered dominant. When you want strong coffee, you ask for black coffee. If you want it light, you want it weak, integrated with white milk. Just like these Negroes who weaken themselves and their race by this integrating and intermixing with whites. If you want bread with no nutritional value, you ask for white bread. All the good that was in it has been bleached out of it, and it will constipate you. If you want pure flour, you ask for dark flour, whole-wheat flour. If you want pure sugar, you want dark sugar.

PLAYBOY: If all whites are devilish by nature, as you have alleged, and if black and white are essentially opposite, as you have just stated, do you view all black men—with the exception of their non-Muslim leaders—as fundamentally angelic?

MALCOLM X: No, there is plenty wrong with Negroes. They have no society. They're robots, automatons. No minds of their own. I hate to say that about us, but it's the truth. They are a black body with a white brain. Like the monster Frankenstein. The top part is your bourgeois Negro. He's your integrator. He's not interested in his poor black brothers. He's usually so deep in debt from trying to copy the white man's social habits that he doesn't have time to worry about nothing else. They buy the most expensive clothes and cars and eat the cheapest food. They act more like the white man than the white man does himself. These are the ones that hide their sympathy for Mr. Muhammad's teachings. It conflicts with the sources from which they get their white-man's crumbs. This class to us are the fence-sitters. They have one eye on the white man and the other eye on the

Muslims. They'll jump whichever way they see the wind blowing. Then there's the middle class of the Negro masses, the ones not in the ghetto, who realize that life is a struggle, who are conscious of all the injustices being done and of the constant state of insecurity in which they live. They're ready to take some stand against everything that's against them. Now, when this group hears Mr. Muhammad's teachings, they are the ones who come forth faster and identify themselves, and take immediate steps toward trying to bring into existence what Mr. Muhammad advocates. At the bottom of the social heap is the black man in the big-city ghetto. He lives night and day with the rats and cockroaches and drowns himself with alcohol and anesthetizes himself with dope, to try and forget where and what he is. That Negro has given up all hope. He's the hardest one for us to reach, because he's the deepest in the mud. But when you get him, you've got the best kind of Muslim. Because he makes the most drastic change. He's the most fearless. He will stand the longest. He has nothing to lose, even his life, because he didn't have that in the first place. I look upon myself, sir, as a prime example of this category—and as graphic an example as you could find of the salvation of the black man.

PLAYBOY: Could you give us a brief review of the early life that led to your own "salvation"?

MALCOLM X: Gladly. I was born in Omaha on May 19, 1925. My light color is the result of my mother's mother having been raped by a white man. I hate every drop of white blood in me. Before I am indicted for hate again, sir—is it wrong to hate the blood of a rapist? But to continue: My father was a militant follower of Marcus Garvey's "Back to Africa" movement. The Lansing, Michigan, equivalent of the Ku Klux Klan warned him to stop preaching Garvey's message, but he kept on and one of my earliest memories is of being snatched awake one night with a lot of screaming going on because our home was afire. But my father got louder about Garvey, and the next time he was found bludgeoned in the head, lying across streetcar tracks. He died soon and our family was in a bad way. We were so hungry we were dizzy and we had nowhere to turn. Finally the authorities came in and we children were scattered about in different places as public wards. I happened to become the ward of a white couple who ran a correctional school for white boys. This family liked me in the way they liked their house pets. They got me enrolled in an all-white school. I was popular, I played sports and everything, and studied hard, and I stayed at the head of my class through the eighth grade. That summer I was 14, but I was big enough and looked old enough to get away with telling a lie that I was 21, so I got a job working in the dining car of a train that ran between Boston and New York City.

On my layovers in New York, I'd go to Harlem. That's where I saw in the bars all these men and women with what looked like the easiest life in the world. Plenty of money, big cars, all of it. I could tell they were in the rackets and vice. I hung around those bars whenever I came in town, and I kept my ears and eyes open and my mouth shut. And they kept their eyes on me, too. Finally, one day a numbers man told me that he needed a runner, and I never caught the night train back to Boston. Right there was when I started my life in crime. I was in all of it that the white police and the gangsters left open to the black criminal, sir. I was in numbers, bootleg liquor, "hot" goods, women. I sold the bodies of black women to white men, and white women to black men. I was in dope, I was in everything evil you could name. The only thing I could say good for myself, sir, was that I did not indulge in hitting anybody over the head.

PLAYBOY: By the time you were 16, according to the record, you had several men working for you in these various enterprises. Right?

MALCOLM X: Yes, sir. I turned the things I mentioned to you over to them. And I had a good working system of paying off policemen. It was here that I learned that vice and crime can only exist, at least the kind and level that I was in, to the degree that the police cooperate with it. I had several men working and I was a steerer myself. I steered white people with money from downtown to whatever kind of sin they wanted in Harlem. I didn't care what they wanted, I knew where to take them to it. And I tell you what I noticed here—that my best customers always were the officials, the top police people, businessmen, politicians and clergymen. I never forgot that. I met all levels of these white people, supplied them with everything they wanted, and I saw that they were just a filthy race of devils. But despite the fact that my own father was murdered by whites, and I had seen my people all my life brutalized by whites, I was still blind enough to mix with them and socialize with them. I thought they were gods and goddesses—until Mr. Muhammad's powerful spiritual message opened my eyes and enabled me to see them as a race of devils. Nothing had made me see the white man as he is until one word from the Honorable Elijah Muhammad opened my eyes overnight.

PLAYBOY: When did this happen?

MALCOLM X: In prison. I was finally caught and spent 77 months in three different prisons. But it was the greatest thing that ever happened to me, because it was in prison that I first heard the teachings of the Honorable Elijah Muhammad. His teachings were what turned me around. The first time I heard the Honorable Elijah Muhammad's statement, "The white man is the devil," it just clicked. I am a good example of why Islam is spreading so rapidly across the land. I was nothing but another convict, a semi-illiterate criminal. Mr. Muhammad's teachings were able to reach into prison, which is the level where people are considered to have fallen as low as they can go. His teachings brought me from behind prison walls and placed me on the podiums of some of the leading colleges and universities in the country. I often think, sir, that in 1946, I was sentenced to 8 to 10 years in Cambridge, Massachusetts, as a common thief who had never passed the eighth grade. And the next time I went back to Cambridge was in March 1961, as a guest speaker at the Harvard Law School Forum. This is the best example of Mr. Muhammad's ability to take nothing and make something, to take nobody and make somebody.

PLAYBOY: Your rise to prominence in the Muslim organization has been so swift that a number of your own membership have hailed you as their articulate exemplar, and many anti-Muslims regard you as the real brains and power of the movement. What is your reaction to this sudden eminence?

MALCOLM X: Sir, it's heresy to imply that I am in any way whatever even equal to Mr. Muhammad. No man on earth today is his equal. Whatever I am that is good, it is through what I have been taught by Mr. Muhammad. If Mr. Muhammad and every identifiable follower he has, certainly including myself, were tomorrow removed from the scene by more of the white man's brutality, there is one thing to be sure of: Mr. Muhammad's teachings of the naked truth have fallen upon fertile soil among 20,000,000 black men here in this wilderness of North America.

PLAYBOY: Has the soil, in your opinion, been as fertile for Mr. Muhammad's teachings elsewhere in the world—among the emerging nations of black Africa, for instance?

MALCOLM X: I think not only that his teachings have had considerable impact even in Africa but that the Honorable Elijah Muhammad has had a greater impact on the world than the rise of the African nations. I say this as objectively as I can, being a Muslim. Even the Christian missionaries are conceding that in black Africa, for every Christian conversion, there are two Muslim conversions.

PLAYBOY: Might conversions be even more numerous if it weren't for the somewhat strained relations which are said by several Negro writers to exist between the black people of Africa and America?

MALCOLM X: Perhaps. You see, the American black man sees the African come here and live where the American black man can't. The Negro sees the African come here with a sheet on and go places where the Negro— dressed like a white man, talking like a white man, sometimes as wealthy as the white man—can't go. When I'm traveling around the country, I use my real Muslim name, Malik Shabazz. I make my hotel reservations under that name, and I always see the same thing I've just been telling you. I come to the desk and always see that "here-comes-a-Negro" look. It's kind of a reserved, coldly tolerant cordiality. But when I say "Malik Shabazz," their whole attitude changes: they snap to respect. They think I'm an African. People say what's in a name? There's a whole lot in a name. The American black man is seeing the African respected as a human being. The African gets respect because he has an identity and cultural roots. But most of all because the African owns some land. For these reasons he has his human rights recognized, and that makes his civil rights automatic.

PLAYBOY: Do you feel this is true of Negro civil and human rights in

South Africa, where the doctrine of apartheid is enforced by the government of Prime Minister Verwoerd?

MALCOLM X: They don't stand for anything different in South Africa than America stands for. The only difference is over there they *preach* as well as practice apartheid. America preaches freedom and practices slavery. America preaches integration and practices segregation. Verwoerd is an honest white man. So are the Barnetts, Faubuses, Eastlands and Rockwells. They want to keep all white people white. And we want to keep all black people black. As between the racists and the integrationists, I highly prefer the racists. I'd rather walk among rattlesnakes, whose constant rattle warns me where they are, than among those Northern snakes who grin and make you forget you're still in a snake pit. Any white man is against blacks. The entire American economy is based on white supremacy. Even the religious philosophy is, in essence, white supremacy. A white Jesus. A white Virgin. White angels. White everything. But a black Devil, of course. The "Uncle Sam" political foundation is based on white supremacy, relegating non-whites to second-class citizenship. It goes without saying that the social philosophy is strictly white supremacist. And the educational system perpetuates white supremacy.

PLAYBOY: Are you contradicting yourself by denouncing white supremacy while praising its practitioners, since you admit that you share their goal of separation?

MALCOLM X: The fact that I prefer the candor of the Southern segregationist to the hypocrisy of the Northern integrationist doesn't alter the basic immorality of white supremacy. A devil is still a devil whether he wears a bed sheet or a Brooks Brothers suit. The Honorable Elijah Muhammad teaches separation simply because any forcible attempt to integrate America completely would result in another Civil War, a catastrophic explosion among whites which would destroy America—and still not solve the problem. But Mr. Muhammad's solution of separate black and white would solve the problem neatly for both the white and black man, and America would be saved. Then the whole world would give Uncle Sam credit for being something other than a hypocrite.

PLAYBOY: Do you feel that the Administration's successful stand on the integration of James Meredith into the University of Mississippi has demonstrated that the Government—far from being hypocritical—is sympathetic with the Negro's aspirations for equality?

MALCOLM X: What was accomplished? It took 15,000 troops to put Meredith in the University of Mississippi. Those troops and $3,000,000—that's what was spent—to get one Negro in. That $3,000,000 could have been used much more wisely by the Federal Government to elevate the living standards of all the Negroes in Mississippi.

PLAYBOY: Has *any* American President, in your opinion—Lincoln, FDR, Truman, Eisenhower, Kennedy—accomplished anything for the Negro?

MALCOLM X: None of them have ever done anything for Negroes. All of them have tricked the Negro, and made false promises to him at election times which they never fulfilled. Lincoln's concern wasn't freedom for the blacks but to save the Union.

PLAYBOY: Wasn't the Civil War fought to decide whether this nation could, in the words of Lincoln, "endure permanently half slave and half free"?

MALCOLM X: Sir, many, many people are completely misinformed about Lincoln and the Negro. That war involved two thieves, the North and the South, fighting over the spoils. The further we get away from the actual incident, the more they are trying to make it sound as though the battle was over the black man. Lincoln said that if he could save the Union without freeing the slaves, he would. But after two years of killing and carnage he found out he would *have* to free the slaves. He wasn't interested in the slaves but in the Union. As for the Emancipation Proclamation, sir, it was an empty document. If it freed the slaves, why, a century later, are we still battling for civil rights?

PLAYBOY: Despite the fact that the goal of racial equality is not yet realized, many sociologists—and many Negro commentators—agree that no minority group on earth has made as much social, civil and economic progress as the American Negro in the past 100 years. What is your reaction to this view?

MALCOLM X: Sir, I hear that everywhere almost exactly as you state it. This is one of the biggest myths that the American black man himself believes in. Every immigrant ethnic group that has come to this country is now a genuinely first-class citizen group—every one of them but the black man, who was here when they came. While everybody else is sharing the fruit, the black man is just now starting to be thrown some seeds. It is our hope that through the Honorable Elijah Muhammad, we will at last get the soil to plant the seeds in. You talk about the progress of the Negro—I'll tell you, mister, it's just because the Negro has been in America while *America* has gone forward that the Negro appears to have gone forward. The Negro is like a man on a luxury commuter train doing 90 miles an hour. He looks out of the window, along with all the white passengers in their Pullman chairs, and he thinks *he's* doing 90, too. Then he gets to the men's room and looks in the mirror—and he sees he's not really getting anywhere at all. His reflection shows a black man standing there in the white uniform of a dining-car steward. He may get on the 5:10, all right, but he sure won't be getting off at Westport.

PLAYBOY: Is there anything then, in your opinion, that could be done—by either whites or blacks—to expedite the social and economic progress of the Negro in America?

MALCOLM X: First of all, the white man must finally realize that *he's* the one who has committed the crimes that have produced the miserable condition that our people are in. He can't hide this guilt by reviling us

today because we answer his criminal acts—past and present—with extreme and uncompromising resentment. He cannot hide his guilt by accusing us, his victims,of being racists, extremists and black supremacists. The white man must realize that the sins of the fathers are about to be visited upon the heads of the children who have continued those sins, only in more sophisticated ways. Mr. Elijah Muhammad is warning this generation of white people that they, too, are also facing a time of harvest in which they will have to pay for the crime committed when their grandfathers made slaves out of us.

But there *is* something the white man can do to avert this fate. He must atone—and this can only be done by allowing black men, those who choose, to leave this land of bondage and go to a land of our own. But if he doesn't want a mass movement of our people away from this house of bondage, then he should separate this country. He should give us several states here on American soil, where those of us who wish to can go and set up our own government, our own economic system, our own civilization. Since we have given over 300 years of our slave labor to the white man's America, helped to build it up for him, it's only right that white America should give us everything *we* need in finance and materials for the next 25 years, until our own nation is able to stand on its feet. Then, if the Western Hemisphere is attacked by outside enemies, we would have both the capability and the motivation to join in defending the hemisphere, in which we would then have a sovereign stake.

The Honorable Elijah Muhammad says that the black man has served under the rule of all the other peoples of the earth at one time or another in the past. He teaches that it is now God's intention to put the black man back at the top of civilization, where he was in the beginning—before Adam, the white man, was created. The world since Adam has been white— and corrupt. The world of tomorrow will be black—and righteous. In the white world there has been nothing but slavery, suffering, death and colonialism. In the black world of tomorrow, there will be *true* freedom, justice and equality for all. And that day is coming—sooner than you think.

PLAYBOY: If Muslims ultimately gain control as you predict, do you plan to bestow "*true* freedom" on white people?

MALCOLM X: It's not a case of what would we do, it's a case of what would God do with whites. What does a judge do with the guilty? Either the guilty atone, or God executes judgment.

Playboy Interview Interludes

What is proper for a man is proper for a woman. There is no particular work which is specifically feminine. Women can choose their work according to their own purpose and premises in the same manner as men do.

Ayn Rand, March 1964

Will Dali have children? I don't like the child. I don't like the dog, the cat, nothing small. Only the flounder—and only in my dreams, where the flounder is living in the carpet and not in the sea.

Salvador Dali, July 1964

My philosophy is the same as Hugh Hefner's. Whatever he says in his "Philosophy" is my philosophy. I'm a hip urban male, and he's about my age. So how come I don't make out like he does?

Art Buchwald, April 1965

The main reason I surround myself with women is simply that I prefer their company to that of men. As a rule I find men boring. They have specialized sensibilities and they talk shop.

Jean-Paul Sartre, May 1965

Some of the whites that I witnessed participating in this civil rights struggle—these sex perverts and beatniks and pinkos, tennis-shoe wearers and all—are in all probability perverts just as oddball as some nigras.

Robert Shelton, August 1965
(Imperial Wizard of the Ku Klux Klan)

ALBERT SCHWEITZER

December 1963

Interviewer: James Biddulph

In the summer of 1963, British reporter James Biddulph wrote to Fisher proposing an interview with the legendary jungle doctor Albert Schweitzer. Biddulph said he'd had some correspondence with Schweitzer and might be able to elicit his almost unheard-of agreement to speak for publication. Fisher felt it was worth the gamble, and cabled Biddulph the expense money for a 1500-mile trek into then-darkest Africa.

He emerged with the shortest interview published in PLAYBOY, as well as one of the most unusual. Although it doesn't say so in the original introduction (the magazine being still protective about its "voice"), the interview took place without a tape recorder or visible written notes.

Upon arrival in Lambaréné, Biddulph met with Schweitzer, who said that he had no objection to being interviewed by PLAYBOY, but couldn't stand those infernal taping machines, and couldn't tolerate reporters taking notes, either. So amid the huts of Schweitzer's jungle clinic, jogging alongside the doctor as he made his hospital rounds, Biddulph asked a couple of questions, listened to the answers, and then excused himself—to run behind a hut and scribble down what he could remember on pieces of paper. He then caught up with Schweitzer, asked a few more questions, and disappeared again. It may well have been the only major interview in history conducted by memory in a little African village, with goats and chickens as an audience.

Albert Schweitzer is a quadruple doctor—of music, theology, philosophy and medicine. He had authored several definitive religious texts and had been named principal of Strasbourg Theological College before he reached 30. He was also—and still is—recognized as the world's foremost authority on organ architecture, as an eminent Bach scholar, and as a celebrated interpreter of Bach's organ music. At the age of 38, in the full maturity of his multifaceted intellectual powers—culminating an eight-year period of spiritual stock-taking—Schweitzer elected to renounce the personal rewards and material blandishments of the Continent for a life of dedication to the sick in the jungles of French Equatorial Africa. Today, at a vigorous 88, he is acknowledged as one of the foremost philosophers of our age— and perhaps its most controversial medical figure.

A man of Schweitzer's stature might seem inhumanly Olympian if his towering intellectual and moral virtues did not shadow all-too-human short-comings. He himself concedes that he is "arrogant" and "lacking in love"; he has been accused of riding his tropical mission as a benevolent dictator; of countenancing the most unsanitary hospital conditions in Africa; of being more interested in the welfare of animals than that of human beings; and of clinging to Kiplingesque tradition of big-brother colonialism. Few, however, will deny that he is one of the handful of great men our century has produced.

Our three-day interview began at the hospital, where "le grand docteur" was supervising construction of a new residence building; it continued in the dining room where he and the staff shared dinner at a long refectory table, and where evenings he played his antique piano and read the Bible aloud in German by the light of a green-shaded paraffin-oil lamp. It resumed the following day at the nearby leper colony—built with his Nobel Peace Prize winnings—en route to which he insisted on walking ahead of the car to shoo chickens out of harm's way; and concluded in the hospital dispensary, where he sits for several hours each day attempting to diminish a mountainous backlog of unanswered correspondence from the outside world, while behind him a tattered little delegation of natives queued up for pills and potions. We first queried him about his half-century of isolation in his adopted homeland.

PLAYBOY: Dr. Schweitzer, in the last few key years in African history you have been silent about African affairs with the exception of a statement on Katanga. Some persons have said your life in a small and isolated corner of Africa has prevented you from seeing the full course of African development. Do you feel that living here in the forest divorces you from outside events?

SCHWEITZER: No, I am not at all cut off; but you will probably agree that it is sometimes better to maintain silence. I spoke out on the Congo because it is an important matter and I was horrified to see what was happening. The Congo has always been a mess, ever since the days of King Leopold. It is altogether too big, too artificial a creation of the Europeans of the 19th Century ever to survive as a single entity, a complete and living country. Even now, even with the assistance he is receiving, Adoula is not in control. Not by any means. The Congo is cracking and disintegrating and nothing anyone can do can hold it together indefinitely. Nor should it be held together. It is doomed by its own artificiality. It is strange, but these things do not seem to worry other people. The United States, for example, is compulsively pouring money into such a country. Why? After all, this is not just token aid, not just the sort of money sent to show dispassionate good will. It is vast sums of money and huge assemblies of equipment which are involved. I can only think that this is being done because the United States has this fixed idea, this obsession, that if it does not flood Africa with money, then all Africans will immediately become Communists. But, my friend, Africans will never become Communists. Because communism is too artificial—too much like the Congo itself in a way—too much an affair of foreign disciplines which are totally alien to the African spirit. No, no, communism is not for Africa—certainly not the communism people comprehend in other parts of the world.

PLAYBOY: Some people see Africa as a microcosm reflecting the difficulties confronting the rest of the world. Do you?

SCHWEITZER: On a certain plane, yes, I suppose so. Basically, men in Africa are looking for the same things as men in India or China or the United States of America. The surroundings differ and the manifestations, of course, may be more violent at a time of immense political change. But really, all people want is a way of life, a religion.

PLAYBOY: You have repeatedly stated that one of your guiding principles is "reverence for life." As we understand it, this is a respect for *all* forms of life, from the highest to the lowest. Isn't this doctrine incompatible with the daily needs of men? And isn't it particularly at odds with your own work as a doctor?

SCHWEITZER: Who is to say which is the highest form and which is the lowest? Are you going to draw a line and say "Below this, life does not matter"? You cannot have a scale of values making that chicken higher than this goat. Mankind must accept that mystery of our life which sometimes makes the taking of life inevitable. Yes, it is true that a doctor is faced with continual and puzzling difficulties. A man has life, but so does a microbe. And sometimes it is necessary to kill that microbe to save the man and this involves a decision. The man with reverence for life must accept the responsibility for destroying that life. A man must think and meditate not only about the mysteries of his own life but about the links between his own life and the multitude of other lives around him. He must learn not only to consider and have *respect* for his own life but for all other life forms. And this need not be difficult. Because the man who thinks, and keeps thinking, is almost bound to progress from awareness and respect for his own life to sharp awareness of the lives around him.

PLAYBOY: Was this basic principle of your philosophy—respect for life, as you just called it—always in the back of your mind, or does it date only from your years at Lambaréné?

SCHWEITZER: Whether it was always in my mind, who can say? But certainly it was here that it became clear, while I was on the river, that this one phrase came into my mind which clarified my thoughts and resolved my struggle to give coherence to my point of view. It seemed, I remember, incredible to me that it had not been thought of by others, but only by an imbecile like me.

PLAYBOY: You have long said man should be governed by the rule of reason, and you have added that civilized man must follow four principles: he must not lie, must not steal, must learn to value property, and to be kind to animals. Don't you feel that this quartet should be expanded to include, say, kindness to human beings?

SCHWEITZER: Surely respect for human beings follows naturally from respect for animals. The principles you have mentioned are merely an outline, not a complete philosophy of life. But if you follow through the deep implications, for example, of kindness to animals, the love of God must surely follow.

PLAYBOY: Do you feel that formal religion, and in particular, Christianity, is still a major force in the world?

SCHWEITZER: No, it is not; not in a true sense. You have only to look at the wars in which mankind is now and then engaged to see that this could not happen if religion in any absolute way was a force. But there is a longing for religion among many people. Especially since the War, the letters I receive show a longing for religion. Christianity in the last century and at present is often untrue to itself. It has lost the essential element of willingness to love, and of reaching communion with God through that willingness.

PLAYBOY: If Christianity has in the last century become untrue to itself, would you say that the ideals of the last century are now worthless?

SCHWEITZER: An ideal which has true merit cannot be worthless or out-of-date. Time has no impact on the true ideal. But it can become obscured, and that is often what has happened. Mankind today is technically brilliant but often spiritually empty because the habit of fundamental thought has been abandoned. Yet fundamental and rational thinking is essential for mankind to reach true awareness. Men must discover for themselves, in their own minds, the truth of existence. Or they must *try* to discover it and up here, here in their minds, explore the mysteries of the world. They must struggle against that spirit of the age which tries to submerge independent thought under a blanket. This struggle is supremely important.

PLAYBOY: Dr. Schweitzer, at the moment of your greatest recognition in the academic worlds you had chosen, you suddenly embarked on a new career. Was this—as some persons have suggested—because of an unrequited love affair or a feeling of inadequacy in theology and music? Or was it your reaction to what you just called the "spirit of the age"?

SCHWEITZER: These suggestions have been made before; but really, the story is a simple one although a little long. I decided early that my life up to the age of about 30 would be to do as I wished; but after that, it would be for my fellow men. As to why I chose to be a doctor, here in Lambaréné, this I have explained in *Out of My Life and Thought*. I wanted to apply in a material way a Christian concept of love, and medicine seemed the obvious course. Lambaréné was not, of course, always part of my ambition. It was only after I read about the difficulties the Paris Missionary Society was having here in finding a staff, after the mission had been established by some Americans, that I chose Equatorial Africa. I think it was the right choice, because, here, human beings were struggling to exist and needed help.

PLAYBOY: Dr. Schweitzer, your hospital is now 50 years old. In the past few years, it has been severely criticized by some visitors who say it is dirty, primitive and inefficient. It has been alleged that crates of modern drugs have been left to spoil in the open and never used.

SCHWEITZER: I never reply to that sort of criticism. But so far as drugs are concerned you can look for yourself—here, in the dispensary. You see, every consignment of drugs is carefully put on the shelves and issued as needed. I have here about four hundred patients, not many nurses and only about six doctors—sometimes more, sometimes less, because many doctors come as visitors for a short time from all over the world. This year we have had a great American dentist, for example, and there is a Japanese doctor running the leper village two kilometers away. I have tried to create a hospital suitable to the circumstances of the forest. Many of the people who come here have never seen anything of civilization before and to throw them into a European type of hospital would make them feel strange and shocked. Here, they are surrounded by their families, by people they know. At the same time, the relatives who come with them can look after many of their physical needs.

PLAYBOY: Looking back on a long, full life, do you have any regrets?

SCHWEITZER: No, I have no regrets. I never have regrets because they are pointless and negative.

PLAYBOY: It is some time since your last book was published. Are you writing another at the moment?

SCHWEITZER: Oh now, my friend, you do not ask a woman if she is pregnant . . . ! There are many things I wish to say still, especially about nuclear disarmament. But a book? You had better wait and see.

PLAYBOY: You have said that the great secret of success is to go through life "as a man who never gets used up." Though you have achieved much, what do you feel you still have to do?

SCHWEITZER: All the time I am allowed to remain here on earth I want to continue building my hospital. There is so much to do; always so much. And building with the hands is satisfying—and creative. Apart from that, there is the bomb. I want, before I die, to see all atomic weapons banned, no matter who makes them or what especial name they give them. This is the only possible hope for mankind if we are to avoid self-destruction. Already I have fought against this insanity for several years with my friend Bertrand Russell and others.

PLAYBOY: What you are asking for is not just a ban on tests, but a ban on atomic weapons altogether. Do you think there is a prospect of achieving this?

SCHWEITZER: It is not just a question of hope: we *must* achieve it. Do you want mankind to be obliterated?

PLAYBOY: You have said that you do not intend to leave Lambaréné again. Don't you think you would be more effective if you personally urged this ban during a visit to Europe or America?

SCHWEITZER: No, I shall not go away. An English university wanted me to go there this year but I told them the same thing. This is my home, this is where I am needed most and in any case, there is no difficulty in communicating with people. I spend several hours a day writing letters and my staff helps me. I am in almost constant touch with others regarding the bomb and I cannot see how my physical presence away from Lambaréné could be of particular help.

PLAYBOY: Let us assume for a moment that the world does succeed in banning atomic weapons. We would still possess many means of waging war, and would still be possessed of many causes which might provoke conflict. Considering the differences which split the world, do you think war can be averted?

SCHWEITZER: My friend, we must hope so. But deep-down among men, you know, the differences are not always as great as they appear on the surface. Look—quick!—look at those two chickens fighting under the tree. See how they rush at one another, make a big noise and ruffle their feathers . . . and now, what? You see, it's all over. It was just bluff, just noise. Big nations are like those chickens. They also like to make big noises. But very often it means no more than two chickens, squabbling under a tree.

PLAYBOY: But in today's world, innocent bluffs and squabbles—through misunderstanding or miscalculation—can quickly explode into global war, so much so that some persons have come to judge man's progress solely in terms of weapons. Do you think that man's historical predilection toward warfare belies the concept that he is basically good?

SCHWEITZER: Why should man exist if he is bad? All living things have an elemental goodness, but in mankind, his true nature is often largely submerged, like a log in the river, by the environment he has created about him. But simply because it is submerged does not mean that idealism does not exist and despite times of pessimism I think the day will come when that idealism is allowed its full function and flowering.

VLADIMIR NABOKOV

January 1964

Interviewer: Alvin Toffler

Although PLAYBOY interviews try to meet a single standard, most of them have individual styles. If Malcolm X's is an example of angry, street-talk craft, Vladimir Nabokov's is an example of the jeweler's fine art.

When Alvin Toffler was sent to Switzerland to interview the formidable author of *Lolita*, he knew very well of Nabokov's painstaking way with words and language, and that this was therefore going to be no off-the-cuff chat. So he prepared himself by writing out hundreds of elaborately worded questions, knowing he would not be able to rely on spontaneous give-and-take. What he didn't know was how far from spontaneous the conversation would be.

The magazine introduction colorfully describes the erudite, almost intimidating atmosphere of Nabokov's suite in a Swiss hotel. What it just misses saying, although it's there if you look for it, is that there wasn't a conversation in any conventional sense. Across the room from where Toffler and Nabokov met and chatted was a high lectern, at which Nabokov stood to write his novels and essays. Toffler suggested they begin the interview, asked some opening questions—but Nabokov stopped him. He stuck his hand out, demanded the first stack of written questions Toffler had prepared, then walked across to his lectern. There he stood in silence, writing out his answers, until he'd gotten through the first stack. He then returned to Toffler, tried out some spoken conversation, and went back to his lectern with another group of written questions—some of which he would rewrite himself.

During much of his "candid conversation," Toffler amused himself by looking at books on Nabokov's shelves, as both the questions and answers of this interview were exquisitely refined by the most gifted unpaid editor PLAYBOY ever had.

Of course, it wasn't *all* as lofty as that. During one of his writing breaks, Nabokov admitted to Toffler that along with his other interests—poetry, philosophy, butterfly collecting, multilingual anagrams—he also happened to be a nut about PLAYBOY's Party Jokes. Never missed them, he said. He remained a friend of the magazine's through the years, contributing fiction and even sending PLAYBOY's art director one of his drawings—a butterfly shaped like a rabbit head, which was used on a PLAYBOY cover after his death.

Few authors of this generation have sparked more controversy with a single book than a former Cornell University professor with the resoundingly Russian name of Vladimir Vladimirovich Nabokov. "Lolita," his brilliant tragicomic novel about the nonplatonic love of a middle-aged man for a 12-year-old nymphet, has sold 2,500,000 copies in the United States alone.

It has also been made into a top-grossing movie, denounced in the House of Commons, and banned in Austria, England, Burma, Belgium, Australia and even France. Fulminating critics have found it to be "the filthiest book I've ever read," "exquisitely distilled sewage," "corrupt," "repulsive," "dirty," "decadent" and "disgusting." Champions of the book, in turn, have proclaimed it "brilliantly written" and "one of the great comic novels of all time."

His amused indifference to the most erudite appraisal of his work and worth has served merely to enhance the legend of his inscrutability. Shunning personal publicity, he grants interviews only rarely—having consented to see PLAYBOY only after satisfying himself that the subjects we proposed to discuss were worthy of his attention.

Tweedy, bespectacled, absent-mindedly professorial in mien, the 64-year-old author greeted our interviewer, free-lance writer Alvin Toffler, at the door of Nabokov's quiet apartment on the sixth floor of an elegant old hotel on the banks of Switzerland's Lake Geneva, where he has lived and worked for the past four years—most recently producing "Pale Fire," the extraordinary story of a gifted poet as seen darkly through the eyes of his demented editor; and a belated English translation of "The Gift." In a weeklong series of conversations which took place in his study, Nabokov parried our questions with a characteristic mixture of guile, candor, irony, astringent wit and eloquent evasiveness. Speaking in a curiously ornate and literary English lightly tinctured with a Russian accent, choosing his words with self-conscious deliberation, he seemed somewhat dubious of his ability to make himself understood—or perhaps skeptical about the advisability of

*doing so. Despite the good humor and well-bred cordiality which marked
our meetings, it was as though the shadowed universe within his skull was
forever beckoning him away from a potentially hostile world outside. Thus
his conversation, like his fiction—in which so many critics have sought
vainly to unearth autobiography—veils rather than reveals the man; and
he seems to prefer it that way. But we believe our interview offers a fascinating glimpse of this multileveled genius.*

PLAYBOY: With the American publication of *Lolita* in 1958, your fame
and fortune mushroomed almost overnight from high repute among the
literary *cognoscenti*—which you had enjoyed for more than 30 years—to
both acclaim and abuse as the world-renowned author of a sensational best
seller. In the aftermath of this *cause célébre*, do you ever regret having
written *Lolita*?

NABOKOV: On the contrary, I shudder retrospectively when I recall that
there was a moment, in 1950, and again in 1951, when I was on the point
of burning Humbert Humbert's little black diary. No, I shall never regret
Lolita. She was like the composition of a beautiful puzzle—its composition
and its solution at the same time, since one is a mirror view of the other, depending on the way you look. Of course she completely eclipsed my other
works—at least those I wrote in English: *The Real Life of Sebastian Knight,
Bend Sinister,* my short stories, my book of recollections; but I cannot grudge
her this. There is a queer, tender charm about that mythical nymphet.

PLAYBOY: Though many readers and reviewers would disagree that her
charm is tender, few would deny that it is queer—so much that when director Stanley Kubrick proposed his plan to make a movie of *Lolita*, you were
quoted as saying, "Of course they'll have to change the plot. Perhaps they
will make Lolita a dwarfess. Or they will make her 16 and Humbert 26."
Though you finally wrote the screenplay yourself, several reviewers took
the film to task for watering down the central relationship. Were you satisfied with the final product?

NABOKOV: I thought the movie was absolutely first-rate. The four main
actors deserve the very highest praise. Sue Lyon bringing that breakfast
tray or childishly pulling on her sweater in the car—these are moments of
unforgettable acting and directing. The killing of Quilty is a masterpiece,
and so is the death of Mrs. Haze. I must point out, though, that I had
nothing to do with the actual production. If I had, I might have insisted
on stressing certain things that were not stressed—for example, the different motels at which they stayed. All I did was write the screenplay, a
preponderating portion of which was used by Kubrick.

PLAYBOY: Do you feel *Lolita*'s two-fold success has affected your life for the better or for the worse?

NABOKOV: I gave up teaching—that's about all in the way of change. Mind you, I loved teaching, I loved Cornell, I loved composing and delivering my lectures on Russian writers and European great books. But around 60, and especially in winter, one begins to find hard the physical process of teaching, the getting up at a fixed hour every other morning, the struggle with the snow in the driveway, the march through long corridors to the classroom, the effort of drawing on the blackboard a map of James Joyce's Dublin or the arrangement of the semi-sleeping car of the St. Petersburg-Moscow express in the early 1870s—without an understanding of which neither *Ulysses* nor *Anna Karenin*, respectively, makes sense. For some reason my most vivid memories concern examinations. Big amphitheater in Goldwin Smith. Exam from 8 A.M. to 10:30. About 150 students—unwashed, unshaven young males and reasonably well-groomed young females. A general sense of tedium and disaster. Half-past eight. Little coughs, the clearing of nervous throats, coming in clusters of sound, rustling of pages. Some of the martyrs plunged in meditation, their arms locked behind their heads. I meet a dull gaze directed at me, seeing in me with hope and hate the source of forbidden knowledge. Girl in glasses comes up to my desk to ask: "Professor Kafka, do you want us to say that . . . ? Or do you want us to answer only the first part of the question?" The great fraternity of C-minus, backbone of the nation, steadily scribbling on. A rustle arising simultaneously, the majority turning a page in their bluebooks, good teamwork. The shaking of a cramped wrist, the failing ink, the deodorant that breaks down. When I catch eyes directed at me, they are forthwith raised to the ceiling in pious meditation. Windowpanes getting misty. Boys peeling off sweaters. Girls chewing gum in rapid cadence. Ten minutes, five, three, time's up.

PLAYBOY: Citing in *Lolita* the same kind of acid-etched sense you've just described, many critics have called the book a masterful satiric social commentary on America. Are they right?

NABOKOV: Well, I can only repeat that I have neither the intent nor the temperament of a moral or social satirist. Whether or not critics think that in *Lolita* I am ridiculing human folly leaves me supremely indifferent. But I am annoyed when the glad news is spread that I am ridiculing America.

PLAYBOY: But haven't you written yourself that there is "nothing more exhilarating than American Philistine vulgarity?"

NABOKOV: No, I did not say that. That phrase has been lifted out of context, and like a round, deep-sea fish, has burst in the process. If you look up my little afterpiece, "On a Book Entitled Lolita," which I appended to the novel, you will see that what I really said was that in regard to Philistine vulgarity—which I do feel is most exhilarating—no difference exists between American and European manners. I go on to say that a proletarian from Chicago can be just as Philistine as an English duke.

PLAYBOY: Many readers have concluded that the Philistinism you seem to find the most exhilarating is that of America's sexual mores.

NABOKOV: Sex as an institution, sex as a general notion, sex as a problem, sex as a platitude—all this is something I find too tedious for words. Let us skip sex.

PLAYBOY: Not to belabor the subject, some critics have felt that your barbed comments about the fashionability of Freudianism, as practiced by American analysts, suggest a contempt based upon familiarity.

NABOKOV: Bookish familiarity only. The ordeal itself is much too silly and disgusting to be contemplated even as a joke. Freudism and all it has tainted with its grotesque implications and methods appear to me to be one of the vilest deceits practiced by people on themselves and on others. I reject it utterly, along with a few other medieval items still adored by the ignorant, the conventional, or the very sick.

PLAYBOY: Speaking of the very sick, you suggested in *Lolita* that Humbert Humbert's appetite for nymphets is the result of an unrequited childhood love affair; in *Invitation to a Beheading* you wrote about a 12-year-old girl, Emmie, who is erotically interested in a man twice her age; and in *Bend Sinister,* your protagonist dreams that he is "surreptitiously enjoying Mariette [his maid] while she sat, wincing a little, in his lap during the rehearsal of a play in which she was supposed to be his daughter." Some critics, in poring over your works for clues to your personality, have pointed to this recurrent theme as evidence of an unwholesome preoccupation on your part with the subject of sexual attraction between pubescent girls and middle-aged men. Do you feel that there may be some truth in this charge?

NABOKOV: I think it would be more correct to say that had I not written *Lolita,* readers would not have started finding nymphets in my other works and in their own households. I find it very amusing when a friendly, polite person says to me—probably just in order to be friendly and polite—"Mr. Naborkov," or "Mr. Nabahkov," or "Mr. Nabkov" or "Mr. Nabohkov," depending on his linguistic abilities, "I have a little daughter who is a regular Lolita." People tend to underestimate the power of my imagination and my capacity of evolving serial selves in my writings. And then, of course, there is that special type of critic, the ferrety, human-interest fiend, the jolly vulgarian. Someone, for instance, discovered telltale affinities between Humbert's boyhood romance on the Riviera and my own recollections about little Colette, with whom I built sand castles in Biarritz when I was 10. Somber Humbert was, of course, 13 and in the throes of a pretty extravagant sexual excitement, whereas my own romance with Colette had no trace of erotic desire and indeed was perfectly commonplace and normal. And, of course, at 9 and 10 years of age, in that set, in those times, we knew nothing whatsoever about the false facts of life that are imparted nowadays to infants by progressive parents.

PLAYBOY: Why false?

NABOKOV: Because the imagination of a small child—especially a town child—at once distorts, stylizes or otherwise alters the bizarre things he is told about the busy bee, which neither he nor his parents can distinguish from a bumblebee, anyway.

PLAYBOY: What one critic has termed your "almost obsessive attention to the phrasing, rhythm, cadence and connotation of words" is evident even in the selection of names for your own celebrated bee and bumblebee— Lolita and Humbert Humbert. How did they occur to you?

NABOKOV: For my nymphet I needed a diminutive with a lyrical lilt to it. One of the most limpid and luminous letters is "L." The suffix "-ita" has a lot of Latin tenderness, and this I required too. Hence: Lolita. However, it should not be pronounced as you and most Americans pronounce it: Low-lee-ta, with a heavy, clammy "L" and a long "o." No, the first syllable should be as in "lollipop," the "L" liquid and delicate, the "lee" not too sharp. Spaniards and Italians pronounce it, of course, with exactly the necessary note of archness and caress. Another consideration was the welcome murmur of its source name, the fountain name: those roses and tears in "Dolores." My little girl's heart-rending fate had to be taken into account together with the cuteness and limpidity. Dolores also provided her with another, plainer, more familiar and infantile diminutive: Dolly, which went nicely with the surname "Haze," where Irish mists blend with a German bunny—I mean a small German hare.

PLAYBOY: You're making a word-playful reference, of course, to the German term for rabbit—*Hase*. But what inspired you to dub Lolita's aging inamorato with such engaging redundancy?

NABOKOV: That, too, was easy. The double rumble is, I think, very nasty, very suggestive. It is a hateful name for a hateful person. It is also a kingly name, and I did need a royal vibration for Humbert the Fierce and Humbert the Humble. Lends itself also to a number of puns. And the execrable diminutive "Hum" is on a par, socially and emotionally, with "Lo," as her mother calls her.

PLAYBOY: Another critic has written of you that "the task of sifting and selecting just the right succession of words from that multilingual memory, and of arranging their many-mirrored nuances into the proper juxtapositions, must be psychically exhausting work." Which of all your books, in this sense, would you say was the most difficult to write?

NABOKOV: Oh, *Lolita,* naturally. I lacked the necessary information— that was the initial difficulty. I did not know any American 12-year-old girls, and I did not know America; I had to invent America and Lolita. It had taken me some 40 years to invent Russia and Western Europe, and now I was faced by a similar task, with a lesser amount of time at my disposal. The obtaining of such local ingredients as would allow me to inject average "reality" into the brew of individual fancy proved, at 50, a much more difficult process than it had been in the Europe of my youth.

PLAYBOY: Though born in Russia, you have lived and worked for many years in America as well as Europe. Do you feel any strong sense of national identity?

NABOKOV: I am an American writer, born in Russia and educated in England, where I studied French literature, before spending 15 years in Germany. I came to America in 1940 and decided to become an American citizen, and make America my home. It so happened that I was immediately exposed to the very best in America, to its rich intellectual life and to its easygoing, good-natured atmosphere. I immersed myself in its great libraries and its Grand Canyon. I worked in the laboratories of its zoological museums. I acquired more friends than I ever had in Europe. My books—old books and new ones—found some admirable readers. I became as stout as Cortez—mainly because I quit smoking and started to munch molasses candy instead, with the result that my weight went up from my usual 140 to a monumental and cheerful 200. In consequence, I am one-third American—good American flesh keeping me warm and safe.

PLAYBOY: You spent 20 years in America, and yet you never owned a home or had a really settled establishment there. Your friends report that you camped impermanently in motels, cabins, furnished apartments and the rented homes of professors away on leave. Did you feel so restless or so alien that the idea of settling down anywhere disturbed you?

NABOKOV: The main reason, the background reason, is, I suppose, that nothing short of a replica of my childhood surroundings would have satisfied me. I would never manage to match my memories correctly—so why trouble with hopeless approximations? Then there are some special considerations: for instance, the question of impetus, the habit of impetus. I propelled myself out of Russia so vigorously, with such indignant force, that I have been rolling on and on ever since. True, I have lived to become that appetizing thing, a "full professor," but at heart I have always remained a lean "visiting lecturer." The few times I said to myself anywhere: "Now, that's a nice spot for a permanent home," I would immediately hear in my mind the thunder of an avalanche carrying away the hundreds of far places which I would destroy by the very act of settling in one particular nook of the earth. And finally, I don't much care for furniture, for tables and chairs and lamps and rugs and things—perhaps because in my opulent childhood I was taught to regard with amused contempt any too-earnest attachment to material wealth, which is why I felt no regret and no bitterness when the Revolution abolished that wealth.

PLAYBOY: You lived in Russia for 20 years, in West Europe for 20 years, and in America for 20 years. But in 1960, after the success of *Lolita,* you moved to France and Switzerland and have not returned to the U.S. since.

Does this mean, despite your self-identification as an American writer, that you consider your American period over?

NABOKOV: I am living in Switzerland for purely private reasons—family reasons and certain professional ones too, such as some special research for a special book. I hope to return very soon to America—back to its library stacks and mountain passes. An ideal arrangement would be an absolutely soundproofed flat in New York, on a top floor—no feet walking above, no soft music anywhere—and a bungalow in the Southwest. Sometimes I think it might be fun to adorn a university again, residing and writing there, not teaching, or at least not teaching regularly.

PLAYBOY: Meanwhile you remain secluded—and somewhat sedentary, from all reports—in your hotel suite. How do you spend your time?

NABOKOV: I awake around seven in winter: my alarm clock is an Alpine chough—big, glossy, black thing with big yellow beak—which visits the balcony and emits a most melodious chuckle. For a while I lie in bed mentally revising and planning things. Around eight: shave, breakfast, meditation and bath—in that order. Then I work till lunch in my study, taking time out for a short stroll with my wife along the lake. Practically all the famous Russian writers of the 19th Century have rambled here at one time or another. Zhukovski, Gogol, Dostoievsky, Tolstoy—who courted the hotel chambermaids to the detriment of his health—and many Russian poets. But then, as much could be said of Nice or Rome. We lunch around one P.M. and I am back at my desk by half-past one and work steadily till half-past six. Then a stroll to a newsstand for the English papers, and dinner at seven. No work after dinner. And bed around nine. I read till half-past eleven, and tussle with insomnia from that time till one A.M. About twice a week I have a good, long nightmare with unpleasant characters imported from earlier dreams, appearing in more or less iterative surroundings—kaleidoscopic arrangements of broken impressions, fragments of day thoughts, and irresponsible mechanical images, utterly lacking any possible Freudian implication or explication, but singularly akin to the procession of changing figures that one usually sees on the inner palpebral screen when closing one's weary eyes.

PLAYBOY: Is it true that you write standing up, and that you write in longhand rather than on a typewriter?

NABOKOV: Yes. I never learned to type. I generally start the day at a lovely old-fashioned lectern I have in my study. Later on, when I feel gravity nibbling at my calves, I settle down in a comfortable armchair at an ordinary writing desk; and finally, when gravity begins climbing up my spine, I lie down on a couch in a corner of my small study. It is a pleasant solar routine. But when I was young, in my 20s and early 30s, I would often stay all day in bed, smoking and writing. Now things have changed. Horizontal prose, vertical verse, and sedent scholia keep swapping qualifiers and spoiling the alliteration.

PLAYBOY: Can you tell us something more about the actual creative process involved in the germination of a book—perhaps by reading a few random notes for or excerpts from a work in progress?

NABOKOV: Certainly not. No foetus should undergo an exploratory operation. But I can do something else. This box contains index cards with some notes I made at various times more or less recently and discarded when writing *Pale Fire*. It's a little batch of rejects. I'll read a few [Reading from cards]:

"Selene, the moon. Selenginsk, an old town in Siberia: moon-rocket town" . . . "Berry: the black knob on the bill of the mute swan" . . . "Dropworm: a small caterpillar hanging on a thread" . . . "In *The New Bon Ton Magazine,* volume five, 1820, page 312, prostitutes are termed 'girls of the town' " . . . "Youth dreams: forgot pants; old man dreams: forgot dentures" . . . "Student explains that when reading a novel he likes to skip passages 'so as to get his own idea about the book and not be influenced by the author' " . . . "Naprapathy: the ugliest word in the language."

PLAYBOY: What inspires you to record and collect such disconnected impressions and quotations?

NABOKOV: All I know is that at a very early stage of the novel's development I get this urge to collect bits of straw and fluff, and to eat pebbles. Nobody will ever discover how clearly a bird visualizes, or if it visualizes at all, the future nest and the eggs in it. When I remember afterwards the force that made me jot down the correct names of things, or the inches and tints of things, even before I actually needed the information, I am inclined to assume that what I call, for want of a better term, inspiration, had been already at work, mutely pointing at this or that, having me accumulate the known materials for an unknown structure. After the first shock of recognition—a sudden sense of "*this* is what I'm going to write"—the novel starts to breed by itself: the process goes on solely in the mind, not on paper; and to be aware of the stage it has reached at any given moment, I do not have to be conscious of every exact phrase. I feel a kind of gentle development, an uncurling inside, and I know that the details are there already, that in fact I would see them plainly if I looked closer, if I stopped the machine and opened its inner compartment; but I prefer to wait until what is loosely called inspiration has completed the task for me. There comes a moment when I am informed from within that the entire structure is finished. All I have to do now is take it down in pencil or pen. Since this entire structure, dimly illumined in one's mind, can be compared to a painting, and since you do not have to work gradually from left to right for its proper perception, I may direct my flashlight at any part or particle of the picture when setting it down in writing. I do not begin my novel at the beginning, I do not reach chapter three before I reach chapter four, I do not go dutifully from one page to the next, in consecutive order; no, I pick out a bit here and a bit there, till I have filled all the gaps on paper. This is why I like writing my stories and novels on index cards, numbering them later when the whole set is complete. Every card is rewritten many times. About three cards make one typewritten page, and when finally I feel that the conceived picture has been copied by me as faithfully as physically possible—a few vacant lots always remain, alas—then I dictate the novel to my wife, who types it out in triplicate.

PLAYBOY: In what sense do you *copy* "the conceived picture" of a novel?

NABOKOV: A creative writer must study carefully the works of his rivals, including the Almighty. He must possess the inborn capacity not only of recombining but of re-creating the given world. In order to do this adequately, avoiding duplication of labor, the artist should *know* the given world. Imagination without knowledge leads no farther than the back yard of primitive art, the child's scrawl on the fence, and the crank's message in the market place. Art is never simple. To return to my lecturing days: I automatically gave low marks when a student used the dreadful phrase "sincere and simple"—"Flaubert writes with a style which is always simple and sincere"—under the impression that this was the greatest compliment payable to prose or poetry. When I struck the phrase out, which I did with such rage in my pencil that it ripped the paper, the student complained that this was what teachers had always taught him: "Art is simple, art is sincere." Someday I must trace this vulgar absurdity to its source. A schoolmarm in Ohio? A progressive ass in New York? Because, of course, art at its greatest is fantastically deceitful and complex.

PLAYBOY: What do you regard as your principal failing as a writer?

NABOKOV: Lack of spontaneity; the nuisance of parallel thoughts, second thoughts, third thoughts; inability to express myself properly in any language unless I compose every damned sentence in my bath, in my mind, at my desk.

PLAYBOY: You're doing rather well at the moment, if we may say so.

NABOKOV: It's an illusion.

PLAYBOY: Your reply might be taken as confirmation of critical comments that you are "an incorrigible leg puller," "a mystificator" and "a literary *agent provocateur*." How do *you* view yourself?

NABOKOV: I think my favorite fact about myself is that I have never been dismayed by a critic's bilge or bile, and have never once in my life asked or thanked a reviewer for a review. My second favorite fact—or shall I stop at once?

PLAYBOY: No, please go on.

NABOKOV: The fact that since my youth—I was 19 when I left Russia—my political outlook has remained as bleak and changeless as an old gray rock. It is classical to the point of triteness. Freedom of speech, freedom of thought, freedom of art. The social or economic structure of the ideal state is of little concern to me. My desires are modest. Portraits of the head of the government should not exceed a postage stamp in size. No torture and no executions. No music, except coming through earphones, or played in theaters.

PLAYBOY: Why no music?

NABOKOV: I have no ear for music, a shortcoming I deplore bitterly. When I attend a concert—which happens about once in five years—I endeavor gamely to follow the sequence and relationship of sounds but cannot keep it up for more than a few minutes. Visual impressions, reflections of hands in lacquered wood, a diligent bald spot over a fiddle, take over, and soon I am bored beyond measure by the motions of the musicians. My knowledge of music is very slight; and I have a special reason for finding my ignorance and inability so sad, so unjust: There is a wonderful singer in my family—my own son. His great gifts, the rare beauty of his bass, and the promise of a splendid career—all this affects me deeply, and I feel a fool during a technical conversation among musicians. I am perfectly aware of the many parallels between the art forms of music and those of literature, especially in matters of structure, but what can I do if ear and brain refuse to cooperate? But I have found a queer substitute for music in chess—more exactly, in the composing of chess problems.

PLAYBOY: Another substitute, surely, has been your own euphonious prose and poetry. As one of few authors who have written with eloquence in more than one language, how would you characterize the textural differences between Russian and English, in which you are regarded as equally facile?

NABOKOV: In sheer number of words, English is far richer than Russian. This is especially noticeable in nouns and adjectives. A very bothersome feature that Russian presents is the dearth, vagueness and clumsiness of technical terms. For example, the simple phrase "to park a car" comes out—if translated back from the Russian—as "to leave an automobile standing for a long time." Russian, at least polite Russian, is more formal than polite English. Thus, the Russian word for "sexual"—*polovoy*—is slightly indecent and not to be bandied around. The same applies to Russian terms rendering various anatomical and biological notions that are frequently and familiarly expressed in English conversation. On the other hand, there are words rendering certain nuances of motion and gesture and emotion in which Russian excels. Thus by changing the head of a verb, for which one may have a dozen different prefixes to choose from, one is able to make Russian express extremely fine shades of duration and intensity. English is, syntactically, an extremely flexible medium, but Russian can be given even more subtle twists and turns. Translating Russian into English is a little easier than translating English into Russian, and 10 times easier than translating English into French.

PLAYBOY: You have said you will never write another novel in Russian. Why?

NABOKOV: During the great, and still unsung, era of Russian intellectual expatriation—roughly between 1920 and 1940—books written in Russian by *émigré* Russians and published by *émigré* firms abroad were eagerly bought or borrowed by *émigré* readers but were absolutely banned in Soviet Russia—as they still are, except in the case of a few dead authors such as Kuprin and Bunin, whose heavily censored works have been recently reprinted there—no matter the theme of the story or poem. An *émigré* novel, published, say, in Paris and sold over all free Europe, might have, in those years, a total sale of 1000 or 2000 copies—that would be a best seller— but every copy would also pass from hand to hand and be read by at least 20 persons, and at least 50 annually if stocked by Russian lending libraries, of which there were hundreds in West Europe alone. The era of expatriation can be said to have ended during World War II. Old writers died, Russian publishers also vanished, and worst of all, the general atmosphere of exile culture, with its splendor, and vigor, and purity, and reverberative force, dwindled to a sprinkle of Russian-language periodicals, anemic in talent and provincial in tone. Now to take my own case: It was not the financial side that really mattered; I don't think my Russian writings ever brought me more than a few hundred dollars per year, and I am all for the ivory tower, and for writing to please one reader alone—one's own self. But one also needs some reverberation, if not response, and a moderate multiplication of one's self throughout a country or countries; and if there be nothing but a void around one's desk, one would expect it to be at least a sonorous void, and not circumscribed by the walls of a padded cell. With the passing of years I grew less and less interested in Russia and more and more indifferent to the once-harrowing thought that my books would remain banned there as long as my contempt for the police state and political oppression prevented me from entertaining the vaguest thought of return. No, I will not write another novel in Russian, though I do allow myself a very few short poems now and then. I wrote my last Russian novel a quarter of a century ago. But today, in compensation, in a spirit of justice to my little American muse, I am doing something else. But perhaps I should not talk about it at this early stage.

PLAYBOY: Please do.

NABOKOV: Well, it occurred to me one day—while I was glancing at the varicolored spines of *Lolita* translations into languages I do not read, such as Japaneses, Finnish or Arabic—that the list of unavoidable blunders in these 15 or 20 versions would probably make, if collected, a fatter volume than any of them. I had checked the French translation, which was basically very good, but would have bristled with unavoidable errors had I not corrected them. But what could I do with Portuguese or Hebrew or Danish? Then I imagined something else. I imagined that in some distant future somebody might produce a Russian version of *Lolita*. I trained my inner telescope upon that particular point in the distant future and I saw that every paragraph could lend itself to a hideous mistranslation, being pockmarked with pitfalls. In the hands of a harmful drudge, the Russian version of *Lolita* would be entirely degraded and botched by vulgar paraphrases or blunders. So I decided to translate it myself. Up to now I have about 60 pages ready.

PLAYBOY: Dostoievsky, who dealt with themes accepted by most readers as universal in both scope and significance, is considered one of the world's great authors. Yet you have described him as "a cheap sensationalist, clumsy and vulgar." Why?

NABOKOV: Non-Russian readers do not realize two things: that not all Russians love Dostoievsky as much as Americans do, and that most of those Russians who do, venerate him as a mystic and not as an artist. He was a prophet, a claptrap journalist and a slapdash comedian. I admit that some of his scenes, some of his tremendous, farcical rows are extraordinarily amusing. But his sensitive murderers and soulful prostitutes are not to be endured for one moment—by this reader anyway.

PLAYBOY: Is it true that you have called Hemingway and Conrad "writers of books for boys"?

NABOKOV: That's exactly what they are. Hemingway is certainly the better of the two; he has at least a voice of his own and is responsible for that delightful, highly artistic short story, *The Killers*. And the description of the fish in his famous fish story is superb. But I cannot abide Conrad's souvenir-shop style, and bottled ships, and shell necklaces of romanticist clichés. In neither of these two writers can I find anything that I would care to have written myself. In mentality and emotion, they are hopelessly juvenile, and the same can be said of some other beloved writers, the pets of the common room, the consolation and support of graduate students, such as ——, but some are still alive, and I hate to hurt living old boys while the dead ones are not yet buried.

PLAYBOY: What did you read when you were a boy?

NABOKOV: Between the ages of 10 and 15 in St. Petersburg, I must have read more fiction and poetry—English, Russian and French—than in any other five-year period of my life. I relished especially the works of Wells, Poe, Browning, Keats, Flaubert, Verlaine, Rimbaud, Chekhov, Tolstoy and Alexander Blok. On another level, my heroes were the Scarlet Pimpernel, Phileas Fogg and Sherlock Holmes. In other words, I was a perfectly normal trilingual child in a family with a large library. At a later period, in Cambridge, England, between the ages of 20 and 23, my favorites were Housman, Rupert Brooke, Joyce, Proust and Pushkin. Of these top favorites, several—Poe, Verlaine, Jules Verne, Emmuska Orczy, Conan Doyle and Rupert Brooke—have faded away, have lost the glamor and thrill they held for me. The others remain intact and by now are probably beyond change as far as I am concerned. I was never exposed in the 20s and 30s, as so many of my coevals have been, to the poetry of Eliot and Pound. I read them late in the season, around 1945, in the guest room of an American friend's house, and not only remained completely indifferent to them, but could not understand why anybody should bother about them. But I suppose that they preserve some sentimental value for such readers as discovered them at an earlier age than I did.

PLAYBOY: What are your reading habits today?

NABOKOV: Usually I read several books at a time—old books, new books, fiction, nonfiction, verse, anything—and when the bedside heap of a dozen volumes or so has dwindled to two or three, which generally happens by the end of one week, I accumulate another pile. There are some varieties of fiction that I never touch—mystery stories, for instance, which I abhor, and historical novels. I also detest the so-called "powerful" novel—full of commonplace obscenities and torrents of dialog—in fact, when I receive a new novel from a hopeful publisher—"hoping that I like the book as much as he does"—I check first of all how much dialog there is, and if it looks too abundant or too sustained, I shut the book with a bang and ban it from my bed.

PLAYBOY: Are there any contemporary authors you *do* enjoy reading?

NABOKOV: I do have a few favorites—for example, Robbe-Grillet and Borges. How freely and gratefully one breathes in their marvelous labyrinths! I love their lucidity of thought, the purity and poetry, the mirage in the mirror.

PLAYBOY: Many critics feel that this description applies no less aptly to your own prose. To what extent do you feel that prose and poetry intermingle as art forms?

NABOKOV: Poetry, of course, includes all creative writing; I have never been able to see any generic difference between poetry and artistic prose. As a matter of fact, I would be inclined to define a good poem of any length as a concentrate of good prose, with or without the addition of recurrent rhythm and rhyme. The magic of prosody may improve upon what we call prose by bringing out the full flavor of meaning, but in plain prose there are also certain rhythmic patterns, the music of precise phrasing, the beat of thought rendered by recurrent peculiarities of idiom and intonation. As in today's scientific classifications, there is a lot of overlapping in our concept of poetry and prose today. The bamboo bridge between them is the metaphor.

PLAYBOY: You have also written that poetry represents "the mysteries of the irrational perceived through rational words." But many feel that the "irrational" has little place in an age when the exact knowledge of science has begun to plumb the most profound mysteries of existence. Do you agree?

NABOKOV: This appearance is very deceptive. It is a journalistic illusion. In point of fact, the greater one's science, the deeper the sense of mystery. Moreover, I don't believe that any science today has pierced any mystery. We, as newspaper readers, are inclined to call "science" the cleverness of an electrician or a psychiatrist's mumbo jumbo. This, at best, is applied science, and one of the characteristics of applied science is that yesterday's neutron or today's truth dies tomorrow. But even in a better sense of "science"—as the study of visible and palpable nature, or the poetry of pure mathematics and pure philosophy—the situation remains as hopeless as ever. We shall never know the origin of life, or the meaning of life, or the nature of space and time, or the nature of nature, or the nature of thought.

PLAYBOY: Man's understanding of these mysteries is embodied in his concept of a Divine Being. As a final question, do you believe in God?

NABOKOV: To be quite candid—and what I am going to say now is something I never said before, and I hope it provokes a salutary little chill: I know more than I can express in words, and the little I can express would not have been expressed, had I not known more.

CASSIUS CLAY/ MUHAMMAD ALI

September 1964 and November 1975
Interviewers: Alex Haley (1964)
and Lawrence Linderman (1975)

One of the few people ever to be interviewed twice by PLAYBOY, but under different names, was Cassius Clay. (The other two repeaters are Jimmy Hoffa and Mel Brooks.) When Ali was first interviewed by Alex Haley, he had just converted to the Muslim faith, announcing that his new name was Muhammad Ali. Altogether, he cut a brash and puzzling swath through people's image of him. He had not yet gone on to his greatest outrage in the eyes of Middle America—his draft resistance— but when he spoke with Haley, his nonstop mouth and his strangely sinister religion had already made him a controversial figure. There is evidence of PLAYBOY's own ambivalence again, in the tone of the introduction ("We approached the mercurial Muslim . . .").

By the time the magazine's editors decided to interview him again eleven years later, Muhammad Ali had become the best-known athlete in the world. Ali was so far past controversy, and the editors so far past nervousness, that it was decided to dispense entirely with an introduction. Free-lance writer Larry Linderman, the interviewer in 1975, expertly caught the rhythms in the champion's speech. This interview is part put-on and part real anger—as is Ali. Both interviews are reprinted here together.

Reaction to the 1964 interview included letters from racists, such as the "doctor" in Alabama who claimed to have scientific proof that boxing's decline began "when the Negro was allowed to enter the ring," and suggesting that "punks like Clay" be put back in their places picking cotton. But the magazine also heard from author Henry Miller, who wrote: "Just a word to say how much I liked the interview. Though it's in another category, it can take its place beside the one with Bertrand Russell—one of your best. . . . That last line, 'Ain't never been *nothing* like me,' is a gem."

As to the second version, it became one of many newsmaking PLAYBOY interviews during the Seventies. Ali had spent a good deal of time telling Linderman (who is white) about the respect in which black women of the Muslim faith are held, about his own happy but chauvinist marriage, about how white *or* black men should be killed for "messing around" on a Muslim woman. As the interview hit the newsstands, the champ was on his way back from the "thrilla in Manila" against Joe Frazier. While he was there, the world's newspapers headlined the scandal involving Ali's abandonment of his Muslim wife in favor of a younger woman. He appeared on a talk show upon his return and was asked about the inconsistencies between his views in PLAYBOY and his behavior in Manila. He chose not to explain his romantic entanglement, and instead denounced the interview, claiming the answers were fabricated. PLAYBOY's editors and interviewer Linderman counterpunched by sending Ali a message that his remarks were on tape, and both the denials and the scandal died down.

As for other reactions to the 1975 interview, Ali did not endear himself to the world's Catholics when he delivered this religious opinion: "A priest saying he'd never touch a woman—that's against nature. What's he gonna do at night? Call upon the hand of the Lord?"

All in all, it was an interview the garrulous Ali probably wished he had passed up. But it was great fun to read.

First Interview, 1964

It wasn't until 9:55 on a night last February that anyone began to take seriously the extravagant boasts of Cassius Marcellus Clay: That was the moment when the redoubtable Sonny Liston, sitting dazed and disbelieving on a stool in Miami Beach's Convention Hall, resignedly spat out his mouthpiece—and relinquished the world's heavyweight boxing championship to the brash young braggart whom he, along with the nation's sportswriters and nearly everyone else, had dismissed as a loudmouthed pushover.

Leaping around the ring in a frenzy of glee, Clay screamed, "I am the greatest! I am the king!"—the strident rallying cry of a campaign of self-celebration, punctuated with rhyming couplets predicting victory, which had rocketed him from relative obscurity as a 1960 Olympic Gold

Medal winner to dubious renown as the "villain" of a title match with the least lovable heavyweight champion in boxing history. Undefeated in 100 amateur fights and all 18 professional bouts, the cocky 22-year-old had become, if not another Joe Louis, at least the world's wealthiest poet (with a purse of $600,000), and one of its most flamboyant public figures.

Within 24 hours of his victory, he also became sports' most controversial cause célèbre when he announced at a press conference that he was henceforth to be billed on fight programs only as Muhammad Ali, his new name as a full-fledged member of the Black Muslims, the militant nationwide Negro religious cult that preaches racial segregation, black supremacy and unconcealed hostility toward whites.

Amidst the brouhaha that ensued—besieged by the world press, berated by more temperate Negro leaders, threatened with the revocation of his title—Cassius preened and prated in the limelight, using his world-wide platform as a pulpit for hymns of self-adulation and sermons on the virtues of Islam. Still full of surprises, he then proceeded to appoint himself as an international goodwill ambassador and departed with an entourage of six cronies on an 8000-mile tour of Africa and the Middle East, where he was received by several heads of state (including Ghana's Nkrumah and Egypt's Nasser), and was accorded, said observers, the warmest reception ever given an American visitor.

We approached the mercurial Muslim with our request for a searching interview about his fame, his heavyweight crown and his faith. Readily consenting, he invited us to join him on his peripatetic social rounds of New York's Harlem, where he rents a three-room suite at the Hotel Theresa (in which another celebrated guest, Fidel Castro, hung his hat and plucked his chickens during a memorable visit to the UN).

For the next two weeks, we walked with him on brisk morning constitutionals, ate with him at immaculate Muslim restaurants (no pork served), sat with him during his daily shoeshine, rode with him in his chauffeured, air-conditioned Cadillac limousine on leisurely drives through Harlem. We interjected our questions as the opportunities presented themselves—between waves and shouts exchanged by the champion and ogling pedestrians, and usually over the din of the limousine's dashboard phonograph, blaring Clay's recording of "I Am the Greatest." We began the conversation on our own blaring note.

PLAYBOY: Are you really the loudmouthed exhibitionist you seem to be, or is it all for the sake of publicity?

CLAY: I been attracting attention ever since I been able to walk and talk. When I was just a little boy in school, I caught onto how nearly everybody likes to watch somebody that acts different. Like, I wouldn't ride the school bus, I would *run* to school alongside it, and all the kids would be waving and hollering at me and calling me nuts. It made me somebody special. Or at recess time, I'd start a fight with somebody to draw a crowd. I always liked drawing crowds. When I started fighting serious, I found out that grown people, the fight fans, acted just like those school kids. Almost from my first fights, I'd bigmouth to anybody who would listen about what I was going to do to whoever I was going to fight, and people would go out of their way to come and see, hoping I would get beat. When I wasn't no more than a kid fighter, they would put me on bills because I was a drawing card, because I run my mouth so much. Other kids could battle and get all bloody and lose or win and didn't hardly nobody care, it seemed like, except maybe their families and their buddies. But the minute I would come in sight, the people would start to hollering "Bash in his nose!" or "Button his fat lip!" or something like that. You would have thought I was some well-known pro ten years older than I was. But I didn't care what they said, long as they kept coming to see me fight. They paid their money, they was entitled to a little fun.

PLAYBOY: How did your first fight come about?

CLAY: Well, on my twelfth birthday, I got a new bicycle as a present from my folks, and I rode it to a fair that was being held at the Columbia Gymnasium, and when I come out, my bike was gone. I was so mad I was crying, and a policeman, Joe Martin, come up and I told him I was going to whip whoever took my bike. He said I ought to take some boxing lessons to learn how to whip the thief better, and I did. That's when I started fighting. Six weeks later, I won my first fight over another boy twelve years old, a white boy. And in a year I was fighting on TV. Joe Martin advised me against trying to just fight my way up in clubs and preliminaries, which could take years and maybe get me all beat up. He said I ought to try the Olympics, and if I won, that would give me automatically a number-ten pro rating. And that's just what I did.

PLAYBOY: When did you hit upon the gimmick of reciting poetry?

CLAY: Somewhere away back in them early fights in Louisville, even before I went to the Olympics, I started thinking about the poetry. I told a newspaperman before a fight, "This guy must be done/I'll stop him in one." It got in the newspaper, but it didn't catch on then. Poetry didn't even catch on with *me* until a lot later, when I was getting ready to fight Archie Moore. I think the reason then was that *he* talked so much, I had to figure up something new to use on him. That was when I told different reporters, "Moore will go in four." When he *did* go down in four, just like I said, and the papers made so much of it, I knew I had stumbled on something good. And something else I found out was how it had bugged Archie Moore. Before the fight, some people got it to me that he was walking around and around in the Alexandria Hotel in Los Angeles, saying over and over, "He's not going to get me in no four, he's not going to get me in no four"—and the next thing he knew, he was getting up off the floor. I been making up things that rhyme for every fight since.

PLAYBOY: Your poetry has been described by many critics as "horrible." Do you think it is?

CLAY: I bet my poetry gets printed and quoted more than any that's turned out by the poem writers that them critics like. I don't pay no attention to no kind of critics about nothing. If they knew as much as they claim to about what they're criticizing, they ought to be doing that instead of just standing on the side lines using their mouth.

PLAYBOY: As your own best critic, what do you consider your finest poem?

CLAY: I don't know. The one the newspapers used the most, though, was the time I covered the water front with a poem I wrote before my fight with Doug Jones. I said, "Jones likes to mix/So I'll let it go six./If he talks jive/I'll cut it to five./And if he talks some more/I'll cut it to four./ And if he talks about me/I'll cut it to three./And if that don't do/I'll cut it to two./And if you want some fun/I'll cut it to one./And if he don't want to fight/He can stay home that night."

PLAYBOY: How often have you been right in predicting the round of a knockout?

CLAY: I ain't missed but twice. If you figure out the man you're up against, and you know what you can do, then you can pretty much do it whenever you get ready. Once I call the round, I plan what I'm going to do in the fight. Like, you take Archie Moore. He's a better fighter than Sonny Liston. He's harder to hit, the way he bobs and weaves, and he's smart. You get careless and he'll drop you. I guess he knows more tricks in the ring than anybody but Sugar Ray. But he was fat and forty-five, and he had to be looking for a lucky punch before he got tired.

PLAYBOY: In that fight, you were twenty and Moore was forty-five. It's often been said that you got to the top by beating a succession of carefully picked setups. What's your response?

CLAY: I didn't beat nobody that wasn't trying to beat me. I don't care who I fought fair and beat, but they said something was wrong. Archie Moore, yeah, they said he was an old man. Doug Jones, he was one of the toughest fights I ever had. He was one of them what-round calls that I missed. I had said just before the fight, "I'll shut the door on Jones in four," but it went the limit, ten rounds. When the judges and referee gave me the decision, everybody was calling it a fix. Then Henry Cooper in London, after he caught me in the fourth with a right that sent me through the ropes, I took him out in the fifth just like I had said I would; I had said, "It ain't no jive/Henry Cooper will go in five." But sure enough, people said that Cooper hadn't been in shape. I'm surprised they haven't been saying Liston was underage, or something, since I whipped *him* good.

PLAYBOY: To get back to Archie Moore for a moment: Do you give him any credit, as a master of self-promotion, for helping you develop your own ballyhoo technique?

CLAY: I learned a lot from the old man, yeah. He showed me some proof of what I had already figured out myself, that talking is a whole lot easier than fighting, and it was a way to get up fast. It's a shame he wasn't fighting big time when he was in his prime. It would have been like a young Satchel Paige in the big leagues. I picked up quick how the old man would talk up a fight to make a gate, how he'd talk it up that the guy he wanted next didn't want no part of him. But the big difference between the old man and me is I'm bigger and louder and better. He believed in whispering something to reporters for them to print—but I believe in yelling.

PLAYBOY: At what joint in your career did you first put this yelling technique into practice?

CLAY: Right after I had won the Olympic Gold Medal. One day, back home in Louisville, I was riding on a bus. I was reading a paper about Patterson and Ingemar Johansson. I didn't have no doubt I could beat either one of them, if I had a chance to fight them. But Machen, Folley, Jones and all of them other bums were standing in the way, and I decided I wasn't just about to stand around like them. I'd won the Olympic title, that was all in the papers, but hadn't nobody really heard of me, though, and they never would as long as I just sat thinking about it. Right there on that bus is where I figured I'd just open up my big mouth and start people listening and paying attention to me. Not just talking, but really screaming, and acting like some kind of a nut. That day was when I started out after getting in the ring with the champion.

PLAYBOY: Even though you never fought him officially, you did have a run-in of sorts with Ingemar Johansson, didn't you?

CLAY: Yeah. Boy, I sure made him mad! He hired me as his sparring partner in Miami, and by the end of the first round I had him pinned against the ropes, all shook up and very mad. And he hadn't put a glove on me at the end of the second round. You talk about somebody upset! He was so mad he wanted me to go to Palm Beach, where we could spar in private. Not me! I wanted the newspapermen to see me if I did anything great and sensational.

PLAYBOY: Do you feel that you could have beaten Johansson?

CLAY: I just finished telling you I did beat him. The only difference between that and a regular fight was that we had on headgear and we didn't have no big fight crowd, and I didn't have no contract.

PLAYBOY: After you had scored victories over Archie Moore, Charley Powell, Doug Jones and Henry Cooper, how did you go about your campaign to get a match with Liston?

CLAY: Well, the big thing I did is that until then, I had just been loudmouthing mostly for the *public* to hear me, to build up gates for my fights. I hadn't never been messing personally with whoever I was going to fight—and that's what I started when it was time to go after Liston. I had been studying Liston careful, all along, ever since he had come up in the rankings, and Patterson was trying to duck him. You know what Patterson was saying—that Liston had such a bad police record, and prison record and all that. He wouldn't be a good example for boxing like Patterson would—the pure, clean-cut American boy.

PLAYBOY: You were saying you had been studying Liston . . .

CLAY: Yeah. His fighting style. His strength. His punch. Like that—but that was just part of what I was looking at. Any fighter will study them things about somebody he wants to fight. The big thing for me was observing how Liston acted *out* of the ring. I read everything I could where he had been interviewed. I talked with people who had been around him, or had talked with him. I would lay in bed and put all of the things together and think about them, to try to get a good picture of how his mind worked. And that's how I first got the idea that if I would handle the thing right, I could use psychology on him—you know, needle him and work on his nerves so bad that I would have him beat before he ever got in the ring with me. And that's just what I did!

PLAYBOY: How?

CLAY: I mean I set out to make him think what I wanted him thinking: that all I was was some clown, and that he never would have to give a second thought to me being able to put up any real fight when we got to the ring. The more out of shape and overconfident I could get him to be, the better. The press, everybody—I didn't want nobody thinking nothing except that I was a joke. Listen here, do you realize that of all them ring "experts" on the newspapers, wasn't hardly one that wasn't as carried away with Liston's reputation as Liston was himself? You know what everybody was writing? Saying I had been winning my fights, calling the rounds, because I was fighting "nothing" fighters. Like I told you already, even with people like Moore and Powell and Jones and Cooper, the papers found some excuse; it never was that maybe I could fight. And when it come to Liston, they was all saying it was the end of the line for me. I might even get killed in there; he was going to put his big fist in my big mouth so far they was going to have to get doctors to pull it out, stuff like that. You couldn't read nothing else. That's how come, later on, I made them reporters tell me I was the greatest. They had been so busy looking at Liston's record with Patterson that didn't nobody stop to think about how it was making Liston just about a setup for me.

PLAYBOY: Would you elaborate?

CLAY: What made it even better for me was when Liston just half-trained for the Patterson rematch, and Patterson looked worse yet—and Liston signed to fight me, not rating me even as good as he did Patterson. He felt like he was getting ready to start off on some bum-of-the-month club like Joe Louis did. He couldn't see nothing at all to me but mouth. And you know

I didn't make no sound that wasn't planned to keep him thinking in that rut. He spent more time at them Las Vegas gambling tables than he did at the punching bag. He was getting fatter and flabbier every day, and I was steady hollering louder to keep him that way: "I'm going to skin the big bear!" . . . "I'm the greatest!" . . . "I'm so pretty I can't hardly stand to look at myself!" Like that. People can't stand a blowhard, but they'll always listen to him. Even people in Europe and Africa and Asia was hearing my big mouth. I didn't miss no radio or television show or newspaper I could get in. And in between them, on the street, I'd walk up to people and they'd tell one another about what "that crazy Cassius Clay" said. And then, on top of this, what the public didn't know was that every chance I got, I was needling Liston *direct.*

PLAYBOY: How?

CLAY: I don't see no harm in telling it now. The first time, it was right after Liston had bought his new home in Denver, and my buddies and me was driving from Los Angeles to New York in my bus. This was Archie Robinson, who takes care of business for me, and Howard Bingham, the photographer, and some more buddies. I had bought this used thirty-passenger bus, a 1953 Flexible—you know, the kind you see around airports. We had painted it red and white with WORLD'S MOST COLORFUL FIGHTER across the top. Then I had LISTON MUST GO IN EIGHT painted across the side right after Liston took the title. Anyway, this time, when we started out for New York, we decided it would be a good time to pay Liston a visit at his new house.

We had the address from the newspapers, and we pulled up in his front yard in the bus about three o'clock in the morning and started blowing: *"Oink! Oink! Oink! Oink!"* In other houses, lights went on and windows went up. You know how them white people felt about that black man just moved in there anyway, and we sure wasn't helping it none. People was hollering things, and got out with the headlights blazing and went up to Liston's door, just about as Liston got there. He had on nylon shorty pajamas. And he was mad. He first recognized Howard Bingham, the photographer, whom he had seen in Los Angeles. "What you want, black mother?" he said to Howard. I was standing right behind Howard, flinging my cane back and forth in the headlights, hollering loud enough for everybody in a mile to hear me, "Come on out of there! I'm going to whip you right now! Come on out of there and protect your home! If you don't come out of that door, I'm going to break it down!"

You know that look of Liston's you hear so much about? Well, he sure had it on standing in that door that night. Man, he was tore up! He didn't know what to do. He wanted to come out there after me, but he was already in enough troubles with the police and everything. And you know, if a man figures you're crazy, he'll think twice before he acts, because he figures you're liable to do *anything.* But before he could make up his mind, the police came rushing in with all their sirens going, and they broke it up, telling us we would be arrested for disturbing the peace if we didn't get out of there. So we left. You can bet we laughed all the way to New York.

PLAYBOY: What other direct confrontations did you have with Liston before the fight?

CLAY: Well, another time was just before we signed to fight. It was in Las Vegas. I was there to be on *David Brinkley's Journal,* and it didn't take me no time to find Liston at a gambling table. People was standing around watching him. He was shooting craps, and I walked up behind him and reached and took some of his chips. He turned around, and I said, "Man, you can't shoot dice!" But he was good-humored. Maybe it was because the people were watching, and maybe he was seeing me helping build up a gate for the fight we were about to sign for—or maybe he was *winning* something for a change. I don't know *what* it was that put him in good spirits, but I just kept right on him. I'd snatch up the dice from him. I could see I was beginning to get to him a little, but not enough. Finally, I had to shoot a loaded water pistol on him. That did it. But he still played it cool, trying to show the people he was trying to humor me. Naturally, the word had spread and people were piling around us. But then very suddenly, Liston *froze* me with that look of his. He said real quiet, "Let's go on over here," and he led the way to a table, and the people hung back. I ain't going to lie. This was the only time since I have known Sonny Liston that he really scared me. I just felt the power and the meanness of the man I was messing with. Anybody tell me about how he has fought cops and beat up tough thugs and all of that, I believe it. I saw that streak in him. He told me, "Get the hell out of here or I'll wipe you out."

PLAYBOY: What did you do?

CLAY: I got the hell out of there. I told you, he had really scared me.

PLAYBOY: Did you consider giving up your campaign to rattle him?

CLAY: Oh, no, I never did think about that. Soon as I got time to think about how he had reacted, I saw I had started for the first time to really get under his skin, and I made up my mind right then that by the time we got to Miami in training, I was going to have him so mad that he would forget everything he knew about fighting, just trying to kill me.

PLAYBOY: Was the scene you made at the airport, when Liston arrived in Miami, part of the plan?

CLAY: You know it. They were making such a big thing of his arriving, you would have thought the Cubans was landing. Well, I wasn't just about to miss *that*! Liston came down off the plane, all cool, and the press was ganged around waiting for an interview. That was when I rushed in the scene, hollering, "Chump! Big ugly bear! I'm going to whip you right now!" Stuff like that. Police were grabbing for me and holding me and I was trying to break loose, and finally I did. I could see I was really turning Liston on.

I got up close enough to him and he gave me that evil look again, but I wasn't even thinking about him. "Look, this clowning, it's not cute, and I'm not joking," he said. And I nearly threw a fit. "Joking? Why, you big chump, I'll whip you right here!" And people were grabbing me again, and somebody had rushed up one of them little VIP cars they have at airports. They got Liston, his wife and his bodyguard in it. Joe Louis and Jack Nilon were trying to calm things down. I saw the little car taking off down the tunnel. So I broke loose and took out after it. I was waving my cane, and hollering at Liston. In the tunnel, I guess he told the driver to stop, and he hopped off. Was he *mad*! He hollered, "Listen, you little punk, I'll punch you in the mouth—this has gone too far!" Then people was rushing in and hollering at both of us, and I was throwing off my coat and shouting, "Come on, chump, right here!" Finally Liston swung at me, and I ducked. He didn't know he'd had his preview of the fight right then.

PLAYBOY: Who won?

CLAY: I bet you it went on two hours before it really got settled. There weren't no more swings, but Joe Louis and Jack Nilon and the cops and bodyguards got Liston in the airport lounge, and they were guarding the doors to keep me out. I was banging my cane on the door, hollering, "Free! I'll fight you free!" I knew everybody inside could hear me. They couldn't hear nothing else *but* me. "Free! You think I'm jiving, chump? I'll fight you free, right here!"

PLAYBOY: And, of course, it was all an act?

CLAY: Completely—and it was also building the gate. At least, if it hadn't been for the reporters, it would have been a better gate. But right then I didn't want nobody in Miami, except at my camp, thinking I wasn't crazy. I didn't want nobody never thinking nothing about I had any fighting ability.

PLAYBOY: Why do you say that if it hadn't been for the reporters, the gate would have been better?

CLAY: They made people think that Liston was so mean and I was so nothing that they would be throwing away money to buy a ticket. There was over sixteen thousand seats in that Convention Hall, and it was only about half full. I read where the promoter, Bill MacDonald, lost something like three hundred thousand dollars. But he sure can't blame *me* for it. I was the one that let him get seat prices up as high as two hundred and fifty dollars. I was the first fighter who ever talked a fight into being bounced off Telstar to fifty nations. I got more publicity than any fight ever had. I'm colorful when I rumble. But the people listened to the so-called "experts." If they had listened to me, that Convention Hall would have been overflowing even if they had charged twice the prices.

PLAYBOY: But the reporters' attitudes, you have said, were in the best interests of your strategy.

CLAY: It's six of one and half a dozen of the other. They still made me mad. But, lookahere, I wasn't nearly about done with Liston yet. I mean, right up to the fight I was messing with him. Everybody in my camp carried canes and wore jackets with BEAR-HUNTING across the back. Guys from my camp went into Liston's camp, standing around, watching him training, until Liston quit to personally order them out. We put out the word that we was going to raid Liston's camp. He got so jumpy and under strain that every day, different reporters would come telling me, serious, "Stop angering that man—he will literally kill you!" It was music to my ears. It meant if he was that mad, he had lost all sense of reasoning. If he wasn't thinking nothing but killing me, he wasn't thinking fighting. And you got to think to fight.

PLAYBOY: The press was generally unimpressed with your workouts, and the Liston camp knew it. Was that part of your plan, too?

CLAY: You ain't so stupid. I made sure nobody but my people saw me *really* working out. If anybody else was around, I didn't do no more than go through motions. But look, I'm going to tell you where Liston really lost the fight. Or *when* he lost it. Every day we had been leaking word over there that we were going to pull our raid that day. The Liston people got to the mayor and the police, and we got cautioned that we'd be arrested if we did it. So we made a court case out of it. We requested legal permission to picket Liston's camp, but we were told that a city ordinance prevented carrying signs. We had paid, I remember, three hundred and twenty-five dollars for signs like BIG UGLY BEAR, BEAR-HUNTING SEASON, TOO PRETTY TO BE A FIGHTER, BEAR MUST FALL, and like that. So we taped the signs all over my bus. It wasn't no ordinance against signs on a bus. And we loaded the bus up with people from my camp, and screaming teen-age girls, and we drove over there and caused such a commotion that people left off from watching Liston train, and we heard he nearly had a fit. One of his men—I knew his name, but I guess I better not call it—even pulled a knife on Howard Bingham. Joe Louis run and asked the guy what in the world was the matter with him. But that's the day Liston lost. We heard he went to pieces. It wasn't long before the weigh-in, where they said *I* was the one went to pieces.

PLAYBOY: One doctor described your conduct at the weigh-in as "dangerously disturbed." Another said you acted "scared to death." And seasoned sportswriters used such terms as "hysterical" and "schizophrenic" in reporting your tantrum, for which you were find twenty-five hundred dollars. What was the real story?

CLAY: I would just say that it sounds like them doctors and sportswriters had been listening to each other. You know what they said and wrote them things for—to match in what they expected was about to happen. That's what I keep on telling you. If all of them had had their way, I wouldn't have been allowed in the ring.

PLAYBOY: Had you worked out a fight plan by this time?

CLAY: I figured out my strategy and announced it *months* before the fight: "Float like a butterfly, sting like a bee," is what I said.

PLAYBOY: We read that. But what specifically did you mean?

CLAY: To start with, I knew that Liston, overconfident as he was, and helped by reading what all of the newspapers were saying, he never was going to train to fight more than two rounds. I don't know if you happened to read it later that some of his handlers admitted, after the fight, that this was exactly what he did. So that was my guide how to train, to pace myself. You know, a fighter can condition his body to go hard certain rounds, then to coast certain rounds. Nobody can *fight* fifteen rounds. So I trained to fight the first two rounds, and to protect myself from getting hit by Liston. I knew that with the third, he'd start tiring, then he'd get worse every round. So I trained to coast the third, fourth and fifth rounds. I had two reasons for that. One was that I wanted to prove I had the ability to stand up to Liston. The second reason was that I wanted him to wear himself out and get desperate. He would be throwing wild punches, and missing. If I just did that as long as he lasted on his feet, I couldn't miss winning the fight on points. And so I conditioned myself to fight full steam from the sixth through the ninth round, if it lasted that long. I never did think it would go past nine rounds. That's why I announced I'd take him in eight. I figured I'd be in command by the sixth. I'd be careful—not get hit—and I'd cut him up and shake him up until he would be like a bull, just blind, and missing punches until he was nearly crazy. And I planned that some time in the eighth, when he had thrown some punch and left himself just right, I'd be all set, and I'd drop him.

Listen here, man, I *knew* I was going to upset the world! You know the only thing I was scared of? I was scared that some of them newspaper "experts" was going to quit praising Liston's big fists long enough to wake up and see what was just as clear as day to me and my camp; and if they printed it, that Liston's camp people might be able to get it into his skull. But I was lucky; that didn't happen. Them newspaper people couldn't have been working no better for me if I had been paying them.

PLAYBOY: Then the fight went about as you had planned?

CLAY: Almost. He came in there at two hundred and twenty pounds, and untrained to go more than two rounds, and as old as he is—too old—against a kid, and I didn't have an ounce of fat on me. And he didn't have *no* respect for me as a fighter. He was figuring on killing me inside of two rounds. He was a perfect setup. If you remember, I didn't throw many punches, but when I did, they made their mark. I have vicious combinations, and just like I had planned, I hurt his body and I closed his eyes.

PLAYBOY: But Liston did do you some damage, too.

CLAY: You don't expect to fight no fighter without getting hit sometime. But you don't want to get hurt bad, and knocked out—that's the point.

Yeah, he hit me some damaging punches. With all the talking I been doing, ain't nobody never heard me say Liston can't hit. He got me in the first with a right to the stomach. In the second, I made the mistake of getting maneuvered on the ropes, and he got in some good shots. And in the last of that second round, after I had cut his eye, he really staggered me there for a minute with a long, hard left. In fact, he did me more damage with that than any other punch. In the fifth, when that stuff—rosin, I guess it was—was in my eyes, and I couldn't see, he hit me with a good left hook to the head. But in the corner after that fifth round, the stuff pretty well washed out of my eyes. I could see again, and I was ready to carry the fight to Liston.

PLAYBOY: Tell us about the end of the fight.

CLAY: I was gaining my second wind now, as I had conditioned myself, to pace the fight, like I was telling you. My corner people knew it, and they were calling to me, "Get mad, baby!" They knew I was ready to go the next three rounds at top steam, and I knew I was going to make Liston look terrible. I hit him with eight punches in a row, until he doubled up. I remember thinking something like, "Yeah, you old sucker! You try to be so big and bad!" He was gone. He knew he couldn't last. It was the first time in the fight that I set myself flat-footed. I missed a right that might have dropped him. But I jabbed and jabbed at that cut under his eye, until it was wide open and bleeding worse than before. I knew he wasn't due to last much longer. Then, right at the end of the round, I rocked back his head with two left hooks.

I got back to my stool, and under me I could hear the press like they was gone wild. I twisted around and hollered down at the reporters right under me, "I'm gonna upset the world!" I never will forget how their faces was looking up at me like they couldn't believe it. I happened to be looking right at Liston when that warning buzzer sounded, and I didn't believe it when he spat out his mouthpiece. I just couldn't believe it—but there it was laying there. And then something just told me he wasn't coming out! I give a whoop and come off that stool like it was red hot. It's a funny thing, but I wasn't even thinking about Liston—I was thinking about nothing but that hypocrite press. All of them down there had wrote so much about me bound to get killed by the big fists. It was even rumors that right after the weigh-in I had been taken to the asylum somewhere, and another rumor that I had caught a plane and run off. I couldn't think about nothing but all that. I went dancing around the ring, hollering down at them reporters, "Eat your words! Eat! Eat!" And I hollered at the people, "I am the *king*!"

PLAYBOY: Despite your victory, the fight ended under a cloud of doubt about the genuineness of Liston's arm injury. What's your own opinion?

CLAY: Eight doctors said his arm was hurt. I ain't going to argue with no eight doctors' opinion. And I don't mean that I think nothing different at all. You take a man punching with the strength and force Liston has in a punch; if all he connects with is air—because wherever he hit, I wasn't there—then, yeah, I think it explains how he could have torn a muscle.

PLAYBOY: There was another controversy about the honesty of your failure to pass the three Army preinduction qualification tests that you took shortly after the fight. Any comment?

CLAY: The truth don't hurt nobody. The fact is I never was too bright in school. I just barely graduated. I had a D-minus average. I ain't ashamed of it, though. I mean, how much do school principals make a month? But when I looked at a lot of the questions they had on them Army tests, I just didn't know the answers. I didn't even know how to *start* after finding the answers. That's all. So I didn't pass. It was the Army's decision that they didn't want me to go in the service. They're the boss. I don't want to say no whole lot about it.

PLAYBOY: Was it embarrassing to be declared mentally unfit?

CLAY: I have said I am the greatest. Ain't nobody ever heard me say I was the smartest.

PLAYBOY: What is your feeling about the fact that your purse was withheld after the fight?

CLAY: I don't understand it. I'm not involved in any tax problems. How can they justify holding up my money? But let me tell you something: Money and riches don't mean nothing to me. I don't care nothing about being no rich individual. I'm not living for glory or for fame; all this is doomed for destruction. You got it today, tomorrow it's gone. I got bigger things on my mind than that. I got Islam on my mind.

PLAYBOY: Speaking of Islam, the National Boxing Association announced that it was considering the revocation of your heavyweight title because of your membership in the Black Muslims, which you announced just after the fight. Have you heard any official word on their decision?

CLAY: It just fizzled out. But until it did, the N.B.A. was going to condemn me, try me, sentence me and execute me, all by themselves. Ain't this country supposed to be where every man can have the religion he wants, even *no* religion if that's what he wants? It ain't a court in America that would take a man's job, or his title, because of his religious convictions. The Constitution forbids Congress from making any laws involving a man's religion. But the N.B.A. would take it on itself to take away my title—for what? What have I done to hurt boxing? I've *helped* boxing. I don't smoke, I don't drink, I don't bother with nobody. Ain't it funny they never said nothing about Liston? He's been arrested for armed robbery, beating up cops, carrying concealed weapons, and I don't know *what* all. And how come they didn't lift Gene Fullmer's title? He was a Mormon. His religion believes Negroes are inferior; they ban Negroes from membership. But I guess that's all right. The N.B.A. don't have no power noway. They can't stop nobody from fighting. And even if they could, it wouldn't matter, because I don't put that much value on no heavyweight crown anyway. Time was when I did, but that was before I found the religious convictions that I have. When I started getting attacked so bad because I am a Muslim, I had to decide, if it would come to me having to give up one or the other, what was most important to me, my religion or my fighting. I made up my mind that I could give up fighting and never look back. Because it's a whole pile of other ways I could make a living. Me being the world heavyweight champion feels very small and cheap to me when I put that alongside of how millions of my poor black brothers and sisters are having to struggle just to get their human rights here in America. Maybe God got me here for a sacrifice. I don't know. But I do know that God don't want me to do down for standing up.

PLAYBOY: What or who made you decide to join the Muslims?

CLAY: Nobody or nothing *made* me decide. I make up my mind for myself. In 1960, in Miami, I was training for a fight. It wasn't long after I had won the 1960 Olympic Gold Medal over there in Rome. Herb Liler was the fellow I was going to fight, I remember. I put him on the floor in four. Anyway, one day this Muslim minister came to meet me and he asked me wouldn't I like to come to his mosque and hear about the history of my forefathers. I never had heard no black man talking about no forefathers, except that they were slaves so I went to a meeting. And this minister started teaching, and the things he said really shook me up. Things like that we twenty million black people in America didn't know our true identities, or even our true family names. And we were the direct descendants of black men and women stolen from a rich black continent and brought here and stripped of all knowledge of themselves and taught to hate themselves and their kind. And that's how us so-called "Negroes" had come to be the only race among mankind that loved its enemies. Now, I'm the kind that catches on quick. I said to myself, listen here, this man's *saying* something! I hope don't nobody never hit me in the ring hard as it did when that brother minister said the Chinese are named after China, Russians after Russia, Cubans after Cuba, Italians after Italy, the English after England, and clear on down the line everybody was named for somewhere he could call home, except us. He said, "What country are we so-called 'Negroes' named for? *No* country! We are just a lost race." Well, *boom*! That really shook me up.

PLAYBOY: Was that when you joined the Muslims?

CLAY: Not right then, no. Before I joined, I attended a lot of mosque meetings in different places I went. I never did come out of a meeting not understanding something I hadn't known or even thought about before. Everywhere I looked, I started seeing things in a new light. Like, I remember right in our house back in Louisville, all the pictures on the walls were white people. Nothing about us black people. A picture of a white Jesus Christ. Now, what painter ever *saw* Jesus? So who says Jesus was white? And all my life, I had been seeing the black man getting his head whipped by the white man, and stuck in the white man's jails, and things like that. And myself, I had to admit that up to then, I had always hated being black, just like other Negroes, hating our kind, instead of loving one another. The more I saw and thought, the more the truth made sense to me. Whatever I'm for, I always have believed in talking it up, and the first thing you know I was in Muslim meetings calling out just like the rest, "Right, brother! Tell it, brother! Keep it coming!" And today my religion is Islam, and I'm proud of it.

PLAYBOY: How has it changed your life?

CLAY: In every way. It's pulled me up and cleaned me up as a human being.

PLAYBOY: Can you be more explicit?

CLAY: Well, before I became a Muslim, I used to drink. Yes, I did. The truth is the truth. And after I had fought and beat somebody, I didn't hardly go nowhere without two big, pretty women beside me. But my change is one of the things that will mark me as a great man in history. When you can live righteous in the hell of North America—when a man can control his life, his physical needs, his lower self, he elevates himself. The downfall of so many great men is that they haven't been able to control their appetite for women.

PLAYBOY: But you have?

CLAY: We Muslims don't touch a woman unless we're married to her.

PLAYBOY: Are you saying that you don't have affairs with women?

CLAY: I don't even kiss a woman. I'm ashamed of myself, but sometimes I've caught myself wishing I had found Islam about five years from now, maybe—with all the temptations I have to resist. But I don't even kiss none, because you get too close, it's almost impossible to stop. I'm a young man, you know, in the prime of life.

PLAYBOY: You mention temptations. What are they?

CLAY: All types of women—white women, too—make passes at me. Girls find out where I live and knock at the door at one and two in the morning. They send me their pictures and phone numbers, saying please just telephone them, they would like to meet me, do I need a secretary? I've even had girls come up here wearing scarves on their heads, with no make-up and all that, trying to act like young Muslim sisters. But the only catch is a Muslim sister never would do that.

PLAYBOY: Did you have any other religious affiliation before Muslim?

CLAY: When I was twelve years old, and didn't know what I was doing, I was baptized in the Centennial Baptist Church in Louisville.

PLAYBOY: Have you given up Christianity, then?

CLAY: The Christian religion has just been used to brainwash the black man here in America. It has just taught him to look for his heaven in the sky, in the hereafter, while the white man enjoys his heaven here on earth.

PLAYBOY: As the owner of four Cadillacs and the recipient of a six-hundred-thousand-dollar purse earned largely from white patronage of your fight with Liston, do you think that assertion is entirely true in your own case?

CLAY: Have you heard anybody complaining he didn't get his money's worth? No! All of the noise is about my religion, something that has nothing to do with fighting. They didn't mind my being champion until they found out I was a Muslim. Then they didn't want nothing to do with me. White people, they worry more about Islam than they do about the championship.

PLAYBOY: Don't you feel that whites have some reason for concern that the heavyweight champion belongs to an organization that is alleged to teach hatred of whites?

CLAY: Look, the black man that's trying to integrate, he's getting beat up and bombed and shot. But the black man that says he don't want to integrate, he gets called a "hate teacher." Looka-here, now Chubby Checker is catching hell with a white woman. And I'm catching hell for *not* wanting a white woman. The followers of Mr. Elijah Muhammad, we're not trying to marry no white man's sisters and daughters. We're not trying to force our way into no white neighborhoods. It looks like to me that the white people who are so against integrated schools and restaurants and hotels ought to be *glad* about what Mr. Muhammad is teaching his followers. The only way for peace between the races is a separation of the races.

PLAYBOY: Are you against the Civil Rights Act, then?

CLAY: I think that the Civil Rights Act will lead to bloodshed. It already has. It won't change people's hearts. But I don't call it hate. I call it human nature. I don't think that white people hate colored people. You just don't never see a rabbit eating with a lion. I think that all of this "integration" started backfiring when it put the white man on the spot. It ain't going to go on much further. I think that the black man needs to get together with his own kind. He needs to say, "Let's don't go where we're not wanted." You take Sonny Liston. He was the champion of the world, and that's supposed to include America. But when he tried to buy a house in a segregated neighborhood in Miami, he was turned down. The white people don't want integration: I don't believe in forcing it and the Muslims don't either.

PLAYBOY: Is that why you've chosen to live in Harlem?

CLAY: Right. I could be living all exclusive, downtown, in some skyscraper hotel. I could be living right up in the hotel's penthouse, with my friends in rooms all around me. But I don't want none of that. I stay right in the heart of Harlem, in a place that a workingman with a good job could afford. I'm just used to being around my own people. I like being around my own people.

PLAYBOY: What do you have to say about the fact that many Negroes, including several Negro leaders, have said that they have no desire to be identified with a heavyweight champion who is a Black Muslim?

CLAY: It's ridiculous for Negroes to be attacking somebody trying to stand up for their own race. People are always telling me "what a good example I could set for my people" if I just wasn't a Muslim. I've heard over and over how come I couldn't have been like Joe Louis and Sugar Ray. Well, they're gone now, and the black man's condition is just the same, ain't it? We're still catching hell. The fact is that my being a Muslim moved me from the sports pages to the front pages. I'm a whole lot bigger man than I would be if I was just a champion prizefighter. Twenty-four hours a day I get offers—to tour somewhere overseas, to visit colleges, to make speeches. Places like Harvard and Tuskegee, television shows, interviews, recordings. I get letters from all over. They are addressed to me in ways like "The Greatest Boxer in the World, U.S.A." and they come straight to me wherever they're mailed from. People want to write books about me. And I ought to have stock in Western Union and cable companies, I get so many of them. I'm trying to show you how I been elevated from the normal stature of fighters to being a world figure, a leader, a statesman.

PLAYBOY: Statesman?

CLAY: That's what I said. Listen, after I beat Liston, some African diplomats invited me to the United Nations. And because I'm a Muslim, I was welcomed like a king on my tour of Africa and the Middle East. I'm the first world champion that ever toured the world that he is champion of.

PLAYBOY: Your Muslim activities will soon have to be interrupted long enough to defend your title against Sonny Liston in your upcoming rematch. Now that he's familiar with your strategy and skills, do you think he'll be a tougher opponent?

CLAY: I know one thing: He would have to think he could put up a better fight than he did the last time. Liston has been through quite a bit.

PLAYBOY: Do *you* think he'll put up a better fight?

CLAY: Maybe, but I'll have the edge again. Liston will be fighting a comeback. He'll be in the position of having to *prove* he can beat me. So he'll come in that ring scared he's going to lose. A lot of people still refuse to accept it, but Liston *knows* he was whipped by a better boxer. Another thing, don't never forget that boxing is for young men. How old is Liston?

PLAYBOY: According to published reports, around thirty-two.

CLAY: Well, I hear he's pushing forty. He ain't physically *capable* of forcing a body that old through four and a half months of the strong training a fighter would need to meet a young, strong fighter like me.

PLAYBOY: How about Patterson? Do you think he has a chance to regain his title a second time?

CLAY: Patterson! Don't make me laugh. I'm a natural heavyweight, and he was never anything but a blown-up light-heavy. He could never take my punches. I could play with him, cut him up and take him out whenever

I got ready. And he knows it. That's why he always ducked me when he was champ. He ain't no fool. You know, at the Olympic games in Rome, I told Patterson, "Two, three years from now, I'm going to take your title." He said, "You're a good kid, keep trying, kid." Well, I bet you he has since thought that over many a day.

PLAYBOY: If he knows he couldn't beat you, how do you explain his recent campaign to meet you in a title match?

CLAY: Only reason he's decided to come out of his shell now is to try and make himself a big hero to the white man by saving the heavyweight title from being held by a Muslim. I wish you would print for Patterson to read that if he ever convinces my managers to let him in the same ring with me, it's going to be the first time I ever trained to develop in myself a brutal killer instinct. I've never felt that way about nobody else. Fighting is just a sport, a game to me. But Patterson I would want to beat to the floor for the way he rushed out of hiding after his last whipping, announcing that he wanted to fight me because no Muslim deserved to be the champ. I never had no concern about his having the Catholic religion. But he was going to jump up to fight me to be the white man's champion. And I don't know no sadder example of nobody making a bigger fool of himself.

PLAYBOY: Are you the greatest now fighting, or the greatest in boxing history?

CLAY: Now, a whole lot of people ain't going to like this. But I'm going to tell you the truth—you asked me. It's too many great old champions to go listing them one by one. But ain't no need to. I think that Joe Louis, in his prime, could have whipped them all—I mean anyone you want to name. And I would have beat Louis. Now, look—people don't like to face the facts. All they can think about is Joe Louis' punch. Well, he did have a deadly punch, just like Liston has a deadly punch. But if Louis didn't hit nothing but air, like Liston didn't with me, then we got to look at other things. Even if Louis did hit me a few times, remember they all said Liston was a tougher one-punch man than even Joe Louis. And I took some of Liston's best shots. Remember that. Then, too, I'm taller than Louis. But I tell you what would decide the fight: I'm *faster* than Louis was. No, Louis and none of the rest of them couldn't whip me. Look—it ain't *never* been another fighter like me. Ain't never been no *nothing* like me.

Second Interview, 1975

As we go to press, Muhammad Ali is in training for his third match with Joe Frazier, slated for Manila; whether or not he retains his title will be known by the time this issue appears. But whatever the outcome, interviewer

Lawrence Linderman feels "they ought to retire the title with Ali, anyway." So, without further ado, we're pleased to introduce a man who needs no introduction.

PLAYBOY: The last time we interviewed you, 11 years ago, you were still Cassius Clay. What would the old Cassius be doing today?

ALI: Cassius Clay would now be training in Paris, France, because French promoters would've offered me—like they've done—free rooms in a hotel on some beach. If not, I'd probably be in Jamaica, training in a plush hotel. When I see a lady now, I do my best to try to teach her about the Honorable Elijah Muhammad so I can help her. Cassius Clay would carry her to some hotel room and use her.

If I was Cassius Clay today, I'd be just like Floyd Patterson. I'd probably have a white wife and I wouldn't represent black people in no way. Or I'd be like Charley Pride, the folk singer. Nothin' bad about him—he's a good fella and I met his black wife, but Charley stays out of controversy. It's not only him, because I could name Wilt Chamberlain and others who just don't get involved in struggle or racial issues—it might jeopardize their position. I'd be that kind of man.

If I was Cassius Clay *tonight*, I'd probably be staying in a big hotel in New York City, and I might say, "Well, I got time to have a little fun. I'm going out to a big *discothèque* full of white girls and I'll find the prettiest one there and spend the night with her."

PLAYBOY: Is that what Cassius Clay used to do?

ALI: I was on my way to it.

PLAYBOY: You never got there?

ALI: Before I was a Muslim, I had one white girlfriend for two days, that's all. I wasn't no Muslim then, but I just felt it wasn't right. I *knew* it wasn't right, 'cause I had to duck and hide and slip around, and I thought, "Man, it's not *worth* all this trouble." Black men with white women just don't *feel* right. They may think it's all right, and that they're in love, but you see 'em walking on the street and they're ashamed—they be duckin' and they be cold. They're not *proud*. Once you get a knowledge of yourself, you see how stupid that is. I don't even think about nothin' like that, chasing white women. I'm married and in love with a pretty black one. But if I wasn't, I'd run after the next pretty black girl I saw.

PLAYBOY: Let's change the subject. Since a lot of people are wondering about this, level with us: Do you write all the poetry you pass off as your own?

ALI: Sure I do. Hey, man, I'm so good I got offered a professorship at

Oxford. I write late at night, after the phones stop ringin' and it's quiet and nobody's around—all great writers do better at night. I take at least one nap during the day, and then I get up at two in the morning and do my thing. You know, I'm a worldly man who likes people and action and I always liked cities, but now when I find myself in a city, I can't wait to get back to my training camp. Neon signs, traffic, noise and people—all that can get you crazy. It's funny, because I was supposed to be torturing myself by building a training camp out in the middle of nowhere in northern Pennsylvania, but this is good livin'—fresh air, well water, quiet and country views. I thought I wouldn't like it at all but that at least I'd work a lot instead of being in the city, where maybe I wouldn't train hard enough. Well, now I like it better than being in *any* city. This is a real good setting for writin' poetry and I write all the time, even when I'm in training. But poems aren't the only thing I've been writing. I've also been setting my mind to sayings. You want to hear some?

PLAYBOY: Do we have a choice?

ALI: You listen up and maybe I'll make you as famous as I made Howard Cosell. "Wars on nations are fought to change maps, but wars on poverty are fought to map change." Good, huh? "The man who views the world at 50 the same as he did at 20 has wasted 30 years of his life." These are words of wisdom, so pay attention, Mr. PLAYBOY. "The man who has no imagination stands on the earth—he has no wings, he cannot fly." Catch this: "When we are right, no one remembers, but when we are wrong, no one forgets. Watergate!" I really like the next one: "Where is man's wealth? His wealth is in his knowledge. If his wealth was in the bank and not in his knowledge, then he don't possess it—because it's in the bank!" You got all that?

PLAYBOY: Got it, Muhammad.

ALI: Well, there's more. "The warden of a prison is in a worse condition than the prisoner himself. While the body of the prisoner is in captivity, the mind of the warden is in prison!" Words of wisdom by Muhammad Ali. This is about beauty: "It is those who have touched the inner beauty that appreciate beauty in all its forms." I'm even going to explain that to you. Some people will look at a sister and say, "She sure is ugly." Another man will see the same sister and say, "That's the most beautiful woman I ever did see."

How do you like *this* one: "Love is a net where hearts are caught like fish"?

PLAYBOY: Isn't that a little corny?

ALI: I knew you wasn't smart as soon as I laid eyes on you. But I know you're gonna like this one, which is called *Riding on My Horse of Hope*: "Holding in my hands the reins of courage, dressed in the armor of patience, the helmet of endurance on my head, I started on my journey to the land of love." Whew! Muhammad Ali sure goes deeper than *boxing*.

PLAYBOY: That's for sure. But let's talk about boxing anyway. What's the physical sensation of really being nailed by hitters like Foreman and Frazier?

ALI: Take a stiff tree branch in your hand and hit it against the floor and you'll feel your hand go *boingggggg.* Well, getting tagged is the same kind of jar on your whole body, and you need at least 10 or 20 seconds to make that go away. You get hit again before that, you got another *boingggggg.*

PLAYBOY: After you're hit that hard, does your body do what you want it to do?

ALI: No, because your mind controls your body and the moment you're tagged, you can't think. You're just numb and you don't know where you're at. There's no *pain,* just that jarring feeling. But I automatically know what to do when that happens to me, sort of like a sprinkler system going off when a fire starts up. When I get stunned, I'm not really conscious of exactly where I'm at or what's happening, but I always tell myself that I'm to dance, run, tie my man up or hold my head way down. I tell myself all that when I'm conscious, and when I get tagged, I automatically do it. I get hit, but all great fighters get hit—Sugar Ray got hit, Joe Louis got hit and Rocky Marciano got hit. But they had something other fighters didn't have: the ability to hold on until they cleared up. I got that ability, too, and I had to use it once in each of the Frazier fights. That's one reason I'm a great defensive fighter. The other is my rope-a-dope defense—and when I fought Foreman, he was the dope.

PLAYBOY: If you prepared that tactic for your fight with Foreman in Zaïre, then why was Angelo Dundee, your trainer, so shocked when you suddenly went to the ropes?

ALI: Well, I didn't really *plan* it. After the first round, I felt myself getting too tired for the pace of that fight, but George wasn't gonna get tired, 'cause he was just cutting the ring off on me. I stayed out of the way, but I figured that after seven or eight rounds of dancing like that, I'd be really tired. Then, when I'd go to the ropes, my resistance would be low and George would get one through to me. So while I was still fresh, I decided to go to the ropes and try to get George tired.

PLAYBOY: What was your original Foreman fight plan?

ALI: To dance every round. I had it in mind to do what I did when I was 22, but I got tired, so I had to change my strategy. George didn't change his strategy, 'cause he can't do nothin' but attack—that's the *only* thing he knows. All he wants to do is get his man in the corner, so in the second round, I gave him what he wanted. He couldn't do *nothin'!*

PLAYBOY: Did Foreman seem puzzled when he had you cornered but couldn't land any punches?

ALI: Nope, he just figured he'd get me in the next round. When he didn't do it in the third, he thought he'd get me in the fourth. Then he thought it would be the fifth, and then the sixth. But in the sixth round, George was so *tired*. All of a sudden, he knew he'd threw everything he had at me and hadn't hurt me at all. And he just lost all his heart.

PLAYBOY: How could you tell?

ALI: He stopped attacking the way he'd been doin'. He had shots to take and didn't take 'em, and then I purposely left him some openings and he wouldn't take *them*. George knew he'd been caught in my trap and there wasn't but one way he could get out of it: by knocking me out. He kept trying with his last hope, but he was too tired, and a man of his age and talent shouldn't get used up that quick. George was *dead* tired; he was throwing wild punches, missing and falling over the ropes. So I started tellin' him how bad he looked: "Lookatcha, you're not a champ, you're a tramp. You're fightin' just like a sissy. C'mon and *show* me somethin', boy."

PLAYBOY: You also called him all kinds of names before the fight. How does that help?

ALI: You mean when I called him The Mummy, 'cause he walks like one? Listen, if a guy loses his temper and gets angry, his judgment's off and he's not thinking as sharp as he should. But George wasn't angry. No, sir. George had this feeling that he was *supreme*. He believed what the press said—that he was unbeatable and that he'd whup me easy. The first three rounds, he still believed it. But when I started throwing punches at him in the fourth, George finally woke up and thought, "Man, I'm in trouble." He was *shocked*.

PLAYBOY: Do you think Foreman was so confident of beating you that he didn't train properly?

ALI: No, George didn't take me lightly. He fought me harder than he fought Frazier or Norton. *Whoever* I fight comes at me harder, because if you beat Muhammad Ali, you'll be the big man, the legend. Beating me is like beating Joe Louis or being the man who shot Jesse James. George just didn't realize how hard I am to hit and how hard I *can* hit. He thought he was greater than me. Well, George is humble now. I did just what I told him I'd do when the ref was giving us instructions. There was George, trying to scare me with his serious look—he got that from his idol, Sonny Liston. And there I was, tellin' him, "Boy, you in *trouble*! You're gonna meet the greatest fighter of all time! We here now and there ain't no way for you to get out of this ring—I *gotcha*! You been readin' about me ever since you were a little boy and now you gonna see me in action. Chump, I'm gonna show you how great I am—I'm gonna eat you up. You don't stand a *chance*! You lose the crown tonight!"

PLAYBOY: Did you like the idea of Zaïre as the fight site?

ALI: I wanted my title back so bad I would've fought George in a telephone booth. World heavyweight champion, that's a big title. When you're the champ, whatever you say or do is news. George would go to Las Vegas and the newspapers are writin' about it. I turn on the television and there's George. It was Foreman this and Foreman that, and I was sitting here in my Pennsylvania training camp, thinkin', "Dadgummit, I really had somethin'. People looked up to *me* that way." That really got me down and made me want to win that title *bad*.

Now that I got it back, every day is a sunshiny day: I wake up and I know I'm the heavyweight champion of the world. Whatever restaurant I walk into, whatever park I go to, whatever school I visit, people are sayin', "The *champ*'s here!" When I get on a plane, a man is always sayin' to his little boy, "Son, there goes the heavyweight champion of the world." Wherever I go, the tab is picked up, people want to see me and the TV wants me for interviews. I can eat all the ice cream, cake, pudding and pie I want to and still get $100,000 for an exhibition. That's what it means to be champ, and as long as I keep winning, it'll keep happenin'. So before I fight, I think, "Whuppin' this man means everything. So many good things are gonna happen if I win I can't even imagine what they'll *be*!"

When I first won the championship from Sonny Liston, I was riding high and I didn't realize what I had. Now, the second time around, I appreciate the title, and I would've gone anywhere in the world to get it back. To be honest, when I first heard the fight would be in Africa, I just hoped it would go off right, being in a country that was supposed to be so undeveloped. Then, when we went down to Zaïre, I saw they'd built a new stadium with lights and that everything would be ready, and I started getting used to the idea and liking it. And the more I thought about it, the more it grew on me, and then one day it just hit me how *great* it would be to win back my title in Africa. Being in Zaïre opened my eyes.

PLAYBOY: In what way?

ALI: I saw black people running their own country. I saw a black president of a humble black people who have a modern country. There are good roads throughout Zaïre and Kinshasa has a nice downtown section that reminds you of a city in the States. Buildings, restaurants, stores, shopping centers— I could name you 1000 things I saw that made me feel good. When I was in training there before the fight, I'd sit on the riverbank and watch the boats going by and see the 747 jumbo jets flying overhead, and I'd know there were black pilots and black stewardesses in 'em, and it just seemed so nice. In Zaïre, *everything* was black—from the train drivers and hotel owners to the teachers in the schools and the pictures on the money. It was just like any other society, except it was all black, and because I'm black oriented and a Muslim, I was *home* there. I'm not home *here*. I'm trying to make it home, but it's not.

PLAYBOY: Why not?

ALI: Because black people in America will never be free so long as they're on the white man's land. Look, birds want to be free, tigers want to be free, everything wants to be free. We can't be free until we get our own land and our own country in North America. When we separate from America and take maybe ten states, then we'll be free. Free to make our own laws, set our own taxes, have our own courts, our own judges, our own schoolrooms, our own currency, our own passports. And if not here in America, the Honorable Elijah Muhammad said the white man should supply us with the means to let us go back somewhere in Africa and build up our own country. America, rich as it is, was made rich partly through the black man's labor. It can afford to supply us for 25 years with the means to make our own nation work, and we'll build it up, too. We can't be free if we can't control our own land. I own this training camp, but it ain't really *my* land, not when some white lady comes up and gives me a $4000 tax bill to pay if I want to stay here. If I thought the taxes I paid was really going to benefit my people, I wouldn't mind paying up. But that ain't what's happening. Black people need to have their own nation.

PLAYBOY: Since it's unlikely they'll get one carved out of—or paid for by—the U.S., are you pessimistic about America's future race relations?

ALI: America don't *have* no future! America's going to be destroyed! Allah's going to divinely chastise America! Violence, crimes, earthquakes—there's gonna be all *kinds* of trouble. America's going to pay for all its lynchings and killings of slaves and what it's done to black people. America's day is over—and if it doesn't do justice to the black man and separate, it gonna *burn*! I'm not the leader, so I can't tell you how the separation will take place or whether it will happen in my lifetime or not, but I believe there's a divine force that will make it happen.

PLAYBOY: Elijah Muhammad preached that all white men are blue-eyed devils. Do you believe that?

ALI: We know that every individual white ain't devil-hearted, and we got *black* people who are devils—the worst devils I've run into can be my own kind. When I think about white people, it's like there's 1000 rattlesnakes outside my door and maybe 100 of them want to help me. But they all look alike, so should I open my door and hope that the 100 who want to help will keep the other 900 off me, when only one bite will kill me? What I'm sayin' is that if there's 1000 rattlesnakes out there and 100 of them mean good—I'm still gonna shut my door. I'm gonna say, "I'm sorry, you nice 100 snakes, but *you don't really matter*."

Yeah, every Negro can say, "Oh, here's a white man who means right." But if that's true, where are the 25,000,000 whites standing next to the 25,000,000 blacks? Why can't you even get 100 of them together who are ready to stand up and fight and maybe even die for black freedom? Hey, we'd *look* if you did that.

PLAYBOY: Didn't white freedom riders of the Sixties—at least four of whom were murdered—demonstrate that many whites were ready to risk their lives for black civil rights?

ALI: Look, we been told there's gonna be whites who help blacks. And we also know there's gonna be whites who'll escape Allah's judgment, who won't be killed when Allah destroys this country—mainly some Jewish people who really mean right and do right. But we look at the situation as a whole. We *have* to. OK, think about a white student who's got long hair and who wants minority people to have something and so he's against the slave white rule. Well, other whites will beat his behind and maybe even kill him, because they don't want him helping us. But that doesn't change what happens to the black man. If white boys get beat up, am I supposed to say, "Oh, some white folks are good. Let's forget our whole movement and integrate and join up in America"?

Yes, a lot of these white students get hurt 'cause they want to help save their country. But listen, your great-granddaddy told my great-granddaddy that when *my* granddaddy got grown, things would be better. Then your granddaddy told my granddaddy that when *my* daddy was born, things would be better. Your daddy told my daddy that when *I* got grown, things would be better. But they ain't. Are you tellin' me that when *my* children get grown, things'll be better for black people in this country?

PLAYBOY: No, we're just trying to find out how you honestly feel about whites.

ALI: White people are good thinkers, man, but they're crazy. Whoever makes the commercials shown on Johnny Carson's TV show and whoever makes all them movies, well, they're smart, they're planners and they can rule the world. Mostly 'cause they always got a story to tell. Is Martin Luther King marching and causing trouble? OK, we'll let the blacks use the public toilets, but let's make 'em fight six months for it, and while they're fighting, we'll make another plan. They wanna come in the supermarket next week? OK, let's make 'em fight two years for that. Meanwhile, we're still trying to get into schools in *Boston*, of all places. I'm telling you, the same men who write movies *must* be writing these plans. It's like, OK, the airlines will give jobs to a few black pilots and black stewardesses—but by the time they're finally hired, white folks are on the moon in *spaceships*.

If I could be President of the U.S. tomorrow and do what I can to help my people or be in an all-black country of 25,000,000 Negroes and my job would be to put garbage in the truck, I'd be a garbageman. And if that included not just me but also my children and all my seed from now till forever, I'd still rather have the lowest job in a black society than the highest in a white society. If we got our own country, I'd empty trash ahead of being President of the U.S.—or being Muhammad Ali, the champion.

PLAYBOY: You've earned nearly $10,000,000 in fight purses in the past two years alone. Would you really part with all your wealth so easily?

ALI: I'd do it in a minute. Last week, I was out taking a ride and I thought, "I'm driving this Rolls-Royce and I got another one in the garage that I hardly ever use that cost $40,000. I got a Scenicruiser Greyhound bus that sleeps 14 and cost $120,000 and another bus that cost $42,000—$162,000 just in mobile homes. My training camp cost $350,000 and I just spent $300,000 remodeling my house in Chicago. I got all that and a lot more."

Well, I was driving down the street and I saw a little black man wrapped in an old coat standing on a corner with his wife and little boy, waiting for a bus to come along—and there I am in my Rolls-Royce. The little boy had holes in his shoes and I started thinkin' that if he was *my* little boy, I'd break into tears. And I started crying.

Sure, I know I got it made while the masses of black people are catchin' hell, but as long as they ain't free, *I* ain't free. You think I need to hire all people I do to help me get in shape? Listen, I can go down to Miami Beach with my cook and my sparring partners and get three hotel rooms and live it up—and I'd save money. I spent $850,000 training for George Foreman, most of it employing the few black people I could. In two months of training for Chuck Wepner, I spent $30,000. I wasn't doing it for me. See, once you become a Muslim, you want for your brother what you want for yourself. Being a Muslim wakes you up to all kinds of things.

PLAYBOY: Such as?

ALI: Black people in America never used to know that our religion was Islam or that Jesus was a black man—we always made him white. We never knew we were the original people. We thought black was bad luck. We never thought that Africans would own their own countries again and that they were our brothers. God is white, but we never knew that the proper name of God is Allah—and Allah ain't white. We never even knew our names, because in slavery we were named what our white masters were named. If our master's name was Robinson, we were Robinson's property. If they sold you to Jones, you were Jones's property. And if you were then auctioned off to Mr. Williams, you were Williams' property. So we got identified by our masters' names. Well, today there's no chains on us, yet we still got names like George *Washington*. But as we wake up, we want our own beautiful names back. If a black man and woman have their first son, name him somethin' pretty like Ahad, which means the beginning.

See how our teaching wakes you up? And not only are our names beautiful, they also have beautiful meanings.

PLAYBOY: What does *your* name mean?

ALI: Muhammad means worthy of all praises, Ali means the most high. And a lot of brothers today are doing like me and giving up their old slave name and taking new first and last names, nice-soundin' ones like Hassan Sharif or Kareem Shabazz. Those *were* our names before we were brought over here and named after George Washington. It's important we get them back, too, because if black folks don't know God's name, which is Allah, or their own name, they're starting too far behind. So the first step is to get out of that old slave name and start you a new family name—every time I hear about another black family doin' that, I get happier and happier. And if you know truth when *you* hear it, then you know how joyful I am to be a Muslim.

PLAYBOY: Will you assume a place in the Muslim movement when your boxing career is over?

ALI: Yes, sir. If I'm blessed to and they allow me, I'm gonna be a minister. I'm goin' to work with our new spiritual leader, brother Wallace D. Muhammad, son of Elijah Muhammad.

PLAYBOY: How has Elijah Muhammad's death affected the Black Muslims?

ALI: Naturally, it was saddening, because it's bad to lose him physically, but if we should lose him in ourselves, that's worse. So we just have to keep pushing, and we now follow his son, who's taking up just where his father left off. And we're 100 percent behind him. We were taught by Elijah Muhammad not to fear or grieve, and we don't.

You've seen the peace and unity of my training camp—it's all Elijah Muhammad's spirit and his teachings. Black people never acted like this before. If every one of us in camp was just like we were before we heard Elijah Muhammad, you wouldn't be able to see for all the smoke. You'd hear things like, "Hey, man, what's happenin', where's the *ladies*? What we gonna *drink* tonight? Let's get that music on and *party!*" And hey, this isn't an Islamic center. We're *happy* today. And we're better off than if we talked Christianity and said, "Jesus loves you, brother, Jesus died for your sins, accept Jesus Christ."

PLAYBOY: You find something wrong with that?

ALI: Christianity is a good philosophy if you live it, but it's controlled by white people who preach it but don't practice it. They just organize it and use it any which way they want to. If the white man lived Christianity, it would be different; but I tell you, I think it's against *nature* for European people to live Christian lives. Their nations were founded on killing, on wars. France, Germany, the bunch of 'em—it's been one long war ever since they existed. And if they're not killing each other over there, they're shooting Indians over here. And if they're not after the Indians, they're after the reindeer and every other living thing they can kill, even elephants. It's always violence and war for Christians.

Muslims, though, live their religion—*we* ain't hypocrites. We submit entirely to Allah's will. We don't eat ham, bacon or pork. We don't smoke. And everybody knows that we honor our women. You can see our sisters on the street from ten miles away, their white dresses dragging along the ground. Young women in this society parade their bodies in all them freak clothes—miniskirts and pants suits—but our women don't wear them. A woman who's got a beautiful body covers it up and humbles herself to Allah and also turns down all the modern conveniences. Nobody else do that but Muslim women. You hear about Catholic sisters—but they do a lot of screwing behind doors. Ain't nobody gonna believe a woman gonna go all her life and say, "I ain't never had a man," and is happy. She be *crazy*. That's against nature. And a priest saying he'd never touch a woman—

that's against nature, too. What's he gonna do at night? Call upon the hand of the Lord?

PLAYBOY: Catholic readers will no doubt provide you with an answer, but, meanwhile, perhaps you could tell us why restrictions on Muslim women are far more stringent than upon Muslim men.

ALI: Because they should be. Women are sex symbols.

PLAYBOY: To whom?

ALI: To me.

PLAYBOY: And aren't you a sex symbol to women?

ALI: Still, men don't walk around with their chests out. Anyway, I'd rather see a man with his breasts showing than a woman. Why should she walk around with half her titties out? There gotta be restrictions that way.

PLAYBOY: But why should men formulate those restrictions?

ALI: Because in the Islamic world, the man's the boss and the woman stays in the background. She don't *want* to call the shots.

PLAYBOY: We can almost hear women's liberation leaders saying, "Sisters, you've been brainwashed. You should control your *own* lives."

ALI: Not Muslim women—Christian women. Muslim women don't think like that. See, the reason we so powerful is that we don't let the white man control *our* women. They obey *us*. And when a Muslim girl becomes a woman, she don't *want* to walk around with her behind hanging out. Horses and dogs and mules walk around with their behinds out. Humans hide their behinds.

PLAYBOY: Are Muslim women allowed to have careers or are they supposed to stay in the kitchen?

ALI: A lot of 'em got careers, working for and with their brothers, but you don't find 'em in no white man's office in downtown New York working behind secretarial desks. Too many black women been *used* in offices. And not even in bed—on the floor. We know it because we got office Negroes who've told us this. So we protect our women, 'cause women are the field that produces our nation. And if you can't protect your women, you can't protect your nation. Man, I was in Chicago a couple of months ago and saw a white fella take a black woman into a motel room. He stayed with her two or three hours and then walked out—and a bunch of brothers saw it and didn't even *say* nothin'. They should have thrown rocks at his car or kicked down the door while he was in there screwing her—do *something* to let him know you don't like it. How can you be a man when another man can come get your woman or your daughter or your sister—and take her to a room and screw her—and, nigger, you don't even *protest*?

But nobody touches our women, white *or* black. Put a hand on a Muslim sister and you are to *die*. You may be a white or black man in an elevator with a Muslim sister and if you pat her on the behind, you're supposed to die right there.

PLAYBOY: You're beginning to sound like a carbon copy of a white racist. Let's get it out front: Do you believe that lynching is the answer to interracial sex?

ALI: A black man *should* be killed if he's messing with a white woman. And white men have always done that. They lynched niggers for even looking at a white woman; they'd call it reckless eyeballing and bring out the rope. Raping, patting, mischief, abusing, showing our women disrespect—a man should die for that. And not just white men—black men, too. We will kill you, and the brothers who don't kill you will get their behinds whipped and probably get killed themselves if they let it happen and don't do nothin' about it. Tell it to the President—*he* ain't gonna do nothin' about it. Tell it to the FBI: We'll kill anybody who tries to mess around with our women. Ain't *nobody* gonna bother them.

PLAYBOY: And what if a Muslim woman wants to go out with non-Muslim blacks—or white men, for that matter?

ALI: Then *she* dies. Kill her, too.

PLAYBOY: Are Muslim women your captives?

ALI: Hey, our women don't want no white men, period. Can you picture me, after what I been talking and thinking, wanting a white woman? Muslims think about 300 years of slavery and lynching, and you think we want to *love* our slave masters? No *way* we think about that. And no, our women aren't captives. Muslim women who lose their faith are free to leave. I'm sure that if all the black men and women who started following Elijah Muhammad were still with us, we'd have an easy 10,000,000 followers. That many came through the doors but didn't stay. They free to go if they want to.

PLAYBOY: If all the blacks in America became Muslims by the end of the year, what do you think would happen as a result?

ALI: President Ford would call our leaders to the White House and negotiate about what states he wants to give us or what country we want to be set up in. Can you imagine 25,000,000 Negroes all feeling the way I do? There'd be nothing you could do with them but let 'em go.

PLAYBOY: "Let 'em go" doesn't mean handing over a group of states to Muslim religious leaders.

ALI: Maybe, maybe not. You could rope off Georgia, Alabama, Tennessee, Kentucky, we could go in there and live, and whites could have passports to come in, do business and leave. Or a mass exodus from America. I wish I can see it before I die. Let me ask *you* something.

PLAYBOY: Shoot.

ALI: You think I'm as pretty as I used to me? I was *so* pretty. Somebody took some pictures of me and they're in an envelope here, so let me stop talking for a few seconds, 'cause I want you to take a look at 'em. . . .

Hey, I'm *still* pretty! What a wonderful face! Don't I look *good* in these pictures? I can see I gotta stay in shape if I want to stay pretty, but that's so *hard*. I've been fighting for 21 years and just *thinkin'* about it makes me tired. I ain't 22 anymore—I'm 33 and I can't fight like I did eight or ten years ago. Maybe for a little while, but I can't keep it up. I used to get in a ring and dance and jump and hop around for the whole 15 rounds. Now I can only do that for five or six, and then I have to slow down and rest for the next two or three rounds. I might jump around again in the 11th and 12th rounds, or I might even go the whole rest of the fight like I used to, but I have to work much more to be able to do it now; weight is harder to get off and it takes more out of me to lose it. That means getting out every day and running a couple of miles, coming into the gym and punching the bags four days a week and eatin' the right foods. But I like to eat the *wrong* foods. I'll go to a coffee shop and order a stack of pancakes with strawberry preserves, blueberry preserves, whipped cream and butter, and then hit them hot pancakes with that good maple syrup and then drink a cold glass of milk. At dinnertime, I'll pull into a MacDonald's and order two big double cheeseburgers and a chocolate milk shake—and the next day I weigh ten pounds more. Some people can eat and not gain weight, but if I just *look* at food, my belly gets bigger. That's why, when I'm training, about all I eat is broiled steaks, chicken and fish, fresh vegetables and salads. I don't even get to *see* them other things I like.

PLAYBOY: How much longer do you intend to defend your title?

ALI: I'd like to give up the championship and retire today, but there's too many things I've got to do. We're taught that every Muslim has a burden to do as much as he can to help black people. Well, my burden is real big, for I'm the heavyweight champion and the most famous black man on the whole planet, so I got to do a whole lot. That's why I just bought a shopping center in a black part of Cleveland, Ohio, for $500,000. It's got room for 40 stores and we'll rent them out for just enough money to pay the upkeep and taxes—I'm not looking to make a quarter off it. That's gonna create jobs for black people. I'm also buying an A&P supermarket in Atlanta that will employ 150 black people. Then I'm going down to Miami, Florida, which doesn't have one nice, plush restaurant for black people; I'm goin' to get one built. You know, there used to be a sign along Miami Beach that said, NO JEWS ALLOWED. Well, the Jews got mad, united and bought up the whole damn beach. That's what *we* got to start doin'—uniting and pooling our money—and I hope to get black celebrities and millionaires behind me, because the Muslim movement is the onliest one that's really going to get our people together. I may be just one little black man with a talent for fightin', but I'm going to perform miracles: When black people with money see what I can do with my pennies, they'll begin to see what can be done with their millions.

People might read all this and say it's easy to talk, but I'm not just talkin'. You watch: I'm goin' to spend the next five years of my life takin' my fight money and settin' up businesses for the brothers to operate. That's the *only* reason why I'll hold on to my title.

PLAYBOY: Since you've already told us that age has been steadily eroding your skills, what makes you think you'll still be champion when you're 38?

ALI: Hey, Jersey Joe Walcott *won* his title when he was 37. Sugar Ray Robinson fought till he was in 40s and Archie Moore went until he was 51.

PLAYBOY: At which point you took him apart with ease. Would you want to wind up your career the same way?

ALI: Archie didn't end up hurt and he's still intelligent—in spite of thinking Foreman could beat me. Going five more years don't mean going till I'm 51, and I can do it just by slowing down my style. You also got to remember I spent three and a half years in exile, when they took away my title because I wouldn't be drafted. That's three and a half years less of tusslin', trainin' and fightin', and if not for all that rest, I don't think I'd be in the same shape I am today. Because of my age, I don't have all of those three and a half years coming to me, but I have *some* of them.

PLAYBOY: Was that period of enforced idleness a bitter part of your life?

ALI: I wasn't bitter at *all*. I had a good time speaking at colleges and meeting the students—whites, blacks and all kinds, but mainly whites, who supported me a hundred percent. They were as much against the Vietnam war as I was.

In the meantime, I was enjoying everything I was doin'. As a speaker, I was makin' $1500 and $2500 at every stop, and I was averaging $5000 a week, so I had money in my pocket. I was also puttin' pressure on the boxing authorities. I'd walk into fight arenas where contenders for my title were boxing and I'd interrupt everything, because I wanted to show everybody that I was still the Man. The people would jump up and cheer for me and the word soon got out that the authorities would have to reckon with me. When I won the Supreme Court decision and they had to let me go back to work, a lot of people came around saying, "Why don't you sue the boxing commission for unjustly taking your title away?" Well, they only did what they thought was right and there was no need for me to try to punish them for that. It's just too bad they didn't recognize that I was sincere in doing what *I* thought was right at the time.

PLAYBOY: Did you receive a lot of hate mail during those years?

ALI: Only about one out of every 300 letters. And I kinda liked those, so I put 'em all away in a box. When I'm 90 years old, they'll be something to show my great-grandson. I'll tell him, "Boy, here's a letter your great-granddaddy got when he fought the draft way back when they had wars." Anyway, there's good and bad in every race. People got their own opinions and they free to talk.

PLAYBOY: Considering your feelings about white America, did it surprise you that so many whites agreed with your stand against the draft?

ALI: Yes, it did. I figured it would be worse and that I'd meet with a lot more hostility, but that didn't happen. See, that war wasn't like World War

Two or like America being attacked. I actually had a lot going for me at the time: The country was halfway against it, the youth was against it and the world was saying to America, "Get out." And there I was, among people who are slaves and who are oppressed by whites. I also had a platform, because the Muslim religion and the Koran preaches against such wars. I would've caught much more hell if America was in a declared war and I didn't go.

PLAYBOY: Would you have served if America had been in a declared war?

ALI: The way I feel, if America was attacked and some foreign force was prowling the streets and shooting, naturally I'd fight. I'm on the side of America, not them, because I'm fighting for myself, my children and my people. Whatever foreigners would come in, if they saw some black people with rifles, I'm sure they'd start shooting. So, yeah, I'd fight if America was attacked.

PLAYBOY: When you returned to the ring in 1970, most boxing observers felt you'd lost a good deal of your speed and timing. Did you think so?

ALI: Nope, I thought I was about the same, maybe even better. My first bout when I came back was with Jerry Quarry, who I'd fought before. It was the strangest thing, but when I watched films of the first Quarry fight, I looked fast; yet when I looked at the second Quarry fight I was *superfast*. Then, after I lost to Frazier, I studied the films and even though I wasn't in great shape and clowned a lot, look at how *sharp* I was, how much I *hit* Joe. Anyway, you saw what Foreman did to Frazier and then what I did to Foreman, so what could I have lost by resting for three and a half years? Couldn't be much, could it? That's why I can stay champ for a long time, and if I fight just twice a year, my title can't be taken away. And those'll be big, big fights worth at least $5,000,000 apiece. That's $10,000,000 a year for five years, which means I'll split $50,000,000 with the Government. I'll wind up with $25,000,000 after taxes. Whew!

PLAYBOY: That kind of money wasn't around when you began boxing professionally. Are you ever astonished by the fact that you can make $5,000,000 in the course of an hour?

ALI: No, and when I leave boxing, there will never be that kind of money for fighters again. I can get $5,000,000 or $7,500,000 a fight because I got a world audience. The people who are puttin' up that money are the richest people in the world—black oilmen. It was a rich black man who paid me and George Foreman, and he did it because he wanted some publicity for his little country, and he got it. For 15 years after the white Belgians had to get out of there, no one—including me—ever heard of Zaïre. No one knew it was a country of more than 22,000,000 people, but now we do.

I just got offered $7,500,000 to fight Foreman in Djakarta, Indonesia, by a black oilman who wants to promote *his* country. How to do it? Call Muhammad Ali over and have him fight for the title and the *world* will read about where he's fighting. But after I'm out of boxing and the title goes back to a fighter like a George Foreman or any good American, title fights won't travel no further than America and England. And that'll be the end of the big, big money.

PLAYBOY: Do you think you'll miss boxing when you finally retire?

ALI: No, because I realize you got to get old. Buildings get old, people get old and we're all goin' to die. See the fat I have around my stomach? Ten years ago, it would come off in two weeks, but not anymore. I can't exactly *feel* myself getting old, but I ain't like I was ten years ago, so time equips me to face the facts of life. When I get to be 50, I won't really miss boxing at all, because I'll know I can't do it anymore.

But when I quit, I sure ain't goin' out like the old-time fighters. You ain't gonna hear it said about me that when I was champ I bought me a Cadillac, had me a couple of white girls on my arm, and that when I retired I went broke. You'll *never* read articles about me that say, "Poor Muhammad Ali, he made so much money and now he's working in a car wash." No, sir.

PLAYBOY: Will you continue to associate yourself with boxing after you retire?

ALI: I don't think so. I'm the champion right now and I can't even find time for training because of other things. I talk to Senators like John Tunney of California, and black bourgeois Congressmen who like to act so *big,* and black doctors and lawyers who have white friends and who no longer want to be black—and who act like they're too good for any of the brothers. I can always say to them, "Why do you-all act like this? I don't act like that, and *you* can't get no bigger than Muhammad *Ali.*"

That's the truth, too. I was over in Ireland and had dinner with Jack Lynch, the prime minister. I was in Cairo and stayed at Sadat's palace for two days. I wined and dined with King Faisal of Saudi Arabia. I might not've been that happy around all of those leaders, but people who look up to them see *them* looking up to *me.* Now when I bring my program down, they'll listen. See, you got to have something going in front for you. A smart fella might go down the street, but if people look at him and think, "Oh, just an ordinary fella," he won't get things done. But when a guy in a Rolls-Royce drives up and says, "Hey, I want to make a deal," people will talk money with him. Same thing with me: My money and my title give me influence.

And I also have something to say. You notice that when we talk, 85 percent of our conversation is away from boxing? Interview some other fighters and see what *they* can talk about: nothing. We couldn't talk this long—you couldn't *listen* this long—if we just talked boxing.

PLAYBOY: Agreed; but let's stick with that 15 percent a bit longer. Many people believe that after you retire, boxing will disappear in America. Do you believe that?

ALI: Boxing will never die. There will always be boxing in schools and clubs, and the fight crowd will always follow the pros. And every once in a while, a sensational fighter will come through.

PLAYBOY: People close to you say that in the past year you've grown visibly weary of boxing. Is that true?

ALI: Well, I started fighting in 1954, when I was just 12, so it's been a long time for me. But there's always a new fight to look forward to, a new publicity stunt, a new *reason* to fight. Now I'm fighting for this charities thing, and it helps me get ready. When I think of all the money and the jobs winning means, I'll run those two miles on mornings when I'd rather sleep.

PLAYBOY: With the possible exceptions of a few of our politicians, you're probably the most publicized American of this century. What kinds of problems does fame on such a grand scale create?

ALI: None. It's a blessing if you use publicity for the right thing, and I use it to help my brothers and to promote truth around the world. It's still an honor for me to talk to TV reporters who come all the way from Germany and Australia just to interview me. And when we're talking, I don't see a man from Germany, I see millions of Germans. The reporter will go back home and show his film to his entire nation, which keeps me popular and sells fight tickets, which is how I earn my living—and also how I can keep buying up buildings for my people. That's why talkin' so much don't bother me, but I'll be bothered when the reporters quit coming around, because on that day I'll realize I'm not newsworthy anymore, and that's when it all ends. So I enjoy it while it's happening.

PLAYBOY: Still, aren't there times when living in the public eye becomes slightly unbearable?

ALI: Yeah, and when that happens, I get into my bus, stock up on food and take my wife and four children and drive somewhere near the ocean and just rest for four or five days.

The times when it all gets me down. I just want to get away—from the commercials and TV and college appearances and airline flights and friends asking for loans and people begging for money that they need. I don't like to do it, but I wind up ducking: "When the phone rings, tell 'em I'm not here." It never lets up, so if I can just get away for a day every once in a while, I'm happy. Yet I don't let that stuff get me *too* bothered, because I have only one cause—the Islamic cause—and my mission is to spread the works and faith that Elijah Muhammad taught me.

PLAYBOY: For a man who's become more and more of a missionary, boxing must occasionally seem like a particularly brutal and inappropriate way to make a living. Did you ever consider a career in any other sport?

ALI: About the onliest other sport I ever thought about was football, but I didn't like it, because there was no personal publicity in it; you have to wear too much equipment and people can't see you. Folks sitting back in the bleachers can't hardly pick you out of a field of 22 men and a bunch of other guys shufflin' in and out, but in a boxing ring there's only two men. I made my decision about sports when I was a 12-year-old kid, and I went with boxing because fighters can make more money than other athletes and the sport isn't cut off by a season, like football. And I've never regretted that decision, 'cause when you're the greatest at what you're doing, how can you question it?

PLAYBOY: Does your claim of being the greatest mean that you think you could have beaten every heavyweight champion in modern ring history?

ALI: I can't really say. Rocky Marciano, Jack Johnson, Joe Louis, Jack Dempsey, Joe Walcott, Ezzard Charles—they *all* would have given me trouble. I can't know if I would've beaten them all, but I do know this: I'm the most talked-about, the most publicized, the most famous and the most colorful fighter in history. And I'm the fastest heavyweight—with feet and hands—who ever lived. Besides all that, I'm the onliest poet laureate boxing's ever had. One other thing, too: If you look at pictures of all the former champions, you know in a flash that I'm the best-looking champion in history. It all adds up to being the greatest, don't it?

PLAYBOY: Do you think you'll be remembered that way?

ALI: I don't know, but I'll tell you how I'd *like* to be remembered: as a black man who won the heavyweight title and who was humorous and who treated everyone right. As a man who never looked down on those who looked up to him and who helped as many of his people as he could— financially and also in their fight for freedom, justice and equality. As a man who wouldn't hurt his people's dignity by doing anything that would embarrass them. As a man who tried to unite his people through the faith of Islam that he found when he listened to the Honorable Elijah Muhammad. And if all that's asking too much, then I guess I'd settle for being remembered only as a great boxing champion who became a preacher and a champion of his people.

And I wouldn't even mind if folks forgot how pretty I was.

MARTIN LUTHER KING, JR.

January 1965

Interviewer: Alex Haley

Getting the first in-depth interview granted by Martin Luther King, Jr., was not easy, as was the case with most Haley assignments. As a candidate for the Nobel Prize (which he received shortly before the magazine went to press), as a minister and the leader of America's blacks, King first expressed his concern about PLAYBOY as a "proper" publication. Haley was able to talk to one of King's advisers and give him the demographic breakdown of the magazine's burgeoning readership. "I told him the readers were crucial to King's cause, and that whatever he thought about the nude photography, he couldn't ignore the audience."

Haley remembered how the interview took place after King agreed to it: "His schedule was so hectic that I made three trips to his Atlanta headquarters, waiting for days at a time without being able to talk to him. On my fourth trip, I was ready to give up when his secretary suggested I show up at a barbecue supper being sponsored by the men's club of Dr. King's church. I spotted Dr. King ambling about, eating from a paper plate, greeting people. When he got to me, he learned I was the one who had failed to meet him so many times. He laughed and said, 'Look, I've gone without sleep before. Come over to my office and we'll talk.' We did just that—far into the night, until he simply nodded off at his desk from exhaustion. Feeling pity for him, I awakened him gently and left—with an exclusive interview on tape."

On December 5, 1955, to the amused annoyance of the white citizens of Montgomery, Alabama, an obscure young Baptist minister named Martin

Luther King, Jr., called a city-wide Negro boycott of its segregated bus system. To their consternation, however, it was almost 100 percent success-ful; it lasted for 381 days and nearly bankrupted the bus line. When King's home was bombed during the siege, thousands of enraged Negroes were ready to riot, but the soft-spoken clergyman prevailed on them to channel their anger into nonviolent protest—and became world-renowned as a champion of Gandhi's philosophy of passive resistance. Within a year the Supreme Court had ruled Jim Crow seating unlawful on Montgomery's buses, and King found himself, at 27, on the front lines of a nonviolent Negro revolution against racial injustice.

Dissatisfied with the slow pace of the protest movement, King decided to create a crisis in 1963 that would "dramatize the Negro plight and galvanize the national conscience." He was abundantly successful, for his mass nonviolent demonstration in arch-segregationist Birmingham resulted in the arrest of more than 3300 Negroes, including King himself; and mil-lions were outraged by front-page pictures of Negro demonstrators being brutalized by the billy sticks, police dogs and fire hoses of police chief Bull Connor.

In the months that followed, mass sit-ins and demonstrations erupted in 800 Southern cities; President Kennedy proposed a Civil Rights Bill aimed at the enforcement of voting rights, equal employment opportunities, and the desegregation of public facilities; and the now-famous march on Washington, 200,000 strong, was eloquently addressed by King on the steps of the Lincoln Memorial. By the end of that "long hot summer," America's Negroes had won more tangible gains than in any year since 1865—and Martin Luther King had become their acknowledged leader and most re-spected spokesman.

This interview is the longest he has ever granted to any publication. Though he spoke with heartfelt and often eloquent sincerity, his tone was one of businesslike detachment. And his mood, except for one or two flickering smiles of irony, was gravely serious—never more so than the moment, during a rare evening with his family on our first night in town, when his four children chided him affectionately for "not being home enough." After dinner, we began the interview on this personal note.

PLAYBOY: Dr. King, are your children old enough to be aware of the issues at stake in the civil rights movement, and of your role in it?
KING: Yes, they are—especially my oldest child, Yolanda. Two years ago, I remember, I returned home after serving one of my terms in the Albany, Georgia, jail, and she asked me, "Daddy, why do you have to go to jail

so much?" I told her that I was involved in a struggle to make conditions better for the colored people, and thus for *all* people. I explained that because things are as they are, someone has to take a stand, that it is necessary for someone to go to jail, because many Southern officials seek to maintain the barriers that have historically been erected to exclude the colored people. I tried to make her understand that someone had to do this to make the world better—for *all* children. She was only six at that time, but she was already aware of segregation because of an experience that we had had.

PLAYBOY: Would you mind telling us about it?

KING: Not at all. The family often used to ride with me to the Atlanta airport, and on our way, we always passed Funtown, a sort of miniature Disneyland with mechanical rides and that sort of thing. Yolanda would inevitably say, "I want to go to Funtown," and I would always evade a direct reply. I really didn't know how to explain to her why she couldn't go. Then one day at home, she ran downstairs exclaiming that a TV commercial was urging people to come to Funtown. Then my wife and I had to sit down with her between us and try to explain it. I have won some applause as a speaker, but my tongue twisted and my speech stammered seeking to explain to my six-year-old daughter why the public invitation on television didn't include her, and others like her. One of the most painful experiences I have ever faced was to see her tears when I told her that Funtown was *closed* to colored children, for I realized that at that moment the first dark cloud of inferiority had floated into her little mental sky, that at that moment her personality had begun to warp with that first unconscious bitterness toward white people. It was the first time that prejudice based upon skin color had been explained to her. But it was of paramount importance to me that she not grow up bitter. So I told her that although many white people were against her going to Funtown, there were many others who *did* want colored children to go. It helped somewhat. Pleasantly, word came to me later that Funtown had quietly desegregated, so I took Yolanda. A number of white persons there asked, "Aren't you Dr. King, and isn't this your daughter?" I said we were, and she heard them say how glad they were to see us there.

PLAYBOY: As one who grew up in the economically comfortable, socially insulated environment of a middle-income home in Atlanta, can you recall when it was that you yourself first became painfully and personally aware of racial prejudice?

KING: Very clearly. When I was 14, I had traveled from Atlanta to Dublin, Georgia, with a dear teacher of mine, Mrs. Bradley; she's dead now. I had participated there in an oratorical contest sponsored by the Negro Elks. It turned out to be a memorable day, for I had succeeded in winning the contest. My subject, I recall, ironically enough, was "The Negro and the

Constitution." Anyway, that night, Mrs. Bradley and I were on a bus returning to Atlanta, and at a small town along the way, some white passengers boarded the bus, and the white driver ordered us to get up and
give the whites our seats. We didn't move quickly enough to suit him, so
he began cursing us, calling us "black sons of bitches." I intended to stay
right in that seat, but Mrs. Bradley finally urged me up, saying we had to
obey the law. And so we stood up in the aisle for the 90 miles to Atlanta.
That night will never leave my memory. It was the angriest I have ever
been in my life.

PLAYBOY: Wasn't it another such incident on a bus, years later, that thrust
you into your present role as a civil rights leader?

KING: Yes, it was—in Montgomery, Alabama, in 1955. E. D. Nixon, a
Pullman porter long identified with the NAACP, telephoned me late one
night to tell me that Mrs. Rosa Parks had been arrested around seven-thirty
that evening when a bus driver demanded that she give up her seat, and she
refused—because her feet hurt. Nixon had already bonded Mrs. Parks out
of prison. He said, "It's time this stops; we ought to boycott the buses." I
agreed and said, "Now." The next night we called a meeting of Negro
community leaders to discuss it, and on Saturday and Sunday we appealed
to the Negro community, with leaflets and from the pulpits, to boycott the
buses on Monday. We had in mind a one-day boycott, and we were banking
on 60-percent success. But the boycott saw instantaneous 99-percent success. We were so pleasantly surprised and impressed that we continued, and
for the next 381 days the boycott of Montgomery's buses by Negroes was
99%10 successful.

PLAYBOY: Were you sure you'd win?

KING: There was one dark moment when we doubted it. We had been
struggling to make the boycott a success when the city of Montgomery successfully obtained an injunction from the court to stop our car pool. I
didn't know what to say to our people. They had backed us up, and we
had let them down. It was a desolate moment. I saw, all of us saw, that the
court was leaning against us. I remember telling a group of those working
closest with me to spread in the Negro community the message, "We must
have the faith that things will work out somehow, that God will make a
way for us when there seems no way." It was about noontime, I remember, when Rex Thomas of the Associated Press rushed over to where I
was sitting and told me of the news flash that the U.S. Supreme Court had
declared that bus segregation in Montgomery was unconstitutional. It had
literally been the darkest hour before the dawn.

PLAYBOY: Can you recall any mistakes you've made in leading the movement?

KING: Well, the most pervasive mistake I have made was in believing that
because our cause was just, we could be sure that the white ministers of

the South, once their Christian consciences were challenged, would rise to our aid. I felt that white ministers would take our cause to the white power structures. I ended up, of course, chastened and disillusioned. As our movement unfolded, and direct appeals were made to white ministers, most folded their hands—and some even took stands *against* us.

PLAYBOY: Their stated reason for refusing to help was that it was not the proper role of the church to "intervene in secular affairs." Do you disagree with this view?

KING: Most emphatically. The essence of the Epistles of Paul is that Christians should *rejoice* at being deemed worthy to suffer for what they believe. The projection of a social gospel, in my opinion, is the true witness of a Christian life. This is the meaning of the true *ekklēsia*—the inner, spiritual church. The church once changed society. It was then a thermostat of society. But today I feel that too much of the church is merely a thermometer, which measures rather than molds popular opinion.

PLAYBOY: Are you speaking of the church in general—or the white church in particular?

KING: The white church, I'm sorry to say. Its leadership has greatly disappointed me. Let me hasten to say there are some outstanding exceptions. As one whose Christian roots go back through three generations of ministers—my father, grandfather and great-grandfather—I will remain true to the church as long as I live. But the laxity of the white church collectively has caused me to weep tears of love. There cannot be deep disappointment without deep love. Time and again in my travels, as I have seen the outward beauty of white churches, I have had to ask myself, "What kind of people worship there? Who is their God? Is their God the God of Abraham, Isaac and Jacob, and is their Savior the Savior who hung on the cross at Golgotha? Where were their voices when a black race took upon itself the cross of protest against man's injustice to man? Where were their voices when defiance and hatred were called for by white men who sat in these very churches?"

My personal disillusionment with the church began when I was thrust into the leadership of the bus protest in Montgomery. I was confident that the white ministers, priests and rabbis of the South would prove strong allies in our just cause. But some became open adversaries, some cautiously shrank from the issue, and others hid behind silence. My optimism about help from the white church was shattered; and on too many occasions since, my hopes for the white church have been dashed.

PLAYBOY: Do you feel that the Negro church has come any closer to "the projection of a social gospel" in its commitment to the cause?

KING: The role of the Negro church today, by and large, is a glorious example in the history of Christendom. For never in Christian history, within a Christian country, have Christian churches been on the receiving end of such naked brutality and violence as we are witnessing here in

America today. Not since the days of the Christians in the catacombs has God's house, as a symbol, weathered such attack as the Negro churches.

I shall never forget the grief and bitterness I felt on that terrible September morning when a bomb blew out the lives of those four little, innocent girls sitting in their Sunday-school class in the 16th Street Baptist Church in Birmingham. I think of how a woman cried out, crunching through broken glass, "My God, we're not even safe in church!" I think of how that explosion blew the face of Jesus Christ from a stained-glass window. It was symbolic of how sin and evil had blotted out the life of Christ. I can remember thinking that if men were this bestial, was it all worth it? Was there any hope? Was there any way out?

PLAYBOY: Do you still feel this way?

KING: No, time has healed the wounds—and buoyed me with the inspiration of another moment which I shall never forget: when I saw with my own eyes over 3000 young Negro boys and girls, totally unarmed, leave Birmingham's 16th Street Baptist Church to march to a prayer meeting—ready to pit nothing but the power of their bodies and souls against Bull Connor's police dogs, clubs and fire hoses. When they refused Connor's bellowed order to turn back, he whirled and shouted to his men to turn on the hoses. It was one of the most fantastic events of the Birmingham story that these Negroes, many of them on their knees, stared, unafraid and unmoving, at Connor's men with the hose nozzles in their hands. Then, slowly the Negroes stood up and advanced, and Connor's men fell back as though hypnotized, as the Negroes marched on past to hold their prayer meeting. I saw there, I felt there, for the first time, the pride and the *power* of nonviolence.

Another time I will never forget was one Saturday night, late, when my brother telephoned me in Atlanta from Birmingham—that city which some call "Bombingham"—which I had just left. He told me that a bomb had wrecked his home, and that another bomb, positioned to exert its maximum force upon the motel room in which I had been staying, had injured several people. My brother described the terror in the streets as Negroes, furious at the bombings, fought whites. Then, behind his voice, I heard a rising chorus of beautiful singing: "We shall overcome." Tears came into my eyes that at such a tragic moment, my race still could sing its hope and faith.

PLAYBOY: Your detractors in the Negro community often refer to you snidely as "De Lawd" and "Booker T. King." What's your reaction to this sort of Uncle Tom label?

KING: I hear some of those names, but my reaction to them is never emotional. I don't think you can be in public life without being called bad names. As Lincoln said, "If I answered all criticism, I'd have time for nothing else." But with regard to both of the names you mentioned, I've always tried to be what I call militantly nonviolent. I don't believe that anyone could seriously accuse me of not being totally committed to the breakdown of segregation.

PLAYBOY: What do you mean by "militantly nonviolent"?

KING: I mean to say that a strong man must be militant as well as moderate. He must be a realist as well as an idealist. If I am to merit the trust invested in me by some of my race, I must be both of these things. This is why nonviolence is a powerful as well as a *just* weapon. If you confront a man who has long been cruelly misusing you, and say, "Punish me, if you will; I do not deserve it, but I will accept it, so that the world will know I am right and you are wrong," then you wield a powerful and a just weapon. This man, your oppressor, is automatically morally defeated, and if he has any conscience, he is ashamed. Wherever this weapon is used in a manner that stirs a community's, or a nation's, anguished conscience, then the pressure of public opinion becomes an ally in your just cause.

We should not forget that, although nonviolent direct action did not originate in America, it found a natural home where it has been a revered tradition to rebel against injustice. This great weapon, which we first tried out in Montgomery during the bus boycott, has been further developed throughout the South over the past decade, until by today it has become instrumental in the greatest mass-action crusade for freedom that has occurred in America since the Revolutionary War. The effectiveness of this weapon's ability to dramatize, in the world's eyes, an oppressed peoples' struggle for justice is evident in the fact that of 1963's top ten news stories after the assassination of President Kennedy and the events immediately connected with it, nine stories dealt with one aspect or another of the Negro struggle.

PLAYBOY: One of the highlights of your campaign was your celebrated "Letter from a Birmingham Jail"—written during one of your jail terms for civil disobedience—an eloquent reply to eight Protestant, Catholic and Jewish clergymen who had criticized your activities in Birmingham. Do you feel that subsequent events have justified the sentiments in your letter?

KING: I would say yes. Two or three important and constructive things have happened which can be at least partially attributed to that letter. By now, nearly a million copies of the letter have been widely circulated in churches of most of the major denominations. It helped to focus greater international attention upon what was happening in Birmingham. And I am sure that without Birmingham, the march on Washington wouldn't have been called—which in my mind was one of the most creative steps the Negro struggle has taken. The march on Washington spurred and galvanized the consciences of millions. It gave the American Negro a new national and international stature. The press of the world recorded the story as nearly a quarter of a million Americans, white and black, assembled in grandeur as a testimonial to the Negro's determination to achieve freedom in this generation.

It was also the image of Birmingham which, to a great extent, helped to bring the Civil Rights Bill into being in 1963. Previously, President Kennedy had decided not to propose it that year, feeling that it would so arouse the South that it would meet a bottleneck. But Birmingham, and subsequent developments, caused him to reorder his legislative priorities.

One of these decisive developments was our last major campaign before the enactment of the Civil Rights Act—in St. Augustine, Florida. We received a plea for help from Dr. Robert Hayling, the leader of the St. Augustine movement. St. Augustine, America's oldest city, and one of the most segregated cities in America, was a stronghold of the Ku Klux Klan and the John Birch Society. Such things had happened as Klansmen abducting four Negroes and beating them unconscious with clubs, brass knuckles, ax handles and pistol butts. Dr. Hayling's home had been shot up with buckshot, three Negro homes had been bombed and several Negro night clubs shotgunned. A Negro's car had been destroyed by fire because his child was one of the six Negro children permitted to attend white schools. And the homes of two of the Negro children in the white schools had been burned down. Many Negroes had been fired from jobs that some had worked on for 28 years because they were somehow connected with the demonstrations. Police had beaten and arrested Negroes for picketing, marching and singing freedom songs. Many Negroes had served up to 90 days in jail for demonstrating against segregation, and four teenagers had spent six months in jail for picketing. Then, on February seventh of last year, Dr. Hayling's home was shotgunned a second time, with his pregnant wife and two children barely escaping death; the family dog was killed while standing behind the living-room door. So S.C.L.C. decided to join in last year's celebration of St. Augustine's gala 400th birthday as America's oldest city—by converting it into a nonviolent battleground. This is just what we did.

PLAYBOY: But isn't it true, Dr. King, that during this and other "nonviolent" demonstrations, violence has occurred—sometimes resulting in hundreds of casualties on both sides?

KING: Yes, in part that is true. But what is always overlooked is how few people, in ratio to the numbers involved, have been casualties. An army on maneuvers, against no enemy, suffers casualties, even fatalities. A minimum of whites have been casualties in demonstrations solely because our teaching of nonviolence disciplines our followers not to fight even if attacked. A minimum of Negroes are casualties for two reasons: Their white oppressors know that the world watches their actions, and for the first time they are being faced by Negroes who display no fear.

PLAYBOY: It was shortly after your St. Augustine campaign last summer, as you mentioned, that the Civil Rights Bill was passed—outlawing many of the injustices against which you had been demonstrating. Throughout the South, predictably, it was promptly anathematized as unconstitutional and excessive in its concessions to Negro demands. How do you feel about it?

KING: I don't feel that the Civil Rights Act has gone far *enough* in some of its coverage. In the first place, it needs a stronger voting section. You will never have a true democracy until you can eliminate *all* restrictions. We need to do away with restrictive literacy tests. I've seen too much of native intelligence to accept the validity of these tests as a criterion for voting qualifications. Our nation needs a universal method of voter registration— one man, one vote, literally. Second, there is a pressing, urgent need to give the attorney general the right to initiate Federal suits in any area of civil rights denial. Third, we need a strong and strongly enforced fair-housing section such as many states already have. President Kennedy initiated the present housing law, but it is not broad enough. Fourth, we need an extension of FEPC to grapple more effectively with the problems of poverty. Not only are millions of Negroes caught in the clutches of poverty, but millions of poor whites as well. And fifth, conclusive and effective measures must be taken immediately at the Federal level to curb the worsening reign of terror in the South—which is aided and abetted, as everyone knows, by state and local law-enforcement agencies. It's getting so that anybody can kill a Negro and get away with it in the South, as long as they go through the motions of a jury trial. There is very little chance of conviction from lily-white Southern jurors. It must be fixed so that in the case of interracial murder, the Federal Government can prosecute.

PLAYBOY: Your dissatisfaction with the Civil Rights Act reflects that of most other Negro spokesmen. According to recent polls, however, many whites resent this attitude, calling the Negro "ungrateful" and "unrealistic" to press his demands for more.

KING: This is a litany to those of us in this field. "What more will the Negro want?" "What will it take to make these demonstrations end?" Well, I would like to reply with another rhetorical question: Why do white people seem to find it so difficult to understand that the Negro is sick and tired of having reluctantly parceled out to him those rights and privileges which all others receive upon birth or entry in America? I never cease to wonder at the amazing presumption of much of white society, assuming that they have the right to bargain with the Negro for his freedom. This continued arrogant ladling out of pieces of the rights of citizenship has begun to generate a *fury* in the Negro. Even so, he is not pressing for revenge, or for conquest, or to gain spoils, or to enslave, or even to marry the sisters of those who have injured him. What the Negro wants—and will not stop until he gets—is absolute and unqualified freedom and equality here in this land of his birth, and not in Africa or in some imaginary state. The Negro no longer will be tolerant of anything less than his due right and heritage. He is pursuing only that which he knows is honorably his. He knows that he is right.

But every Negro leader since the turn of the century has been saying this in one form or another. It is because we have been so long and so conscientiously ignored by the dominant white society that the situation has now reached such crisis proportions. Few white people, even today, will face the clear fact that the very future and destiny of this country are tied up in what answer will be given to the Negro. And that answer must be given soon.

PLAYBOY: Relatively few dispute the justness of the struggle to eradicate racial injustice, but many whites feel that the Negro should be more patient, that only the passage of time—perhaps generations—will bring about the sweeping changes he demands in traditional attitudes and customs. Do you think this is true?

KING: No, I do not. I feel that the time is always right to do what is right. Where progress for the Negro in America is concerned, there is a tragic misconception of time among whites. They seem to cherish a strange, irrational notion that something in the very flow of time will cure all ills. In truth, I feel that time has been used destructively by people of ill will much more than it has been used *con*structively by those of *good* will.

If I were to select a timetable for the equalization of human rights, it would be the *intent* of the "all deliberate speed" specified in the historic 1954 Supreme Court decision. But what has happened? A Supreme Court decision was met, and balked, with utter defiance. Ten years later, in most areas of the South, less than one percent of the Negro children have been integrated in schools, and in some of the deepest South, not even one tenth of one percent. Approximately 25 percent of employable Negro youth, for another example, are presently unemployed. Though many would prefer not to, we must face the fact that progress for the Negro—to which white "moderates" like to point in justifying gradualism—has been relatively insignificant, particularly in terms of the Negro masses. What little progress has been made—and that includes the Civil Rights Act—has applied primarily to the middle-class Negro. Among the masses, especially in the Northern ghettos, the situation remains about the same, and for some it is worse.

PLAYBOY: It would seem that much could be done at the local, state and Federal levels to remedy these inequities. In your own contact with them, have you found Government officials—in the North, if not in the South—to be generally sympathetic, understanding, and receptive to appeals for reform?

KING: On the contrary, I have been dismayed at the degree to which abysmal ignorance seems to prevail among many state, city and even Federal officials on the whole question of racial justice and injustice. Particularly, I have found that these men seriously—and dangerously—underestimate the explosive mood of the Negro and the gravity of the crisis. Even among those whom I would consider to be both sympathetic and sincerely intellectually committed, there is a lamentable lack of under-standing. But this white failure to comprehend the depth and dimension of the Negro problem is far from being peculiar to Government officials. Apart from bigots and backlashers, it seems to be a malady even among those whites who like to regard themselves as "enlightened." I would especially refer to those who counsel, "Wait!" and to those who say that they sympa-thize with our goals but cannot condone our methods of direct-action pursuit of those goals. I wonder at men who dare to feel that they have some paternalistic right to set the timetable for another man's liberation. Over the past several years, I must say, I have been gravely disappointed with such white "moderates." I am often inclined to think that they are more of a stumbling block to the Negro's progress than the White Citizen's Counciler or the Ku Klux Klanner.

PLAYBOY: Haven't both of these segregationist societies been implicated in connection with plots against your life?

KING: It's difficult to trace the authorship of these death threats. I seldom go through a day without one. Some are telephoned anonymously to my office; others are sent—unsigned, of course—through the mails. Drew Pear-son wrote not long ago about one group of unknown affiliation that was committed to assassinate not only me but also Chief Justice Warren and President Johnson. And not long ago, when I was about to visit in Missis-sippi, I received some very urgent calls from Negro leaders in Mobile, who had been told by a very reliable source that a sort of guerrilla group led by a retired major in the area of Luceyville, Mississippi, was plotting to take my life during the visit. I was strongly urged to cancel the trip, but when I thought about it, I decided that I had no alternative but to go on into Mississippi.

PLAYBOY: Why?

KING: Because I have a job to do. If I were constantly worried about death, I couldn't function. After a while, if your life is more or less constantly in peril, you come to a point where you accept the possibility philosophically. I must face the fact, as all others in positions of leadership must do, that America today is an extremely sick nation, and that something could well happen to me at any time. I feel, though, that my cause is so right, so moral, that if I should lose my life, in some way it would aid the cause.

PLAYBOY: That statement exemplifies the total dedication to the civil rights movement for which you are so widely admired—but also denounced as an "extremist" by such segregationist spokesmen as Alabama's Governor Wallace. Do you accept this identification?

KING: It disturbed me when I first heard it. But when I began to consider the true meaning of the word, I decided that perhaps I would *like* to think of myself as an extremist—in the light of the spirit which made Jesus an extremist for love. If it sounds as though I am comparing myself to the

Savior, let me remind you that all who honor themselves with the claim of being "Christians" *should* compare themselves to Jesus. Thus I consider myself an extremist for that brotherhood of man which Paul so nobly expressed: "There is neither Jew nor Greek, there is neither bond nor free, there is neither male nor female: for ye are all one in Christ Jesus." Love is the only force on earth that can be dispensed or received in an extreme manner, without any qualifications, without any harm to the giver or to the receiver.

PLAYBOY: Perhaps. But the kind of extremism for which you've been criticized has to do not with love, but with your advocacy of willful disobedience of what you consider to be "unjust laws." Do you feel you have the right to pass judgment on and defy the law—nonviolently or otherwise?

KING: Yes—morally, if not legally. For there are two kinds of laws: man's and God's. A man-made code that squares with the moral law, or the law of God, is a just law. But a man-made code that is inharmonious with the moral law is an unjust law. And an unjust law, as St. Augustine said, is no law at all. Thus a law that is unjust is morally null and void, and must be defied until it is legally null and void as well. Let us not forget, in the memories of 6,000,000 who died, that everything Adolf Hitler did in Germany was "legal," and that everything the Freedom Fighters in Hungary did was "illegal." In spite of that, I am sure that I would have aided and comforted my Jewish brothers if I had lived in Germany during Hitler's reign, as some Christian priests and ministers did do, often at the cost of their lives. And if I lived now in a Communist country where principles dear to the Christian's faith are suppressed, I know that I would openly advocate defiance of that country's anti-religious laws—again, just as some Christian priests and ministers are doing today behind the Iron Curtain. Right here in America today there are white ministers, priests and rabbis who have shed blood in the support of our struggle against a web of human injustice, much of which is supported by immoral man-made laws.

PLAYBOY: Segregation laws?

KING: Specifically, court injunctions. Though the rights of the First Amendment guarantee that any citizen or group of citizens may engage in peaceable assembly, the South has seized upon the device of invoking injunctions to block our direct-action civil rights demonstrations. When you get set to stage a nonviolent demonstration, the city simply secures an injunction to cease and desist. Southern courts are well known for "sitting on" this type of case; conceivably a two- or three-year delay could be incurred. At first we found this to be a highly effective subterfuge against us. We first experienced it in Montgomery when, during the bus boycott, our car pool was outlawed by an injunction. An injunction also destroyed the protest movement in Talladega, Alabama. Another injunction outlawed the oldest civil rights organization, the NAACP, from the whole state of Alabama. Still another injunction thwarted our organization's efforts in Albany, Georgia. Then in Birmingham, we felt that we had to take a stand and disobey a court injunction against demonstrations, knowing the consequences and being prepared to meet them—or the unjust law would break our movement.

We did not take this step hastily or rashly. We gave the matter intense thought and prayer before deciding that the right thing was being done. And when we made our decision, I announced our plan to the press, making it clear that we were not anarchists advocating lawlessness, but that in good conscience we could not comply with a misuse of the judicial process in order to perpetuate injustice and segregation. When our plan was made known, it bewildered and immobilized our segregationist opponents. We felt that our decision had been morally as well as tactically right—in keeping with God's law as well as with the spirit of our nonviolent direct-action program.

PLAYBOY: If it's morally right for supporters of civil rights to violate segregation laws which they consider unjust, why is it wrong for segregationists to resist the enforcement of integration laws which *they* consider unjust?

KING: Because segregation, as even the segregationists know in their hearts, is morally wrong and sinful. If it weren't, the white South would not be haunted as it is by a deep sense of guilt for what it has done to the Negro— guilt for patronizing him, degrading him, brutalizing him, depersonalizing him, thingifying him; guilt for lying to itself. This is the source of the schizophrenia that the South will suffer until it goes through its crisis of conscience.

PLAYBOY: Is this crisis imminent?

KING: It may not come next week or next year, but it is certainly more imminent in the South than in the North. If the South is honest with itself, it may well outdistance the North in the improvement of race relations.

PLAYBOY: Why?

KING: Well, the Northern white, having had little actual contact with the Negro, is devoted to an abstract principle of cordial interracial relations. The North has long considered, in a theoretical way, that it supported brotherhood and the equality of man, but the truth is that deep prejudices and discriminations exist in hidden and subtle and covert disguises. The South's prejudice and discrimination, on the other hand, has been applied against the Negro in obvious, open, overt and glaring forms—which make the problem easier to get at. The Southern white man has the advantage of far more actual contact with Negroes than the Northerner. A major problem is that this contact has been paternalistic and poisoned by the myth of racial superiority.

PLAYBOY: Many Southern whites, supported by the "research" of several Southern anthropologists, vow that white racial superiority—and Negro inferiority—are a biological fact.

KING: You may remember that during the rise of Nazi Germany, a rash of books by respected German scientists appeared, supporting the master-race theory. This utterly ignorant fallacy has been so thoroughly refuted by the social scientists, as well as by medical science, that any individual who goes on believing it is standing in an absolutely misguided and diminishing circle. The American Anthropological Association has unanimously adopted a resolution repudiating statements that Negroes are biologically, in innate mental ability or in any other way inferior to whites. The collective weight and authority of world scientists are embodied in a Unesco report on races which flatly refutes the theory on innate superiority among *any* ethnic group. And as far as Negro "blood" is concerned, medical science finds the same four blood types in all race groups.

When the Southern white finally accepts this simple fact—as he eventually must—beautiful results will follow, for we will have come a long way toward transforming his master-servant perspective into a person-to-person perspective. The Southern white man, discovering the "nonmyth" Negro, exhibits all the passion of the new convert, seeing the black man as a man among men for the first time. The South, if it is to survive economically, must make dramatic changes, and these must include the Negro. People of good will in the South, who are the vast majority, have the challenge to be open and honest, and to turn a deaf ear to the shrill cries of the irresponsible few on the lunatic fringe. I think and pray they will.

PLAYBOY: Whom do you include among "the irresponsible few"?

KING: I include those who preach racism and commit violence; and those who, in various cities where we have sought to peacefully demonstrate, have sought to goad *Negroes* into violence as an excuse for violent mass reprisal. In Birmingham, for example, on the day it was flashed about the world that a "peace pact" had been signed between the moderate whites and the Negroes, Birmingham's segregationist forces reacted with fury, swearing vengeance against the white businessmen who had "betrayed" them by negotiating with Negroes. On Saturday night, just outside of Birmingham, a Ku Klux Klan meeting was held, and that same night, as I mentioned earlier, a bomb ripped the home of my brother, the Reverend A. D. King, and another bomb was planted where it would have killed or seriously wounded anyone in the motel room which I had been occupying. Both bombings had been timed just as Birmingham's bars closed on Saturday midnight, as the streets filled with thousands of Negroes who were not trained in nonviolence, and who had been drinking. Just as whoever planted the bombs had *wanted* to happen, fighting began, policemen were stoned by Negroes, cars were overturned and fires started.

PLAYBOY: Were none of your S.C.L.C. workers involved?

KING: If they had been, there would have been no riot, for we believe that only just means may be used in seeking a just end. We believe that lasting gains can be made—and they *have* been made—only by practicing what we preach: a policy of nonviolent, peaceful protest. The riots, North and South, have involved mobs—not the disciplined, nonviolent, direct-action demonstrators with whom I identify. We do not condone lawlessness, looting and violence committed by the racist or the reckless of *any* color.

I must say, however, that riots such as have occurred do achieve at least one partially positive effect: They dramatically focus national attention upon the Negro's discontent. Unfortunately, they also give the white majority an excuse, a provocation, to look away from the cause of the riots—the poverty and the deprivation and the degradation of the Negro, especially in the slums and ghettos where the riots occur—and to talk instead of looting, and of the breakdown of law and order. It is never circulated that some of the looters have been white people, similarly motivated by their own poverty. In one riot in a Northern city, aside from the Negroes and Puerto Ricans who were arrested, there were also 158 white people—including mothers stealing food, children's shoes and other necessity items. The poor, white and black, were rebelling together against the establishment.

PLAYBOY: Whom do you mean by "the establishment"?

KING: I mean the white leadership—which I hold as responsible as anyone for the riots, for not removing the conditions that cause them. The deep frustration, the seething desperation of the Negro today is a product of slum housing, chronic poverty, woefully inadequate education and substandard schools. The Negro is trapped in a long and desolate corridor with no exit sign, caught in a vicious socioeconomic vise. And he is ostracized as is no other minority group in America by the evil of oppressive and constricting prejudice based solely upon his color. A righteous man has no alternative but to resist such an evil system. If he does not have the courage to resist nonviolently, then he runs the risk of a violent emotional explosion. As much as I deplore violence, there is one evil that is *worse* than violence, and that's cowardice. It is still my basic article of faith that social justice can be achieved and democracy advanced only to the degree that there is firm adherence to *nonviolent* action and resistance in the pursuit of social justice. But America will be faced with the ever-present threat of violence, rioting and senseless crime as long as Negroes by the hundreds of thousands are packed into malodorous, rat-plagued ghettos; as long as Negroes remain smothered by poverty in the midst of an affluent society; as long as Negroes are made to feel like exiles in their own land; as long as Negroes continue to be dehumanized; as long as Negroes see their freedom endlessly delayed and diminished by the head winds of tokenism and small handouts from the white power structure. No nation can suffer any greater tragedy than to cause millions of its citizens to feel that they have no stake in their own society.

Understand that I am trying only to explain the *reasons* for violence and the threat of violence. Let me say again that by no means and under no circumstance do I condone outbreaks of looting and lawlessness. I feel that every responsible Negro leader must point out, with all possible vigor, that anyone who perpetrates and participates in a riot is immoral as well as impractical—that the use of immoral means will not achieve the moral end of racial justice.

PLAYBOY: Still, doesn't the very fact that riots have occurred tend to indicate that many Negroes are no longer heeding the counsels of nonviolence?

KING: Not the majority, by any means. But it *is* true that some Negroes subscribe to a deep feeling that the tactic of nonviolence is not producing enough concrete victories. We have seen, in our experience, that nonviolence thrives best in a climate of justice. Violence grows to the degree that injustice prevails; the more injustice in a given community, the more violence, or potential violence, smolders in that community. I can give you a clear example. If you will notice, there have been fewer riots in the South. The reason for this is that the Negro in the South can see some visible, concrete victories in civil rights. Last year, the police would have been called if he sat down at a community lunch counter. This year, if he chooses to sit at that counter, he is served. More riots have occurred in the North because the fellow in Harlem, to name one Northern ghetto, can't see any victories. He remains throttled, as he has always been, by vague, intangible economic and social deprivations. Until the concerned power structures begin to grapple creatively with these fundamental inequities, it will be difficult for violence to be eliminated. The longer our people see no progress, or halting progress, the easier it will be for them to yield to the counsels of hatred and demagoguery.

PLAYBOY: The literature of the John Birch Society, accusing you of just such counsels, has branded you "a conscious agent of the Communist conspiracy."

KING: As you know, they have sought to link many people with communism, including the Chief Justice of the Supreme Court and a former President of the United States. So I'm in good company, at least. The Birchers thrive on sneer and smear, on the dissemination of half-truths and outright lies. It would be comfortable to dismiss them as the lunatic fringe—which, by and large, they are; but some priests and ministers have also shown themselves to be among them. They are a very dangerous group—and they could become even more dangerous if the public doesn't reject the un-American travesty of patriotism that they espouse.

PLAYBOY: Was there any basis in fact for the rumors, still circulating in some quarters, that last summer's riots were fomented and stage-directed by Communist agitators?

KING: I'm getting sick and tired of people saying that this movement has been infiltrated by Communists. There are as many Communists in this freedom movement as there are Eskimos in Florida. The FBI provided the best answer to this absurd rumor in its report to the President after a special investigation which he had requested. It stated that the riots were not caused or directed by any such groups, although they did try to capitalize upon and prolong the riots. All Negro leaders, including myself, were most happy with the publication of these findings, for the public whisperings had troubled us. We knew that it could prove vitally harmful to the Negro struggle if the riots had been catalyzed or manipulated by the Communists or some other extremist group. It would have sown the seed of doubt in the public's mind that the Negro revolution is a genuine revolution, born from the same womb that produces all massive social upheavals—the womb of intolerable conditions and unendurable situations.

PLAYBOY: Is it destined to be a violent revolution?

KING: God willing, no. But white Americans must be made to understand the basic motives underlying Negro demonstrations. Many pent-up resentments and latent frustrations are boiling inside the Negro, and he must release them. It is not a threat but a fact of history that if an oppressed people's pent-up emotions are not nonviolently released, they will be violently released. So let the Negro march. Let him make pilgrimages to city hall. Let him go on freedom rides. And above all, make an effort to understand why he must do this. For if his frustration and despair are allowed to continue piling up, millions of Negroes will seek solace and security in black-nationalist ideologies. And this, inevitably, would lead to a frightening racial nightmare.

PLAYBOY: One of the most articulate champions of black Afro-American brotherhood has been Malcolm X, the former Black Muslim leader who recently renounced his racist past and converted to orthodox Mohammedanism. What is your opinion of him and his career?

KING: I met Malcolm X once in Washington, but circumstances didn't enable me to talk with him for more than a minute. He is very articulate, as you say, but I totally disagree with many of his political and philosophical views—at least insofar as I understand where he now stands. I don't want to seem to sound self-righteous, or absolutist, or that I think I have the only truth, the only way. Maybe he *does* have some of the answer. I don't know how he feels now, but I know that I have often wished that he would talk less of violence, because violence is not going to solve our problem. And in his litany of articulating the despair of the Negro without offering any positive, creative alternative, I feel that Malcolm has done himself and our people a great disservice. Fiery, demagogic oratory in the black ghettos, urging Negroes to arm themselves and prepare to engage in violence, as he has done, can reap nothing but grief.

PLAYBOY: For them or for whites?

KING: For everyone, but mostly for them. Even the extremist leaders who preach revolution are invariably unwilling to lead what they know would certainly end in bloody, chaotic and total defeat; for in the event of a violent revolution, we would be sorely outnumbered. And when it was all over, the Negro would face the same unchanged conditions, the same squalor and deprivation—the only difference being that his bitterness would be even more intense, his disenchantment even more abject. Thus, in purely practical as well as moral terms, the American Negro has no rational alternative to nonviolence.

PLAYBOY: You categorically reject violence as a tactical technique for social change. Can it not be argued, however, that violence, historically, has effected massive and sometimes constructive social change in some countries?

KING: I'd be the first to say that some historical victories have been won by violence; the U.S. Revolution is certainly one of the foremost. But the Negro revolution is seeking integration, not independence. Those fighting for independence have the purpose to *drive out* the oppressors. But here in America, we've got to live together. We've got to find a way to reconcile ourselves to living in community, one group with the other. The struggle of the Negro in America, to be successful, must be waged with resolute efforts, but efforts that are kept strictly within the framework of our democratic society. This means reaching, educating and moving large enough groups of people of both races to stir the conscience of the nation.

PLAYBOY: The B'nai B'rith, a prominent social-action organization which undertakes on behalf of the Jewish people many of the activities that you ask the Government to perform for Negroes, is generously financed by Jewish charities and private donations. All of the Negro civil rights groups, on the other hand—including your own—are perennially in financial straits and must rely heavily on white philanthropy in order to remain solvent. Why do they receive so little support from Negroes?

KING: We have to face and live with the fact that the Negro has not developed a sense of stewardship. Slavery was so divisive and brutal, so molded to break up unity, that we never developed a sense of oneness, as in Judaism. Starting with the individual family unit, the Jewish people are closely knit into what is, in effect, one big family. But with the Negro, slavery separated families from families, and the pattern of disunity that we see among Negroes today derives directly from this cruel fact of history. It is also a cruel fact that the Negro, generally speaking, has not developed a responsible sense of financial values. The best economists say that your automobile shouldn't cost more than half of your annual income, but we see many Negroes earning $7000 a year paying $5000 for a car. The home, it is said, should not cost more than twice the annual income, but we see many Negroes earning, say, $8000 a year living in a $30,000 home. Negroes, who amount to about 11 percent of the American population, are reported to consume over 40 percent of the Scotch whisky imported into the U.S., and to spend over $72,000,000 a year in jewelry stores. So when we come asking for civil rights donations, or help for the United Negro College Fund, most Negroes are trying to make ends meet.

PLAYBOY: The widespread looting that took place during last summer's riots would seem to prove your point. Do you agree with those who feel that this looting—much of which was directed against Jewish-owned stores—was anti-Semitic in motivation?

KING: No, I do not believe that the riots could in any way be considered expressions of anti-Semitism. It's true, as I was particularly pained to learn, that a large percentage of the looted stores were owned by our Jewish friends, but I do not feel that anti-Semitism was involved. A high percentage of the merchants serving most Negro communities simply happen to be Jewish. How could there be anti-Semitism among Negroes when our Jewish friends have demonstrated their commitment to the principle of tolerance and brotherhood not only in the form of sizable contributions, but in many other tangible ways, and often at great personal sacrifice? Can we ever express our appreciation to the rabbis who chose to give moral witness with us in St. Augustine during our recent protest against segregation in that unhappy city? Need I remind anyone of the awful beating suffered by Rabbi Arthur Lelyveld of Cleveland when he joined the civil rights workers there in Hattiesburg, Mississippi? And who can ever forget the sacrifice of two Jewish lives, Andrew Goodman and Michael Schwerner, in the swamps of Mississippi? It would be impossible to record the contribution that the Jewish people have made toward the Negro's struggle for freedom—it has been so great.

PLAYBOY: In conspicuous contrast, according to a recent poll conducted by *Ebony,* only one Negro in ten has ever participated physically in any form of social protest. Why?

KING: It is not always sheer numbers that are the measure of public support. As I see it, every Negro who does participate represents the sympathy and the moral backing of thousands of others. Let us never forget how one photograph, of those Birmingham policemen with their knees on that Negro woman on the ground, touched something emotionally deep in most Negroes in America, no matter who they were. In city after city, where S.C.L.C. has helped to achieve sweeping social changes, it has been not only because of the quality of its members' dedication and discipline, but because of the moral support of many Negroes who never took an active part. It's significant, I think, that during each of our city struggles, the usual average of crimes committed by Negroes has dropped to almost nothing.

But it is true, undeniably, that there are many Negroes who will *never* fight for freedom—yet who will be eager enough to accept it when it comes. And there are millions of Negroes who have never known anything but oppression, who are so devoid of pride and self-respect that they have resigned themselves to segregation. Other Negroes, comfortable and complacent, consider that they are *above* the struggle of the masses. And still others seek personal profit from segregation.

PLAYBOY: Your schedule of speaking engagements and civil rights commitments throughout the country is a punishing one—often 20 hours a day, seven days a week, according to reports. How much time do you get to spend at home?

KING: Very little, indeed. I've averaged not more than two days a week at home here in Atlanta over the past year—or since Birmingham, actually. I'm away two and three weeks at a time, mostly working in communities across the South. Wherever I am, I try to be in a pulpit as many Sundays as possible. But every day when I'm at home, I break from the office for dinner and try to spend a few hours with the children before I return to the office for some night work. And on Tuesdays when I'm not out of town, I don't go to the office. I keep this for my quiet day of reading and silence and meditation, and an entire evening with Mrs. King and the children.

PLAYBOY: If you could have a week's uninterrupted rest with no commitments whatever, how would you spend it?

KING: It's difficult to imagine such a thing, but if I had the luxury of an entire week, I would spend it meditating and reading, refreshing myself spiritually and intellectually. I have a deep nostalgia for the periods in the past that I was able to devote in this manner. Amidst the struggle, amidst the frustrations, amidst the endless work, I often reflect that I am forever *giving*—never pausing to take in. I feel urgently the need for even an hour of time to get away, to withdraw, to refuel. I need more time to think through what is being done, to take time out from the mechanics of the movement, to reflect on the *meaning* of the movement.

PLAYBOY: If you were marooned on the proverbial desert island, and could have with you only one book—apart from the Bible—what would it be?

KING: That's tough. Let me think about it—one book, not the Bible. Well, I think I would have to pick Plato's *Republic*. I feel that it brings together more of the insights of history than any other book. There is not a creative idea extant that is not discussed, in some way, in this work. Whatever realm of theology or philosophy is one's interest—and I am deeply interested in both—somewhere along the way, in this book, you will find the matter explored.

PLAYBOY: If you could send someone—anyone—to that desert island in your stead, who would it be?

KING: That's another tough one. Let me see, I guess I wouldn't mind seeing Mr. Goldwater dispatched to a desert island. I hope they'd *feed* him and everything, of course. I *am* nonviolent, you know. Politically, though, he's already on a desert island, so it may be unnecessary to send him there.

PLAYBOY: We take it you weren't overly distressed by his defeat in the Presidential race.

KING: Until that defeat, Goldwater was the most dangerous man in America. He talked soft and nice, but he gave aid and comfort to the most vicious racists and the most extreme rightists in America. He gave respectability to views totally alien to the democratic process. Had he won, he would have led us down a fantastic path that would have totally destroyed America as we know it.

PLAYBOY: Until his withdrawal from the race following Goldwater's nomination, Alabama's Governor Wallace was another candidate for the Presidency. What's your opinion of *his* qualifications for that office?

KING: Governor Wallace is a demagog with a capital D. He symbolizes in this country many of the evils that were alive in Hitler's Germany. He is a merchant of racism, peddling hate under the guise of States' rights. He wants to turn back the clock, for his own personal aggrandizement, and he will do literally *anything* to accomplish this. He represents the misuse, the corruption, the destruction of leadership. I am not sure that he believes all the poison that he preaches, but he is artful enough to convince others that he does. Instead of guiding people to new peaks of reasonableness, he intensifies misunderstanding, deepens suspicion and prejudice. He is perhaps the most dangerous racist in America today.

PLAYBOY: One of the most controversial issues of the past year, apart from civil rights, was the question of school prayer, which has been ruled unlawful by the Supreme Court. Governor Wallace, among others, has denounced the decision. How do you feel about it?

KING: I endorse it. I think it was correct. Contrary to what many have said, it sought to outlaw neither prayer nor belief in God. In a pluralistic society such as ours, who is to determine what prayer shall be spoken, and by whom? Legally, constitutionally or otherwise, the state certainly has no such right. I am strongly opposed to the efforts that have been made to nullify the decision. They have been motivated, I think, by little more than the wish to embarrass the Supreme Court. When I saw Brother Wallace going up to Washington to testify against the decision at the Congressional hearings, it only strengthened my conviction that the decision was right.

PLAYBOY: Governor Wallace has intimated that President Johnson, in championing the cause of civil rights only since he became Vice-President, may be guilty of "insincerity."

KING: How President Johnson may or may not have felt about or voted on civil rights during his years in Congress is less relevant, at this point, than what he has said and done about it during his tenure as President of the United States. In my opinion, he has done a good job up to now. He is an extremely keen political man, and he has demonstrated his wisdom and his commitment in forthrightly coming to grips with the problem. He does not tire of reminding the nation of the moral issues involved. My impression is that he will remain a strong President for civil rights.

PLAYBOY: In well-earned recognition of your dedication to and leadership of the struggle to achieve these goals, you became, in October of last year, the youngest man ever to receive the Nobel Peace Prize. What was your reaction to the news?

KING: It made me feel very humble indeed. But I would like to think that the award is not a personal tribute, but a tribute to the entire freedom movement, and to the gallant people of both races who surround me in the drive for civil rights which will make the American dream a reality. I think that this internationally known award will call even more attention to our struggle, gain even greater sympathy and understanding for our cause, from people all over the world. I like to think that the award recognizes symbolically the gallantry, the courage and the amazing discipline of the Negro in America, for these things are to his eternal credit. Though we have had riots, the bloodshed that we would have known without the discipline of nonviolence would have been truly frightening. I know that many whites feel the civil rights movement is getting out of hand; this may reassure them. It may let them see that basically this is a disciplined struggle, let them appreciate the *meaning* of our struggle, let them see that a great struggle for human freedom can occur within the framework of a democratic society.

PLAYBOY: Do you feel that this goal will be achieved within your lifetime?

KING: I confess that I do not believe this day is around the corner. The concept of supremacy is so imbedded in the white society that it will take many years for color to cease to be a judgmental factor. But it is certainly my hope and dream. Indeed, it is the keystone of my faith in the future that we will someday achieve a thoroughly integrated society. I believe that before the turn of the century, if trends continue to move and develop as presently, we will have moved a long, long way toward such a society.

PLAYBOY: Do you intend to dedicate the rest of your life, then, to the Negro cause?

KING: If need be, yes. But I dream of the day when the demands presently cast upon me will be greatly diminished. I would say that in the next five years, though, I can't hope for much letup—either in the South or in the North. After that time, it is my hope that things will taper off a bit.

PLAYBOY: If they do, what are your plans?

KING: Well, at one time I dreamed of pastoring for a few years, and then of going to a university to teach theology. But I gave that up when I became deeply involved in the civil rights struggle. Perhaps, in five years or so, if the demands on me have lightened, I will have the chance to make that dream come true.

PLAYBOY: In the meanwhile, you are now the universally acknowledged leader of the American civil rights movement, and chief spokesman for the nation's 20,000,000 Negroes. Are there ever moments when you feel awed by this burden of responsibility, or inadequate to its demands?

KING: One cannot be in my position, looked to by some for guidance, without being constantly reminded of the awesomeness of its responsibility. I live with one deep concern: Am I making the right decisions? Sometimes I am uncertain, and I must look to God for guidance. There was one morning I recall, when I was in Birmingham jail, in solitary, with not even my lawyers permitted to visit, and I was in a nightmare of despair. The very future of our movement hung in the balance, depending upon capricious turns of events over which I could have no control there, incommunicado, in an utterly dark dungeon. This was about ten days after our Birmingham demonstrations began. Over 400 of our followers had gone to jail; some had been bailed out, but we had used up all of our money for bail, and about 300 remained in jail, and I felt personally responsible. It was then that President Kennedy telephoned my wife, Coretta. After that, my jail conditions were relaxed, and the following Sunday afternoon—it was Easter Sunday—two S.C.L.C. attorneys were permitted to visit me. The next day, word came to me from New York that Harry Belafonte had raised $50,000 that was available immediately for bail bonds, and if more was needed, he would raise that. I cannot express what I felt, but I knew at that moment that God's presence had never left me, that He had been with me there in solitary.

I subject myself to self-purification and to endless self-analysis; I question and soul-search constantly into myself to be as certain as I can that I am fulfilling the true meaning of my work, that I am maintaining my sense of purpose, that I am holding fast to my ideals, that I am guiding my people in the right direction. But whatever my doubts, however heavy the burden, I feel that I must accept the task of helping to make this nation and this world a better place to live in—for *all* men, black and white alike.

I never will forget a moment in Birmingham when a white policeman accosted a little Negro girl, seven or eight years old, who was walking in a demonstration with her mother. "What do you want?" the policeman asked her gruffly, and the little girl looked him straight in the eye and answered, "Fee-dom." She couldn't even pronounce it, but she knew. It was beautiful! Many times when I have been in sorely trying situations, the memory of that little one has come into my mind, and has buoyed me.

Similarly, not long ago, I toured in eight communities of the state of Mississippi. And I have carried with me ever since a visual image of the penniless and unlettered, and of the expressions on their faces—of deep and courageous determination to cast off the imprint of the past and become free people. I welcome the opportunity to be a part of this great drama, for it is a drama that will determine America's destiny. If the problem is not solved, America will be on the road to its self-destruction. But if it *is* solved, America will just as surely be on the high road to the fulfillment of the founding fathers' dream, when they wrote: "We hold these truths to be self-evident . . ."

Playboy Interview Interludes

Before my marriage, I was very much a 20th Century modern young woman. I was very independent, which I enjoyed very much. But too much independence for a woman I don't think brings so much happiness.

Princess Grace, January 1966

The Communists need not invade the United States. Pro-Communist sentiment in the U.S. is already greater than when the Bolsheviks overthrew the Kerensky government and took over Russia.

H. L. Hunt, August 1966

There should be a regime in Vietnam that will be genuinely independent and neutral. The only regime I can think of that would be capable of doing this is a united Vietnam under Ho Chi Minh. . . . The Palestinian Arabs have a right to their homes, and I feel that Zionism, by evicting them, has become guilty of colonialism.

Arnold Toynbee, April 1967

Joanne and I have been very fortunate in that we haven't had to be separated that much. I know this is going to sound corny, but there's no reason to roam. I have steak at home; why should I go out for hamburger?

Paul Newman, July 1968

MADALYN MURRAY

October 1965
Interviewer: Richard Tregaskis

The headline read: "A candid conversation with the most hated woman in America"—and she may well have been. Madalyn Murray was the tough, uncompromising woman who challenged organized religion, school prayer, and belief in God, and so became the best-known, most detested atheist in the country. At that time Hefner and the magazine were doing their own questioning of religion, particularly as it applied to legal statutes governing private behavior. So it was not inappropriate that Murray be given her first lengthy interview in PLAYBOY.

Richard Tregaskis, the author of *Guadalcanal Diary*, was given the assignment, and first encountered Murray in a Honolulu hospital, where she was recovering from what she claimed was a beating delivered by God-fearing police in Baltimore. When the interview was delivered to Chicago, Fisher felt that some added questions were necessary, so he conducted the final portion of the interview himself. "I found her an amiable, plump housewife with a bawdy sense of humor," Fisher said. "She was a woman who took her own liberation for granted."

Indeed, her description of herself as a "militant feminist" came as a surprise to the editors, who thought they were getting an interview about atheism. Her freewheeling, raunchy descriptions of her sex life and her calls for equality at all levels for women may mark this interview—along with Ayn Rand's in 1964—as among the earliest such discussions in any mass publication.

The interview drew a near-record response, split predictably between those who thought she was undermining the moral fiber of the country and those delighted to read such radical opinions. But perhaps the most ironic after-the-fact event came in 1979, when Murray's son Bill, whose intellectual curiosity about atheism she credits in the interview with having triggered her own antireligious crusade, announced he had found God and was joining a fundamentalist church to preach the word *against* his mother's beliefs.

Until June 17, 1963, she was dismissed by many people as a litigious, belligerent, loudmouthed crank. On that day, however, the Supreme Court upheld her contention that prayer and Bible study should be outlawed in U.S. public schools, and Madalyn Murray became the country's best-known, and most-hated, atheist. She also became the churches' most formidable enemy when, undaunted, she promptly proceeded to launch another broadside at religion: a suit aimed at eliminating from tax exemption the churches' vast nationwide property holdings—a case which many lawyers concede she will probably win if it gets to the Supreme Court, and which, if she wins it, may be what one attorney has called "the biggest single blow ever suffered by organized religion in this country." Organized religion could hardly have an unlikelier nemesis.

PLAYBOY called the embattled 46-year-old atheist (and onetime socialist) at her home in Honolulu with its request for an exclusive interview. Consenting readily, she invited us to meet her at Honolulu's Tripler Veterans' Hospital, where she was being treated for nerve injuries which she claims were inflicted by the beating she says she sustained at the hands of the police during a melee that precipitated her departure from Baltimore.

Our first two tape sessions took place at her hospital bedside, where she proceeded to hold forth on her various suits, trials and tribulations, on church and state, and on sex and marriage, with a pungent, four-letter vehemence undiminished by her bedridden condition. Our conversations continued some weeks later in the modest frame house which she shares with her mother, her brother and her 11-year-old son Garth on Honolulu's Spencer Street.

No one can predict what the next chapter in the continuing melodrama of Madalyn Murray's life will be; but at this juncture, we feel that an exploration of her intransigent convictions, and of her continuing confrontations with the church, the law and the public, may shed some timely light on the issues involved in her private war on religion.

PLAYBOY: Why are you an atheist, Mrs. Murray?
MURRAY: Because religion is a crutch, and only the crippled need crutches.

I can get around perfectly well on my own two feet, and so can everyone else with a backbone and a grain of common sense. One of the things I did during my 17 years as a psychiatric social worker was go around and find people with mental crutches, and every time I found one, I kicked those goddamn crutches until they flew. You know what happened? Every single one of those people has been able to walk without the crutches—better, in fact. Were they giving up anything intrinsically valuable? Just their irrational reliance upon superstitions and supernatural nonsense. Perhaps this sort of claptrap was good for the Stone Age, when people actually believed that if they prayed for rain they would get it. But we're a grown-up world now, and it's time to put away childish things. But people don't, because most of them don't even know what atheism is. It's not a negation of anything. You don't have to negate what no one can prove exists. No, atheism is a very positive affirmation of man's ability to think for himself, to do for himself, to find answers to his own problems. I'm thrilled to feel that I can rely on myself totally and absolutely; that my children are being brought up so that when they meet a problem they can't cop out by foisting it off on God. Madalyn Murray's going to solve her own problems, and nobody's going to intervene. It's about time the world got up off its knees and looked at itself in the mirror and said: "Well, we are men. Let's start acting like it."

PLAYBOY: What led you to become an atheist?

MURRAY: Well, it started when I was very young. People attain the age of intellectual discretion at different times in their lives—sometimes a little early and sometimes a little late. I was about 12 or 13 years old when I reached this period. It was then that I was introduced to the Bible. We were living in Akron and I wasn't able to get to the library, so I had two things to read at home: a dictionary and a Bible. Well, I picked up the Bible and read it from cover to cover one weekend—just as if it were a novel—very rapidly, and I've never gotten over the shock of it. The miracles, the inconsistencies, the improbabilities, the impossibilities, the wretched history, the sordid sex, the sadism in it—the whole thing shocked me profoundly. I remember I looked in the kitchen at my mother and father and I thought: Can they really *believe* in all that? Of course, this was a superficial survey by a very young girl, but it left a traumatic impression. Later, when I started going to church, my first memories are of the minister getting up and accusing us of being full of sin, though he didn't say why; then they would pass the collection plate, and I got it in my mind that this had to do with purification of the soul, that we were being invited to buy expiation from our sins. So I gave it all up. It was too nonsensical.

A few years later, I went off to college, a good, middle-class, very proper college, where I studied with, and under, good, middle-class, very proper people; which is to say, the kind who regard sex as distasteful and religious doubts as unthinkable; the kind to whom it would never occur to scrutinize the mores of society, who absolutely and unquestioningly accept the social system.

PLAYBOY: What school was it?

MURRAY: Ashland College in Ashland, Ohio—a Brethren institution, where two years of Bible study are required for graduation. One year I studied the Old Testament and one year the New Testament. It was a good, sound, thorough, but completely biased evaluation of the Bible, and I was delighted with it, because it helped to document my doubts; it gave me a framework within which I could be critical. But I can't deny that I was an intellectual prostitute along the way many, many times. I can remember one examination where they said, "Describe the Devil," and in order to get 12 points on that question one had to say that the Devil was red and had a forked tail and cloven hoofs and fangs and horns on his head. So I merrily wrote this answer down and got my 12 points. I always got straight hundreds in Bible study. My independent study continued for 20 years after this. So I do know the Bible very well from a Protestant point of view—which is what, along with my reason, entitles me to refute it. You can't rationally reject something until you know all about it. But at this time, of course, my convictions hadn't yet crystallized intellectually. I didn't know where my doubts were leading me.

I recall that I had a terrible struggle finding anything antireligious in the school libraries. But many years later, the family returned to Pittsburgh and moved into a house where a woman had left a box of books containing 20 volumes on the history of the Inquisition.

It was then that I found out there was a word for people like me: "heretic." I was kind of delighted to find I had an identity. And then, as I grew a little bit older and got interested in law, I read that Clarence Darrow didn't believe in the Bible either. So I read everything he had ever written, all of his trials, everything—to search out the philosophy of his disbelief. But I couldn't find it. Then I went into the Army, and one day, in the middle of a bull session, somebody called me an atheist. Believe it or not, it was the first time I'd ever heard the word. It goes to show you how a person can grow up in America and have a college education and still not know a goddamned thing. Anyway, when I learned that there was such a thing as an atheist, I looked it up—and found out that the definition fitted me to a tee. Finally, at the age of 24, I found out who—and what—I was. Better late than never.

PLAYBOY: Do you think everyone should believe as you do—or rather, disbelieve?

MURRAY: I think this would be the best of all possible worlds if everybody were an atheist or an agnostic or a humanist—his or her own particular brand—but as for compelling people to this, absolutely not. That would be just as infamous as their imposing Christianity on me. At no time have I ever said that people should be stripped of their right to the insanity of belief in God. If they want to practice this kind of irrationality, that's their business. It won't get them anywhere; it certainly won't make them happier or more compassionate human beings; but if they want to chew that particular cud, they're welcome to it.

PLAYBOY: Even as an atheist, would you concede that religion, at its best, can be and has been a constructive force, a source of strength and comfort for many people?

MURRAY: If you're talking about Christianity, absolutely not. I don't think the Church has ever contributed anything to anybody, anyplace, at any time.

PLAYBOY: How about the welfare and charity work to which many Catholic, Protestant and Jewish organizations dedicate themselves?

MURRAY: Oh, they love to point to their hospitals and orphanages—most of which are restricted, by the way. But what do these "good works" amount to? They're nothing but a sop to the clerical conscience, a crumb thrown to the populace, alleviating some of the miseries which the Church itself—particularly the Catholic Church—has helped to instigate and perpetuate. I can't pinpoint a period in history or a place in the universe where religion has actually helped the welfare of man. On the contrary, the history of the Church has been a history of divisiveness, repression and reaction. For almost 2000 years, Christianity has held mankind back in politics, in economics, in industry, in science, in philosophy, in culture. Anyone who has even a surface knowledge of the Middle Ages, when the Church held unchallenged sway, can recognize this. But if any one age could be singled out as the worst in the history of Christendom, it would be the administration of Pope Pius XII, the most reactionary head of the most reactionary single force in the world—a force that binds men's minds, a force that divides them, a force that chains them so that they are unable to think and act for themselves.

PLAYBOY: How do you feel about Pope John XXIII? Don't you think his humanitarian views, as enunciated in his *Pacem in Terris,* testify to the fact that enlightenment can flourish within the confines of the Church?

MURRAY: There are good, humanitarian people everywhere—occasionally even in the Church. But John was an amoeba of goodness in a sea of waste, mistakenly believing that the Holy See could or would really change in any fundamental way. He was a tragic figure, for he raised a false hope, cast a brief ray of light that was snuffed out when he died. With Pope Paul in the saddle, the Church is firmly back in the hands of archconservative reaction.

PLAYBOY: When you say that organized religion has contributed nothing to human welfare, do you include those many clergymen, such as Reverend Reeb, who have risked, and in some cases lost, their lives participating in civil rights demonstrations?

MURRAY: Of course not. Reverend Reeb, by the way, was a well-known atheist, a Unitarian, and was not even buried with a religious ceremony. But those priests, nuns and ministers who aren't afraid to stand up and be counted are very much in the minority. They're the exception that proves the rule. Archbishop Toolen of Mobile-Birmingham has forbidden his priests to participate in Alabama civil rights demonstrations, and Cardinal McIntyre of California has punished priests in his diocese for getting involved in civil rights. These are the men who represent the Church mind —not the poor maverick priest who defies them by marching.

But the most heinous crime of the Church has been perpetrated not against churchmen but against churchgoers. With its poisonous concepts of sin and divine punishment, it's warped and brainwashed countless millions. It would be impossible to calculate the psychic damage this has inflicted on generations of children who might have grown up into healthy, happy, productive, zestful human beings but for the burden of antisexual fear and guilt ingrained in them by the Church. This alone is enough to condemn religion.

PLAYBOY: How do you feel about such Catholic canons as the vow of celibacy for priests, and the spiritual "marriage" of Catholic sisters to Christ?

MURRAY: Sick, sick, sick! You think *I've* got wild ideas about sex? Think of those poor old dried-up women lying there on their solitary pallets yearning for Christ to come to them in a vision some night and take their maidenheads. By the time they realize he's not coming, it's no longer a maidenhead; it's a poor, sorry tent that *nobody* would be able to pierce— even Jesus with his wooden staff. It's such a waste. I don't think *anybody* should be celibate—and that goes for priests as well as nuns. I don't even like to alter a cat. We should all live life to the fullest, and sex is a part of life.

PLAYBOY: As an atheist, do you also reject the idea of the virgin birth?

MURRAY: Even if I believed there was a real Jesus, I wouldn't fall for that line of hogwash. The "Virgin" Mary should get a posthumous medal for telling the biggest goddamn lie that was ever told. Anybody who believes that will believe that the moon is made out of green cheese. If she could get away with something like that, maybe I should have tried it myself. I'm sure she played around as much as I have, and certainly was capable of an orgasm. Let's face it: If a son of God was ever born, it was because of this wonderful sex act that Joseph and Mary enjoyed one night.

PLAYBOY: A moment ago, you said, "Even if I believed there was a real Jesus . . ." Are you saying that you don't believe that there was such a person as Christ, or are you denying his divinity?

MURRAY: I'm saying that there's absolutely no conclusive evidence that he ever really existed, even as a mortal. I don't believe he was a historical figure at all.

PLAYBOY: Do you dismiss all the Biblical records of his life?

MURRAY: Those so-called records were written by devout ecclesiasts who wanted to believe, and wanted others to believe, in the coming of a Messiah. Until someone *proves* otherwise, therefore, these stories must be considered nothing more than folk tales consisting in equal parts of legend and wish fulfillment. But there's never going to be any way of verifying them one way or the other. Scholars have found that references to Christ in Josephus were deliberately planted in the translation long after it was written, and the Latin references to Christ are not to a person of that name. In the Dead Sea Scrolls there *was* mention of a particular "teacher of righteousness" who had characteristics somewhat like those attributed to Christ, but it might easily have been someone else. About six years ago, *Life* magazine ran an article on the historicity of Jesus, and I was floored to find that they conceded the only evidence we have for his existence is in the Gospels. But don't take *Life's* word for it. In his book *The Quest of the Historical Jesus*, the most definitive study that's ever been done on the subject, Albert Schweitzer admitted that there isn't a shred of conclusive proof that Christ ever lived, let alone was the son of God. He concludes that one must therefore accept both on faith. I *reject* both for the same reason.

PLAYBOY: Do you also reject the idea of a life hereafter on the same grounds?

MURRAY: Do you know anybody who's come back with a firsthand report on heaven? If you do, let me know. Until then, you'll pardon me if I don't buy it. If a humanist or an atheist or an agnostic says, "We'll bake you a pie," we can go right into the kitchen and bake it, and you can eat it an hour later. We don't promise you a pie in the sky by and by. It's charlatanry to promise people something that no one can be sure will ever be delivered. But it's even worse to offer people a reward, like children, for being good, and to threaten them with punishment if they're not. I'm reminded of the joke about Saint Peter sitting at the golden gate questioning a new arrival: "Well, my son, what good deeds have you done to get into heaven?" Well, the guy casts about for something to tell him and finally remembers that he gave five cents to a charwoman one night, and once he tipped a bootblack a nickel when he got his shoes shined, and another time he gave a beggar five shiny new pennies. And that's all he can think of that he's ever done for his fellow man. Well, Saint Peter looks at him and says, "Here's your fifteen cents back. You can go to hell."

That guy didn't know how lucky he was. I agree with Mark Twain, who wrote about the hereafter that there's no sex in it; you can't eat anything in it; there is absolutely nothing physical in it. You wouldn't have your brain, you wouldn't have any sensations, you wouldn't be able to enjoy anything—unless you're queer for hymn singing and harp playing. So who needs it? Speaking for myself, I'd rather go to hell.

PLAYBOY: Because of your success in persuading the Supreme Court to outlaw school prayer in public schools, many outraged Christians seem to feel that's just where you belong. What made you decide to pursue your suit in the face of this predictable indignation?

MURRAY: I was shamed into it by my son, Bill, who came to me in 1960— he was 14 then—and said: "Mother, you've been professing that you're an atheist for a long time now. Well, I don't believe in God either, but every day in school I'm forced to say prayers, and I feel like a hypocrite. Why should I be compelled to betray my beliefs?" I couldn't answer him. He quoted the old parable to me: "It is not by their words, but by their deeds that ye shall know them"—pointing out that if I was a true atheist, I would not permit the public schools of America to force him to read the Bible and say prayers against his will. He was right. Words divorced from action supporting them are meaningless and hypocritical. So we began the suit. And finally we won it. I knew it wasn't going to make me the most popular woman in Baltimore, but I sure as hell didn't anticipate the tidal wave of virulent, vindictive, murderous hatred that thundered down on top of me and my family in its wake.

PLAYBOY: Tell us about it.

MURRAY: God, where should I begin? Well, it started fairly predictably with economic reprisals. Now, I'd been a psychiatric social worker for 17 years, but within 24 hours after I started the case, I was fired from my job as a supervisor in the city public welfare department. And I was unable to find another one, because the moment I would go in anywhere in town and say that my name was Madalyn Murray, no matter what the job opening, I found the job filled; no matter how good my qualifications, they were never quite good enough. So my income was completely cut off. The second kind of reprisal was psychological. The first episode was with our mail, which began to arrive, if at all, slit open and empty—just empty envelopes. Except for the obscene and abusive letters from good Christians all over the country, calling me a bitch and a Lesbian and a Communist for instituting the school-prayer suit—they somehow arrived intact, and by the bushel-basketful. Hundreds of them actually threatened our lives; we had to turn a lot of them over to the FBI, because they were obviously written by psychopaths, and you couldn't be sure whether or not they were going to act on their very explicit threats. None did, but it didn't help us sleep any better at night.

Neither did the incredible anonymous phone calls we'd get at every hour of the day and night, which were more or less along the same lines as the letters. One of them was a particular gem. I was in the VA hospital in Baltimore, and I had just had a very critical operation; they didn't think I was going to make it. They had just wheeled me back to my bed after two days in the recovery room when this call came in for me, and somebody who wouldn't give his name told me very seriously and sympathetically that my father had just died and that I should be prepared to come home and take care of my mother. Well, I called home in a state of shock, and my mother answered, and I asked her about Father, and she said, "What are you talking about? He's sitting here at this moment eating bacon and eggs." Obviously, that call had been calculated to kill me, because whoever it was knew that I was at a low ebb there in the hospital.

Then they began to take more direct action. My Freethought Society office was broken into; our cars were vandalized repeatedly; every window in the house was broken more times than I can count, every flower in my garden trampled into the ground, all my maple trees uprooted; my property looked like a cyclone had hit it. This is the kind of thing that went on constantly, *constantly,* over a three-year period. But it was just child's play compared to the reprisals visited upon my son Bill. He'd go to school every day and hand in his homework, and a couple of days later many of his teachers would say to him, "You didn't hand in your homework." Or he'd take a test and about a week later many of his teachers would tell him, "You didn't hand in your test paper. You'll have to take the test again this afternoon." This was a dreadful reprisal to take against a 14-year-old boy. It got to the point where he had to make carbon copies of all his homework and all his tests to prove that he had submitted them But that's nothing to what happened *after* school, both to him and to his little brother, Garth. I lost count of the times they came home bloodied and beaten up by gangs of teenage punks; five and six of them at a time would gang up on them and beat the living hell out of them. Many's the time I've stood them off myself to protect my sons, and these fine young Christians have spat in my face till spittle dripped down on my dress. Time and again we'd take them into magistrate's court armed with damning evidence and eyewitness testimony, but the little bastards were exonerated every time.

But I haven't told you the worst. The neighborhood children, of course, were forbidden by their parents to play with my little boy, Garth, so I finally got him a little kitten to play with. A couple of weeks later we found it on the porch with its neck wrung. And then late one night our house was attacked with stones and bricks by five or six young Christians, and my father got very upset and frightened. Well, the next day he dropped dead of a heart attack. The community knew very well that he had a heart condition, so I lay a murder to the city of Baltimore.

I decided that we'd have to take our chances with the law and get the hell out of Baltimore. I thought of seeking asylum in Canada or Australia or England, but I didn't want to leave the United States, because for better or worse I'm an American, and this is my land; so I decided to fight it out on home ground, and finally we hit upon Hawaii, because of the liberal atmosphere created by its racial admixture, and because of its relatively large population of Buddhists, who are largely nontheistic, and might therefore be more tolerant of our views. So we packed up all the worldly possessions we could carry with us and took the next flight to Hawaii from Washington.

PLAYBOY: How many were in your party?

MURRAY: Six of us—my mother, my brother, my two sons, Bill's wife and me. And I can tell you, it took just about every cent we had to our name just to pay the plane fare. When we arrived, we had about $15 left among us. We were really in pitiful shape. But we were together, and we were alive, and this was all that mattered.

PLAYBOY: How did you find a place to stay?

MURRAY: Well, we were just floored by the kindness of the people here. The minister of the Unitarian Church in Honolulu invited us over to his office the day we arrived and told us to make it our headquarters while we looked for a permanent residence. When we couldn't find a place for about a week, he let us live in the church; that's ironic, isn't it? But it points up the vastly different intellectual atmosphere that prevails here in Hawaii. Anyway, we rustled up some mattresses and put them on the floor and slept there, cooked there and ate there until we found a home. I was overwhelmed by the number of calls we got from people offering to rent us houses, to take us out to dinner, to drive us around house hunting. Everyone was just indescribably kind. Finally we moved into a house offered to us for an incredible $125 a month by a man who feels that the separation of church and state is a valid constitutional issue which should be fought for.

PLAYBOY: Considering the repercussions of the school-prayer case, why did you decide to take on the tax-the-churches suit?

MURRAY: Once involved in the school-prayer fight, I rapidly became aware of, and appalled by, the political and economic power of the Church in America—all based on the violation of one of our nation's canon laws: the separation of church and state. The churches rose to power on the income from tax-free property. What earthly—or heavenly—right have they got to enjoy a privilege denied to everyone else, even including non-profit organizations? None! My contention is that with the churches exempted from property taxation, you and I have to pay that much more in taxes—about $140 a year per family, according to a recent survey—to make up for what they're not contributing. If this exemption were rescinded, our property taxes would be substantially lowered, and those who rent houses and apartments would consequently be able to pass along this savings in the form of lowered rents. It could have a profoundly salubrious effect on the entire economy. I decided that if nobody else was going to do anything to rectify this colossal inequity, I'd have to do it myself. So I instituted a suit against the city of Baltmore demanding that the city assessor be specifically ordered to assess the Church for its vast property holdings in the city, and that the city tax collector then be instructed to collect the taxes once the assessment has been made.

PLAYBOY: Have you made any estimate of approximately how many annual tax dollars the churches will have to pay if you win your suit?

MURRAY: On a nationwide basis, I would guess that the various churches would have to pay annually an amount at least equal to the national debt. But it's impossible for me to make an exact estimate, because the churches hide their wealth in every way they can—deliberate falsification as to the value of property, registering it under phony names in order to obscure the fact that the Church owns the property. In Baltimore alone, I know that the Roman Catholic Church alone would have to pay taxes of almost $3,000,000 a year. This is why the Roman Catholic Church has become a codefendant with the city in the suit—an unprecedented occurrence in a case of this nature. I'm going after them where they live—in their pocketbooks— and they're fighting for their lives. They have a tremendous amount at stake—more than any other church, because they're the biggest property owners and they've dabbled in business more than any other church. More than any other church, they've been greedy about grabbing up land and property—not just in Baltimore, but all over the country. According to a Catholic priest writing in *The Wall Street Journal,* the assets and real-estate holdings of the Church "exceed those of Standard Oil, A.T.&T. and U. S. Steel combined." I'd make an educated guess that 20 to 25 percent of the taxable property in the U.S. is Church-owned. In a recent book, *Church Wealth and Business Income*, it was estimated that this property—all of it tax-exempt—is worth upwards of 80 billion dollars. I know that's a fantastic, unbelievable figure, but there's every reason to believe that it's on the con-servative side; and this amount is increasing yearly at a geometric rate. They're moving into everything—gas stations, banks, television stations, supermarket chains, hotels, steel mills, resort areas, farms, wine factories, warehouses, bottling works, printing plants, schools, theaters—everything you could conceivably think of that has nothing to do with religion, they are moving into big. They're even coming in as stockholders in the big oil companies, and the Bank of America is almost entirely owned by the Catholic Church. And mind you—they don't pay a penny in taxes on any of it, even on the income from rentals. The Roman Catholic Knights of Columbus, for example, pays *no* income tax on any of its vast rental revenue—which comes from such sources as the land on which Yankee Stadium stands. Almost every constitutional authority has spoken on this issue, and the overwhelming consensus is that we will *win* if we can get it to the U.S. Supreme Court. But we won't unless thousands of people help me raise the money to pay the legal fees—at least $40,000.

PLAYBOY: You've been quoted as saying that the Catholic Church in Baltimore was behind a conspiracy to have you and your family jailed on some pretext so that you would be unable to pursue this suit, and that this is why you were subjected to a "campaign of extralegal harassment" by the police, the courts and the citizens of Baltimore. Do you really believe that?

MURRAY: I can't think of any other plausible explanation for this vendetta. But quite apart from the Church's financial self-interest in getting me out of the way, Baltimore is an overwhelmingly Catholic city and, like most good Christians, they felt we ought to be punished for our unorthodox views. Intolerance has always been one of the cornerstones of Christianity— the glorious heritage of the Inquisition. It's no coincidence that most of my abusive mail—sentencing me to exquisite Oriental tortures and relegating me to hell-fire and damnation—comes from self-admitted Catholics.

PLAYBOY: Are you still receiving that kind of mail here in Hawaii?

MURRAY: For some reason, the letters we've been getting here have been just a little bit more rational; I wonder what's happened to our lunatic fringe. I kind of miss them.

PLAYBOY: Is it true that you received a letter in Baltimore composed only of the word "Kill" clipped from dozens of magazines and newspapers, and pasted onto a sheet of paper in the style of a blackmail note?

MURRAY: Absolutely. It was from a man who had written to me over a period of about two years. He started out in his first letter with something innocuous like: "You're a damn fool!" But each successive letter got more and more violent, until he came to the point where he was very explicit in his threats. We turned that whole series of letters over to the FBI. One of the things this guy said he was going to do to me was put a gun up my ass and blow the crap out between my eyes. Nice? But that's mild compared to some of them. I've gotten literally thousands in the same vein. Someday I'd like to publish a book of these mash notes. It would be an extraordinary document. I'd call it *Letters from Christians*.

PLAYBOY: Would you include the photograph of yourself which you received smeared with feces?

MURRAY: That would be the frontispiece. This was a picture of my mother and me coming out of the United States Supreme Court, with fecal matter smeared across our faces. They wrapped it in wax paper so that when I received it I'd get the full impact of the message. Though I haven't gotten anything quite that original lately, there's still never a dull moment in my mailbox. Shall I read you excerpts from a random sampling?

PLAYBOY: Please.

MURRAY: You asked for it. Here goes: "You should be shot!" . . . "Why don't you go peddle your slop in Russia?" . . . "YOU WICKID ANAMAL" . . . "I will KILL you!" . . . "Commie, Commie, Commie!" . . . "Somebody is going to put a bullet through your fat ass, you scum, you masculine Lesbian bitch!" . . . "You will be killed before too long. Or maybe your pretty little baby boy. The queer-looking bastard. You are a bitch and your son is a bastard" . . . "Slut! Slut! Slut! Bitch slut from the Devil!"

That'll give you the general idea. Oh—just one more; I love this one: "May Jesus, who you so vigorously deny, change you into a Paul."

Isn't that lovely? Christine Jorgensen had to go to Sweden for an operation, but me they'll fix with faith—painlessly and for nothing. I hate to disappoint them, but I'm not the least bit interested in being a man. I'm perfectly satisfied with the female role.

PLAYBOY: What *is* the proper female role, in your opinion?

MURRAY: Well, as a militant feminist, I believe in complete equality with men: intellectual, professional, economic, social and sexual; they're all equally essential, and they're all equally lacking in American society today.

PLAYBOY: According to many sociologists, American women have never enjoyed greater freedom and equality, sexually and otherwise, than they do today.

MURRAY: Let's distinguish between freedom and equality. The modern American woman may be more liberated sexually than her mother was, but I don't think she enjoys a bit more sexual equality. The American male continues to use her sexually for one thing: a means to the end of his own ejaculation. It doesn't seem to occur to him that she might be a worthwhile end in herself, or to see to it that *she* has a proper sexual release. And, to him, sex appeal is directly proportional to the immensity of a woman's tits. I'm not saying that all American men are this way, but nine out of ten are breast-fixated, wham-bam-thank-you-ma'am cretins who just don't give a damn about anyone's gratification but their own.

If you're talking about intellectual and social equality for women, we're not much better off. We're just beginning to break the ice. America is still very much a male-dominated society. Most American men feel threatened sexually unless they're taller than the female, more intellectual, better educated, better paid and higher placed statuswise in the business world. They've got to be the authority, the final word. They say they're looking for a girl just like the girl who married dear old dad, but what they really want, and usually get, is an empty-headed little chick who's very young and very physical—and very submissive. Well, I just can't see either a man or a woman in a dependency position, because from this sort of relationship flows a feeling of superiority on one side and inferiority on the other, and that's a form of slow poison. As I see it, men wouldn't want somebody inferior to them unless they felt inadequate themselves. They're intimidated by a mature woman.

PLAYBOY: Like yourself?

MURRAY: Yes, as a matter of fact. I think I actually *frighten* men. I think I scare the hell out of them time after time. It's going to take a pretty big man to tame this shrew. I need somebody who can at least stand up to me and slug it out, toe to toe. I don't mean a physical battle. I mean a man who would lay me, and when he was done, I'd say: "Oh, brother, I've been *laid*." Or if we had an argument, he would stand up and engage in intellectual combat and not go off and mope in the corner, or take reprisals, or go to drink. I want somebody who's whole and wholesome and has as much zest for living as I have. But I haven't found *one* who fills the bill; you can't hardly find them kind no more. And I know many women my size, psychologically and intellectually, who have the same problem.

PLAYBOY: How many lovers have you had, if you don't mind our asking?

MURRAY: You've got a hell of a nerve, but I don't really mind. I've had— if you count my marriage as an affair, which I would like to do rather than count it as a marriage, because I'm not proud of having been married— I've had five affairs, all of them real wingdings. I've enjoyed every god-damned minute of them, but sooner or later I've outgrown every one of them, and when I did I got fed up and threw them out. If they can't keep up with me, the hell with them.

PLAYBOY: Suppose a man were to get fed up with you first. What then?

MURRAY: Well, then *he* should be the one to pick up and leave. No hard feelings. I don't feel that people should glom onto other people. I feel that relationships should be nice and easy and convenient and happy and not strictured with legality or jealousy.

PLAYBOY: When you say "not strictured with legality," are you saying that you don't think people ought to get married?

MURRAY: Well, I've found that most people who are bound together legally would be a damn sight happier together—or apart—if they were released from the contract. A man-woman relationship is physical and emotional, not legal. Legality can't create love if it isn't there, or preserve it if it's dying, but it can *destroy* love by making it compulsory. You don't need a marriage license to live with someone, to have the security of a home, to rear any number of children, to have years of companionship; it's not illegal, But the moment you want to screw somebody, you have to get a license from the state to use your genital organs—or run the risk of being charged with any number of crimes carrying sentences up to and including death. So sex is really the only sensible reason for getting married. But I'd suggest pulling down the shades instead. In the long run, it's cheaper—and more fun.

PLAYBOY: How do you feel about the heritage of puritanical sexual guilt which many social scientists assert precipitates early marriages in this country?

MURRAY: It's shit for the birds. When will we grow up? Sex is where you find it. I say take it and enjoy it. Give and receive freely, without fear, without guilt and without contractual obligations.

PLAYBOY: Starting at what age?

MURRAY: Let nature decide. When a cow is biologically ready to have sex relations, she mates with the nearest well-hung bull. When a flower is ready to scatter its seed, it pollinates. It's the same way throughout nature— except with man, who tries to postpone consummation of his sex drive, unsuccessfully, for the most part, for six or eight years after he reaches puberty. By the time it's considered socially acceptable to start screwing, most of us are sexually constipated, and this is often an incurable condition. I think young people should be able to have their first sexual love affair whenever they feel like it. In the case of most girls, this would be around 13 or 14; with most boys, around 15 or 16.

PLAYBOY: What about VD and pregnancy?

MURRAY: They should be taught about sex, sex hygiene and contraceptive methods starting in the sixth grade, and whenever they want to try it, they should be allowed to go at it without supervision or restriction—in their parents' bedroom, on the grass in a park, in a motel; it doesn't matter, as long as the setting is private and pleasant. If we did all this, our kids would grow up into happier, healthier human beings. But we won't, of course. It would make too much sense.

PLAYBOY: Would you call yourself an advocate of free love?

MURRAY: I'd describe myself as a sexual libertarian—but I'm not a libertine. "To each his own" is my motto. If anybody wants to engage in any kind of sexual activity with any consenting partner, that is their business. I don't feel that I can sit in judgment on them, or that society can sit in judgment on them. Anybody can do anything they damn well please, as long as the relationship isn't exploitive. And I don't feel that legality should have anything to do with it. There are certain bodily functions of mine which I will not allow to be supervised. One of these is eating. Nobody's going to license me to do this. Another one is bodily disposals. I will defecate and urinate when I damn well please and as the spirit—and the physical necessity—moves me. And my sex life is peculiarly my own. I will engage in sexual activity with a consenting male any time and any place I damn well please.

PLAYBOY: Do you have any immediate plans along these lines?

MURRAY: It's none of your business, but as a matter of fact, I do. I've been completely without a sex life for about five years now—ever since I began the school-prayer suit—and if you don't think that's a hardship for a hot-blooded woman in her prime, just try it. I'm taking applications for stud service at this address—care of Good and Haffner, Attorneys, 1010 Standard Building, Cleveland 13, Ohio—as well as contributions for our tax-the-churches suit. Please enclose photograph, vital statistics, and a check for the lawsuit.

PLAYBOY: Are there any particular qualifications you're looking for?

MURRAY: No, I just want a man—a real, two-balled masculine guy—and there aren't many of them around, believe me. But I do want somebody my own age, and somebody who has brains enough to keep me interested and to earn enough money to support me in the style to which I've become accustomed. And I want a big man physically as well as intellectually. I want a man with the thigh muscles to give me a good frolic in the sack, the kind who'll tear hell out of a thick steak, and yet who can go to the ballet with me and discuss Hegelian dialectic and know what the hell he's talking about. I want a strong man, but a gentle one. And, most unlikely of all, but most essential, I want a man with a capacity for love—to give it generously and accept it joyously. I also want somebody who, when I say, "Let's call it quits," won't hang on; who'll say, "All right, it was fun while it lasted. So long and good luck."

PLAYBOY: Have you ever known a man like that?

MURRAY: No, but there was one who came close, and I loved him madly for some time. I don't think anybody in the world thought he was gentle, but he was gentle with *me*. And he treated me like a woman, which is all I really ask or want. I felt *handled* by him, and this is a good feeling. But, unfortunately, he never outgrew his particular intellectual commitment, so I outgrew *him*. He was an engineer and he was almost totally involved in his work; engineers have a very limited education and background, I think. You need to move into the broader humanities in order to become a total person. But I loved him very much.

PLAYBOY: Was he the one you loved most?

MURRAY: I think so. He's a damned Dago. That's a term of affection.

PLAYBOY: Of the men you've had affairs with, how many others were foreigners?

MURRAY: None of them. But they were of different extractions. This particular guy was of Italian parentage; another had English blood; one was a real upper-class Bostonian; one had a Russian background, and one was Irish; he was the one that was best in bed. Did you know that we ladies have bull sessions like this among ourselves, and we talk about which of you fellows are good stud service and which ones aren't? If you boys knew what you sound like when you and your bedroom manners are dissected by a bunch of WACs, it would curl your hair, because we talk about exactly the same things you do among yourselves—and just as graphically.

Say, I wonder why I'm telling you all this. I know I'm being indiscreet, because this kind of thing could be used against me nationwide; it'll just add fuel to the fire, which is already hot enough for me. But you know something? It just so happens that I don't give a damn. I'm going to be damned anyway. If they haven't destroyed me yet, I'd say I'm indestructible.

Five years ago, before I opened Pandora's box by starting the school-prayer case, I was doing all right financially; I had my health, a good job, a nice brick Colonial home, beautiful furniture, three cars; we were a happy close-knit, well-adjusted family. Well, brother, look at me now, as the saying goes: Here I am in a termite-ridden bungalow in Hawaii; my savings are gone; my job is gone; my health is gone—thanks to the beating I got in Baltimore, which has lost me almost all the use of two fingers in my right hand. I'm bothered by a continuous low-grade pain in that same hand

and arm, which distracts me from my work and keeps me awake nights. My Baltimore home is in jeopardy; I may lose it. I've lost my furniture and my cars. My brother can't find a job, though he's been looking for work ever since we arrived here; so he's just a nice, educated bum at this point. I've lost my father by a heart attack, and my son Bill has broken down emotionally to the extent that he's under psychiatric care. My aged mother is with me, and she can't even be buried next to Dad, whose grave is back in Baltimore. And my son and I are living under the Damoclean sword of imminent extradition back to Maryland, where we are certain to be convicted and sentenced to several years in the state penitentiary for assault—a crime which we not only didn't commit, but which was perpetrated against *us*. So my life and the life of my family has been completely disrupted in absolutely every way. But it's been worth it. It's uncovered a vast cesspool of illegitimate economic and political power in which the Church is immersed right up to its ears, and I intend to dive in headfirst and pull it out of there dripping wet for all the world to see—no matter how long it takes, no matter whose feet get stepped on in the process, no matter how much it costs, no matter how great the personal sacrifice.

PLAYBOY: It sounds as if you intend to make this cause your *raison d'être*.

MURRAY: No, this crusade to separate church and state is only one expression of my *raison d'être*. I'm an atheist, but I'm also an anarchist, and a feminist, and an integrationist, and an internationalist—and all the other "ists" that people seem to find so horrible these days. I embrace all of them.

Long ago, when I was a very young girl, I said that I wanted to go everywhere, see everything, taste everything, hear everything, touch everything, try everything before I died. Well, I've been a model, I've been a waitress, I've been a hairdresser, I've been a stenographer, I've been a lawyer, I've been an aerodynamics engineer, I've been a social worker, I've been an advertising manager, I've been a WAC. There isn't anything you can name that a woman can do that I haven't done. Before they put me under, I'm going to get involved in everything there is to get involved in. That's what I want from life. I don't intend to stand by and be a spectator. I want to be right in there in the midst of it, right up to my nose—totally involved in the community, in the world, in the stream of history, in the human image. I want to drink life to the dregs, to enlarge myself to the absolute limits of my being—and to strive for a society in which everyone—regardless of race, creed, color and especially religious conviction—has the same exhilarating *raison d'être*, and the same opportunity to fulfill it. In other words, to paraphrase Jack Kennedy and John Paul Jones, from this day forward, let the word go forth, to friend and foe alike: I have not yet begun to fight.

GEORGE LINCOLN ROCKWELL

April 1966
Interviewer: Alex Haley

It may have been one of the most dramatic moments in the magazine's history: Alex Haley, sitting across from the "führer" of the American Nazi party, a revolver on the desk between them, as George Lincoln Rockwell explained his intentions to ship "niggers" back to Africa, exile "queers," and exterminate Jews. Haley's first-person account in the introduction sets the scene memorably, so the introduction is reprinted in full, omitting only Rockwell's biographical summary.

What the public did not learn from the introduction, however, was of the odd relationship that had grown up between Haley and Rockwell. After their initial confrontation, described below, the interview continued for several weeks, and when they were alone, Rockwell would drop his guard and ask Haley's advice about writing and show business. Fisher recalls: "Rockwell wanted to be an actor or an author, but he was constantly surrounded by illiterate storm troopers. Alex traveled in a world Rockwell always wanted to be a part of." The attempts at friendship would take place only when they were alone; the bluster and racism would return as soon as Rockwell was in earshot of his followers.

After the interview was completed, but before it was published, the two men struck up a correspondence. Haley would be traveling on assignment, and would write to Rockwell that he was off to Monaco or Dakar—to provoke him. Rockwell would write back long, touching letters with the initials V.I.N. on the envelope—Very Important Nigger, which Haley found sad and funny. "There was so much of the child in that man," he later said.

Perhaps the most dramatic development to come out of this interview was its inclusion in the script of "Roots II" on ABC television in 1978. The story of Haley's family ends with his own personal history, and includes the assignment he was given by PLAYBOY to interview Rockwell. In a climactic scene, James Earl Jones, playing Haley, sits across from Rockwell, who is played by Marlon Brando.

In real life, however, Haley later brooded that Rockwell was his third Playboy Interview subject—after Malcolm X and Martin Luther King, Jr.—to have died by assassins' bullets. He said he knew it was morbid, but he wondered if his assignments didn't have a curse on them. (Other Haley interviews, not reprinted here, included athlete-actor Jim Brown and entertainer Johnny Carson.) It was a coincidence, of course, but it is a fact that with his PLAYBOY interviews, Haley chronicled some tragic chapters in contemporary American history.

Publishing footnote: This is the only time that a PLAYBOY interviewer uses the word "I" in the interview—for reasons that will be evident. And again, the reader will note in the introduction the efforts made to put some distance between the magazine and the subject.

"Genocidal maniac!" "Barnum of the bigots!" These are among the more temperate epithets hurled regularly—along with eggs, paint, pop bottles, rocks and rotten vegetables—at George Lincoln Rockwell, self-appointed Führer *of the American Nazi Party and self-styled messiah of white supremacy and intransigent anti-Semitism. Reveling in his carefully cultivated role as a racist bogeyman, he has earned—and openly enjoys—the dubious distinction of being perhaps the most universally detested public figure in America today; even the Ku Klux Klan, which shares his Jew-hating, segregationist convictions, has officially disowned and denounced him.*

Unlike controversial past interviewees, such as atheist Madalyn Murray, Rockwell could not be called a spokesman for any socially or politically significant minority; indeed, his fanatical following is both motley and minuscule (estimates of Nazi Party membership range from 25 to 100). But we felt that the very virulence of Rockwell's messianic master-racism could transform a really searching conversation with the 48-year-old Führer *into a revealing portrait of both rampant racism and the pathology of fascism. The results—obtained for us by interviewer Alex Haley— explosively exceeded our expectations. Of the experience, Haley writes:*

"I called Rockwell at his Arlington, Virginia, headquarters and relayed PLAYBOY's request for an exclusive interview. After assuring himself that I wasn't Jewish, he guardedly agreed. I didn't tell him I was a Negro. Five days later, as my taxi pulled up in front of Rockwell's 'International Head-quarters,' a nine-room white frame house in Arlington (since padlocked by the Internal Revenue Service, which is currently investigating the labyrinth of Nazi financial backing), I noticed a billboard-sized sign on the roof reading: WHITE MAN FIGHT—SMASH THE BLACK REVOLUTION! I couldn't help wondering what kind of welcome I'd receive when they got a look at my non-Aryan complexion. I didn't have long to wait; the khaki-clad duty guard at the door stiffened as I stepped out of the cab and up the front stairs. When I identified myself, he ushered me uncertainly inside and told me to wait nearby in what he called 'the shrine room,' a small, black-walled chamber dimly lit by flickering red candles and adorned with American and Nazi flags, adjoining portraits of Adolf Hitler and George Washington, and a slightly larger, rather idealized painting of Rockwell him-self—a self-portrait. On the table beside my chair sat a crudely bound and printed copy of Rockwell's self-published autobiography, 'This Time the World'; I was leafing through it when a pair of uniformed 'storm troopers' loomed suddenly in the doorway, gave the Nazi salute and informed me coolly that Commander Rockwell had ordered them to take me in one of the Party staff cars to his nearby personal headquarters.

"Fifteen minutes later, with me and my tape recorder in the back and my two chaperones in the front, the car turned into a narrow, tree-lined road, slowed down as it passed a NO TRESPASSING sign (stamped with a skull and crossbones) and a leashed Doberman watchdog, and finally pulled up in front of a white, 16-room farmhouse emblazoned at floor- and second-story levels with four-foot-high red swastikas. About a dozen Nazis stared icily as the guards walked me past them and up the stairs to Rockwell's door, where a sidearmed storm trooper frisked me expertly from head to toe. Within arm's reach, I noticed, was a wooden rack holding short combat lengths of sawed-off iron pipe. Finding me 'clean,' the guard ceremoniously opened the door, stepped inside, saluted, said, 'Sieg heil!'—echoed brusquely from within—then stood aside and nodded permission for me to come ahead. I did.

"As if for dramatic effect, Rockwell was standing across the room, corn-cob pipe in hand, beneath a portrait of Adolf Hitler. Warned about my Negritude, he registered no surprise nor did he smile, speak or offer to shake hands. Instead, after surveying me up and down for a long moment, he motioned me peremptorily to a seat, then sat down himself in a nearby easy chair and watched silently while I set up my tape machine. Rockwell al-ready had one of his own, I noticed, spinning on a nearby table. Then, with the burly guard standing at attention about halfway between us, he *took out a pearl-handled revolver, placed it pointedly on the arm of his chair, sat back and spoke for the first time: 'I'm ready if you are.' Without any further pleasantries, I turned on my machine."*

PLAYBOY: Before we begin, Commander, I wonder if you'd mind telling me why you're keeping that pistol there at your elbow, and this armed bodyguard between us.

ROCKWELL: Just a precaution. You may not be aware of the fact that I have received literally thousands of threats against my life. Most of them are from cranks, but some of them *haven't* been; there are bullet holes all over the outside of this building. Just last week, two gallon jugs of flaming gasoline were flung against the house right under my window. I keep this gun within reach and a guard beside me during interviews because I've been attacked too many times to take any chances. I haven't yet been jumped by an impostor, but it wasn't long ago that 17 guys claiming to be from a university came here to "interview" me; nothing untoward happened, but we later found out they were armed and planned to tear down the flag, burn the joint and beat me up. Only the fact that we were ready for that kind of rough stuff kept it from happening. We've never yet had to hurt anybody, but only because I think they all know we're ready to fight any time. If you're who you claim to be, you have nothing to fear.

PLAYBOY: I don't.

ROCKWELL: Good. Just so we both know where we stand, I'd like to make something else crystal clear before we begin. I'm going to be honest and direct with you. You're here in your professional capacity; I'm here in *my* professional capacity. While here, you'll be treated well—but I see you're a black interviewer. It's nothing personal, but I want you to understand that I don't mix with your kind, and we call your race "niggers."

PLAYBOY: I've been called "nigger" many times, Commander, but this is the first time I'm being *paid* for it. So you go right ahead. What have you got against us "niggers"?

ROCKWELL: I've got nothing against you. I just think you people would be happier back in Africa where you came from. When the pilgrims got pushed around in Europe, they didn't have any sit-ins or crawl-ins; they got out and went to a wilderness and built a great civilization.

PLAYBOY: It was built with the help of Negroes.

ROCKWELL: Help or no, the white people in America simply aren't going to allow you to mix totally with them, whether you like it or not.

PLAYBOY: The purpose of the civil rights movement is equality of rights and opportunity, Commander—not miscegenation, as you seem to be implying.

ROCKWELL: Equality may be the *stated* purpose, but race mixing is what it boils down to in practice; and the harder you people push for that, the madder white people are going to get.

PLAYBOY: Do you think you're entitled to speak for white people?

ROCKWELL: Malcolm X said the same thing I'm saying.

PLAYBOY: He certainly was in no position to speak for white people.

ROCKWELL: Well, I think I *am* speaking for the majority of whites when I say that race mixing just isn't going to work. I think, therefore, that we should take the billions of dollars now being wasted on foreign aid to Communist countries which hate us and give that money to our own niggers to build their own civilized nation in Africa.

PLAYBOY: Apart from the fact that Africa is already spoken for territorially by sovereign nations, all but a few of the 20,000,000 Negroes in this country are native-born Americans who have just as much right to remain here as you do, Commander.

ROCKWELL: That's not my point. When two people prove incompatible in marriage and they can't live together, they separate; and the mass of average niggers simply don't "fit" in modern American society. A leopard doesn't change his spots just because you bring him in from the jungle and try to housebreak him and turn him into a pet. He may learn to sheathe his claws in order to beg a few scraps off the dinner table, and you may teach him to be a beast of burden, but it doesn't pay to forget that he'll always be what he was born: a wild animal.

PLAYBOY: We're talking about human beings, not animals.

ROCKWELL: We're talking about niggers—and there's no doubt in my mind that they're basically animalistic.

PLAYBOY: In what way?

ROCKWELL: Spiritually. Our white kids are being perverted, like Pavlov's dogs, by conditioned-reflex training. For instance, every time a white kid is getting a piece of ass, the car radio is blaring nigger bebop. Under such powerful stimuli, it's not long before a kid begins unconsciously to connect these savage sounds with intense pleasure and thus transfers his natural pleasurable reactions in sex to an unnatural love of the chaotic and animalistic nigger music, which destroys a love of order and real beauty among our kids. This is how you niggers corrupt our white kids—without even laying a dirty hand on them. Not that you wouldn't like to.

PLAYBOY: It's sometimes the other way around, Commander.

ROCKWELL: Well, I'll have to admit one great failing of my own people: The white man is getting too soft. The niggers are forced to do hard manual labor, and as a result, most nigger bucks are healthy animals—rugged and tough, the way nature intended a male to be. When you take a look at how the average, bourgeois white man spends his time, though—hunched over a desk, going to the ballet, riding around on his electric lawn mower or squatting on his fur-lined toilet seat—you can't help but observe how soft and squishy a lot of white men allow themselves to become; especially some of the skinny, pasty-faced white peace creeps with their long hair, their fairy-looking clothes and the big yellow stripe up their spineless back. What normal woman would want one of *these* cruds? Unfortunately, some of our white women, especially in the crazy leftist environment on our college campuses, get carried away by Jewish propaganda into betraying their own instincts by choosing a healthy black buck instead of one of these skinny, pansified white peace creeps who swarm on our college campuses.

PLAYBOY: Are you implying that the Negro male is sexually superior to the white man?

ROCKWELL: Certainly not. The average white workingman, the vast majority of white men, are just as tough and ballsy as any nigger who ever lived. It's the white *intellectuals* who have allowed themselves to be degenerate physically, mentally and especially spiritually, until I am forced to admit that a healthy nigger garbage man is certainly superior physically and sexually to a pasty-faced skinny white peace creep.

PLAYBOY: Do you consider Negroes superior to white men in any other way?

ROCKWELL: On the contrary—I consider them *inferior* to the white man in *every* other way.

PLAYBOY: That's a fairly sweeping generalization. Can you document it?

ROCKWELL: When I speak at colleges, they often ask me the same question. I always answer with a question of my own: How do colleges determine the superior and inferior students? By *performance*, that's how! Look at history; investigate the different races. The Chinese perform; they've created a great civilization. And the white races certainly perform. But the nigger race, until very recently, has done absolutely nothing.

PLAYBOY: How recently?

ROCKWELL: The past 20 or 30 years.

PLAYBOY: What about the contribution of those millions of African Negroes and their descendants—along with that of migrants of every color from all over the world—who helped found and build this country?

ROCKWELL: I don't dismiss it, but the fact is that any contribution of the niggers has been almost entirely manual and menial. *Horses* could have done most of it, or well-trained monkeys from the same trees *they* were flushed out of back in Africa. They've picked up a few more tricks since then—but only what they've learned from the white man.

PLAYBOY: Recent archaeological findings have documented the existence of advanced black African civilizations centuries before the dawn of comparable cultures in Europe.

ROCKWELL: If they were so far ahead of us then, why are they still shooting blow darts at each other while we're launching rockets to the moon?

PLAYBOY: The American space program isn't a segregated project, Commander. There are many Negroes working for NASA and in the space industry.

ROCKWELL: This only proves my point. A few niggers, like trained chimpanzees, have been pushed and jammed into such things as the space program by our race-mixing Presidents and the Federal Government; but niggers didn't originate any of the ideas or develop the fantastic organizations capable of putting men into space. The niggers in NASA are like chimpanzees who have learned to ride bicycles. A few trained monkeys riding bicycles doesn't prove that chimpanzees could invent or build or even *think about* a bicycle. The fact is that the average nigger is not as intelligent as the average white man.

PLAYBOY: There's no genetic or anthropological evidence to substantiate that.

ROCKWELL: I know you're going to say you can show me thousands of intelligent niggers and stupid white men. I'm well aware that there are exceptions on both sides. All I'm saying is that the *average* of your people is below the *average* of my people; and the pure-black ones are even *further* below us. I have living evidence of this sitting right in front of me.

PLAYBOY: If you mean me, I'm far from pure black—as you can see.

ROCKWELL: That's just it. You're an intelligent person; I enjoy talking to you. But, you're not pure black like your ancestors in the Congo. Now, this may insult you, but we're not here to throw pansies at each other: There *had* to be some white people in your background somewhere, or you wouldn't be brown instead of black. Right?

PLAYBOY: Right.

ROCKWELL: Well, I'm saying that your intelligence comes from the blood of my people. Whenever they trot out some smart nigger and say, "See? Look how brilliant niggers are," what they usually show you is a part-*white* man with some nigger blood in him. This doesn't prove that niggers *are* great. On the contrary; it proves that white blood can make a part-nigger more intelligent.

PLAYBOY: That's not proof, Commander. Can you offer any authoritative documentation to support your view?

ROCKWELL: A psychologist named G. O. Ferguson made a definitive study of the connection between the amount of white blood and intelligence in niggers. He tested all the nigger school children in Virginia and proved that the pure-black niggers did only about 70 precent as well as the white children. Niggers with one white grandparent did about 75 percent as well as the white children. Niggers with two white grandparents did still better, and niggers with *three* white grandparents did almost as well as the white kids. Since all of these nigger children shared exactly the same environment as niggers, it's impossible to claim that environment produced these tremendous changes in performance.

[Ferguson's study, conducted in 1916, we later learned, has since been discredited by every major authority on genetics and anthropology; they call it a pseudoscientific rationale for racism, based on an inadequate and unrepresentative sampling, predicated on erroneous assumptions, and statistically loaded to prove its point.—*Ed.*]

PLAYBOY: In his book *A Profile of the Negro American*, the world-famed sociologist T. F. Pettigrew states flatly that the degree of white ancestry does not relate in any way to Negro I.Q. scores. According to Pettigrew, the brightest Negro yet reported—with a tested I.Q. of 200—had no traceable Caucasian heritage whatever.

ROCKWELL: The fact that you can show me one very black individual who is superior to me doesn't convince me that the *average* nigger is superior. The startling fact I see is that the lighter they are, the smarter they are, and the blacker they are, the dumber they are.

PLAYBOY: That's an opinion, Commander, not a fact. Can you back it up with any concrete evidence?

ROCKWELL: The evidence of lifelong experience. I've never met a black nigger—I mean a real *black* one, so black he looks purple—that can talk, and think as, say, you can. When I do, then maybe I'll change my opinion. All the really black niggers are either what you call Uncle Toms, or they're revolutionists, or they want to loaf, loot and rape.

PLAYBOY: Most sociologists would agree that the vast majority of Negroes—dark-skinned or otherwise—don't fit into any of those categories.

ROCKWELL: Like I said, there are always exceptions—but everybody knows that they prove the rule. Evolution shows that in the long run, if the superior mixes with the inferior, the product is halfway between, and inferior to what you started with in the original superior group—in other words, mongrelized.

PLAYBOY: The words superior and inferior have no meaning to geneticists, Commander—and neither does mongrelization. Every authority in the field has attested that the world's racial groups are genetically indistinguishable from one another. All men, in other words—including hybrids—are created equal.

ROCKWELL: You're bringing tears to my eyes. Don't you know that all this equality garbage was started by a Jew anthropologist named Franz Boas from Columbia University? Boas was followed by another Jew from Columbia named Gene Weltfish. And our present Jew expert preaching equality is another Jew named Ashley Montagu. Any anthropologist who dares to preach the facts known by any farmer in the barnyard—that breeds differ in quality—is simply not allowed to survive in the universities or in publishing, because he can't earn a living. You never hear from that side. But Carleton Putnam has written a wonderful book called *Race and Reason,* showing that there is plenty of scholarly evidence to back up my contention that the nigger race is inherently inferior to the white race in-

tellectually. [Putnam, a former president of Delta Airlines, has no academic credentials in sociology, anthropology or genetics. Explaining its
"Not Recommended" classification for his book—fully titled *Race and
Reason: A Yankee View—Book Review Digest* writes: "At no time does
the author show himself qualified to speak as a scientist."—*Ed.*] This
equality garbage is straight Soviet, Lysenkian biology—direct from the
Communist Lysenko, who preached that by changing the environment you
could grow one plant from another plant's seeds. This is the doctrine that's
destroying our society—because it's not true. You can't grow wheat from
corn by changing the environment.

PLAYBOY: You can't grow wheat from corn by changing *anything*. In any
case, we're discussing human beings, not foodstuffs.

ROCKWELL: I don't feel like quibbling. What I'm saying is that I believe the
Jews have consciously *perverted* the study of anthropology and biology and
human genetics in order to reach this phony conclusion—and thus destroy
the great white race.

PLAYBOY: What phony conclusion?

ROCKWELL: The totally erroneous notion that heredity has nothing to do
with why, for example, the niggers have lower scholastic averages and
higher illegitimacy rates than whites.

PLAYBOY: According to geneticists, it doesn't. In any case, how would
acceptance of this notion lead to the destruction of the white race?

ROCKWELL: By deluding people into believing that the nigger is only
"underprivileged" rather than inherently inferior; into believing, therefore,
that he can be cleaned up and smartened up by letting him eat in our
restaurants, study in our schools, move into our neighborhoods. The next
inevitable step is to take him into our beds—and this would lead to the
mongrelization, and hence the destruction, of the white race.

PLAYBOY: You said that the Jews are behind this plot. Since they're whites
themselves, how would they benefit from their own destruction?

ROCKWELL: They won't be mingling like the rest of us. They believe they're
too pure to mix; they think they're "the chosen people"—chosen to rule
the world. But the only world they could rule would be a world of inferior
beings. And as long as the white man is pure, they cannot succeed. But
when the white man permits himself to be mixed with black men, then the
Jews can master him.

PLAYBOY: How?

ROCKWELL: They *already* run the niggers. Except for the Black Muslims,
the Jews run practically all the big civil rights organizations.

PLAYBOY: You're misinformed, Commander. The key posts in all but one
of the major civil rights groups—the NAACP—are held entirely by
Negroes.

ROCKWELL: They're just the front men. The Jews operate behind the
scenes, pulling the strings and holding the moneybags.

PLAYBOY: The Jews who belong and contribute to these groups serve strictly in an advisory capacity.

ROCKWELL: *You're* misinformed. As I started to say, Jews want to run the white people just the way they run the niggers. Once they get the white people mixed with the black people, the white people will be just as easy to run as the niggers.

PLAYBOY: Why?

ROCKWELL: Because when you mix superior and inferior, like I told you, the product is inferior—halfway between the two. The Jews would be able to outwit and outmaneuver and thus manipulate the mongrelized white man just the way he already does the niggers. That's what the whole so-called civil rights movement is all about; and they're just liable to get away with it if the good white Christians of this country don't wake up and get together before it's too late to restore the natural order of things.

PLAYBOY: And what's that?

ROCKWELL: Separation. In nature, all things of a similar being tend to group together. Chimpanzees do not run with baboons; they run with chimpanzees. This is the natural order of people, too. Even in thoroughly integrated colleges, when I visit them, I notice that niggers usually sit and eat at tables with other niggers—even though they don't have to. And the white people sit with other white people. I think this is the natural tendency, and to attempt to pervert this is to fight nature.

PLAYBOY: You fail to make an important moral and constitutional distinction between *choosing* to associate with one's own race and being *forced* to do so. Left to themselves, some people will mingle and some won't; and most Americans think this is just the way it ought to be.

ROCKWELL: That's all very noble-sounding; it brings a lump to my throat. But what does it boil down to in practice? Every time your people move into my neighborhood, the white people move out; and often there's violence—by peaceful, decent white men who never before committed any, but are outraged at the black invasion.

PLAYBOY: That's an exaggeration, Commander. The record shows that fewer and fewer white people are moving out when Negroes move into white neighborhoods; and the fact is that violence very seldom occurs because of Negro "block-busting." In most instances, after an initial period of strain, the newcomers are being quietly accepted.

ROCKWELL: I don't know what neighborhoods you've been hanging around in, but my own experience has been that violence and animosity are the rule rather than the exception. And that goes double when one of *my* guys moves into a place like Watts. Your people don't just riot; they try to kill him. This is natural. Their instincts are coming out, and they always will. And any effort to override these instincts, or deny they exist, will inevitably be unsuccessful. Nature will prevail.

PLAYBOY: Negro hostility toward Nazis could hardly be offered as proof that integration is unnatural. Nor is anti-Nazi violence confined to Negroes.

ROCKWELL: You're right—the Jews are even better at it.

PLAYBOY: You've been quoted as saying that the Watts, Harlem and Rochester riots, among others, were actually instigated by Jews. Do you have any evidence to substantiate that charge?

ROCKWELL: I didn't say they started them; I said they *engineered* them. First of all, they tell the niggers, "You people don't have to obey the laws you don't like"—just like Martin Luther Coon preaches. If a cop arrests a nigger, it's "police brutality." And he's told he should fight back. Whenever a policeman tries to do his duty, the Jew-oriented niggers have been told to try and take the prisoner away from this brutal cop. The Jews turn him into a psychological bomb—so that when a cop comes along and does his duty it's just like touching a match to a fuse. *Boom*—up it goes! Like it did in Watts. Like they do in Harlem.

PLAYBOY: In both the Watts and Harlem riots, the bulk of the property damage was suffered by Jewish-owned stores and businesses. Why would the Jews foment violence that's bound to result in the destruction of their own property?

ROCKWELL: It just happens that most of the businessmen making money off the niggers in the ghettos are Jews. The big Jews in charge are willing to sacrifice the little Jews just as a general sacrifices some troops to win a war.

PLAYBOY: But what could *any* Jews possibly win by engineering riots?

ROCKWELL: They're just natural-born agitators. They just can't help coming in and getting everybody all stirred up—and they're always the ones to suffer for it. Every time! But they just can't quit. It's irrational as hell. With all their liberalism and their preaching about equal rights for niggers, they've promoted disorder and chaos that's eventually going to bury them. The liquor dealers are getting it now. Last summer, all those kike store owners in Watts kept screaming, "Oy! Stop! Listen! We're your friends!"— while the coons beat their brains out. And that's just the beginning, just a sample of things to come. This summer I predict that racial violence even more terrible than Watts will erupt—all because of these two trouble-making inferior races.

PLAYBOY: In judging Negroes "inferior" to whites, you said a while ago that you made this appraisal on the basis of "performance." Do you find Jews inferior for the same reason?

ROCKWELL: I've never accused the Jews of being incapable of performing. As a matter of fact, I think there's a good chance they're *superior* to everybody else in terms of actual mental capabilities. I think the average Jew is probably sharper intellectually than the average gentile, because for years and years he's had to live by his wits. Consequently, there has evolved a race of Jews who are more agile mentally than the rest of us.

PLAYBOY: In what way do you consider Jews inferior, then?

ROCKWELL: Spiritually. I believe that a human being, in order to be a successful person, in addition to performing—inventing a rocket or something—has got to have something he *believes* in, something more than his own survival, something that's a little bigger than himself. The Jews don't. They've even got a rabbi now who admits he's an atheist—Rabbi Sherwin Wine of Birmingham, Michigan.

PLAYBOY: Perhaps you didn't know that the current Church movement toward disbelief in God originated among the Protestant clergy. In any case, Rabbi Wine's convictions are a minority voice and could not in any way be said to represent those of the Jewish faith in general. Most Jews continue to believe in God, as set down in the Torah.

ROCKWELL: Jews *talk* a lot about God. But actually their god, just like Marx said, is money. Cash! This is where the Jews fail—in their lack of idealism. Most of them are strictly materialists at heart. Wherever the Jews have gone, they've moved into a friendly, unsuspecting country and promptly started to glut on its people and resources. They think they're engaging in business, but actually what they're doing is eating the country up alive. And when people begin to resent their viciousness and greed, and either kick the Jews out or kill them, they always scream "Persecution!" That's not persecution. It's self-defense.

PLAYBOY: Are you implying that Hitler was justified in exterminating 6,000,000 European Jews?

ROCKWELL: I don't believe for one minute that any 6,000,000 Jews *were* exterminated by Hitler. It never happened. You want me to prove it to you?

PLAYBOY: Go ahead.

ROCKWELL: We have the figures for the number of Jews in the world in 1939, before World War Two: 15,688,259; and the figures for the number living after World War Two: 18,000,000. Now, if you take the number of Jews for after World War Two and add the 6,000,000 you say were gassed, you get a total of 24,000,000—which means that there would have to have been a 50-percent increase in the Jewish population during a period of about five years. Even people as good at sex as the Jews couldn't possibly reproduce that fast. So you see, the Jews' own figures convict them as liars!

PLAYBOY: What's your source for these statistics?

ROCKWELL: The pre-War figures came from the 1947 *World Almanac,* page 219; and the post-War figures from *The New York Times,* February 22, 1948, in an article by Hanson Baldwin.

[Subsequent investigation revealed that the *World Almanac* figure of 15,688,259 is correct as claimed. The post-War figures cited by Hanson Baldwin in *The New York Times* were in the following context: "In these countries (Palestine and Egypt), the Jews are tied by bonds of religion to the rest of the 15 to 18 million Jews of the world." According to every official source, however, Baldwin's estimates are in error. The figures compiled by the Population Reference Bureau in Washington, D.C., show that the world's Jewish population declined from 16,600,000 to 11,400,000 between 1939 and 1945—while' European Jewry decreased 6,000,000 during that same period, from 9,700,000 to 3,700,000.—*Ed.*]

PLAYBOY: Population figures aside, do you deny the validity of documentary photographic evidence showing the gas chambers themselves, and the thousands of bodies piled up in concentration-camp trenches?

ROCKWELL: I emphatically deny that there is any valid proof that innocent Jews were systematically murdered by the Nazis. The photographs you've seen that have been passed off as pictures of dead Jews have been identified as pictures of the corpses of German civilians—mostly women and children and refugees—who were killed in the one-night Allied bombing of Dresden, which slaughtered 350,000 innocent people.

PLAYBOY: By whom have these pictures been so identified?

ROCKWELL: By Matt Koehl, my research chief, who says that you can recognize the buildings in the background of these so-called Nazi atrocity photographs as buildings in Dresden.

PLAYBOY: We don't accept the findings of your research chief as authoritative.

ROCKWELL: I have conclusive evidence to *prove* that some of these "documentary" photographs are frauds, pure and simple. In a magazine published by the Jews and sold all over America, they show a bottle supposedly containing soap made by the Germans out of the poor, dead, gassed Jews.

PLAYBOY: What evidence do you have for claiming that it's fradulent?

ROCKWELL: Common sense. That soap could have been made out of *anything*; it could have been melted down from a dozen bars of Lifebuoy. But here's my ultimate proof of just how utterly ridiculous all the anti-Nazi literature you've read really is: an article in *Sir* magazine, March 1958, on how the Nazis gassed and burned and murdered everybody. It's by "a former corporal of the SS" as told to an American Army master sergeant who signs himself "Lew Cor." Well, "Lew Cor" is simply Rockwell spelled backward. I wrote it *myself*—as a test. I wrote the vilest lies I could think of! And here they all are in print in this magazine. Look at the photographs! These are supposed to be actual shots of Nazi victims mentioned in the article—victims that I invented!

PLAYBOY: Your own willingness to lie about Nazi atrocities doesn't prove that the Jews have done the same thing, Commander. Do you also dismiss the testimony of hundreds of prison-camp survivors who have given eyewitness testimony about Nazi atrocities?

ROCKWELL: I have an affidavit from a Jewish doctor, a prisoner at Auschwitz, who says there *were* no gas chambers.

PLAYBOY: Do you have that affidavit?

ROCKWELL: I'll send you a photostat. [It has not arrived.—*Ed.*] I believe the gas chambers in these concentration camps were built *after* the War—by Jewish Army officers. We know this for sure: It was mostly Jewish Army officers who went in there to liberate these camps. And it was mostly

Jewish Army CIC officers who were in charge of the Nuremberg trials. It was they who tortured innocent Nazis, using any kind of vile method they could to cook up phony evidence.

PLAYBOY: Can you prove these charges?

ROCKWELL: I know of several cases where American personnel resigned in disgust at the methods used.

PLAYBOY: That doesn't prove that torture was used to extract false testimony. In any case, you still haven't said whether you dismiss eyewitness testimony of Nazi atrocities.

ROCKWELL: Certainly I do. I've lost count of the times I've been in court, after being assaulted and beaten by gangs of Jews, and seen these same Jews get up on the witness stand, with tears pouring down their faces, and tell how *I* attacked *them*! The Jews are the world's master liars! They are geniuses at it. Why, when a kike is up on a witness stand, he doesn't even need *onions* to start the tears pouring.

PLAYBOY: It's said that you keep a model gas chamber here at your headquarters. Is that true?

ROCKWELL: No, but we have an electric chair at Sing Sing that's already done a great deed for America in frying the Rosenbergs; and there are hundreds of thousands *more* Rosenbergs running around America who need frying—or gassing.

PLAYBOY: By "more Rosenbergs," do you mean more Jews or more Communist spies?

ROCKWELL: More Communist Jews. They're practically the same thing.

PLAYBOY: Are you saying that many Jews are Communists, or that many Communists are Jewish?

ROCKWELL: I use the term "Communist Jews" in exactly the same sense that I would say "Italian gangsters." Most Italians are not gangsters, but everybody knows that the Mafia is mostly Italians. Well, my experience is that communism is as Jewish as the Mafia is Italian. It's a fact that almost all of the convicted spies for communism have been atheist Jews like the Rosenbergs. And international communism was invented by the Jew Karl Marx and has since been led mostly by Jews—like Trotsky.

PLAYBOY: Stalin, Khrushchev, Brezhnev, Kosygin and Mao Tse-tung, among many others, certainly aren't Jews.

ROCKWELL: The Jews operate nowadays mostly as spies and agitators for the Reds. Mind you, I'm not saying that there aren't vast numbers of Jews who *despise* communism.

PLAYBOY: Yet you say there are hundreds of thousands of Jewish Communists in America?

ROCKWELL: Perhaps more.

PLAYBOY: What evidence do you have to back up that figure?

ROCKWELL: Plain statistics. Fourteen of the 16 Americans convicted in U.S. courts of treason as Communist spies have been racial Jews and one of them was a nigger. Of the 21 Communist leaders convicted in Judge Medina's court, 19 were racial Jews. Of the so-called "second-string Politburo" Communist leaders rounded up, more than 90 percent were racial Jews.

PLAYBOY: The total number of convicted spies who you say are Jewish comes to 33. That's far from hundreds of thousands.

ROCKWELL: There's also evidence in black and white. Even in their own publications, the Jews do not hide from the Jewishness of communism. It's there for anybody to see. For instance, the largest-circulation Communist newspaper in America is not *The Worker*, but a paper published in Yiddish called *The Morning Freiheit*. Any American can get a copy of this Jewish Communist newspaper and read, in the English portions, the open Communist treason they're preaching.

PLAYBOY: The views of *The Morning Freiheit* certainly can't be said to reflect those of most American Jews, Commander. Can you give a specific example of a pro-Marxist statement by any recognized spokesman for American Jewry?

PLAYBOY: Just one? That's easy. Let's take a statement made by Rabbi Stephen Wise; he's one of the leading spokesmen for American Jewry.

PLAYBOY: He died in 1949.

ROCKWELL: Well, before he died, he wrote, "Some call it communism; I call it Judaism." That's a direct quote. I'd say that's putting it pretty unequivocally, wouldn't you?

PLAYBOY: Can you produce proof of that statement?

ROCKWELL: Certainly. I'll send it to you. [The proof has not arrived, nor was Commander Rockwell able to tell us the name of the publication in which the alleged statement appeared. An official at Manhattan's Hebrew Union College, where Rabbi Wise's entire works are kept in archive, later said that no such statement appears anywhere in the late rabbi's writings. Rabbi Edward Kline, Wise's successor at New York's Free Synagogue, told us further that no such quote appears in any of Wise's speeches; nor could he, as a lifelong foe of communism, said Kline, have been capable of making such a remark. Confronted with this evidence, Rockwell later retracted the allegation.—*Ed.*]

PLAYBOY: Do you have any tangible evidence to substantiate your charges?

ROCKWELL: Would you accept evidence based on a statistical sampling?

PLAYBOY: Let's hear it.

ROCKWELL: Out of the number of Jews that I have known personally, a tremendous proportion—at least 50 percent, maybe as high as 85 or 90 percent—have been pro-Red; either card-carrying Communists or accessories before or after the fact, either openly and knowingly aiding and abetting communism and promoting the Communist overthrow of this Government, or assisting the Communist enemies who are killing Americans, or consciously suppressing legal evidence which would tend to convict such traitors.

PLAYBOY: Your own conjectures about the political sympathies of Jews you've known personally, Commander, could hardly be accepted as evidence to support your allegations about them, let alone the "hundreds of thousands" you say are pro-Red. In any case, you say they "need frying—or gassing." On what grounds?

ROCKWELL: Treason. Everybody—not just Jews—with suspicious records of procommunism, or treasonable Zionism, or any subversive attack on this country or its people, should be investigated and arrested and the evidence placed before a grand jury. If they're indicted, they should be tried for treason, and if they're convicted, they should be killed.

PLAYBOY: How?

ROCKWELL: Well, there are going to be hundreds of thousands of Jewish traitors to execute, don't forget. I don't see how you can strap that many people in electric chairs and get the job done before they all die of old age; so it seems to me that mass gas chambers are going to be the only solution for the Communist traitor problem in America.

PLAYBOY: Your suggestion of gas chambers as a "solution for the Communist traitor problem" is reminiscent of the "final solution for the Jewish problem" instituted by the Nazis in Germany. Are you planning to lead another anti-Semitic crusade along the lines laid down by Hitler?

ROCKWELL: The crusade I plan to lead will be much broader in scope than that. In Germany, Hitler produced a local "lab experiment"; he provided me with an ideology in the same way that Marx provided one for Lenin. My task is to turn this ideology into a *world* movement. And I'll never be able to accomplish that by preaching pure Aryanism as Hitler did—by glorifying the Nordic-Germanic people as a "master race." There *is* an easily identifiable master race, however: the *white* race. You can find it all over the world. This is what I'm fighting for—not Aryanism, but white Christian solidarity. In the long run, I intend to win over the people of Greece, of Germany, of Italy, of England, of Canada, of France, of Spain, of Latin America, of Rhodesia, of South Africa—the people of every white Christian country in the world. All the white Christian countries of the earth I would try to mold into one racial, religious, political and military entity. I want them eventually to have hegemony.

PLAYBOY: Over the nonwhite, non-Christian nations?

ROCKWELL: Over the Afro-Asian bloc, which is to me the ultimate danger the earth faces. Worse than the bomb! These people have something both communism and democracy have lost. They're fanatics! They're full of this wild-eyed belief and vitality that the white man has gradually been losing. If they ever unite, there will be almost a billion of them against the white man—a ratio of seven to one. They're breeding so fast that the odds could easily be ten or fifteen to one before too long. When these billions of primitive colored people are able to control an atom or an H-bomb, as Red China may soon be able to do, we could wipe out a hundred million of them, and there would still be plenty more who kept coming. The white race couldn't take that kind of a bloodletting for long. We'd be wiped out! The huge masses of semi-animal colored people would simply sweep over us, and there'd be nothing we could do about it. It would be the ultimate victory of quantity over quality—unless the white people unite first. We're in real trouble if *they* get together first. But make no mistake: There's going to be a battle of Armageddon, and it's going to be not between communism and democracy, but between the colored millions of the world and the small but elite corps of white men; ideological, economic and philosophical issues will play little or no part in it. When the time comes— and it's later than we think—I plan to be ready not only to defend myself, but to lead the millions of whites all over the world who today are foolishly pretending they don't know what's going on.

PLAYBOY: Estimates of your nationwide membership range from 25 to 100. Do you propose to lead the white Christian nations with this handful of followers?

ROCKWELL: In the first place, we're a *world* movement, just as communism is a world movement rather than a local or a national organization. We've launched a world union of National Socialists, of which I am the international commander. In the second place, you've got those figures wrong. In this country alone, we've got about 500 storm troopers—that's men ready for street action—plus about 1500 Party members. Also about 15,000 correspondents—people sympathetic to our cause who write in and donate. And our membership abroad numbers in the thousands.

PLAYBOY: Where abroad?

ROCKWELL: Let me name you countries. Argentina: Horst Eichmann, Adolf Eichmann's son, is our leader there; he's either in jail or disappeared, but our movement is growing there. In Australia, our movement is temporarily busted up, but my leader—an American—is running around under cover, trying to get his group back together again. In Spain, we've got a pretty good undercover movement, but Franco doesn't appreciate it, so we have to stay under cover. In England, Colin Jordan is operating wide open—and doing *very* well. In France, we've got a damned good group; they were all arrested just a while back. In Belgium, I've got an ex-SS paratrooper in charge, and he's doing very well. In Sweden, we've got a tremendous group; they were all just arrested. In Austria—our guy is in jail, so things are pretty well broken up there. In Canada, John Beattie is leading a tremendous and successful movement. Our leader in Chile is in jail. In Germany, we've gone under cover; our leader is going to jail shortly. In Holland, we're doing fine. In Ireland, they're coming along fast. In Italy, we've got a real tremendous movement. In Japan, one of our guys stabbed the Socialist deputy. Remember? New Zealand is coming along fine. But Norway isn't doing too good. We've a fine group in South Africa now, though, and we've got a group in Rhodesia now, too.

So you see, we've got groups all over the world. They're still little. But after all, it's only been 20 years since Hitler died. Twenty years after Christ was crucified, there were almost no Christians. Right now, the followers of the swastika are in the catacombs, like the original followers of the cross were then. I can't say we're a Christian movement in the ordinary sense; in fact, I personally am an agnostic. But I deeply believe that there is a power greater than ours that's helping us in our fight to keep the world natural and racially pure—as opposed to perverted and mongrelized. We've got an ideology, a dedication, a belief, a vitality to match the zealotry of the fanatical Asian-African bloc. That's why we're going to grow; that's why—eventually—we're going to prevail.

PLAYBOY: Can you tell us just how you plan to go about fulfilling this destiny—with or without divine intervention?

ROCKWELL: I have a four-phase plan. The first phase is to reach the masses; you can do nothing until you've reached the masses. In order to reach them—without money, without status, without a public platform— you have to become a dramatic figure. Now in order to achieve that, I've had to take a lot of garbage: being called a nut and a monster and everything else. But by hanging up the swastika, I reach the masses. The second phase is to disabuse them of the false picture they have gotten of me, to educate them about what my real program is. The third phase will be to organize the people I've educated into a political entity. And the fourth phase will be to use that political entity as a machine to win political power.

That's the plan. They all overlap, of course. Right now we're about 50 percent involved in phase two; we're actually beginning to educate people—in interviews like this one, in speaking engagements at colleges and the like. The other 50 percent is still phase one—just raising hell to keep people aware that there's such a thing as the American Nazi Party, not caring what they call us, as long as they call us *something*.

PLAYBOY: What kind of hell-raising?

ROCKWELL: Well, I haven't done it yet, but one of my ambitions is to rent me a plane and skywrite a big smoke swastika over New York City—on Hitler's birthday. That sort of thing. Or I might get one plane to do the Star of David, and I'll come in another plane and squat and do brown smoke all over it—on Ben-Gurion's birthday. I've checked Federal regulations, and they couldn't do a thing about it. All I need is the money to do it. But that's in the future. One of the biggest things we've already done to propagandize ourselves is our "Coon-ard Lines Boat Tickets to Africa." It's our most popular mail-order item; white high school students order them by the thousands. Would you like me to read you what a ticket entitles one nigger to?

PLAYBOY: Go ahead.

ROCKWELL: Six things. One: a free trip to Africa on a Cadillac-shaped luxury liner. Two: choice cuts of all the bananas and missionaries desired en route, and a free jar of meat tenderizer. NAACP members may sit up front and twist to Martin Luther Coon's jazz band. Three: a barrel of hair-grease axle grease delicately scented with nigger sweat. Four: a framed picture of Eleanor Roosevelt and Harry Golden. Five: an unguarded chicken coop and watermelon patch on deck, plus fish and chips for breakfast. And six: plenty of wine, marijuana, heroin and other refreshments. On the reverse side, we offer white liberal peace creeps a year's supply of "Instant Nigger." It's described as "Easy-mixing powder! Just sprinkle this dingy black dust on any sidewalk! Just make water on it, and presto! Hundreds of niggers spring up—little niggers, big niggers, fat niggers, skinny niggers, light niggers, midnight-black niggers, red niggers, even Jew niggers." It reads here, "Why wait? With this Instant Nigger Powder, any nigger-loving beatnik peace creep can have all the niggers he can stand!" Want one? Compliments of the house.

PLAYBOY: Is mail-order hate literature your main source of income?

ROCKWELL: That, plus initiation fees from new members; plus small donations from those who believe in what we're trying to do; plus the proceeds from special events like one of our "hate-nannies."

PLAYBOY: What are they?

ROCKWELL: Big musical jamborees. We hold them on patriotic holidays.

PLAYBOY: Would you give an example of a hate-nanny lyric?

ROCKWELL: Sure. Remember, you asked for it: "Ring that bell, shout for joy/White man's day is here/Gather all those equals up/Herd them on the pier/America for whites/Africa for blacks/Send those apes back to the trees/Ship those niggers back/Twenty million ugly coons are ready on their pier/America for whites/Africa for blacks/Ring that bell, shout for joy/The white man's day is here/Hand that chimp his ugly stick/Hand that buck his spear . . ." That's just the first part of that song. Do you want to hear more of it?

PLAYBOY: No, we get the general idea.

ROCKWELL: Well, I believe a man ought to hoist up his flag and tell you what he is. And that's just what we do here.

PLAYBOY: Are there any anti-Jewish ballads in your hate-nanny song bag?

ROCKWELL: Oh, yes! One of our favorites is *The Jews are Through in '72*. It goes to the tune of *Mademoiselle from Armentières*. Want to hear it?

PLAYBOY: We'll listen.

ROCKWELL: "The Jews are through in '72, *parlez-vous*/The Jews are through in '72, *parlez-vous*/We'll feed them bacon till they yell/And send them all to kosher hell/Hinky dinky, *parlez-vous* . . ." The chorus repeats, and then comes the next verse: "We'll steal the rabbi's knife and sheath/And make him do it with his teeth/Hinky dinky, *parlez-vous*." The rest of it I don't remember.

PLAYBOY: The song says the Jews will be "through in '72." Is that date significant in some way?

ROCKWELL: 1972 is the year I'm going to be elected President on the National Socialist ticket. Five years of the Johnson Administration will leave the country so torn with racial tensions that some Republican will be a cinch to win in 1968. Then, in 1969, a great economic catastrophe is going to hit this country.

PLAYBOY: The nation's economy has never been healthier than it is today, and most economists predict that the end of the boom is not in sight.

ROCKWELL: Nevertheless, there *will* be an economic catastrophe, though of what nature I'm not sure. It could be an inflation. I say so because all this buildup is based on sand. America's so-called prosperity is based on debt, war and inflationary money which has no backing and is bound to collapse. Along about 1969, it's all going to come tumbling down like a house of cards, and the President is going to be blamed for it. In the ensuing economic chaos, plus all the racial warfare, the people will welcome a man who stands unequivocally for the white Christian majority.

PLAYBOY: What makes you think so?

ROCKWELL: As I travel, I find that people everywhere, from the smallest towns to the biggest cities, are looking for what I offer. Most of them won't agree with me openly, but if you take them aside, ask them privately, they'd probably tell you "Rockwell has the right idea: White Christian people should dominate." By 1972, with the economy coming apart at the seams, with the niggers pushing, with the Communists agitating, with all of this spiritual emptiness, with all this cowardice and betrayal by our Government, the masses of common, ordinary white people will have had it up to *here*. They'll want a real *leader* in the White House—no more spineless jellyfish, no more oily, two-faced demagogs, no more queers in the White House like Walter Jenkins and his friends. They'll be looking for a white leader with the guts of a Malcolm X, with the guts to stand up and say, "I'm going to completely separate the black and white races and preserve white Christian domination in this country, and I'm going to have the Jew Communists and any other traitors gassed for treason. And if you don't like it, you know what you can do about it."

PLAYBOY: Do you seriously think you can be elected on that platform?

ROCKWELL: I know so. Things are going to be so desperate by then that it won't matter whether I've got two horns and a tail; I'll be swept into office.

PLAYBOY: If you *are* elected, who from among contemporary public figures would you appoint to your Cabinet?

ROCKWELL: If he were still alive, I'd have General Douglas MacArthur as Secretary of State. For Secretary of Defense, Retired General of the Marine Corps "Chesty" Puller. For Attorney General, J. Edgar Hoover. For Secretary of the Interior, Governor George Wallace of Alabama. Let me think, now, others: Senators William Jenner and Harry Byrd, Charles Lindbergh—and William Buckley; he won't appreciate that, but I think his brilliance could certainly be valuable. You'll have to agree that this is a Cabinet to give nightmares to any Jew alive. They'd start swimming for Israel even before I was sworn in. But I don't think there's a man in that Cabinet who is known as anti-Semitic.

PLAYBOY: How about anti-Negro?

ROCKWELL: Well, I'd prefer to call them pro-white.

PLAYBOY: If you had carte-blanche power to do so as the Chief Executive, would you create a dictatorship along the lines of Hitler's?

ROCKWELL: No, I'd reinstitute the American Constitutional Republic the way it was set up by our *authoritarian* forefathers—who were, in essence, nothing more than National Socialists just like me.

PLAYBOY: In no way did the founding fathers attempt to abridge the democratic right to "liberty and justice for all." How can you call them Nazis?

ROCKWELL: In the first place, I don't believe in democracy. In the second place, neither did our white forefathers. I believe, as they did, in a republic—an authoritarian republic with a limited electorate—just like the one the writers of our Constitution meant this country to be. When these white Christian patriots sat down to write the Declaration of Independence, there were no black citizens for them to worry about. In those days, all the niggers were slaves; but today, thanks to several misguided amendments, our Constitution provides even the blackest of savages with the same rights as his former white masters.

PLAYBOY: Then you advocate the disenfranchisement of Negroes?

ROCKWELL: And the revocation of their citizenship.

PLAYBOY: And the restoration of slavery?

ROCKWELL: No, we have machines to do their work now. I would simply revoke their citizenship and then offer them the alternatives of either returning to Africa with our generous help and assistance in establishing a modern industrial nation, or being relocated on reservations like the Indians were when they became a problem to the survival of the white people. This will apply to *you,* too, by the way. Nothing personal, you understand; I *like* you, personally; but I can't make any exceptions.

PLAYBOY: Of course not. What would you do with America's 6,000,000 Jews?

ROCKWELL: I think the Jews can be dealt with individually rather than as a group—like the niggers must be because of their race. As I said earlier, I think all Jews—in fact, all those connected in any way with treason, whether Jews or not—should be investigated and their cases put before grand juries; if they're indicted, they should then be tried, and if convicted, they should be killed.

PLAYBOY: Having disposed of Jews and Negroes, would that complete your list of those slotted for removal?

ROCKWELL: Not quite. I'd also purge the queers. I despise them worst of all. They're one of the ugliest problems of our society, and they must be removed—I don't know if with gas, or what, just so they don't poison society. If they insist on being queers, put them on some island maybe—but certainly not around the rest of society. They're the ultimate symbol of a decaying civilization.

PLAYBOY: Since you're concerned about the problem, Commander, would you like to reply to a frequent charge by psychiatrists that the womanless atmosphere of military asceticism and institutionalized hostility that characterize your "hate monastery," as you've called your headquarters here, make it an ideal sanctuary for those with repressed homosexual tendencies?

ROCKWELL: My reply is that this is the standard Jewish charge. The biggest charger that we are a bunch of homosexuals is Walter Winchell, whose real name is Isadore Israel Lipshitz, or something like that. [Winchell's real name is Walter Winchel.—*Ed*.] He's always calling me "George Lincoln Ratwell, Queen of the Nazis," saying I'm a fairy, and so forth. Universally, I have found that the Jews themselves, as Hitler said, are the greatest people in the world for accusing others of their own crimes.

PLAYBOY: You haven't answered the charge that your Party is a haven for homosexuals.

ROCKWELL: Well, I do think there is a tendency for queers to come here, because to a queer, this place is as tempting as a girls' school would be to me. Whenever I catch any of them in here, I throw them out; and I *have* caught quite a few of them in here. We had one case where we had reason to believe that the police would catch two guys in the act. The two of them left here hand in hand. I tried to get them prosecuted. We won't tolerate that sort of thing.

PLAYBOY: How about heterosexual relations? Are they *verboten*, too?

ROCKWELL: Absolutely not. Any man who didn't vigorously enjoy normal sex could never be a National Socialist. One of the best American Nazis I've ever known used to use a vulgar expression, "Those who won't fuck won't fight." I wouldn't put it so crudely myself, but I heartily subscribe to that doctrine. I never knew a good fighting man who didn't enjoy a lusty sex life.

PLAYBOY: Are any of your men married?

ROCKWELL: A few, but most are either single or divorced, like myself. I believe very strongly in the importance of basic morals to protect civilization, but it's almost impossible for a guy in this kind of work to have a normal marriage and family; so most of us have no choice but to make other arrangements. And I might add, to paraphrase a French bon mot, *vive les arrangements*. But I must admit that it's damn difficult—especially for me—to have any sort of normal contacts with women, since I'm so often approached in this regard for political blackmail.

PLAYBOY: Is it true that you require your Party members to swear an oath against drinking, smoking and cursing?

ROCKWELL: All my officers take an oath against drinking, including myself. Most have also taken an oath against smoking. I, myself, would not smoke except that the corncob pipe I've smoked for so long has become sort of a trademark. As for cursing, it's hard to stop cursing in the rough situations in which we live, just like in the Armed Services; but I do all I can to discourage it.

PLAYBOY: You've used swearwords in this interview. Is this setting a good example for your men?

ROCKWELL: Well, I exempt myself from that oath for professional appearances such as this. In talking to you, I've used words like "nigger" and "kike" because this is a big interview in a national magazine, and I want to attract attention—to shock people into listening to what I have to say. If I were discussing, say, the favorite word of niggers—"mother-fucker"— I'd say it strictly as a factual observation and to make a point. But in private conversation, neither I nor any of my members ever use that word—or any other foul language.

PLAYBOY: Do you also forbid the use of drugs?

ROCKWELL: Certainly. I've had a few guys in here who I think were marijuana smokers, but I've thrown them out and turned them in. Addiction to any drug is degenerative mentally as well as physically, and we're dead serious about our dedication to the healthy-body-healthy-mind philosophy.

PLAYBOY: Is karate or judo instruction part of your training program?

ROCKWELL: Not so much of that. I've found that unless you're a real expert at karate or judo, it doesn't help you much. Unless you use it instinctively, it's no use at all. So we concentrate on physical education, boxing and weapons training.

PLAYBOY: What sort of weapons?

ROCKWELL: Rifles and pistols.

PLAYBOY: For what purpose?

ROCKWELL: Self-defense. I believe the white people of America should learn methods of surviving in the event of racial anarchy and general bedlam in this country, which I think is likely.

PLAYBOY: Do you share the belief of the Minutemen in the importance of being prepared for an armed Communist invasion of the U.S. mainland?

ROCKWELL: The Minutemen are kidding themselves. If there *is* a total Communist take-over, they haven't got a prayer in the world of *surviving* it, let alone stopping it—running around in the weeds with a few guns like little boys playing cops and robbers. All they're doing is giving themselves an emotional catharsis. They're wasting millions of dollars, and in the process they're getting a lot of good kids sent to jail for illegal possession of weapons. I think it's like the Klan. Their aim, insofar as being ready is concerned, I'm for. I'm for the Klan's principles, ideas and so forth—except the anti-Catholicism—but from my point of view, their methods stink!

PLAYBOY: What methods?

ROCKWELL: Their *partial* terrorism. I feel that terrorism is a valid weapon in guerrilla warfare, or any kind of warfare; and under the circumstances in which our country finds itself, I would *favor* terrorism if it could be *complete*—if it would *work*. A hundred years ago, I'd have been a Klansman with a rope and a gun and the whole business. I'd have really gone all out during the Reconstruction to save the white South. And make no mistake about the terrorism: It did the job. But today, it plays directly into the hands of Martin Luther Coon; it manufactures martyrs for the Northern press, for the liberals, and it doesn't scare the niggers out of hell-raising anymore.

PLAYBOY: But apart from your belief that racial violence against Negroes has become self-defeating, you have no moral objection to it?

ROCKWELL: None at all. What I object to is war among *white* men. This is what we're been doing for centuries—fighting among ourselves and wiping each other out. The North versus the South is a perfect example: the biggest bloodletting we've had, the cream of the white population wiped out, all because of the niggers. It solved nothing; it really changed nothing—except that a lot of good white kids got killed. I'm *agin* that! If we have any more wars, I want to fight the Red Chinese or the Jews, or go over to Africa and fight the niggers. This I can see some point to. As far as violence on an individual basis is concerned, well, when I come to power I plan to have dueling for officers in the Armed Forces. I'll have two purposes in that: first, to maintain a corps of officers unafraid to face death—not just in case of war; and second, to restore the concept of personal honor. I don't think going to court and suing somebody is really a deterrent to libelous, vicious talk. But people don't flap their mouths quite so freely when they're liable to have to back it up with a gun. Right now dueling isn't legal, but the moment it is, I would be eager to face Billy James Hargis and Robert "Rabbit" Welch on a field of honor for going around calling me a Communist.

PLAYBOY: Have you considered the possibility that you might be killed in such a confrontation?

ROCKWELL: I've not only considered it; I expect it. And I'm ready for it. Being prepared to die is one of the great secrets of living. I know I'm going to go—probably in some violent manner; the only question is when and how. But I don't think that's going to happen to me until I complete my mission. I know this is irrational, but I believe that I was placed here for a purpose and I think God has something to do with it: Our country needs a leader. So I think I'll be spared. As Rommel said, "Stand next to me; I'm bulletproof."

PLAYBOY: Do you think you're bulletproof, too?

ROCKWELL: Not literally, of course, but I firmly believe that the more arrogant and defiant you are of danger, the safer you are from harm. I think that's the reason I've survived so many times when people have shot at me. If you're fearless enough, it implants a certain psychology in the guy that's trying to shoot at you. It's almost as if he could *smell* your fearlessness, the way an animal smells fear. But the effect is the opposite: Instead of being emboldened to attack, he's so unsettled that his hand shakes when he goes to pull the trigger; and this makes it almost impossible for him to hit you. Either that, or he'll back down entirely. When I go out in the street and toughs come up threatening to whip me, I look them straight in the eye and say, "Go ahead. Start." Maybe they *could* whip me, but so far nobody's tried.

PLAYBOY: We read a newspaper interview a few years ago in which you claimed you were being "gagged and slandered by the Jewish press," sabotaged by a nationwide journalistic conspiracy in your fight to put your case before the nation. When "the Jewish press" wasn't pretending that you didn't exist, you said, it was either deliberately misquoting you or doctoring your public statements to remove the sense and retain the shock value—in order to make you sound simple-minded or to portray you as a racist monster. Only this conspiracy of silence and misrepresentation, you claimed, was preventing you from getting your revolutionary message across to the white, gentile masses and rallying them to your flag. To some people, Commander, these might sound like the remarks of a man who's trying to blame his failures on someone else.

ROCKWELL: You think I'm being paranoid, is that it?

PLAYBOY: Some people might.

ROCKWELL: In the *Columbia Journalism Review* about three months ago, Ben Bagdikian, a frequent writer for the Anti-Defamation League, wrote an article called "The Gentle Suppression" which asked the question, "Is the news quarantine of Rockwell a good thing?" Bagdikian openly reveals that the press maintains as much silence as possible about our activities. So you see, the Jew blackout on us is as real as a hand over my mouth. They know we're too poor to buy air time or advertising space, so they ban our publications from all channels of distribution, and they refuse to report our activities in the daily press. I could run naked across the White House lawn and they wouldn't report it. I'm being facetious. But I'm dead serious when I say that the only kind of free speech left in this country is that speech that doesn't criticize the Jews. If you criticize the Jews, you're either smeared or silenced. They have that same kind of "free speech" in Cuba, Red China and Russia and every other Communist country: You can say anything you like as long as it doesn't criticize the dictator. The Jews are *never* going to let me reach the people with my message in the American press; they can't afford to.

PLAYBOY: How do you reconcile that statement with the fact that you're being interviewed at this moment for a national magazine?

ROCKWELL: I've been interviewed, taped and photographed thousands of times for just such presentations as these, but they never appear. The fact that you come here and get this interview doesn't prove that you'll print it, or that if you do, you'll print it straight. After the editors read over the transcript, they'll decide it's too hot to handle, and they'll chicken out rather than risk getting bombed by the Jews and the niggers when it comes out.

PLAYBOY: We'll take our chances, Commander—if you will.

ROCKWELL: I'll take *any* chances to get my message read. But it's never going to happen. We've been kept out of the news too many times before. I'll bet you a hundred dollars this whole thing has been nothing but a waste of my time, because it's never going to reach the people who read your magazine.

TIMOTHY LEARY

September 1966
Interviewer: Bernard Gravzer

It was just one year before the "Summer of Love" in Haight-Ashbury. The bizarre spectacle of a middle-aged former Harvard professor urging America's youth to "turn on, tune in, and drop out" was horrifying to most of the public. There had been a great deal of publicity by mid-1966 about the dangers of LSD and other hallucinogens, but their chief spokesman, Tim Leary, had never been accorded a chance to state his case fully—whatever the merits or faults of that case.

As Thomas Weyr put it in *Reaching for Paradise*:

> Publication of Leary's 1966 Playboy Interview was a newsworthy event. Leary had become everybody's devil. He had been chased from Harvard, cited during congressional hearings on LSD, arrested and convicted for marijuana possession and transportation. That spring, G. Gordon Liddy had led a force of Dutchess County sheriff's deputies in a postmidnight raid on Leary's borrowed estate in Millbrook, New York, and arrested the guru and three of his followers. The threat of a second conviction and yet longer jail term made him an even more romantic figure.

When free-lancer Bernard Gravzer delivered a rough draft of the interview to PLAYBOY, the editors began to have second thoughts. Were they being tough enough? Was it responsible to let Leary state that LSD was the most powerful aphrodisiac ever discovered by man—and risk tripping out an entire generation of turned-on young men? Fisher decided to make a trip himself to Millbrook to toughen up some of the questions and rebut what points he could. He recalled:

I drove up the driveway to find a nude girl passed out on the high edge of the swimming pool. I wondered if she was going to fall into the sharp gravel on one side or fall into the pool and drown. But suddenly my guide appeared: a six-foot-six behemoth with blond hair, a glazed look in his eye, carrying a double-edged ax. He smiled sweetly, and led me into the house and up-stairs into Leary's lair. Leary greeted me warmly and, instead of sitting down in an easy chair, he stepped out of the window onto a small tin roof and proceeded to stretch out on a giant mattress a few feet from the edge of the roof. I squatted at the other end of the mattress, watched him open his shirt, and began my ques-tions.

Fisher also remembers that he refused the drinks Leary offered. "I was afraid of what Leary might have spiked them with."

Hefner and Spectorsky agreed to publish the interview once the questions were sharper, and there was an outpouring of mail when the interview appeared. Much of it was from true believers praising PLAYBOY for its "hipness" and "courage." But the magazine also published a long, sober letter from two UCLA research psychiatrists who per-suasively challenged Leary's claims about the drug's safety and charged that "emphasizing the sexual areas is very misleading."

In retrospect, Fisher believed the interview was "too much celebra-tion of drugs, not enough cerebration," though it remains an interesting look at a subject that fascinated a generation. As for Leary himself, he was later convicted on drug charges and then escaped from prison to lead a shabby fugitive's life in exile. As of this writing he had returned to the United States, served out his sentence, and had last surfaced attempting to earn a living in Los Angeles as a stand-up comic and disc jockey.

On a sunny Saturday afternoon in 1960, beside the swimming pool of his rented summer villa in Cuernavaca, a 39-year-old American ate a handful of odd-looking mushrooms he'd bought from the witch doctor of a nearby village. Within minutes, he recalled later, he felt himself "being swept over the edge of a sensory niagara into a maelstrom of transcendental visions and hallucinations. The next five hours could be described in many extrav-agant metaphors, but it was above all and without question the deepest religious experience of my life." The implications of that fateful first com-munion are as yet unmeasured; that they are both far-reaching and pro-

found, however, is generally conceded—for the fungi were the legendary "sacred mushrooms" that have since become known, and feared by many, as one of the psychedelic (literally, mind-manifesting) chemicals that have created a national fad among the nation's young and a scandal in the press. The American was a Harvard psychotherapist named Timothy Leary, who has since found himself transmogrified from scientist and researcher into progenitor and high priest of a revolutionary movement spawned not by an idea but by a substance that's been called "the spiritual equivalent of the hydrogen bomb."

When Leary returned to Harvard in 1960 from his pioneering voyage into inner space—beside the swimming pool in Cuernavaca—he began experimenting on himself, his associates and hundreds of volunteer subjects with measured doses of psilocybin, the chemical derivative of the sacred mushrooms. Vowing "to dedicate the rest of my life as a psychologist to the systematic exploration of this new instrument," he and his rapidly multiplying followers began to turn on with the other psychedelics: morning-glory seeds, nutmeg, marijuana, peyote, mescaline—and a colorless, odorless, tasteless but incredibly potent laboratory compound called LSD 25, first synthesized in 1938 by a Swiss biochemist seeking a pain killer for migraine headaches. A hundred times stronger than psilocybin, LSD sent its hallucinated users on multihued, multileveled roller-coaster rides so spectacular that it soon became Leary's primary tool for research. And as word began to circulate about the fantastic, phantasmagorical "trips" taken by his students, it soon became a clandestine campus kick, and by 1962 had become an underground cult among the young avant-garde from London to Los Angeles.

By 1963, it had also become something of an embarrassment to Harvard, however, which "regretfully" dismissed Leary, and his colleague Dr. Richard Alpert, in order to stem the rising tide of avid undergraduate interest in the drug. Undaunted, they organized a privately financed research group called the International Foundation for Internal Freedom (IFIF), and set up a psychedelic study center in Zihuatanejo, Mexico; but before they could resume full-scale LSD sessions, the Mexican government stepped in, anticipating adverse popular reaction, and demanded that they leave the country.

Leary had now become not only the messiah but the martyr of the psychedelic movement. But soon afterward came a dramatic 11th-hour reprieve from a young New York millionaire named William Hitchcock, a veteran LSD voyager who believed in the importance of Leary's work— by now a mission—and toward that end turned over to him a rambling mansion on his 4000-acre estate in Millbrook, New York, which has since become not only Leary's home and headquarters but also a kind of shrine and sanctuary for psychedelic pilgrims from all over the world. On April 16 of this year, it also became a target for further harassment by what

Leary calls "the forces of middle-aged, middle-class authority." Late that night, a squad of Dutchess County police descended on the place, searched it from top to bottom, found a minute quantity of marijuana, and arrested four people—including Leary. If convicted, he could be fined heavily and sent to prison for 16 years. Already appealing another conviction, Leary had been arrested in Laredo the previous December as he was about to enter Mexico for a vacation, when Customs officials searched his car and found a half ounce of marijuana in the possession of his 18-year-old daughter. Despite his claim that the drug was for scientific and sacramental use in the furtherance of his work and his spiritual beliefs (as a practicing Hindu), he was fined $30,000 and sentenced to 30 years in prison for transporting marijuana and failing to pay the Federal marijuana tax.

In the months since then, the LSD controversy has continued to escalate along with Leary's notoriety—spurred by a spate of headline stories about psychedelic psychoses, dire warnings of "instant insanity" from police and public health officials, and pious editorials inveighing against the evils of the drug. In May and June, two Senate subcommittees conducted widely publicized public hearings on LSD; and three states—California, Nevada and New Jersey—enacted laws prohibiting its illicit use, possession, distribution or manufacture. With a ringing appeal for still more stringent legislation on a Federal level, Ronald Reagan even dragged the issue into his successful campaign for the Republican gubernatorial nomination in California.

It was amid this mounting outcry against the drug that PLAYBOY *asked Dr. Leary to present his side of the psychedelic story—and to answer a few pertinent questions about its putative promise and its alleged perils. Consenting readily, he invited us to visit him in Millbrook, where we found him a few days later reciting Hindu morning prayers with a group of guests in the kitchen of the 64-room mansion.*

PLAYBOY: How many times have you used LSD, Dr. Leary?

LEARY: Up to this moment, I've had 311 psychedelic sessions.

PLAYBOY: What do you think it's done for you—and to you?

LEARY: That's difficult to answer easily. Let me say this: I was 39 when I had my first psychedelic experience. At that time, I was a middle-aged man involved in the middle-aged process of dying. My joy in life, my sensual openness, my creativity were all sliding downhill. Since that time, six years ago, my life has been renewed in almost every dimension. Most of my colleagues at the University of California and at Harvard, of course, feel that I've become an eccentric and a kook. I would estimate that fewer than 15 percent of my professional colleagues understand and support what I'm doing. The ones who do, as you might expect, tend to be among the younger psychologists. If you know a person's age, you know what he's going to think and feel about LSD. Psychedelic drugs are the medium of the young. As you move up the age scale—into the 30s, 40s and 50s—fewer and fewer people are open to the possibilities that these chemicals offer.

PLAYBOY: Why is that?

LEARY: To the person over 35 or 40, the word "drug" means one of two things: doctor-disease or dope fiend-crime. Nothing you can say to a person who has this neurological fix on the word "drug" is going to change his mind. He's frozen like a Pavlovian dog to this conditioned reflex. To people under 25, on the other hand, the word "drug" refers to a wide range of mind benders running from alcohol, energizers and stupefiers to marijuana and the other psychedelic drugs. To middle-aged America, it may be synonymous with instant insanity, but to most Americans under 25, the psychedelic drug means ecstasy, sensual unfolding, religious experience, revelation, illumination, contact with nature. There's not a teenager or young person in the United States today who doesn't know at least one person who has had a good experience with marijuana or LSD. The horizons of the current younger generation, in terms of expanded consciousness, are light-years beyond those of their parents. The breakthrough has occurred; there's no going back. The psychedelic battle is won.

PLAYBOY: What do you say to the standard charge that LSD is too powerful and dangerous to entrust to the young?

LEARY: Well, none of us yet knows exactly how LSD can be used for the growth and benefit of the human being. It is a powerful releaser of energy as yet not fully understood. But if I'm confronted with the possibility that a 15-year-old or a 50-year-old is going to use a new form of energy that he doesn't understand, I'll back the 15-year-old every time. Why? Because a 15-year-old is going to use a new form of energy to have fun, to intensify sensation, to make love, for curiosity, for personal growth. Many 50-year-olds have lost their curiosity, have lost their ability to make love, have dulled their openness to new sensations, and would use any form of new energy for power, control and warfare. So it doesn't concern me at all that young people are taking time out from the educational and occupational assembly lines to experiment with consciousness, to dabble with new forms of experience and artistic expression. The present generation under the age of 25 is the wisest and holiest generation that the human race has ever seen. And, by God, instead of lamenting, derogating and imprisoning them, we should support them, listen to them and turn on with them.

PLAYBOY: If we wanted to take you up on that last suggestion, how would we go about it?

LEARY: Find a beloved friend who knows where to get LSD and how to run a session; or find a trusted and experienced LSD voyager to guide you on a trip.

PLAYBOY: Is it necessary to have a guide?

LEARY: Yes. Unless you have an experienced guide—at least for your first 10 or 15 sessions—it would be extremely reckless.

PLAYBOY: What if a person can't find either a guide or a source of LSD among his friends? Where does he go?

LEARY: LSD is against the law, and I certainly would not advise anyone to violate the law. I will say this, however: Throughout human history, men who have wanted to expand their consciousness, to find deeper meaning inside themselves, have been able to do it if they were willing to commit the time and energy to do so. In other times and countries, men would walk barefooted 2000 miles to find spiritual teachers who would turn them on to Buddha, Mohammed or Ramakrishna.

PLAYBOY: If you can't say where one could buy LSD, can you tell us the formula for making it? We understand it can be synthesized in any well-equipped chemical laboratory.

LEARY: That's true. But it would be irresponsible of me to reveal it. The unauthorized manufacture of LSD is now against the law.

PLAYBOY: Assuming you can get it, how do you take it? Can it be injected, or is it mostly just swallowed in a sugar cube?

LEARY: It can be injected or it can come in the form of powder or pills or in a solution, which is odorless, tasteless and colorless. In any case, you're dealing with a very minute quantity. One hundred micrograms is a moderate dose.

PLAYBOY: For a session lasting how long?

LEARY: Eight to twelve hours.

PLAYBOY: What's it like? What happens to you?

LEARY: If we're speaking in a general way, what happens to everyone is the experience of incredible acceleration and intensification of all senses and of all mental processes—which can be very confusing if you're not prepared for it. Around a thousand million signals fire off in your brain every second; during any second in an LSD session, you find yourself tuned in on thousands of these messages that ordinarily you don't register consciously. And you may be getting an incredible number of simultaneous messages from different parts of your body. Since you're not used to this, it can lead to incredible ecstasy or it can lead to confusion. Some people are freaked by this niagara of sensory input. Instead of having just one or two or three things happening in tidy sequence, you're suddenly flooded by hundreds of lights and colors and sensations and images, and you can get quite lost.

You sense a strange, powerful force beginning to unloose and radiate through your body. In normal perception, we are aware of static symbols. But as the LSD effect takes hold, everything begins to *move*, and this relentless, impersonal, slowly swelling movement will continue through the several hours of the session. It's as though for all of your normal waking life you have been caught in a still photograph, in an awkward, stereotyped posture; suddenly the show comes alive, balloons out to several dimensions and becomes irradiated with color and energy.

The first thing you notice is an incredible enhancement of sensory awareness. Take the sense of sight. LSD vision is to normal vision as normal vision is to the picture on a badly tuned television set. Under LSD, it's as though you have microscopes up to your eyes, in which you see jewellike, radiant details of anything your eye falls upon. You are really seeing for the first time—not static, symbolic perception of learned things, but patterns of light bouncing off the objects around you and hurtling at the speed of light into the mosaic of rods and cones in the retina of your eye. Everything seems alive. Everything *is* alive, beaming diamond-bright light waves into your retina.

PLAYBOY: Is the sense of hearing similarly intensified?

LEARY: Tremendously. Ordinarily we hear just isolated sounds: the rings of a telephone, the sound of somebody's words. But when you turn on with LSD, the organ of Corti in your inner ear becomes a trembling membrane seething with tattoos of sound waves. The vibrations seem to penetrate deep inside you, swell and burst there. You hear one note of a Bach sonata, and it hangs there, glittering, pulsating, for an endless length of time, while you slowly orbit around it. Then, hundreds of years later, comes the second note of the sonata, and again, for hundreds of years, you slowly drift around the two notes, observing the harmony and the discords, and reflecting on the history of music.

But when your nervous system is turned on with LSD, and all the wires are flashing, the senses begin to overlap and merge. You not only hear but *see* the music emerging from the speaker system—like dancing particles, like squirming curls of toothpaste. You actually *see* the sound, in multicolored patterns, while you're hearing it. At the same time, you *are* the sound, you are the note, you are the string of the violin or the piano. And every one of your organs is pulsating and having orgasms in rhythm with it.

PLAYBOY: What happens to the sense of taste?

LEARY: Taste is intensified, too, although normally you won't feel like eating during an LSD session, any more than you feel like eating when you take your first solo at the controls of a supersonic jet. Although if you eat after a session, there is an appreciation of all the particular qualities of food—its texture and resiliency and viscosity—such as we are not conscious of in a normal state of awareness.

PLAYBOY: How about the sense of smell?

LEARY: This is one of the most overwhelming aspects of an LSD experience. It seems as though for the first time you are breathing life, and you remember with amusement and distaste that plastic, odorless, artificial gas that you used to consider air. During the LSD experience, you discover that you're actually inhaling an atmosphere composed of millions of microscopic strands of olfactory ticker tape, exploding in your nostrils with ecstatic meaning. When you sit across the room from a woman during an LSD session, you're aware of thousands of penetrating chemical messages floating from her through the air into your sensory center: a symphony of a thousand odors that all of us exude at every moment—the shampoo she uses, her cologne, her sweat, the exhaust and discharge from her digestive system, her sexual perfume, the fragrance of her clothing—grenades of eroticism exploding in the olfactory cell.

PLAYBOY: Does the sense of touch become equally erotic?

LEARY: Touch becomes electric as well as erotic. I remember a moment during one session in which my wife leaned over and lightly touched the palm of my hand with her finger. Immediately a hundred thousand end cells in my hand exploded in soft orgasm. Ecstatic energies pulsated up my arms and rocketed into my brain, where another hundred thousand cells softly exploded in pure, delicate pleasure. The distance between my wife's finger and the palm of my hand was about 50 miles of space, filled with cotton candy, infiltrated with thousands of silver wires hurtling energy back and forth. Wave after wave of exquisite energy pulsed from her finger. Wave upon wave of ethereal tissue rapture—delicate, shuddering—coursed back and forth from her finger to my palm.

PLAYBOY: And this rapture was erotic?

LEARY: Transcendentally. An enormous amount of energy from every fiber of your body is released under LSD—most especially including sexual energy. There is no question that LSD is the most powerful aphrodisiac ever discovered by man.

PLAYBOY: Would you elaborate?

LEARY: I'm saying simply that sex under LSD becomes miraculously enhanced and intensified. I don't mean that it simply generates genital energy. It doesn't automatically produce a longer erection. Rather, it increases your sensitivity a thousand percent. Let me put it this way: Compared with sex under LSD, the way you've been making love—no matter how ecstatic the pleasure you think you get from it—is like making love to a department-store-window dummy. In sensory and cellular communion on LSD, you may spend a half hour making love with eyeballs, another half hour making love with breath. As you spin through a thousand sensory and cellular organic changes, she does, too. Ordinarily, sexual communication involves one's own chemicals, pressure and interactions of a very localized nature—in what the psychologists call the erogenous zones. A vulgar, dirty concept, I think. When you're making love under LSD, it's as though every cell in your body—and you have trillions—is making love with every cell in her body. Your hand doesn't caress her skin but sinks down into and merges with ancient dynamos of ecstasy within her.

PLAYBOY: How often have you made love under the influence of LSD?

LEARY: Every time I've taken it. In fact, that is what the LSD experience is all about. Merging, yielding, flowing, union, communion. It's all lovemaking. You make love with candlelight, with sound waves from a record player, with a bowl of fruit on the table, with the trees. You're in pulsating harmony with all the energy around you.

PLAYBOY: Including that of a woman?

LEARY: The three inevitable goals of the LSD session are to discover and make love with God, to discover and make love with yourself, and to discover and make love with a woman. You can't make it with yourself unless you've made it with the timeless energy process around you, and you can't make it with a woman until you've made it with yourself. The natural and obvious way to take LSD is with a member of the opposite sex, and an LSD session that does not involve an ultimate merging with a person of the opposite sex isn't really complete. One of the great purposes of an LSD session is sexual union. The more expanded your consciousness—the farther out you can move beyond your mind—the deeper, the richer, the longer and more meaningful your sexual communion.

PLAYBOY: We've heard about sessions in which couples make love for hours on end, to the point of exhaustion, but never seem to reach exhaustion. Is this true?

LEARY: Inevitably.

PLAYBOY: Can you describe the sensation of an orgasm under LSD?

LEARY: Only the most reckless poet would attempt that. I have to say to you, "What does one say to a little child?" The child says, "Daddy, what is sex like?" and you try to describe it, and then the little child says, "Well, is it fun like the circus?" and you say, "Well, not exactly like that." And the child says, "Is it fun like chocolate ice cream?" and you say, "Well, it's like that but much, much *more* than that." And the child says, "Is it fun like the roller coaster, then?" and you say, "Well, that's part of it, but it's even more than that." In short, I can't tell you what it's like, because it's not like anything that's ever happened to you—and there aren't words adequate to describe it, anyway. You won't know what it's like until you try it yourself—and then I won't *need* to tell you.

PLAYBOY: We've heard that some women who ordinarily have difficulty achieving orgasm find themselves capable of multiple orgasms under LSD. Is that true?

LEARY: In a carefully prepared, loving LSD session, a woman will inevitably have several hundred orgasms.

PLAYBOY: Several *hundred*?

LEARY: Yes. Several hundred.

PLAYBOY: What about a man?

LEARY: This preoccupation with the number of orgasms is a hang-up for many men and women. It's as crude and vulgar a concept as wondering how much she paid for the negligee.

PLAYBOY: Still, there must be some sort of physiological comparison. If a woman can have several hundred orgasms, how many can a man have under optimum conditions?

LEARY: It would depend entirely on the amount of sexual—and psychedelic—experience the man has had. I can speak only for myself and about my own experience. I can only compare what I was with what I am now. In the last six years, my openness to, my responsiveness to, my participation in every form of sensory expression has multiplied a *thousandfold*.

PLAYBOY: This aspect of LSD has been hinted at privately but never spelled out in public until now. Why?

LEARY: The sexual impact is, of course, the open but private secret about LSD, which none of us has talked about in the last few years. It's socially dangerous enough to say that LSD helps you find divinity and helps you discover yourself. You're already in trouble when you say that. But then if you announce that the psychedelic experience is basically a *sexual* experience, you're asking to bring the whole middle-aged, middle-class monolith down on your head. At the present time, however, I'm under a 30-year sentence of imprisonment, which for a 45-year-old man is essentially a life term; and in addition, I am under indictment on a second marijuana offense involving a 16-year sentence. Since there is hardly anything more that middle-aged, middle-class authority can do to me—and since the secret is out anyway among the young—I feel I'm free at this moment to say what we've never said before: that sexual ecstasy is the basic reason for the current LSD boom. When Dr. Goddard, the head of the Food and Drug Administration, announced in a Senate hearing that ten percent of our college students are taking LSD, did you ever wonder why? Sure, they're discovering God and meaning; sure, they're discovering themselves; but did you really think that sex wasn't the fundamental reason for this surging, youthful social boom? You can no more do research on LSD and leave out sexual ecstasy than you can do microscopic research on tissue and leave out cells.

LSD is not an automatic trigger to sexual awakening, however. The first ten times you take it, you might not be able to have a sexual experience at all, because you're so overwhelmed and delighted—or frightened and confused—by the novelty; the idea of having sex might be irrelevant or incomprehensible at the moment. But it depends upon the setting and the partner. It is almost inevitable, if a man and his mate take LSD together, that their sexual energies will be unimaginably intensified, and unless clumsiness or fright on the part of one or the other blocks it, it will lead to a deeper experience than they ever thought possible.

From the beginning of our research, I have been aware of this tremendous personal power in LSD. You must be very careful to take it only with someone you know really well, because it's almost inevitable that a woman will fall in love with the man who shares her LSD experience. Deep and lasting neurological imprints, profound emotional bonds, can develop as a result of an LSD session—bonds that can last a lifetime. For this reason, I have always been extremely cautious about running sessions with men and women. We always try to have a subject's husband or wife present during his or her first session, so that as these powerful urges develop, they are directed in ways that can be lived out responsibly after the session.

PLAYBOY: Are you preaching psychedelic monogamy?

LEARY: Well, I can't generalize, but one of the great lessons I've learned from LSD is that every man contains the essence of all men and every woman has within her *all* women. I remember a session a few years ago in which, with horror and ecstasy, I opened my eyes and looked into the eyes of my wife and was pulled into the deep blue pools of her being, floating softly in the center of her mind, experiencing everything that she was experiencing, knowing every thought that she had ever had. As my eyes were riveted to hers, her face began to melt and change. I saw her as a young girl, as a baby, as an old woman with gray hair and seamy, wrinkled face. I saw her as a witch, a Madonna, a nagging crone, a radiant queen, a Byzantine virgin, a tired, worldly-wise Oriental whore who had seen every sight of life repeated a thousand times. She was *all* women, all *woman*, the essence of female— eyes smiling, quizzically, resignedly, devilishly, always inviting: "See me, hear me, join me, merge with me, keep the dance going."

PLAYBOY: A great deal of what is said about LSD by its proponents, including you, has been couched in terms of religious mysticism. You spoke earlier, in fact, of discovering "divinity" through LSD. In what way is the LSD experience religious?

LEARY: It depends on what you mean by religion. For almost everyone, the LSD experience is a confrontation with new forms of wisdom and energy that dwarf and humiliate man's mind. This experience of awe and revelation is often described as religious. I consider my work basically religious, because it has as its goal the systematic expansion of consciousness and the discovery of energies within, which men call "divine." From the psychedelic point of view, almost all religions are attempts—sometimes limited temporally or nationally—to discover the inner potential. Well, LSD is Western yoga. The aim of all Eastern religions, like the aim of LSD, is basically to get high: that is, to expand your consciousness and find ecstasy and revelation within.

PLAYBOY: Dr. Gerald Klee, of the National Institute of Mental Health, has written: "Those who say LSD expands consciousness would have the task of defining the terms. By any conventional definition, I don't think it does expand the consciousness." What do you think?

LEARY: Well, he's using the narrow, conventional definition of consciousness that psychiatrists have been taught: that there are two levels of consciousness—sleep and symbolic normal awareness. Anything else is insanity. So by conventional definition, LSD does *not* expand symbolic consciousness; thus, it creates psychosis. In terms of his conventional symbol game, Dr.

Klee is right. My contention is that his definition is too narrow, that it comes from a deplorable, primitive and superstitious system of consciousness. My system of consciousness—attested to by the experience of hundreds of thousands of trained voyagers who've taken LSD—defines *many* different levels of awareness.

PLAYBOY: What are they?

LEARY: The lowest level of consciousness is sleep—or stupor, which is produced by narcotics, barbiturates and our national stuporfactant, alcohol. The second level of consciousness is the conventional wakeful state, in which awareness is hooked to conditioned symbols: flags, dollar signs, job titles, brand names, party affiliations and the like. This is the level that most people—including psychiatrists—regard as reality; they don't know the half of it. There is a third level of awareness, and this is the one that I think would be of particular interest to PLAYBOY readers, because most of them are of the younger generation, which is much more sensual than the puritanical Americans of the older generation. This is the sensory level of awareness. In order to reach it, you have to have something that will turn *off* symbols and open up your billions of sensory cameras to the billions of impulses that are hitting them. The chemical that opens the door to this level has been well known for centuries to cultures that stress delicate, sensitive registration of sensory stimulation: the Arab cultures, the Indian cultures, the Mogul cultures. It is marijuana. There is no question that marijuana is a sensual stimulator—and this explains not only why it's favored by young people but why it arouses fear and panic among the middle-aged, middle-class, whiskey-drinking, bluenosed bureaucrats who run the narcotics agencies. If they only knew what they were missing.

But we must bid a sad farewell to the sensory level of consciousness and go on to the fourth level, which I call the cellular level. It's well known that the stronger psychedelics such as mescaline and LSD take you *beyond* the senses into a world of cellular awareness. Now, the neurological fact of the matter is that every one of your 13 billion brain cells is hooked up to some 25,000 other cells, and everything you know comes from a communication exchange at the nerve endings of your cells. During an LSD session, enormous clusters of these cells are turned on, and consciousness whirls into eerie panoramas for which we have no words or concepts. Here the metaphor that's most accurate is the metaphor of the microscope, which brings into awareness cellular patterns that are invisible to the naked eye. In the same way, LSD brings into awareness the cellular conversations that are inaudible to the normal consciousness and for which we have no adequate symbolic language. You become aware of processes you were never tuned in to before. You feel yourself sinking down into the soft tissue swamp of your own body, slowly drifting down dark red waterways and floating through capillary canals, softly propelled through endless cellular factories, ancient fibrous clockworks—ticking, clicking, chugging, pumping relentlessly. Being swallowed up this way by the tissue industries and the bloody, sinewy carryings-on inside your body can be an appalling experience the first time it happens to you. But it can also be an awesome one—fearful, but full of reverence and wonder.

PLAYBOY: Is there a fifth level of awareness?

LEARY: Yes, and this one is even more strange and terrifying. This is the *pre*cellular level, which is experienced only under a heavy dosage of LSD. Your nerve cells are aware—as Professor Einstein was aware—that all matter, all structure, is pulsating energy; well, there is a shattering moment in the deep psychedelic session when your body, and the world around you, dissolves into shimmering latticeworks of pulsating white waves, into silent, subcellular worlds of shuttling energy. But this phenomenon is nothing new. It's been reported by mystics and visionaries throughout the last 4000 years of recorded history as "the white light" or the "dance of energy." Suddenly you realize that everything you thought of as reality or even as life itself— including your body—is just a dance of particles. You find yourself horribly alone in a dead, impersonal world of raw energy feeding on your sense organs. This, of course, is one of the oldest Oriental philosophic notions, that nothing exists except in the chemistry of your own consciousness. But when it first really happens to you, through the experience of LSD, it can come as a terrorizing, isolating discovery. At this point, the unprepared LSD subject often screams out: "I'm dead!" And he sits there transfigured with fear, afraid to move. For the experienced voyager, however, this revelation can be exalting: You've climbed inside Einstein's formula, penetrated to the ultimate nature of matter, and you're pulsing in harmony with its primal, cosmic beat.

PLAYBOY: Has this happened to you often during a session?

LEARY: It's happened to me about half of the 311 times I've taken LSD. And every time it begins to happen, no matter how much experience you've had, there is that moment of terror—because nobody likes to see the comfortable world of objects and symbols and even cells disintegrate into the ultimate physical design.

PLAYBOY: Do you think there may be a deeper level of consciousness beyond the precellular?

LEARY: I hope so. We know that there are many other levels of energy within and around us, and I hope that within our lifetimes we will have these opened up to us, because the fact is that there is no form of energy on this planet that isn't recorded somewhere in your body. Built within every cell are molecular strands of memory and awareness called the DNA code— the genetic blueprint that has designed and executed the construction of your body. This is an ancient strand of molecules that possesses memories of every previous organism that has contributed to your present existence. In your DNA code, you have the genetic history of your father and mother. It goes back, back, back through the generations, through the eons. Your body carries a protein record of everything that's happened to you since the moment you were conceived as a one-cell organism. It's a living history of every form of energy transformation on this planet back to that thunderbolt in the Pre-Cambrian mud that spawned the life process over two billion years ago. When LSD subjects report retrogression and reincarnation visions, this is not mysterious or supernatural. It's simply modern biogenetics.

PLAYBOY: According to a spokesman for the student left, many former campus activists who've gone the LSD route are "more concerned with what's happening in their heads than what's happening in the world." Any comment?

LEARY: There's a certain amount of truth in that. The insight of LSD leads you to concern yourself more with internal or spiritual values; you realize that it doesn't make any difference what you do on the outside unless you change the inside. If all the Negroes and left-wing college students in the world had Cadillacs and full control of society, they would still be involved in an anthill social system unless they opened themselves up first.

PLAYBOY: Aren't these young ex-activists among an increasing number of students, writers, artists and musicians whom one critic has called "the psychedelic dropouts"—LSD users who find themselves divested of motivation, unable to readjust to reality or to resume their roles in society?

LEARY: There *is* an LSD dropout problem, but it's nothing to worry about. It's something to cheer. The lesson I have learned from over 300 LSD sessions, and which I have been passing on to others, can be stated in six syllables: Turn on, tune in, drop out. "Turn on" means to contact the ancient energies and wisdoms that are built into your nervous system. They provide unspeakable pleasure and revelation. "Tune in" means to harness and communicate these new perspectives in a harmonious dance with the external world. "Drop out" means to detach yourself from the tribal game. Current models of social adjustment—mechanized, computerized, socialized, intellectualized, televised, Sanforized—make no sense to the new LSD generation, who see clearly that American society is becoming an air-conditioned anthill. In every generation of human history, thoughtful men have turned on and dropped out of the tribal game, and thus stimulated the larger society to lurch ahead. Every historical advance has resulted from the stern pressure of visionary men who have declared their independence from the game: "Sorry, George III, we don't buy your model. We're going to try something new"; "Sorry, Louis XVI, we've got a new idea. Deal us out"; "Sorry, L.B.J., it's time to mosey on *beyond* the Great Society."

The reflex reaction of society to the creative dropout is panic and irritation. If anyone questions the social order, he threatens the whole shaky edifice. The automatic, angry reaction to the creative dropout is that he will become a parasite on the hard-working, conforming citizen. This is not true. The LSD experience does not lead to passivity and withdrawal; it spurs a driving hunger to communicate in new forms, in better ways, to express a more harmonious message, to live a better life. The LSD cult has already wrought revolutionary changes in American culture. If you were to conduct a poll of the creative young musicians in this country, you'd find that at least 80 percent are using psychedelic drugs in a systematic way. And this new psychedelic style has produced not only a new rhythm in modern music but a new decor for our *discothèques*, a new form of film making, a new kinetic visual art, a new literature, and has begun to revise our philosophic and psychological thinking.

Remember, it's the college kids who are turning on—the smartest and most promising of the youngsters. What an exciting prospect: a generation of creative youngsters refusing to march in step, refusing to go to offices, refusing to sign up on the installment plan, refusing to climb aboard the treadmill.

PLAYBOY: Are any of the scare statements true? According to a recent report on narcotics addiction published by the Medical Society of the County of New York, for example, "those with unstable personalities may experience LSD-induced psychoses." Is that true?

LEARY: In over 3000 people that I have personally observed taking LSD, we've had only four cases of prolonged psychoses—a matter of, say, two or three weeks after the session. All of these had been in a mental hospital before, and they were people who could not commit themselves to any stable relationship. And all of these people had nothing going in their lives. They were drifting or floating, with no home or family or any roots, no stable, ongoing life situation to return to. It's dangerous to take a trip if you have no internal trust and no external place to turn to afterward.

PLAYBOY: The same New York Medical Society report also stated that "normal, well-adjusted persons can undergo an acute psychotic break under the influence of LSD." Is there any truth to that?

LEARY: Everyone, normal or neurotic, experiences some fear and confusion during the high-dose LSD session. The outcome and duration of this confusion depends upon your environment and your traveling companions. That's why it's tremendously important that the LSD session be conducted in a protected place, that the person be prepared and that he have an experienced and understanding guide to support and shield him from intrusion and interruption. When unprepared people take LSD in bad surroundings, and when there's no one present who has the skill and courage to guide them through it, then paranoid episodes are possible.

PLAYBOY: Will you describe them?

LEARY: There are any number of forms a paranoid episode can take. You can find yourself feeling that you've lived most of your life in a universe completely of your own, not really touching and harmonizing with the flow of the people and the energies around you. It seems to you that everyone else, and every other organism in creation, is in beatific communion, and only you are isolated by your egocentricity. Every action around you fits perfectly into this paranoid mosaic. Every glance, every look of boredom, every sound, every smile becomes a confirmation of the fact that everyone knows that you are the only one in the universe that's not swinging lovingly and gracefully with the rest of the cosmic dance. I've experienced this myself.

I've also sat with hundreds of people who have been panicked because they were trapped at the level of cellular reincarnation, where they looked out and saw that their body had scales like a fish or felt that they had turned into an animal. And I've sat with people who were caught on the fifth level, in that eerie, inhuman world of shuttling vibrations. But all these episodes can be dealt with easily by an experienced guide who recognizes where the LSD tripper is caught. He can bring you back down quite simply by holding a candle in front of you, or getting you to concentrate on your breathing, or having you lie down and getting you to feel your body merging with the mattress or the floor. If he understands the map of consciousness, it's very easy to bring you back to a more recognizable and less frightening level. With his help, you'll be able to exult in and learn from the experience.

If he's frightened or uncomprehending, however, or if he acts so as to protect his own social interests, your own terror and confusion are naturally increased. If he treats you as a psychotic rather than as one who is seriously groping with basic problems that you should be encouraged to face and work through, you may be forced into a psychotic state. Every case of prolonged LSD psychosis is the fault not of the drug nor of the drug taker but of the people around him who lose their cool and call the cops or the doctors. The lesson here is to fear neither LSD nor your own psychological nature—which is basically OK—but to fear the diagnosing mind of the psychiatrist. Ninety percent of the bad LSD trips are provoked by psychiatric propaganda, which creates an atmosphere of fear rather than of courage and trust. If the psychiatrists had their way, we'd *all* be patients.

PLAYBOY: Speaking of patients, a recent *Time* essay reported that a survey in Los Angeles "showed as many as 200 victims of bad trips in the city's hospitals at one time." Does that sound to you like a realistic figure?

LEARY: I'd like to know who conducted that survey and where they got their figures, because it's contradicted by the known facts. I was recently told by the director of a large California hospital, which handles LSD cases, that most LSD panic subjects are given a tranquilizer and sent home without even being admitted. The same is true at Bellevue and throughout the country.

PLAYBOY: In the same essay, *Time* wrote: "Under the influence of LSD, nonswimmers think they can swim, and others think they can fly. One young man tried to stop a car on Los Angeles' Wilshire Boulevard and was hit and killed. A magazine salesman became convinced that he was the Messiah." Are these cases, and others like them, representative reactions to LSD, in your opinion?

LEARY: I would say that one case in 10,000 is going to flip out and run out into the street and do something bizarre. But these are the cases that get reported in the papers. There are 3000 Americans who die every year from barbiturates and it never hits the papers. Thousands more die in car crashes and from lung cancer induced by smoking. That isn't news, either. But one LSD kid rushes out and takes off his clothes in the street and it's headlines in the New York *Daily News*. If one nut who's a member of the narcotics squad from the Los Angeles police force gets drunk and climbs into an airplane and threatens the pilot, that's no reason for grounding all airplanes, calling alcohol illegal, outlawing guns and dissolving the narcotics bureau of the Los Angeles police force. So one episode out of 10,000 LSD cases is no reason for any kind of hand wringing and grandmotherly panic.

PLAYBOY: A recent case of this nature involved a young man who contended that he killed his mother-in-law while he was on LSD. Isn't that a cause for concern?

LEARY: Yes—but only because this one episode has led to some psychiatrists and police calling LSD a homicidal drug. Actually, there's no evidence that that unfortunate boy ever took LSD. He was obviously attempting a cop-out when he talked to the police about it afterward.

PLAYBOY: There have also been reports of suicide under the influence of LSD. Does this happen?

LEARY: In 23 years of LSD use, there has been one definite case of suicide during the LSD session. This was a woman in Switzerland who'd been given LSD without her knowledge. She thought she was going crazy and jumped out of the window. But it wasn't that the LSD poisoned her. The unexpected LSD led to such panic and confusion that she killed herself. There have been other rumors about LSD panics leading to suicide, but I am waiting for the scientific evidence. In more than a million LSD cases, there haven't been more than one or two documented cases of homicide or suicide attributable to the LSD experience.

PLAYBOY: Though it hasn't led to any reported deaths, a number of LSD panics have been attributed to the experience of many users, in the midst of a session, that they're about to have a heart attack. Is this a common occurrence?

LEARY: Fairly common. When somebody says to us in an LSD session, "My heart's going to stop!" we say, "OK, fine. That's a new experience, nothing to be afraid of. Let it stop." There is no physiological change in your heart, but the experience is that the heart is stopping. On LSD, you see, you may actually hear the thump of your heartbeat. You become aware of its pulsing nerves and muscle fibers straining for the next beat. How can they possibly do this over and over again? If you're unprepared for it, this can become a terror that it cannot continue. Because of LSD's distention of the time dimension, you may wait what seems like five hours for the second beat. Then you wait again, and you wait, and you are aware of the millions of cells that must be tiring out; they may not have the strength to beat again.

You're afraid that your heart is going to burst. Then finally—thump! At last! But did it come slower this time? Is it stopping? You feel the blood throbbing in your heart. You feel the ventricles opening and closing; there's a hole in your heart! The blood is flooding your body! You're drowning in your own blood! "Help! Get me a doctor!" you may shout. If this kind of episode occurs, of course, all that's necessary to allay your fears are a few words of understanding and reassurance from an experienced guide and companion, who should be with you at all times.

PLAYBOY: Dr. Jonathan Cole, of the National Institute of Mental Health, has said that psychedelic drugs "can be dangerous. . . . People go into panic states in which they are ready to jump out of their skins. . . . The benefits are obscure." What do you say?

LEARY: Based on the evidence that Dr. Cole has had at hand, he is justified in saying that. Dr. Cole undoubtedly has never taken LSD himself. He *has* sponsored research that has been done—indeed, must be done—in mental hospitals, under psychiatric supervision. But this is the worst possible place to take LSD. Take LSD in a nuthouse and you'll have a nuthouse experience. These poor patients are usually not even told what drugs they're given; they're not prepared. I consider this psychological rape. So I'm not surprised that the cases Dr. Cole has heard about from his researchers are negative.

But Dr. Cole doesn't listen to the hundreds of thousands of people who have taken LSD under intelligent, aesthetic, carefully planned circumstances and have had their lives changed for the better. He doesn't receive the hundred letters a week that I receive from people who are profoundly grateful to have been dramatically opened up by LSD. He hears only the horror stories. If you talk to a mortician, you'll come to the conclusion that everyone who is of any importance is dead. If you talk to a law-enforcement officer, you'll find that practically everyone is a criminal, actual or potential. And if you talk to a psychiatrist, you'll hear nothing but gloomy lexicons of psychopathology. What Dr. Cole thinks about LSD is irrelevant, because for every case that his Federal researchers have studied, there are 5000 serious-minded, courageous young laymen out in the universities and out in the seminaries and in their own homes and on the beaches who are taking LSD and having fantastically beautiful experiences.

PLAYBOY: Have you allowed or encouraged your own children to use marijuana and LSD?

LEARY: Yes. I have no objection to them expanding their consciousness through the use of sacramental substances in accord with their spiritual growth and well-being. At Harvard, in Mexico and here at Millbrook, both of my children have witnessed more psychedelic sessions than any psychiatrist in the country.

PLAYBOY: At most of the psychedelic sessions you've conducted in the course of research, as you've said elsewhere, you and your associates have turned on with your subjects—and not in the laboratory but on beaches, in meadows, living rooms and even Buddhist temples. In the opinion of most authorities, this highly unconventional therapeutic technique is not only impractical but irrational and irresponsible. How do you justify it?

LEARY: This sort of criticism has ruined my reputation in conventional research circles, but it simply betrays ignorance of the way LSD works. You have to take it with your patient—or at least to have taken it yourself—in order to empathize with and follow him as he goes from one level to another. If the therapist has never taken it, he's sitting there with his sticky molasses Freudian psychiatric chessboard attempting to explain experiences that are far beyond the narrow limits of that particular system.

PLAYBOY: You've also been criticized for being insufficiently selective in the screening of subjects to whom you've administered LSD.

LEARY: We have been willing and eager to run LSD sessions with anyone in any place that made collaborative sense to me and the subject. We've never given LSD to anyone for our own selfish purposes, or for selfish purposes of his own; but if any reasonably stable individual wanted to develop his own consciousness, we turned him on. This ruined our reputation with scientists, of course, but it also made possible a fantastically successful record: 99 percent of the people who took LSD with us had fabulous experiences. None of our subjects flipped out and went to Bellevue; they walked out of the session room with messianic gleams in their eyes.

PLAYBOY: Even if only one percent of your subjects had bad experiences, is it worth the risk?

LEARY: That question can be answered only by the individual. When men set out for Plymouth in a leaky boat to pursue a new spiritual way of life, of course they were taking risks. But the risks of the voyage were less than the risks of remaining in a spiritual plague area, immobilized from the possibility of change by their fears of taking a risk. No Government bureau or Big Brother doctor can be allowed to decide who is going to take the risks involved in this 20th Century voyage of spiritual discovery.

PLAYBOY: Yet restrictive and prohibitive laws against the use of LSD have already been passed in California, Nevada and New Jersey, and several members of Congress have urged Federal legislation outlawing its manufacture or possession.

LEARY: Such laws are unrealistic and unconstitutional. Over 15 percent of college students are currently using LSD. Do the hard-arteried politicians and police types really want to put our brightest and most creative youngsters in prison for possession of a colorless, odorless, tasteless, nonaddictive, mind-opening substance? Irrational, senile legislation preventing people from pursuing private, intimate experiences—sexual or spiritual—cannot and will not be obeyed. We are currently planning to appeal any conviction for possession of LSD on constitutional grounds. But the Federal Government is opposed to laws penalizing possession of LSD, because it recognizes the impossibility of enforcement and the unconstitutionality of such statutes. Of course, this ambiguous situation is temporary. In 15 years, the bright kids who are turning on now will be shaping public opinion, writing our novels, running our universities and repealing the hysterical laws that are now being passed.

PLAYBOY: In what way are they hysterical?

LEARY: They're hysterical because the men who are passing them have allowed their ignorance of LSD to escalate into irrationality. Instinctively, they put LSD in the same bag with heroin. They think of drug taking as a criminal activity practiced by stuporous escapists and crazed, deranged minds. The daily diatribes of police officials and many legislators to that effect completely ignore the fact that the use of LSD is a white-collar, upper-middle-class, college-educated phenomenon. The LSD user is not a criminal type. He's not an underground character or a junkie. He doesn't seek to hide, or to apologize for, his activities. But while more and more laws are being passed restricting these activities, more and more people are engaging in them. LSD is being manufactured by people in their own homes and in small laboratories. If this continues, in ten years the LSD group will constitute one of our largest minorities. Then what are the lawmakers going to do?

PLAYBOY: What *should* they do, in your opinion?

LEARY: As they learn more about LSD, I think—I hope—they will recognize that there will have to be special legislation. There *should* be laws about the manufacture of LSD. It is incredibly powerful and can be a frightening experience. It is not a narcotic and not a medical drug; it doesn't cure any illness. It is a new form of *energy*. Just as a new form of legislation had to be developed for radioactive isotopes, so will there need to be something comparable for LSD. And I think some LSD equivalent of the Atomic Energy Commission and some special licensing procedures should be set up to deal with this new class of drugs.

PLAYBOY is among the rare institutions that will tackle an issue of this sort. There is an enormous amount of peripheral harassment. For example, I couldn't get bail bond after my indictment in Laredo, and I had to put up cash. This issue has generated so much hysteria that the normal processes of democratic debate are consistently violated. When several million Americans can't have their voices heard and can't get objective and scientific consideration of their position, I think that the Constitution is in danger.

PLAYBOY: There are some who see the appeal of your conviction in Laredo as a step leading to legalization of marijuana. Do you think that's possible?

LEARY: If I win my case in the higher courts—and my lawyers believe I will—this will have wide implications. It will suggest that future arrests for marijuana must be judged on the merits of the individual case rather than a blanket, arbitrary implementation of irrational and excessive regulation. I consider the marijuana laws to be unjust laws. My 30-year sentence and $30,000 fine simply pointed up in a rather public way the severity and harshness of the current statutes, which are clearly in violation of several amendments to the Constitution.

PLAYBOY: Which amendments?

LEARY: The First Amendment, which guarantees the right of spiritual exploration; and the Fifth Amendment, which guarantees immunity from self-incrimination. The fact that I'm being imprisoned for not paying a tax on a substance that, if I had applied for a license, would have led to my automatic arrest, is clearly self-incrimination. The current marijuana statutes are also in violation of the Eighth Amendment, which forbids cruel and unusual punishments; and of the Ninth Amendment, which guarantees certain personal liberties not specifically enumerated in the other amendments.

PLAYBOY: Dr. Humphrey Osmond of the New Jersey Neuropsychiatric Institute—the man who coined the word "psychedelic"—has described you as "Irish and revolutionary, and to a good degree reckless." He was suggesting that if you had been more careful, you might not have been arrested in Laredo.

LEARY: I plead guilty to the charges of being an Irishman and a revolutionary. But I don't think I'm careless about anything that's important.

PLAYBOY: Wasn't it careless to risk the loss of your freedom by carrying a half ounce of marijuana into Mexico?

LEARY: Well, that's like saying: Wouldn't it be careless for a Christian to carry the Bible to Russia? I just can't be bothered with paranoias about wire tapping, surveillance and police traps. It's been well known for several years that I'm using psychedelic drugs in my own home and in my own center for the use of myself and my own family. So at any time the Government wanted to make an issue of this, it certainly could. But I can't live my life in secrecy or panic paranoia. I've never bothered to take a lot of elementary precautions, for example, about my phone was being bugged or my actions being under surveillance—both of which the police admit. I would say that if there was carelessness in Laredo, it was carelessness on the part of the Government officials in provoking a case that has already changed public attitudes and will inevitably change the law on the possession and use of marijuana by thoughtful adults in this country. The Narcotics Bureau is in trouble. I'm not.

PLAYBOY: Do you dread the prospect of imprisonment?

LEARY: Well, I belong to one of the oldest trade unions in human civilization—the alchemists of the mind, the scholars of consciousness. The threat of imprisonment is the number-one occupational hazard of my profession. Of the great men of the past whom I hold up as models, almost every one of them has been either imprisoned or threatened with imprisonment for their spiritual beliefs: Gandhi, Jesus, Socrates, Lao-tse. I have absolutely no fear of imprisonment. First of all, I've taken LSD over 40 times in a maximum-security prison as part of a convict rehabilitation project we did in Boston; so I know that the only real prisons are *internal*. Secondly, a man who feels no guilt about his behavior has no fear of imprisonment; I have not one shred of guilt about anything I've done in the last six years. I've made hundreds of mistakes, but I've never once violated my own ethical or moral values. I'm the freest man in America today. If you're free in mind and heart, you're not in trouble. I think that the people who are trying to put other people in jail and to control basic evolutionary energies like sex and psychedelic chemicals are in trouble, because they're swimming upstream against the two-billion-year tide of cellular evolution.

PLAYBOY: What would you say is the most important lesson you've learned from your personal use of LSD?

LEARY: First and last, the understanding that basic to the life impulse is the question, "Should we go *on* with life?" This is the only real issue, when you come down to it, in the evolutionary cosmic sense: whether to make it with a member of the opposite sex and keep it going—or not to. At the deepest level of consciousness, this question comes up over and over again. I've struggled with it in scores of LSD sessions. How did we get here and into this mess? How do we get out? There are two ways out of the basic philosophic isolation of man: You can ball your way out—by having children, which is immortality of a sort. Or you can step off the wheel. Buddhism, the most powerful psychology that man has ever developed, says essentially that. My choice, however, is to keep the life game going. I'm Hindu, not Buddhist.

Beyond this affirmation of my own life, I've learned to confine my attention to the philosophic questions that hit on the really shrieking, crucial issues: Who wrote the cosmic script? What does the DNA code expect of me? Is the big genetic-code show live or on tape? Who is the sponsor? Are we completely trapped inside our nervous systems, or can we make *real* contact with anyone else out there? I intend to spend the rest of my life, with psychedelic help, searching for the answers to these questions—and encouraging others to do the same.

Playboy Interview Interludes

I'm not sure I've ever really been single since my divorce. The terms of my divorce were extremely just, almost detrimental to the woman. When a guy's been balling a chick, his responsibility toward her ought to be up to him. . . . Marriage is an obligation in which you must consider the other person. Whatever happens in cohabitation, you're still free.

Lee Marvin, January 1969

Once, sitting next to Jack Kennedy at a horse show, I remarked how easy it would be for someone to shoot him. "Only," I said, "they'd probably miss and hit me." "No great loss," he observed cheerfully.

Gore Vidal, June 1969

If I get hurt playing football tomorrow and I can't come back, it's good to feel that I won't have to change the way I live. The bread and all the fame hasn't loused me up, and I don't think it ever will.

Joe Namath, December 1969

I have discovered a new sensual treat, which, appropriately, the readers of PLAYBOY should be the first to know about. It is to have the President of the U.S. take notes while you are speaking to him, even though you run the risk that he is scribbling, "Get this bore out of here."

William F. Buckley, May 1970

MEL BROOKS

October 1966 and February 1975
Interviewers: Larry Siegel (1966) and Brad Darrach (1975)

The first Mel Brooks interview, conducted by satirist Larry Siegel, catches the comedy writer on his way up: He had done a cult album, *The 2000-Year-Old Man*, and had written a hit TV series, "Get Smart," but he was as yet largely unknown to the public. The interview was pure put-on, and is reprinted here in a shortened version without the introduction.

The second interview—conducted by author Brad Darrach after Brooks had completed *Blazing Saddles* and *Young Frankenstein*—is no less a put-on, but contains a few glints of what makes Brooks shtick. The introduction to this interview is reprinted here, following the 1966 interview. No one will claim there is a speck of socially redeeming value to either of the two interviews, but, together, they just may be among the funniest articles ever published in PLAYBOY.

First Interview, 1966

PLAYBOY: Mel, we'd like to ask you—

BROOKS: Who's *we*? I see one person in the room. Not counting me.

PLAYBOY: By "we" we mean PLAYBOY.

BROOKS: In other words, you're asking questions for the entire sexually liberated PLAYBOY organization?

PLAYBOY: Yes.

BROOKS: By the way, how much are you paying me for this?

PLAYBOY: We don't pay our interview subjects.

BROOKS: How about *you,* Mr. We? Do *you* get paid for this thing?

PLAYBOY: Well, yes. But that's because we're employed by PLAYBOY. With the help of the editors, we prepare the questions and conduct the interview.

BROOKS: I'll tell you what. I'll ask *you* questions. Let them pay *me.*

PLAYBOY: Mel, can we begin now?

BROOKS: Fine, do you gavotte?

PLAYBOY: Let's sit this one out. You've recently completed a series of radio commercials as Ballantine Beer's "2500-year-old Brewmaster." It's a character quite similar to your famous 2000-year-old man, in that once again you jog satirically through the pages of history. But the big difference is: Now you're peddling beer. Why did you sell out to Madison Avenue, like they say?

BROOKS: I decided that I had given enough of myself to mankind. After all, my definitive 12-volume series on enlightened penology was completed; my staff and I had UNESCO running in apple-pie order; and of course I had just come up with the vaccine to wipe out cystic fibrosis. So I felt I could afford to allow myself a few monetary indulgences.

PLAYBOY: Why Madison Avenue?

BROOKS: Frankly, they made me the best offer.

PLAYBOY: What were some of the other offers you received?

BROOKS: Well, Fifth Avenue offered me $4000 a week, Lexington Avenue offered me $3500, and the Bowery's offer was insulting.

PLAYBOY: The Brewmaster has a thick German accent. The 2000-year-old man has a Jewish accent. Why do you use dialects when you perform?

BROOKS: It's easier to hide behind accents. Once you're playing a character you have more mobility, more freedom. I suppose it's also cowardice on my part. I can say anything I want, and then if people question me, I say, "Don't blame me. Blame the old Jew. He's crazy."

PLAYBOY: Aren't you a lot like your old boss, Sid Caesar, in this respect?

BROOKS: Yes. When I began working with Sid on *Your Show of Shows,* I noticed that he always had trouble expressing himself as Sid Caesar. So I'd always try to provide him with an accent or a character to hide behind. Once in character, Sid is the funniest man in the world.

PLAYBOY: What made you decide to give the 2000-year-old man a Jewish accent?

BROOKS: It's not a Jewish accent. It's an *American*-Jewish accent. And in 50 years it will disappear. I think it'll be a great loss.

PLAYBOY: You're obviously proud of being Jewish.

BROOKS: Proud and scared.

PLAYBOY: How do you feel about the current Jewish kick in American humor?

BROOKS: Unless Jews do Jews accurately, I consider the whole thing to be in questionable taste.

PLAYBOY: Then the character of the 2000-year-old man is never in questionable taste?

BROOKS: I don't think so. He may be pompous at times; he may be a nut, but he's always honest and compelling. And the accent is always accurate.

PLAYBOY: Why are so many top comedians and comedy writers Jewish?

BROOKS: When the tall, blond Teutons have been nipping at your heels for thousands of years, you find it enervating to keep wailing. So you make jokes. If your enemy is laughing, how can he bludgeon you to death?

PLAYBOY: Mel, you're co-creator of *Get Smart*. Since it violates every standard of tested TV comedy—a bumbling antihero, far-out satire, and so on—why is it so successful?

BROOKS: I'd say because of a bumbling antihero, far-out satire, and so on.

PLAYBOY: What do you mean by "and so on"?

BROOKS: What do *you* mean by "and so on"?

PLAYBOY: Well, we meant that the public could identify with, and yet feel superior to, a nitwit like Maxwell Smart.

BROOKS: That's what *I* meant.

PLAYBOY: How does a clod like Smart differ from the bird-brained protagonists in situation comedies such as *Ozzie and Harriet*?

BROOKS: Guys like Ozzie Nelson are lovable boobs. There's nothing lovable about Don Adams' Max Smart. He's a dangerously earnest nitwit who deals in monumental goofs. He doesn't trip over skates; he loses whole *countries* to the Communists.

PLAYBOY: And standard situation comedies, on the other hand, deal with dull people in petty situations?

BROOKS: Right. And in their supposedly true-to-life little episodes, they avoid anything approaching reality. For years I've always wanted to see an honest family TV series—maybe something called *Half of Father Knows Best*. The other half of him was paralyzed by a stroke in 1942 when he suspected we might lose the War.

PLAYBOY: Did you have any trouble selling the series to NBC?

BROOKS: Plenty. ABC put up the original money to develop the thing, but when we took them our first script, they thought it was too wild. They wanted something more "warm and lovable."

PLAYBOY: What did they mean by "warm and lovable"?

BROOKS: Who knows? Maybe a nice mother in a print dress, with undulant fever.

PLAYBOY: Did you make changes for them?

BROOKS: Yes, we figured we'd try to make them happy. So we threw in a dog. But they didn't like it.

PLAYBOY: Why not?

BROOKS: The dog was asthmatic.

PLAYBOY: Why did they object to that?

BROOKS: I suppose they felt we might offend some important dogs.

PLAYBOY: Do you think *Get Smart* will spawn wittier comedy series in the future?

BROOKS: There's certainly an audience for them. Somewhere between those who sop up the gelatinous, brain-scrambling nonsense of *Petticoat Junction* and the intellectuals who catch *Basic Hungarian* at six A.M. is a vast segment of the population that wants intelligent entertainment. Without morals.

PLAYBOY: You mean the public wants amoral TV?

BROOKS: No, I mean they want TV without little sermons. For years *The Danny Thomas Show* was doing the Ten Commandments. Every episode had a little message to deliver: Don't lie, don't kill your neighbor, don't covet your neighbor's wife, don't uncovet your neighbor's wife. . . .

PLAYBOY: Living in New York, with a hit TV show being filmed on the Coast, you must be doing a lot of traveling these days.

BROOKS: I spend a lot of time in L.A. on business, but I also travel for pleasure. I just got back from Europe.

PLAYBOY: How did you like it?

BROOKS: I love it. Europe is very near and dear to my heart. Would you like to see a picture of it?

PLAYBOY: You carry a picture of Europe?

BROOKS: Sure, right here in my wallet. Here it is.

PLAYBOY: It's very nice.

BROOKS: Of course, Europe was a lot younger then. It's really not a very good picture. Europe looks much better in person.

PLAYBOY: It's a fine-looking continent.

BROOKS: It gives me a good deal of pleasure, but it's always fighting, fighting. I tell you, I'll be so happy when it finally settles down and gets married.

PLAYBOY: Mel, there's a rumor going around that you invented the popular expression "pussycat" on one of your records.

BROOKS: I didn't invent it. It's an old Jewish-American expression. When anyone was dear and sweet, they would call him a pussycat. But I think I was the first one to use it in show business. In our first 2000-year-old-man record, Carl asked me if I knew Shakespeare. I said, "What a pussycat he was! What a cute beard!"

PLAYBOY: Have you thought up a new expression to replace "pussycat"?

BROOKS: Yes, I have. "Water rat." "Look at him. What a nice water rat!" You know something? It doesn't work as well as "pussycat."

PLAYBOY: You're right. Can you think of any other funny expressions?

BROOKS: "Confusion to the French."

PLAYBOY: What the hell is that?

BROOKS: It was a toast that Horatio Hornblower used aboard his flagship. It's always been one of my favorites. Good old Horatio! What a water rat.

PLAYBOY: Would you ever like to be a director of films?

BROOKS: I'd love to be one. I think I'd be a great comedy director. As a matter of fact, I have just finished a screenplay called *Marriage Is a Dirty, Rotten Fraud.* I'd like very much to direct it.

PLAYBOY: Is it based on your own personal experience?

BROOKS: No, it's based on a very important conversation I overheard once while waiting for a bus at the Dixie Hotel terminal.

PLAYBOY: What are the chances of a studio assigning you to direct it?

BROOKS: Very, very good. Well, let me amend that slightly: None.

PLAYBOY: What else are you working on?

BROOKS: *Springtime for Hitler.*

PLAYBOY: You're putting us on.

BROOKS: No, it's the God's honest truth. It's going to be a play within a play, or a play within a film—I haven't decided yet. It's a romp with Adolf and Eva at Berchtesgaden. There was a whole nice side of Hitler. He was a good dancer—no one knows that. He loved a parakeet named Bob—no one knows that either. It's all brought out in the play.

PLAYBOY: What was the first funny thing you ever said?

BROOKS: "Lieutenant Faversham's attentions to my wife were of such a nature I was forced to deal him a lesson in manners."

PLAYBOY: That's pretty funny. Do you recall to whom you said that?

BROOKS: Very vividly. It was an elderly Jewish woman carrying an oilcloth shopping bag on the Brighton Beach Express.

PLAYBOY: What was her reaction to the remark?

BROOKS: She immediately got up and gave me her seat.

PLAYBOY: Who makes *you* laugh?

BROOKS: It's very hard to get me to laugh at a comic. What I want is something really funny. But how can I verbalize what I think is really funny? Now, Harry Ritz of the Ritz Brothers—there's someone who makes me laugh. To me he is the father of modern American visual comedy. He sired Caesar, Berle, Lewis, all of them. Jonathan Winters is another guy who can break me up.

PLAYBOY: But he's a gentile.

BROOKS: I love gentiles. In fact, one of my favorite activities is Protestant spotting.

PLAYBOY: How do you do that?

BROOKS: It's not difficult. First you look for a family, the members of which address each other as "Mother" and "Dad." What I mean is, the father calls the mother "Mother" and the mother calls the father "Dad." Not just the kids.

PLAYBOY: Are they easy to spot?

BROOKS: Oh, yes, they're always in a white Ford station wagon filled with hundreds of jars of mayonnaise and tons of white bread. Say, who's that guy that just walked into the room with a camera?

PLAYBOY: That's one of our photographers. He's going to take a few shots of you to run with the interview.

BROOKS: Should I undress?

PLAYBOY: It's not for the gatefold, Mel. You'll be shot fully dressed. But while we're on the subject, do you think there's a sexual revolution going on in this country?

BROOKS: Yes, I do think there's a sexual revolution going on, and I think that with our current foreign policy, we'll probably be sending troops in there any minute to break it up.

PLAYBOY: In where?

BROOKS: How do I know? We always send in troops when there's a revolution.

PLAYBOY: We hate to get personal, but, speaking of sex, why haven't you asked us to introduce you to a Playmate or a Bunny?

BROOKS: Three reasons: It would be impolite; it would be beneath my dignity; and besides, I'm a fag. Anyway, the trouble with Playmates and Bunnies is that they're too openly sexy and clean-cut. I've been taught ever since I was a kid that sex is filthy and forbidden, and that's the way I think it *should* be. The filthier and more forbidden it is, the more exciting it is.

PLAYBOY: By those criteria, can you give us an example of someone you consider sexy?

BROOKS: To me *anyone* is sexy if they're not obvious about it. A 71-year-old man in a fur collar and spats could be enormously sexy under the right circumstances.

PLAYBOY: What would be the right circumstances?

BROOKS: Well, if you're in the moonlight, if you're by a lazy lagoon—and if you're a 71-year-old *woman* in a fur collar and spats.

PLAYBOY: Is it true that you're always on?

BROOKS: No, I'm only on when the people I'm with are worth it. If they're superperceptive. Or if they're just good.

PLAYBOY: Which would you rather do—perform or write?

BROOKS: Performing is easier. Writing is more durable.

PLAYBOY: We usually wind up our interviews with a question like this one: What do you think will prove to be the most important legacy of our age?

BROOKS: Carl Reiner once asked me a similar question on one of our records, and in jocular fashion I said, Saran Wrap. But I've become a lot more mature since then. I suppose I've also grown with the times.

PLAYBOY: So *now* what do you think will prove to be the most important legacy of our age?

BROOKS: Glad Bags.

PLAYBOY: Well, Mel, thanks very much for taking the time to talk to us.

BROOKS: I would have been much happier gavotting.

Second Interview, 1975

"The rich," according to a Spanish proverb, "laugh carefully." They have a lot to lose. The poor, on the other hand, need to laugh in order to forget how little they have to laugh about—which may be why the Depression was the last golden age of comedy in American movies. Will the current economic recession bring on another comedy boom? Movie producers think so; the 1975 production docket is packed with laugh-it-up scripts. Film producers also acknowledge that the strongest creative impulse behind the boom is the maniacal imagination and energy of one of the very few moviemakers since Charlie Chaplin who is unarguably a comic genius—Mel Brooks.

Brooks is an American Rabelais. Short and blocky, he has a nose once described as "a small mudslide," a grin that loops almost from ear to ear like a tenement laundry line and the flat-out energy of a buffalo stampede. His imagination is violent and boundless; and in the opinion of other comedy writers, no brain on the planet contains such a churning profusion of wildly funny ideas.

Brad Darrach, a free-lance journalist, was assigned by PLAYBOY *to interview Brooks. Brooks was flattered by our request. As the subject of a previous "Playboy Interview" (October 1966), he was about to become the first person ever interviewed twice by the magazine. Nevertheless, though always friendly and charming, Brooks flatly refused at first to discuss any aspect of his private life and, for more than a month after Darrach arrived in Hollywood, said he was too busy editing "Young Frankenstein" to take any time out for formal interviews. He allowed Darrach to watch the editing process, however, and gradually admitted him to his working family. Here is Darrach's report:*

"After five weeks, the interviews began. They were held at Brooks's office, a large smog-soiled rectangle in 20th Century-Fox's main office building. We had 12 sessions in all, over a period of three weeks, beginning every day at about 11:45 and lasting until about one. For the first session, Brooks's secretary, Sherry Falk, and I assembled an audience of writers, directors, producers and their secretaries. After that, there was no need to stimulate attendance. Swiveling and grinning behind his big curved paper-cluttered desk, leaping up and shouting and mugging and scrambling around the room as he spouted sense and nonsense, Brooks had his listeners literally falling out of their chairs almost from the first word of the interview. Hearing the ruckus, people came running from all over the building. During every session, 15 or 20 people would wander in and out, while a half-dozen stood grinning at the door. To preserve the frenetic flavor of the scene, I have left in the interview a few of these interruptions. In the

last two recording sessions, which were conducted in private, Brooks finally revealed details of his personal life and made the powerful statements about himself and his philosophy that conclude the interview. 'I hope you got enough,' he said when the last session was over. 'My tongue just died. PLAYBOY's gonna have to pay for the funeral and put up a statue of Mel Brooks's tongue in Central Park.' "

BROOKS (*sucking up a fistful of chocolate-covered Raisinets and chomping them behind a Brooklyn-street-kid grin*): All right, ask away, Jew boy, or whatever you pretend you are.

PLAYBOY: As one Episcopalian to another, how about giving our readers some idea of what you really look like? There will be three pictures of you on the first page of this interview, but they won't do you justice.

BROOKS: I don't want to be vain, but I might as well be honest. I'm crowding six-one. Got a mass of straight blond hair coming to a widow's peak close to the eyes. Sensational steel-blue eyes, bluer than Newman's. Muscular but whippy, like Redford. The only trouble is I have no ass.

PLAYBOY: What happened to it?

BROOKS: It fell off during the war. Now I have a United Fruit box in the back and I shit pears.

PLAYBOY: Tell us about your ears.

BROOKS: My ears are very much like Leonard Nimoy's—you know, Mr. Spock on *Star Trek*, the guy whose ears come to a point. It happened like this: One night Leonard and I went out and before dinner we had 35 margaritas. We woke up in a kennel. There were four great Danes, two on each side of us. Their ears had already been clipped. And so had Leonard's. I reached up, felt my ears and, alas, mine had, too.

PLAYBOY: What about your nose?

BROOKS: What about *yours*? Mine is aquiline, lacking only a little bulb at the end.

PLAYBOY: You wish you had a bulb?

BROOKS: I do; I do—one that said 60 watts on it and lit up. It would attract moths. And it would help me read at night under the blankets at summer camp. Care for a Raisinet? We mentioned Raisinets in *Blazing Saddles* and now the company sends me a gross of them every month. A *gross* of Raisinets! Take 50 boxes. My friends are avoiding me. I'm the leading cause of diabetes in California. Seriously, they make great earplugs. Or you could start a new school of Raisinet sculpture. No? Did you know that PLAYBOY in Yiddish is *Spielboychick*? Is it true that I am the only person who has ever been interviewed twice (*ear-piercing whistle*) by PLAYBOY?

PLAYBOY: Yes, and we're beginning to think we've made a terrible mistake. To what, by the way, do you attribute this distinction?

BROOKS: To my height. And the lack of it.

PLAYBOY: Since you've brought it up, why are you so short?

BROOKS: You mean all of me or parts of me? OK, you want me to admit I'm a four-foot, six-inch freckle-faced person of Jewish extraction? I admit it. All but the extraction. But being short never bothered me for three seconds. The rest of the time I wanted to commit suicide.

PLAYBOY: Now we know what you look like. What do you do for a living?

BROOKS: I make people laugh for a living. I believe I can say objectively that what I do I do as well as anybody. Just say I'm one of the best broken-field runners that ever lived. I started in '38 and I'm hot in '75. For 35 years I was a cult hero, an underground funny. First I was a comic's comic, then I was a comedy writer's comedy writer. When I'd go to where they were working, famous comedians would turn white. "My God, he's here! The Master!" But I was never a big name to the public. And then suddenly I surfaced. *Blazing Saddles* made me famous. Madman Brooks. More laughs per minute than any other movie ever made—until *Young Frankenstein,* that is.

PLAYBOY: What's so special about your comedy?

BROOKS (*snatching up the receiver as the phone rings*): This is Mel Brooks. We want 73 party hats, 400 balloons, a cake for 125 and any of the girls that are available in those costumes you sent up before. Thank you! (*Slams the receiver down*) You were saying?

PLAYBOY: What's so special about—

BROOKS: My comedy is midnight blue. Not black comedy—I *like* people too much. Midnight blue, and you can make it into a peacoat if you're on watch on the bow of a ship plowing through the North Atlantic. The buttons are very black and very shiny and very large.

PLAYBOY: Speaking of blue, you've been accused of vulgarity.

BROOKS: Bullshit!

PLAYBOY: And of being undisciplined in the comedy you write and direct.

BROOKS: Anarchic, the crickets call it. My mother says, "An archic?" She think I'm an architect. My comedy is big-city, Jewish, whatever I am. Energetic. Nervous. Crazy. Anyway, what do PLAYBOY readers care about comedy? They're not reading this interview. They're all sitting on the toilet with the centerfold open, doing God knows what.

PLAYBOY: How did you come by your sense of humor?

BROOKS: Found it at South Third and Hooper. It was in a tiny package wrapped in electrical tape and labeled GOOD HUMOR. When I opened it up, out jumped a big Jewish genie. "I'll give you three wishes," he said. "Uh, make it two."

PLAYBOY: Where was South Third and Hooper?

BROOKS: Brooklyn. I was born in Brooklyn on June 28, 1926, the 12th anniversary of the blowing up of Archduke Ferdinand of Austria. We lived at 515 Powell Street, in a tenement. I was born on the kitchen table. We were so poor my mother couldn't afford to have me; the lady next door gave birth to me. My real name was Melvin Kaminsky. I changed it to Brooks because Kaminsky wouldn't fit on a drum. My mother's maiden name was Kate Brookman. She was born in Kiev. My father was born in Danzig. Maximilian Kaminsky. He was a process server and he died when I was two and a half—tuberculosis of the kidney. They didn't know how to knock it out, no antibiotics then. To this day, my mother feels guilty about us being orphans at such early ages.

PLAYBOY: What's your mother like?

BROOKS: Mother is very short—four-eleven. She could walk under tables and never hit her head. She was a true heroine. She was left with four boys and no income, so she got a job in the Garment District. Worked the normal ten-hour day and then brought work home. Turned out bathing-suit sashes until daylight, grabbed a few hours of sleep, got us up and off to school and then went to work again.

PLAYBOY: Did your mother have time to look after you?

BROOKS: I was adored. I was always in the air, hurled up and kissed and thrown in the air again. Until I was six, my feet didn't touch the ground. "Look at those eyes! That nose! Those lips! That tooth! Get that child away from me, quick! I'll eat him!" Giving that up was very difficult later on in life.

My mother was the best cook in the world. "I make a matzoh ball," she used to say, "that will sweep you off your feet!" And she did her piecework in the kitchen, too. All night she would sit up sewing, pressing rhinestones, going blind. Wonderful woman! She's 78 now and still running to catch planes. I took her to Las Vegas not long ago. She loved the lobbies, to hell with the big stars and the gambling. She liked the lobbies. Jews like lobbies.

PLAYBOY: Did you get your sense of humor from your mother?

BROOKS: More from my grandmother. She could hardly speak English, but she made up bilingual jokes. "Melbn? *Es var a yenge mann gegange* for a physical, OK?" A young man went for his Army physical. *"Geht zurick und sagt,* 'Momma, *ich bin Vun-A!'* " Tells his mother he's One-A. "Momma *hat gejumped* in the air *mit* joy. *'Vunderbar!* You vouldn't go!' " "But, Momma! One-A means perfect! I go!" *"Bubele!* Vat you talking? How dey can teck you *mit* Vun-A?" Well, the joke was, I discovered finally, that A sounds like *ei* in Yiddish. *Ei* means egg, and egg means testicle. How 'bout *that* for Grandma?

PLAYBOY: Not bad. Do you have any other—

BROOKS: Freeze! Don't move! Time for a well-known Quotation from Chairman Mel's *2013-Year-Old Man* record. *Ta-daaaa!* "IF PRESIDENTS

DON'T DO IT TO THEIR WIVES—THEY'LL DO IT TO THE COUNTRY!" You were saying?

PLAYBOY: Any other memorable relatives?

BROOKS: Yes, Uncle Joe. Uncle Joe was a philosopher, very deep, very serious. "Never eat chocolate after chick'n," he'd tell us, wagging his finger. "Don't buy a cardboard belt," he'd say. Or he'd warn us—we're five years old—"Don't invest. Put da money inna bank. Even the land could sink." He'd come up and tap you on the arm while you were playing stickball. "Marry a fat goil," he'd whisper. "They strong. Woik f'ya. Don't marry a face. Put ya under." He had great similes. "Clever as a chick'n" was one of them. "That guy's got da eyes of a bat. Never misses!" Later, we're in our teens, we're horsing around outside the candy store, he'd come up to us. "What you talk' 'bout, boys?" "New cars." "Hmmmm." He'd stroke his chin. "As far as I'm consoined," he'd say finally, "dey all good!"

PLAYBOY: Did you ever run away from home?

BROOKS: I don't think Jewish boys did that. Run away to *what?* But we hitchhiked a lot across the Williamsburg Bridge in search of jobs. We're 11 and we're going to get jobs in New York. So we'd walk around the Lower East Side and for four cents we'd buy a ton of sauerkraut and gorge ourselves and be very sick. Then we'd walk back; nobody would give you a ride at night. It was a 20-minute walk over the bridge. Somewhere over the middle, we'd get scared and begin running. Six hundred feet below is water—right—and Jews on both sides. If you fell in, who would rescue you? Jews in those days couldn't swim.

PLAYBOY: Why not?

BROOKS: Only place to swim was McCarren Park, which was in a gentile region of Brooklyn. We could only go there if there were six to twelve of us. Otherwise, we'd be attacked. Like, we'd be in the locker room and a gang of Irish or Polish or Italian kids would be there and they'd inspect you. They'd see you were circumcised, so they knew who was what. In those days, gentile kids were not circumcised. Then they'd follow you out and pick on you.

PLAYBOY: Did you carry weapons?

BROOKS: Never. Because then they'd panic and get a hundred people. No weapons in those days.

PLAYBOY: Did you ever commit a crime?

BROOKS: Yes. I stole salt off pretzels in Feingold's candy store.

PLAYBOY: You *were* a wild kid.

BROOKS: Not only that, there were Penny Picks—chocolate-covered candy, white inside. If you got one that was pink inside, you got a nickel's worth of candy free. We would scratch the bottom of the chocolate with our thumbnails until we found a pinkie. Poor Mr. Feingold. He could never figure out how we found so many pink ones. Which reminds me—Raisinet? Take two.

PLAYBOY: No, thanks. No juvenile offenders in your neighborhood?

BROOKS: Sure, me! There were these Japanese yo-yo experts who used to do exhibitions at the Woolworth. They were great and even the managers would take their eyes off the counters to watch them "walk the dog" and "skinny up a pole" and all that. "Ok," we'd say, "the coast is clear." Then we'd steal something. One time I was with Muscles Mandel and I was caught lifting a 20-cent cap pistol. The manager grabbed me and said, "Gotcha!" I ripped the gun around and said, "Stand back or I'll blow your head off!" He jumped back. Everybody jumped back, and with this toy gun I made my getaway—stealing the gun at the same time! Those idiots! They *knew* it was a cap gun and still they backed up! I used that gag later in *Blazing Saddles*. What the —— (*Brooks looks up, startled. An actor wearing a "Planet of the Apes" mask is strolling down the corridor outside Brooks's office, as though there were nothing in the least unusual about his appearance. He glances casually into Brooks's office. Just as casually, Brooks gives him a nod.*)

Hiya, kid. Workin'? (*The actor does a startled take, then moves on.*)

PLAYBOY: What were you good at in school?

BROOKS: Emoting. When I had to read a composition, I would turn into a wild-eyed maniac, fling out my arms and announce in a ringing soprano: "MY DAY AT CAMP!"

PLAYBOY: What were your favorite books?

BROOKS: Dirty comics. Eight pagers. Short attention span. No. Actually, I liked *Robinson Crusoe, Black Beauty,* the usual things. But I wasn't a big reader. Couldn't sit still long enough.

PLAYBOY: How about Hebrew school?

BROOKS: Shul, we called it. I went for a little while. About 45 minutes. We were the children of immigrants. They told us religious life was important, so we bought what they told us. We faked it, nodded like we were praying. Learned enough Hebrew to get through a *bar mitzvah*. Hebrew is a very hard language for Jews. And we suffered the incredible breath of those old rabbis. They'd turn to you and they'd say, "Melbn, make me a *brüche*. A *brüüüüüüüche*!" You never knew what they said. Three words and you were on the floor because their breath would wither your face. There was no surviving rabbi breath. God knows what they ate—garlic and young Jewish boys. Terrible!

PLAYBOY: Did you go to the movies much?

BROOKS: Are you kidding? The dumps would open at ten o'clock Saturday morning and I'd be there. We'd get in for 11 cents, loaded down with Baby Ruths and O'Henrys and Mars bars. No Raisinets in those days. Sherreee! Bring Raisinets! PLAYBOY is looking a little peaked! No? Goy bastard! No offense. So, anyway, in the movies, even before the lights went out, paper clips would start to slingshot all over the place. You'd get a shot in the back of your head—it would lodge in your brain—and you'd hear them hitting the screen like rain through the whole movie. Then about 11 o'clock at night, there'd be a light in my eye. An usher would be slapping me awake and a Jewish woman screaming behind him, "Melvin! You have to eat!"

PLAYBOY: What was your favorite movie?

BROOKS: Horror movies. *Frankenstein* gave me nightmares. I'd be sleeping on the fire escape in the summer and the monster would climb up to get me. And just when he'd put his hand on my face and I couldn't breathe, I'd see the gleam of that metal rod in his neck and I'd wake up screaming "Frankensteiiiiiiiin!" I'd yell. Scare everybody in the house. I'm still yelling it. Don't tell anybody, but I watch *Young Frankenstein* from behind my fingers. (*Phone rings*) I've got it, Sherry. Hello? Cleavon Little! The talented black star of *Blazing Saddles*! I love your face! Your obedient Jew here. How are you? What can I do for you? . . . You're looking for a part that will make you a millionaire? I've got it! Play Blanche du Bois. Right, in *A Streetcar Named Desire*. You'd be the first black guy ever to play Blanche. Tennessee would love it. But do it right. Go to Denmark, have the operation. You could open in Mobile, Alabama, to sensational reviews. Police dogs. Sirens. With a little luck, you could become the first transsexual martyr! . . . Yes, Cleavon, yes! Don't be strange! I love your feet! (*Hangs up*) Speak, PLAYBOY.

PLAYBOY: When did you find out that you could be funny?

BROOKS: I was always funny. But the first time I remember was at Sussex Camp for Underprivileged Children. I was seven years old and whatever the counselors said, I would turn it around. "Put your plates in the garbage and stack the scraps, boys!" "Stay at the shallow end of the pool until you learn to drown!" "Who said that? Kaminsky! Grab him! Hold him!" Slap! But the other kids liked it and I was a success. I needed a success. I was short. I was scrawny. I was the last one they picked to be on the team. "Oh, all right, we'll take him. Put him in the outfield." Now, I wasn't a bad athlete, but the other kids were *champs*. In poor Jewish neighborhoods, every kid could hit a mile. They could be on their back and throw a guy out at first. They were great and I was just good. But I was brighter than most kids my age, so I hung around with guys two years older. Why should they let this puny kid hang out with them? I gave them a reason. I became their jester. Also, they were afraid of my tongue. I had it sharpened and I'd stick it in their eye. I read a little more than they did, so I could say, "Touch me not, leper!" "Hey! Mel called me a leopard!" "Schmuck! Leper!" Words were my equalizer.

PLAYBOY: Where did you hang around? In the schoolyard?

BROOKS: Are you kidding? We couldn't wait to get *away* from school. We hung out in the street—and on the corner. I mean, we didn't hang out there just because the street came to a corner. We weren't driven sexually crazy by a building coming to a point. We met there because there was a drugstore or a candy store on the corner. We'd all stand out on the sidewalk in warm weather and duel verbally, tell jokes, laugh it up. Girl watching was part of it, and so was having an egg cream. But the main thing was corner shtick, we called it, and in our gang, I was the undisputed champ at corner shtick.

PLAYBOY: Would you give us a sample?

BROOKS: The corner was tough. You had to score on the corner—no bullshit routines, no slick laminated crap. It had to be, "Lemme tell ya what happened today. . . ." And you really had to be good on your feet. "Fat Hymie was hanging from the fire escape. His mother came by. 'Hymie!' she screamed. He fell two stories and broke his head." Real stories of tragedy we screamed at. The story had to be real and it had to be funny. Somebody getting hurt was wonderful. "You hear what happened with Miltie and the Buick?" "What? What?" "He was doing an eagle turn on his skates. . . ." "Yeah? Yeah?" "*Oogah! Oogah!* Miltie thought it was applause, didn't bother to look. *Bam!* Buick got him right in the ass. Did a somersault. *Crunncchh!* Out like a light, took him away, Saint Catherine's Hospital. The nuns are with him now." The *nuns* are with this little Jewish kid, right? And then you visit Miltie, propped up on pillows, very cool. "Who are these penguins?" he says. "And why do they want me to pee all the time?"

PLAYBOY: We've heard that medicine is kind of a hobby with you. How did you get interested in it?

BROOKS: I always thought it was great to be able to make people feel better. It was a little like being God. So I started to take charge when anybody got hurt playing ball. "Get the Mercurochrome. Put a Band-Aid on. Quick! Flappy fainted. Bring an egg cream!"

PLAYBOY: An egg cream has healing properties?

BROOKS: An egg cream can do anything. An egg cream to a Brooklyn Jew is like water to an Arab. A Jew will kill for an egg cream. It's the Jewish malmsey.

PLAYBOY: But there's no egg in an egg cream.

BROOKS: That's the best part. That's the wonder and the mystery of it. Talmudic sages for generations have pondered this profound question. Why is there no egg in an egg cream? Well, 1000 years ago there may have been egg in egg creams. Joe Heller is very bright and he thought so. But Georgie Mandel and Speed Vogel are bright, too, and they applauded Julie Green's reasoning. He said, "Egg creams are called egg creams because the top of a well-made egg cream looks like whipped egg white." I can't offer you an egg cream right now, but how about a Raisinet? If you scrape the chocolate off 5000 of them, you could have an egg cream.

PLAYBOY: What does an egg cream do for you?

BROOKS: Physically, it contributes mildly to your high blood sugar.

Psychologically, it is the opposite of circumcision. It *pleasurably* reaffirms your Jewishness. But what is all this with egg creams? Isn't this a *Playboy Interview*? When are you going to ask me about sex?

PLAYBOY: Mr. Brooks, what is your attitude toward sex?

BROOKS: How *dare* you ask me such a filthy question? What do you take me for—an animal? Kindly change the subject!

PLAYBOY: Were there any Jewish princesses in Brooklyn in those days?

BROOKS: Sheila Rabinowitz. Jewish princesses are a second-generation thing. First-generation girls were scrubbing floors and helping out. Second-generation parents could afford to support royalty. But Sheila's father was a coriander importer; he made it big in coriander; so Shelia was a *first-generation* Jewish princess. She lived two blocks away from school and she took a cab. She had four chain bracelets with different names on them, two on her wrists and two on her ankles. And all the names were gentile, just to put you in your place: Bob, Dick, Peter and Steve. They happened to be Jewish guys, but the names were gentile. Sheila came to class in a Pucci, and Pucci wasn't even in business yet. Sixteen years old and she wore a turban with a rhinestone in the middle of it. And the accent! "Why, helloooo, theahhh. How aahh you?" What the hell *is* coriander, anyway?

PLAYBOY: What became of Sheila?

BROOKS: Don't know. She was dreaming of the great world beyond the ghetto. I was happy where I was. When I was a kid, I was very confused by what the Jew was in the outer world. I knew what he was in Williamsburg. He was a runner and a rat and scared as hell. But Jews in the outside world I heard different, conflicting things about. First of all, I heard that they were the Communists, overthrowing all the governments in the world. When I was in high school, I thought a Jew's job in life was to throw over every government. The other thing I heard was that the Jews were capitalists and had all the gold and the banks and that the Jews' job was to kill all the socialists and the radicals. So I never really figured out what the Jewish mission was. Should I kill the capitalists and take their money? No, I'd be killing Jews. Should I stamp out the radicals so that we could keep our money? No, I'd be killing Jews. Very confusing. BUT (*leaps to his feet*) ENOUGH OF JEWS! I WILL SPEAK NO MORE OF JEWS! IN FACT, I WILL SPEAK NO MORE OF ANYTHING! (*Ripping off several strips of Scotch tape, he seals his lips tight and then, in a frenzy, rolling his eyes and squealing wordlessly, slaps sticky ribbons of tape over his ears, over his nostrils, over his hair and finally, eyelids stuck shut, goes staggering around the room, dragging one leg, gurgling and mumbling*) Look! Look wha' th' G'rm'ns did t' me! (*He tears off the tape*) They stole into my foxhole at night and covered my face with Scotch tape.

PLAYBOY: In your movies, you make fun of Germans. Don't you like them?

BROOKS: Me? Not like Germans? Why should I not like Germans? Just because they're arrogant and have fat necks and do anything they're told so long as it's cruel, and killed millions of Jews in concentration camps and made soap out of their bodies and lamp shades out of their skins? Is that any reason to hate their fucking guts?

PLAYBOY: Certainly not. Have you ever been in Germany?

BROOKS: Only to kill Germans. I was in the Army, World War Two. Seventeen, I enlisted. Fort Sill, Oklahoma. Basic training, right? Make a soldier out of the Jew boy. Left, right. I tried to explain to the sergeant, walking is not good for Jews. He felt otherwise. Then one day they put us all in trucks, drove us to the railroad station, put us in a locked train with the windows blacked out. We get off the train, we get on a boat. We get off the boat, we get into trucks. We get out of the trucks, we start walking. Suddenly, all around us, *Waauhwaauhwaauh!* Sirens! Tiger tanks! We're surrounded by Germans. It's the Battle of the Bulge! Hands up! "Wait!" I say. "We just left Oklahoma! We're Americans! We're supposed to win!" *Very* scary, but we escaped.

I spent a lot of time in the artillery. Too noisy. Could *not* take the noise. All through the war, two cigarette butts stuck in my ears. Couldn't read, couldn't think, couldn't even make a phone call. *Bagharrroooooommmmm! Brrllaggghhaarrooooooooooommmmm!* And they *they* started shooting. "Incoming mail!" Bullshit. Only Burt Lancaster says that. We said, "Oh, God! Oh, Christ!" Who knows, he might help. He was Jewish, too. "MOTHER!"

PLAYBOY: What did you do when you got out of the Army?

BROOKS: Wait! You're going too fast! At the end of the war, I did Army shows. First for the Germans, then at Fort Dix I did some camp shows. We all rolled up our pants and were the Andrews Sisters. One of us is still doing LaVerne in the East Village. Anyway, after I got out, I had three choices. I could go to college and hang out a shingle and make $10,000 a year. Another thing for a Jew to do would be to become a salesman. Hipsy, pipsy, lotsa pep, you know? White-on-white shirt, black-mohair suit, Swank cuff links, and, if you made it, a cat-eye ring on the pinkie. And on the other pinkie, your *bar mitzvah* ring. That was the big Brooklyn jewelry artillery. Shine in everybody's eyes at a party.

PLAYBOY: And the third thing?

BROOKS: Show business. But you got to understand something: Jews don't do comedy in winter. In summer, all right. You're a kid, you work in the mountains. That's how I got started years before—as a pool *tumeler.* A pool *tumeler* is a busboy with tinsel in his blood. For eight bucks a week and all you can eat, you do dishes, rent out rowboats, clean up the tennis courts and, if you beg hard enough, they let you try to be funny around the pool. I'm 14 years old and I walk out on the diving board wearing a black derby and a big black-alpaca overcoat. I'm carrying two suitcases filled with rocks. "Business is terrible!" I yell. "I can't go on!" And I jump in the pool. Big laugh—the Jews love it. But I don't laugh—because the suitcases weigh a ton and like a shot I go to the bottom. The overcoat soaks up 20 gallons of water instantly. I run out of air, but I can't lift the suitcases—and I can't leave them in the water. They're made of cardboard, in two minutes they'll dissolve, and I need them for tomorrow's act. God bless Oliver, that big goy! He was the lifeguard—Jews don't swim, remember?—and every day he'd do a little swan dive and haul me up.

PLAYBOY: What happened after pool *tumeling*?

BROOKS: I joined a Borscht Belt stock company. They let me play the district attorney in *Uncle Harry,* a straight melodrama. I'm 14 and a half, but I'm playing a 75-year-old man. My only line was, I pour some water from a carafe into a glass and say, "Here, Harry, have some water and calm down." But on opening night, I'm a little nervous, right? So I dropped the carafe on the table and it smashed and this flood rushed in all directions and made a waterfall off the table and all over the stage—such a mess! The audience gasped. I don't waste a minute; I walk right down to the footlights and take off my gray toupee and say, "I'm 14, what do you want?" Well, I got a 51-minute laugh, but the director of the play came running down the aisle and chased me through five Jewish resorts.

PLAYBOY: So how did you become a comedian?

BROOKS: I became a drummer, that's how. When we moved to Brighton Beach, I was 13 and a half and only a few houses away lived the one and only Buddy Rich. Buddy was just beginning with Artie Shaw then, and once in a while he would give me and my friend Billy half a lesson. When I went back to the mountains after the war, I played drums and sang. (*Eyes suddenly dreamy, begins to patter rhythmically on his desk with fingertips as he sings*) "It's not the pale moooon that excites me, that thrills and delights me. Oh, nooooo. . . ." Oh, I was so shitty. You've no idea.

Anyway, one time in the mountains I was playing drums behind a standard mountain comedian. Wonderful delivery, but all the usual jokes. "I just flew in from Chicago and, boy, are my arms tired." "Was that girl skinny—when I took her to a restaurant, the waiter said, 'Check your umbrella?' " Anyway, one night the comic got sick and they asked me to go on for him. Wow! But I didn't want to do those ancient jokes, so I decided to go out there and make up stuff. I figured, I'll just talk about things we all know and see if they turn out funny. Now, that day a chambermaid named Molly got shut in a closet and the whole hotel had heard her screaming, *"Los mir arois!"* Let me out! So when I went on stage, I stood there with my knees knocking and said, "Good evening, ladies and gentlemen . . . *LOS MIR AROIS!*" They tore the house down.

PLAYBOY: You continued to improvise your act, night after night?

BROOKS: Crazy, huh? But I did. Look, I had to take chances or it wasn't fun being funny. And you know, there was a lot of great material lying around in the Catskills, waiting to be noticed. Like Pincus Cantor. He was the manager where I was working, an old-fashioned Jew from the Polish *shtetl*. He couldn't handle the loudspeaker system at the hotel. Technology was beyond him. He was never sure if he had the speaker off or on and he usually had it on at the wrong time. It's a peaceful sunny day in the mountains, right? People are snoozing in deck chairs, people are rowing slowly across the lake. Suddenly, a tremendous shout booms out. For ten miles in the mountains, you could hear it: "SON OF BITCH BASTARD! FILT'Y ROTTEN! HOW DEY CAN LEAVE A SHEET SO FILT'Y! THAT SON OF BITCH! LAT HIM SLEEP IN IT! I VUDN'T. . . . IT'S VAAAAT? IT'S ON? OYYYYY!" Click.

So I did Pincus Cantor onstage—big hit. But *I* wasn't a big hit, not at first. The Jews in the tearoom, the Jewish ladies with blue hair, would call me over and say, "Melvin, we enjoyed certain parts of your show, but a trade would be better for you. Anything with your hands would be good. Aviation mechanics are very well paid." I'd walk by a bald guy, Sol Yasowitz. "Well, what did you think, Mr. Yasowitz?" I'd ask him. "Stunk." With a little smile. You could never get a kind word out of the Jews. And you know, maybe I *was* terrible. I had this theme song, wrote it myself (*Does a Donald O'Connor walk-on as he sings*) "Dadadadat dat daaaa! Here I am./I'm Melvin Brooks!/I've come to stop the show./Just a ham who's minus looks/But in your hearts I'll grow!/I'll tell you gags, I'll sing you songs./Just happy little snappy songs that roll along./Out of my mind,/Won't you be kind?/And please . . . love . . . *Melvin Brooooooooks!*" Terrible, right? After that, you surely need a Raisinet, right? Wrong. But think it over. Believe me, there are very few things that work as well when covered with chocolate. Anyway, I wanted to entertain so badly that I kept at it until I was good. I just browbeat my way into show business.

PLAYBOY: Is it true that everybody hated you on *Your Show of Shows*?

BROOKS: Everybody hated everybody. We robbed from the rich and kept everything. There was tremendous hostility in the air. A highly charged situation, but very good. We were all spoiled brats competing with each other for the king's favor, and we all wanted to come up with the funniest joke. I would be damned if anybody would write anything funnier than I would and everybody else felt the same way. There were seven comedy writers in that room, seven brilliant comedic brains. There was Mel Tolkin and Lucille Kallen. Then I came in. And spoiled everything. Then Joe Stein, who later wrote *Fiddler on the Roof,* and Larry Gelbart, who writes and produces *M*A*S*H*. Mike Stewart typed for us. Imagine! Our *typist* later wrote *Bye Bye Birdie* and *Hello, Dolly!* Later on, Mike was replaced at the typewriter by somebody named Woody Allen. Neil and Danny Simon were there, too, but Doc was so quiet we didn't know how good he was. Seven rats in a cage. The pitch sessions were lethal. In that room, you had to fight to stay alive.

PLAYBOY: From what we've heard, your competitive relationship with the other writers was nothing compared with your troubles with Max Liebman, the producer of the show.

BROOKS: Max hated me. I was a pretty snotty kid. But I hated him right back. When Sid first asked Max to hire me, Max wouldn't do it. So Sid gave me $50 a week himself and I'd wait in the hallway outside where Sid and Max and Mel and Lucille were writing the show. After a while, Sid would stick his head out and say, "We need three jokes." So I'd give him three jokes, but Max wouldn't let me in.

PLAYBOY: What didn't he like about you?

BROOKS: He didn't like my fast mouth. When I'd sass him back, he'd throw a lighted cigar at me—right at my face! I'd duck. One day, we were standing on the stage. I yelled, "Pepper Martin sliding into second! Watch your ass!" And I ran straight at him at full speed and then threw myself into a headfirst slide. Slid right between his legs, sent him flying in the air, scared the shit out of him. We laugh about it now, but it was rough then. He's a great showman, though; unconsciously, I think I still copy him.

PLAYBOY: Didn't you once scare the shit out of General Sarnoff?

BROOKS: True! One day they had a big conference in the RCA Building. All the big shots. General Sarnoff, the chairman of the board of RCA; Pat Weaver, the president of NBC; Max Liebman and Sid. When I tried to walk into the room with them, the door was slammed in my face. But I wanted to know what they were planning. Would there be a new show? Should I buy a new car? So I put on a white duster and a straw hat and I crashed through the door into the meeting and jumped up on the conference table. "Hurray!" I yelled. "Hurray! Lindy has landed at Le Bourget!" This was 1950. And I whipped off my straw hat and skimmed it across the room and it sailed right out the window and has never been seen since. Then I burst into the *Marseillaise* while General Sarnoff clutched his heart and Liebman picked his eyes up off the floor. Weaver was white as a sheet. Sid was the only one who laughed; staggered around, holding his gut. Liebman said, "And now, if you will kindly leave us, Mr. Brooks!" But I said, "Don't you understand? Lindy made it!"

PLAYBOY: So much for your offscreen material. What did you write for the show?

BROOKS: Masterpieces. Best work I ever did. We did eight comedy items a week. Live. No taping. Big classy items.

PLAYBOY: Would you run through a skit?

BROOKS: I remember the first one I wrote for Sid. *Jungle Boy.* "Ladies and gentlemen, now for the news. Our roving correspondent has just discovered a jungle boy, raised by lions in Africa, walking the streets of New York City." Sid played this in a lionskin, right? "Sir, how do you survive in New York City?" "Survive?" "What do you eat?" "Pigeon." "Don't the pigeons object?" "Only for a minute." "What are you afraid of more than any-

thing?" "Buick." "You're afraid of a Buick?" "Yes. Buick can win in death struggle. Must sneak up on parked Buick, punch grille hard. Buick die."
PLAYBOY: Who were the show's other stars?
BROOKS: Imogene Coca, brilliant lady. Carl Reiner, greatest straight man in the world. And Howie Morris! Howie had the best nose ever given to a Jew. No job. His own nose. A miracle! On the nose alone he could pass. Also a genius. Didn't know a word except in English but could speak any language—German gibberish, Italian gibberish, Russian gibberish. Amazing ear for accents. You'd think it was the real thing. But the best thing about Howie was that he was the only guy on the show who was shorter than me! Gave me this incredible feeling of power.

So one night, just after he came on the show, we were walking along MacDougal Alley in the Village, chatting about the show, getting acquainted. Lovely evening, just getting dark. So I decided to rob him. No, really. I slapped him around, knocked him against a yellow Studebaker. "This is a stick-up!" I said. I had my hand in my coat pocket with my finger pointed like a pistol. "Gimme everything you got or I'll kill ya!" My eyes were glittering. I looked crazy. He went white. I took his wallet, his watch, even his wedding ring. Cleaned him out. Then I ran away in the night. He staggered to a phone booth, called Sid. Sid said, "Oh, he's started *that* again, has he? Whatever you do, don't call him up or go to his house, he'll kill ya." Howie said, "But when do I get my stuff back?" Sid said, "Ya gotta wait till he comes to his senses."

Well, for three weeks, Howie waited. No wallet, no watch. Had to buy another wedding ring. I'd say hello to him every morning like nothing had happened. "Hi, Howie. How ya doing? D'ya like the sketch?" He'd say, "Very good, Mel. Like it a lot." Then he'd go to Sid and say, "When's he going to remember? My license was in my wallet. I haven't been able to drive for three weeks." And Sid would say, "Wait." And then one day I stared at Howie and hit my head. "Howie! Oh, my God! I robbed you! I'm so sorry! Here's your wallet! Here's your money! Here's your ring!"

Well, it was the longest practical joke in history, because three years later—by now we're the best of friends—we're rowing on the lake in Central Park at lunchtime. Lovely sunny day. Butterflies making love, the splash of the oars. Howie is rowing. We go under a secluded bridge. Perfect place for a holdup. I stand up, put my hand in my pocket, slap him in the face. Howie's smart. The prey always respects the predator's prerogatives. So without a word, he forks over his wallet, his watch, his ring, takes off his shoes, ties them around his neck, jumps overboard—the water's up to his chin—and wades ashore. Well, that time I gave him his stuff back in a few days. But I intend to rob him again someday, ladies and gentlemen, because robbing Howie is what I do best.
PLAYBOY: Over the years, what was your main contribution to the show?
BROOKS: Energy and insanity. I mean, I would take terrifying chances. I

was totally willing to be an idiot. I would jump off into space, not knowing where I would land. I would run across tightropes, no net. If I fell, blood all over. Pain. Humiliation. In those pitch sessions, I had an audience of experts and they showed no mercy. But I had to go beyond. It wasn't only competition to be funnier than they were. I had to get to the ultimate punch line, you know, the cosmic joke that all the other jokes came out of. I had to hit all the walls. I was immensely ambitious. It was like I was screaming at the universe to pay attention. Like I had to make *God* laugh.

Funny, I remember one year at the Emmy-awards ceremony, they gave the award for comedy writing to the writers of *The Phil Silvers Show,* and they had never ever given an Emmy to the writers of *Your Show of Shows.* So I jumped up on a table and started screaming, right there in front of the cameras and everybody. "Coleman Jacoby and Arnie Rosen won an Emmy and Mel Brooks didn't! Nietzsche was right! *There is no God! There is no God!"*

PLAYBOY: You know, you've described a lot of really wild behavior. Are you sure some of it wasn't actually a little crazy?

BROOKS: I'm sure it *was.* I went through some disastrous times when I was a young man. After I was hired by *Your Show of Shows,* I started having acute anxiety attacks. I used to vomit a lot between parked Plymouths in midtown Manhattan. Sometimes I'd get so anxiety-stricken I'd have to run, because I'd be generating too much adrenaline to do anything *but* run or scream. Ran for miles through the city streets. People stared. No joggers back then. Also, I couldn't sleep at night and I'd get a lot of dizzy spells and I was nauseated for days.

PLAYBOY: What brought on all this anxiety?

BROOKS: Fear of heights. Look at what had happened. I was a poor kid from a poor neighborhood, average family income $35 a week. I felt lucky to be making $50 a week, which is what Sid was paying me. And then, on top of that, I got a screen credit! "Additional dialog, Mel Brooks." Wow! But when I was listed as a regular writer and my pay went to $250 a week, I began to get scared. Writer! I'm not a writer. Terrible penmanship. And when my salary went to $1000 a week, I really panicked. Twenty-four years old and $1000 a week? It was unreal. I figured any day now they'd find me out and fire me. It was like I was stealing and I was going to get caught. Then, the year after that, the money went to $2500 and finally I was making $5000 a show and going out of my mind. In fact, the psychological mess I was in began to cause a real physical debilitation. To wit: low blood sugar and underactive thyroid.

PLAYBOY: You—underactive thyroid?

BROOKS: Everybody thinks, Mel Brooks, that maniac! The energy of that man! He must be hyperthyroid. *Au contraire, mon frère.* To this day, I take a half grain of thyroid—and an occasional Raisinet. Now, seriously, have you got kids? How's about taking a couple boxes Raisinets for the kids? They'll love 'em, and—

PLAYBOY: But chocolate is terrible for their teeth.

BROOKS: Are teeth so good for chocolate? Let's be fair.

PLAYBOY: Thanks, but—

BROOKS: Take your time. It's a big decision. Maybe you should call your lawyer. Use my phone, OK? Where were we?

PLAYBOY: What straightened you out emotionally?

BROOKS: Mel Tolkin sent me to an analyst. Strictly Freudian. On the couch—no peeking. But the man himself was kind and warm and bright. Most of my symptoms disappeared in the first year, and then we got into much deeper stuff—whether or not one should live and why.

PLAYBOY: Did you find any answers to that?

BROOKS: The main thing I remember from then is bouts of grief for no apparent reason. Deep melancholy, incredible grief where you'd think that somebody very close to me had died. You couldn't grieve any more than I was grieving.

PLAYBOY: Why?

BROOKS: It was connected with accepting life as an adult, getting out in the real world. I was grieving about the death of childhood. I'd had such a happy childhood, my family close to me and loving me. Now I really had to accept the mantle of adulthood—and parenthood. No more cadging quarters from my older brothers or my mother. Now I was the basic support of the family unit. I was proud of doing my bit, but it meant no longer being the baby, the adorable one. It meant being a father figure. Deep, deep shock. But finally I went on to being a mature person.

You often hear, you know, that people go into show business to find the love they never had when they were children. Never believe it! Every comic and most of the actors I know had a childhood full of love. Then they grew up and found out that in the grown-up world, you don't get all that love, you just get your share. So they went into show business to re-capture the love they had known as children when they were the center of the universe.

PLAYBOY: Are you saying that analysis changed you from the wild man who did a Pepper Martin slide at Max Liebman into the mature man who wrote and directed *Blazing Saddles*?

BROOKS: I'm saying that you should stop trying to be funnier than the Jew. What changed me was success and having to solve the problems of success. At that time of life, no matter what you do, you're getting your education, what Joseph Conrad called the bump on the head. I got mine from the analyst and from Mel Tolkin. Between them, they were the father I never had. *Sherreeeeee!* Bring me some Trident gum! I gave up smoking, folks, on January 3, 1974. In lieu of eating my desk, I chew gum. 'Cause the mouth still wants to inhale. Already I've inhaled a Bell telephone; that's how fierce the desire is.

PLAYBOY: Can you give some advice to someone who is trying to quit smoking?

BROOKS: Suck somebody else's nose.

PLAYBOY: Thank you. Now about Tolkin . . .

BROOKS: Tolkin is a big, tall, skinny Jew with terribly worried eyes. He looks like a stork that dropped a baby and broke it and is coming to explain to the parents. Very sad, very funny, very widely read. When I met him, I had read nothing—*nothing!* He said, "Mel, you should read Tolstoy, Dostoievsky, Turgenev, Gogol." He was big on the Russians. So I started with Tolstoy and I was overwhelmed. Tolstoy writes like an ocean, in huge, rolling waves, and it doesn't look like it was processed through his thinking. It feels very natural. You don't question whether Tolstoy's right or wrong. His philosophy is housed in interrelating characters, so it's not up for grabs. Dostoievsky, on the other hand, you can dispute philosophical points with, but he's good, too. *The Brothers Karamazov* ain't chopped liver.

PLAYBOY: So you got rich, cultured, secure—then what happened?

BROOKS: And then the roof fell in. There I am, strolling around in silk shirts and thinking, I'm cut out for greatness. Television's too small for me. How am I going to get out of this lousy racket? And suddenly I *am* out of it. The show is off the air. One day it's $5000 a week, the next day it's zilch. I couldn't get a job anywhere! Comedy shows went out of style and the next five years I averaged $85 a week. Five thousand a week to $85 a week! It was a terrifying nose dive.

PLAYBOY: What about the money you had saved?

BROOKS: What money? Are you kidding? I was *married*! I was so much in debt I couldn't believe it! All I had was a limited edition of *War and Peace* and an iron skate key. I kissed the skate key four times a day just to have something to do.

PLAYBOY: How about the record? Didn't you and Reiner record *The 2000-Year-Old Man* not long after the show folded?

BROOKS: A year later, the record came out. Saved me. Sold maybe 1,000,000 copies. And we did two others, *2001* and the *Cannes Film Festival.* We'd been doing the act for nothing at parties. We'd go to Danny's Hide-A-Way in New York and Carl would say, "Sir, I understand that you were living at the time of Christ." I'd say, "Christ? Can't place him. Thin, nervous fella? Yeah. Came in the store, never bought anything. Little beard, cute. Wore sandals, right?" We did it once at a big party at Carl's house and Steve Allen said we ought to make a comedy record, there was money in it. *"What?* Money in it?" So we got a shipment of black Russian health bread—you know, the round, flat kind. Ripped the shit out of it trying to make grooves, but the reproduction is pretty good, don't you think? And if you don't like the jokes, you can put cream cheese on them and eat them. Anyway, it was a good thing the record took off. In the meantime, my marriage had fallen apart and alimony and child support were eating me up.

PLAYBOY: How did you meet Anne Bancroft?

BROOKS: Anne Bancroft? Never heard of her.

PLAYBOY: Famous actress, beauty of stage and screen, star of *The Miracle Worker, Two for the Seesaw, The Pumpkin Eater,* featured in the forthcoming film version of *The Prisoner of Second Avenue,* married to some Jewish comedian.

BROOKS: Oh, *that* Anne Bancroft. Yes, I am a great fan of hers—and of her husband's. When did I meet her? Let's go back to February 5, 1961, four o'clock in the afternoon. I went to the rehearsal of a Perry Como special, and there she was, singing in a beautiful white gown. Strangely enough, she was singing *Married I Can Always Get,* and when she finished the song, I stood up and clapped loudly in this empty theater. "Bravo!" I shouted. "Terrific!" Then I rushed down the aisle and up onto the stage. "Hi," I said, "I'm Mel Brooks." I was really a pushy kid. And I shook her hand and she smiled and laughed.

Anyway, she said she was going to the William Morris office to see her agent, so I said, "Oh, by chance I happen to be going there, too." Big lie. "Let's all take a cab together." *Vrrrrreeeeeet!* I gave this great New York whistle. It stopped a cab. Later she said that really impressed me. We went to her agent's office. I said, "I haven't seen *The Miracle Worker* yet, but I hear it's great." She said, "Want me to do it for you?" I said, "The whole play?" She said, "Yes." She obviously liked me, too. Well, she did the whole play! A one-hour version right there in the office! The fight scene and everything. And then *Waaaa! Waaaa!* The screaming at the end, the buckets of water, she did everything. I was on the floor. I was in tears, screaming with laughter, stunned.

I called and called her that night. She wasn't in. Next day I called her and went over with my record album and we sat for six hours in the living room and talked. That night she was going to Village Vanguard. I managed to be there. Then I went to a closing party for *The Miracle Worker.* Everybody was crazy about her. Me, too. I really loved her. I just fell in love. I hadn't fallen in love since I was a schoolboy. She was just radiant and beautiful and when we talked, I saw how bright she was. And her humor!

I asked her about dates and she said that very few men asked her to go out. And I realized that a man had to be pretty sure of himself, because she was quite an illustrious person. Just normal males who wanted to be big shots, wanted to hold their own, they couldn't deal with that. She was a very hard woman to dominate if you wanted to be Mr. Male. But I wasn't interested in dominating.

So we started going out and I told her, "OK, you're very bright. You're

going to be my foreign-movie date. We'll go see foreign movies together."
We went to the Thalia because it was 99 cents, and to dozens of recording
sessions. All I could get into for nothing was recording sessions. Sometimes
we ate in Chinatown for a buck-twenty-five. We walked, we held hands. I
saw her every day. She would cook a lot, to save money. Great cook. Egg-
plant *parmigiana* and lasagna, wonderful Italian dishes. After a while, we
just didn't see anybody else. Not because we said "Let's go steady" but because nobody else was as fascinating as we were to each other. Finally,
I got a couple of TV spectaculars, as they were called then. An Andy
Williams show, a Jerry Lewis show. Then the record began to save my life.
But it was *Get Smart!,* a TV series I did with Buck Henry, that made it
possible for us to get married.

PLAYBOY: Was it tough to bring yourself to the point of asking?

BROOKS: I never did. We were staying out at Fire Island and my mother
had come to visit us, and her parents, too, and we were staying in separate
rooms but still living in the same house. Didn't look nice for the parents.
So suddenly Annie said, "Why don't we get married? It'll be so much easier
for the folks to deal with our relationship." And I said, "Oh, absolutely.
Fine." And she nearly fainted. Then she got scared. "Well, I don't know
if I want to do this—really get *married.*" She had been married before and
it hadn't been good.

Anyway, we got married in 1964, on my lunch hour. It was a civil
ceremony. Annie is Italian and I'm Jewish. We were married by a Presby-
terian. There was a black kid waiting in the anteroom and I asked him if
he would stand up for us. His name was Andrew Boone. He had no idea
that it was Mel Brooks marrying Anne Bancroft, because her maiden name
is Italiano and she was married under that name. I didn't even have a
wedding ring for her. Annie had an old earring. It was made of very thin,
bendable silver, looked like a piece of wire. I just twisted that around and
gave her that. The clerk was very upset about that; he liked regular rings.
Afterward, I had to go back to work and that night I went to her apartment
for our wedding dinner. Annie made me spaghetti. It was great. Just the
two of us.

It's been like that to this day. My wife is my best friend, and I can't think
of anybody I'd rather be with, chat with. We live way out here in California
now, in a foreign place, so we need each other a little more. We're even
closer. We have plenty of fights; I mean we're *married,* right? But for me,
this is it.

PLAYBOY: Isn't it about time we discussed sex?

BROOKS (*rising indignantly*): I beg your pardon. We hardly know each
other, and besides, I'm already married. You *were* proposing? Anyway,
I'm not in favor of miscegenation. Later for sex. Let's keep that guy on
the toilet turning the pages. I think I'd rahthah discuss AHT. Why don't
we talk about *The Producers*?

PLAYBOY: Your first movie, 1967. How did you get *The Producers* off the ground?

BROOKS: With 12,000 German slaves and lots of ropes. I had this idea about two schnooks on Broadway who set out to produce a flop and swindle the backers, and the flop was to be called *Springtime for Hitler*. I wrote the script in nine months, with the help of my secretary, Betty Olsen, and then couldn't think of anybody to direct it. So it had to be me. But I hated the idea of directing, and after four pictures I hate it even more. Directing is a terrible, anxious process. It's all collaboration, and if you have a dream, it's diluted very quickly by the slightest ineptness in any of your collaborators. They're supposed to help you, but too often they help you into your grave. Your vision can never achieve perfection. If you want to be a moviemaker, you've got to say, "All right, I'll chop the dream down. I'll be very happy if I get 60 percent of my vision on the screen."

PLAYBOY: Why do you direct if you don't like it?

BROOKS: In self-defense. Basically, I'm a writer. I'm the proprietor of the vision. I alone know what I eventually want to happen on the screen. So if you have a valuable idea, the only way to protect it is to direct it.

PLAYBOY: How did you get to direct *The Producers*?

BROOKS: I went to all the big studios with Sidney Glazier, my producer, and said, "I'm going to have to direct this." They said, "Please get out of here before you get hurt." There were physical threats. Finally, someone at Universal Pictures said, "You can direct, but it has to be called *Springtime for Mussolini*. Nazi movies are out." I said, "I think you missed the point." Then I met Joseph E. Levine, a plain person from the street. "You think you can direct it?" "Yes." "OK." Shook hands. That was it! In the middle of the night, I woke up in a cold sweat. "Foolish person! You had to open your big mouth."

PLAYBOY: Still, you brought it in on schedule.

BROOKS: And under budget: $941,000. I won an Oscar for the Best Screenplay of 1968. And the picture died at the box office. Anyway, that's what Avco-Embassy said. Their motto is emblazoned in Hebrew letters on the office wall. WE MAKE THE MONEY, YOU TRY AND FIND IT.

PLAYBOY: But *The Producers* was a critical success, wasn't it?

BROOKS: Never believe it. Today everybody calls *The Producers* a classic. But at the time, you never saw such vitriolic reviews. What can I tell you? Some critics are emotionally desiccated, personally about as attractive as a year-old peach in a single girl's refrigerator. It's easy to say shit is shit, and it should be said. But the real function of a critic is to see what is truly good and go bananas when he sees it.

PLAYBOY: With your first picture a financial flop, how did you finance *The Twelve Chairs*?

BROOKS: Minimally. I got $50,000 for writing and coproducing the picture and it took three years to make. After the tax bite, I got about half of the

$50,000, so that means I was living on $8000 a year and the good nature of several banks. We shot the picture in Yugoslavia, which saved us a lot of money but gave us a lot of headaches. When I went to Yugoslavia, my hair was black. When I came back, nine months later, it was gray. Truly. To begin with, it's a very long flight to Yugoslavia and you land in a field of full-grown corn. They figure it cushions the landing. The first thing they tell you is that the water is death. The only safe thing to drink is *Kieselavoda,* which is a mild laxative. In nine months, I lost 71 pounds. Now, at night, you can't do anything, because all of Belgrade is lit by a ten-watt bulb, and you can't go anywhere, because Tito has the car. It was a beauty, a green '38 Dodge. And the food in Yugoslavia is either very good or very bad. One day we arrived on location late and starving and they served us fried chains. When we got to our hotel rooms, mosquitoes as big as George Foreman were waiting for us. They were sitting in armchairs with their legs crossed.

The Yugoslav crew was very nice and helpful, but you had to be careful. One day in a fit of pique, I hurled my director's chair into the Adriatic. Suddenly I heard *"Halugchik! Kakdivmyechisnybogdanblostrov!"* On all sides, angry voices were heard and clenched fists were raised. "The vorkers," I was informed, "have announced to strike!" "But why?" "You have destroyed the People's chair!" "But it's mine! It says Mel Brooks on it!" "In Yugoslavia, everything is property of People." So we had a meeting, poured a lot of vodka, got drunk, started to cry and sing and kiss each other. Wonderful people! If they had another ten-watt bulb, I'd go there to live.

PLAYBOY: What happened when *Twelve Chairs* was released?

BROOKS: The movie was released at Meyer Roberts' apartment in Evanston, Illinois. Sixteen people attended the world premiere. Meyer himself couldn't make it; he had a date. We were all fingerprinted and booked by the police. No, the picture did pretty well in New York, but it couldn't get across the George Washington Bridge. Taught me something. There is no room in the business now for a special little picture. You either hit 'em over the head or stay home with the canary.

PLAYBOY: And *Blazing Saddles* was designed to hit 'em over the head.

BROOKS: No. Actually, it was designed as an esoteric little picture. We wrote it for two weirdos in the balcony. For radicals, film nuts, guys who draw on the washroom wall—my kind of people. I had no idea middle America would see it. What would a guy who talks about white bread, white Ford station wagons and vanilla milk shakes on Friday night see in that *meshugaas*?

PLAYBOY: How did you hit on the idea for *Blazing Saddles*?

BROOKS: It's an interesting story; I don't think I'll tell it. Can I interest you in a Raisinet? No? Maybe you'd like a chocolate-covered Volkswagen? Do you have a dollar on you? I hate to answer questions for nothing. (*Accepts a dollar*) Thank you. For two more I'll sell you my T-shirt. See this little alligator on the pocket? I understand that in the Everglades, there are alligators with little Jews on their shirt pockets.

We were talking about *Blazing Saddles*. It was Andy Bergman's idea. He sent Warner Bros. a rough draft of a screenplay called *Tex-X*. What grabbed me were the possibilities of a modern black man arriving in the traditional West. Like, he'd say, "Right on, baby!" And they'd say, "Consarnit!" Then I realized that at the same time I could make fun of Westerns and the West. So I called Bergman and said, "Do you mind if I despoil your script?" And he said, "Can I help ?" David Brown at Warner's called me and I told him I wanted to write it the way we wrote *Your Show of Shows*—lock a bunch of weirdos up together and come out with a great script. We called in Norman Steinberg and Alan Uger, a Jewish comedy team, and Richard Pryor, a black person of *outré* imagination. Then we turned on the tape recorder and started bullshitting. Pryor wrote the Jewish jokes, the Jews wrote the black jokes. Nine months later, we had a finished script.

Blazing Saddles was a breakthrough comedy. It carried the audience into territory that film comedy had never entered before—kinds of satire, kinds of special vulgarity—and some critics felt confused and disoriented. So they thought that because *they* were confused, *we* were confused. We weren't.

PLAYBOY: What was the point of the vulgarity—the farting scene, for example?

BROOKS: The farts were the point of the farting scene. In real life, people fart, right? In the movies, people don't. Why not? When I was in high school, I knew a kid, won't mention his name—Robert Weinstein—who when he let one go, you could get in it and drive it away, that's how firm. But before *Blazing Saddles*, America had not come to terms with the fart. Wind was never broken across the prairie in a Ken Maynard picture. In every cowboy picture, the cowboys sit around the campfire and eat 140,000 beans, and you never hear a burp, let alone a bloozer.

PLAYBOY: Oh. Was anything cut out in the interest of good taste?

BROOKS: Yes. A scene between Cleavon Little, the black sheriff, and Madeline Kahn. The scene takes place in the dark. "Is it twue vot zey say," Madeline asks him seductively, "about how you people are built?" Then you hear a zipper. Then you hear her say, "Oh! It's twue! It's twue! It's *twue!*" That much is in the picture. But then comes the line we cut. Cleavon says, "Excuse me, ma'am. I hate to disillusion you, but you're sucking my arm."

PLAYBOY: What happened to your life and your career after *Blazing Saddles*?

BROOKS: I became John Carradine. Aquiline nose, face long and aristocratic, voice deep and vibrant. Thinking of running for the U.S. Senate. . . .

Frankly, I'm in demand and it's great. I can take my best shot and take it under the best conditions. I have a three-picture deal at Fox that gives me everything I want.

PLAYBOY: Which brings us to *Young Frankenstein*. But first, a little bone to pick. Why, why do you always have so little sex in your movies?

BROOKS: What? Who? Avoid *sex*? Oh, that *word*! To whom are you speaking, sir? My name is Kaminsky.

PLAYBOY: In *The Producers*, for example, the closest thing you had to sex was a Swedish secretary with big boobs.

BROOKS: Ya gotta admit that's pretty close.

PLAYBOY: And looking at *Twelve Chairs*, you'd think the Soviet Union was populated by 250,000 people without glands. Even in *Blazing Saddles*, which is obviously intended as a comic saturnalia, there are plenty of anal jokes but hardly any genital jokes.

BROOKS: What about Lili von Shtupp? We almost called the picture *She Shtupps to Conquer*.

PLAYBOY: German sex is the best you can do? Mr. Brooks, some people say your humor is prepubescent. What do you say to that?

BROOKS: I say, if I may quote a comedy writer named Joe Schrank, I can hardly believe my hearing aid. I say in a couple hundred years cabs will be so low to the ground you'll have to step over them and get in from the other side.

PLAYBOY: We say let's talk about *Young Frankenstein*.

BROOKS: I've got a better idea. I'm surprised you haven't asked me. Let's talk about *sex*! Are you ready out there, all you goys? Lock the bathroom door! The Jew is going to talk dirty! Speaking of pornographic movies, the trouble with them is, you're watching them do all these wild things on the screen, six girls with big tits and a guy with a *schwanstucker* like the Chrysler Building, and you get all hot and bothered, but you can't do anything about it. I'd like to see a porno flick if I could do something about it. Like, if there was an intermission at dirty movies, so you could go get your Goobers—or Raisinets, for that matter. Tell me, have you ever considered the possibilities of a Raisinet as a sex object?

PLAYBOY: Did your mother ever discuss sex with you boys?

BROOKS: Never. Completely taboo. There *was* no sex. Children arrived because of affection. You had a terrific bout of affection with each other and suddenly there in the kitchen was a baby at the table, eating. Wonderful! A miracle! I really believed that until Morris Steinberg told me in seven B. His nose is not the same, because I gave it a punch and said, "Not *my* mother! No, sir!" It was a tough thing to hear. But once I knew the score, I got busy.

Most sex in Brooklyn was in the back of a Buick; a Ford was too small to move around in. And most sex was petting. A lot of hallway jobs. Banging against each other in those hallways was terrible and you gotta watch hitting the bells, because you'd get the whole tenement shouting down the stairs at you. So we sneaked up to the roof. My first affair was on the roof of 365 South Third Street. And there was a guy flying pigeons who we saw later watching us. It was late at night, but I heard—ha-ha-ha—a little laughing. Very embarrassing. But there wasn't very much sex for teenagers. We were shy and it was taboo. You got married and had sex.

PLAYBOY: Was there anything kinky going on in those days?

BROOKS: Not that I knew or heard of. Nothing hip or weird or sensational like today. It was thrilling because we were very young, but it was very straight. I mean, no two guys and a girl, none of that.

PLAYBOY: What about Jewish girls—are they puritanical?

BROOKS: The best thing about Jewish girls is, they can tell real jade. No, I don't go for those jokes about "What do you mean, she's dead? I thought she was Jewish!" Jewish women are very exciting, as exciting sexually as any other group. Even so, my advice to a young man marrying a Jewish girl would be to have three and a half years of foreplay. Of course, most girls in every group are reserved about getting down to it. They don't usually do it right away. But once they do it, women are bananas. They don't wanna do it, you can't make them do it, there's no way they'll do it—but once they do it, they don't let you alone. Then it's "OK, Murray, let's do it till we die!"

But PLAYBOY readers, I think, are different. I think they're either single or have single dreams. Singles bars, single girls. They have sultan fantasies, 26 chicks coming at them, screaming and biting them. In real life, I mean, you're lucky if your *wife* will do it with you.

PLAYBOY: What about orgies?

BROOKS: No, I'm Jewish. Besides, at orgies there are too many people. You're naked and you hardly know each other. "Are you Mel Brooks?" "Yes." "I loved *Springtime for Hitler.*" "Thank you." "Did you write the lyrics as well as the music?" Who cares? And orgies would be embarrassing. You meet somebody later that you've seen at an orgy; you don't want that. Maybe in Romania you'd never see anybody again. But think of the plane fare.

PLAYBOY: What about sexual apparatus—such as vibrators and dildos and electrical—

BROOKS: Please, you're talking to a Jewish person. Electrical apparatus would scare me. God gave us enough apparatus to get the thing done. I understand in Japan, though, they make rubber people you can go to bed with. A whole rubber person, supposed to be sensational. Costs as much as a Toyota, but you can't back up in it. OK? Enough sex? Would you like me to expose myself, Mr. Filth?

PLAYBOY: Thank you, no. But there *is* one side of sex we haven't discussed. Your pictures all have happy endings, but you may have noticed that boy never gets girl.

BROOKS: True. At the end of the first three pictures, boy gets boy. Zero Mostel get Gene Wilder, Frank Langella gets Ron Moody, Gene Wilder gets Cleavon Little. It's a remarkable coincidence, and I'm not sure what it means. But I'm pretty sure my need to have my male characters come together and be close is not some sort of a sexual need I've displaced into these people. I think it goes back a lot further than sex. All the way back to my father, whom I never really knew and can't remember. I can't tell you what sadness, what pain it is to me never to have known my own father, who died when I was two and a half. All I know is what they've told me. He was lively, peppy, sang well. Isn't it sad that that's all a son should know about his father? If only I could look at him, touch his face, see if he had eyebrows! Maybe in having the male characters in my movies find each other, I'm expressing the longing I feel to find my father and be close to him.

PLAYBOY: But in *Young Frankenstein*, even the monster gets a girl.

BROOKS: Yes. I'm turning straight. In fact, there's a lot of heterosex in *Young Frankenstein*. There's lust on a lab table, rape in a cave and a big double-wedding-night sequence. But sex isn't the point. What we had in mind was a picture that played on two main levels. One, we wanted to make a hilarious pastiche of the old black-and-white horror films of the Thirties. Two, we wanted to offer sincere and reverent homage to those same beautifully made movies.

PLAYBOY: What's the difference between directing comedy and directing a serious picture?

BROOKS: I'll tell you that after I call Sherry. *Sherreeee!* Take a letter, please, to this guy who calls *Blazing Saddles* "an artless and vulgar display" and says he and his wife saw it only because they were "unwary tagalongs." "Dear sir: *Blazing Saddles* has been rated R. The R is there to protect people like you and your wife from unwittingly attending adult movie fare. I don't think it's fair of you to walk into an R-rated film and then criticize it for containing sophisticated material. I also don't think that the excuse of tagging along relieves anyone of culpability. One doesn't wander into a brothel and then attack the establishment for not being Howard Johnson's. Sincerely yours, Mel Brooks." Where were we?

PLAYBOY: Directing comedy.

BROOKS: There's one thing you've got to understand before you can direct comedy. Comedy is serious—deadly serious. Never, never try to be funny! The actors must be serious. Only the situation must be absurd. Funny is in the writing, not in the performing. If the situation isn't absurd, no amount of hoke will help. And another thing, the more serious the situation, the funnier the comedy can be. The greatest comedy plays against the greatest tragedy. Comedy is a red rubber ball and if you throw it against a soft, funny wall, it will not come back. But if you throw it against the hard wall of ultimate reality, it will bounce back and be very lively. *Vershteh*, goy bastard? No offense. Very, very few people understand this.

PLAYBOY: Does Woody Allen understand it?

BROOKS: Woody Allen is a genius. His films are wonderful. I liked *Sleeper* very, very much. It's Woody's best work to date. The most imaginative and the best performed. I was on the floor, and very few people can put me on the floor. He's poetic, but he's also a critic. He artfully steps back from a social setting and criticizes it without—I suspect—without letting himself be vulnerable to it.

PLAYBOY: And you?

BROOKS: I'm not a critic. I like to hop right in the middle, right into the vortex. I can't just zing a few arrows at life as it thunders by! I have to be down on the ground and shouting at it, grabbing it by the horns, biting it! Look, I really don't want to wax philosophic, but I will say that if you're alive, you got to flap your arms and legs, you got to jump around a lot, you got to make a lot of noise, because life is the very opposite of death. And therefore, as I see it, if you're quiet, you're not living. I mean you're just slowly drifting into death. So you've got to be noisy, or at least your *thoughts* should be noisy and colorful and lively. My liveliness is based on an incredible fear of death. In order to keep death at bay, I do a lot of "Yah! Yah! Yah!" And death says, "All right. He's too noisy and busy. I'll wait for someone who's sitting quietly, half asleep. I'll nail *him*. Why should I bother with this guy? I'll have a lot of trouble getting him out the door." There's a little door they gotta get you through. "This will be a fight," death says. "I ain't got time."

Most people are afraid of death, but I really *hate* it! My humor is a scream and a protest against goodbye. Why do we have to die? As a kid, you get nice little white shoes with white laces and a velvet suit with short pants and a nice collar, and you go to college, you meet a nice girl and get married, work a few years—and then you have to *die*? What is that shit? They never wrote *that* in the contract. So you yell against it, and if you yell seriously, you can be a serious playwright and everybody can say, "Very nice." But I suspect you can launch a little better artillery against death with humor.

PLAYBOY: But it's a battle you can't win.

BROOKS: You can win a conditional victory, I think. It all boils down to scratching your name in the bark of a tree. You write M. B. in the bark of a tree. *I was here.* When you do that—whatever tree you carve it in—you're saying, "Now, there's a record of me!" I won't be erased by death. Any man's greatness is a tribute to the nobility of all mankind, so when we celebrate the genius of Tolstoy, we say, "Look! One of our boys made it! Look what we're capable of!"

So I try to give my work everything I've got, because when you're dead or you're out of the business or you're in an old actors' home somewhere, if you've done a good job, your work will still be 16 years old and dancing and healthy and pirouetting and arabesquing all over the place. And they'll say, "That's who he is! He's not this decaying skeleton."

I once had this thought that was so corny, but I loved it. It was that infinitesimal bits of coral, by the act of dying upon each other, create something that eventually rises out of the sea—and there it is, it's an island and you can stand on it, live on it! And all because they died upon each other. Writing is simply one thought after another dying upon the one before. Where would I be today if it wasn't for Nikolai Gogol? You wouldn't be laughing at *Young Frankenstein*. Because he showed me how crazy you could get, how brave you could be. Son of a bitch bastard! I love him! I love Buicks! I love Dubrovnik! I love Cookie Lavagetto! I love Factor's Deli at Pico and Beverly Drive! I love Michael Hertzberg's baby boy! I love rave reviews! I love my wife! I love not wearing suits! I love New York in June! I love Raisinets! Which brings me, Mr. Interlocutor, for the last time, to the question: Would you or would you not care for a Raisinet?

PLAYBOY: Sure. Why not?

BROOKS: Sorry, kid. They're all gone.

FIDEL CASTRO

January 1967
Interviewer: Lee Lockwood

Giving a forum to radical American figures was one thing, and that hadn't come easily to all the editors at PLAYBOY. But letting Fidel Castro have *his* say, in the atmosphere of 1966, was another. Lee Lockwood, an author and journalist, was in Cuba at the time interviewing Castro for a book. When Fisher spoke with him by telephone, he told Lockwood to see if he could persuade Castro to give him a full-length interview for PLAYBOY. As it turned out, it was not Castro who was the problem, but Spectorsky. Nonetheless, Castro *was* a chief of state, and to the magazine that meant something. So Hefner gave the go-ahead, and Spectorsky eventually agreed as well.

It should be noted that, with respect to chiefs of state, PLAYBOY had reason to be cautious. In 1964 Fisher had purchased an already completed interview by a staffer at *Wisdom,* a hard-cover magazine that at the time counted among its contributors heads of state, foreign ministers, and the like. The interview was with India's prime minister Jawaharlal Nehru. When it was published as a Playboy Interview, the Indian Embassy issued an immediate denial: It was a fraud, a scissors-and-paste job put together from clippings. PLAYBOY ran a retraction in the next issue, and Fisher vowed never again to buy an interview not assigned especially by the magazine. It was the only fake interview ever published in PLAYBOY, and it made the editors wary of anyone purporting to have access to a chief of state.

In Castro's case, Lockwood's access was genuine, but so was the nervousness at editorial headquarters when the interview was edited. It was a reasonable exposition of the Cuban leader's views, and it was done without jingoistic bias, something rare by then-prevailing standards in the American press. The nervousness was dissipated when

Spectorsky reverted to an old habit—and to the prevailing standards—by directing that a tough, anti-Communist introduction be written. And the headline that month read: "A Candid Conversation with the Bellicose Dictator of Communist Cuba." In addition, editorial insertions were peppered through the interview, correcting Castro on his facts.

Reader reaction was predictably strong, with one letter writer stating, "It is easy to see why Castro has limited his communication with the press of the outside world. Only in PLAYBOY could he have been guaranteed such a comprehensive record of his statements." But another reader apparently detected tension at the home office when he wrote that he considered the interview "scrupulously fair" except for "a little needling by that Ed. fellow."

Partly because this was one of the first attempts to show Castro outside his image as a bearded madman, and partly because he explained for the first time in this interview his resentment of Khrushchev for backing down during the 1963 Missile Crisis, this was one of the few PLAYBOY interviews of the era to receive press coverage.

Footnote: In early 1968, just after President Carter's inauguration, an American reporter asked Castro what he thought of the new American president. The conversation was taking place in Havana, and Castro had never permitted PLAYBOY to be sold in Cuba. Castro replied that he had carefully read the interview with Carter in PLAYBOY and had been convinced that the American leader was "a sincere man," and that he hoped relations would improve as a result.

Fidel Castro, the tempestuous, charismatic fomenter and continuing prime mover of the Cuban revolution, may be the most hated dictator in the Western Hemisphere, but he is his country's indispensable man, a ubiquitous despot who supplies the energy for nearly every phase of contemporary Cuban life.

Although the negative aspects of his regime are usually emphasized in the American press, just as propagandistic blasts against American life are trumpeted in Cuba's press, Castro's revolution has achieved some undeniable reforms affecting the lives of the peasants and the proletariat. It has virtually wiped out illiteracy, provided free education and medical care for all, instituted revisions of land and rent laws, and claims to have achieved a higher standard of living for the masses, whose support was instrumental in sweeping him to power. There is no one at large and alive in Cuba today, either in the zealous cadre of revolutionaries that surrounds him or among the Cuban people, who is capable of opposing Castro. He is larger than life size; his image dominates Cuba. For better or worse, he is contemporary Cuba.

Castro's Communist regime could not have survived this long without the Soviet Union's military and financial backing. But it must also be recognized that enough of Cuba's 7,336,000 people have either supported or paid lip service to Castro's dictatorship to keep him in power—despite eight years of internal hardship, the counterrevolutionary campaigns of 1962 and 1963, the sectarian disputes within his own party, the disparity between promised goals and actual progress to date, the exodus of hundreds of thousands of dissident Cubans to the U.S., and the severe economic shortages that continue to plague the country. Whether putative gains from his leadership will offset Cuba's past blunders, present bellicosity, and the drastic curtailment of individual freedom imposed by its new ideology, whether history will ultimately "absolve" Castro as he prophesies, are questions for posterity. This much, however, is clear: He is one of the most feared political figures of our time, and as such, he wields a power disproportionate to the size of his tiny island nation.

Not the least logical of reasons for this fear in the U.S. is ignorance of Castro's own view of himself and his goals, of his role in world politics, of his aspirations for his country, his personal motivations for the stormy course on which he is embarked—and for this lack, the American press and he himself are not blameless. Of propagandistic boasts, as of pro-Communist and anti-U.S. diatribes, there has been more than enough. But Castro has been elusively chary of interviews by members of the American press, perhaps because the majority may be presumed to be something less than objective. It was PLAYBOY's belief that an unexpurgated interview —despite the evasions it might contain—would do much to clarify the thoughts and actions at work behind the Cuban curtain, and thus to illuminate a darkly threatening presence in our hemisphere.

To this end, we contacted old Havana hand and author-journalist Lee Lockwood, who had already been granted an audience with Castro as preparation for a forthcoming book, "Castro's Cuba, Cuba's Fidel," to be published by Macmillan in March, and of which an expanded version of this interview will be one part. When the two met at Castro's Isle of Pines home, the result was the longest and most revealing conversation the Cuban leader has ever held with a member of the American press.

Lounging at a card table on the veranda in his green fatigues, wearing socks but no boots, his hair matted, and smoking a succession of long Cuban cigars, the Cuban dictator spoke with Lockwood volubly and inexhaustibly—often through the night and into the dawn. At the end of a week, their conversations (conducted in Spanish) had filled nearly 25 hours of tape.

"An interview with Castro," writes Lockwood, "is an extraordinary experience, and until you get used to it, an unnerving one. Unless you stand *your ground, it's seldom a conversation at all, but more like an extended monolog with occasional questions from the audience. When replying to a question, he would usually begin in a deceptively detached, conversational tone of voice, with his eyes fixed on the table, while his hands fidgeted compulsively with a lighter, a ballpoint pen or anything else at hand. As he warmed to his subject, Castro would start to squirm and swivel in his chair. The rhythm of his discourse would slowly quicken, and at the same time he would begin drawing closer to me little by little, pulling his chair with him each time, until—having started out at right angles to my chair—he would finally be seated almost alongside me. His foot, swinging spasmodically beneath the table, would touch my foot, then withdraw. Then his knee would wedge against mine as he leaned still closer, oblivious of all but the point he was making, his voice becoming steadily more insistent. As he bent forward, his hands would move gracefully out and back in emphatic cadence with his words, then begin reaching toward me, tapping my knee to punctuate a sentence, prodding my chest with an emphatic forefinger, still in the same hypnotizing rhythm. Finally, I would become aware of his dark-brown eyes, glittering in the frame of his tangled beard, peering fervently into my own eyes, in true Latin style, from only inches away as he continued speaking. He would remain thus sometimes for as long as a quarter of an hour, fixing me with his messianic gaze."*

Regarding the frankness of the Cuban leader's replies, Lockwood adds: "Naturally, you cannot expect a man in Castro's position to answer every question for publication as openly as if he were having a private chat with a friend. Nevertheless, as one who has spent a good deal of time in Cuba, I believe that his answers were generally honest—however ideologically inimical his views."

PLAYBOY: When you came to power in 1959, did you think that Cuba and the U.S. were going to get along better than they actually have?

CASTRO: Yes, that was one of my illusions. At that time, we believed that the revolutionary program could be carried out with a great degree of comprehension on the part of the people of the United States. We believed that because it was just, it would be accepted. True, we didn't think about the Government of the United States. We thought about the *people* of the United States, that in some way their opinion would influence the decisions of the Government. What we didn't see clearly was that the North American interests affected by the revolution possessed the means to bring about a change of public opinion in the United States and to distort everything that was happening in Cuba and present it to the U.S. public in the worst form.

PLAYBOY: Is that why you went to the United States in April of that year?

CASTRO: Precisely—in an effort to keep public opinion in the United States better informed and better disposed toward the revolution in the face of the tremendous campaign that was being waged against us. When I went to the U.S., I had practically no contact with the Government. It was with public opinion.

PLAYBOY: You did meet with Vice-President Nixon, though.

CASTRO: Yes. But my trip was not an official one. I had been invited by an organization of editors. There were some—I would say—"acts of protocol," however, because diplomatic relations were being maintained. There was a luncheon with the then Secretary of State [Christian Herter—*Ed.*] and an invitation to speak with some Senators. Nixon, too, wanted to talk with me; we had a long conversation. He has written his version of that talk, and he maintains that from then on he came to the conclusion that I was a dangerous character.

PLAYBOY: Did the subsequent hostility of the American Government have much to do with creating a receptive atmosphere for communism in Cuba?

CASTRO: I think so, in the same way that the friendly acts of the Soviet Union also helped. The connections we established with the U.S.S.R. in 1960 very much matured the minds of both the people and the leaders of the revolution. Undoubtedly, it taught us something we had not clearly understood at the beginning: that our true allies, the only ones that could help us make our own revolution, were none other than those countries that had recently had their own. We had an opportunity to see what proletarian internationalism was, to learn that it was something more than a phrase; we saw it in deeds.

PLAYBOY: Yet some observers have characterized your development as a Communist as having been largely a series of reactions on your part to a series of hostile acts by the U.S.; that is, that the U.S., in effect, forced you and Cuba into the Communist camp.

CASTRO: The United States, with its imperialist foreign policy, constitutes part of the contemporary circumstances that make revolutionaries out of people everywhere. It is not the only cause, but it is certainly one of the many factors. It can be said that the policy of the United States is accelerating the radicalization process of revolutionary movements not only in Cuba but throughout the world.

PLAYBOY: Do you think that you personally would have become a Communist in any case, that U.S. actions and attitudes only hastened the process?

CASTRO: It could be said that just as the United States was then and had to continue being imperialistic, we were destined inevitably to become Communists.

PLAYBOY: Were you personally a Communist when you seized power in 1959?

CASTRO: It is possible that I appeared less radical than I really was at that time. It is also possible that I was more radical than even I myself knew. Nobody can say that he reaches certain political conclusions except through a process. Nobody reaches those convictions in a day, often not in a year. Long before I became a Marxist, my first questionings of an economic and social kind arose when I was a student at the university, studying political economy and especially capitalist economics—the problems posed by over-production and the struggle between the workers and the machines. They aroused my attention extraordinarily and led me to turn my mind to these problems for the first time. How could there exist a conflict between man's technical possibilities and his needs for happiness, and why did it have to exist? How could there be overproduction of some goods, causing un-employment and hunger? Why did there have to be a contradiction be-tween the interests of man and of the machine, when the machine should be man's great aid, precisely that aid which could free him from privation, misery and want?

In this way, I began to think of different forms of the organaztion of production and of property, although in a completely idealistic way, without any scientific basis. You might say that I had begun to transform myself into a kind of utopian Socialist. At that time I had not read the *Communist Manifesto.* I had read hardly anything by Karl Marx. This was when I was a student in the second or third year of law. Later on, I did read the *Manifesto,* and it made a deep impression on me; for the first time I saw a historical, systematic explanation of the problem, phrased in a very militant way that captivated me completely.

In the succeeding years, I read a number of works by Marx, Engels and Lenin that gave me many additional theoretical insights. This encounter with revolutionary ideas helped me orient myself politically. But there is a big difference between having a theoretical knowledge and considering oneself a Marxist revolutionary. Unquestionably, I had a rebellious tempera-ment and at the same time felt a great intellectual curiosity about those problems. Those insights inclined me more and more toward political struggle. However, I still could not have been considered a true Marxist.

PLAYBOY: Did you become one as a result of Batista's *coup d'état?*

CASTRO: No, but I already had some very definite political ideas about the need for structural changes. Before the *coup,* I had been thinking of utilizing legal means, of using the Parliament as a point of departure from which I might establish a revolutionary platform and motivate the masses in its favor—not as a means of bringing about those changes directly. I was now convinced that it could be done only in a revolutionary way. I had acquired enough sense of reality to understand that.

Nonetheless, I was still in some ways ingenuous and deluded. In many ways I was still not a Marxist, and I did not consider myself a Communist. In spite of having read theoretically about imperialism as a phenomenon, I didn't understand it very well. I didn't thoroughly appreciate the relation that existed between the phenomenon of imperialism and the situation in Cuba. It is possible that I was then still very much influenced by the habits and ideas of the *petit bourgeois* education I had received. As the son of a landowner, educated in a Jesuit secondary school, I had brought nothing more than a rebellious temperament and the uprightness, the severe character that they had inculcated in me in the Jesuit school. When I graduated from the university, I still didn't have a very good political training. Even so, one might say that I had advanced extraordinarily, since I had been a political illiterate when I entered the university.

In fact, my political consciousness was already much greater than that of the political party with which I had been associated during my student years. That party, which had begun from very popular origins, had, over a period of years, been falling into the hands of landowners and opportunistic politicians; great property owners who lived lavishly on the rents they received from their holdings. Of course, the revolution compensated them, but the law affected them. Many of those people began to feel dissatisfaction with the revolution. That same year, the Agrarian Reform Law was passed; this also affected them. Also, many other laws were passed relating to mortgage loans, debts, etc.—a whole series of social laws that very much affected the interests of the middle class. So they became disaffected because the revolution passed laws affecting their interests as an exploiting class, not because the revolution made a political proclamation.

PLAYBOY: In your speech at the Moncada trial, you promised free elections, a free press, respect for private enterprise, the restoration of the 1940 Constitution, and many other democratic reforms when you came to power. Isn't that correct?

CASTRO: That is true, because that was our program at that moment. Every revolutionary movement, in every historical epoch, proposes the greatest number of achievements possible. We would have been deluding ourselves to have attempted at that moment to do more than we did. But no program implies a renunciation of new revolutionary stages, of new objectives that may pre-empt the old. An initial program can set forth the immediate objectives of a revolution, but not *all* the objectives, not the ultimate objectives. During the subsequent years of prison, of exile, of war in the mountains, the alignment of forces changed so extraordinarily in favor of our movement that we could set goals that were much more ambitious.

PLAYBOY: Yes, but to return to our original question: Wouldn't you admit that many of those middle- and upper-class Cubans who followed you because they believed in your Moncada program later had the right to feel deceived?

CASTRO: I told no lies in the Moncada speech. That was how we thought at the moment; those were the honest goals we set ourselves. But we have since gone beyond that program and are carrying out a much more profound revolution.

PLAYBOY: In the five years since you announced the true nature of the revolution and began to institute its sweeping social changes, several hundred thousand Cubans have renounced their country and fled to the United States. If the revolution is really for the good of the people, how do you account for this mass exodus?

CASTRO: There were many different reasons. Many of those who emigrated were declassed, *Lumpen* elements who had lived from gambling, prostitution, drug traffic and other illicit activities before the revolution. They have gone with their vices to Miami and other cities in the United States, because they couldn't adapt themselves to a society that has eradicated those social ills. Before the revolution, many stringent requirements were imposed on people applying for emigration to the United States; but after the revolution, even such unsavory parasites as these were admitted for the asking. All they had to do was say they were against communism.

Others of the emigrants were those with a very clear class position, who had been in the forefront against any change in social structure and felt themselves tricked when changes came about. Even though we had proclaimed them in our initial program, they didn't believe we would implement them, either because they had gotten used to changes never occurring or because they thought such changes would not be possible in Cuba because they would affect the American interests, and that any government that tried this was destined to be rapidly swept away. Others left out of opportunism, because they believed that if a great many of their class left, the revolution wouldn't last very long. Some also left out of fear of war or from personal insecurity. There were even some who left after a whole series of revolutionary laws had been passed, when counterrevolutionaries spread a rumor that a new law was going to be passed that would take away the right of parents to bring up their own children. This absurd campaign succeeded in convincing many people, especially those who already had a lot of doubts. They sent their children out of the country and later left themselves. They had no alternative, once their children were in the United States, for they were not permitted to bring them back.

There were also many cases of emigration that had nothing to do with politics. There have always been people who wanted to leave Cuba and live in a country like the United States, which has a much higher standard of living. Before the revolution, many people had worked for North American businesses such as banks, refineries, the electric company, the telephone company—a certain working-class aristocracy with better salaries than the rest of the workers—and some of them were attracted by the North American way of life and wanted to live like a middle-class family in the United States. Naturally, that wasn't the case with those who did the hardest and poorest-paid work, like the cutting of sugar cane. It would be interesting to know how many sugar-cane workers have gone to the United States. It would be very difficult to find any.

PLAYBOY: If there had been active opposition to the revolution from the middle and upper classes, do you think you might have lost?

CASTRO: I don't think so. It would have been a longer struggle, more violent, keener from the beginning; but, together with the poor peasants and the workers, we would have overthrown Batista even if he had had their solid support.

PLAYBOY: Given Batista's vast superiority of troops and armaments—with or without middle- and upper-class support—some American military strategists feel you could have been defeated if it hadn't been for his ineptitude. Do you think that's true?

CASTRO: Unquestionably, if Batista had been a wiser and a braver man, a man of different characteristics, he would have been able to to instill more spirit in his soldiers. Instead, he tried to ignore the war, following the tactic of minimizing the importance of our force, believing that any gesture of his, such as visiting the front, would have meant giving more political importance to our movement. By leading his troops more skillfully, he could have prolonged the war, but he would not have won it. He would have lost just the same, and not long after.

He had his only opportunity right at the beginning, when we were few and inexperienced. By the time we had gained a knowledge of the terrain and had increased our force to a little more than 100 armed men, there was already no way of destroying us with a professional army. The only way he could have contained us then would have been by fighting us with an army of peasants from the mountains where we were operating. For that, it would have been necessary to obtain the genuine support of the exploited peasant class. But how could he have gained that support? An army that served the landowners would never have been able to get the exploited farmers on their side. Only a revolutionary movement can organize that force. It is our thesis that no revolutionary movement, no guerrilla movement that is supported by the peasant population can be defeated—unless, of course, the revolutionary leaders commit very grave errors.

You know, people in the United States seem to spend a great deal of time writing elaborate literary works about how the revolution could have been prevented or defeated. This means that most of them think simply as counterrevolutionaries; they feel a genuine terror of revolutions and prefer intermediate formulas. We cannot agree with that reactionary point of view. At the present time, the major concern of the United States seems to be to find a way by which revolutions outside of the United States can be avoided. Unquestionably, the United States today represents the most reactionary ideas in the world. And I think that they cause grave danger both to the world and to the people of the United States themselves.

PLAYBOY: What do you mean by "reactionary ideas"?

CASTRO: I mean especially its self-appointed role of world gendarme, its desire to impose outside its frontiers the kind of government system it thinks other states and other peoples should have. The fact that the United States was itself at one time in the revolutionary avant-garde and had established the best and the most advanced political institutions of its time is one of the historical factors that greatly contributed to the eminence and development of that country. That, plus the natural advantages of being situated in an extraordinarily rich territory. Many North Americans still hark back to 1776, declaring that theirs is still a progressive country. But this is to pretend that the realities of the world and ideas have not changed in 200 years. The fact is that they have changed profoundly.

Apart from this, although the United States arose as a nation based on the most revolutionary political principles of its time, this doesn't mean that its history has been characterized by a profound humanism. As a matter of fact, capitalist society deforms individuals greatly. It entangles them in an egotistical struggle for existence. What is the philosophical foundation of free enterprise? That the most competent, the most able, the most audacious will triumph. Success is the goal of each individual. And he has to achieve it in competition, in a war to the death with everybody else, in a pitiless struggle for existence. Capitalism presupposes that men are moved exclusively by material interests. It assumes that man is capable of acting rightly and correctly only when he can derive an advantage or a profit from it.

PLAYBOY: Isn't that a misleading oversimplification?

CASTRO: I don't think so. In your country, the majority of people do have an opportunity to study and to work; but the majority do not have the *best* opportunities for study, the *best* opportunities for work or for genuine participation in the direction of public affairs and the economy of the country. There are many who are born destined to be presidents of companies or already occupying privileged places in the society. Under capitalism there is a much higher productivity of work, a much greater social yield, and much better living conditions than there were under feudalism; but without the slightest doubt, they are far inferior to the conditions of life that socialism permits.

For example, even though the Northern part of the United States, directed by Lincoln, struggled sucessfully for the liberation of the slaves, discrimination has endured there for a century and today still takes its toll in the blood of Negro citizens of the U.S. Why don't you ask yourselves whether perhaps a relation doesn't exist between racial discrimination and the egoistic feelings that are developed under capitalism? Why hasn't the United States been able to eradicate discrimination? It is because racial discrimination and the economic exploitation of man by man are two things intimately joined.

PLAYBOY: If that's so, why have there been reports of discrimination against Cuba's Negro population by the white majority?

CASTRO: That was true before the revolution, but since the revolution all racial discrimination has disappeared, along with the exploitation of man by man—a lesson you could profit from. I don't say this with the intention of hurting anybody or of wounding the feelings of the North American public. I am simply reasoning and meditating on this subject. I don't consider any people evil. What I do consider evil are certain *systems* that inculcate feelings of hatred in people.

PLAYBOY: Is it your conviction, then, that the U.S. would be better off under socialism or communism?

CASTRO: No. I am a Marxist, and as a Marxist, I believe that revolutions are engendered by a state of misery and desperation among the masses. And that is not the situation of all the people of the United States, but of only a minority, especially the Negroes. Only the masses can bring about a change of social structure, and the masses decide to make those great changes only when their situation is one of desperation. Many years could pass without that happening to the masses of the United States.

In reality, the struggle between the classes is not being conducted inside the United States. It is being conducted outside U.S. borders, in Vietnam, in Santo Domingo, in Venezuela and in certain other countries, including Cuba. Though I understand that a certain amount of protest and dissent is being heard in some North American universities, it is not the masses of the U.S. who fight today against the North American capitalists, because U.S. citizens have a relatively high standard of living and they are not suffering from hunger or misery. The ones who are fighting against the capitalists of the United States are the masses in the rest of the world who *do* live in conditions of hunger and poverty. And just as I say to you that nobody can imagine a social revolution in the United States in the near future, in the same way nobody can deny that a social revolution is taking place in the rest of the poor and underdeveloped world against the North American capitalists. In all parts of the world you see that the most repressive and reactionary governments are backed by the political and military power of the North American capitalists.

This foreign policy, which monopolistic capital imposes, is a ruinous one for the people of the United States. The United States had some 30 billion dollars in gold in its reserves at the end of the Second World War; in 20 years it has used up more than half of those reserves. [According to the Treasury Department, U.S. gold reserves diminished from \$20,083,000,000 to \$14,587,000,000 between 1945 and 1965.—*Ed.*] What has it been used for? With what benefits for the people of the United States? Does the United States perhaps have more friends now than before? In the United States, many people proclaim that they are defending liberty in other countries.

But what kind of liberty is it that they are defending, that nobody is grateful to them, that nobody appreciates this alleged defense of their liberties? What has happened in Korea, in Formosa, in South Vietnam? What country has prospered and has achieved peace and political stability under that protection from the United States? [Japan, West Germany and Formosa, among others.—*Ed.*] What solutions has it found for the great problems of the world? The United States has spent fabulous resources pursuing that policy; it will be able to spend less and less, because its gold reserves are being exhausted. Is the influence of the United States greater now, perhaps, than it was 20 years ago, when the War ended? Nobody could say so. It is a certainty that for 20 years, under the pretext of the struggle against communism, the United States has been carrying out a repressive and reactionary policy in the international field, without having resolved the problems of a single underdeveloped country in the world.

PLAYBOY: Wherever the U.S. has intervened militarily since World War Two, it has been to defend the underdeveloped nations from the threat of Communist subversion or aggression.

CASTRO: Why does it regard communism as a threat?

PLAYBOY: To put it simply, our Government's position is that the goal of international communism is to enslave peoples, not to liberate them.

CASTRO: That is an absolutely erroneous point of view. Look at the case of Cuba: The United States wants to "liberate" Cuba from communism; but in reality, Cuba doesn't *want* to be "liberated" from communism. In order to "liberate" Cuba from communism, the United States organized the followers of Batista, the most reactionary people of this country—torturers, conspirators, thieves, exploiters of all types. It organized them, trained them and armed them in order to come to "liberate" the people of Cuba. But none of those counterrevolutionaries had ever considered the needs of the Cuban people. They hadn't solved the problem of unemployment, ignorance, the lack of medical care, the poverty and misery that existed before the revolution.

Tell me, for what purpose did the United States come to "liberate" us at the Bay of Pigs? To re-establish the power of the landowners, of thieves, of torturers, of the managers of its monopolistic businesses? In what sense can that be called liberty? The United States says that it fights to defend liberty in Vietnam. Can anyone believe that if the people of Vietnam did not support the revolution, they could have resisted as they have? What kind of liberty is that which the United States wants to impose on people at the point of a bayonet? What kind of liberty is that which the United States wants to impose in Santo Domingo, invading the country with its Marines, violating the sovereignty of the country? What kind of liberty is that which the United States seeks to impose upon people against their will? What right does the United States have to impose that kind of liberty on anybody? It seems to me that these lofty rationales for U.S. inerventionism are simply words. Perhaps there are many people in the United States who believe them in good faith; but outside the United States, *nobody* believes them.

PLAYBOY: Speaking of interventionism, why does Cuba actively aid and abet revolutionary movements in other countries?

CASTRO: I believe it is the duty of all revolutionary governments to help all the forces of liberation in whatever part of the world.

PLAYBOY: What kind of aid does your country give to such movements?

CASTRO: Each country helps in whatever way it can. I don't think that anybody ought to say how he does it.

PLAYBOY: In a 1964 newspaper interview, you said that one of the points you would consider as a basis for negotiations with the United States would be the question of abandoning Cuban assistance to revolutionary movements in other Latin-American countries. Is this no longer your position?

CASTRO: What I said at that time was that our country was ready to live by norms of an international character, obeyed and accepted by all, of non-intervention in the internal affairs of the other countries. But I believe that this formula should not be limited to Cuba. Bringing that concept up to date, I can say to you that we would gladly discuss our problems with the United States within the framework of a *world* policy of peace, but we have no interest in discussing them independently of the international situation. We are not interested in negotiating our differences while the U.S. is intervening in Santo Domingo, in Vietnam and elsewhere, while it is playing the role of repressive international policeman against revolutionary movements.

Before long, the United States will find itself required to overextend its forces in order to fight interventionist wars of a universally hateful nature against the revolutionary movements in Asia, in Africa, in Latin America. It will find itself increasingly alone, isolated and repudiated by world opinion. The revolutionary movement will break out sooner or later in *all* oppressed and exploited countries, and even if "nuclear equilibrium" creates a situation in which thermonuclear war would really be increasingly difficult, because neither side wants it, the United States will inevitably lose the fight against the revolutionary movement anyway, simply because objective social and historical conditions extraordinarily favor that struggle of the under-developed peoples.

PLAYBOY: Since you've brought up the subject of "nuclear equilibrium," perhaps we could discuss the Missile Crisis of October 1962. At what point was the decision taken, and upon whose initiative, to install Russian ground-to-ground nuclear missiles in Cuba?

CASTRO: Naturally, the missiles would not have been sent in the first place if the Soviet Union had not been prepared to send them. But they wouldn't have been sent if we had not felt the need for some measure that would unquestionably protect the country. We made the decision at a moment when we thought that concrete measures were necessary to paralyze the plans of aggression of the United States, and we posed this necessity to the Soviet Union.

PLAYBOY: And the Soviet response was simply that the missiles would be sent immediately?

CASTRO: Yes.

PLAYBOY: In retrospect, thinking about all that ensued as a result of that move, have you any regrets about the decision?

CASTRO: Actually, no.

PLAYBOY: When the U.S. and Russia came to an agreement that the missiles would be removed, did Cuba have any influence by which she might have kept them?

CASTRO: It would have been at the cost of a complete break with the Soviet Union, and that would have been really absurd on our part.

PLAYBOY: But wasn't there great popular sentiment in Cuba for keeping the missiles?

CASTRO: All of us were advocates of keeping the missiles in Cuba. Furthermore, the possibility that the Soviet Union would withdraw them was an alternative that had never entered our minds. That doesn't mean that we would have opposed to the death any solution whatsoever, but we would have preferred a more satisfactory solution, with the participation of Cuba in the discussions.

PLAYBOY: What might have been an alternative solution?

CASTRO: At that moment, we were advocates of confronting the events. We felt that we had a clear right as a sovereign country to adopt measures that were pertinent to our defense, and we were absolutely opposed to accepting the demands of the United States, which in our view curtailed the rights of our country. I asked myself: What right does the United States have to protest against those installations here, while in Italy, in Turkey, in the vicinity of the Soviet Union, the U.S. maintains similar bases? Didn't this give the Soviet Union the right to do the same? Not only were we acting within our rights but they were defensive measures similar to those that the United States takes in other parts of the world.

PLAYBOY: But why did you feel it was necessary to defend Cuba with nuclear missiles? You say that you feared an American invasion—but there was no invasion of Cuba being mounted at that time; this was well known. And you must have realized that by allowing the admission of nuclear missiles into Cuba at that moment, you were creating a strong possibility of a nuclear conflict.

CASTRO: The danger of aggression existed, just as it now exists and will exist for a long time. Why did the missiles constitute security for us? Because the United States strategy was, and is, based on nuclear equilibrium.

Within that concept, the presence of missiles in Cuba would have kept us protected. They insured us against the danger of a local war, of something similar to what the United States is doing in Vietnam—a war that, for a small country, can mean almost as much destruction and death as that of a nuclear war.

PLAYBOY: You felt that it made little difference whether Cuba was involved in a conventional or a thermonuclear war?

CASTRO: On an island our size, conventional weapons with the employment of masses of airplanes are equivalent to the use of atomic weapons. We are certain that such an aggression by the United States against our country would cost us millions of lives, because it would mean the initiation of a struggle that would be indefinitely prolonged, with its sequel of destruction and death.

PLAYBOY: Are you convinced that this is going to happen sooner or later?

CASTRO: I cannot be sure of what is going to happen sooner or later, but we are very much aware that the danger exists. If this were not so, we would not spend so much effort and money in preparing our defenses.

PLAYBOY: Can you state unequivocally that there are no ground-to-ground nuclear missiles in Cuba now?

CASTRO: I don't have to perform that service for the North American Intelligence. They get enough information through their own channels.

PLAYBOY: Then you might do it as a service for the American people, who don't have access to classified reports of U.S. Intelligence.

CASTRO: I do not want to make a declaration that might be interpreted as a renunciation of a right. But if this, as you say, can be useful to the North American people, for the sake of their tranquillity, I have no objection to declaring that those weapons do *not* exist in Cuba. Unfortunately, there are none.

PLAYBOY: Do you think Khrushchev acted in a highhanded manner toward Cuba during the Missile Crisis?

CASTRO: Yes. Khrushchev had made great gestures of friendship toward our country. He had done things that were extraordinarily helpful to us. But the way in which he conducted himself during the October crisis was to us a serious affront.

PLAYBOY: Until that time, you had enjoyed rather close personal relations with Khrushchev, hadn't you?

CASTRO: Yes, I had had very good relations with him, and we maintained those relations as much as possible afterward, because we believed, in spite of the wrong we had been done on that occasion, that the maintenance of the best relations with the Soviet state and people was vital to our revolution. Khrushchev was still prime minister of the Soviet Union. On a personal level, he was always kind to all of us. I have no doubt that he was sympathetic toward the Cuban revolution. But he found himself in a great dilemma, facing factors related to peace and war, and those factors were what decided him. It was really a very grave responsibility that he had. In the end, it will be history that judges his decisions.

PLAYBOY: After the Bay of Pigs fiasco, do you really think the United States will support another invasion of Cuba?

CASTRO: The policy of the United States is modeled on interventionism and aggression. It is logical that we should always be very suspicious. On that account, we have to behave as if that could happen any day. We are also conscious, however, that it is not an easy thing for the United States to launch an attack against us. First, because it would have to employ large forces and cope with a long war in our country, to become entangled in a struggle that would never end. In the second place, because it would expose them to very serious international complications, and they must know very well the things that can happen as a result of an invasion of Cuba, for the Soviet Union has a very firm, very definite stand regarding Cuba. So the U.S. would have much more to lose than to win, and in the long run it would not be able in so doing to stop the revolutionary movement in other areas.

PLAYBOY: If that is so, why do you feel there is a danger of a U.S. invasion?

CASTRO: The United States also knows how risky the intervention is in Vietnam; it knows the disadvantages and the dangers to which it exposes itself in having to battle against an association of superior forces on the other side of the world. Nevertheless, against all logic, contrary to the simplest common sense and despite the advice of many of their allies, they have gone farther and farther down that one-way street that is the war in South Vietnam. When a government behaves like that, what security can anyone have that it will not make a similar error in some other part of the world—perhaps much closer to home?

PLAYBOY: Has there been any diminution of counterrevolutionary activities in Cuba since the Missile Crisis?

CASTRO: No, the CIA maintains its activities incessantly and with all possible resources. It works systematically with all the Cubans who are now in the United States, with the relatives and friends of the counter-revolutionaries who are there, trying constantly to organize webs of information, espionage and counterrevolution. That is unceasing and daily. Much of the news related to the activities of the CIA we do not make public. Many times we know when agents come. We are always capturing agents, launches, boats, radio-communication equipment. We simply don't give out the news, in order to keep them in a state of the greatest insecurity and confusion. They use many different means. For example, they use mother ships to introduce speedboats full of agents, then later come back to rescue them. But because of our improved organization, that tactic has become more and more uncertain. They are now using the method of infiltrating people. When they come to pick them up, they don't come straight from the outside, but place a well-camouflaged launch at a rendezvous along the coast with the fuel and all written instructions concerning its handling and the route to follow. Later, they tell the pepole where they have to go to find the launch. We have captured quite a number of these launches.

PLAYBOY: What do you do with the agents you capture?

CASTRO: The same thing we did with the prisoners captured at the Bay of Pigs.

PLAYBOY: How many political prisoners are you holding at the present time?

CASTRO: Although we usually do not give this kind of information, I am going to make an exception with you. I think there must be approximately 20,000. [According to *Time* (October 8, 1965), the number is closer to 50,000.—*Ed.*] This number comprises all those sentenced by revolutionary tribunals, including not only those sentenced on account of counter-revolutionary activities but also those sentenced for offenses against the people during Batista's regime, and many cases that have nothing to do with political activities, such as embezzlement, theft or assault, which because of their character were transferred to revolutionary tribunals. Unfortunately, we are going to have counterrevolutionary prisoners for many years to come.

PLAYBOY: You once stated that if the U.S. Government would agree to cease fostering counterrevolution in Cuba, you would consider freeing the majority, if not all, of your political prisoners. Has your position changed on this matter?

CASTRO: We made that proposal because we believe that the counter-revolutionary activity directed and encouraged by the United States is the fundamental cause of the existing tensions and, therefore, of the measures that we find ourselves obliged to take. I am certain that without the support of the United States, there would *be* no counterrevolution. If the counterrevolution ends, the necessity of keeping many of the counter-revolutionaries in prison will end, too. Thanks to our rehabilitation program, I have no doubt that many of these men will come to be revolutionaries themselves.

PLAYBOY: What have been the effects of the U.S. blockade on Cuban overseas trade?

CASTRO: The effect of the American blockade has been to require us to work harder and better.

PLAYBOY: Has it been effective?

CASTRO: It has been effective in favor of the revolution.

PLAYBOY: Aren't you now trading with France, Japan, Canada, England, Italy and other non-Communist countries, and even planning to expand this commerce?

CASTRO: Yes, we are—and the United States utilizes all the pressures it can, both against the governments of those countries and against the commercial companies that trade with us, to cut off this trade. [Not confirmable—*Ed.*] But what happens? Why do all the other countries trade with us? Because they understand that the policy of the U.S. is a policy of suicide. Because those countries, far from following the United States in not trading with the Socialist camp, are trading more and more with it, and are filling the vacuum the United States leaves with its restrictive policy on such trade.

PLAYBOY: But except for Red China, Albania, North Vietnam, North Korea and Cuba, the U.S. does trade with the Communist nations.

CASTRO: Those are fairly significant exceptions. The Socialist camp, including China, is made up of more than a billion human beings. It is a gigantic market. It is absurd that any country that has maturity and experience should abandon such an opportunity. By renouncing the fullest possibilities of selling to the vast markets in the Socialist camp, the U.S. is following a course contrary to its own economic interests. The United States doesn't want to trade with China, so Japan increases its trade with China; England increases its trade with China; France increases its trade with China. The United States doesn't want to trade with the Soviet Union; yet one of the reasons for the high level of the European economy, one of the major factors that has supported the redevelopment of the European economy, is the increasing trade of Western Europe with the Soviet Union. [The U.S. does trade nonstrategic goods with the Soviet Union, but the amount is minuscule. Late last year, however, President Johnson asked Congress to further reduce existing restrictions on trade with the U.S.S.R.—*Ed.*]

I wonder whether the United States considers doing with the rest of the world what it has done with Cuba every time a revolution takes place. If so, the time will come when it will have to break off trade relations with the largest part of the world, with two or three billion human beings. No less self-destructively, the United States engages in a species of international aid that makes it the victim of blackmail. In support of its repressive policy against liberation movements, it finds itself required to expend enormous sums. The beneficiaries of that aid, understanding the U.S. panic about revolutions, make the classic demand, "Your money or communism," and almost always get their pay-off—much of which goes to line the pockets of the blackmailers rather than to help their people.

The only thing that can resolve the problems of hunger and misery in the underdeveloped countries is revolution—revolution that really changes social structures, that wipes out social bonds, that puts an end to unnecessary costs and expenditures, to the squandering of resources; revolution that allows the people of underdeveloped nations to devote themselves to planned and peaceful work. A time will come when the United States will understand that only those countries in which a revolution has taken place are in a position to fulfill their international financial obligations.

PLAYBOY: Havana today looks to most visitors like a crumbling relic. Its streets, which have fallen into disrepair, are almost empty of traffic; its buildings are run-down; its public utilities are inefficient; its housing shortages are acute. If Cuba can't maintain its own capital city, how can it be expected to fulfill its international financial obligations?

CASTRO: A modern city has many expenses; to maintain Havana at the same level as before would be detrimental to what has to be done in the interior of the country. For that reason, Havana must necessarily suffer this process of disuse, of deterioration, until enough resources can be provided. Of course, everything that's essential will be taken care of in Havana: the public services—transportation, water, sewerage, streets, parks, hospitals, schools, etc. But construction of new buildings—like those lavish skyscrapers that were built before the revolution, to the detriment of the interior of the country—has been discontinued for the time being. Moreover, under the Urban Reform Law of 1960, all rents were reduced and many people are now paying no rent at all.

PLAYBOY: To what extent does the curriculum in Cuban schools include political indoctrination?

CASTRO: What you call political indoctrination would perhaps be more correctly called social education; after all, our children are being educated to live in a Communist society. From an early age, they must be discouraged from every egotistical feeling in the enjoyment of material things, such as the sense of individual property, and be encouraged toward the greatest possible common effort and the spirit of cooperation. Therefore, they must receive not only instruction of a scientific kind but also education for social life and a broad general culture.

PLAYBOY: Is this "culture" to which they are exposed selected from a political point of view?

CASTRO: Of course, some knowledge is of a universal kind, but other subjects that are taught may be influenced by a definite conception. For instance, history cannot be taught as a simple repetition of events that have occurred without any interrelationship, in an accidental way. We have a scientific conception of history and of the development of human society, and, of course, in some subjects there is and will be influence by our philosophy.

PLAYBOY: Is there an attempt to teach such subjects as art and literature, and their criticism, from the Marxist point of view?

CASTRO: We have very few qualified people as yet who could even try to give a Marxist interpretation of the problems of art. But as a revolutionary, it is my understanding that one of our fundamental concerns must be that all the manifestations of culture be placed at the service of man, developing in him all the most positive feelings. For me, art is not an end in itself. Man is its end; making man happier, making man better. I do not conceive of any manifestation of culture, of science, of art, as purposes in themselves. I think that the purpose of science and culture is man.

PLAYBOY: The words "happier" and "better" can be interpreted very broadly.

CASTRO: They *should* be interpreted in a broad sense. I don't think there has ever existed a society in which all the manifestations of culture have not been at the service of some cause or concept. Our duty is to see that the whole is at the service of the kind of man we wish to create. But does this mean that every work must have a political message in itself? No. That is not necessary.

PLAYBOY: Is there any attempt to exert control over the production of art in Cuba—of literature, for example?

CASTRO: No—but a book that we did not believe to be of some value wouldn't have a chance of being published.

PLAYBOY: In other words, an author who wrote a novel that contained counterrevolutionary sentiments couldn't possibly get it published in Cuba?

CASTRO: At present, no. The day will come when all the paper and printing resources will be available; that is, when such a book would not be published to the detriment of a textbook or of a book having universal value in world literature. One will then be able to argue whatever one wishes about any theme. I am a partisan of the widest possible discussion in the intellectual realm. Why? Because I believe in the free man, I believe in the well-educated man, I believe in the man who is able to think, in the man who acts always out of conviction, without fear of any kind. And I believe that ideas must be able to defend themselves. I am opposed to black lists of books, prohibited films and the like. For I believe in a people sufficiently cultivated and educated to be capable of making a correct judgment about anything without fear of coming into contact with ideas that could confound or deflect their fundamental beliefs. May all the men and women of our country be like this in the future. That is the kind of man we wish to shape. If we did not feel this way, we would be men with no faith in their own convictions, in their own philosophy.

PLAYBOY: Why isn't such an atmosphere possible at the present time?

CASTRO: It would be an illusion to think it was. First, on account of the economic problems involved, and second, because of the struggle in which we are engaged.

PLAYBOY: Is it also in the name of that "struggle" that the Cuban press writes so one-sidedly about the United States?

CASTRO: I'm not going to tell you that we don't do that. It's true, everything that we say about the United States refers essentially to the worst aspects, and it is very rare that things in any way favorable to the United States will be published here. We simply have a similar attitude to the attitude of your country toward Cuba. I mean that we always try to create the worst opinion of everything there is in the United States, as a response to what it has always done with us. The only difference is that we do not write falsehoods about the United States. I told you that we emphasize the worst things, that we omit things that could be viewed as positive, but we do not invent any lies.

PLAYBOY: Doesn't that amount to the same thing, in the largest sense?

CASTRO: That depends on what you mean by "lie." I agree that it is a distortion. A lie is simply the willful invention of facts that do not exist. There is a difference between a distortion and a lie, although unquestionably they have some effects of a similar kind. Now, I know this is not ideal. But it is the result of realities that have not been imposed by us. In a world of peace, in which genuine trust and respect prevailed among peoples, this wouldn't happen.

PLAYBOY: But if you persist in promoting these distortions, which encourage only hostile feelings in your citizens, how can you ever expect to have peace or trust between Cuba and the U.S.?

CASTRO: Again, we are not the ones responsible. It is the United States who cut all relations with Cuba.

PLAYBOY: Still, wouldn't you have more to gain by keeping your society open to knowledge of all kinds about the United States than by persisting in creating a distorted image of it? For example, in recent years, as you know better than your people, there has been an increasing effort on the part of our Government to aid the Negro in his fight for civil rights, and strong supportive legislation has been passed. Isn't this historic story one that should be covered by the Cuban press—in addition to its usual headlined accounts of Negro rioting in California and Ku Klux Klan violence in Alabama, which is the only kind of race story you ever publish here?

CASTRO: It is my understanding that news of civil rights legislation *has* been published here, although, naturally, we have a substantially different point of view about it than you do. We believe that the problem of discrimination has an economic basis appropriate to a class society in which man is exploited by man. But this is clearly a difficult, complex problem. We ourselves went through the experience of discrimination. Discrimination disappeared when class privileges disappeared, and it has not cost the revolution much effort to resolve that problem. I don't believe it could have been done in the United States. It would be a little absurd to speak at this moment of a revolution there. Perhaps there will *never* be a revolution in the United States, in the classic sense of the word, but rather evolutionary changes. I am sure, for example, that within 500 years North American society will bear no similarity to the present one. Probably by that time they won't have problems of discrimination.

PLAYBOY: But why not speak of these evolutionary changes that are taking place in the U.S.? Why not tell the Cuban people the whole story?

CASTRO: Because altogether there have not yet *been* any evolutionary changes in a positive sense in the United States. But rather, politically speaking, a true regression. From our general point of view, the policy of the United States—above all, its foreign policy—has veered more and more toward an ultrareactionary position.

PLAYBOY: There is a commonly held view in the U.S. that you are an absolute dictator, that not only intellectuals but the Cuban people have no voice in their government, and that there is no sign that this is going to change. Would you comment?

CASTRO: As far as the people having a voice in government is concerned, we are Marxists and look upon the state as an instrument of the ruling class to exercise power. In Cuba, the ruling class consists of the workers and peasants; that is, of the manual and intellectual workers, directed by a party that is composed of the best men from among them. We organize our party with the participation of all the workers in all the fields of labor, who express their opinions in a completely free way, in assemblies, proposing and supporting those they believe should be members of the party or opposing those they believe should not be. You also asked about power concentrated in one person. The question is: In leading the people, have I acted in a unilateral manner? Never! All the decisions that have been made, absolutely all of them, have been discussed among the principal leaders of the revolution. Never would I have felt satisfied with a single measure if it had been the result of a personal decision. Furthermore, I have learned from experience that one must never be absolutely certain that the decisions he makes or the ideas he cherishes are always correct. Often one can have a point of view that leaves out certain factors or considerations. And there is nothing more useful or positive or practical, when a decision is going to be made on an important issue, than hearing everybody else's opinions.

If we are going to speak about personal power, I might point out that in no other country in the world, not even under absolute monarchies, has there ever been such a high degree of power concentrated in one person as is concentrated in the Presidency of the United States. If he chose to, that officeholder whom you call President could even take the country into a thermonuclear war without having to consult the Congress. There is no case like it in history. He intervened in Vietnam on his own decision. He intervened in Santo Domingo on his own decision. Thus, that functionary you call President is the most complete expression of the dictatorship of a class that on occasion exercises itself by conceding truly absolute powers to one man. Why don't you North Americans think a little about *these* questions, instead of accepting as an irrefutable truth your own definition of democracy? Why don't you analyze the realities and the meaning of your catch phrases, instead of repeating them mechanically? We honestly consider our system infinitely more democratic than that of the United States, because it is the genuine expression of the will of the vast majority of the country, made up not of the rich but of the poor.

PLAYBOY: The American system of government expresses the will of the majority through a President and a Congress elected by rich and poor alike. How do Cuba's people express *their* will?

CASTRO: By struggling and fighting against oppression. They revealed it in the Sierra Maestra by defeating the well-equipped army of Batista. They revealed it on Girón Beach [the Bay of Pigs—*Ed.*] by destroying the mercenary invaders. They revealed it in the Escambray in wiping out the counterrevolutionary bands. They reveal it constantly, in every public demonstration that the revolution organizes with the multitudinous support of the masses. They have revealed it with their firm support of the revolutionary government in the face of America's economic blockade, and by the fact that there are hundreds of thousands of men ready to die in the defense of their revolution.

PLAYBOY: But if Cuba is not a dictatorship, in what way are your people able to effectively influence the leadership?

CASTRO: There is a mutual influence of the people over the leaders and of the leaders over the people. The first and most important thing is to have genuine affection and respect for the people. The people can feel that, and it wins them over. Sometimes the leaders have to take responsibilities on their own; sometimes they have to walk at the head of the people. The important thing is the identification of the leaders with the aspirations and the emotions of the people. There are many ways of establishing this identification. The best way of all is to maintain the most immediate contact possible with the masses.

PLAYBOY: The hero worship they feel for you, in the opinion of many outsiders who have seen the fervid reception you receive at huge public rallies, has a mystical, almost religious intensity about it. Do you feel that's true?

CASTRO: To some extent, perhaps principally among the farmers; but in personal contact they do not treat me like that. I visit many places; I talk a great deal with the farmers; I go to their homes, and they treat me with great naturalness in a very friendly and informal way—which means that this mystical business really doesn't exist in person. Far from any kind of reverence, there is a certain feeling of familiarity.

PLAYBOY: Is this familiarity enhanced by the thousands of idealized, inspirational portraits and photographs of you posted prominently in nearly every Cuban home and public building?

CASTRO: I don't know whether you are aware that one of the first laws passed by the revolutionary government, following a proposal of mine, was an edict against erecting statues to any living leader or putting his photograph in government offices. That same law prohibited giving the name of any living leader to any street, to any park, to any town in Cuba. I believe that nowhere else, under circumstances such as ours, has a similar resolution been passed, and it was one of the first laws approved by the revolution.

Now you *will* see, in many homes and schools and public places, a small photograph in a little frame on the bookshelf or a corner of the desk. But where do most of these photographs come from? From magazines, from newspapers, from posters connected with some public meeting. Some people have even done a business in photographs, printing the ones they like and selling them in the street. But all of this has taken place—and anybody can verify it—without any official initiative whatever. The fact that there are photographs in homes has been a completely voluntary and spontaneous thing among the people. We could have selected some photographs and printed hundreds of thousands of them and distributed them systematically, but this has not been done, because I am not interested in it.

And permit me to say, finally, that I don't experience any personal satisfaction whatsoever when I read some of the flattering qualities that are attributed to me in the press. I have never spent a single second of pleasure over such things. I can tell you in all sincerity that they have no importance for me. And I think this is a positive thing. Because, as a general rule, power corrupts men. It makes them egotistical; it makes them selfish. Fortunately, this has never happened to me, and I don't think it will. Very honestly, I can say that nothing satisfies me more than seeing that every day things depend less and less on me, and more and more upon a collective spirit grounded in institutions. What importance can a man's accomplishments have if they are going to last only as long as *he* lasts? If we really love the revolution, if we hope that the revolution will always continue upon its road, if we wish for our people the greatest happiness in the future, what value would all our good intentions have if we didn't take steps to ensure that they would not depend wholly on the will of only one man, if we didn't take steps to make it depend on the collective will of the nation?

I'm not trying, out of modesty, to diminish the role it has been my fortune to play. But I sincerely believe that the merits of the individual are always few, because there are always external factors that play a much more important role than his own character in determining what he does. It would be hypocrisy for me to tell you that I don't have a high opinion of myself. Most men do. But I can say with all sincerity that I am also very self-critical. The masses bestow upon certain men a heroic stature—perhaps out of necessity, perhaps because it cannot happen in any other way. There is a kind of mechanism in the human mind that tends to create symbols in which it concentrates its sentiments. By transforming men into symbols, the people manifest a greater gratitude; they attribute to the individual what is not deserved by him alone but by the many. Often I think of the hundreds, even thousands of men who are working anonymously, making possible all those things for which the people are grateful. Recognition is not divided in an equitable way. It would be an error for any man—and I say this sincerely—to be unconscious of this, to believe himself truly deserving of all that recognition and affection. One must have a proper appreciation of the things he has accomplished, but he should never consider himself deserving of the recognition that belongs to the many.

PLAYBOY: Under the new constitution that you have said will be promulgated soon, will the people have any electoral voice in determining who the collective leadership will be?

CASTRO: We will have a system of permanent participation by the mass of workers in the formation of the party, in the election of its members and in the replacement of those members of the party who do not deserve the trust of the masses. The party will be something like a combined parliament of the workers and interpreter of their will.

PLAYBOY: And will that parliament in turn choose the leadership of the party?

CASTRO: It will be chosen by assemblies or delegates who in turn are elected by the mass membership of the party.

PLAYBOY: Will there be more than one slate of candidates for whom the people may vote?

CASTRO: It can happen that in the party congress there would be more than one candidate. In your country, people are accustomed to thinking there is only one kind of democracy possible. I would say that there are two forms of democracy: bourgeois democracy and workers' democracy. We think that our democracy is much more functional than yours, because it is the constant expression of the true majority will. We think that the participation of our masses in political, economic and social problems will become infinitely greater than that which the North American citizen has in his bourgeois democracy, where he is reduced to voting once every four years for one of the candidates that only two parties designate.

We have to create our own forms of socialist democracy. One of the postulates of Marxism is the ultimate disappearance of the state as a coercive institution, once the Communist society is established. To all those who are suspicious of the state, who fear it as the coercive instrument it has been throughout history, we offer this ultimate prospect of a stateless society. I believe that we must continue working toward the fulfillment of that Marxist ideal.

PLAYBOY: What role do you yourself expect to play in the government of the future, once the party is fully established and the constitution is in effect?

CASTRO: I think that for a few more years I will figure as the leader of the party. If I were to say that I didn't want that, people would think I was crazy. But you want me to speak sincerely? I will try to make it the least amount of time possible. I am attracted to many other things that are not official activities. I believe that all of us ought to retire relatively young. I don't propose this as a duty, but as something more—a right.

PLAYBOY: Can you really picture yourself as a retired "elder statesman"?

CASTRO: It is more difficult for me to imagine myself as an old man than as a retired statesman, because of the hardship it will be for me not to be able to climb mountains, to swim, to go spear-fishing and to engage in all the other pastimes that I enjoy. But there is one thing to which I am very much attracted that old age will not deter me from: studying, experimenting and working in agriculture. When I retire, I will be able to devote all my working time to that. So I don't think I will be bored. But perhaps I will fall into the habit that comes to all of us, of thinking that the younger generation is bungling everything. That is a mania characteristic of all old people—but I'm going to try to remain alert against it.

JOHN WAYNE

May 1971

Interviewer: Richard Warren Lewis

After several years of interviews that emphasized the liberal, or leftist, point of view (such figures as John Kenneth Galbraith, William Sloane Coffin, Ralph Nader, Ramsey Clark, and William Kunstler, not reprinted here), the interview with John Wayne in the spring of 1971 must have come as a surprise—and in some cases a relief—to PLAYBOY readers. Although people knew vaguely that the Duke was a strongly conservative man, this interview drove home the point colorfully.

Wayne speaks here, after the tumult of the late Sixties, as an unreconstructed hawk, an unashamed anti-Communist, a movie cowboy who thought the Indians were "selfish" to hold on to their land in the old days. Most startling is his assertion of white supremacy, which came as news to young men and women who were willing to overlook his strictly political views. But it may have been movie buffs who were most shattered—by his assertion here that *High Noon* was the most un-American movie of all time.

One thing that the Duke was not conservative about was PLAYBOY. Because of his trips to Vietnam, when he found the magazine to be the most widely read publication among servicemen, he welcomed the opportunity to talk with interviewer Richard Warren Lewis. Asked in 1977 by a student at Northwestern's Medill School of Journalism what he thought of this interview, Wayne, then in poor health, said the interview was the most thorough and accurate ever done with him, but that the magazine had not been as explicit then.

For more than 41 years, the barrel-chested physique and laconic derring-do of John Wayne have been prototypical of gung-ho virility, Hollywood style. In more than 200 films Wayne has charged the beaches of Iowa Jima, beaten back the Indians at Fort Apache and bloodied his fists in the name of frontier justice so often—and with nary a defeat—that he has come to occupy a unique niche in American folklore. The older generation still remembers him as Singing Sandy, one of the screen's first crooning cowpokes; the McLuhan generation has grown up with him on "The Late Show." With Cooper and Gable and Tracy gone, the last of the legendary stars survives and flourishes as never before.

His milieu is still the action Western, in which Wayne's simplistic plotlines and easily discernible good and bad guys attest to a romantic way of life long gone from the American scene—if indeed it ever really existed. Even his screen name—changed from Marion Michael Morrison—conveys the man's plain, rugged cinematic personality. Fittingly, he was the first of the Western movie heroes to poke a villain in the jaw. Wearing the symbolic white Stetson—which never seemed to fall off, even in the wildest combat—he made scores of three-and-a-half-day formula oaters such as "Pals of the Saddle" in the Thirties before being tapped by director John Ford to star in "Stagecoach"—the 1939 classic that paved the way for his subsequent success in such milestone Westerns as "Red River," the ultimate epic of the cattle drive, and "The Alamo," a patriotic paean financed by Wayne with $1,500,000 of his own money.

By 1969, having made the list of Top Ten box-office attractions for 19 consecutive years, Wayne had grossed more than $400,000,000 for his studios—more than any other star in motion-picture history. But because of his uncompromising squareness—and his archconservative politics— he was still largely a profit without honor in Hollywood. That oversight was belatedly reflected when his peers voted the tearful star a 1970 Oscar for his portrayal of Rooster Cogburn, the tobacco-chewing, hard-drinking, straight-shooting, patch-eyed marshal in "True Grit"—a possibly unwitting exercise in self-parody that good-naturedly spoofed dozens of his past characterizations.

Long active in Republican politics, Wayne has vigorously campaigned and helped raise funds for Nixon, Ronald Reagan, George Murphy, Barry Goldwater and Los Angeles' maverick Democratic mayor Sam Yorty, Before the 1968 campaign, a right-wing Texas billionaire had urged Wayne to serve as Vice-Presidential running mate to George Wallace, an overture he rejected. Not least among the Texan's reasons for wanting to draft Wayne was the actor's obdurately hawkish support of the Indochina war—as glorified in his production of "The Green Berets," which had the dubious distinction of being probably the only pro-war movie made in Hollywood during the Sixties.

Last year Wayne was named one of the nation's most admired entertainers in a Gallup Poll. Assigned by PLAYBOY *shortly afterward to interview the superstar, Contributing Editor Richard Warren Lewis journeyed to Wayne's sprawling (11-room, seven-bath) $175,000 bayfront residence on the Gold Coast of Newport Beach, California, where he lives with his third Latin wife—Peruvian-born Pilar Pallete—and three of his seven children. Of his subject, Lewis writes:*

"Wayne greeted me on a manicured lawn against a backdrop of sailboats, motor cruisers and yachts plying Newport harbor. Wearing a realistic toupee, Wayne at first appeared considerably younger than he is; only the liver spots on both hands and the lines in his jut-jawed face told of his 63 years. But at six feet, four and 244 pounds, it still almost seems as if he could *have single-handedly mopped up all those bad guys from the Panhandle to Guadalcanal. His sky-blue eyes, though somewhat rheumy from the previous night's late hours, reinforced the image.*

" 'Christ, we better get going,' he said shortly before one o'clock. 'They're holding lunch for us.' He led the way past a den and trophy room stacked with such memorabilia as photos of his 18 grandchildren and the largest collection of Hopi Indian kachina *dolls west of Barry Goldwater. Outside the house, past jacaranda and palm trees and a kidney-shaped swimming pool, we reached a seven-foot-high concrete wall at the entryway and boarded Wayne's dark-green Bonneville station wagon, a production model with only two modifications—a sun roof raised six inches to accommodate the driver's ten-gallon hat, and two telephone channels at the console beside him.*

"At Newport harbor, we boarded Wayne's awesome Wild Goose II, a converted U.S. Navy mine sweeper that saw service during the last six months of World War Two and has been refitted as a pleasure cruiser. After a quick tour of the 136-foot vessel—which included a look at the twin 500-horsepower engines, clattering teletype machines (A.P., U.P.I., Reuter's, Tass) on the bridge disgorging wire dispatches, and the lavishly appointed bedroom and dressing suites—we were seated at a polished-walnut table in the main saloon.

"Over a high-protein diet lunch of char-broiled steak, lettuce and cottage cheese, Wayne reminisced about the early days of Hollywood, when he was making two-reelers for $500 each. Later that afternoon, he produced a bottle of his favorite tequila. One of the eight crew members anointed our glasses with a dash of fresh lemon juice, coarse salt and heaping ice shards that, Wayne said, had been chopped from a 1000-year-old glacier on a recent Wild Goose visit to Alaska. Sustained by these potent drinks, our conversation—ranging from Wayne's early days in film making to the

current state of the industry—continued until dusk, and resumed a week later in the offices of Wayne's Batjac Productions, on the grounds of Paramount Pictures—one of the last of Hollywood's rapidly dwindling contingent of major studios."

PLAYBOY: How do you feel about the state of the motion-picture business today?

WAYNE: I'm glad I won't be around much longer to see what they do with it. The men who control the big studios today are stock manipulators and bankers. They know nothing about our business. They're in it for the buck. The only thing they can do is say, "Jeez, that picture with what's-her-name running around the park naked made money, so let's make another one. If that's what they want, let's give it to them." Some of these guys remind me of high-class whores. Look at 20th Century-Fox, where they're making movies like *Myra Breckinridge*. Why doesn't that son of a bitch Darryl Zanuck get himself a striped silk shirt and learn how to play the piano? Then he could work in any room in the house. As much as I couldn't stand some of the old-time moguls—especially Harry Cohn—these men took an interest in the future of their business. They had integrity. There was a stretch when they realized that they'd made a hero out of the goddamn gangster heavy in crime movies, that they were doing a discredit to our country. So the moguls voluntarily took it upon themselves to stop making gangster pictures. No censorship from the outside. They were responsible to the public. But today's executives don't give a damn. In their efforts to grab the box office that these sex pictures are attracting, they're producing garbage. They're taking advantage of the fact that nobody wants to be called a bluenose. But they're going to reach the point where the American people will say, "The hell with this!" And once they do, we'll have censorship in every state, in every city, and there'll be no way you can make even a worthwhile picture for adults and have it acceptable for national release.

PLAYBOY: Won't the present rating system prevent that from happening?

WAYNE: No. Every time they rate a picture, they let a little more go. Ratings are ridiculous to begin with. There was no need for rated pictures when the major studios were in control. Movies were once made for the whole family. Now, with the kind of junk the studios are cranking out—and the jacked-up prices they're charging for the privilege of seeing it—the average family is staying home and watching television. I'm quite sure that within two or three years, Americans will be completely fed up with these perverted films.

PLAYBOY: What kind of films do you consider perverted?

WAYNE: Oh, *Easy Rider, Midnight Cowboy*—that kind of thing. Wouldn't you say that the wonderful love of those two men in *Midnight Cowboy*, a story about two fags, qualifies? But don't get me wrong. As far as a man and a woman is concerned, I'm awfully happy there's a thing called sex. It's an extra something God gave us. I see no reason why it shouldn't be in pictures. Healthy, lusty sex is wonderful.

PLAYBOY: How graphically do you think it should be depicted on the screen?

WAYNE: When you get hairy, sweaty bodies in the foreground, it becomes distasteful, unless you use a pretty heavy gauze. I can remember seeing pictures that Ernst Lubitsch made in the Thirties that were beautifully risqué—and you'd certainly send your children to see them. They were done with *intimation.* They got over everything these other pictures do without showing the hair and the sweat. When you think of the wonderful picture fare we've had through the years and realize we've come to this shit, it's disgusting. If they want to continue making those pictures, fine. But my career will have ended. I've already reached a pretty good height right now in a business that I feel is going to fade out from its own vulgarity.

PLAYBOY: Don't gory films like *The Wild Bunch* also contribute to that vulgarity?

WAYNE: Certainly. To me, *The Wild Bunch* was distasteful. It would have been a good picture without the gore. Pictures go too far when they use that kind of realism, when they have shots of blood spurting out and teeth flying, and when they throw liver out to make it look like people's insides. *The Wild Bunch* was one of the first to go that far in realism, and the curious went to see it. That may make the bankers and the stock promoters think this is a necessary ingredient for successful motion pictures. They seem to forget the one basic principle of our business—illusion. We're in the business of magic. I don't think it hurts a child to see anything that has the *illusion* of violence in it. All our fairy tales have some kind of violence— the good knight riding to kill the dragon, etc. Why do we have to show the knight spreading the serpent's guts all over the candy mountain?

PLAYBOY: Proponents of screen realism say that a public inured to bloody war-news footage on television isn't going to accept the mere illusion of violence in movies.

WAYNE: Perhaps we *have* run out of imagination on how to effect illusion because of the satiating realism of a real war on television. But haven't we got *enough* of that in real life? Why can't the same point be made just as effectively in a drama without all the gore? The violence in my pictures, for example, is lusty and a little bit humorous, because I believe humor nullifies violence. Like in one picture, directed by Henry Hathaway, this heavy was sticking a guy's head in a barrel of water. I'm watching this and I don't like it one bit, so I pick up this pick handle and I yell, "Hey!" and cock him across the head. Down he went—with no spurting blood. Well, that got a hell of a laugh because of the way I did it. That's my kind of violence.

PLAYBOY: Audiences may like your kind of violence on the screen, but they'd never heard profanity in a John Wayne movie until *True Grit*. Why did you finally decide to use such earthy language in a film?

WAYNE: In my other pictures, we've had an explosion or something go off when a bad word was said. This time we didn't. It's profanity, all right, but I doubt if there's anybody in the United States who hasn't heard the expression son of a bitch or bastard. We felt it was acceptable in this instance. At the emotional high point in that particular picture, I felt it was OK to use it. It would have been pretty hard to say "you illegitimate sons of so-and-so!"

PLAYBOY: In the past, you've often said that if the critics liked one of your films, you must be doing something wrong. But *True Grit* was almost unanimously praised by the critics. Were you doing something wrong? Or were they right for a change?

WAYNE: Well, I knew that *True Grit* was going to go—even with the critics. Once in a while, you come onto a story that has such great humor. The author caught the flavor of Mark Twain, to my way of thinking.

PLAYBOY: The reviewers thought you set out to poke fun at your own image in *True Grit*.

WAYNE: It wasn't really a parody. Rooster Cogburn's attitude toward life was maybe a little different, but he was basically the same character I've always played.

PLAYBOY: Do you think *True Grit* is the best film you've ever made?

WAYNE: No, I don't. Two classic Westerns were better—*Stagecoach* and *Red River*—and a third, *The Searchers*, which I thought deserved more praise than it got, and *The Quiet Man* was certainly one of the best. Also the one that all the college cinematography students run all the time—*The Long Voyage Home*.

PLAYBOY: Which was the worst?

WAYNE: Well, there's about 50 of them that are tied. I can't even remember the names of some of the leading ladies in those first ones, let alone the names of the pictures.

PLAYBOY: At what point in your career were you nicknamed Duke?

WAYNE: That goes back to my childhood. I was called Duke after a dog— a very good Airedale out of the Baldwin Kennels. Republic Pictures gave me a screen credit on one of the early pictures and called me Michael Burn. On another one, they called me Duke Morrison. Then they decided Duke Morrison didn't have enough prestige. My real name, Marion Michael Morrison, didn't sound American enough for them. So they came up with John Wayne. I didn't have any say in it, but I think it's a great name. It's short and strong and to the point. It took me a long time to get used to it, though. I still don't recognize it when somebody calls me John.

PLAYBOY: After giving you a new name, did the studio decide on any particular screen image for you?

WAYNE: They made me a singing cowboy. The fact that I couldn't sing—or play the guitar—became terribly embarrassing to me, especially on personal appearances. Every time I made a public appearance, the kids insisted that I sing *The Desert Song* or something. But I couldn't take along the fella who played the guitar out on one side of the camera and the fella who sang on the other side of the camera. So finally I went to the head of the studio and said, "Screw this, I can't handle it." And I quit doing those kind of pictures. They went out and brought the best hillbilly recording artist in the country to Hollywood to take my place. For the first couple of pictures, they had a hard time selling him, but he finally caught on. His name was Gene Autry. It was 1939 before I made *Stagecoach*—the picture that really made me a star.

PLAYBOY: Like *Stagecoach*, most of the 204 pictures you've made—including your latest, *Rio Lobo*—have been Westerns. Don't the plots all start to seem the same?

WAYNE: *Rio Lobo* certainly wasn't any different from most of my Westerns. Nor was *Chisum*, the one before that. But there still seems to be a very hearty public appetite for this kind of film—what some writers call a typical John Wayne Western. That's a label they use disparagingly.

PLAYBOY: Does that bother you?

WAYNE: Nope. If I depended on the critics' judgment and recognition, I'd never have gone into the motion-picture business.

PLAYBOY: Did last year's Academy Award for *True Grit* mean a lot to you?

WAYNE: Sure it did—even if it took the industry 40 years to get around to it. But I think both of my two previous Oscar nominations—for *She Wore a Yellow Ribbon* and *Sands of Iwo Jima*—were worthy of the honor. I know the Marines and all the American Armed Forces were quite proud of my portrayal of Stryker, the Marine sergeant in *Iwo*. At an American Legion convention in Florida, General MacArthur told me, "You represent the American Serviceman better than the American Serviceman himself." And, at 42, in *She Wore a Yellow Ribbon*, I played the same character that I played in *True Grit* at 62. But I really didn't need an Oscar. I'm a box-office champion with a record they're going to have to run to catch. And they won't.

PLAYBOY: A number of critics claim that your record rests on your appeal to adolescents. Do you think that's true?

WAYNE: Let's say I hope that I appeal to the more carefree times in a person's life rather than to his reasoning adulthood. I'd just like to be an image that reminds someone of joy rather than of the problems of the world.

PLAYBOY: Do you think young people still feel strongly about you?

WAYNE: Luckily, so far, it seems they kind of consider me an older friend, somebody believable and down-to-earth. I've avoided being mean or petty, but I've never avoided being rough or tough. I've only played one cautious part in my life, in *Allegheny Uprising*. My parts have ranged from that rather dull character to Ralls in *Wake of the Red Witch*, who was a nice enough fella sober, but bestial when he was drunk, and certainly a rebel. I was also a rebel in *Reap the Wild Wind* with De Mille. I've played many parts in which I've rebelled against something in society. I was never much of a joiner. Kids do join things, but they also like to consider themselves individuals capable of thinking for themselves. So do I.

PLAYBOY: And you think liberals aren't?

WAYNE: Well, the liberals seem to be quite willing to have Communists teach their kids in school. The Communists realized that they couldn't start a workers' revolution in the United States, since the workers were too affluent and too progressive. So the Commies decided on the next-best thing, and that's to start on the schools, start on the kids. And they've managed to do it. They're already in colleges; now they're getting into high schools. I wouldn't mind if they taught my children the basic philosophy of communism, in theory and how it works in actuality. But I don't want somebody like Angela Davis inculcating an enemy doctrine in my kids' minds.

PLAYBOY: Angela Davis claims that those who would revoke her teaching credentials on ideological grounds are actually discriminating against her because she's black. Do you think there's any truth to that?

WAYNE: With a lot of blacks, there's quite a bit of resentment along with their dissent, and possibly rightfully so. But we can't all of a sudden get down on our knees and turn everything over to the leadership of the blacks. I believe in white supremacy until the blacks are educated to a point of responsibility. I don't believe in giving authority and positions of leadership and judgment to irresponsible people.

PLAYBOY: Are you equipped to judge which blacks are irresponsible and which of their leaders inexperienced?

WAYNE: It's not my judgment. The academic community has developed certain tests that determine whether the blacks are sufficiently equipped scholastically. But some blacks have tried to force the issue and enter college when they haven't passed the tests and don't have the requisite background.

PLAYBOY: How do they get that background?

WAYNE: By going to school. I don't know why people insist that blacks have been forbidden their right to go to school. They were allowed in public schools wherever I've been. Even if they don't have the proper credentials for college, there are courses to help them become eligible. But if they aren't academically ready for that step, I don't think they should be allowed in. Otherwise, the academic society is brought down to the lowest common denominator.

PLAYBOY: But isn't it true that we're never likely to rectify the inequities in our educational system until some sort of remedial education is given to disadvantaged minority groups?

WAYNE: What good would it do to register anybody in a class of higher algebra or calculus if they haven't learned to count? There has to be a standard. I don't feel guilty about the fact that five or ten generations ago these people were slaves. Now, I'm not condoning slavery. It's just a fact of life, like the kid who gets infantile paralysis and has to wear braces so he can't play football with the rest of us. I will say this, though: I think any black who can compete with a white today can get a better break than a white man. I wish they'd tell me where in the world they have it better than right here in America.

PLAYBOY: Many militant blacks would argue that they have it better almost *anywhere* else. Even in Hollywood, they feel that the color barrier is still up for many kinds of jobs. Do you limit the number of blacks you use in your pictures?

WAYNE: Oh, Christ no. I've directed two pictures and I gave the blacks their proper position. I had a black slave in *The Alamo,* and I had a correct number of blacks in *The Green Berets.* If it's supposed to be a black character, naturally I use a black actor. But I don't go so far as hunting for positions for them. I think the Hollywood studios are carrying their tokenism a little too far. There's no doubt that ten percent of the population is black, or colored, or whatever they want to call themselves; they certainly aren't Caucasian. Anyway, I suppose there should be the same percentage of the colored race in films as in society. But it can't always be that way. There isn't necessarily going to be ten percent of the grips or sound men who are black, because more than likely, ten percent haven't trained themselves for that type of work.

PLAYBOY: Can blacks be integrated into the film industry if they are denied training and education?

WAYNE: It's just as hard for a white man to get a card in the Hollywood craft unions.

PLAYBOY: That's hardly the point, but let's change the subject. For years American Indians have played an important—if subordinate—role in your Westerns. Do you feel any empathy with them?

WAYNE: I don't feel we did wrong in taking this great country away from them, if that's what you're asking. Our so-called stealing of this country from them was just a matter of survival. There were great numbers of people who needed new land, and the Indians were selfishly trying to keep it for themselves.

PLAYBOY: Weren't the Indians—by virtue of prior possession—the rightful owners of the land?

WAYNE: Look, I'm sure there have been inequalities. If those inequalities are presently affecting any of the Indians now alive, they have a right to a court hearing. But what happened 100 years ago in our country can't be blamed on us today.

PLAYBOY: Indians today are still being dehumanized on reservations.

WAYNE: I'm quite sure that the concept of a Government-run reservation would have an ill effect on anyone. But that seems to be what the socialists are working for now—to have *everyone* cared for from cradle to grave.

PLAYBOY: Indians on reservations are more neglected than cared for. Even if you accept the principle of expropriation, don't you think a more humane solution to the Indian problem could have been devised?

WAYNE: This may come as a surprise to you, but I wasn't alive when reservations were created—even if I *do* look that old. I have no idea what the best method of dealing with the Indians in the 1800s would have been. Our forefathers evidently thought they were doing the right thing.

PLAYBOY: Do you think the Indians encamped on Alcatraz have a right to that land?

WAYNE: Well, I don't know of anybody else who wants it. The fellas who were taken off it sure don't want to go back there, including the guards. So as far as I'm concerned, I think we ought to make a deal with the Indians. They should pay as much for Alcatraz as we paid them for Manhattan. I hope they haven't been careless with their wampum.

PLAYBOY: How do you feel about the Government grant for a university and cultural center that these Indians have demanded as "reparations"?

WAYNE: What happened between their forefathers and our forefathers is so far back—right, wrong or indifferent—that I don't see why we owe them anything. I don't know why the Government should give them something that it wouldn't give me.

PLAYBOY: Do you think they've had the same advantages and opportunities that you've had?

WAYNE: I'm not gonna give you one of those I-was-a-poor-boy-and-I-pulled-myself-up-by-my-bootstraps stories, but I've gone without a meal or two in my life, and I still don't expect the Government to turn over any of its territory to me. Hard times aren't something I can blame my fellow citizens for. Years ago, I didn't have all the opportunities, either. But you can't whine and bellyache 'cause somebody else got a good break and you didn't, like these Indians are. We'll *all* be on a reservation soon if the socialists keep subsidizing groups like them with our tax money.

PLAYBOY: In your distaste for socialism, aren't you overlooking the fact that many worthwhile and necessary Government services—such as Social Security and Medicare—derived from essentially socialistic programs evolved during the Thirties?

WAYNE: I know all about that. In the late Twenties, when I was a sophomore at USC, I was a socialist myself—but not when I left. The average college kid idealistically wishes everybody could have ice cream and cake for every meal. But as he gets older and gives more thought to his and his fellow man's responsibilities, he finds that it can't work out that way—that some people just won't carry their load.

PLAYBOY: What about welfare recipients?

WAYNE: I believe in welfare—a welfare *work* program. I don't think a fella should be able to sit on his backside and receive welfare. I'd like to know why well-educated idiots keep apologizing for lazy and complaining people who think the world owes them a living. I'd like to know why they make excuses for cowards who spit in the faces of the police and then run behind the judicial sob sisters. I can't understand these people who carry placards to save the life of some criminal, yet have no thought for the innocent victim.

PLAYBOY: Who are "these people" you're talking about?

WAYNE: Entertainers like Steve Allen and his cronies who went up to Northern California and held placards to save the life of that guy Caryl Chessman. I just don't understand these things. I can't understand why our national leadership isn't willing to take the responsibility of leadership instead of checking polls and listening to the few that scream. Why are we allowing ourselves to become a mobocracy instead of a democracy? When you allow unlawful acts to go unpunished, you're moving toward a government of men rather than a government of law; you're moving toward anarchy. And that's exactly what we're doing. We allow dirty loudmouths to publicly call policemen pigs; we let a fella like William Kunstler make a speech to the Black Panthers saying that the ghetto is theirs, and that if police come into it, they have a right to shoot them. Why is that dirty, no-good son of a bitch allowed to practice law?

PLAYBOY: Why do you think many young people—black and white—support the Panthers?

WAYNE: They're standing up for what they *feel* is right, not for what they *think* is right—'cause they don't think. As a kid, the Panther ideas probably would have intrigued me. When I was a little kid, you could be adventurous like that without hurting anybody. There were periods when you could blow the valve and let off some steam. Like Halloween. You'd talk about it for three months ahead of time, and then that night you'd go out and stick the hose in the lawn, turn it on and start singing *Old Black Joe* or something. And when people came out from their Halloween party, you'd lift the hose and wet them down. And while you were running, the other kids would be stealing the ice cream from the party. All kinds of rebellious actions like that were accepted for that one day. Then you could talk about it for three months afterward. That took care of about six months of the year. There was another day called the Fourth of July, when you could go out and shoot firecrackers and burn down two or three buildings. So there were two days a year. Now those days are gone. You can't have firecrackers, you can't have explosives, you can't have this—don't do this, don't do that. Don't . . . don't . . . don't. A continual *don't* until the kids are ready to do almost anything rebellious. The Government makes the rules, so now the running of our Government is the thing they're rebelling against. For a lot of those kids, that's just being adventurous. They're not deliberately setting out to undermine the foundations of our great country.

PLAYBOY: Is that what you think they're doing?

WAYNE: They're doing their level worst—without knowing it. How 'bout all the kids that were at the Chicago Democratic Convention? They were conned into doing hysterical things by a bunch of activists.

PLAYBOY: What sort of activists?

WAYNE: A lot of Communist-activated people. I know communism's a horrible word to some people. They laugh and say, "He'll be finding them under his bed tomorrow." But perhaps that's because their kid hasn't been inculcated yet. Dr. Herbert Marcuse, the political philosopher at the University of California at San Diego, who is quite obviously a Marxist, put it very succinctly when he said, "We will use the anarchists."

PLAYBOY: Why do you think leftist ideologues such as Marcuse have become heroes on so many of the nation's campuses?

WAYNE: Marcuse has become a hero only for an articulate clique. The men that give me faith in my country are fellas like Spiro Agnew, not the Marcuses. They've attempted in every way to humiliate Agnew. They've tried the old Rooseveltian thing of trying to laugh him out of political value to his party. Every comedian's taken a crack at him. But I bet if you took a poll today, he'd probably be one of the most popular men in the United States. Nobody likes Spiro Agnew but the people. Yet he and other responsible Government leaders are booed and pelted when they speak on college campuses.

PLAYBOY: Beyond the anti-Administration demonstrations on campuses, do you think there's any justification for such tactics as student occupation of college administrative offices?

WAYNE: One or two percent of the kids is involved in things like that. But they get away with it because ten percent of the teaching community is behind them. I see on TV how, when the police are trying to keep the kids in line, like up at the University of California at Berkeley, all of a sudden there's a bunch of martyr-professors trying to egg the police into violent action.

PLAYBOY: If you were faced with such a confrontation, how would you handle it?

WAYNE: Well, when I went to USC, if anybody had gone into the president's office and shit in his wastepaper basket and used the dirt to write vulgar words on the wall, not only the football team but the average kid on campus would have gone to work on the guy. There doesn't seem to be respect for authority anymore; these student dissenters act like children who have to have their own way on everything. They're immature and living in a little world all their own. Just like hippie dropouts, they're afraid to face the real competitive world.

PLAYBOY: What makes you, at the age of 63, feel qualified to comment on the fears and motivations of the younger generation?

WAYNE: I've experienced a lot of the same things that kids today are going through, and I think many of them admire me because I haven't been afraid to say that I drink a little whiskey, that I've done a lot of things wrong in my life, that I'm as imperfect as they all are. Christ, I don't claim to have the answers, but I feel compelled to bring up the fact that under the guise of doing good, these kids are causing a hell of a lot of irreparable damage, and they're starting something they're not gonna be able to finish. Every bit of rampant anarchy has provoked a little more from somebody else. And when they start shooting policemen, the time has come to start knocking them off, as far as I'm concerned.

PLAYBOY: What do you mean by "knocking them off"?

WAYNE: I'd throw 'em in the can if I could. But if they try to kill you, I'd sure as hell shoot back. I think we should break up those organizations or make 'em illegal. The American public is getting sick and tired of what these young people are doing. But it's really partly the public's own fault for allowing the permissiveness that's been going on for the past 15 or 20 years. By permissiveness, I mean simply following Dr. Spock's system of raising children. But that kind of permissiveness isn't unique to young people. Our entire society has promoted an "anything goes" attitude in every area of life and in every American institution. Look at the completely irresponsible editorship of our country's newspapers. By looking for provocative things to put on their front pages, they're encouraging these kids to act the way they're acting. I wonder even more about the responsibility of the press when I read about events like the so-called My Lai massacre in Vietnam. The press and the communications system jumped way ahead of the trials. At the time, they made accusations that I doubted they could back up; frankly, I hoped they couldn't. Well, it turns out there may have been something to it. But I could show you pictures of what the North Vietnamese and the Viet Cong are doing to our people over there. I was at a place called Dak Song, where the children were all burned to death by the V.C., and that's not an unusual thing. But for some reason, our newspapers have never printed pictures or stories about it. With all the terrible things that are being done throughout the world, it has to be one little incident in the United States Army—and the use of the word massacre—that causes the uproar.

PLAYBOY: Don't you deplore what happened at My Lai?

WAYNE: Not only do I deplore it, but so does the Army—which conducted an extensive investigation and charged everyone connected with the alleged crime.

PLAYBOY: Does the fact that the Viet Cong have systematically engaged in atrocities excuse our forces for resorting to the same thing?

WAYNE: No, absolutely not. But if your men go to a supposedly peaceful village and the occupants start shooting at them, they're going to have to shoot back to defend their own lives.

PLAYBOY: Do you think there's a credibility gap between the way the war has been reported and the way it's actually being fought—on both sides?

WAYNE: It's obvious to me, because I've been there. And you'll find that the young veterans who come back from Vietnam have a lot to say that the media haven't told us—even about our allies. These young men know what they're talking about, because they own a piece of that war, and you should ask the man who owns one.

PLAYBOY: Many of those young men who "own a piece of that war" never wanted to go to Vietnam in the first place. Do you think our Government is justified in sending them off to fight in an undeclared war?

WAYNE: Well, I sure don't know why we send them over to fight and then stop the bombing so they can get shot that much more. We could easily stop the enemy from getting guns and ammunition that we know are being sent by Chinese and Soviet Communists. But we won't do anything to stop it because we're afraid of world opinion. Why in hell should we worry about world opinion when we're trying to help out a country that's asked for our aid?

I honestly believe that there's as much need for us to help the Vietnamese as there was to help the Jews in Germany. The only difference is that we haven't had any leadership in this war. All the liberal Senators have stuck their noses in this, and it's out of their bailiwick. They've already put far too many barriers in the way of the military. Our lack of leadership has gone so far that now no one man can come in, face the issue and tell people that we ought to be in an all-out war.

PLAYBOY: Why do you favor an all-out war?

WAYNE: I figure if we're going to send even one man to die, we ought to be in an all-out conflict. If you fight, you fight to win. And the domino theory is something to be reckoned with, too, both in Europe and in Asia. Look at what happened in Czechoslovakia and what's happened all through the Balkans. At some point we have to stop communism. So we might as well stop it right now in Vietnam.

PLAYBOY: You're aware, of course, that most military experts, including two recent Secretaries of State, concede that it would be an unwinnable war except at a cost too incalculable to contemplate.

WAYNE: I think you're making a misstatement. Their fear is that Russia would go to war with us if we stopped the Vietnamese. Well, I don't think Russia wants war any more than we do.

PLAYBOY: Three Presidents seem to have agreed that it would be unwise to gamble millions of lives on that assumption. Since you find their leadership lacking, who would you have preferred in the highest office?

WAYNE: Barry Goldwater would at least have been decisive. I know for a fact that he's a truthful man. Before the '64 election, he told me that he said to the Texan, "I don't think we ought to make an issue out of Vietnam because we both know that we're going to probably end up having to send a half a million men over there." Johnson said, "Yeah, that's probably true, Barry, but I've got an election to win." So Barry told the truth and Johnson got elected on a "peace" platform—and then began to ease them in, a few thousand at a time. I wish our friend Fulbright would bring out those points.

If Douglas MacArthur were alive, he also would have handled the Vietnam situation wtih dispatch. He was a proven administrator, certainly a proven leader. And MacArthur understood what Americans were and what Americans stood for. Had he been elected President, something significant would have happened during his Administration. He would have taken a stand for the United States in world affairs, and he would have stood by it, and we would have been respected for it. I also admired the tie salesman, President Truman. He was a wonderful, feisty guy who'll go down in history as quite an individual. It's a cinch he had great guts when he decided to straighten things out in Korea; it's just too bad that the State Department was able to frighten him out of doing a complete job. Seems to me, politics have entered too much into the decisions of our leadership. I can't understand politicians. They're either yellowing out from taking a stand or using outside pressure to improve their position.

PLAYBOY: Is that why you've refused to run for public office yourself?

WAYNE: Exactly.

PLAYBOY: Is that what you told George Wallace when you were asked to be his running mate on the 1968 American Independent ticket?

WAYNE: No, I explained that I was working for the other Wallis—Hal Wallis—the producer of *True Grit,* and that I'd been a Nixon man.

PLAYBOY: What do you think of Nixon's performance since then?

WAYNE: I think Mr. Nixon is proving himself his own man. I knew he would. I knew him and stuck with him when he was a loser, and I'm sticking with him now that he's a winner. A lot of extreme rightists are saying that he isn't doing enough, but I think he's gradually wading in and getting control of the reins of Government.

PLAYBOY: What impressed you about him when you first met him?

WAYNE: His reasonableness. When he came into office, there was such a hue and cry over Vietnam, for instance, that it didn't seem possible for a man to take a stand that would quiet down the extreme leftists. He came on the air and explained the situation as it was from the beginning, and then he told the American people—in a logical, reasoning way—what he was going to do. And then he began to do it.

PLAYBOY: What he began to do, of course, was "Vietnamize" the war and withdraw American troops. How can you approve of these policies and also advocate all-out war?

WAYNE: Well, I don't advocate an all-out war if it isn't necessary. All I know is that we as a country should be backing up whatever the proposition is that we sent one man to die for.

PLAYBOY: If that view is shared by as many Americans as you seem to think, then why was *The Green Berets*—which has been labeled as your personal statement on the Vietnam war—so universally panned?

WAYNE: Because the critics don't like my politics, and they were condemning the war, not the picture. I don't mean the critics as a group. I mean the irrationally liberal ones. Renta Adler of *The New York Times* almost foamed at the mouth because I showed a few massacres on the screen. She went into convulsions. She and other critics wouldn't believe that the Viet Cong are treacherous—that the dirty sons of bitches are raping, torturing gorillas.

PLAYBOY: Did you resent the critics who labeled it a shameless propaganda film?

WAYNE: I agreed with them. It was an American film about American boys who were heroes over there. In that sense, it *was* propaganda.

PLAYBOY: *The Alamo* was another of your patriotic films. What statement did this picture make?

WAYNE: I thought it would be a tremendous epic picture that would say "America."

PLAYBOY: Borden Chase, the screenwriter, has been quoted as saying: "When *The Alamo* was coming out, the word of mouth on it was that it was a dog. This was created by the Communists to get at Wayne. Then there were some bad reviews inspired by the Communists. . . . It's a typical Communist technique and they were using it against Duke for what he did in the early Fifties at the Motion Picture Alliance for the Preservation of American Ideals." Is that true?

WAYNE: Well, there's always a little truth in everything you hear. The Alliance thing was used pretty strongly against me in those days.

PLAYBOY: Was the Motion Picture Alliance formed to black list Communists and Communist sympathizers?

WAYNE: Our organization was just a group of motion-picture people on the right side, not leftists and not Commies. I was the president for a couple of years. There was no black list at that time, as some people said. That was a lot of horseshit. Later on, when Congress passed some laws making it possible to take a stand against these people, we were asked about Communists in the industry. So we gave them the facts as we knew them. That's all. The only thing our side did that was anywhere near black listing was just running a lot of people out of the business.

PLAYBOY: That sounds a good deal worse than black listing. Why couldn't you permit all points of view to be expressed freely on the screen?

WAYNE: Because it's been proven that communism is foreign to the American way of life. If you'd read the official Communist doctrine and then listened to the arguments of these people we were opposing, you'd find they were reciting propaganda by rote. Besides, these Communist sympathizers ran a lot of *our* people out of the business. One of them was a

Pulitzer Prize winner who's now a columnist—Morrie Ryskind. They just never used him again at MGM after Dore Schary took charge of the studio, even though he was under contract.

PLAYBOY: What was the mood in Hollywood that made it so fashionable to take such a vigorous stand against communism?

WAYNE: Many of us were being invited to supposed social functions or house parties—usually at well-known Hollywood writers' homes—that turned out to be Communist recruitment meetings. Suddenly, everybody from make-up men to stagehands found themselves in seminars on Marxism. Take this colonel I knew, the last man to leave the Philippines on a submarine in 1942. He came back here and went to work sending food and gifts to U.S. prisoners on Bataan. He'd already gotten a Dutch ship that was going to take all this stuff over. The State Department pulled him off of it and sent the poor bastard out to be the technical director on my picture *Back to Bataan,* which was being made by Eddie Dmytryk. I knew that he and a whole group of actors in the picture were pro-Reds, and when I wasn't there, these pro-Reds went to work on the colonel. He was a Catholic, so they kidded him about his religion: They even sang the *Internationale* at lunchtime. He finally came to me and said, "Mr. Wayne, I haven't anybody to turn to. These people are doing everything in their power to belittle me." So I went to Dmytryk and said, "Hey, are you a Commie?" He said, "No, I'm not a Commie. My father was a Russian. I was born in Canada. But if the masses of the American people want communism, I think it'd be good for our country." When he used the word "masses," he exposed himself. That word is not a part of Western terminology. So I knew he was a Commie. Well, it later came out that he was.

I also knew two other fellas who really did things that were detrimental to our way of life. One of them was Carl Foreman, the guy who wrote the screenplay for *High Noon,* and the other was Robert Rossen, the one who made the picture about Huey Long, *All the King's Men.* In Rossen's version of *All the King's Men,* which he sent me to read for a part, every character who had any responsibility at all was guilty of some offense against society. To make Huey Long a wonderful, rough pirate was great; but, according to this picture, everybody was a shit except for this weakling intern doctor who was trying to find a place in the world. I sent the script back to Charlie Feldman, my agent, and said, "If you ever send me a script like this again, I'll fire you." Ironically, it won the Academy Award.

High Noon was even worse. Everybody says *High Noon* is a great picture because Tiomkin wrote some great music for it and because Gary Cooper and Grace Kelly were in it. So it's got everything going for it. In that picture, four guys come in to gun down the sheriff. He goes to the church and asks for help and the guys go, "Oh well, oh gee." And the women stand up and say, "You're rats. You're rats. You're rats." So Cooper goes out alone. It's the most un-American thing I've ever seen in my whole life. The last thing in the picture is ole Coop putting the United States marshal's badge under his foot and stepping on it. I'll never reget having helped run Foreman out of this country.

PLAYBOY: What gave you the right?

WAYNE: Running him out of the country is just a figure of speech. But I did tell him that I thought he'd hurt Gary Cooper's reputation a great deal. Foreman said, "Well, what if I went to England?" I said, "Well, that's your business." He said, "Well, that's where I'm going." And he did.

PLAYBOY: You seem to have a very blunt way of dealing with people. Why?

WAYNE: I've always followed my father's advice: He told me, first, to always keep my word and, second, to never insult anybody unintentionally. If I insult you, you can be goddamn sure I intend to. And, third, he told me not to go around looking for trouble.

PLAYBOY: A turning point for you was your cancer operation in 1964. At the time, were you optimistic about the outcome of the surgery?

WAYNE: Well, I had two operations six days apart—one for a cancer that was as big as a baby's fist, and then one for edema. I wasn't so uptight when I was told about the cancer. My biggest fear came when they twisted my windpipe and had to sew me back together a second time. When my family came in to see me and I saw the looks on their faces, I figured, "Well, Jeez, I must be just about all through."

PLAYBOY: How did you keep your spirits up?

WAYNE: By thinking about God and my family and my friends and telling myself, "Everything will be all right." And it was. I licked the big C. I know the man upstairs will pull the plug when he wants to, but I don't want to end up my life being sick. I want to go out on two feet—in action.

PLAYBOY: Does the loss of one lung restrict you from doing those rough-house movie stunts?

WAYNE: The operation hasn't impeded anything except that I get short of breath quickly. Particularly in the higher altitudes, that slows me down. I still do my own fights and all that stuff. I'd probably do a little bit more if I had more wind, but I still do more than my share. Nobody else does anything any more than I do, whether they're young or old.

PLAYBOY: Is it a matter of *machismo* for you to continue fighting your own fights?

WAYNE: I don't have to assert my virility. I think my career has shown that I'm not exactly a pantywaist. But I do take pride in my work, even to the point of being the first one on the set in the morning. I'm a professional.

PLAYBOY: In recent years, you've fallen off horses rather unprofessionally on a couple of occasions—once dislocating a shoulder during the production of *The Undefeated*. Wasn't that embarrassing?

WAYNE: What the hell, in my racket I've fallen off a lot of horses. I even fell off on purpose in *True Grit*. But that fall in *The Undefeated* was irritating because I tore some ligaments in my shoulder. I don't have good use of one arm anymore, and it makes me look like an idiot when I'm getting on a horse.

PLAYBOY: Is that an unfamiliar experience?

WAYNE: Getting on a horse?

PLAYBOY: Looking like an idiot.

WAYNE: Not hardly. One of the times I really felt like a fool was when I was working on my first important film, *The Big Trail,* in Yuma, Arizona. I was three weeks flat on my back with *turistas*—or Montezuma's revenge, or the Aztec two-step, whatever you want to call it. You know, you get a little grease and soap on the inside of a fork and you've got it. Anyway, that was the worst case I ever had in my life. I'd been sick for so long that they finally said, "Jeez, Duke, if you can't get up now, we've got to get somebody else to take your place." So, with a loss of 18 pounds, I returned to work. My first scene was carrying in an actor named Tully Marshall, who was known to booze it up quite a bit. He had a big jug in his hand in this scene, and I set him down and we have a drink with another guy. They passed the jug to me first, and I dug back into it; it was straight rotgut bootleg whiskey. I'd been puking and crapping blood for a week and now I just poured that raw stuff right down my throat. After the scene, you can bet I called him every kind of an old bastard.

PLAYBOY: You've long been known for your robust drinking habits, whether it's rotgut bootleg or imported Scotch. How great is your capacity?

WAYNE: Well, I'm full grown, you know. I'm pretty big and got enough fat on me, so I guess I can drink a fair amount.

PLAYBOY: What kind of liquor has provided your most memorable hangovers?

WAYNE: *Conmemorativo* tequila. That's as fine a liquor as there is in the world. Christ, I tell you it's better than any whiskey; it's better than any schnapps; it's better than any drink I ever had in my life. You hear about tequila and think about a cheap cactus drink, but this is something extraordinary.

PLAYBOY: Many people argue that alcohol may be a more dangerous health hazard than marijuana. Would you agree?

WAYNE: There's been no top authority saying what marijuana does to you. I really don't know that much about it. I tried it once, but it didn't do anything to me. The kids say it makes them think they're going 30 miles an hour when they're going 80. If that's true, marijuana use should definitely be stopped.

PLAYBOY: Have you had any other experience with illegal drugs?

WAYNE: When I went to Hong Kong, I tried opium once, as a clinical thing. I heard it didn't make you sick the first time, and Jesus, it just didn't affect me one way or the other, either. So I'm not a very good judge of how debasing it is.

PLAYBOY: Do you think such drugs are debasing?

WAYNE: It's like water against a cliff. Each wave deteriorates it a little more. I'm quite sure that's the same thing that happens to human beings when they get hooked on drugs. What bothers me more is society's attitude toward drugs. We allowed all the hippies to stay together in Haight-Ashbury and turn it into a dirty, filthy, unattractive place. We allow the glorifying of drugs in our business—like in *Easy Rider,* where the guy says, "Jesus, don't you smoke pot?"—as if smoking pot is the same as chewing Bull Durham.

PLAYBOY: You chew tobacco, don't you?

WAYNE: I learned to do that in college. During football season, when we couldn't smoke, we always used to chew. When I was a kid, if you wore a new pair of shoes, everybody would spit on them. I haven't practiced spitting lately, so don't wear your new shoes and expect me to hit them with any accuracy. I'm not the marksman I used to be.

PLAYBOY: You chew, but you don't use drugs. Do you still have as much drink, food and sex as you used to?

WAYNE: I drink as much as I ever did. I eat more than I should. And my sex life is none of your goddamn business.

PLAYBOY: Sexuality, however, seems a large part of your magnetism. According to one Hollywood writer, "Wayne has a sexual authority so strong that even a child could perceive it." Do you feel you still convey that onscreen?

WAYNE: Well, at one time in my career, I guess sexuality was part of my appeal. But God, I'm 63 years old now. How the hell do I know whether I still convey that? Jeez. It's pretty hard to answer a question like, "Are you attractive to broads?" All that crap comes from the way I walk, I guess. There's evidently a virility in it. Otherwise, why do they keep mentioning it? But I'm certainly not conscious of any particular walk. I guess I must walk different than other people, but I haven't gone to any school to learn how.

PLAYBOY: Another integral ingredient of your image is a rugged manliness, a readiness to mix it up with anyone who gets in your way. Have you ever run into situations in a restaurant or a bar in which someone tried to pick a fight with you?

WAYNE: It never happens to me anymore. Whatever my image is, it's friendly. But there was one time, a number of years ago, that I did get a little irritated. I was wearing long hair—the exception then, not the rule— and I was, if I say so myself, a fairly handsome kid. Anyway, I'm dancing with my wife-to-be and I'm saying to her, quietly, "You're beautiful enough to marry." Some punk alongside pipes up, "Forget about him, lady; not with that hair." So I sat her down and went over and explained very gently to him that if he would step outside, I'd kick his fuckin' teeth down his throat. That ended that.

PLAYBOY: Having once worn long hair yourself, how do you feel about long-haired young people?

WAYNE: They don't bother me. If a guy wants to wear his hair down to his ass, I'm not revolted by it. But I don't look at him and say, "Now there's a fella I'd like to spend next winter with."

PLAYBOY: Many pessimists say that our nation has lost its dignity and is headed toward self-destruction. Some, in fact, compare the condition of our society to the decline and fall of the Roman Empire and the last days of Sodom and Gomorrah. Are you that gloomy about the future of America?

WAYNE: Absolutely not. I think that the loud roar of irresponsible liberalism, which in the old days we called radicalism, is being quieted down by a reasoning public. I think the pendulum's swinging back. We're remembering that the past can't be so bad. We built a nation on it. We must also look always to the future. Tomorrow—the time that gives a man or a country just one more chance—is just one of many things that I feel are wonderful in life. So's a good horse under you. Or the only campfire for miles around. Or a quiet night and a nice soft hunk of ground to sleep on. Or church bells sending out their invitations. A mother meeting her first-born. The sound of a kid calling you Dad for the first time. There's a lot of things great about life. But I think tomorrow is the most important thing. Comes in to us at midnight very clean, ya know. It's perfect when it arrives and it puts itself in our hands. It hopes we've learned something from yesterday. As a country, our yesterdays tell us that we have to win not only at war but at peace. So far we haven't done that. Sadly, it looks like we'll have to win another war to win a peace. All I can hope is that in our anxiety to have peace, we remember our clear and present dangers and beware the futility of compromise; only if we keep sight of both will we have a chance of stumbling forward into a day when there won't be guns fired anymore in anger.

PLAYBOY: Contrasting the America you grew up in and the America of today, is it the same kind of country, or has it changed?

WAYNE: The only difference I can see is that we now have an enemy within our borders fighting with propaganda and coloring events in a manner that belittles our great country. But all in all, it's practically the same.

PLAYBOY: In retrospect, would you have wanted your life to have been any different?

WAYNE: If I had it to do over again, I'd probably do everything I did. But that's not necessarily the right thing to do.

PLAYBOY: What legacy do you hope to leave behind?

WAYNE: Well, you're going to think I'm being corny, but this is how I really feel: I hope my family and my friends will be able to say that I was an honest, kind and fairly decent man.

ALBERT SPEER

June 1971

Interviewer: Eric Norden

This brings together the best that the Playboy Interview is capable of doing: an important theme, a fascinating personality, thoughtful questioning, and a thorough exploration of the subjects it touches upon. It is editor Murray Fisher's personal favorite of the nearly one hundred and fifty interviews he supervised in his fourteen years at the magazine. "If anything ever captured the Wagnerian tragedy that was Albert Speer, this did," Fisher said years later. "I believe it raised questions of guilt and responsibility that Speer had never faced—not in his book, perhaps not at Nuremberg."

It was interviewer Eric Norden's finest work, and he spent the better part of a year putting the interview together. It is also one of the longest interviews published. Norden's background sketch of Speer, and his own impressions of him, set the scene without need for amplification.

At the stroke of midnight on September 30, 1966, the giant iron gates of Berlin's Spandau prison creaked open and a tall, silver-haired man walked uncertainly out into the glare of flashbulbs and TV floodlights. Prisoner number five of the four-power-administered penitentiary greeted his wife without visible emotion, shook hands cordially with the governor of the Spandau district and spoke briefly to the press, first in German and then in fluent French and English. "My sentence was just," he said quietly. "We were treated correctly and properly the whole time. I have no complaints." He turned and walked with his wife to a waiting car. Rudolf Hess, Adolf

Hitler's executive secretary, now 77, lay inside alone in his cell—Spandau's only remaining prisoner—as Albert Speer, Hitler's architect, friend and second-in-command throughout World War Two, sped off to freedom after 20 years' imprisonment.

After Germany's unconditional surrender, Speer was arrested by the Allies and tried before the International Military Tribunal at Nuremberg, along with 21 other surviving Nazi leaders. He was charged with having brought more than 5,000,000 slave laborers to the Reich, "many of them under terrible conditions of cruelty and suffering." To the fury of his co-defendants, the opposition of his own lawyer and the surprise of the judges, Speer accepted full responsibility for the most telling count against him: the forced-labor charges. On September 30, 1946, he was found not guilty on two counts of the indictment relating to conspiracy to initiate aggressive war, but was convicted on crimes-against-humanity charges, although the court took note of such extenuating circumstances as his efforts to provide better food, clothing and housing for the forced laborers and his defiance of Hitler in the last year of the war. Overriding Russian demands for the death penalty, the court sentenced Speer to 20 years' imprisonment and he was transported to Spandau prison.

He settled down to the harsh regimen of prison life with surprising adaptability; but as the years dragged on and his children grew older, Speer began to become concerned about their assessment of his role in the Third Reich. Would they despise him as a mass murderer—or would a sense of misplaced loyalty pervert their filial devotion into neo-Nazi political sympathies? Speer realized that he must somehow try to explain to them why and how he had become involved with Hitler and the Nazi movement, and in greater length and detail than he was permitted in his two single-page monthly letters. That need to explain—if not to justify—was the origin of his memoirs.

Upon publication in Germany, the book was an instant best seller and has already sold over 200,000 copies in the German edition. Rapidly translated into a dozen languages, "Inside the Third Reich" has soared to the top of the best-seller lists in the United States, England and western Europe and precipitated both lavish critical praise and bitter controversy. Writing in The Nation, *Lincoln Kirstein predicted that "Inside the Third Reich" "may, in its somber logic, be the prose masterpiece from World War Two," and in a review in* The Wall Street Journal, *critic Frank Gannon suggested that, "At its deepest level," Speer's memoirs define "20th Century Western man's dilemma and potential in a way that Saint Augustine and Rousseau did for their own times when they wrote their confessions . . . a staggering and monumental book." And Thomas Mann's son Golo, in a German review praising Speer's honesty in confronting his own guilt, declared: "Speer consecrated himself to self-accusation as he had consecrated himself to serving Hitler; such a man does not do things by halves."*

But while no critics doubted the intensity of Speer's mea culpas, *a few reviewers challenged their integrity. According to this view, Speer's acceptance of personal responsibility for the crimes of the Reich is more propaganda than penitence, a cynical device to disarm his critics and justify both himself and the majority of Germans who supported Hitler. In a devastating essay in* The New York Review of Books, *historian Geoffrey Barraclough not only cast doubt on the sincerity of Speer's repentance but also accused him of doctoring the statistics of his own ministry in order to put "the whole story of German war production in a falsely dramatic light." Barraclough warns against the growth of what he terms the "Speer legend," fostered by uncritical book reviews and savants ignorant of the realities of the Third Reich. "The picture the Speer legend presents," he concludes, "both of Speer himself and of the regime he served, is a distorted picture."*

To evaluate the origins and outlines of the Speer legend, and to probe the complexities and contradictions of Speer's own character, PLAYBOY *sent Eric Norden to interview the 66-year-old ex–Reich minister in his pleasant timbered villa on a wooded hill overlooking the Neckar River, three miles from the picturesque university town of Heidelberg. Norden writes of their meeting:*

"Speer greeted me amiably and escorted me into the richly furnished living room of his spacious home. He was still handsome in a distinguished, company-director manner, and his beetling black eyebrows reminded me of the younger man I had seen in photographs strolling through occupied Paris with his friend and patron, Adolf Hitler. As we sat over Scotch and sodas by a roaring fire, snow began to fall lightly outside and his three-year-old Saint Bernard, Bello, snored contentedly at her master's feet as Speer's attractive wife, Margarethe, served us heaping plates of home-baked cakes and rich German pastries.

"For six weeks, I had studied this man, poring over his book and published interviews, as well as the voluminous reviews and polemical articles in the American and European press. But as I leaned forward to switch on the tape recorder, I felt no closer to the real man behind the public façade than I ever had. I had been frustrated throughout my research by a certain vague opacity, an insubstantiality, about Speer; and as we began talking, I experienced some of the same doubts I had had while reading his book and studying his published statements: As forthright as he appeared on the surface, there seemed to me to be a veil drawn between him and the truth.

"I suspected, as some reviewers had, that the litany of his self-recrimination was in itself an evasion of ultimate responsibility. Now, as I began the interview—which was to extend into almost ten days of relentless day-and-night question-and-answer sessions, ending with both Speer and myself on the brink of exhaustion—this uneasiness persisted, intensified at first by his curiously detached manner. As my interrogations proceeded late into that

*night and resumed over breakfast the next morning, I began to realize that
what disturbed me most about Speer was his tranquillity, the way in which he
could accuse himself of terrible crimes in the same tone he would use to
offer me a piece of* Apfel Torte.

*"But as I listened to Speer recount the terrors and triumphs of the Third
Reich in German and the fluent English he learned in Spandau, as I saw
the patient concern with which he tried to express and explain himself and
his era in the course of our tiring sessions, I realized that this interview and
all his other confrontations with press and public were part of the burden
he bore, part of his penance—way stations to a salvation he himself recognized as unattainable." Norden began the interview by asking Speer about
the harsh judgment of his critics.*

PLAYBOY: Critical acclaim for *Inside the Third Reich* has not been universal. Rebecca West, dismissing the book as a cynical whitewash, brands you
a "repulsive criminal," and historian Gudrun Tempel writes that "Speer
may easily have been as brutal, as ruthlessly ambitious and almost as sick
as Hitler . . . one puts his book away with a greater fear of men like him
than of any Hitler." How would you respond to such critics?
SPEER: Perhaps they are right. After what I have done, it is not for me to
call them wrong. But I think many reviewers, including those who liked the
book, miss the point when they place their emphasis on me as an individual.
My guilt can never be erased, nor should it be, but that guilt is only the
frame for a larger picture. I wrote the memoirs to describe and explain what
happened from 1933 to 1945 and to warn people so that it will not happen
again, in Germany or anywhere else. I suppose that in a personal sense, it
was also an attempt to understand myself, to see how and why I could have
been a part of such things. But so many seem to expect me to offer justi-
fications for what I did. I cannot. There is no apology or excuse I can ever
make. The blood is on my hands. I have not tried to wash it off—only to
see it.
PLAYBOY: At Nuremberg, you accepted responsibility for the crimes of the
Third Reich. But did you then, and do you now, consider yourself *personally*
responsible?
SPEER: Yes, for everything that happened. For the forced labor, obviously—
that was directly under my jurisdiction. But I was also responsible for acts
about which I knew nothing at the time they were committed, such as the
atrocities against the Jews and the mass executions of Russian civilians
and prisoners of war. There was no way, legally or morally, for me to evade
this guilt. I took that position at the Nuremberg trial, although there was
a great temptation to try to save my life by mitigating guilt, by offering

excuses, by blaming others, by claiming I was only obeying orders. But whenever I wavered, I would think of the mass of evidence presented before the tribunal—the photographs and testimony and documents about what had happened. In particular, there was one photograph of a Jewish family going to its death, a husband with his wife and children being led to the gas chamber. I couldn't rid my mind of that photograph; I would see it in my cell at night. I see it still. It has made a desert of my life. But also, in a strange way, it freed me. When you finally comprehend that you have devoted 15 years of your life to building a graveyard, the only thing left is to accept responsibility for your actions. From that moment of recognition, I felt for the first time in my life a sense of inner calm.

PLAYBOY: It's strange to hear such compassionate sentiment from the second most powerful man in Nazi Germany. Historian Hugh Trevor-Roper, who interrogated you at Nuremberg, conceded that you were a "civilized, sensitive, intelligent man," but said he failed to comprehend how you could "so long and so faithfully serve, at such close quarters, such vulgar tyranny." Do you have an answer?

SPEER: No. I have been living with the question for 25 years and I have found many reasons—but no adequate reply. Of course, for a while, I tried to soothe my conscience with pseudo truths, rationalizations that would make me look better to myself. I tried to persuade myself that, in a totalitarian system such as Nazi Germany, a man's isolation increases as his position rises and he is not aware of crimes committed by underlings. I would tell myself that, in this modern technological age, genocide becomes an assembly-line process, with the number of murdered rising even as the number of murderers decreases, that under such circumstances, it is easy to be ignorant. I argued that in such a system, the mania for secrecy is self-justifying and self-perpetuating and, therefore, I could not be blamed for not knowing what happened. In each of those arguments, there is a considerable measure of objective truth. But in the larger moral sense, they are all lies, evasions of my responsibility as a human being. If I was isolated, I determined the degree of my own isolation. If I was ignorant, I ensured my own ignorance. If I did not see, it was because I did not want to see.

PLAYBOY: Trevor-Roper writes, "It is this remarkable contrast between perception and blindness, between sensitivity and insensitivity, between moral standards and moral neutrality, which makes Speer psychologically so interesting." And, to some critics, so frightening. What accounted for this moral schizophrenia?

SPEER: The answer is not pleasant for me to contemplate, because it is so banal. I was blinded by the glory and authority of my position, by the great plans I was making, the great events I helped to shape. It was a classic case of *hubris,* the affliction of the ancient Greeks. I stood at the pinnacle of power and I was intoxicated by the distant landscapes I saw—while all the time a charnel house reeked at my feet. My own pride and ambition

made me an accomplice in the extermination of millions of human beings.
PLAYBOY: An extermination you did nothing to prevent and—by successfully prolonging the war as armaments minister—actually assisted.
SPEER: I could not have prevented it short of assassinating Hitler before his "final solution" was under way, and at that time, I had neither the courage nor the vision to do so. But it was my duty to *confront* it, to assert my individual and collective responsibility for it. That was my greatest failure. From the very beginning, I should have seen where Hitler's hatred of the Jews would lead. But slowly, at first almost imperceptibly, I accommodated myself to his mania. When I first joined the party, I viewed Hitler's anti-Semitism with distaste but thought it was just a cheap propaganda weapon that he would abandon when he came to power. Once Hitler was in office and unleashed the full power of the state against the Jews—and the Socialists and the Communists and the Freemasons and the Jehovah's Witnesses—I just stood aside and said to myself that as long as I did not personally participate, it had nothing to do with me. I believe there is a saying in English—"We first endure, then pity, then embrace." My toleration of the anti-Semitic campaign made me responsible for it.
PLAYBOY: You've said you weren't an anti-Semite when you joined the party and you write in your book that you had many Jewish friends in your school days. How *could* you tolerate their persecution?
SPEER: By depersonalizing them. The people who were deprived of their jobs, who were hounded from the professions, whose property was confiscated and who were finally dragged off to the concentration camps gradually became abstractions to me, not human beings with families and aspirations and worries and needs like anyone else. It shames me to admit that these people disappeared from my life and my thoughts as if they had never existed. If I had continued to see them as human beings, I could not have remained a Nazi. I did not hate them; I was indifferent to them. My crime was far worse because I was *not* an anti-Semite.
PLAYBOY: You never had any qualms of conscience whatever about the treatment of the Jews?
SPEER: No. As the anti-Semite campaign escalated, my conscience was progressively calloused and blunted. Of course, one's conscience does not just cease to exist overnight; it is slowly eroded over the years, eaten away day by day, anesthetized by a multiplicity of little crimes. Things that would have shocked and horrified me in 1934, such as the assassination of opposition leaders, the persecution of the Jews, the incarceration and torture of innocent men in concentration camps, I tolerated as unfortunate excesses in 1935; and things I couldn't have stomached in 1935 were palatable a few years later. This happened in one way or another to all of us in Germany. As the Nazi environment enveloped us, its evils grew invisible—because we were part of them.
PLAYBOY: How could a man of your intelligence and sensibility allow

himself to remain part of so evil a system, however gradually it enveloped you?

SPEER: There is, unfortunately, no necessary correlation between intelligence and decency; the genius and the moron are equally susceptible to corruption. Almost 200 years ago, Goethe wrote in *Iphigenie auf Tauris* that even "the best man" finally "becomes accustomed to cruelty" and "in the end makes a law of that which he despises." As far as sensibility is concerned, I would have been shocked and outraged if I had seen some hoodlum throw a brick through a Jewish store window in 1930. But on the day after *Kristallnacht* in 1938, the great pogrom in which dozens of synagogues and thousands of Jewish homes and businesses were burned and looted, I strolled by the smoldering ruins of a Berlin synagogue, and my only reaction was to be aesthetically offended by the ruins' spilling over onto the *Fasanenstrasse*. That was all; I was bothered only by the litter. The memory of that day is one of the most painful of my life. What makes it worse is that on *Kristallnacht*, Hitler crossed a Rubicon; barbarous as his treatment of the Jews had been, I don't think even he had contemplated their physical extermination until then. More was shattered than glass that night.

PLAYBOY: When was it finally decided to annihilate the Jews?

SPEER: I am sure Hitler had it in his mind since *Kristallnacht*, but I learned from evidence introduced at Nuremberg that the actual decision was made at the Wannsee Conference in 1942, once he knew the war was going to be total, with either absolute victory or absolute defeat at the end. I think that knowledge eliminated the last remaining political and diplomatic restraints and liberated his most terrible instincts. It wasn't a ministerial decision; most of Hitler's government associates, including me, never even knew about it till they were told at the end of the war. Himmler was placed in charge of the extermination program, and his henchmen Eichmann and Kaltenbrunner and Heydrich organized and implemented it. But even within the SS, relatively few people were involved—the top administrators, plus the actual concentration-camp commandants and guards and logistics and transport personnel. I know that many people outside Germany believe that everyone in the country knew of the extermination, but that just wasn't the case, as historians of the period will tell you.

PLAYBOY: Since Hitler's power was absolute, why did he bother to keep his "final solution" secret—if, in fact, it was as secret as you indicate?

SPEER: It was. I think, in a sense, the last residue of humanity in Hitler prevented him from boasting about it to any but his most fanatic and degenerate followers; and then, too, on a more pragmatic level, it's possible he was afraid of the army's reaction if they had learned what was happening. His power was not completely absolute; in the final analysis, he was still dependent on the military. The generals were subservient to Hitler—until the July 20 plot, at any rate—but I doubt if the *Wehrmacht* could have stomached the horrors of Auschwitz. Despite all the crimes in which it tacitly acquiesced, the army still prided itself on possessing a military code of honor which would have prevented it from accepting the wholesale massacre of unarmed men, women and children. But they didn't know until it was too late—too late for the Jews, too late for all of us. In my own case, I did not know what was happening until 1945, when I learned with horror at Nuremberg precisely what monstrous acts our regime had been committing—a horror that has never left me.

PLAYBOY: This is the point that has aroused the greatest suspicion among your critics about your integrity. They argue that you were a member of Hitler's inner circle, by your own admission the closest thing to a friend he ever had. You were intimately involved with all aspects of Nazi military and political strategy. How, they ask, can you expect people to believe that you remained ignorant until the end of the war of the systematic extermination of 6,000,000 Jews—an extermination carried out all around you?

SPEER: I know this is difficult for many people to believe, but I think that if they really understood the machinations of the Nazi state, they would see how it could happen—and did. You must remember that pervasive interdepartmental rivalries and a fetish for secrecy affected every aspect of the Nazi state; both major policy decisions and relatively innocuous operations were shrouded in deception and evasion. Everything was compartmentalized; there was a bureaucracy even of murder.

PLAYBOY: But even in a totalitarian state, crimes are committed by *people*—people with families and friends and neighbors who must have been aware of their activities. The extermination of the Jews was on a huge scale, the most massive genocide in the history of man. How *could* it have been kept secret?

SPEER: Before this century, it would have been impossible. But no longer. This is the true horror of the technological age—that a handful of men, in utmost secrecy, have the power by virtually the push of a button to dispatch millions to their deaths. In my own case, there is no way I can avoid responsibility for the extermination of the Jews. I was as much their executioner as Himmler, because they were carried past me to their deaths and I did not see. It is surprisingly easy to blind your moral eyes. I was like a man following a trail of bloodstained footprints through the snow without realizing someone had been injured.

PLAYBOY: But in your capacity as minister of armaments, you traveled all over Germany and the occupied territories, inspecting industrial and military facilities. Do you mean to say that you never came across a concentration camp?

SPEER: Of course I knew there were camps; everyone knew that. It was what was going *on* in them we did not know. Beatings, perhaps even torture, we knew the Gestapo to be capable of; but systematic mass slaughter—no, in our worst dreams, we could not conceive the reality of that.

PLAYBOY: You were in regular contact with Himmler and his top aides, and yet they never let anything slip and you never attempted to question them?

SPEER: No. I had a chance to find out in the summer of 1944, when I was visited by one of my old friends, Karl Hanke, the gauleiter, or district governor, of Lower Silesia. Hanke was a fanatic Nazi, but he had some lingering human instincts; I remember that he had come back from the Polish and French fronts and spoken with sympathy and concern about the dead and wounded and maimed on both sides. On this occasion, he came into my office and just slumped down into my green-leather armchair and was silent for a long time. There was a strange expression on his face, and when he finally began to speak, he was quite unlike his normal hearty self. He told me he had just visited a concentration camp in Upper Silesia and he urged me in a faltering voice never, under any circumstances whatsoever, to accept an invitation to inspect that camp. He had seen horrible things there, things he was not allowed to discuss—things he could not bring himself to discuss. I had never seen Hanke in such a state.

PLAYBOY: What did you do?

SPEER: Nothing. There he was, sitting in my office, hinting at things that it was my duty as a minister of the Reich to discover—not to mention my duty as a human being. But I did not question him. I did not question Himmler. I did not question Hitler. I did not speak with any of my friends or acquaintances in the government or party who might have known something; I did not investigate; I did nothing. Hanke, of course, was speaking of Auschwitz. From that point on, I had irrevocably condemned myself. My moral contamination was complete. That moment was very much in my mind when I accepted responsibility for the crimes of the Reich at Nuremberg. It has never left me. Because of my failure at that moment, my utter moral abdication, I still feel directly responsible for Auschwitz in a completely personal sense.

PLAYBOY: The sins you admit were all of omission—not acting on *Kristallnacht,* not eliciting the truth about Auschwitz from Hanke. But what would you have done if you *had* known that 6,000,000 Jewish men, women and children were being exterminated?

SPEER: This is a crucial question, and one I have asked myself many times. The answer does not help me to sleep at night. I might have resigned from the government; of that much, at least, I was capable even then. But would I have fought, protested, tried to stop the slaughter, risked my life? In all honesty, I must say I doubt it. Looking back over the decades at the man I was then, I can expect no moral courage from him.

PLAYBOY: If Hitler had admitted to you that he was annihilating the Jews, what would you have said to him?

SPEER: That, too, I have asked myself, and the answer is equally dispiriting. I would have said, "You are killing them? That is insane! I need them to work in our factories." That would have been, I am afraid, my first reaction at the time.

PLAYBOY: No moral outrage? No revulsion?

SPEER: The man who left Spandau was not the same man who entered. That other Speer—I hate to think of him as me, but he is me, of course, my *Doppelgänger*—would have thought only in terms of efficiency and the war effort. The killing of the Jews would have seemed to me a waste. A crime, perhaps, if I had thought about it abstractly, but first and foremost a *waste*. I had no thought other than oiling the war machine. Even with blood.

PLAYBOY: One historian has written that you loved machines more than people. Was he right?

SPEER: Yes. That is why I could serve Hitler so long and so faithfully and so blindly. Sometimes I think, in despair, if only I could go back to the beginning and change it all, become a professor of architecture in some small university town. But I can never escape the consequences of that betrayal of my conscience.

PLAYBOY: What were your original motivations for joining the Nazi Party?

SPEER: They were not in themselves base. I sincerely believed that the Nazis offered the only salvation for a Germany torn by social and economic chaos and that it was thus my duty to assist them to come to power. You must remember the conditions in Germany following World War One: inflation followed by deflation and massive unemployment, great human suffering and despair, decadence and moral decay, the apparent disintegration of all our traditional institutions and values. It seemed that the democratic system had hopelessly failed to provide answers for the problems of the nation, and people with a social conscience tended to gravitate to the extremes of either right or left. Some became Nazis, others Communists—often for the very same reasons. The sound and constructive thing would have been to try working within the system to solve the economic crisis. But to the idealistic and impetuous young, that seemed sterile and ineffectual.

At that time, I still could not make up my mind politically. Conditions had become so bad in Germany that I felt drastic measures were required to restructure the entire social and economic system—but I did not know how to translate this disaffection into concrete political action. Then, toward the end of 1930, some of the Nazi students in Tessenow's seminars invited me to attend a rally, where Hitler would address the students of both the Institute and Berlin University. I had hitherto rather halfheartedly resisted their attempts to convert me to National Socialism, but I wanted to hear their leader, so I attended.

PLAYBOY: Was this the first time you had seen Hitler in person?

SPEER: Yes, till then, I had tended to view him as a vulgar, rabble-rousing fanatic in a comic-opera Brownshirt uniform. But that meeting in a dirty, ill-lit beer hall drastically altered my image of him. He entered wearing a well-cut blue suit and after the tumultuous ovation died down, he spoke earnestly, persuasively, almost shyly. His manner was completely sincere, more like a dedicated professor delivering a lecture than a screaming demagog.

Within a few minutes, he had the entire audience in his grip—and by no means was everyone there his supporter. Soon his low-key manner disappeared, his voice rose to a hypnotic pitch and there was a palpable aura of tension and excitement in the hall, a crackling emotional voltage, the kind of supercharged atmosphere I'd encountered before only at dramatic sporting events. Hitler's dynamic presence filled the room, his voice swelled, his eyes transfixed the audience. It was not so much what he said—I hardly remembered afterward—but the mood he cast over the entire hall: It had an almost orgiastic quality.

Hitler always said that the masses are essentially feminine, and his aggressiveness and charisma elicited an almost masochistic surrender and submission in his audience—a form of psychic rape. I believe there may be a tendency of man, perhaps rooted in Jung's concept of the collective unconscious, to surrender himself to the yoke of a stronger personality, and this was certainly true of Hitler's mass meetings. He didn't convince his audiences; he conquered them.

PLAYBOY: Yourself included.

SPEER: Yes. I left that meeting quite overwhelmed. Here, at last, it appeared to me, were hope for the future, imaginative new concepts, new goals to be achieved, a new beginning. Hitler, I thought then, could save Germany, end unemployment, rebuild the economy, rectify the injustices of Versailles, check the Communist threat, give our people a new mission and purpose. The very simplicity with which he approached complex problems both perplexed and impressed me, as did the magic of his rhetoric. I did not translate my ideas into action for several weeks, but my mind was made up that very night. In January 1931, I became member number 474,481 in the National Socialist Party.

PLAYBOY: What brought you to the attention of the Nazi hierarchy?

SPEER: While I was in Berlin, I was a courier for the party and, in that capacity, I met Karl Hanke, whom I mentioned earlier; he was then a minor party functionary. When he learned I was an architect, he gave me the modest assignment of redecorating his district headquarters. A few other small commissions followed, but when I left Berlin for Mannheim, Hanke and I lost touch. Then, on January 30, 1933, von Hindenburg appointed Hitler as chancellor in the hope that a strengthened and unified right-wing government might quiet labor and left-wing dissent and stabilize the economy.

In March 1933, immediately after national elections had strengthened Hitler's hand, I received a call from Hanke, asking me to come to Berlin right away, where he introduced me to Dr. Goebbels, a small man with intense, flashing eyes and a pronounced limp from his clubfoot. Goebbels commissioned me to rebuild and redecorate his propaganda ministry, instructing me to begin at once. I left Goebbels and walked through Berlin, thrilled at the prospect of my first major commission. The atmosphere in the city was excited, exhilarating. Everyone realized that Germany had reached her hour of decision. People gathered on street corners to discuss the *Führer's* latest moves; strangers exchanged Nazi salutes and comradely *"Heil* Hitlers," storm troopers and military bands paraded through the streets; people proudly flew the swastika flag from their windows.

PLAYBOY: Was Goebbels your patron from that point on?

SPEER: No, he was shortly replaced by Hitler himself. Once again, Karl Hanke played a pivotal role in my life. He had now risen to the influential position of Goebbels' ministerial secretary, and one day, as I sat in his elegant new office, I noticed on his desk a sketch of decorations for a forthcoming night rally at Tempelhof Field. I was appalled by those drawings. "They look like the decorations for some rifle-club meeting," I told Hanke. He just tossed me the designs and said, "If you can do better, do it." I rushed home and worked through the evening, designing a huge platform backed by three tremendous swastika banners stretched across wooden struts, each one taller than a ten-story building, all illuminated by giant air-raid searchlights. The design was snapped up the next day and I learned that Hitler was delighted with it.

I was subsequently called to Nuremberg, where plans were under way for the next party rally—a particularly important one, because it would mark the first anniversary of the party's coming to power. I designed a free-form giant eagle with a 100-foot wingspread to dominate the Zeppelin Field. The local party leader arranged for me to submit my plans to Rudolf Hess, Hitler's secretary; but when I entered Hess's office with my folio of sketches under one arm, he cut me off before I could speak. "Only the *Führer* himself can decide this kind of thing," he said, then picked up a telephone and spoke briefly. He hung up and turned to me. "The *Führer* is in his apartment. I'll have you driven over there." A chauffeur drove me to a middle-class apartment house and led me two flights up and into an anteroom piled with cheap mementos and presents sent to Hitler by his worshipful female followers. An adjutant entered, opened an adjacent door casually and told me to go in. I entered, my knees trembling, and stood before Adolf Hitler, the leader of my country and my party, the man I had admired from afar for three years. He was sitting in an armchair in his shirt sleeves, cleaning a revolver.

"Put the drawings here," he said abruptly, pointing to a table in front of him, barely looking at me. He placed the dismantled gun onto the table and examined my designs closely, but with no comment. My heartbeat seemed to ring in my ears; surely he can hear it, I thought. And then, still without so much as glancing at me, he shoved the sketches back across the table. "Agreed," he said curtly and turned back to his revolver. I left the room in confusion, my pulse racing. I had met my destiny. Looking back, it was significant that he should have been cleaning a gun at the time.

PLAYBOY: You are generally credited—or blamed—for creating the decor and stage settings that made the mass party rallies so chillingly effective. Do you accept the responsibility for those demagogic mass rallies?

SPEER: Oh, yes, although in those days, I did not really understand the larger implications of the rallies; I was part of the machine by then and no longer questioned its operation. In any case, it was a grueling job. I was responsible for virtually every aspect of these marathon meetings, from building maintenance to lighting and stage setting. My most arduous task was the "choreography" of the rally, drilling the thousands of party members who appeared in parades and paramilitary processions.

We had a particularly vexing problem with the *Amtswalter,* the lower and middle party functionaries whose newfound power had gone to their bellies as well as to their heads; the sight of several thousand beer paunches wobbling across the parade ground was hardly awe-inspiring. So I designed the rallies so that the *Amtswalter* would cross the Zeppelin Field in darkness, through a sea of thousands of Nazi banners. I divided the flag-bearers into ten massive columns, forming lanes through which they could march to the speakers' platform. Spotlights illuminated the massed banners, as well as the huge eagle crowning the stadium; and to highlight the effect, I asked Hitler to requisition 130 anti-aircraft searchlights—virtually all the *Luftwaffe* had at the time. I positioned these around the field at 40-foot intervals, their beams slashing into the night sky, visible up to 25,000 feet, at which point they dissolved into a luminous glow.

The dramatic effect was breath-taking, beyond anything I had anticipated. The floodlit stadium gave the impression of a giant hall ringed by titanic gleaming white pillars, with an occasional cloud floating surrealistically through the majestic wall of light, like a translucent anemone drifting through the sea. British ambassador Neville Henderson wrote later that the effect was like being in a cathedral of ice.

PLAYBOY: Nuremberg was perhaps history's most impressive example of propaganda through scenic display. Countless young and impressionable Germans must have been first enraptured and then converted by your pageantry—the same young men who a few years later fought and died in Hitler's war. How can you rhapsodize about the beauty of your light shows when their cumulative effect was to lead a generation to its death?

SPEER: At the time, I gave no thought to such considerations; I rarely even concerned myself about politics, save in the most perfunctory fashion. I deluded myself that I was an artist and that, as Hitler's architect, I was above politics, whether I was directing party rallies or designing government buildings. This is folly, of course. I was a technician, but a technician of death. It took me many years to see that, however. From the day Troost died in 1934 to the last days of the war, I was completely engrossed in my work and totally under Hitler's domination. He became the center of my life, to the exclusion of my family, my children and my own individuality. I was part of the Nazi juggernaut as it gained momentum and gave no more thought to it than a fish does to the water in which it swims.

I could easily have seen if I had really wanted to, of course, because by 1934, the true nature of the Nazi system had already been indelibly stamped on Germany by two events: On June 30, 1934, in the so-called Roehm *Putsch,* Hitler bloodily purged the party of his archrival Ernst Roehm and Roehm's radical Brownshirt followers, along with prominent conservative opposition leaders; and on August second, President von Hindenburg died, clearing the way for Hitler's assumption of absolute dictatorial control.

I was close to Hitler throughout this period, and the emerging pattern should have been clear to me, particularly after the Roehm *Putsch,* when the Nazis murdered several hundred people, at the very least. Perhaps to justify himself, Hitler stressed the homosexuality of Roehm and his circle and the perverted atmosphere of his headquarters: "In one room, we found two naked boys!" But Roehm's death and the deaths of all the others— old party comrades and conservative democrats alike—had no effect on him whatsoever. To Hitler, the June 30 purge was just a difficult but necessary political move.

PLAYBOY: Did the bloodiness of the purge repel you?

SPEER: No, I hate to admit it did not. Right after the purge, I was assigned to renovate the vice-chancellor's office in Berlin. When I entered Vice-Chancellor von Papen's office, I saw a large circle of dried blood on the floor of one room where his aide, Herbert von Bose, had been shot to death by the SS. I instantly averted my eyes and from that moment on, I stayed away from the room. But that was the only effect the incident had on me; it was as if I'd drawn a curtain inside my mind, blocking the incident off. All I was concerned with in those days was my ambition to excel as Hitler's architect.

PLAYBOY: Your ambitions seemed to grow proportionately with the crimes committed by your benefactors.

SPEER: Yes, I suppose so. I think from the very beginning Hitler was preparing to entrust me with tasks he had dreamed of undertaking ever since his adolescence. The first time he met my wife, at a state reception, he told her solemnly: "Your husband is going to erect buildings for me such as have not been created for 4000 years." Even then, I had no idea of the megalomaniac scale of his plans, nor of what they heralded for Germany and the rest of Europe.

PLAYBOY: Do you have any lingering regrets that those plans never came to fruition?

SPEER: I must admit that, despite their absurdity and madness, I still find it difficult to completely free myself of the power they exerted over me for so many years. Intellectually, I can now despise them—but on a deeper level, they still have a hold on me. Perhaps, apart from everything else, that is one reason why I so deeply hate Hitler: He not only enabled me to destroy my conscience, he also drained and perverted the creative energies of my youth.

But even though those plans still have a visceral fascination for me, I am grateful that they never came into being, because I can see now, as I never could then, that they were profoundly immoral in conception. Their proportions were alien, inhuman, reflecting the coldness and inhumanity of the Nazi system. "I am building for eternity," Hitler used to tell me, and that was true. But he was never building for people. The size and scale of his monuments were a prophetic symbol of his plans for world domination, and the giant metropolis he envisaged could only serve as the heart of a conquered and enslaved empire. One day in the summer of 1939, we were standing together over the wooden models when Hitler pointed down at the gold German eagle with a swastika in its talons, which would crown the top of the *Kuppelhalle* dome. "That has to be changed," he said intensely. On his instructions, I altered the design so that the eagle held a globe clutched in its claws. Two months later, World War Two broke out.

PLAYBOY: When did Hitler first confide his plans for war to you?

SPEER: Well, he never said in so many words, "Speer, I am planning a world war." But this was clear from his designs for Berlin; and over the years, he never troubled to hide his plans for conquest from his circle of intimates. But I don't think Hitler ever envisioned a general war; he thought the West was so decadent that he could achieve his territorial aspirations piecemeal, seizing one nation at a time, virtually without opposition, until he controlled all of Europe. This had been his intention ever since his remilitarization of the Rhineland in 1936, in clear violation of the Treaty of Locarno, when England and France proved weak and irresolute.

And from that point, too, a subtle change took place in him; he must have understood what an intense drama his life had become, realized that in the game he was playing, the stakes were the life or death of entire nations and the destiny of the world. A few months after his victory in the Rhineland, I was sitting with Hitler in his Berchtesgaden house at twilight, watching the sun fall behind the mountain peaks. He looked out the window silently for some time and then said to me softly, "There are two possibilities for me: to win through with all my plans—or to fail. If I win, I shall be one of the greatest men in history. If I fail, I shall be condemned, despised, damned." Before I could say anything, he rose abruptly and left, apparently embarrassed to have revealed his innermost thoughts and doubts in such a manner.

PLAYBOY: What was his life-style at Berchtesgaden?

SPEER: Relatively modest. This was, after all, his escape from Berlin, and he dispensed with the power and pomp of his official role. His associates, like Goering and Martin Bormann, were always trying to outdo one another with splendid showpiece homes, but Hitler lived unostentatiously in his small house, the *Berghof,* a typical country lodge decorated in the comfortable ersatz-peasant style cherished by the *petit bourgeois.* The lunches and dinners he hosted were informal affairs, with simple, hearty food—no gourmet fare such as graced the tables of Goering and the other Nazi potentates.

PLAYBOY: We've read that Hitler was a vegetarian.

SPEER: He was, in addition to neither drinking nor smoking. He had a special vegetarian chef prepare his dishes. He loved animals and thought their wholesale slaughter for our tables was cruel and barbaric—the same man who could order millions to their deaths without a flicker of pity! But he wasn't a fanatic about his vegetarianism and didn't try to impose his tastes on the rest of us, although he would occasionally chide us as "carrion eaters."

After dinner, the company always followed Hitler into the *salon,* which had been fitted out as a film-projection room. Until the war, when the practice was discontinued. Hitler always saw one or two movies every evening, generally romantic films, historic spectaculars and light musical comedies, particularly those with a lot of leggy chorus girls. Hitler suffered from insomnia and would not let us go until two or three in the morning, when we would finally stagger gratefully off to our own beds to get enough sleep to face another day of stultifying boredom.

PLAYBOY: Was there much infighting among Hitler's entourage?

SPEER: Hitler's circle was like a Byzantine court, seething with intrigue and jealousy and betrayal. The Third Reich was less a monolithic state than a network of mutually warring bureaucracies, with Hitler's satraps staking out their own independent spheres of influence and then unscrupulously seeking to extend them—often at the expense of the national interest.

PLAYBOY: Were Hitler's courtiers corrupt as well as ambitious?

SPEER: Most of them would have made their American contemporary Al Capone look like a benign philanthropist. From the moment they assumed power and got their hands on the state treasury, they lined their own pockets, amassing personal fortunes, profiteering from government contracts, building huge palaces and country villas with public funds, indulging in a lavish life-style more suited to the Borgias than to self-styled revolutionaries. The rot was all-pervasive; like a fish, the Nazi government decayed from the head down.

PLAYBOY: Which Nazi leader was the most corrupt?

SPEER: I would have to accord that dubious accolade to Goering. He was a thief on the grand scale, looting the museums and art collections of Europe for his own private hoards, requisitioning state funds to build luxurious homes, expropriating state land for his vast hunting preserves, extorting huge bribes from leading industrialists to support his estates and palaces and the hundreds of servants who staffed them. To give the devil his due, Goering had great personal charm, and also a very keen intellect. He could be a most engaging bandit. In a sense, he was born out of his time—he was a true *condottiere*, a soldier of fortune, totally amoral, with no ideology beyond personal advancement. His state secretary told me at Nuremberg, "Goering was the last of the Renaissance princes," and he was right.

PLAYBOY: Were you on good personal terms with Goering?

SPEER: Yes, we got along quite well. He frequently invited me out to Karinhall, his grand hunting estate north of Berlin, where he lived like a feudal lord. I remember driving out one night in 1942 after a phone call from Goering asking me to come immediately on a matter of urgent national interest. When I arrived, he greeted me, his corpulent body draped in an emerald-velvet dressing gown with a giant ruby brooch pinned to the satin lapel, his face covered by a thick patina of rouge, his fingernails lacquered a bright red. He told me he had a brilliant idea: In view of the desperate steel shortage, why didn't we build our locomotives out of concrete? I just stared at him. Of course, he went on eagerly, extracting a handful of uncut diamonds and rubies from his pocket and rolling them nervously through his fingers, concrete locomotives obviously wouldn't last as long as steel ones, but we could compensate for this by manufacturing *more* of them. I looked at him for a moment, sighed and said nothing. He kept elaborating on this new brain storm as he escorted me around Karinhall, expansively pointing out the latest artworks he had "liberated" from occupied France, Italy, the Netherlands and Russia, and he was still rambling on about it when I pleaded pressing business and left.

Goering loved to revel in his illicit riches and it was a ritual with him to show his guests through his cellars, where some of the world's most priceless art treasures were stored. But it was the money and power his collection represented that thrilled him, not its beauty, and he derived the same pleasure from showing guests his huge stock of confiscated French soaps and perfumes or his vulgarly impressive hoards of diamonds, rubies and emeralds, worth millions of dollars. By the end of the war, Goering must have been the richest man in Germany. Perhaps that's why he thought up the weird idea of concrete locomotives—to carry more of his loot! Of course, by that time, Goering was no longer completely rational; his mental and physical energies had been sapped by his addiction to heroin.

PLAYBOY: He was a drug addict, too?

SPEER: Yes, he'd been addicted since the Twenties. But his deterioration was gradual. When the Nazis first came to power, he demonstrated great energy and ability; but by the beginning of the war, his drug habit dominated him completely and he began to lose his grip. After his *Luftwaffe* had been cleared from English skies in the Battle of Britain, he became completely incapacitated by drugs, stagnating in a near-comatose state of narcotic stupor. Every once in a while, he would burst out of his torpor with an impressive display of euphoric energy, but it never lasted long. As the bad news got worse, Goering retreated more and more into his drug-induced womb, bestirring himself only to engage in an intrigue against his perennial rival, Martin Bormann.

PLAYBOY: There have been reports that not only Bormann but Hitler as well survived the war and escaped to South America. Do you believe either of them could still be alive?

SPEER: Well, I haven't received any postcards. Hitler certainly did not escape; the proofs of his death are irrefutable. The facts surrounding Bormann's fate are less certain, but I tend to be a bit skeptical about reports of his survival; he seems to surface and then disappear in Paraguay or Brazil with the same regularity as sightings of the Loch Ness monster. Of course, I suppose it is possible that in those chaotic last days, he could have made his way out of Berlin and found passage to South America or the Middle East or some other distant refuge. But even if he had, I doubt strongly that he would be alive today; he would have drunk himself to death years ago. Bormann was as addicted to alcohol as Goering was to drugs. When I knew him, he had the look of a man suffering from liver disease, and I think he had only a few years of life left, in any case. If he had reached South America, the hot climate and the isolation would doubtless have accelerated his drinking and finished him off even earlier.

PLAYBOY: What sort of man was Goebbels?

SPEER: He was a very capable and intelligent man, a dedicated worker and gifted administrator, a very well organized and systematic thinker, with a great gift for abstracting problems from their context, examining them clearly and incisively and arriving at sound and objective judgments. He was the kind of man who would have made his mark even in a normal society. He towered over the mental pygmies in Hitler's entourage; he was one of the few men in the inner circle with a university education and was thus openly contemptuous toward most of his associates, whom he correctly regarded as his intellectual inferiors. Despite the fanatic rhetoric of his speeches, he had a cold, calculating mind and was quite sophisticated and cultivated. He was a bit of a martinet and had a waspish tongue, but we tended to respect each other and got along well.

PLAYBOY: Was Goebbels as corrupt as the other Nazi leaders?

SPEER: I'd place him in the middle rank of corruption, not as bad as Goering and Himmler, worse than some others. He wasn't averse to using his position for personal advancement, building palaces and lavish country homes and inflating his bank account. But even though Goebbels did feather his own nest, I suspect that material benefits were not a dominant motivating factor in his life. At heart, he was an ideologue, a dedicated Nazi, although more clear-thinking than most. He belonged to the radical wing of the party and wanted to sweep away the existing order and replace it with a socialist utopia. This could have been due to reformist idealism, but deep down, I think he may have been something of a nihilist. During the war, he often said that the greatest mistake we had made was not joining up with Stalin and the Communists to jointly crush the West, and he pointed out the similarities between our ideologies; he used to say that ex-Communists made the best Nazis. He was not personally ambitious or power hungry, in the sense that Bormann was, and intellectually, he was a revolutionary ascetic, not a greedy hedonist like Goering. Goebbels was more interested in using his exalted position to blackmail girls into his bed than to transport gold into his vaults.

PLAYBOY: Goebbels, too, was a womanizer?

SPEER: That's something of an understatement. As minister of propaganda, he was czar of the German motion-picture industry and theater, and his casting couch must have been the envy of the Hollywood directors of that day. Most of the leading German actresses owed their careers to Goebbels, and he was not altruistic about repayment.

PLAYBOY: Did Hitler disapprove of Goebbels' private life?

SPEER: Not as long as it didn't create a public scandal. In his own way, of course, Hitler exploited women as callously as Goebbels did.

PLAYBOY: Are you referring to his relationship with Eva Braun?

SPEER: Yes. He treated her very badly. He never publicly acknowledged their relationship and went to absurd lengths to disguise it, even within his own circle of intimates. When she accompanied Hitler on trips or public appearances, she was never allowed to be seen in the motorcade or in close proximity to Hitler; and at Berchtesgaden, she was banished from the *Führer*'s presence whenever official guests arrived. On these occasions, Hitler exiled her to her small room on the second floor, with a connecting door to his own bedroom, where she would sit in sad isolation while the festivities carried on downstairs. Why Hitler kept up this transparent pretext, I don't know. Everyone knew she was his mistress. He never displayed any consideration for her feelings and was consistently callous toward her in public. This was painful to witness, because she was obviously devoted to him and easily hurt by his indifference.

PLAYBOY: What kind of person was she?

SPEER: Neither a dim-witted slut nor a scheming Madame Pompadour, but a sweet, gentle and quiet woman. She was completely apolitical and never attempted to intervene in affairs of state or influence any of Hitler's decisions. She loved sports, particularly skiing, and had a pleasant, unmalicious sense of humor; she teasingly referred to herself as "Mother of the Country." She came from a simple lower-middle-class Munich family, and neither she nor her parents ever seemed to benefit financially from her relationship with Hitler. His only gifts to her were birthday and Christmas presents of rather tasteless costume jewelry, and she lived on a frugal allowance doled out begrudgingly by Bormann. She alone of Hitler's inner circle remained unspoiled and unpretentious to the end. She was a sad, lonely person, the one member of that entourage who did not deserve her doom.

PLAYBOY: Why did Hitler treat her so shabbily throughout their relationship?

SPEER: I think there were several reasons. He used to discuss the question of marriage at the dinner table, while Eva sat next to him, her eyes lowered. "I could never marry," he would say with total insensitivity. "Think of the problems if I had children! In the end, they would try to make my son my successor, and the chances are slim for someone like me to have a capable son. That is almost always how it goes in such cases." He always cited the example of Goethe's son, who was a cretin, to explain his distrust of a hereditary succession. On other occasions, he would expound on his cynical disregard for women in general, just as if Eva were not there: "A highly intelligent man should take a primitive and stupid woman. Imagine if, on top of everything else, I had a woman who interfered with my work!" Eva's face would remain expressionless; only her eyes betrayed her pain. There was never any outward manifestation of tenderness or regard for her in his manner.

PLAYBOY: There were stories that Hitler was a homosexual. Do you think there was any truth to them?

SPEER: I think that was just wartime propaganda, rather like the stories that he was of Jewish ancestry or chewed the carpets in epileptic fits or was a syphilitic. No, Hitler was sexually normal; his perversion was of the soul, not of the body. But I don't believe he was capable of real love. Perhaps once in his life he may have been. As a young man, he had an incestuous affair with his niece, Geli Raubal, whom he drove to suicide. But as long as I knew Hitler, there was an ultimate coldness about him; on a deep level, he was devoid of all feelings of empathy and tenderness. He was an inhuman being.

PLAYBOY: And yet you said at Nuremberg, "If Hitler had ever had a friend, I would have been that friend."

SPEER: Yes, but the operative word there is *if*. I think at times that Hitler longed for the kind of human contact he could never achieve. I sensed this occasionally at Berchtesgaden, when I sat with him at teatime before his open fireplace; on these occasions, he would strive so hard to create a *gemütlich* atmosphere, serving cake to his secretaries with exaggerated gallantry, attempting to strike an easy and relaxed conversational tone with his guests, trying to play the friendly host. I felt a pang of pity for him on these occasions; he was like a ghost pretending he was alive, trying desperately to convince himself that he was, after all, a normal human being with normal feelings. But even Hitler's will could not fill that vacuum deep inside him, that pervasive quality of intangibility, of insubstantiality. I have never met anyone else in my life with whom I felt this sense of something vital missing, this impression that at the core of his being there was just a deadness. It is true that I probably came nearer to seeing this inner self than anyone else in his entourage. The only times I saw him behave with genuine vivacity and pleasure and spontaneity were when we were together, poring over architectural plans or inspecting his cherished scale models of the Berlin of the future. On such occasions, he came as close as he ever could to being human. One of my friends, after witnessing one of our work sessions, said of our relationship: "Do you know what you are? You are Hitler's unrequited love."

PLAYBOY: Could there have been an element of latent homosexuality in Hitler's relationship with you?

SPEER: Not in any conventional psychological sense. It was something deeper and darker. In *Beyond the Pleasure Principle,* Freud discusses the eternal struggle between the life and death urges within man; and in Hitler, the death force held almost uncontested sway. But it's possible that, at times, he struggled unconsciously against his own evil, and the last vestiges of his humanity reached out in search of the life principle. At such times, he may have sensed in me a reincarnation of the vanished hopes of his youth. But whatever our remarkable relationship was, it was not friendship. Our rapport lasted only as long as I was his architect; once I entered his government as minister of armaments, everything began to change. The war was the real turning point in our relationship.

PLAYBOY: Were you with Hitler the day the war began?

SPEER: No, at that time, I was still excluded from high-level military-strategy meetings. For weeks before he gave the order to invade Poland, the atmosphere at headquarters had been tense, and whenever I saw Hitler, he appeared withdrawn and distracted. This was the most desperate gamble of his life, of course; for the first time, it seemed possible that his territorial acquisitions would have to be sealed in blood. But he still hoped the Western powers would cave in without a fight, as they had over the Rhineland and Austria and Czechoslovakia.

Some kind of *rapprochement* with the Russians was a vital prerequisite to his Polish gamble. On August 21, 1939, I learned that Ribbentrop was in Moscow for some delicate negotiations with Stalin and Molotov. That night at dinner, a wire was handed to Hitler. He read it, stared vacantly out the window for a moment and then flushed a deep red. He slammed both fists on the table so hard that glasses rattled, and he cried out in an emotion-choked voice: "I have them! I have them!" His composure returned and he slumped back into his chair without elaborating. None of us dared to ask him any questions and the meal resumed in silence. Shortly after dinner, Hitler assembled his guests and told us: "We are going to conclude a non-aggression pact with Russia. Here, read this. A telegram from Stalin." He handed around the message he'd received at the table, which tersely informed him of Stalin's agreement to the terms of the proposed treaty. Hitler was euphoric, convinced that nothing now stood in the way of his mastery of Europe.

Around three in the morning, Hitler and I stood on the *Berghof* terrace, witnessing a rare and beautiful natural phenomenon. Northern lights of a remarkable intensity crackled across the night sky in a shimmering explosion of colors, bathing the mountains in a strange red glow. Our hands and faces were illuminated by this flickering red light, like cold flame, and there was something about the display that suddenly chilled me. Hitler stared out across the valley at the scarlet slopes of the *Untersberg,* then down at the red light dancing over his hands. He said abruptly: "Looks like a great deal of blood. This time we won't bring it off without violence." Even Hitler couldn't foresee how much blood.

PLAYBOY: When was the decision made to violate the treaty with Stalin and invade Russia?

SPEER: Hitler had always intended to expand to the East, to seek *Lebensraum* for Germany in Russia; you can see this quite explicitly stated in *Mein Kampf*. This was his grand strategy; but in tactics he was quite flexible and pragmatic, and I think that when he signed the Nazi-Soviet pact, he did not envision a showdown with Russia for several years, until he had absorbed Poland and, if necessary, brought England and France to their knees. But the scope and speed of his victories in the West made him overconfident and undermined his old resolve never to fight a war on two fronts. Russia's earlier poor showing in the Russo-Finnish War, and the outdated and deficient state of Soviet equipment, led him to a fatal underestimation of Soviet military strength.

He knew that the Russians had signed their pact with us mainly to buy time; our alliance was a marriage of convenience from the start, and the break was just a question of timing. On June 21, 1941, Hitler took me into his chancellery *salon* in Berlin after supper and played a few bars from Liszt's *Les Préludes* on the phonograph. "You'll hear that often in the near future," he smiled, "because it's going to be our victory fanfare for the Russian campaign." The next day, Operation Barbarossa, the German onslaught against Russia, began.

PLAYBOY: What was your own role in the war effort at that time?

SPEER: In the late summer of 1939, Hitler, who still liked to think of himself as grand patron of the arts, had personally exempted all artists—actors, painters, musicians, sculptors and architects—from military conscription. He ordered the army to send the draft records of all artists to him and he just tore them up and threw them away. But I felt it was my duty to contribute something to the war effort, so I visited General Fromm of the army's high command and volunteered my services and those of my team of engineers and workers. Our most important military task was the development of a new twin-motored medium-range Junkers dive bomber for the *Luftwaffe*. Toward the end of 1941, I visited the Junkers general manager, *Herr* Koppenberg, at their plant in Dessau to synchronize our construction with his production plans. He took me into a room, locked the door behind him and showed me a comparative graph of projected German and American bomber production over the following three years. The figures were overwhelmingly in favor of the Americans. I asked him how Goering and Hitler had reacted to these unnerving statistics. "That's just it," he whispered, "they won't believe them."

PLAYBOY: How long did you yourself remain blind to the realities of the military situation?

SPEER: Not for long; events were soon to open my eyes in the most brutal fashion. At the end of January 1942, I learned that Sepp Dietrich, formerly commander of Hitler's personal guard and now leading an SS Panzer corps on the Eastern front, was scheduled to fly to Dnepropetrovsk in the southern Ukraine, where my staff had made its headquarters for railroad reconstruction work. I was anxious to check firsthand on their progress, particularly after Todt's disturbing report, so I asked Dietrich to take me along. I will never forget that trip; it was my first foretaste of the end. As we flew over Russia, a vast empty landscape of devastation stretched out before me—desolate snow-covered fields with no signs of life other than the burned-out remnants of farms and railroad installations, the few roads empty save for an occasional gutted vehicle strewn along the roadside like the bones of some prehistoric animal. There was a terrible silence over everything, the silence of death, broken only by the sound of our motors and the rattle of sleet-driven snow on the fuselage. As I looked down on this endless lunar landscape, I knew what it must be like for a soldier struggling across it on foot, cut off from supplies, blinded by the snow and numbed by frostbite. I thought of Napoleon's terrible march from Moscow and I suddenly realized that the same disaster could befall us.

When we landed at Dnepropetrovsk, I was deeply relieved to see again some evidences of organized human activity. But even there, conditions were harsh; my crew of technicians was quartered in an abandoned railroad sleeping car, kept from freezing only by an occasional puff of steam running through the heating coils from an attached locomotive. Most of the city was in rubble and our makeshift headquarters was in an icy dining car. I soon discovered that the rail situation was even worse than we had feared. In their retreat, the Russians had adopted a scorched-earth policy, destroying all stations, repair sheds, switching yards, signal systems and water tanks. As we desperately tried to mobilize our slender and overextended resources to effect at least emergency repairs, the great blizzards of the Russian winter descended on us. All highway as well as rail traffic was brought to a standstill and our crude airstrip was snowed in, cutting us off from the outside world. As the weather continued to deteriorate, our situation grew graver by the hour. We learned that a Soviet tank corps had penetrated our defenses and was rapidly approaching Dnepropetrovsk.

There was only a small *Wehrmacht* contingent in the city to hold them off, so my technicians and I anxiously foraged around for weapons to defend ourselves. We came up with nothing but a few old rifles and an antique artillery piece without shells. So we broke open our remaining supply of liquor and spent the evening drinking with Sepp Dietrich and some of his men.

PLAYBOY: How was their morale?

SPEER: Very low, except for Dietrich, who, as a professional military man, would never show any outward manifestation of concern. During that evening of socializing, the soldiers poured out many of their fears and anxieties. As we sat through the night, listening to the booming of Russian artillery in the distance, songs were sung—sad and despairing songs echoing the men's loneliness and homesickness and the bleak horror of a death on the barren Russian steppes. These were the soldiers' favorite songs, not any of the familiar martial melodies, and they expressed more than a thousand words. As I sang with them, I thought what a different world this was from Berlin, where right now the night clubs and restaurants, as yet unfettered by austerity decrees, were full, the laughter high, the music gay, the champagne bubbling—a Berlin so many of these men around me would never see again.

For the moment, however, we were spared when the Russian offensive inexplicably turned back in one of those critical blunders both sides were guilty of throughout the war; and the next day, the weather cleared enough for me to fly back to Germany. I had one final impression before entering the plane. I was forced to wait on the airstrip in freezing cold for several hours while Soviet POWs strove to clear the snow and ice from the runway, and, at one point, several Russians in padded jackets surrounded me and gesticulated animatedly. They spoke no German and I no Russian, but finally, one scooped up some snow and rubbed my face with it. I realized he was warning me of frostbite. Another of the Russians reached into the filthy, tattered remnants of his Red Army uniform and handed me a clean, folded white handkerchief to wipe my face. Later, that image stuck in my mind: Here was one of a race we were determined to turn into helots, a people whom we already regarded with utter contempt and indifference as little more than pack animals, giving me what was probably the last of his personal possessions—and for no reason other than that I was a fellow human being threatened by the elements.

Though, once again, I did not draw the proper conclusions from this incident, it remained with me. But soon the plane took off and the Russian workers were left behind—ants on the snow-swept waste. Within hours, I would be at the "Wolf's Lair," the *Führer*'s command headquarters in Rastenburg, back in the "real world" of pomp and power and glory— and inhumanity. As I arrived, Todt emerged from a conference with Hitler, appearing exhausted and depressed. He sat with me, drinking a glass of wine, glumly reticent, and then excused himself for a few hours' sleep. He was flying back to Berlin, he said, and asked me if I'd like to accompany him. I accepted eagerly, glad to avoid the grueling train journey, and agreed to meet him at the airport later.

But when my own meeting with Hitler ended, it was after three o'clock in the morning and I was totally exhausted, mentally and physically. I sent Todt a message that I could not fly with him to Berlin and was assigned a small bedroom where I could get some sleep. I was awakened the next morning by the harsh ringing of the telephone. I picked it up groggily and Dr. Brandt, Hitler's personal physician, came on the line, his voice charged with excitement: "Todt's plane has just crashed and he has been killed." He hung up and I sat there numbly for several minutes while the news sank in.

PLAYBOY: Did you expect Hitler to appoint you as Todt's successor?

SPEER: That was the last thought in my mind. Todt's position was, after Hitler himself, the most important in the Reich. I expected that a small proportion of Todt's construction tasks would be shifted to me, but I never even dreamed that I would become his successor. I assumed that his duties would be transferred to other ministers, with the bulk of his work probably falling to Goering. This was what I expected when Hitler summoned me to his office at one o'clock in the afternoon on the day of Todt's death. Unlike our meeting of the previous evening, he greeted me formally, in his capacity as chief of state, and his manner was businesslike. He replied to my expression of condolences and then said abruptly: "*Herr* Speer, I appoint you successor to Minister Todt in all his capacities."

I was rooted to the ground, unable to speak. I could not believe I was hearing right. "I've selected you for the whole task. I have confidence in you. I know you will manage it." I stood there in silence, unable to think of anything to say, and Hitler ignored me, coolly returning to his paperwork. When I left, he had no personal word for me, none of the friendly goodbyes I'd grown accustomed to. I'd had my first taste of our new relationship. I was no longer his personal friend and architect but an underling in his government. But at the time, I did not recognize the significance of this change in Hitler's manner. As I left his office, my thoughts were reeling in confusion—and some apprehension. I had been transformed from an architect to the number-two man in the government, with complete responsibility for the efficient functioning of our war effort. I had been entrusted, in effect, with the destiny of the entire nation.

PLAYBOY: By all accounts, your successes, at least in the early days, were quite phenomenal.

SPEER: Yes, once we had restructured the war economy under a central planning control and mobilized our industrial reserves and resources, the production results were remarkable. Within six months of my appointment, production had soared in every area under our control. In the period from February to August 1942, production increased by a ratio of 27 percent for guns and 25 percent for tanks, while ammunition output rose by 97 percent. Our armaments production in that half year rose by 59.6 percent. By 1943, our factories were producing seven times the weapons produced in 1942 and over five times the amount of ammunition; our total munitions production rose from 540,000 tons in 1941 to 2,558,000 tons in 1943. Even as the Allied air onslaught grew in ferocity, our production figures continued to skyrocket. The Allies were quite amazed by the way our arms industry kept going almost to the end.

When I was arrested after the war, General Frederick L. Anderson, commander of the U.S. Eighth Air Force, visited me in my cell and talked to me for some time about the way our arms industry had continued functioning despite his bomber attacks. He told some reporters afterward, "Had I known what this man was achieving, I would have sent out the entire American Eighth Air Force merely to put him underground." So it is true that we had some startling successes. But they only served to delay the inevitable. The forces arrayed against us were too overwhelming for even the most brilliant industrial planning to overcome.

PLAYBOY: But you did succeed in delaying the inevitable; without your efforts, according to some historians, Hitler might have had to admit defeat as early as 1942 or 1943. Hundreds of thousands of soldiers and civilians on both sides died in that period, and yet you still speak of your achievements with apparent pride.

SPEER: I am not proud of my role in prolonging the war—just the opposite. It would have been far better for Germany and the world if the collapse had come in 1943, when the human sacrifice would have been far less and many victims would have been spared. So, in that sense, my successes were really failures—crimes, in fact. But, of course, in those years, I did not think in ethical or humanitarian terms. All I was interested in was increasing our war production.

PLAYBOY: And yet there is still that note of pride in your voice when you discuss these technical achievements.

SPEER: I cannot help feeling stirrings of pride. This is my weakness—a human weakness, perhaps. Those were the days of my youth, and I achieved things which many people predicted were impossible, and I suppose my ego still takes pleasure in those accomplishments. Then I think of all the cities destroyed, the soldiers killed, the Jews butchered between 1943 and 1945—and my pride turns to sickness. But I will not be a hypocrite and say the pride is not there. Intellectually, I have accepted that it is wrong to be proud of such things, but emotionally, I still feel a surge of pride when I think of the obstacles I overcame and the goals we achieved. I would be dishonest if I said otherwise.

PLAYBOY: When did the slave-labor policy begin?

SPEER: As early as November 1941, Hitler told me when I stressed our manpower problems, "The area working directly for us embraces more than

250,000,000 people [and] we will succeed in involving every one of these millions in the labor process." Hitler ordered Sauckel to recruit labor from the occupied countries, by force, if necessary, and Sauckel enthusiastically agreed, promising to provide millions of workers for our factories. Sauckel went ahead with brutal procurement of forced labor, and millions of foreign laborers, Soviet POWs and concentration-camp inmates were sent to work in my armaments factories, often under the most appalling conditions.

PLAYBOY: If only for reasons of economic efficiency, you could have improved the barbaric conditions under which these men worked and lived —and died.

SPEER: I actually did try to improve conditions. In fact, this was one of the reasons the judges at Nuremberg gave for reducing the severity of my sentence. But even when I did do the right thing, it was for all the wrong reasons. I saw the conditions under which these prisoners worked on several occasions and it is burned into my memory—and my conscience. In December 1943, I inspected a huge rocket-production complex built in air-raid-proof caves in the desolate Harz Mountain range. The foreign workers there had been provided by the SS, which was then my rival in manpower procurement, and I remember vividly walking through those bleak, echoing caverns where thousands of slave laborers worked on V-2 assembly lines.

These men went about their work like zombies, and as I passed among them, they looked at and through me blankly with drowned eyes and mechanically plucked their blue prison caps from their shaven skulls until I had passed by them. They walked and worked like men swimming under water, immersed in their private horrors. They were skeletal, under-nourished and brutally treated. I learned that sanitary facilities were virtually nonexistent, disease was everywhere and the mortality rate was tremendous; the men were forced to sleep in the wet, chilly caves and they died like flies from dysentery, tuberculosis and pneumonia. After I left the caves, which reeked with human illness, I almost vomited, and I had to down several stiff brandies before I could carry on. I knew that we were ruthlessly exploiting slave labor, but I had not been prepared for this sickening human reality.

PLAYBOY: What did you do about it?

SPEER: I immediately dispatched the labor force to build a large barracks camp on a nearby hill to quarter the workers and instructed the overseers to improve sanitary and health conditions and improve their diet. I sent Dr. Poschmann, the medical supervisor for my ministry, to inspect the site and see that all hygienic precautions were taken and that henceforth the men would be well fed, clothed and housed and provided with civilian doctors stationed at the camp. Whenever I tried to improve living and working conditions for foreign laborers, of course, I was faced with stiff opposition from the SS, whose declared policy was to treat these men as no more than beasts of burden. But don't get me wrong; I took such measures only for reasons of maximizing efficiency and production. As I said to Hitler so often, what good to our war effort is a sick or dead worker? I helped these men rather as one would keep livestock well fed, not out of any sympathy for their plight as human beings.

PLAYBOY: In a review of your book, Willi Frischauer writes, "I have come across nothing quite as repugnant as the tears Speer sheds" for your slave laborers. How would you answer him?

SPEER: What can I say to him? My behavior on this question *was* repugnant and there is no way I can convince anyone of the sincerity of my guilt. It is something I must live with. I suppose, to be honest, that the tears I shed are for myself as well as for my victims, for the man I could have been but was not, for a conscience I so easily destroyed.

PLAYBOY: How many slave laborers died in your factories?

SPEER: There are no precise figures, but thousands must have perished from disease, malnutrition and, in some cases, the brutality of SS guards. And, of course, the casualty figures among both forced laborers and German workers mounted with the increasing tempo of Allied air attacks on our industrial installations. By the end of the war, our factories were taking a tremendous pounding from the air.

PLAYBOY: Some observers, such as playwright Rolf Hochhuth, have charged that the Allied "terror bombings" of such German cities as Dresden were immoral and inhumane and actually constituted a war crime in themselves. Do you agree with them?

SPEER: I think you have a saying in English about the pot calling the kettle black, so after all my own sins, I am not going to accuse others; if my own hands were clean, perhaps I could do otherwise. All I can say is that these raids certainly did not achieve their stated objective of shortening the war. There is no doubt that the air attacks were terrifying, but their final result was to engender more hatred than fear among the survivors.

I was in my ministry in Berlin when the Royal Air Force began its great bomber offensive against the city on November 22, 1943. We were in the midst of a staff conference when the air-raid siren sounded; and when I was informed that a huge fleet of Allied bombers had reached Potsdam, I adjourned the meeting and drove to a flak tower in the vicinity, where I intended to witness the attack from the platform, as I had done previously. I had just reached the top when direct hits nearby forced me to take refuge inside; the heavy concussions were shaking the thick concrete tower like a leaf. All around me staggered dazed and bleeding anti-aircraft gunners; the terrific air pressure from the detonations of the bombs had flung them against the walls and down the stairs like rag dolls. For 20 minutes, we huddled together in the tower while bombs rained down on the city and we were choked by a haze of cement dust from the crumbling walls.

As the sound of the exploding bombs began to recede from our immediate vicinity, I reeled out onto the observation tower and looked out over the besieged city. Berlin appeared to be one giant inferno. Fierce conflagrations raged everywhere and there was a sinister, seductive quality of beauty about the terrible scene; if one could forget the death and suffering in the streets below, it was quite visually entrancing. The night sky was shattered by the explosion of countless parachute flares, which the Berliners dubbed "Christmas trees," casting a fitful illumination over the burning city. Anti-aircraft shells exploded in bursts of flame amid the roiling black smoke, and the sky was slashed by searchlights, like gigantic swords in some medieval duel. Occasionally, an enemy bomber would be trapped in a probing searchlight and I would watch as it struggled to escape the cone of light like a moth trying to wriggle free of its pin, until the anti-aircraft gunners zeroed in on it and the bomber dissolved in a blossom of flame, its debris plummeting to earth, lost in the sea of fire that was sweeping the city.

The spectacle was strangely choreographed and somehow unreal. It was only when the raid was over and I ventured forth into the streets that its apocalyptic splendor dissolved into the screaming and sobbing of the maimed and bereaved and the grim finality of death. I got hold of my staff car and drove to the sections of the city where key factories were situated, driving over streets thick with rubble, past rows of flaming buildings. Dispossessed families stood or sat before their burning homes, pathetic bundles of salvaged possessions piled around them. The air was filled with suffocating clouds of soot and smoke and the sound of crackling fire was everywhere, as if some giant carnivore were rending the city in its jaws. A huge pall of smoke hovered over Berlin, extending up to 20,000 feet in height, and even when day came, everything remained as dark as night. There was a *Walpurgisnacht* atmosphere about the city, heightened by the near-hysterical laughter and gaiety of people dazed and stunned by the disaster and unable to comprehend its full dimensions. From that point on, Berlin was subjected to relentless and devastating Allied air attack, until, at the end of the war, the city was reduced to rubble.

PLAYBOY: How did Hitler react to the systematic destruction of his cities?

SPEER: With a weird, somnambulistic indifference. As reverses accumulated, beginning with the totally unexpected disaster at Stalingrad, Hitler's state of mind began to change, and he withdrew. Increasingly, he sought solace in his delusions of omnipotence and, as Stalingrad was followed by the Allied landings in Africa, the collapse of the Afrika Korps and the steady deterioration of the Eastern front, he progressively blocked himself off from reality. This was particularly true of the air war; as it intensified, Hitler remained in his own dreamworld and, to the end, refused to perceive the enormity of the devastation.

PLAYBOY: Was he afraid to face the consequences of his own miscalculations?

SPEER: That may have been part of it. At first, I tried to tell myself that the devastation of the cities moved Hitler so deeply that he could not bear to confront it; but gradually, I came to suspect that he had no real feeling for the human victims of his blunders, that he could not stand visible confirmation of his failures. From the moment the war began, Hitler shut himself off from his own people, among whom he had once moved with relative impunity—a fact that had contributed to his immense prewar popularity. I recall one evening in the middle of the war, when we were traveling with Hitler on his private railroad train to his headquarters at Rastenburg. We enjoyed a late and lavish meal in his elegant rosewood-paneled dining car, the linen and silverware glistening, the wine in delicate cut-glass goblets. As we ate, our train slowed down and crawled past a freight train halted on a side track. From one open cattle car, wounded German soldiers from the Eastern front—starved, their uniforms in tatters—stared across the few yards to our dining-car window. Hitler recoiled as he saw these injured men regarding us expressionlessly and, without even a wave of his hand in their direction, he sharply ordered an adjutant to lower the window shades.

As we resumed the meal in silence, our train picked up speed and left behind the men who were fighting and dying for Hitler's cause. That encounter was symptomatic of his attitude whenever the question of military or civilian casualties was raised in his presence. I don't know to what extent such blindness was a defensive reaction, or if he actually succeeded in deluding himself. But as the war progressed, Hitler not only ignored the suffering of his populace but made vital military decisions without any consideration of realistic technical and tactical limitations—decisions that determined the destiny of millions of people.

PLAYBOY: Was there a corresponding mental deterioration in Hitler as the war turned against him?

SPEER: Yes, without any doubt. The Hitler of the last three years of the war was a pale shadow of the dynamic peacetime leader of the Thirties. The deterioration first manifested itself in 1942 and grew progressively worse until the end. The keen cutting edge of his intellect seemed blunted; intellectually he was sluggish and torpid; he was permanently irritable and on edge. Where once he had arrived at decisions swiftly and firmly, he now had to drag them painfully from his fatigued mind. Every time I saw him in those days, he seemed to have grown more withdrawn and taciturn. I will say to Hitler's credit that he had fantastic powers of self-control when he was willing to exercise them; and throughout the war, he did force himself to accept a strictly disciplined work schedule. But this was contrary to his character and it imposed severe strains upon him—strains that were reflected in the erratic quality of his judgments.

The military men around Hitler had been accustomed to intense daily work since their youth, and they could not grasp the extent to which Hitler suffered from overwork. It was only years later, when I was imprisoned at

Spandau, that I really understood what it must be like to live every day under such intense psychological pressure. Looking back on Hitler's physical environment in his military bunkers in Berlin and Rastenburg, I realized how similar the atmosphere was to a prison—immense concrete walls and ceilings, harsh electric light instead of daylight, iron doors and iron grilles over the few windows. Even Hitler's brief strolls through the barbed-wire perimeters, surrounded by armed guards and police dogs, resembled a convict's exercise in the jail yard. Hitler had turned all of Europe into a prison, but he was its leading prisoner.

PLAYBOY: How sound was Hitler's health in other respects? It's been said that he was a hypochondriac.

SPEER: I know that Hitler himself was deeply worried about his health for as long as I knew him; but whether this was hypochondria or there was something seriously wrong I never discovered, because he was never specific about the nature of his troubles. As early as 1935, he would complain to me of intense gastric and cardiac pains, as well as of his perpetual insomnia. More and more, throughout the Thirties, he brooded over the possibility of his early death. This is certainly one reason why he pushed forward both his domestic plans and his foreign policies at such a relentless pace.

PLAYBOY: Did he ever confide to you that he feared the war was lost?

SPEER: Never. As a matter of fact, a remarkable transformation came over him during this period. Even as our military situation grew progressively worse, he expressed an unshakable confidence in absolute . victory. Of course, after the Allied demand for unconditional surrender in January 1943, Hitler knew his back was to the wall and he was fighting with all the tenacity of a cornered rat. He used to say to me: "There is no turning back. We can only move forward. We have burned our bridges." Whether or not he believed his own predictions, they were vital to sustaining the enthusiasm and loyalty of his military and political subordinates. But I think he believed that Providence would never fail him. If there ever was an element of insanity in Hitler, it was this abiding faith in his own divine mission. He was essentially a religious man, but his worship had been perverted into self-adulation, and on the altar of his will he was prepared to sacrifice the lives of millions. Perhaps the most frightening thing about Hitler is that he never once recognized his own evil.

After the failure of the July 20, 1944, *Putsch*, Hitler told me, "If the German nation is now defeated in this struggle, it has been too weak. That will mean it has not withstood the test of history and was destined for nothing but doom." I was soon to learn that this was more threat than prophecy.

PLAYBOY: How did you react to it?

SPEER: At first, I didn't realize how deadly serious Hitler was. It was not until the end of 1944 that I recognized the full criminal implications of his scorched-earth policy. I realized then that if Hitler was to go down to defeat, he was determined, like Samson, to carry the entire nation with him. He desired total catastrophe, a Wagnerian *Götterdämmerung* that would prove a genocidal funeral pyre to mark his departure from the stage of history. To accomplish this, he instructed my ministry to effectively annihilate German industry, transportation, communications and food production. Had I obeyed, the entire industrial and productive infrastructure of our nation would have been destroyed and millions of Germans would have perished of starvation in the immediate postwar period. Fortunately, I was able, with the aid of the remaining sane men in the government, to sabotage this criminal policy. But it was not easy and the fight was touch and go. I had to travel the length and breadth of Germany, rallying army officers, civilian administrators and even some responsible gauleiters to my cause. Together with the help of the leaders of German industry, we were able to vitiate this scorched-earth policy not only in Germany but also in France, the Netherlands, Norway and other occupied countries.

PLAYBOY: Did Hitler learn of your insubordination?

SPEER: Yes, he did. After I succeeded in sabotaging the scorched-earth policy in the vital Ruhr industrial area, I returned to Berlin. The roads were jammed with hapless refugees and retreating soldiers and, everywhere along the way, villagers were digging up their gardens to bury the family silverware and other valuables. Late on the night of March 27, I finally reached Berlin, where I was summoned to the *Führer*'s tomblike bunker beneath the chancellery. He received me coldly, without shaking hands or smiling, and did not respond to my greeting. "Bormann has given me a report on your conference with the Ruhr gauleiters," he told me. "You pressed them not to carry out my orders and declared that the war is lost. Are you aware of what must follow from that?" I was, and I could feel the sweat springing out on my brow as I stood there, unable to speak.

The penalty for such treasonous insubordination was death, with or without the formality of a trial. I stood there numbly, waiting for Hitler to issue the orders for my arrest. But suddenly his mood seemed to change and he stared off into the distance for a moment, as if lost in a remote memory. When he resumed speaking, his voice was warmer, gentler: "If you were not my architect, I would take the measures that are called for in such a case."

His words had just reprieved me from a certain death sentence, but some obscure stirring of rebellion forced me to reply rashly: "Take the measures you think necessary and grant no consideration to me as an individual." But he ignored my remark and stood silent, deep in thought. Finally, he said softly: "You are overworked and ill. I have therefore decided that you are to go on leave at once. Someone else will run your ministry as your deputy." Hitler was offering me an easy way out of the situation, but it would have been cowardice to accept it, for I then would have been impotent to preserve our industrial capacity from his orders.

So I remained obdurate: "I cannot keep the responsibility of a minister while another man is acting in my name." Hitler suddenly slumped into his chair and there was another long pause. Finally, he looked up at me and said in more normal tones, "Speer, if you can convince yourself that the war is not lost, you can continue to run your office." This was the crux of the matter; all I had to do was to pay lip service to his fantasies and my position would be restored. For practical considerations, I should have had no hesitation about doing so; but something stopped me. After all the years of accepting this man's delusions, of becoming part of them, of participating in the sycophancy and hypocrisy of his circle, I felt that I now owed both him and myself a measure of honesty, however belated. "You know I cannot be convinced of that," I said quietly but firmly. "The war is lost."

Instead of flaring up at this, Hitler embarked on a series of rambling recollections of the past crises he had overcome. As I continued to regard him steadily, he faltered and broke off, and then spoke in an almost begging tone: "If you would believe that the war can still be won, if you could at least have faith in that, all would be well." Somehow, the sight of Hitler pleading was pitiable and more compelling than his autocratic demands. In the past, I would doubtless have surrendered to such an appeal, but the thought of his scorched-earth plans stiffened my resistance. My voice strident, I replied: "I cannot, with the best will in the world. I do not want to be one of the swine of your entourage who tell you they believe in victory without believing in it."

Hitler did not answer me. For a while, he mused silently; then he launched into another monolog. After all, he said, Frederick the Great had been delivered from defeat in the darkest days of the Seven Years' War, and history could repeat itself. "One must believe that all will turn out well," he muttered desperately. "Do you still hope for a successful continuance of the war, or is your faith shattered?" I could sense that he was exerting all the magnetism of his will to pull me back under his control, but I was able to resist his spell. Finally, he whispered brokenly: "If you could at least *hope* that we have not lost? You must certainly be able to hope—that would be enough to satisfy me." He looked at me imploringly, but my silence told him my answer. There was an uncomfortable pause, and then Hitler jumped to his feet and dismissed me with his old curtness: "You have 24 hours to think over your answer! Tomorrow, let me know whether you hope that the war can still be won." He turned his back on me and I left, shaken by the duel of wills.

PLAYBOY: How did you respond to his ultimatum?

SPEER: I spent a sleepless night. It was vital that I resume some of my lost authority, because otherwise it would be far more difficult to sabotage his plans. Yet something deep within me rebelled at an ultimate act of hypocrisy. Toward midnight the next day, I drove along the rubble-strewn Wilhelmstrasse to the chancellery, still not sure what I was going to tell Hitler. He met me at the door to his office and stood facing me. He seemed strangely uncertain and there was an expression of anxiety on his face. "Well?" he asked me tensely. I stood silent for a few seconds, unable to answer him, my thoughts confused. And then, impulsively, I blurted out: "*Mein Führer*, I stand unreservedly behind you." I had not committed myself to a belief in victory, but this expression of personal loyalty satisfied Hitler and seemed to move him. Tears sprang into his eyes and he shook my hand with trembling fingers, something he had not done for some time. His relief was so strong that it shook me, and I felt a surge of pity and affection for him.

Once again, our old relationship asserted itself; but with an almost physical effort, I shook it off and managed to exploit the situation to my advantage: "If I stand unreservedly behind you, then you must entrust me with the implementation of your demolition decree." He nodded and allowed me to draw up a fresh document for his signature. He would not retreat on the destruction of industry and transport and I knew better by now than to try to change the major provisions of the decree. But I succeeded in undermining its application by slipping in a few key clauses providing that "Implementation will be undertaken solely by the agencies and organs of the ministry of armaments and war production, and the minister of armaments and war production may, with my authorization, issue instructions for implementation." I also inserted a sentence which was to prove of vital importance in preventing the total destruction of large areas of industry: "The same effect can be achieved with industrial installations by crippling them." I added a proviso that the total demolition of key plants would be authorized only by me. Hitler signed the decree without protest. I had regained my lost powers and was once more czar of the scorched-earth policy. No program ever had a director more devoted to its sabotage.

PLAYBOY: Hitler seems to have displayed remarkable tolerance toward you. Did he ever become aware of the full extent of your opposition to him?

SPEER: My rivals at court, such as Himmler and Bormann, would have been all too glad to inform him, if they had discovered it; but in those chaotic final days of the war, it was possible for the first time to defy the *Führer* with relative impunity. While I was playing my dangerous double game, I operated on the sound principle of staying as close to Hitler as I could. By remaining in regular contact with him, I was able to defuse any rumors or planted suspicions.

PLAYBOY: What was Hitler's mood in the last months of the war?

SPEER: He remained capable to the end of deluding himself and those around him that victory was still possible, even as Soviet tanks were rumbling through the outskirts of Berlin. I remember one instance of this very clearly. On April 12, 1945, I look a brief respite from work to attend the last concert of the Berlin Philharmonic, conducted by Wilhelm Fürtwangler. On the occasion of this final concert, arranged by my ministry, we all sat in our overcoats in the unheated Philharmonic Hall, cold winds blowing in through the shattered windows. Electricity was normally canceled at that time of the day, but I had the current kept on for the performance and, as the leaders of the Reich pulled up in their Mercedeses before the brightly lit concert hall, the war-weary Berliners passing by must have thought us all mad. But, somehow, this performance seemed a fitting finale for the Philharmonic, as well as for the Third Reich. I had ordered selections from Wagner's *Götterdämmerung,* followed by Beethoven's violin concerto and concluding with Bruckner's *Romantic Symphony.* As I sat shivering in the hall, I wondered how many weeks—or days—any of us had left to live; at that time, we all expected short shrift from the victorious Allies, and there was a brisk trade in cyanide capsules.

After the concert, I was urgently summoned to Hitler's bunker, where the *Führer* rushed up to me in a state of excitement the moment I arrived, waving a newspaper clipping under my nose. "Here, read it!" he shouted, the words rushing over each other. "Here! You never wanted to believe it! Here it is! Here we have the miracle I always predicted! Who was right? The war isn't lost! Read it! Roosevelt is dead!" He was euphoric, racing around the bunker, buttonholing his courtiers and regaling them with the great news, and Goebbels and others expressed similar delight at the glad tidings. Hitler was convinced that Roosevelt's death was the work of divine providence, that at last the promised turning point was in sight. Now he was sure the Allies would fall out among themselves, the Americans would begin fighting the Russians and they would have to enlist Nazi Germany against the Bolshevik hordes; just as Frederick the Great was saved at the last moment by the death of the czarina, history had now turned the tide for Hitler. Later on, he calmed down somewhat and slumped back into his armchair, exhausted by his frenzy of jubilation, looking vastly relieved. I didn't know whether to pity or despise such escapist fantasies; I suppose they were at least therapeutic—a means of staving off the reality of impending defeat and almost certain death.

PLAYBOY: Did you feel any personal sympathy for Hitler at this point?

SPEER: Again, I could not help but experience pangs of pity for him, although I knew he was the author of all our misfortunes and directly responsible for the devastation of our country and for the death of millions on both sides. If it had not been for the scorched-earth policy, I would certainly have felt far more sympathy for his condition, but his vicious determination to carry the nation with him to destruction had severed my old bonds of loyalty and affection. It was then that I plotted his assassination.

PLAYBOY: Why did you decide on such drastic action?

SPEER: I realized that if Hitler were removed from the leadership of the Reich, our people might still have a chance of survival and postwar regeneration. After much soul-searching throughout a night early in 1945, I came to the decision that I must kill Adolf Hitler.

PLAYBOY: But isn't it true that you never actually lifted a finger against him?

SPEER: Yes, my assassination plot never got beyond the planning stage, and that is one reason I refused to use it as a defense point in Nuremberg and prefer to play it down today. In any case, my plan was never of the same caliber as that of the July 20 plotters; I had no alternative government in mind; I merely wished to eliminate Hitler before he could cause more death and destruction.

PLAYBOY: How did you intend to assassinate him?

SPEER: While strolling through the chancellery gardens, I had observed the ventilation shaft of Hitler's bunker. Hidden by a small shrub was the air-intake opening, which passed air into the bunker through a purifying filter system. In my armaments work, I had developed a close association with Dieter Stahl, the head of munitions production, and we had once discussed a new nerve gas called *Tabun,* which was highly lethal—so lethal and so virulent that the filtration process could not reduce its potency.

I knew that Stahl was no friend of the regime, as I once had to intervene with Gauleiter Sturtz of Brandenburg to save him from arrest by the Gestapo for "defeatist" remarks; and in mid-February, I asked him about *Tabun* as we sat in our air-raid shelter during a heavy raid on Berlin. He must have been bewildered by my request, but he replied frankly, detailing the effectiveness of the gas. Suddenly, as the explosion of bombs rattled in the background, I blurted out: "It is the only way to bring the war to an end. I want to try to conduct the gas into the chancellery bunker." Stahl received this treasonous news calmly and, with no change in his voice or expression, promised to obtain samples of the gas for me.

Unfortunately, he soon discovered that *Tabun* had to be fired by a detonating shell, as it became operational only after an explosion, which was useless in this case, since the blast would have wrecked the air ducts needed to conduct the gas throughout the bunker. Stahl, however, promised to get hold of a stock of ordinary poison gas, which could do the job equally well. I then spoke with Henschel, the bunker's chief engineer, and suggested a complete overhaul of the filtration system to improve the freshness of air in the bunker. To my gratification, he responded swiftly and dismantled the filters, leaving the bunker defenseless to traditional poison gases.

But a few days later, while Stahl was still engaged in requisitioning the gas, our whole scheme fell apart when I reconnoitered the chancellery garden and discovered that the old ventilation shaft had been replaced on Hitler's orders by a ten-foot-high chimney, which made the air intake inaccessible to anyone on the ground level. SS guards with submachine guns now patrolled the garden, too, and the walls were illuminated by search-lights. For a moment, I panicked and thought my plot had been discovered, but it turned out to have been a coincidence; Hitler had been reminiscing about his own temporary blinding by poison gas in the First World War and had decided to order precautions against an enemy gas attack. As a result, my assassination attempt came to nothing.

PLAYBOY: It has a rather halfhearted ring to it, in any case.

SPEER: At the time, it seemed like a desperate and courageous act; but looked at in hindsight, the whole episode does now appear somewhat absurd. Actually, I was far more relieved than upset when it was frustrated. I don't think I would have been able to go through with it.

PLAYBOY: You were alone with Hitler on many occasions and you carried a sidearm. Would you have been incapable of shooting him?

SPEER: That would have required far too much courage. I could never have confronted Hitler with a pistol. I was intellectually free of his thralldom at this point, but not emotionally. Looking back on it, I am glad that circum-stances aborted the plot. Even if I had finally been able to summon up the fortitude to kill Hitler, it would have added just one more stain to my con-science. My plot was actually the culmination of the moral degradation to which my association with the regime had led me; for years I had lived among mass murderers and criminals without ever giving a thought to it. I had been corrupted by my own pride and ambition, and now I was allow-ing my detestation of Hitler's policies to lead me to one more crime. Hitler deserved to die—but not by my hand.

PLAYBOY: When did you last see him alive?

SPEER: Our final meeting clearly expressed my ambivalent emotions. I eagerly anticipated his death, yet I simultaneously mourned his last pathetic hours of life. Once Hitler's scorched-earth orders had been thwarted and he could cause no more wanton waste of human lives, my feelings of pity for his plight grew in intensity. This was certainly naïve, perhaps even in-decent, in view of his crimes, but I had shared too much with him for too long to resist this final emotion. My war work was over; our armaments industry had been wiped out of existence and there was nothing more I could do to affect the course of the war one way or another. Yet I could not rest. It was as if Hitler's will was a palpable force, calling out to me from the rubble of Berlin to the estate near Wilsnack where I paced back and forth in my room. Something of me was still possessed by Hitler, and I knew I must see it to the grave.

I flew to Berlin on April 22. As I approached Hitler's bunker, I was quite aware that his capricious nature might have turned against me since our last meeting, perhaps on the basis of fresh evidence of my sabotage of the scorched-earth policy, and I knew it was quite possible that I was going to my death. Hitler had just executed Eva Braun's brother-in-law for attempting to take his family to safety outside Berlin; the poor devil had been machine-gunned in the chancellery garden. A similar fate might well await me, yet I was strangely calm and not at all unnerved. This was not courage but more a sense of fatalism, of predestination. The thought crossed my mind that if Hitler executed me for refusing to destroy German industry, it might redound to the credit of my family and soften their lot in the post-war years. I suppose I was also somewhat numb and drained by the cumulative strain of the last months; I no longer really cared if I lived or died.

I arrived at the chancellery in late afternoon, after a tortuous ride through the rubble-littered streets. Most of Berlin was in ruins as the result of aerial bombardment and the recent pounding by Soviet heavy artillery. When I was ushered into Hitler's office, his manner was cool, reflecting none of the warmth elicited by my avowal of support several weeks before. He was now obviously keeping his emotions under tight rein. "What do you think?" he asked me. "Should I stay here or fly to Berchtesgaden? Jodl has told me that tomorrow is the last chance for that." I knew that, no matter what he did, his life was numbered in weeks, and I suggested he remain in Berlin rather than prolong the agony on the *Obersalzberg* for a few more days. I told him, "It seems to me better, if it must be, that you end your life here in the capital as the *Führer* rather than in your weekend house." Hitler just nodded wearily and, for once, there was no more talk about the tide turning. I had the strange sensation that I was facing a walking corpse; he was devoid of any spark of life, listless, drained.

He spoke of his death without great interest: "I, too, have resolved to stay here. I only wanted to hear your view once more." He added, in an empty voice: "I shall not fight personally. There is always the danger that I would only be wounded and fall into the hands of the Russians alive. I don't want my enemies to disgrace my body, either. I've given orders that I be cremated." He looked off into space for a moment and when he resumed, his voice was quiet: "*Fräulein* Braun wants to depart this life with me, and I'll shoot Blondi [his Alsatian dog] beforehand. Believe me, Speer, it is easy for me to end my life. A brief moment and I'm freed of everything, liberated from this painful existence." I did not know what to say. I had the sensation that his vital core was already dead, that whatever demon had possessed him for most of his life had now departed, perhaps glutted on the blood and suffering it had wreaked, leaving Hitler's physical shell behind. But as I looked into those dead eyes, I felt that over the years, a part of *me* had died, too; my soul, perhaps.

In any case, I was suddenly possessed by an overwhelming sense of remorse, whether for Hitler, for myself or for all the unknown victims of our mutual madness, I do not know. In a shaking voice, I heard myself admitting to him that I had sabotaged his scorched-earth orders. His eyes briefly filled with tears, but he said nothing. Somehow, it was desperately important to me to make some flicker of human contact with Hitler, even in this lifeless state. I stammered that I was willing to stay in Berlin and share his fate, but he did not react; perhaps he knew I did not really mean it. Sometimes I wonder if he had known all along of my defiance of his demolition orders and had allowed me, for incomprehensible reasons of his own, to obstruct his policies. It was one of the mysteries of his strange personality that I will never unravel. But there is no doubt that he had hundreds shot for far less.

PLAYBOY: What would you have done if Hitler had taken you up on your offer to stay in Berlin to the end?

SPEER: I don't know. It was an irrational and impetuous thing to say, as even in those dark hours I was not suicidally inclined. But I was so swept with conflicting emotions that I was almost incapable of rational thinking. Fortunately, our conversation was interrupted by General Krebs, who delivered the daily situation report to Hitler. I did not see Hitler again for the next few hours, but around midnight, Eva Braun dispatched an SS orderly to invite me to her spare but pleasantly furnished room in the bunker. She was strangely gay and relaxed. "How about a bottle of champagne for our farewell?" she said lightly. "And some sweets? I'm sure you haven't eaten for a long time." I was moved by her thoughtfulness, and we settled down to a late-night snack of Moët et Chandon and cakes. The very normality of the atmosphere was abnormal under the circumstances. She told me, "You know, it was good that you came back once more. The *Führer* had assumed you would be working against him. But your visit has proved the opposite to him, hasn't it?" I could not answer her. "Anyhow," she went on, "he liked what you said to him today. He has made up his mind to stay here, and I am staying with him. And you know the rest, too, of course."

I wish there was something I could have said to her, some argument I could have advanced to save her young life, but of course there was no way I could influence her. "He wanted to send me back to Munich," she continued, "but I refused; I've come to end it here." Eva Braun, Hitler's much-maligned mistress, was the only person in the bunker with a capacity for compassion; she asked me sadly, "Why do so many more people have to be killed? It's all for nothing. . . ." Her words echoed in my mind as we said our goodbyes, Eva maintaining her poignant serenity.

It was three o'clock in the morning when I left her room, but Hitler was still up and I saw him to say goodbye. He stood before me, aged, shrunken, trembling, a human shadow. I was both deeply affected by our last meeting and strangely bewildered. Was this wraith the man I had believed in, revered, loved, hated for so long, the almighty *Führer* to whom I had devoted all my physical and mental powers for the past 15 years? As he said farewell, he was cold and indifferent. He shook my hand perfunctorily and said, "So, you're leaving? Good. *Auf Wiedersehen*." Nothing else—no expression of good wishes, neither thanks nor recrimination, no sentiment whatsoever. Suddenly, I realized I would never see this mysterious man again, and life without him to either love or hate suddenly seemed a dismaying prospect. In both loyal service and bitter opposition, he had become my universe. Shaken, I mumbled some promise to return, but he knew it was our final meeting and, without emotion, turned his back on me. For the last time, I had been dismissed from the *Führer*'s presence.

Dazed and exhausted by the events of the day, I left the bunker and walked through the deserted chancellery, its gutted windows gaping like the eye sockets of some stone skeleton. A spectral silence hung over the city: The normal street noises of Berlin were gone and the only sounds were the muted explosions of distant Soviet shells. Years ago, I had built this chancellery at the peak of my powers and ambition, burning with pride in my accomplishment. Now I left it in ruins, along with the better part of my life. I flew out of Berlin that night and returned to my family in Schleswig-Holstein.

Several days later, on May 1, 1945, the radio announced the news of Hitler's death. I had just moved into a small room at the headquarters of Admiral Doenitz, who had been appointed head of a new provisional government by Hitler in the last few days of his life, and as I unpacked my suitcase, I discovered a silver-framed photograph of himself that Hitler had given me on my 40th birthday. Suddenly, as if a dam had burst inside me, I began weeping uncontrollably. My relationship with Hitler was finally over, but only his death had shattered the spell. His fatal, compelling magic was at last overcome; the flames that consumed his body also freed my soul. But I have not been able to forget the fires of the ovens at Auschwitz, the burning cities, the charred corpses of our millions of victims. Nothing, not even Hitler's death, has freed me of that.

PLAYBOY: How did your codefendants at the Nuremberg War Crimes Trials regard your acceptance of responsibility for the crimes of the Reich?

SPEER: Some of them thought I was mad, and others misunderstood and thought that I was somehow trying to shift the blame onto them. Goering called me a "second Brutus" who had betrayed his oath to the *Führer*, and others were equally bitter. I told the court, "In political life, there is a responsibility for a man's own sector. For that he is, of course, fully responsible. But beyond that, there is a collective responsibility when he has been one of the leaders. Who else is to be held responsible for the course of events, if not the closest associates around the chief of state? Even in an authoritarian system, this collective responsibility of the leaders must exist; there can be no attempting to withdraw from the collective responsibility after the catastrophe. . . . I have this obligation all the more since the chief of government has withdrawn from his responsibility to the German people and to the world." These statements alienated me even further from the majority of my codefendants, but I refused to temper them in private or in the witness box. It was as if I was purging myself.

Flächsner wanted me to play down my coresponsibility with Sauckel for the forced-labor program; but again, I told the court that I shared full guilt with Sauckel. This dismayed my attorney, but it liberated me; with each confession, I felt freer. But I was still deeply depressed throughout the trial. The overwhelming evidence of the atrocities in the concentration camps preyed on my mind, preventing me from sleeping; images of the doomed Jews, especially the women and children, kept recurring in my mind. All this, I thought, was done by a government which I strove with all my energy to keep in power. Four years of tireless effort, and in the end, all that was left in my mind was a mother holding her baby in her arms as she entered the gas chamber. I felt defiled, as if my life had turned to ashes in my mouth. I used to think: What will my own children think of me when they grow up and learn of these crimes for which their father shared responsibility? They will view me as a monster. I sometimes viewed myself as harshly.

PLAYBOY: You were sentenced to 20 years' imprisonment, primarily for your role in the forced-labor program. Do you regard that sentence as fair?

SPEER: I most definitely do—eminently fair and just. After what had happened, any penalty would have been just—even a death sentence, although I wanted to live as much as any man. A few weeks after my sentence, I wrote in my diary, "There are things for which one is guilty even if one might offer excuses—simply because the scale of the crimes is so overwhelming that by comparison, any human excuse pales to insignificance." I believed that then and I believe it now.

PLAYBOY: Some historians have contended that the Nuremberg trial was an act of revenge by the victors on the vanquished and that its establishment of ex post facto crimes was juridically invalid. How do you feel about such criticism?

SPEER: I disagree most emphatically. The principles of international jurisprudence established at Nuremberg are, in my opinion, among the most heartening and noble developments of the 20th Century. They established a moral basis on which to judge the actions of great powers, a principle of vital importance in a world of rockets and hydrogen bombs. I sincerely believe the principles of Nuremberg are of enduring value to humanity.

The main reason I wrote my memoirs was not to rehash history but to hold the past up to present and future generations as a mirror in which they may behold similar seeds of destruction in themselves. The crimes of the Third Reich are essentially *modern* crimes, made possible by 20th Century technology, which holds within it both great promise and great danger for human values.

In my closing speech at the Nuremberg trial, I tried to approach the root of this problem. Speaking as the leading representative of a technocracy which had ruthlessly perverted the tools of technology into instruments of mass destruction, I told the tribunal, "Hitler's dictatorship was the first dictatorship of an industrial state in this age of modern technology, a dictatorship which employed to perfection the instruments of technology to dominate its own people. . . . By means of such instruments of technology as the radio and public-address systems, 80,000,000 persons could be made subject to the will of one individual. Telephone, teletype and radio made it possible to transmit the commands of the highest levels directly to the lowest organs, where, because of their high authority, they were executed uncritically."

I told the tribunal that, in my opinion, nuclear weapons and chemical-bacteriological warfare further compounded the problem: "The more technological the world becomes, the greater is the danger. As the former minister in charge of a highly developed armaments economy, it is my last duty to state: A new great war will end with the destruction of human culture and civilization. There is nothing to stop unleashed technology and science from completing its work of destroying man, which it has so terribly begun in this war. The nightmare shared by many people that someday the nations of the world may be dominated by technology—that nightmare was very nearly made a reality under Hitler's authoritarian system. Every country in the world today faces the danger of being terrorized by technology, but in a modern dictatorship, this seems to me to be unavoidable. Therefore, the more technological the world becomes, the more essential will be the demand for individual freedom and the self-awareness of the human being as a counterpoise to technology." I concluded, "Consequently, this trial must contribute to laying down the ground rules for life in human society. What does my own fate signify, after all that has happened and in comparison with so important a goal?"

PLAYBOY: You paid for your crimes with 20 years' imprisonment. Do you believe you have atoned for your guilt?

SPEER: No, I don't. I don't believe there can be any atonement in this lifetime for sins of such huge dimension. But I also sincerely believe that I am a much different man today than I was in 1945. In the isolation of imprisonment, I learned to look inside myself, to study my own weaknesses and strengths; and for the first time in my life, I had the leisure and opportunity to read and absorb works of philosophy and theology. Perhaps equally important to my own moral development, I was guarded at Spandau for 20 years by citizens of the four Allied powers against whom I had mobilized Hitler's war effort, and through them I was able to discover the direct human results of my armaments efforts. Many of them had lost close relatives in the course of the war, particularly the Soviet guards, every one of whom had lost a wife or child or father or mother; a few of them had seen their entire families perish in the holocaust. But despite this, despite the fact that I had produced the bullets and bombs that killed and maimed their loved ones and devastated their country, not one of the Russians blamed me directly for their bereavement—as, in fact, they would have had every right to do. Throughout those years of imprisonment, these simple soldiers treated me with warmth and friendship and consideration. At my moments of deepest despair, when I felt I would never be reunited with my own wife or children again, they always had a word of comfort for me, a re-assuring smile, a sympathetic pat on the shoulder.

Unless someone has been in prison for a prolonged period, he will not comprehend the importance of such understanding human contact. Their kindness and humanity transcended ideology and nationalism and recrimi-nation; we met not as political enemies or conquerors and conquered but as human beings. If I had to draw one single lesson from the horrors of World War Two, it would be not to depersonalize your enemy. Once this happens—whether it is a case of Nazi and Jew, Communist and capitalist or black and white—the greatest crimes are not only feasible but inevitable. The ideological differences that divide mankind today are, when seen in historical perspective, as transient and evanescent as the religious quarrels of the 16th and 17th centuries; the difference is that in the 20th Century, man has the power to totally destroy the race or nation he views as the enemy.

It is this vast gulf between our technological potential and our moral development that makes this age both so challenging and so terrifying. We now have the power to reach the stars—and to destroy our own planet.

If Adolf Hitler had possessed a button that would destroy the entire world, he would have pushed it at the end. Today, there are such buttons in the war rooms of all the great powers. None of the world's leaders is a Hitler, but the hatreds and fears on which Hitler thrived still persist, and the potential for mass destruction is even greater today. In the 1970s, an executioner never has to see his victims, whether they number in the hundreds or the thousands or the millions. This was the nightmare of Nazi Germany, the first modern state to mechanize murder. It is also the night-mare of a world of H-bombs and high-altitude jet bombers and intercon-tinental ballistic missiles and chemical-bacteriological warfare. In such a world, terrorized by technology, we are *all* in Auschwitz.

I know that these instruments of death are in the hands of sane men, often decent men, but there were sane and decent men in Nazi Germany and they did not avert the greatest bloodbath in recorded history. The automated juggernaut of modern mass destruction can all too easily achieve a momen-tum of its own, carrying the world to total annihilation. Once the beast is loosed, it can travel in only one direction. The descent into hell can be an exhilarating ride, but it is a one-way trip. I know. I have been there. I still am.

Playboy Interview Interludes

At the age of 14 or 15, I believe, youngsters should be isolated and fed little, be purged and frightened, and then given a hallucinogen. While under it, they should be taught the moral rules of life.

Robert Graves, December 1970

I'm never dirty, dear. I'm interestin' without bein' vulgar. I have—taste. I *kid* sex. I was born with sophistication and sex appeal, but I'm never vulgar and I don't like obscenity. I just—*suggest.*

Mae West, January 1971

I have the feeling that Nixon is a very detached man who sees politics as a process in which you manipulate various levers to advance your career, rather than as a process you use to advance certain ideals. . . . I think the Democrats could boot it away in 1972. If they don't call for a fundamental change in priorities, I think a lot of people may well decide to go along with Nixon again.

George McGovern, August 1971

The reporting about Sharon and the murders was virtually criminal. God-*damn* the press! The victims were assassinated two times: once by the murderers, the second time by the press.

Roman Polanski, December 1971

GERMAINE GREER

January 1972
Interviewer: Nat Lehrman

In 1971, probably no single topic received more attention in the press than the women's movement. Not surprisingly, it meant PLAYBOY received a lot of press, too, since the magazine was the splashiest, most visible target for feminists to aim at. Although Hefner and the magazine made a point of stressing the many feminist issues PLAYBOY had supported through the years, it made no difference: PLAYBOY was the enemy.

The editors wanted to present PLAYBOY's readers with a strong argument on the issues, but the problem was that none of the women associated with the movement would talk to PLAYBOY. In the past, the magazine had published interviews with such liberated women as Madalyn Murray, Ayn Rand, and Joan Baez (though admittedly not solely about feminist issues), but now all overtures were rejected. Nat Lehrman, then PLAYBOY's assistant managing editor, who led the search for a spokeswoman from "the other side," recalls that he had hopes of persuading Gloria Steinem to participate in a panel or an interview. "We sent out feelers to her, and she sent back icicles."

Then *The Female Eunuch* was published. Written by Germaine Greer, the outspoken scholar known to the press as the "feminist who likes men," it caused a tremendous sensation and was reviewed glowingly. After a couple of false starts, she agreed to the interview and suggested that Lehrman, who had volunteered to conduct it, question her at her farmhouse in a remote village in Italy.

Most of Lehrman's impressions of the controversial feminist are contained in his personal remarks in the introduction reprinted below. What was not published was the bantering, sometimes hostile, sometimes teasing quality of their relationship. Lehrman, who is now the associate publisher of PLAYBOY, was considered the editorial expert on sexual behavior and social sciences, since he supervised the Playboy Adviser and Forum departments. He was prepared to point out the contradictions in her writings, but he was less prepared for the actress in Greer, who bombastically tore into PLAYBOY, Hefner, and points west—and did so effectively. Since no one in the village spoke English, Lehrman would return to his tiny, hot hotel room and listen to the tapes of Greer excoriating him and the magazine. "It was the only conversation I would have all day—and it was this woman kicking the hell out of me," he remembers.

One afternoon they went out for a drive. The talk was lusty and frank, as it apparently always was with Greer. Lehrman overtook another car and Greer muttered, "You Americans, you get an orgasm every time you pass somebody." Lehrman kept quiet and continued driving. He passed another car, then turned to Greer. "Germaine, I just came," he said. Lehrman remembers thinking it was the only time he topped her during the course of the interview.

What was finally published was one of the liveliest interviews to appear in the magazine. Hefner made the decision to publish intact all of Greer's criticisms of PLAYBOY, and was in fact delighted with her uninhibited remarks about sexuality. Lehrman's responses to Greer in defense of the magazine's positions were in the spirit of equal time.

Greer later wrote to Lehrman that she felt the interview "turned out much better than I expected," but cautioned him not to get carried away: "You don't know what crassness I expected." Writer Nora Ephron said to Lehrman after the interview appeared that it was "unbelievable, the dynamite interview of all time." Ephron conceded that Lehrman might have had a point in saying that it was better for a man to interview Greer than a woman. "And you know how hard it is for me to agree with anything as Hefnerish as that," she concluded.

While the reader will have to draw his own conclusions as to who won the debate between PLAYBOY and the feminist who likes men, Lehrman adds one recollection that may or may not be telling: When he joined Greer for a home-cooked dinner at her home in Italy, the main course was roast rabbit.

"WHO IS GERMAINE GREER?" *headlines the newspaper advertisement. "The most lovable creature to come out of Australia since the koala bear? A feminist leader who admittedly loves men? A brilliant writer, 'extraordinarily entertaining'? Great Britain's Woman of the Year? The author of a perceptive, outrageous, devastating book on women?" McGraw-Hill, publisher of "The Female Eunuch," informs us: "Germaine is all of the above."*

This would seem a large number of roles to play—particularly the feminist-who-loves-men part, which, amid the anti-male rhetoric prevalent in women's lib, is comparable, one observer has said, to being a Nazi leader who loves Jews (or vice versa, depending on one's point of view). But Germaine Greer not only suits these roles, she adds several that weren't even mentioned. She's a linguist—fluent in French and Italian—and a Shakespearean scholar with a Ph.D. in literature, which she teaches at an English university. She's a professional entertainer who has performed in comedy shows on English telly. She's an ardent motorcyclist who tours the Italian countryside on a low-horsepower Garelli. She's even a skilled homemaker.

But all of Dr. Greer's accomplishments might have languished in obscurity were it not for her best-selling book. Published in England in 1970, "The Female Eunuch" was released in America in the spring of 1971 and was an instant smash. New York Times *critic Christopher Lehmann-Haupt dubbed it "the best feminist book so far" and went on to say: "I only wish that the timing . . . had been such that it could have caught the lightning that struck 'Sexual Politics,' for it is everything that Kate Millet's book is not— lively, spontaneous, witty, well organized without being rigid, comfortable with scholarship, personal when biases need explaining, assertive when the evidence is clear—a book with personality, a book that knows the distinction between the self and the other, a book that combines the best of masculinity and femininity."*

The last phrase may contribute to an understanding of "The Female Eunuch's" wide popularity. Women can read it and identify not only with the oppression it describes but with its chronicler, who is both a woman and a winner. Men can read the same book and likewise admire—even desire—its author, while at the same time not feel compelled to burden themselves with guilt for the crimes against women discussed therein. For Greer, while never forgetting her solidarity with her sisters, goes beyond feminism. She recognizes that the sexual polarities of society have been so locked in by economic, political and historical factors that it is pointless— and useless—to blame either sex. Rather, she feels, the liberation of both can be accomplished only by the withering away of authoritarian social structures, whether they be capitalist or Communist.

PLAYBOY *Assistant Managing Editor Nat Lehrman flew to Italy to conduct this interview. "After driving 140 miles north from Rome to her rented farmhouse in Cortona," Lehrman says, "I planned to greet her with: 'I've come a long way, baby,' but I quickly realized that flippancy would be out of place when she stood in her doorway and glared at me icily. No hello, no how—nor even who—are you, just a frigidly phrased, 'I'd planned to sneak out tonight to see a play in Montepulciano. But you would show up on time. Just like a bloody American.' Yet once she'd gotten that initial rude-*

ness out of her system, she was cooperative and good-humored during most—if not all—of the interview.

"In spite of her warmth and candor, she was a very tough interviewee in some ways. I had the feeling she thought I was going to try to do her in journalistically, which may explain why she was occasionally edgy and defensive. Once, she even threatened to cancel the interview. What made her suspicious of me may have been my tendency to confront her with contradictions—a standard interviewing technique—and the fact that I represented the establishment press in general and PLAYBOY in particular.

"In any case, her confidence in her ability to deal with the press allowed her to continue the interview, and her many other qualities more than compensated for any difficulties she presented. A born performer, she's on at all times; in fact, it's often difficult to stop her from talking. What she says is always intelligent, refreshing, colorfully phrased and frequently outrageous, primarily because she loves to give you the answer you least expect. She's generally well informed, but even when lacking facts, is quick and clever enough to talk around them.

"Finally, no statement about Germaine is complete without some reference to her sexuality. She said in the London Times that she never has sex at her home in Tuscany but that she's very 'randy.' She doesn't hide her randiness, often turning her head to look at a passing man and commenting about him the way men generally do about women. This shouldn't be surprising, since she has described herself as a female chauvinist when it comes to sex.

"While she was looking at other men, I was looking at her—thinking that she is a very attractive woman, sexily built and prettier than her TV image and most candid photos, yet not as cosmetically pretty as that plastic book-jacket shot that's made the rounds. She told me over dinner at my hotel that she would consent to pose nude for PLAYBOY under two conditions. The first was that we pay her an enormous amount of money—sum unspecified but enough, I believe, so that she could tell people she'd ripped off Hugh Hefner. The second condition was that she be allowed to pose in the act of swinging a bat at a softball or scrambling on a motorcycle or fucking any one of about 100 men, a list of whose names she promised to give me the next day. She didn't. I guess she wasn't serious. Or maybe we'd had too much to drink.

"After dining at her house another night, I can affirm that she's a superb cook and a gracious hostess. She even made it clear that she wouldn't appreciate an offer to help clear the table. I hope my revealing this does not get her in trouble with the movement, which sometimes behaves as if the kitchen were its real battleground.

"In between all this eating and drinking, we managed five two-hour taping sessions over a period of a week. I began, logically enough, by asking her to discuss the book that had catapulted her to fame."

PLAYBOY: Why did you call your book *The Female Eunuch*?

GREER: The term eunuchs was used by Eldrige Cleaver to describe blacks. It occurred to me that women were in a somewhat similar position. Blacks had been emancipated from slavery but never given any kind of meaningful freedom, while women were given the vote but denied sexual freedom. In the final analysis, women aren't really free until their libidos are recognized as separate entities. Some of the suffragettes understood this. They could see the connection among the vote, political power, independence and being able to express their sexuality according to their own experience, instead of in reference to a demand by somebody else. But they were regarded as crazy and were virtually crucified. Thinking about them, I suddenly realized, Christ, we've been castrated and that's what it's all about. You see, it's all very well to let a bullock out into the field when you've already cut his balls off, because you know he's not going to do anything. That's exactly what happened to women.

PLAYBOY: You're physically imposing, bright, well educated and enormously successful. Nobody would describe *you* as an emasculated woman. Yet you've called yourself a female eunuch. Why?

GREER: Because it's useless to think of liberating oneself in a vacuum. You can't liberate yourself *by* yourself. Women can become free only insofar as circumstances allow them to. It's a slow business and involves constant compromise. Indeed, neither of the sexes is truly liberated at this time.

PLAYBOY: What will make them free?

GREER: Only true equality, which is best understood in terms of Plato's concept of love. You see, it's impossible for superiors and inferiors to love, since the superior can only condescend and the inferior can only admire. Whereas what you really want is recognition between two equals, which means that they don't need to exploit each other. They simply rejoice in each other's presence, because what they see is a reflection of themselves in the other. The brotherhood of man would work only if this were the case—if we became more impressed by our similarities than by our differences.

PLAYBOY: How does this apply to women?

GREER: Women have a deficient sense of self-value and, therefore, cannot love. They cannot accept themselves. They need evidence of value, which they can get only through some man's attachment to them. As an example, take a 50-year-old husband who's going through that sort of male crisis of declining potency and approaching retirement and all the other hard things that can happen to men. He has an affair with a 20-year-old girl that really makes him think he can rule the world, that he's not all finished and he's still got what it takes. It might be mostly a fantasy affair, but whatever it is, I know of no wife who could stand it, even though her husband may be obviously much better for it. She'd rather have him gray and miserable and confused, as long as he is *hers*, since she values her life only through her relationship with him and therefore cannot stand the implied rejection.

PLAYBOY: There's not much of the Platonic concept of love in society today. Do you think there's any prospect of our moving toward love between equals?

GREER: I don't know, but without it, we'll never survive. The true revolutionary, Ché Guevara said, is motivated by great feelings of love. That may not have been true in the past, but I think it may be beginning to happen today. Take those American kids who went to Vietnam with the peace treaty to be signed by the Vietnamese students. They really worked hard. They used the kind of energy and the kind of imagination one would suppose more properly directed to a personal relationship. But the odd thing is that the relationship with humanity on that level becomes personal.

There's the old jive about the revolutionary being one who loves humanity but treats human beings badly in the name of humanity. So he treats his mother like shit and he tramps on his women, and so on. But I don't think this is true anymore. There is really developing a kind of group eroticism. It's a result of individuals' stepping out of the restrictions of sexual roles and trying to become sexually polymorphous and unpossessive; they're attempting to be accepting of all kinds of differences in people and to be able to see in them the lineaments of the beloved self. The outward expression of this is the group grope. The ultimate form of this great hippie ritual would be a never-ending copulation involving hundreds of people participating without shame or fear. This has never happened, of course, and it's not likely to. I've seen things like the beginnings of it, though, and it's extraordinary. But I must say, it can be as awful as it is beautiful. When I was in Amsterdam as a judge at the Wet Dream Film Festival, I was invited to an orgy. It turned out to be a PLAYBOY-type orgy.

PLAYBOY: It must have been some other company's orgy. We don't merchandise them.

GREER: Says you. It was in this really beautiful apartment. Oh, my God, I can see it now, just like the PLAYBOY gatefolds, with all that stained wood and rose-pink lighting and heavy drapes and full cocktail cabinets and bearskin rugs and—sure enough—the door was opened by the host, naked, with a drink in his hand. He said, with wit characteristic of your *Party Jokes* page, "Come in and take your clothes off!" There were two other men and two girls. The girls were blonde and long-legged and lovely. They had taken their clothes off already and you could see that they'd never had any children, which is one of the essential characteristics of your Playmate: No signs of actual *use* of the body have ever interposed themselves, not so much as a callus. I was with a really nice boy and we sort of obediently climbed out of our clothes, because we were supposed to be in favor of that kind of liberated behavior. It was so awful I can't tell you. There was one man too many all the time and he kept pattering about, peering at everybody else and trying to get in somewhere. When he put his hand on my bloke's behind, the poor boy completely lost his erection.

PLAYBOY: Where did you pick up these weird fantasies about PLAYBOY?

GREER: I know what a PLAYBOY pad looks like and I know what a Playmate looks like, too, so they're hardly fantasies. For one thing, your girls are so excessively young. What does this do to the man who looks at them? His wife's legs have been ruined by childbearing or her bum sags. Thanks to your youthful image of female sexuality, he's not expected to fuck his seamy old wife anymore. No one *blames* him for not doing it.

PLAYBOY: Surely you don't believe that any mature man confuses his wife or girlfriend with a Playmate—or with an attractive movie star, for that matter—or that his fantasies about any of these beautiful women impinge on his actual sex life. Don't you think it's true that most mature men know what they have to offer on the sociosexual market—whether it be looks, position, intelligence, charm, wealth or any combination thereof—and that they know pretty much what they can expect in return? If a man is Mr. Perfection, he'll expect to make it with Miss Perfection. But if he's not, he probably won't, and his fantasies are likely to be harmless.

GREER: You've got to be crazy! Men don't know anything about their own value on the market, as you put it. If they do, then why are repulsive, scrawny, half-wit little men coming up to every woman on the street and whispering, "I'll bet you'd like a fuck"?

PLAYBOY: Maybe they're sick.

GREER: No, they're not—it's normal. You don't know about it, because you're a man and no one is going to do it to you. In any case, it's not just the centerfold I disapprove of. It's all the other images of women in PLAYBOY. Why, you even ran a shoe advertisement that showed an Indian squaw stroking some dude's damn shoes! And those Playboy parties are so awful. All those *bleary* faces and those haggard men and those pumped-up women in their see-through dresses, with everyone's nipples poking out and those fixed, glittering, maniacal smiles on all the girls' faces. And I don't like the Vargas cartoon. Or the Femlin on your *Party Jokes* page. Or the jokes themselves—not to mention the cartoons. They all give the illusion that 50-year-old men are entitled to fuck 15-year-old girls—especially if they're given diamond bracelets—while 50-year-old *women* are too repulsive to be seen with. And I don't like the breast fetishism that I see in PLAYBOY. There's no connection between the breasts you show and satisfactory sexual activity. And you display your girls as if they were a commodity. Sex ought not to be that. It ought to be a means of communication between people. It's not something you can buy for whatever an issue of PLAYBOY costs.

PLAYBOY: At first you condemned the fact that our Playmates are young. Then you seemed to be arguing that their figures are too good. Now, when you bring up the commodity argument, you appear to be joining those critics who think we shouldn't publish nude pictures of *any* girls, young or old, beautiful or ugly.

GREER: I'm simply against showing girls as if they were pork chops. Why should women's bodies be this sort of physical fetish? Why can't their bodies just be an extension of their personalities, the way a man supposes *his* body is? No, I'm not against nudity, and I will pay dues to PLAYBOY when it runs a man in the gatefold. You can even keep the Playmate.

PLAYBOY: As a matter of fact, we do on occasion run pictures of nude men. As for putting them in featured spots such as the centerfold, ours is a men's magazine and we assume that our readers aren't terribly interested in looking at nude males. Even if PLAYBOY were a general magazine with a large female circulation, we doubt that pictures of naked men would be a major attraction, since women don't generally turn on to graphic images of sex.

GREER: I know that as well as you do—that women are not voyeurs; but women are not the clients for prostitutes, either—male or female. And this disparity has to be understood. Women do not regard men as a commodity they may have if they pay for it—even to look at.

PLAYBOY: From what direction are you casting stones? As a contributing editor of an underground sex paper called *Suck*, you must have noticed that, among other things, it contains pictures of young children locked in sexual embrace, women copulating with machines, homosexuals penetrating each other while wearing Nazi uniforms and references to people being forced to eat and drink human waste. Do you find these images less offensive than the Playmate?

GREER: I don't approve of the sadomasochistic stuff that appears in *Suck*, and an editorial statement by me was run in a recent issue about that very thing. I said, essentially, that the editors don't approve of censorship, that it's our principal enemy. But that's why we carry things that make us sick. Because contemporary sexuality is sick, because people are twisted and impotent and incapable of straightforward sexual expression. Insofar as we're dedicated to writing a paper about sex actualities, this sort of thing is going to have to appear in it. But we don't endorse it, and we reserve the right to vomit. That's where it's at. The minute we start to apply censorship, we're just in the same bag as everybody else.

PLAYBOY: You may not endorse the pictures published in *Suck*, but except for an occasional disclaimer, the magazine doesn't condemn them either. Moreover, using judgment and taste about what you print in your own magazine is hardly tantamount to censorship. Censorship is what happens when you are told what you can and cannot publish.

GREER: No, it is not. One censors oneself all the time. Freud calls it self-censorship. You just censor out what you don't find acceptable. And none of us has got the Holy Ghost on his side. We don't own the truth about sexuality. We're just as confused as anybody else. And there is some virtue in finding out that you turn on to a Nazi uniform. You've got to discover at some point just what kind of shit you are.

PLAYBOY: But isn't that essentially what you criticize about us—that we perpetuate fantasy-ridden fetishes?

GREER: No, it's not the same, because anybody who's turned on by the pictures in *Suck* is a bit strange; they're such terrible photographs.

PLAYBOY: We agree on that. Perhaps we can move on to some other areas of agreement if we conclude our conversation about PLAYBOY.

GREER: But it's important for me to talk about PLAYBOY, because I'm going to get shit for giving you an interview in the first place. It's got to be very clear with what kind of cynicism I do it.

PLAYBOY: Why *did* you grant the interview? Other feminists won't come this close even to insult us.

GREER: I'm not sure why I did, but basically I guess it's because you seem to be trying to go in a decent direction. Although I disapprove of the entire subliminal message in PLAYBOY, I suppose your editorial matter is more liberal than that of other large-circulation magazines. And I probably feel that some people will read this interview and drop some of their more ridiculous notions about the women's movement. I really think that the basis of every political movement is people. And you have to have some faith in people, even people like your readers who pay money to drool over pink Playmates. If you don't have confidence that these people will understand you when you say something clearly enough and will begin to see how your statements reflect on their own lives, then you've got no reason to be a revolutionary. I suppose I'm really being arrogant, thinking that what I'm about will come across, even if there should be a pinup inter-leaved thickly between every 500 words of discourse.

PLAYBOY: What *are* you about? Do you carry the banner for any particular feminist organization?

GREER: No, I don't belong to anything. My role is simply to preach to the unconverted. I'm the one who talks to PLAYBOY.

PLAYBOY: Given the job of public education you feel has to be done, why have the majority of feminists—unlike yourself—refused to talk not only with PLAYBOY but with almost any representative of the media?

GREER: Most women aren't as articulate nor as brazen as I am. If I get pissed on by the press, I can piss right back. I've been well educated and I can take care of myself. As you know, most members of the movement don't speak alone anywhere. They're always in a group, which they do to protect themselves. But it looks bad—something they don't understand—from the point of view of the media. It looks like a little gang of people bolstering each other's egos.

PLAYBOY: Aren't you violating the movement's rule against the cult of personality by allowing yourself to become such a popular public figure?

GREER: I'm against the cult of personality, too, but I think we have to use whatever weapons we've got. And I've always been a personality. There's nothing new about that.

PLAYBOY: A great deal of your popularity is with men, which led an American feminist to tell us that you can't be all good if so many pigs like you. What's your response?

GREER: I don't give a fuck. Pigs may like honey, but that doesn't stop it from being sweet.

PLAYBOY: Apparently it's not only your sweetness that arouses the ire of your American sisters. There are still grumblings about your put-down of NOW—the National Organization for Women—when you were in the U.S. What prompted those remarks?

GREER: My feelings about the policies of NOW are no secret. I wrote about them in my book. But the grumblings you mentioned may have been the aftereffect of some comments I made at a NOW party on—where else?— Park Avenue. First, let me say that I'd never been to expensive, radical-chic parties to raise funds. I felt like I was in the fucking Kennedy clan. I expected everybody there to burst out in pearls and raw-silk suits, volunteering to give $100-a-head parties to launch a Presidential campaign. And, sure enough, that's what they're going to do next: The women's movement is trying for 50 percent representation in the next Federal election!

But that's not what I talked about at the party. What I said was that all their interest in job opporunities for highly qualified women is basically counterproductive. What will happen is that providing jobs for these women will create a squeeze at the bottom. Those who suffer most will be workingmen who, under the present system, have enormous family responsibilities and who will be pushed out of work. That, unfortunately, will be the result of abolishing discrimination against females. You see, women are a reserve work force, and it's quite right for us to protest the fact that that's what we are. But if we simply fight for increased job opportunities without thinking of what it means in terms of the whole economic structure, then we're paving the way for a bloody confrontation between women and the poor. And we *must* have the poor on our side. In other words, for our own purposes, we must be part of the general pressure for revolution in a capitalist society. We can't just be yet another privileged group applying pressure for our personal interests. That just isn't good enough. But I'm sorry to say that this is pretty much what we're doing at the moment. Another thing that got me put down at that pary was my statement that a very significant factor in the American women's movement is its predominantly middle-class makeup; there is too wide a breach between NOW and poor women. There was an angry outcry and the women said, "No, no, we communicate with the poor." I replied, "Yes, I'm sure you do, but for it to work properly, those poor women have to be on an equal basis with middle-class women in the movement; they have to be officeholders, even though they've never put any money into it, because they haven't got any money."

PLAYBOY: Would you offer any advice that, if followed, might hasten the radicalization of the movement?

GREER: I don't advise people what to do. It's a waste of time. Anyhow, one of the worst results of women's oppression is their propensity for *taking* advice. They're figuring it all out for themselves and they're being radicalized one way or another, but it's a slow, difficult process to go from having been apolitical for your entire life to becoming a committed revolutionary.

PLAYBOY: Presumably, the difficulty is compounded by the fact that women live—as you've said—"in the house of the enemy." We found that phrase a little surprising, because you appear to be holding men responsible for the problems women have, whereas many of your other statements tend to put the blame on society, without singling out either sex.

GREER: When I talk about the house of the enemy, I don't refer only to the husband. Women also live with their children, their families, the door-to-door salesmen, the daily newspapers with their drawings of fantasy women wearing fancy clothes and pictures of men making the news. That's what I mean about living in the house of the enemy. It's quite different with blacks. They live with their own people and they have their own way of talking. They panhandle you and me—it's "Yes, ma'am, no ma'am" and all that crap. But when they're at home, they speak a language you and I have never heard.

Even if women go to a consciousness-raising group once a week, they still identify with another group—the family—and that's much more strongly buttressed and much more cohesive than the group to which they belong politically. When you get down to culture, the entire analogy falls apart, because women have no culture of their own. Theirs is a pale reflection of masculine culture. It's mostly a parody.

PLAYBOY: Does this dependence of women on men account for the hatred you've said exists between the sexes?

GREER: I didn't say it that way. I said women have very little idea of how much men hate them.

PLAYBOY: Isn't the hostility mutual?

GREER: The real sort of sexual hostility is masculine. Women have lots of sexual hatred, but it emerges in petty and destructive behavior at a different level. They just have much less confidence in their way of expressing hatred, yet much less ability to control it, too. So it just keeps leaking out all the time, in destructive acts, petty acts of ego erosion and belittlement. But it's nothing like masculine hostility. Let's face it, rape is a male crime.

PLAYBOY: We gather that you're not limiting rape, as the law generally does, to forcible intercourse.

GREER: Right. I think rape is any coercion of a woman for sexual purposes. If a man takes you out on a motorway and stops the car and says, "Now you can walk or fuck" and you fuck, then you've been raped. He wanted to use your hole and he did it—his way. He didn't care whether you wanted him. That's rape, even though it's not so classified by law.

PLAYBOY: Do you favor the tough penalties we now have for rape?

GREER: Absolutely not. I regard imprisonment as an inappropriate punishment for any crime you can name. It doesn't work. It doesn't deter, it doesn't cure, it doesn't rehabilitate, it does nothing. It costs a lot of money and it shows no returns whatever. In any case, the common attitude toward rape is absurd. First, it's a very frequently committed crime. Second, it's not a terribly serious crime, but it's irritating that a woman can get redress only with great difficulty. Third, when you consider how common rape is and minor it is compared with, let's say, murder, it's ridiculous that the very few people who actually get caught suffer so desperately and for so long. And in the case of a poor man who belongs to a despised minority, he is likely to be charged with a capital crime; a privileged citizen finds it very easy to get the charge thrown out.

PLAYBOY: Do you think a woman who's been raped would have such compassion for her attacker?

GREER: *I am* a woman who has been raped. My men friends were more bitter than I was. Actually, from the woman's point of view, it's better to forget about the rape than to go through the necessary rigamarole to bring the rapist to justice. She actually has to have sperm in her hole to prove her case and she has to have corroborating testimony. But how many rapes are committed in the presence of witnesses? And there's no limit to the charges that the defense may bring in order to discredit a raped woman's testimony. She can be utterly vilified in court, as if *she* were the perpetrator of the crime.

PLAYBOY: What do you suggest in place of the present penal system regarding rape?

GREER: I'm interested in certain programs that provide for psychoanalysis of the rapist. Beyond that, all specific sexual legislation should be abolished.

PLAYBOY: Even laws designed to protect women from being raped?

GREER: Well, I don't know. A lot of women would disapprove of that, but some radical women's groups think that all sexual legislation should be abolished and that there ought to be a rationalization of the laws with regard to sexual assault.

PLAYBOY: Would you elaborate?

GREER: It's a matter of redefining the crimes. I mean, if someone sticks a broom handle up a woman's cunt, she has been sexually assaulted, but she hasn't been raped, according to some versions of the law. As far as I'm concerned, it's a good deal more offensive to have a broom handle up me than a cock. In other words, it should be possible to isolate the violence in a sexual assault and bring action against *that*.

PLAYBOY: If rape is a characteristic expression of male hostility, then abstention might be considered a female one. Accordingly, some segments of women's lib have expressed their anger toward men by avoiding any sexual contact with them—even to the extent, in some cases, of opting for Lesbianism. Do you approve?

GREER: I do my best to understand and I start with the assumption that the institution of heterosex stinks. And either a person tries to change it from within—by playing the rules her own way—or she gets out of it altogether. She makes love in some completely different way to completely different people with completely different sets of claims on her. That, I think, is the rationale for much of the Lesbianism in the movement.

The fact is, of course, that homosexuality quite often follows a neurotic pattern. It's not automatically a spontaneous and generous love relationship just because it happens between people of the same gender. Sometimes it follows a sort of transferred heterosexual pattern, with one of the partners dominating and exploiting the other—although that's not as common among Lesbians as its detractors like to pretend. I think, in the end, Lesbianism will probably be the only way to persuade men that they've got to offer a different deal.

PLAYBOY: Is that a personal conviction?

GREER: Not in the sense that I practice it. The Lesbian way doesn't turn me on sexually, so, politically, it would be a major dishonesty for me to follow it. But I don't think it's something to sneer at, by any means. And one of the reasons men are frightened by this female separatism is that they have to be able to think that cock is important.

PLAYBOY: Most *women* seem to think it's important—including, presumably, you. In your book, you reject the notion of some feminists that penile insertion is irrelevant to sexual pleasure, pointing out that it's "nicer to have a clitoral orgasm with a full cunt than with an empty one."

GREER: Do you think a cock is the only thing I can put in my cunt? Do you think it's the biggest or the pleasantest or the smoothest or the nicest thing I can put in my cunt? You do!

PLAYBOY: A thousand pardons. You have written, however, about the psychosexual satisfaction of making love with a man, so one presumes you'd rather have a cock with a man attached to it than a banana or something else big and pleasant and smooth and nice.

GREER: It's the psychosexual satisfaction of having another *person* that's important. All right, I will concede that in my case, I generally prefer that person to be a man. But what I'm trying to point out to you is that a man's cock is much more important to *him* than it is to a woman. A man whose cock is soft is not useless, but *he* thinks he is. He becomes desperate with images of his own uselessness because he has never got the message that a stiff cock is not all that necessary. Of course, if he could *get* that message, he'd have an erection anyway. There's so much foolish anxiety about erections and premature ejaculation and all the rest of it. You can use *anything* while making love. You can make love without even touching each other. It depends entirely on what the communication ratio is between you.

PLAYBOY: Do you think love is an important component in that ratio?

GREER: I've never understood anybody who could separate love and sex. And yet people do. I don't think most people necking in cars and swapping fraternity pins are in love at all. On the other hand, you can sometimes love a man better in a one-night stand, because you haven't got to the point where you actually *want* anything from him. You can't exploit him. All you can do is respond to him as simply and straightforwardly as possible, knowing he's going to be gone the next day. So it's all unconditional tenderness.

PLAYBOY: Do you love everybody you make it with?

GREER: If I don't, I don't make it. If a man does something shitty, something cruel or fascist or ignorant or whatever, then all his sex appeal falls away from him. He suddenly just doesn't have *anything* anymore.

PLAYBOY: Do you fall in and out of love a lot?

GREER: I think I gave up falling in love when I was about 19. Since then, I've allowed myself to be misled into it again, and when that happens, I become absolutely abject, utterly unscrupulous, totally dishonest, and I can do nothing about it. From being an interesting and independent woman, I just become a complete pain.

PLAYBOY: Are you ever accused of promiscuity?

GREER: Sure, but so what? Promiscuity's an absolutely artificial concept and it's been developed as an expression of the prejudice against women's free sexual activity. I've yet to hear people registering anything like the same amount of disgust at male behavior. It's assumed, you see, that the man *chooses* his sexual object, whereas when a woman fucks a lot of people, it's because she's unable to say no. Well, insofar as this is the case, then it would be a problem. I suppose you could call it nymphomania. It certainly would be if there were some kind of compulsion involved. But insofar as a woman likes to fuck a lot and chooses relatively numerous partners, promiscuity's a meaningless idea.

Of course, I must add that women get promiscuized—to coin a word—by the way men behave. I mean a woman sometimes fucks without discrimination just to get out of a situation. She thinks, "Oh, my God, I really don't want to fuck this man, but if I sit here and argue for the next six hours, trying to talk this turd out of it, I'll be a rag tomorrow." So she says, "I want to go to bed, I'm tired. But if you're fucking going to insist, if you're going to keep me here all night, then I'll lie down on the floor with my legs apart and think of something else and you can fuck me, you stupid swine. Then I'll be able to go to sleep." Men just don't seem to realize that if you don't want to fuck, you shouldn't; and if you think you might want to fuck a man one of these days, you don't fuck him tonight. But men think that by wearing a woman down, they're going to get what they want, and then they wonder why the sex is so bad.

PLAYBOY: The male's ability to turn on at a moment's notice—and at the slightest provocation—is one of those sexual differences that really seems to bother women. Do you think the slower female response is something women are born with, or is it simply retarded by social repression?

GREER: I think it's obvious that female response has been retarded. But if you want to talk about being bothered, there's nothing more bothersome than being a woman in a situation where a man believes he has to work to make you come. He's trying to make a good impression and he wants you to like him, so he tills your vineyard for hours on end. You might just as well be doing something else, because the real sexual excitement comes from a sense of urgency, not from the efforts of a guy who's trying to remember what some sex manual told him about turning women on. Sometimes, you know, a four-hour fuck can be a big drag and a five-minute fuck can be marvelous.

PLAYBOY: Some men are perhaps reluctant to let themselves ejaculate quickly because the sex-manual culture labels this premature.

GREER: Let it be premature, then. There are times when you can *tell* that the man is doing the multiplication tables to avoid coming. He might as well not be doing anything, because it's taken the meaning out of the whole bloody thing. So many guys apologize abjectly for coming too fast. But who says it was too fast? It may have been beautiful. Then there are the guys who go on and on and on and don't come at all. They've said the multiplication tables so often that they can no longer have an ejaculation. That's not my concept of ecstasy.

PLAYBOY: What is?

GREER: It's the combination of what we call the erotic with what Freud called the oceanic impulse—a sort of identification with a huge, cosmic order of things. It doesn't happen when people go around twiddling knobs and trying to give you titillating sensations in the extremities of your body. All the sex in the manuals is localized genitality, and you just isolate it more and more when you play the push-button game. I think the sex manuals that teach marriage partners how to develop a kind of characteristic play, in order to satisfy each other with no sweat and strain, are absolutely counterrevolutionary and deeply arid.

PLAYBOY: What other counsel do you have for men on how not to be boring lovers?

GREER: To tell you the truth, I think every man should be fucked up the arse as a prelude to fucking women, so that he'll know what it's like to be the receiver. Otherwise, he'll forever go about thinking that he's doling out joy unlimited to every woman he fucks.

PLAYBOY: Thank you for the suggestion. Let's change subjects.

GREER: You ol' hetero, you.

PLAYBOY: The fact that such things as we've been talking about can be discussed in a national publication, combined with reported changes in

various kinds of sexual behavior, is considered an indication of an ongoing sexual revolution. Do you agree that we're in the midst of such a revolution?
GREER: No, just call it a fashion.
PLAYBOY: Will things change back to the way they were?
GREER: It depends. If it's tits you're not allowed to show this year, it's ankles you're not allowed to show the next. It's like skirt lengths. Modesty is a curious anthropological phenomenon, because it relates to parts of the body that achieve their significance only by being covered. And I think sexuality is pretty much like that. Permissiveness, as far as I'm concerned, doesn't really exist. It didn't really happen. It's generally agreed there's nothing much wrong with fucking, at least in theory. But it hasn't been agreed that there are a lot of things right with it, that it's something people really ought to be doing. Even though 16-year-old girls have been given the key to the door, they haven't actually been told to bring their blokes home to bed. It's now permissible to do a lot of talking about it and see a lot of pictures about it. It's permissible to have a great many sexual fantasies, but we still haven't endowed sexual activity with positive value.
PLAYBOY: Does there have to be a sexual revolution in order for there to be a female revolution?
GREER: Absolutely. We just won't have one without the other. There will be no wholesale acceptance of women on an equal basis until sexual activity has escaped its neurotic concomitants, until the sort of ambivalence men feel about their own sexual activity has been resolved, so that they don't consider what they fuck degraded. As long as we're at odds with our bodies, as long as excreta is regarded as filthy and semen as unpleasant and cunt as having a nasty smell, and so on, men will be at odds with women, because society in its imagery has made the woman fundamentally a body.
PLAYBOY: You seemed to express some of that self-doubt—or at least squeamishness—yourself when you commented in your book that you still feel certain inhibitions about getting head. Why?
GREER: Some of it does arise from a feeling that my cunt can't possibly be all that pleasant. I could pretend not to have the fear, but most women have it, so it's just as well to recognize it. Men have been taught to glorify their sexual apparatus and we've been taught to despise ours, to pretend it's not there. But that's not the only hang-up about getting head. I mean, there's a kind of man who dives down there because he thinks it's the thing to do, even though you hardly know him. You're sort of miles away and you don't even see him and there he is, ferreting around down there. And then there's always the suspicion that many a man isn't really into it and he's doing it because he thinks he's *supposed* to. Well, that's just a drag, because I'm really not that difficult and nobody has to go to all that trouble—I mean unless the guy really digs it. And there are such guys. Some lucky girls might even be married to them.
PLAYBOY: Haven't you said that girls who are married aren't very lucky?

In fact, you've been quoted as advocating that women leave their husbands.

GREER: I've been misquoted. What I've said is that if a woman feels she cannot live with her husband anymore, then her children ought not to constitute a reason for staying with him. Her misery will only be the misery of the children, because they pick it up loud and clear.

PLAYBOY: Even if you haven't advocated mass walkouts, you've certainly put down the institution of marriage. For what reasons?

GREER: The word institution has something to do with it. The moment you institutionalize a relationship, you completely change its character. Instead of being involved in a situation where you're always relating to each other as warmly and spontaneously as possible, you begin to assume that you're being held together by something external, and you might as well start taking things for granted. Consequently, you lose the delicacy of response to each other's requirements. You don't have to worry. Everything's taken care of.

All that's made even worse by the existence of a contract, an instrument that, I assure you, would not hold up in a court of law for any agreement *except* marriage. What you do when you sign this contract is write yourself into a great body of law about which you know nothing until something goes wrong. The law involves things like property held in common, property held separately, the entitlement of a wife to a portion of her husband's earnings, the entitlement of a wife to spend a proportion of what she gets for housekeeping on something else, etc. And none of that is *in* the contract. You know nothing about it until you go to court, and then you get told, for example, that you're not entitled to anything if you don't keep house according to your husband's satisfaction, depending on where you are and what kind of attitude the judge takes. It's all secrecy and bullshit and confusion. And it's to the disadvantage of the woman, mainly because she has so much less opportunity for independent income.

PLAYBOY: The disadvantages of marriage notwithstanding, wouldn't you agree that it's the best system so far devised for raising children?

GREER: On the contrary, it's the *worst* possible system. I'm passionately opposed to the nuclear family, with its mom and dad and their 2.4 children. I think it's the most neurotic life-style ever developed. There's just no space between the mother and the children. And the husband, on the other hand, is an extraneous element in the household who usually just exacerbates the tension that already exists between the mother and the children. The nuclear family's just too small, too introspective and incestuous a unit. But our socioeconomic situation makes it necessary, because it requires a family that's mobile, that can be uprooted at will. And this means that the relationship of the nuclear family to its community becomes extremely superficial. Consequently, there is no way for the kids to ever learn social responsibility.

PLAYBOY: Perhaps, but the family itself becomes extremely close-knit. Do you consider that a disadvantage?

GREER: Unquestionably. What really develops is an extraordinary relationship of tyranny by the child over the mother. She is ever at his disposal and this is the *sine qua non* for the development of the kind of person we call normal—which is possessive, security-seeking, and so on.

PLAYBOY: What alternatives would you suggest?

GREER: I think we ought to try to enlarge our households somehow. It might be through group marriage, though not necessarily. Preferably, it should be through some sort of group cohabitation. That way, you'd live with your friends and there would be people around who were not concerned in the sexual battle and who could referee when things got bad and when the children were exhausted and bullied by the tension.

PLAYBOY: Have you lived in a commune?

GREER: No. But I think they are the shape of the future, even though they have enormous problems. It's such an unlikely and extraordinary event for a commune to survive in the present social and political setup that one can only regard it as testimony to the greatness of the human spirit. Nothing is in its favor, absolutely nothing—the attitude of neighbors, the attitude of the law and even the difficulties the people inside the commune have with one another. My kind of commune would be with very old and tried friends. People shouldn't join together just for the purpose of cohabiting; it gets a bit too compulsive, like being in a barracks.

PLAYBOY: You envision in *The Female Eunuch* a household setup similar to what you just described. A review of your book, by Naomi Lowinsky in the magazine *Organ,* had this to say about your vision: "My critique of Germaine is a loving one. She has had no children, so it is understandable that all she can offer is a pretty utopian plan for a country nursery, with parents free to come and go. A lovely conceit but little comfort for those of us who are trying to be free and joyous for ourselves and for our children who exist with us now in the cities, amidst money hassles and no free child care." Did you intend for your communal dream to be taken seriously by mothers?

GREER: Well, first of all, the whole point about having children is that there is no *need* for them. The world is in no great need of *my* child. Some people might say, "Well, a woman with your I.Q. should have a baby, because it will be genetically advantageous." I happen to think that's crap. And I hope that when we find out more about genetics, it will be so seen, because I don't think there's all that much inherent difference between one human being and the next. There is no need for me to bring yet another neurotic, unhappy little child into the world, who is likely to have to go and fight some crummy war like the one in Vietnam. Until we've stopped that sort of thing, we have no right to procreate. For women who already have children,

I realize there's a problem, which I have never set out to solve with my communal vision. I said it was a dream. It's a kind of erotic thing to have a baby and I would quite like to do it.

But, you know, contrary to a great deal of popular belief, having an abortion is not the serious and responsible thing having a baby is. Yet these broody women keep having babies all the time. And then they say, "What do we do now? We have no free day-care centers." As long as there *are* no free day-care centers, it's just as well not to behave as if they were there—for the children's sake, at least.

PLAYBOY: American feminists have been clamoring for day-care centers so that mothers can be released for work. Doesn't the cooperative system, by requiring part-time participation of each mother, effectively prevent that?

GREER: Working in the day-care center is itself employment. It is not intended that the center be barren of adults. However, the women's movement seems to assume that the labor market is expanding, that there are more and more jobs. But, as I already said, there simply is no room for a sudden influx of women workers.

PLAYBOY: You've expressed a rather grim view of marriage and the family. Is it possible that your own unhappy experiences with both might have prejudiced your ideas?

GREER: No, I think my family is pretty normal. My parents didn't get on very well, but I don't know very many parents whose relationships are a source of inspiration and enlightenment. That's mainly because of the bullshit: you know, they tell you how to behave and they behave totally without dignity or respect for each other. But my views of marriage and the family are either right or wrong. I obviously cannot put them down by saying they're a subjective reaction to the way I grew up. I'm not so dumb that I can't think beyond a particular personal situation into a general one. Like many other wartime marriages, my parents' marriage had a lot of things against it—so many that it would really be irresponsible of me to make a rule out of it.

When my father returned from the war in 1944, my mother and I went to meet him, and I remember her going up and down the platform unable to find him—that is, to recognize him—because as it turned out, my father had aged so. He'd been in Malta all during its siege, and the famine had caused his gums to shrink and his upper teeth to fall out. He was obviously heartbroken. The war had really disgusted him. I don't think he ever recovered. He's been on sedation ever since. Well, he just withdrew from us, withdrew, withdrew. All he wanted was a quiet life. He spoke quite often of his death as well. Well, you simply can't *leave* a returned serviceman, even though he is a total stranger to you. At the same time, I don't imagine my father had the guts to leave *us*. So it wasn't easy. But my mother had problems long before my father volunteered for the service, because very soon after they'd been married, they found they couldn't get on. They might have made a go of it, though, if it hadn't been for the war.

PLAYBOY: You've been married yourself. How did that relationship fare?

GREER: I got married about three years ago to a man who I thought knew what he was doing, on account of it was his second time. You know, experience and all that. Actually, it turns out experience is the *worst* teacher. I was immensely flattered that he asked me to marry him. I kept thinking, "How extraordinary—this man has decided he wants me around for the rest of his *life!"* It has never occurred to me that marriage is anything but permanent. I don't understand the now-you-see-me, now-you-don't style of marriage. But it shouldn't involve you in eye-to-eye confrontation all the time. I mean, you can be married and be on opposite sides of the earth, but you're still married. You can have lovers, but you're still married. It's a bit like having siblings: you can't lose a brother or a sister. They are always there.

Well, I got it completely wrong. Before we were married, he agreed I could go on working at the university. But once the papers were signed, it was, "Now you're just going to knuckle down, don't give me any more of that jazz. Now you're going to be a wife." So after three weekends—we didn't even live together all the time—I said, "I'm off. Let's have no drama, because I'm not in love with you or anything unhappy like that, and let's have no weeping or sobbing or gnashing of teeth. It was just a mistake and I'm sorry. What did you pay for the license?" But the funny thing is that I still consider myself married to him.

PLAYBOY: You were never divorced?

GREER: Well, he asked me for a divorce just before I went to America to promote my book. But he insisted on paying for it; and as long as he comes on with those masculine gestures, I'll resist him. We even thought at one stage of asking for an annulment on the grounds of nonconsummation. But I thought the judge would take one look at me and one look at him and start laughing. He's such a big, sexy guy—very handsome, very dishy. He's capable of busting his shirt straight down the back just by scratching his nose.

PLAYBOY: If you found a guy, now or in the future, who could give you the kind of marriage you originally thought you would have had the first time, would you get married again?

GREER: Nah. I'll stick with the one I've got, though I don't know where he is or even what *country* he's in.

PLAYBOY: Some American husbands and wives, also disenchanted by one-to-one matrimony, claim that mate swapping provides an escape valve. Do you think there's anything to that?

GREER: All I know about wife swapping is what I read in books. I think it's really like permitted incest. In a community where there's enforced togetherness, where the corporations buy up the land and sell it back to their executives, where everyone's under tacit supervision, where your wife's been looked over and the kids have been looked over and you've taken your little psychometric test that tells the boss whether you'd rather be a cook or a forester, so he can really determine whether you're an extrovert or an introvert—well, in this kind of community, by the time you've been processed by the American machine, you're a white rat. And all your mates are pretty much the same. So wife swapping is a bit like the shared sin of drunkenness. What I mean by that is, in America, drunkenness is a sort of social imperative, which means that no one can squeal on anyone else, because everyone gets sloshed, and you all enjoy a special sort of anarchic behavior that your superiors are prepared to overlook. So, wife swapping is like a form of incest in which nobody's more guilty than anybody else. You make sure that everybody's got the same; no one can say that the other sinned. I think it's probably awful.

PLAYBOY: Swapping sometimes manifests itself in group sex—which you mentioned approvingly before. Do you think it might have any value in that form?

GREER: No. It only amounts to husbands' and wives' gingering up a fairly lifeless sexual relationship by incorporating tits of a different shape and a few new cocks and stuff like that. I think it also probably relates to a kind of sexual uniformity. Undoubtedly, they all do the same things to one another. Group scenes are fine, but there's no reason they should be composed of husbands and wives.

PLAYBOY: What about total strangers?

GREER: That's the other extreme and it's equally unnecessary. I'm not interested in what happens to people who advertise in the papers for personnel for an orgy. I mean they're crazy.

PLAYBOY: But how can you reconcile your own highly developed individualism with a desire to be part of a group?

GREER: We've all paid a very high price for individualism, and the fact is I don't really value mine at all.

PLAYBOY: Yet your whole life seems to belie what you're saying.

GREER: That's my problem. I'm an individualist, but I'm not proud of my individualism. I should add, however, that in a truly cooperative group, where everyone contributes what he has to contribute, there isn't such a great loss of individuality as you might imagine. It depends on your concepts of human interrelationships. If they relate to property—in other words, to people owning other people, and so forth—then you really can't see what cooperation is. Cooperation is working together in a way that brings out the best in all, which is why I believe that clever students do not lose by helping slow ones. When I was at school, I could have helped other people do well and still have done well myself. The competitive impulse is what prevented me from doing that, apart from school discipline. You see, it's individualism that leads you to suppose that the knowledge you've discovered belongs to you. That's mad, because facts are not the property of anybody.

It's the difference between anarchism and fascism. In a fascist group, for example, uniformity is imposed by the dogma of the group, not necessarily by the leader, since the group, to all appearances, may be collective. "Everyone will wear black; everyone will march this way and be beautifully uniformed and everyone will admire us for our precision marching and will blow up the electric power station on the 24th of March because everybody who's on our side is blowing up electric power stations on that day." In a cooperative group under anarchism, on the other hand, no activity would be undertaken without the unanimous agreement of the group, which has been invited to consider the alternatives.

PLAYBOY: Wouldn't the requirement of unanimity immobilize the group?

GREER: It slows it down, more often. That's why anarchists have always been defeated by fascists. Fascism makes for a more efficient military organization.

PLAYBOY: Are you in favor of political as well as interpersonal anarchy?

GREER: I favor a communist form of state structure.

PLAYBOY: How do you reconcile your belief in self-government with your belief in a form of government that is presently as authoritarian as fascism?

GREER: If you're referring to Russia, it's not a communist state. A true communist system is one in which the vital means of production are in the possession of the people, so that profits from the industry go to those who work in it, not to those who own it. That's certainly not true of Russia, where the state owns industry and the profits go to the state. It's a little truer of China, I think, but I'm not sure how much. True communism is, of course, anarchic. It involves the direct participation of workers in their own fate, instead of their doing as they're told.

PLAYBOY: What's been the experience with female equality in Communist countries?

GREER: It's bad. The sexual revolution was betrayed in Russia. Women fought to liberate Cuba, and as soon as the battle was over, Castro told them to put their guns down like good girls and go back to looking after the children, even though the children seem to have got on all right during the liberation. In China, women are better off than they were before; both sexes dress the same in a sort of unisex regime. And Mao doesn't go around giving prizes for motherhood, as they did in post-Stalinist Russia.

PLAYBOY: Do you think that most of the different qualities men and women have are conditioned rather than inborn?

GREER: I think they're substantially conditioned, but I can't really say. We just don't know what the genuine innate sexual differences are, because we've obscured them by cultural sexual differences. There may, indeed, be some biological disparities, but I don't know that they're very pronounced. I mean, do you think you'd be better off being attacked by a lion than a lioness? Or vice versa? In any case, what small differences may exist don't justify the great degree of sexual discrimination we see in our ordinary lives.

PLAYBOY: Would you like to see men and women play pretty much the same roles in society?

GREER: One of the troubles with the world as it exists now is that the number of differences has been decreased. Uniformity is the desideratum. What one would hope for is a world in which there were myriad differences. But these would be *individual* differences rather than deep differences between groups that are pacing out the same kinds of steps according to their sex or class. People would be genuinely developing different psychic possibilities and living in endlessly variable ways. The whole point about abolishing the sexual polarity is not to make the world less interesting but to make it *more* interesting. I'm sure you've noticed here in Italy the kind of behavior you can expect from the average boy. It's so predictable. It's excruciatingly boring and an absolutely off-turning mechanism. I can practically chant to them what their next gambit is going to be. That's the price of sexual polarity. They can act only in one way. Their parts have been written for them by history. What *we're* trying to do is free human inventiveness to a new kind of interplay between the sexes where the rules have not been written by some humorless priest.

PLAYBOY: Even if there weren't unalterable rules for the sexes in your world, would there at least be flexible guidelines?

GREER: What for? Without guidelines, I could pursue *you*. I could climb in your bedroom window in the middle of the night. How do you know you wouldn't like it?

PLAYBOY: If a woman answers, climb down.

GREER: Why?

PLAYBOY: The point is that we've had centuries of experience with men behaving one way, women another. Even if it's undesirable, how is all this going to be deconditioned?

GREER: We're not going to eliminate sex roles by fiat. It's going to be a very gradual process and it's going to be connected with socioeconomic processes that destroy the functions of the sex roles.

PLAYBOY: Once the roles have merged, don't you think there might be a reduction in sexual turn-on?

GREER: I imagine—at least I hope—that if it happens the right way, there will be a bigger sexual turn-on. In a bureaucratic state, where sex roles are formally abolished by a ruling minority, there would be a turnoff, because the people wouldn't know how to cope with it. Women are suddenly allowed to be cosmonauts and lift drivers and manual laborers and all the rest of it. But that represents a new kind of oppression, because the women themselves have never yearned for it nor expected it and they don't find any new way of expressing themselves in it. In short, it's another case of still obeying the rules.

The authoritarian personality is always sexually confused and the sexually liberated person, I think, is anti-authoritarian. So unless we develop some kind of cooperative life-style, and not a bureaucratic one in which we're told we have to fill out forms every time we want to crack a fart, unless we make sure that we create real freedom, then the abolition of sex roles will certainly be a turnoff. From what I gather, that's what's been happening in Sweden. It's otherwise hard to explain why so many Swedish girls come to Italy for summer sex. I think it's because women have become competitive with men without any corresponding increase in real freedom. They've been emancipated by *law*, which is a contradiction in terms.

PLAYBOY: Do you have any particular thoughts about abortion, beyond being against the laws restricting it?

GREER: The question of abortion is very complicated. When it comes to late-term abortions, I don't really think they're any great shakes. They're bad for the women and they're bad for the nurses or midwives who have to take out the child who's almost viable and put it in a rubbish tin. On the other hand, very few women voluntarily have a late-term abortion. They would like an early-term abortion, but they just don't get it. They get grilled and examined and pushed around and bullied and confused for so long that they're six months gone before a decision is made. Certainly, I think birth control is preferable to abortion just from a personal point of view.

PLAYBOY: A currently fashionable method for population control is voluntary sterilization—particularly vasectomy. But you criticize this operation in your book. Why?

GREER: A great many women in the movement think that it's time the men bore the responsibility, but I don't find that the responsibility for my own childbearing is in any way distinct from my claim for control over my own body. And if I'm to rely on some man's goodness in being sterilized, then I've lost control of my body and *he's* got control of it. It also means that he can demand my fidelity, because he's sterilized. I can fuck *him* without problems, but I can't fuck anybody else without some form of contraception. Apart from anything else, it's impossible to tell whether or not a man's sterilized. I'm the one who's going to have the kid, so I'd like to know what the situation is without having to trust his scout's honor.

But my strongest reservation concerns the fact that in many cases, the male is irreversibly sterilized. He's become a kind of fuck machine and there's no way in which he can reassess his position. I tell you, I wouldn't sterilize myself. Apart from everything else, biology is a sort of emergency mechanism. We're designed so that if society does something really stupid, then whoever of us is left alive has got a reasonable chance of repopulating the earth.

PLAYBOY: *The Female Eunuch* was your first book. Do you enjoy writing?

GREER: I have to write. It's a bit like shitting. It's quite nice. Especially if you do it nicely. You know, if a nice well-formed piece emerges. But if it's coming in dribs and drabs or not coming at all, or being forced out, if you're missing the rhythm somewhere, it's no pleasure at all. And yet sometimes there's an enormous pressure to do it. And not much pleasure when it's finished.

PLAYBOY: We understand you have another book in the works.

GREER: Yes. I'm writing a book on the female artistic impulse and what happens to it. It's probably going to be called *The Problem of Waste.*

PLAYBOY: What else does the future hold for you—and for the women's liberation movement?

GREER: The movement will simply get bigger, that's all. I don't know *when* things are going to start to happen. The astounding thing is that in the space of about three years, the movement has got so huge. How else do you explain things like Kate Millet's book becoming a best seller? It's not a very readable book. It's not a book you buy for fun, nor even for curiosity, because it's pretty easy to figure out what it's about. But the buying of that book is a positive act of support. I think the same goes for *The Female Eunuch,* which I don't think is really all that good, either. It's very uneven. Admittedly, McGraw-Hill has sold it pretty well; but even so, I would never have thought it would be a best seller in the U.S. So maybe I'm the wrong person to ask about the future. I just don't know.

It may be that an enormous disappointment is in store for the movement, that a lot of people, say, involved in the equal-rights-amendment business, all that tokenism, are going to be so disgusted by the small difference their considerable efforts have made that there'll be ten years or so of confusion. What did the suffragettes think when they won the vote? They probably thought the whole world was going to change. Well, it didn't. Revolutionary movements give in to disappointment and bitterness when they discover that Rome was not even *destroyed* in a day. I expect all that ebb and flow of revolution, all that waste and confusion, and I expect the fragmentation of the women's movement, which is becoming a serious problem. As it is, its members hardly ever provide a united front even when one is strategically called for. I don't expect that to get appreciably better until women have got used to the hypocrisies of politics. They're got to learn that you just don't wash your dirty linen in public. If you disapprove of Germaine Greer's actions, for example, which quite a few feminists do, you don't write to a pig newspaper and put her down, because it makes things too easy for the pigs. You write to *her* and put her down. Women are going to take a long time to figure out things like that.

Political education is a dreary process, however, and if you try to short-circuit it, you betray your whole scene. Because once you say, "Oh, well, we'll never get these people educated, we'll just tell them what to do," then you spend all your time consolidating your own power, like Macbeth, who seized it unjustly.

As for my own future, my life's work is to make the feminist position more and more comprehensible to more and more people. As I told you, my role is to preach to the unconverted, rather than sitting about cozily developing the line with people who already agree with it. I'm much more interested in the truly anarchist part of the movement, and this involves increasing its grass-roots support as much as possible. That includes people who have been ill educated, because I think everybody in our society is ill educated in one way or another. It means exposing myself to the worst kinds of prejudice and antagonism and doing my best to discredit them. I happen to be better at that than I would be at attempting to organize the women's movement from inside. I'm just trying to make sure there *is* a women's movement. Let somebody else organize it. I don't have any talent in that direction. But I won't submit to being abused because I don't do it. The women who abuse me for not doing it should be doing it themselves. So there you are.

TENNESSEE WILLIAMS

April 1973

Interviewer: C. Robert Jennings

Although the public in 1973 had a tacit knowledge of the homosexuality of some artists and performers, a homosexual simply did not not discuss his preferences in public, and it was journalistic protocol not to bring it up. Even in those liberated times, it wasn't done. Earlier interviews with Gore Vidal and Truman Capote in PLAYBOY—not reprinted here—went by without any personal references to homosexuality. And when David Frost, on television in late 1972, made so bold as to ask Tennessee Williams a blunt question about his sexuality, the flustered playwright could say only, "I cover the waterfront."

A short time later, however, Fisher sent free-lance writer C. Robert Jennings to conduct the first lengthy interview with the playwright. The occasion was the opening of a new play by Williams and the revival of *A Streetcar Named Desire,* and, indeed, a good portion of their conversation was about his theater work. But the editors were also seeking an opportunity to discuss homosexuality in an open, frank manner. Although Williams was suspicious at first, what eventually poured out is one of the most intense and anguished conversations published by the magazine. In the words of John Brady, in *The Craft of Interviewing,* it is "one of the toughest in PLAYBOY's history."

For almost two decades, from 1944 to 1961, Tennessee Williams wrote a series of corrosively eloquent, strangely compelling plays on subjects seldom confronted before outside the nether world of fantasy and nightmare: "A Streetcar Named Desire" (homosexuality, nymphomania, promiscuity, rape), "The Glass Menagerie" (loneliness, sexual frustration), "Summer and

Smoke" (profligacy, frigidity), "Cat on a Hot Tin Roof" (greed, alcoholism, impotence, more homosexuality), "Baby Doll" (crib fetishism, pedophilia), "Orpheus Descending" (blowtorch killing), "Sweet Bird of Youth" (castration, dope addiction, V.D.), "Suddenly, Last Summer" (cannibalism, madness) and "Night of the Iguana" (panty fetishism, masturbation, coprophagy). He got away with it not because he served up aberrant sex and violence with such realistic fervor, as some critics had it, but through shining epiphanies, through his unique vision as a poetic symbolist and mythologer. Not surprisingly, Williams won three New York Drama Critics Circle Awards and two Pulitzer Prizes before he turned 50.

Then something happened. After "The Milk Train Doesn't Stop Here Any More" unceremoniously flopped in 1962, and again in 1963, the critics began to write Williams' obituary. His one great love—Frank Merlo, who had been with him since 1947—died of cancer; his writing powers diminished; and like the psychically emasculated victims in his plays, America's topmost playwright plummeted with tragic force into a snake pit of coronaries, convulsions, pills, liquor, madness and impotence. The circle of his life seemed to have closed, and to his horror he saw manifested in himself the failure he feared he had been born to.

To explore the tortured inner landscape of this shy, scared man who, despite his resurgence, still considers himself a failed artist, PLAYBOY sent free-lancer C. Robert Jennings to interview him in New York and New Orleans, two of Williams' three adopted homes. (The third is Key West).

Jennings reports: "Tennessee Williams was directly responsible for my first and lastingest love: the theater. What passed for my adolescence was just peaking when I saw 'Streetcar'—five times—on Broadway and became riveted to the theater for life. Yet I confess that my awe of the playwright had been diminished by his toxic visions and affectations of the past decade. This, curiously, served me well when I went into this assignment: I found the man and the whomped-up myth to be very different, indeed. I came to see that this was not, as Truman Capote had told me, a 'rather dumb man' with a once-flaming talent, nor even the publicity nut that recently he seemed to have become, but a highly private and complex human being with his poetic if not his personal madness under control. He was at once introverted, thin-skinned, humanistic, obdurate, suspicious and vindictive; as cunning, tough and ageless as a crocodile. At first blush, he was disconcertingly crotchety, self-dramatizing, arch, with some of the sub-human idiosyncrasies of the self-made star manqué on the hard comeback trail, a lame phoenix rising unsteadily from bitter ash. In the grimmer reaches of his paranoia, he harbors ancient grievances, like a long-wounded wife. But I came to know that Williams holds with Gide's warning: 'Do not understand me too quickly.'

"I met him in New York after the final performance of his little motet of a play, 'Small Craft Warnings,' which was made notable by his own quite *believable performance as a hard-drinking, down-at-the-heels doctor in a seedy Southern California beach bar. Backstage, we were introduced by his new manager, Bill Barnes of International Famous Agency, and Williams greeted me warmly. He is short but oddly handsome. As the only character in the play who wore the same clothes offstage as on—white linen suit and white panama hat, a gold cross on his chest—he was the first to arrive at the closing-night cast party. Noting his unease, I began talking about his play in general and his performance in particular, and I asked him if he was a ham. He looked at me with malevolence and flashed: 'And who are you?' Then to Barnes: 'Who is this?' Bristling, I countered: 'I'm the guy who just crossed a continent to see you, with your OK. We just met.' 'Mmm,' he muttered and wandered uncertainly away.*

"As it was already my second day in the city, I assumed that he would get his act together in time to hold our first interview session, which was to have been at dinner, after the party. That turned out to be one of my wilder assumptions. He was so unglued over everyone's tardiness that he dismissed the nonparty as 'poorly organized' and sulked out into the muggy Manhattan night with a beautiful Botticelli boy poet, without saying goodbye to anyone. Later I made the tactical error of having a drink with his producer at the bar of the same beanery in which he was dining with three young men, including the poet. Though we were several leagues out of earshot, he accused me the next day of spying on him. Moreover, he seemed convinced that PLAYBOY *was out to 'get homosexuals.' With two friends in tow, he was 45 minutes late for our first lunch and made no apology. We were seated at one of the tables favored by the fabled Algonquin Round Table, but Williams turned his back to the room with: 'I don't want to be on display, I'm in a death sweat.'*

"Knowing that he drinks mostly wine, I asked if he'd like a cold dry white. Without looking up from the menu, he snapped, 'I think that all depends on what we're eating, don't you?' With which he ordered, all ruffles and flourishes, a Pouilly-Fuissé and chicken pancakes with white meat. When the waiter explained that the meat was mixed, Williams became slightly hysterical and, his noisy drawl turning heads at adjoining tables, said: 'Well, you just have the chef make it all white for me.' When I heard that his sister Rose, long confined to a mental hospital in Ossining, New York, was dining with him at the Plaza, I asked if I might meet her, if only for a minute. He was aghast, rolled his eyes skyward and said: 'Good God, man, you can't be serious.' When later he changed his mind, I had changed mine, too, and he professed to be 'highly disappointed' that I failed to show up. 'She looked so pretty,' he said ruefully. And so it went, achingly.

"Until my third day in New York, just as I was about to split the scene, when I managed somehow to engage his confidence. Though still paranoid, he suddenly dropped his guard and became warm, open, courtly, hospitable, funny—and piteously vulnerable. He never spoke off the record. For

Williams, having virtually stripped himself naked in his work, no longer has anything to hide. He is an open wound. He not only asked me up to his suite at the Hotel Elysée, fittingly shabby-genteel and haunted by the ghost of the great Tallulah Bankhead, who had lived there for many years (as had Ethel Barrymore before her), but he invited me to fly to New Orleans with him. There he would seek a respite from his writing, rewriting and acting labors, and I would be talking to an 'exhausted old man.' Besides, he added, only his French Quarter apartment had a handsome young houseboy named Victor who 'looks like a young Gore Vidal,' its own veranda and a huge, full-lipped bust of Lord Byron 'that I always kiss good night—he's very sympathetic.'

"We were driven by chauffeured limousine to the airport and, when the agent informed Williams that, although he carried a first-class ticket, he had been misbooked in tourist, he flared once more and demanded to see the boss. When another airline agent politely asked for his autograph, he refused. Once in the air, he ordered a vodka martini and, dismayed at the paltry size of it, ordered several more. Relaxed at last, he abruptly changed his manner yet again and, then and for the next six days, gave of himself (and others) intimately, unsparingly and, for the most part, graciously, revealing more, he averred, than he had in his completed but still unpublished, highly personal memoirs—for which Doubleday advanced him $50,000. His ramblings, whether lucid or manic, were almost always accompanied by giggles or a loud, mad cackle. He also gave equal time to the many people who stopped him on the street, one of whom went on at such length and so boringly about a play that I intervened, then said to Williams: 'That is the price of fame.' Said he: 'The price is too high, baby.' "

PLAYBOY: With which of your characters do you identify?

WILLIAMS: All of them—that is my gift. Alma of *Summer and Smoke* is my favorite—because I came out so late and so did Alma, and she had the greatest struggle, you know? Blanche in *Streetcar* was at it like knives from the time of the death of her husband, fucking those soldiers at camp. She had to expiate for feeling responsible for killing him. When he told her about his relations with an older man, she called him digusting; then she just went out and solved her problems with a continuous orgy. *I* didn't even masturbate until I was 27. I only had spontaneous orgasms and wet dreams. But I was never frigid like Miss Alma, not even now, when I most need it. But Miss Alma grew up in the shadow of the rectory, and so did I. Her love was intense but too late. Her man fell in love with someone else and Miss Alma turned to a life of profligacy. I've been profligate, but, being a puritan, I naturally tend to exaggerate guilt. But I'm not a typical homosexual. I can identify completely with Blanche—we are both hysterics—with Alma and even with Stanley, though I did have trouble with some of the butch characters. If you understand schizophrenics, I'm not really a *dual* creature; but I can understand the tenderness of women and the lust and libido of the male, which are, unfortunately, too seldom combined in women. That's why I seek out the androgynous, so I can get both. I couldn't have raped Blanche, as Stanley did. I've never raped anybody in my life. I've *been* raped, yes, by a goddamn Mexican, and I screamed like a banshee and couldn't sit for a week. And once a handsome beachboy, very powerful, swam up on a raft, and he raped me in his beach shack. I had a very attractive ass and people kept wanting to *fuck* me that way, but I can't stand it. I'm not built for it and I have no anal eroticism.

PLAYBOY: What do you mean by seeking out the androgynous?

WILLIAMS: I mean I'm only attracted to androgynous males, like Garbo. Ha! After a few drinks, I can't distinguish between the two. I find women much more interesting than men, but I'm afraid to try to fuck women now. I find sexual *excitement* in women, but I can't complete the act with them. By completing the act I don't mean oral copulation. I'm just as anxious to feel a woman's ass and embrace and kiss her and enter her as I am a boy.

PLAYBOY: Why are you afraid to go through with it?

WILLIAMS: Because women aren't as likely as the androgynous male to give you sexual reassurance. With a boy who has the androgynous quality in spirit, like a poet, the thing is more spiritual. I need that. And the other, too; I always want my member to enter the body of the sexual partner. I'm an aggressive person, I want to give, and I think it should be reciprocal. It's wonderful when they do and *you* do—let's face it.

PLAYBOY: But isn't that somewhat contradictory——

WILLIAMS: I *am* contradictory, baby.

PLAYBOY: What we mean is that women can certainly reciprocate as well as men, be equally spiritual, and there is the obvious physiological advantage.

WILLIAMS: Unfortunately, I cannot combine the two. Until I was 28, I was attracted to girls, but after that I fell in love with a man and felt it was better for me as a writer, for it meant *freedom*. If I were saddled with a wife and family to support—and I'd have had several wives by this time—it'd be disastrous. Oh, I'm very lucky that I've *had* women in my life, as I can write about both sexes equally well. I've loved them very deeply, but I'm shy of women sexually. I'm shy of *men* sexually. I'm very moral. I think it's most likely I'll go back to a woman in the end. Women have always been my deepest emotional root; anyone who's read my writings knows that. But I've never had any feeling of sexual security—except with my longtime secretary Frank Merlo, who served me as I had to be served. He both loved and hated me for it. I've always been terrified of impotence, even when I was very young, and Frank and Bette cured me of it.

PLAYBOY: Bette?

WILLIAMS: Bette was the only woman with whom I ever had a fully realized sexual affair. We were at the University of Iowa together. It lasted three and a half months—and then I found that androgynous boys could give me more. And as an artist, I was better off with a boy because I couldn't *afford* a girl. But at bottom, it doesn't make a goddamn bit of difference who you go to bed with, as long as there's love. I can't get it up without love. Sex is so much an integral part of my work that I must talk about it—but sex isn't the center of my life. Love is a great deal if you can get it, but my work is everything.

PLAYBOY: Did you ever have any kind of sexual contact with another woman?

WILLIAMS: Yes. My great female love was a girl named Hazel from St. Louis. But she was frigid. She'd make me count to ten before she'd let me kiss her; we were both 11 when we met and we were sweethearts until she was in college. She said, "Tom, we're much too young to think about these things." But I constantly thought about sex. In fact, the first time I had a spontaneous ejaculation was when I put my arm around Hazel on a river boat in St. Louis. She had on a sleeveless dress and I put my arm about her and stroked her bare shoulder and I had on white-flannel pants and I *came*, and we couldn't go on dancing. She didn't say anything about it. She was such a dear girl, but I couldn't be as close to her as she needed me to be. I can be a bitch. I was busy with someone else, and so I failed her. I was wise to her—her frigidity, her need—but I couldn't admit her to my life again. Hazel and I both went on pills and liquor. She married another man but killed herself when she was still very young.

PLAYBOY: When was your first homosexual encounter?

WILLIAMS: In college I was deeply in love with my roommate, "Green Eyes," but neither of us knew what to do about it. If he came to my bed, I'd say, "What do you want?" I was so puritanical I wouldn't permit him to kiss me. But he could just touch my arm and I'd come. Nothing planned, just spontaneous orgasms. The only sex we were exposed to was with dreadful old whores with cunts like diseased orchids. But my first real encounter was in New Orleans at a New Year's Eve party during World War Two. A very handsome paratrooper climbed up to my grilled veranda and said, "Come down to my place," and I did, and he said, "Would you like a sunlamp treatment?" and I said, "Fine," and I got under one and he proceeded to do me. That was my coming out and I enjoyed it.

PLAYBOY: Is that how you lost your virginity—or did you really make it with Bette?

WILLIAMS: Oh, Bette and I really did it. I was in my late 20s—a shockingly advanced age. I wasn't very virile, I was just terribly oversexed, baby, and terribly repressed. As I said, I had had orgasms before, but not through penetration of another person's body. And I never masturbated until one year before I lost my virginity. I didn't know what such a thing *was*. Well, I'd heard of it, but it never occurred to me to practice it.

PLAYBOY: Was there a moment in your life when you decided to commit yourself to one sex or the other?

WILLIAMS: No, no. I never thought much in those terms, and I still don't. I'm either in love or not in love. Oh, I've had casual adventures, yes. But, as I said, I don't think there can be truly satisfactory sex without love, even if it's only a one-night stand.

PLAYBOY: Do you consider yourself promiscuous?

WILLIAMS: Decidedly not. I feel right now I'm trying to meet my work, and I don't have energy for both work and sex at the moment. I see you don't believe that statement. Well, I have many people spending the night with me, because I *like* a companion at night; the people at the Hotel Elysée in New York think I'm terrible. But I go mad at night. I can't be alone, because I have this fear of *dying* alone. But they're usually there just for the ceremony of the dropping of the sleeping pill. Every night I take a hot bath and I have a massage if there's someone around who's any good at it.

PLAYBOY: Still, could you live and work long without sex?

WILLIAMS: I don't *want* to live without sex. I need to be touched and held and embraced. I need human contact. I need sexual contact. But at my age, one becomes terrified of impotence. I no longer feel I have the power I had. The problem is to find a partner who won't demand it of you but will offer it when the time is suitable. A really gifted sexual partner can give you complete potency if he wants to—or can deprive you of it totally. So many people just like to tease, you know. Age bothers me only in this area; at my age, one never knows whether one is being used as an easy mark or if there is a true response. But I do know that I shall never cease to be sensual—even on my deathbed. If the doctor is young and handsome, I shall draw him into my arms.

PLAYBOY: Are you afraid of death?

WILLIAMS: Who isn't? I've almost died so many times, but I didn't die because I didn't really want to. I don't think I shall die while I'm happy. I think I can delay death. I don't spend much time thinking about it, though. I've even become rather accustomed to those panicky little heart attacks that I have at times. I've had them most of my life, and how many of them were strictly of nervous origin, I don't know. Of course, if a person with a bad heart gets too agitated, that could trigger an attack, so you have to avoid such circumstances. I have always suffered from claustrophobia and fear of suffocation. It's why I travel first-class. And for a long time, I couldn't walk down a street unless I could see a bar—not because I wanted a drink but because I wanted the security of knowing it was there.

I think a lot of my work has dealt with death. I have a preoccupation at times with death and a preoccupation with sensuality—well, with a number of things. I wouldn't say that death is my main theme. Loneliness is. But I do find it difficult to accustom myself to the death of friends. Unfortunately, most of my close friends are dead. I have a few surviving ones, but not many. I've lost most of them in the last few years, you know? Frank, Diana Barrymore, Carson McCullers, all the doomed people. We did seem to flock together, didn't we?

PLAYBOY: Have you striven consciously for a kind of immortality, as some writers do?

WILLIAMS: Oh, heavens, I've never given it a thought. I just don't want to be a total has-been during my lifetime. That's what I try to avoid, mostly by hard work, baby.

PLAYBOY: You said you'd almost died many times. How?

WILLIAMS: I can't understand why anyone would give a damn about the sex life or the sicknesses of a tired old man.

PLAYBOY: For one thing, you're not just any old man; you're not even old. For another, both may be organic to your work.

WILLIAMS: Oh, all right, then. The Sixties were the worst time for me. At the beginning of one play, *Camino Real,* I quoted Dante: "In the middle of the journey of our life, I came to myself in a dark wood where the straight way was lost." I didn't know then what a prophet I was. The Sixties were no good for me even from the beginning, from *Night of the Iguana* on; everything went to pieces for me. I told Gore Vidal that I didn't remember a thing about the Sixties—that I thought I had *slept* through them. And he said, "Don't worry, you didn't miss a thing." First Frank was taken sick and I didn't know it. It was a harrowing illness and it manifested itself in erratic behavior. I think he went on hard-core-drug stuff, and you try to hide that, you know.

Frank was probably the greatest person I've ever known. He died so nobly. It was 1963 and we had a small apartment on East 65th Street. He was entering the terminal stage of lung cancer, and I moved into the study and he took the master bedroom. Fortunately, I had this huge sofa, which I slept on quite comfortably, except that I would hear him all night being racked with his cough and I would keep wanting to go in there and see if he were all right. I was so afraid he would hemorrhage like my grandmother. She died of a hemorrhage. But I couldn't, because he kept his door locked. He didn't want anyone near him. He was like a cat—they withdraw when they're dying. Well, Frank did not die alone, though *Atlantic* said I was so frightened of death that I deserted him on his deathbed, which is a malicious lie that infuriated me. Frank was very happy to have me there. But the only person he wanted in the room with him was little Gigi, our sprightly bull terrier, and in the morning they would emerge from the bedroom and she would trot at his heels. And they would sit side by side watching television. She would pretend to be watching, too.

I was with Frank the day of his death. The poor boy was put in a ward with patients who had just had brain-cancer operations, brain-tumor operations, and if you've ever seen people who've just had that operation, they're appalling to look at, you know. Their mouths are unnaturally swollen, their eyes are popping, they're sort of vegetables. And I begged him to go to a private room. I said, "Frank, you mustn't be surrounded with this," and he said, "How could it matter to me now?" And then he pointed to little cups of bloody sputum all along his bedside table. He knew he was going to go. But finally they *did* move him to a private room and he was down there gasping for breath. It seemed to me to be at least half an hour before they brought his oxygen to him; hospitals can be so callous. He never voiced any complaint. He never said, "I'm so frightened." But he wouldn't stay in bed. He kept getting up and staggering over to a chair. He'd sit in the chair a minute and then he'd stagger back to the bed. I asked him, "Frank, why won't you stay in one place?" He said, "I'm just so restless today, I've had so many visitors." I said, "Frank, would you like me to go?" And he said, "Oh, no, I'm used to *you*." And then he died.

PLAYBOY: The press always referred to Frank as your secretary. What was your true relationship?

WILLIAMS: Once, when I was working on a screenplay in Hollywood, Jack Warner said to Frank, "And what do *you* do?" Without a moment's hesitation, he said, in his quiet way, "I *sleep* with Mr. Williams." Frank would also put me down like a prize shit when I deserved it, and I often did. One loved him for it. He taught me life. He was my great male lover.

PLAYBOY: Did your decline begin with his death?

WILLIAMS: That wasn't the beginning, no. My professional decline began after *Iguana*. As a matter of fact, I never got a good review after 1961. I suppose it might make an interesting story to say that my breakdown was related to one person's death, but it's not true. I was broken as much by repeated failures in the theater as by Frank's death. Everything went wrong. My life—private and professional—and ultimately my mind broke. But it came back—I trust it's *partly* back. I must say, I still have periods of hysterical behavior, but then I always have had. I do think I'm in my right mind now. I feel no pain anymore, just morning sickness.

PLAYBOY: You mentioned bad reviews. Are you particularly sensitive to criticism of your work?

WILLIAMS: Reviews can be devastating to me. A barrage of bad reviews contributed enormously to my demoralization. The plays weren't that bad— *Slapstick Tragedy* and *Kingdom of Earth* and *In the Bar of a Tokyo Hotel* and *The Seven Descents of Myrtle* and *The Milk Train Doesn't Stop Here Anymore,* in which Hermione Baddeley got fabulous reviews. I don't think the play worked out sufficiently well, but I've seen *worse* plays do much better. Walter Kerr dismissed *Gnadiges Fräulein* in one line. He said, "Mr. Williams should not attempt black comedy." I'd never *heard* of black comedy, though I'd been writing it all my life.

During that period, I was abandoned by friends to a large extent. People ceased to think of me as an existing person. I was, you know, a sort of apparition. I was only interested in work and I had just *three* sexual experiences in four years, which I think was certainly unhealthy. I'm sure I was more depressed than I was aware of being, but when you're under sedation constantly, except when you're working, then things don't bother you terribly. A depression, you know, can easily be obscured by drugs. I think most people who take drugs are covering up depression.

PLAYBOY: What finally precipitated your breakdown? Was the critical disaster of *In the Bar of a Tokyo Hotel* in 1969 the last straw?

WILLIAMS: Yes. *Time,* which is usually kind to me, said it was more deserving of a coroner's report than a review. I was not amused. The reviewers were intolerant of my attempt to write in a freer way. *Life* said I was finished, and its obituary was reproduced in *The New York Times.* I ran off to Japan with Anne Meacham, who starred in the play, to escape the brutality of the critics. But I couldn't escape. I began washing the pills down with liquor and I just went out of my mind. I took sedation every night, and every morning I took something related to speed, so that I could still write. Finally I returned to Key West, and one morning I was preparing coffee at the stove and I was staggering about from the synergistic effect of the pills and liquor, you know. I was falling a great deal in the Sixties. Anyway, I got the boiling coffee off the stove and then I fell and it spilled all over my right shoulder—I was naked—and it gave me very severe burns.

It's almost the last thing I remember before they committed me to the loony bin, except when I was in a doctor's office and he was bandaging my shoulder. And the next thing I knew, my brother Dakin was in town and we were at the airport; and next I was in the basement of the house in St. Louis with a bottle and Dakin had brought me a typewriter and I couldn't hit any of the right keys, and I told him the typewriter was no good and he said, "Tom, you really must check into the hospital *now.*" And I said, "No, I've decided not to. I'll be all right; I'll go back to Key West." So there was a great deal of discussion about *that*, you know.

But finally I conceded that I would go to the hospital, provided they would send an ambulance for me. Well, Mother said this was ridiculous—it would just alarm the neighbors—and so it turned out that my brother drove me over. I spent one day there in a very deluxe ward watching television programs. I was so demented that all the programs seemed to be directed personally at *me*—isn't that fantastic? Even Shirley Booth's little program, *Hazel.* I thought Shirley was making veiled innuendoes about me, and then all of a sudden my brother came in grinning with a bunch of flowers and some crayon pictures drawn by his children, and in came Momma, and I said, "I'm leaving here at once." And they said, "Oh, no, Tom. In fact, you're being transferred to another section." And I said, "Oh, no I'm not."

So I rushed into the closet and somehow got into my clothes and I rushed down into an elevator and noticed a horrible intern—sort of an albino creature, you know—towering over me, and every time I pressed the DOWN button, he would shove the doors open with this great arm of his. I just couldn't escape. And so finally I ran back to my room and I said, "You must get me out of this nuthouse." I was panicky. And my mother sort of pretended to be having a faint. She said, "Oh, some smelling salts, please," and was going into a swoon, a *Southern* swoon.

By this time, my mind was quite clear. The shock of the situation had cleared my senses and so I started toward the door again, thinking I would go down the fire escape or something, and there was this *goon* squad with a wheelchair and they pushed me to the violent ward. I had my little flight bag, containing my pills and my liquor, with me and the last thing I remember is their snatching it from me as I was wheeled into the violent ward. The rest was just a series of wild hallucinations until, I don't know how much later, I woke up and my brother was there and he said, "They say you nearly died. By the way, did you know you had a silent coronary?" I had had three heart attacks while I was having convulsions. I don't know why it was necessary to tell me, but then, Dakin acts by obscure impulses. It's hard to hate him, though; he has a great deal of humor and I think he's one of the great eccentrics of our time.

Anyway, my incarceration in the bin was nothing less than an attempt at legal assassination. I've never cracked up again—I'm too *scared* to. I'm *never* going back to the bin. A physician there loathed me and refused to attend me. He was one of the most evil men I've ever known, a monster. The idea of *not* seeing a patient who had brain convulsions and a coronary is shocking. Eventually, I came under the care of three neurologists who were supposed to be eminent but weren't. Undue risks were taken with my life; I lost 30 pounds and nearly died. Well, that was the end of my long death wish. Now I want to live. That's the main trouble with Key West: I can't get a doctor there. Last year I fell into a fish pond and cut my back and broke a rib and no doctor would see me for a *week*. I had to call my doctor in New Orleans. He said, "Take two aspirins," and I said, "I'm allergic to aspirin!" But I had a fever and took them anyway and I was soon cured.

PLAYBOY: Last year a story was published that you had breast cancer and had gone to Bangkok to die. What was that all about?

WILLIAMS: If I were going to die, I would have been in Rome. I didn't have cancer, I had an old gynecomastia, a swelling in the breast that comes from the liver, from having too much to drink. Of course, I've imagined I've had cancer for 20 years. But that was all *shit*. A military surgeon in Bangkok completely removed the swelling. I have large pectoral muscles from swimming all my life, so it wasn't easy—in fact, it was quite painful, as the anesthesia wore off before he had finished. He said, "Don't worry about your chest, worry about your fucking liver." So I've cut down to drinking mostly wine, with an infrequent vodka martini and a little rum in my tea.

PLAYBOY: What's your latest malady, real or imagined?

WILLIAMS: Well, last summer I had to leave the play when I got thrown from a horse in Montauk. I was riding with a young surfer and we kept *leaping* over arroyos in the woods. A horse is something I should stay off of because of a chronic hemorrhoid condition. Anyway, after falling I developed a thrombosis *and* gangrene. The pain was affecting my heart because of my chronic cardiac condition. Everything *about* me is chronic. Bill Barnes, my agent, booked me into Doctors Hospital and got me the best doctors available. He was like Florence Nightingale. They told me they had to operate. I knew that I was *doomed,* of course, all those surgeons in their dreadful green gowns. The 15 minutes before I went under were the longest of my life. And while I was there, I got hooked on Demerol. I *love* it, but it didn't kill the pain. Anyway, I recovered and I went straight back into *Small Craft Warnings. . . .* But the critics will say I am excessively personal and I pity myself.

PLAYBOY: Can't you forget about the critics?

WILLIAMS: I've forgotten about them, baby. I wish they'd forget about me.

PLAYBOY: It's clear that you haven't. And certainly they won't.

WILLIAMS: Umm, I suppose. I hope I'll never become one of those querulous old writers who go after critics. I shall never answer them. It does no good to criticize the critics. But it's true that sometimes I think they are out to get me; it's an American syndrome. They knock you down with all the ammunition they've got, and they've got plenty. They've got all that power. They pretend they don't, but they know they do, and they love it. *Everybody* loves power. They want to try to judge you on traditional form when you're trying to move to something freer, like presentational theater, when you depart from realism and put style on the presentation itself—as Tom O'Horgan does so well. The critics still want me to be a poetic realist, and I never was. All my *great* characters are larger than life, not realistic. In order to capture the quality of life in two and a half hours, everything has to be concentrated, intensified. You must catch life in moments of crisis, moments of electric confrontation. In reality, life is very *slow*. Onstage, you have only from 8:40 to 11:05 to get a lifetime of living across.

But the personal criticism of me is no better than the criticism of my plays. Some members of the press are still virulently against the outspokenly sensual person. I shall not name them, but they are significantly influential. One of them said I wasn't the sort of person one would take to dinner—that I didn't mind telling people I was an octoroon. Ho! I had just announced to some stuffy, small-minded people that I was an octoroon and I hoped they didn't mind. But I'm *not* white trash; one of my ancestors on my father's side was a scout for the Choctaw and Cherokee. Fortunately, there are also a great many people who don't think of me as a bum; a lot of them think of me as Tennessee Ernie Ford!

PLAYBOY: How does your public image differ from the private person?

WILLIAMS: I think the theater public has an image of me that has very little relation to the truth. I think that I come on very open and corn-pone and hearty and all that, but I'm really a very private person—in a profession where privacy cannot be practiced very easily. But I must say this is a little hypocritical, because I really don't like to practice privacy now. I enjoy being a public figure, more or less. I like people recognizing me and saying hello to me on the street, as they do since I've taken up acting. I think I would miss it if people suddenly didn't know me or talk about me. And I don't mean getting the right table in the right restaurant, either; I don't go to Sardi's because I'm always so afraid they'll send me upstairs. And Elaine's seats me only out of sheer compassion for my condition.

PLAYBOY: You are certainly more visible now than you used to be. Some critics have said that you seem to be implicitly begging for mercy, in a rash of newspaper and TV interviews.

WILLIAMS: I have simply emerged, after that long period of deep depression when I didn't care if I was alive or dead. I am living again and I am glad to be alive and I've been happy to go on TV or *anything*. I suspect it has always been an instinctive thing with me, when being interviewed, to ham it up and be fairly outrageous in order to provide good copy. Why? I have a need to convince the world that I still exist and to make this fact a matter of public interest and amusement. I'm such a ham, you know. Kim Stanley once said to me, "There are actors and there are hams, baby, and I hope you know what *you* are." I could be a screen actor if the part fit me. My appearance on the Oscar show last year was by invitation of the Academy, and I was delighted to attend. I wanted to get the point across that I haven't forgotten what it feels like to receive a public award, one that's presented to you by the official arbiters of excellence in that field of creative work in which you serve.

PLAYBOY: Over the years, you've spent some time in Hollywood. How did you first land there?

WILLIAMS: In 1943, I was ushering at Broadway's Strand Theater for $17 a week. The attraction was *Casablanca* and for several months I was able to catch Dooley Wilson singing *As Time Goes By*. Anyway, one day Audrey Wood informed me I had been sold to MGM for the unheard-of sum of $250 a week. But I had to write a screenplay based on a dreadful novel for Miss Lana Turner—who couldn't act her way out of her form-fitting cashmeres. The producer, Pandro Berman, came back at me with the script and said, "She can't understand such literate dialog," although I had avoided any language that was at all eclectic. They used exactly two lines of mine. Then they asked me to do a screenplay for Margaret O'Brien and I threw in the sponge. Margaret *O'Brien*! I'm *allergic* to child actors and I said, I can't possibly write for her for *any* amount of money. For the next six months, even when I wasn't working, I'd go in once a week just to collect my pay check. I'd never *seen* such money, and I was able to live on half of it and bank the rest. I rather enjoyed it, and I was able to write *The Glass Menagerie* then.

PLAYBOY: Who were your friends in Hollywood?

WILLIAMS: My oldest friend on the Coast is Christopher Isherwood; I met Thomas Mann through him. Gavin Lambert is another old friend out there. But Mae West is the only movie star I went out of my way to meet. I just wanted to pay my respects. I told her that she was one of the three greatest talents ever to come out of the movies, the other two being W. C. Fields and Chaplin. She said, "Umm, well, I don't know about Fields."

PLAYBOY: Your own plays and movies have been filled with beautiful and famous people. Did any of them become friends, or were they important to your life in any way?

WILLIAMS: I was always very shy with actors. They all liked Frank very much, however, and he formed a sort of bond between me and the actors, made it easier for us to have contact. I see Michael York and his wife, Pat; Michael is a charming, charming young man, but to me his importance is that of a great actor. Maureen Stapleton became a good friend; she is a genius. I saw Gerry Page the other day and she looked a *mess;* she's let herself go so and her house was a rat's nest. People like Brando and Paul Newman I merely saw after performances when I dropped in to congratulate them in their dressing rooms. When I'm in Rome, I see Anna Magnani.

PLAYBOY: She was once quoted as saying she wanted to marry you.

WILLIAMS: Well, she was saved. I don't think she ever really thought she was in any danger of it. Besides, I like delicate breasts.

PLAYBOY: Do you have any other favorites?

WILLIAMS: I'm always after Maggie Leighton to star in my plays; she can do anything. And I loved Vivien Leigh. She had this *grace.* Then there was Tallulah: She was never dull, but she could be tiring. It's too bad she destroyed herself so quickly. But one could never accuse her of sweetness, exactly. When they revived *Streetcar,* she pissed on my play. She said to me, looking like a frightened animal, "I'm afraid it wasn't the greatest Blanche you've ever seen." I said, "No, in fact, it was the *worst.*" She just nodded her head very sadly. All the drag queens were out there screaming; she was a riot. But she did quite an amazing job of controlling the faggots; whenever there were lines they'd scream at, she'd draw herself up and try to shut them off. Being a natural camp, it was difficult for her to cut down on it, but she did try. In any case, being at bottom too much of a lady, she wasn't right for the part. For Blanche, an actress has got to be a bit of a *bum.* And during the second production of *Milk Train,* Tallulah no longer had enough strength to project her voice. It was her last appearance on Broadway.

When she visited me in Key West, she raved over Leonzia, my cook, and asked if she might go back to the kitchen, thank her and tell her I didn't deserve her. She said, "Oh, you divine treasure, I've never tasted such divine food in my life, you beautiful creature, you're too great to be *here*." Then she came back into the room and said, "That goddamn cook is the ugliest nigger God ever put guts into." Then she would announce that she was going to take a suppository and, whatever it was, she would just turn into a zombie and pass out on the floor.

PLAYBOY: Did you ever have an affair with any of these stars?

WILLIAMS: I'm not about to allow myself to be turned on by my actors sexually, because it would interfere with the professional thing. I don't approve of a playwright or a director or a producer using actors as sexual objects. I've been to bed with the assistant stage manager, yes, but that was long before he *became* assistant stage manager. I'm overly puritanical in this respect. I realize that many directors have gotten fabulous performances out of actors because they've slept with them.

PLAYBOY: Which of the films that have been based on your works did you like best?

WILLIAMS: I liked *A Streetcar Named Desire* and I liked *Baby Doll,* both of which I wrote for the screen. I also liked *The Roman Spring of Mrs. Stone,* from my novel, and *Sweet Bird of Youth,* which was probably better than the play. Though *Glass Menagerie* may be my best play, *Cat on a Hot Tin Roof* is still my favorite. But I hated the movie. I don't think the movie had the *purity* of the play. It was jazzed up, hoked up a bit. I OKed Burl Ives after he read one line, but Elizabeth Taylor was never my idea of Maggie the Cat.

PLAYBOY: It's been said that you had an extremely hard time writing *Streetcar,* that it "possessed" you.

WILLIAMS: I worked on it on and off for three years or more. I thought it was too *big* for the theater. Its subjects had not been dealt with before. It was Blanche, this lascivious, demonic woman, who possessed me. *Streetcar* contained just about everything but sadism—which is about the only form of sex of which I disapprove. Cruelty may be the only sin. The rape of Blanche was not sadistic, however, but a natural male retaliation. Stanley said of Blanche, "We've had this date with each other from the beginning," and he meant it. He had to prove his dominance over this woman in the only way he knew how.

PLAYBOY: Richard Harris once said he thought that all the great performances Brando might have given after *Streetcar* were buried in the files of his psychiatrist—a judgment that has fortunately since been disproved. But do you feel that psychiatry can dissipate the creative impulse?

WILLIAMS: Potentially, it's possible. I never saw any decline in the quality of Brando's acting, but I thought he was terribly ill-advised in his choice of certain screen vehicles that were not worthy of his great talent.

PLAYBOY: Have you ever been in psychoanalysis?

WILLIAMS: I've gone to analysts only at periods when it was absolutely necessary, and they *did* help me. I don't feel they've hurt my work; after all, you spend 50 minutes just rambling away about anything to them. Writers are paranoid, because they're living two lives—their creative life, which they are most protective of, and their life as a human being. They have to protect *both* lives. I put a premium on the creative life. One risks one's personal life in order to work, and when one cannot work, or when one expects total failure, there is a crisis. In one such crisis, I went to Dr. Lawrence Kubie, who said I'd written nothing but violent melodramas because of the violence of the times. He told me to break up with Frank, whom I suspected was a heroin addict. Kubie thought I should be heterosexual. He was a *strict* Freudian. He was a divine man, but I wouldn't break up with Frank, of course, so I broke up with Kubie. Besides, if I got rid of my demons, I'd lose my angels.

There are times in your life, though, when you reach such a peak of crisis that you *have* to go to a shrink. But even he can't finally solve it. He just gets you through it. Kubie would imitate my father and scream at me— to break the doors down, you know. What he gave me was not forgettable. I actually learned to respect my father, and now that he's dead, I love the old son of a bitch. But I wouldn't get within a mile of a shrink now, if I could help it. I don't even think I'll have another nervous breakdown. I'll become hysterical, but I won't crack. It's a good release to be hysterical— like having an orgasm.

PLAYBOY: Why do you feel you won't have another breakdown, after so many in the past?

WILLIAMS: Because I don't allow myself to feel constant disappointment anymore. I don't hate myself habitually. I try to recognize my limitations and to content myself with what I'm able to do. It's all very banal: I order my coffee and juice and it comes immediately and then I go straight to the typewriter and don't stop until noon. I usually have several things going at once; I can switch to anything.

PLAYBOY: Have any other writers exerted a special influence on your work?

WILLIAMS: The only ones of which I am conscious are Chekhov and D. H. Lawrence. I greatly admire Rimbaud and I love Rilke. Gide always seemed a bit prissy to me. Proust I admire enormously, but he wasn't an influence. Hemingway was, without any question, the greatest; he had a poet's feeling for words, economy. Fitzgerald's early books I thought were shit—I couldn't finish *Gatsby*—but I read *Tender Is the Night* several times. There are very few writers I can stand; isn't that awful? But I'm mad about Jane Bowles and Joan Didion and, of course, I like the Southern writers, Flannery O'Connor and Carson McCullers, a very dear friend who was the only person I could ever write in the same room with. We used to read Hart Crane's poems to each other. Miss Didion's first novel, *Run River*, is good writing, but it begins with a murder and I'm always suspicious of anything that begins with a murder. It's like beginning a novel with fucking your mother—where do you go from that? So I never finished it. But I think *Play It As It Lays* is masterful.

PLAYBOY: What about your friends Gore Vidal and Truman Capote?

WILLIAMS: Friends? Baby, with friends like that . . . Once I was about to go to Ischia with Truman and his good friend Jack Dunphy, who's a *much* better writer than Truman; his *Friends and Vague Lovers* is a better book than anything Truman could ever *dream* of writing. Anyway, Truman said to me, "Anne Jackson tells me that when Margo Jones was directing *Summer and Smoke*, she said, 'Baby, we're doing a play by a dying man. We've got to give it all we've got.' " So I didn't go to Ischia with him. Gore and I were friendly until *Two Sisters* came out; he said that with the passage of time, I had gone mad.

PLAYBOY: Didn't you once write an essay saying that success and security were a kind of death to an artist?

WILLIAMS: Yes, after *Glass Menagerie,* which made me an instant celebrity, I just shut out the world and came to suspect everyone in it, including myself, of hypocrisy. Though I think I am less inclined to hypocrisy than anyone I know. I think hypocrisy is something imposed upon all of us. Maybe it's just exercise of a certain propriety. I wouldn't call it wearing a mask so much as upon occasion, one must just behave in a manner that is not precisely instinctual. But my public self, that artifice of mirrors, has ceased to exist and I have learned that the heart of man, his body and his brain are forged in a white-hot furnace for the purpose of conflict. That struggle for me is creation. Luxury is the wolf at the door and its fangs are the vanities and conceits germinated by success. When an artist learns this, he knows where the dangers lie. Without deprivation and struggle, there is no salvation and I am just a sword cutting daisies.

PLAYBOY: Aren't you making the job of creation tougher for yourself by spending so much time eating in posh places with stylish people and drinking more than one should drink?

WILLIAMS: No, I think I'm making it easier. After some four hours of work every morning seven days a week, you try to spend the rest of your time as pleasantly as possible. I swim at the New York Athletic Club, which I'm not too fond of—or perhaps they're not very fond of me; they gave me hell on the gay thing. If I were a *duck,* I'd be swimming in Central Park. In New Orleans and Key West, I have my own pools. But I feel very depressed if I don't work during the day, *every* day.

PLAYBOY: Being a Catholic, do you take time out for Mass or confession?

WILLIAMS: I would *love* confessionals if I could get up at that time, but *writing* is a confessional, and I feel that I confess everything in these interviews. What is there left to say? My brother Dakin had me converted to Catholicism when he thought I was dying; it did me no harm. I've always been very religious; I was religious as an Episcopalian and I'm still religious as a Catholic, although I do not subscribe to a great many of the things you are supposed to subscribe to, like the belief in individual immortality. Nor in the infallibility of Popes. I think Popes are among the most fallible people on earth, so this is heresy, isn't it? And yet I *love* the poetry of the Church. I love to go into either a high Anglican service or a Roman Catholic service. And I love to receive communion, but I'm usually working Sunday morning—so I take communion at funerals.

PLAYBOY: Is your Catholicism unconventional in any other respects?

WILLIAMS: Well, I wouldn't care for extreme unction at my death, because if they came at you with it, you'd know that you'd had it. And I believe in contraception of every kind. Anybody who doesn't oppose the population explosion is out of his mind. Overpopulation ruins the ecology of all life.

PLAYBOY: You're pretty well off financially, aren't you?

WILLIAMS: Everybody coaxes me into talking about how wealthy I am. My royalties mostly come from abroad, foreign productions, you know, and they add up. I have houses, too, and a considerable amount of stocks. I don't even know their value, though, so I don't know my worth precisely. But it's not as much as President Nixon's, who lists his property alone as $800,000. When I asked my lawyer what my estate amounts to, she said the exact amount of money is not what you're worth, it's your work.

PLAYBOY: What do you feel are your greatest gifts—and your greatest limitations?

WILLIAMS: I'm strongest on characterization, dialog, use of language. And I do have a sense of what is theater, I believe. Oh, but weaknesses, I have so *many*. When we were first reading *Sweet Bird,* I jumped up and said, "Stop it at once. It's dreadfully overwritten." If things are powerfully directed and acted, however, the purple writing becomes true. My greatest weaknesses are structural. And I overdo symbols; they're the natural language of drama, but I use them excessively. I'm also inclined to be overly introspective, but I don't know how to avoid it. I am an introspective person. I don't like writing that doesn't come deeply from the person, isn't deeply revealing *of* the person.

PLAYBOY: When your life story is filmed from the memoirs you've written, who will play Tennessee Williams?

WILLIAMS: Let me see, who's the handsomest young actor around? Michael York? Marjoe is quite charming—he has everything Billy Graham doesn't. Victor, my houseboy in New Orleans, breaks my heart—isn't he beautiful?—but he can't act.

PLAYBOY: So we're back to sex. Do you believe that, in the final analysis, a man follows his phallus?

WILLIAMS: I hope not, baby. I hope he follows his heart, his frightened heart.

WALTER CRONKITE

June 1973

Interviewer: Ron Powers

Since 1971, the Nixon administration had been orchestrating an attack on what it saw as the liberal bias of the press, with the alliterative vice-president, Spiro Agnew, leading the charge. That "the most trusted man in America," CBS's Walter Cronkite, should speak out on the issue meant it was important. That he should do so in PLAYBOY meant he wanted his message to reach an audience larger than the number of viewers who tuned in to the CBS "Evening News." (The CBS news program has an audience of about fourteen million; PLAYBOY's total readership is about twenty-two million.) But what was unusual was how forcefully—even passionately—Cronkite spoke about newsmen's rights. Abandoning his avuncular neutrality, he lashed out at the Nixon spokesmen and defended the independence of the media. The interview remains a rare look at "Uncle Walter" off-camera, and on a podium.

The interview was conducted by Chicago *Sun-Times* TV critic Ron Powers, who later won a Pulitzer Prize for television coverage. Queried by Northwestern's Medill School of Journalism in 1977, Cronkite said that his interview in PLAYBOY was "one of the best ever done with me."

If God had set out to create a prototypical middle American, He could have done little better than limn the image of the sad-eyed 56-year-old man—at his CBS anchor desk in New York—whose military-drum-roll voice, sending modulator needles flickering toward the bass registers, has become part of our collective consciousness.

But while Cronkite is regarded by the public as a fatherly, sympathetic figure, he has a rather more volatile reputation among his colleagues in the broadcast industry, where he's known as a tough, jealous and outspoken guardian of newsmen's rights.

To get a summing up of Cronkite's own feelings about his 40 years in journalism and about the current contretemps between the Government and the press, PLAYBOY *assigned TV critic Ron Powers to interview Cronkite in New York. His report:*

"Walter Cronkite is a Walter Mitty in reverse: He is a famous man who has fantasies of being ordinary. His office—a pristine cubbyhole just off the 'Evening News' set at CBS' big broadcast barn on West 57th Street in New York—proves it. There are the obligatory 'serious books' about Presidents and nations, the plastic-lined wastebasket, the three TV sets and the 'Facts on File.' But there is also a large, sentimental oil painting of a sailing boat (boating is Cronkite's favorite recreation), a box of chocolates and a cardboard-cutout statue of Apollo spacemen, a grade-schooler's gift that Cronkite keeps as a souvenir.

"He never loosened his necktie as we talked, but he propped his feet up on his desk and alternately clasped his hands behind his head and fiddled with his stretch socks.

"His eyes, so penetrating on the screen, seem pale and sensitive in person. He has the old-time journalist's knack of forming his thoughts into cogent, parsable sentences as he speaks, and he displayed a gift for the lyric phrase when talking of his reveries at the helm of his boat or of memories of childhood days in Texas.

"I frequently sensed a mild, resigned puzzlement that the life of a superstar had come to him. He was unfailingly courteous with me, but on the topic that was obviously foremost in his mind—current Government ploys to muffle newsmen in the pursuit of their work—he was neither mild nor resigned. He was visibly steamed, in fact, when we discussed the subject, which I broached in my first question."

PLAYBOY: You are perhaps the most outspoken of all newsmen in defending broadcasters' rights against Government intimidation. In fact, you have used the word conspiracy in describing the Nixon Administration's efforts to discredit the press. How would you characterize this conspiracy?

CRONKITE: Let me say, first of all, that after I used the word conspiracy the first and only time, in a speech to the International Radio and Television Society in New York a couple of years ago, I began to regret the use of the word—only because I found that there were still people who equated conspiracy with some of the witch-hunts of the past. The word has nearly lost its true meaning. Having said that, I still feel that this is basically what has taken place: a well-directed campaign against the press, agreed upon in secret by members of the Administration. I can't see how it's possible to have such an orchestrated, coordinated campaign without some prior plan and agreement—which really comes out to be a conspiracy.

PLAYBOY: Can you trace it to one person in the Administration?

CRONKITE: I certainly think that the President has to be held accountable, since he's the boss.

PLAYBOY: Do you attribute Nixon's hostility toward the press to his personal bitterness about the way the press has treated him?

CRONKITE: I think that may be true, although it's very hard to ascribe motivation to anybody. Circumstantially, the evidence would point to that. Certainly, he's had his bouts with the press before; his disappointments have been shown in public. There is the case of the 1962 gubernatorial concession statement in California. There is his failure just in recent months, at a very critical time in history, to appear more frequently before the press and the public to explain the workings of the Administration. I think all these things point to that general attitude toward the press.

I don't know what happened inside the Administration. I don't know at what point its members decided that it would be wise to attempt to bring down the press's credibility in an attempt to raise their own. But I think that's what has happened. It's sort of like that U tube we used to see in physics class that shows the countereffects of pressure: When you put pressure on one side and the level goes down, the level of the water on the other side has to rise. Extending that theory, if you could lower the credibility of the press, you could raise the credibility of the politicians. That must be the underlying theory in their attack.

PLAYBOY: Nearly all politicians have felt the need to control the press to some degree. Is this Administration simply more sophisticated than its predecessors in the techniques of applying pressure effectively?

CRONKITE: I don't know that they're any more sophisticated, but they're the first ones who have deliberately set out to *use* those techniques.

PLAYBOY: What has been the chronology of this attack? Was Vice-President Agnew's 1969 Des Moines speech—in which he attacked the "tiny, enclosed fraternity of privileged men"—the start of it all?

CRONKITE: I think that was the open declaration in the battle. Before that, it was simply felt that this Administration's antagonism had been about like the antagonism shown by previous Administrations, Democratic as well as Republican—particularly Democratic—toward the press. An adversary relationship, we all agree, is a good thing. But the Agnew attack suddenly became a matter of Administration policy and, more than that, a threat to use Governmental weapons against the press. Then, following Agnew's speech, there was a tightening in attitudes on the part of press-relations people in the Government. It was a subtle thing.

The Administration feels network news must exercise a greater degree of "professional responsibility." I'd have a hard time defining professional responsibility myself. But my hackles rise when I hear it suggested that we're *not* responsible. We in broadcast news have ethics we defend and maintain as strongly as a doctor or a lawyer does; in fact, a lot *more* strongly than some doctors and lawyers I know.

PLAYBOY: Doctors and lawyers have rather well-defined codes of professional standards, but journalists don't. Do you think they should?

CRONKITE: I don't really see that they need to be imposed, and I see some dangers in it. Freedom of press and speech seems to imply that anybody can write or speak out, whether he's literate or not. Erecting standards would also suggest that you're going to legislate against the underground press, and I think that would be a mistake. If you're going to accept journalists only if they conform to some establishment norm, you won't have the new blood and free flow of new ideas that are absolutely essential to a vital press. I don't know that Tom Paine could have passed a journalism-review test.

PLAYBOY: One standard that Government already confers on broadcasters is the so-called fairness doctrine, which requires that both sides of controversial issues be presented. You have said you favor its elimination because it imposes artificial and arbitrary standards of balance and objectivity.

CRONKITE: Yes. I think the only way to free radio and television news broadcasting from the constant danger of Government censorship is to free it from any form of Government control. The only way to do that is to limit the licensing practice to a technical matter of assignment of channels.

PLAYBOY: Insofar as television is bearing the brunt of this attack, do you feel that CBS is the primary target—that the Administration is still vindictive about *The Selling of the Pentagon* and your own news reports last summer on the Watergate affair and the Soviet wheat deal?

CRONKITE: I like to think that we've been in the forefront of the reporting and therefore in the forefront when the flak starts to fly. That doesn't alarm me. I'm not alarmed for CBS. I'm alarmed for the entire country.

PLAYBOY: News analysis on all the networks has dropped off since the Administration's attacks began. There are fewer "instant analyses" of Presidential addresses, for example.

CRONKITE: I'm not sure I agree with you. I think that we at CBS bend over backward to be sure that we get an analysis on after every major address. Even when commercial considerations might have dictated going immediately from the address to the next program, we've cut into the top of that program in order to get a few licks in.

PLAYBOY: But are these licks as tough as they used to be?

CRONKITE: I don't know. I guess I have to be candid and say that it seems to me that on occasion our guys have pulled their punches. But I've talked with them about it—not officially, because that's not part of my function—and I get the impression that they don't feel they have. But they do feel threatened. This question of "instant analysis," though, is one of the major phonies of the whole anti-network, anti-press campaign. As any newspaperman knows, it's rare that the press doesn't have a major Presidential speech several hours in advance. The newspapers must get it set in type, the editorial writers must have a shot at it for the next day's paper. So there's nothing instant about analysis. The network analysts have longer than the print press to study a speech, in fact, because they don't deliver their analysis until after it's given.

PLAYBOY: Do you think that the public's apparent declining interest in documentaries has anything to do with the Administration's success in discrediting the press? Were you surprised, for example, at the low level of outrage following the Watergate exposé?

CRONKITE: I certainly was, very much so. I tie it to the fact that the people say, well, it's just another campaign-year press attack against Nixon.

PLAYBOY: Do you think the public really cares about freedom of the press anymore? Or even about its own freedom of speech or assembly?

CRONKITE: I think people care in the abstract. But they don't understand the specifics. We did a poll on the Bill of Rights at CBS a couple of years ago. We asked people such specific questions as, "As long as there appears to be no danger of violence, do you think any group, no matter how extreme, should be allowed to organize protests against the Government?" Something like 76 percent of the people said no, they don't have that right. But the same people *support* the constitutional guarantee of freedom of assembly. So they believe in the abstract but not in the specific. And this is our problem.

PLAYBOY: Implicit in the Administration's attempts to force the networks to "balance" the news is a conviction that most newscasters are biased against conservatism. Is there some truth in the view that television newsmen tend to be left of center?

CRONKITE: Well, certainly liberal, and possibly left of center as well. I would have to accept that.

PLAYBOY: What's the distinction between those two terms?

CRONKITE: I think the distinction is both clear and important. I think that being a liberal, in the true sense, is being nondoctrinaire, nondogmatic, noncommitted to a cause—but examining each case on its merits. Being left of center is another thing; it's a political position. I think most newspapermen by definition have to be liberal; if they're not liberal, by my definition of it, then they can hardly be good newspapermen. If they're preordained dogmatists for a cause, then they can't be very good journalists; that is, if they carry it into their journalism.

As far as the leftist thing is concerned, that I think is something that comes from the nature of a journalist's work. Most newsmen have spent some time covering the seamier side of human endeavor; they cover police stations and courts and the infighting in politics. And I think they come to feel very little allegiance to the established order. I think they're inclined to side with humanity rather than with authority and institutions. And this sort of pushes them to the left. But I don't think there are many who are *far* left. I think a little left of center probably is correct.

PLAYBOY: Some critics believe that this left-of-center tendency produces a kind of conventional wisdom for liberals—a point of view that's common to most newsmen. During last summer's convention coverage, for example, George McGovern was repeatedly characterized as a likable but conniving bumbler and President Nixon as an unlovable but efficient manager running a closed shop. According to Richard Dougherty, Senator McGovern's press secretary during the 1972 campaign, the press never rests until it has found a convenient tag. Then, unconsciously, it edits its coverage to fit this pre-conception. Is this a legitimate charge?

CRONKITE: God, it worries me more than almost any other single factor. It's a habit that I justify to myself because of the time element. You quickly label a man as a leftist or a conservative or something, because every time you mention him, it's almost impossible to explain precisely where he stands on various issues. But labeling disturbs me at every level of our society. We all have a tendency to do it.

PLAYBOY: Doesn't the fact that the same labels tend to be applied to the same people by all the networks—as well as by the print media—imply that there's a bit too much editorial camp-following in the news business?

CRONKITE: Don't forget that in political campaigns those who cover a candidate are all living and working together in the greatest intimacy. I mean, there's a lot of cross-fertilization, and these reporters become kind of a touchstone for the rest of the press. That's inevitable, I suppose. But the idea that there's some elitist liberal Eastern establishment policy line is absolutely mad.

PLAYBOY: To the extent that there is at least a tendency to group-think, what do you think the effect of it is?

CRONKITE: To the extent that there *is* an effect, I think it's to be deplored. But I don't know that there's anything you can do about it. We're perhaps all conditioned by similar backgrounds, similiar experiences. And you'll find, I think, that if we do, indeed, react in a knee-jerk fashion to news stimuli, so do people in every other business.

PLAYBOY: Isn't that the essence of Vice-President Agnew's charge—that newsmen are conditioned by similar backgrounds and experiences?

CRONKITE: Again, he's thinking of the elitist Eastern establishment as our common background and experience. I'm thinking about covering the police station in Louisiana in Howard K. Smith's case or North Carolina in David Brinkley's case. That's the kind of experience I'm talking about—experience of America, experience with the people, experience with the burgeoning and overburdening bureaucracy, experience with those who have a tough shake in life. That's the experience I'm talking about.

PLAYBOY: How do you feel about advocacy journalism—the kind of reporting that puts the sort of experience you mention in the service of a newsman's own personal convictions? Is it possible that there isn't enough of this—rather than too much, as Agnew claims—in the media?

CRONKITE: I think that in seeking truth you have to get both sides of a story. In fact, I don't merely think, I *insist* that we present both sides of a story. It's perfectly all right to have first-person journalism; I'm all for muckraking journalism; I'm all for the sidebar, the eyewitness story, the impression piece. But the basic function of the press has to be the presentation of all the facts on which the story is based. There are no pros and cons as far as the press is concerned. There shouldn't be. There are only the facts. Advocacy is all right in special columns. But how the hell are you going to give people the basis on which to advocate something if you don't present the facts to them? If you go only for advocacy journalism, you're really assuming unto yourself a privilege that was never intended anywhere in the definition of a free press.

PLAYBOY: In reporting an official statement that a newsman knows to be patently untrue, do you think that in the interest of presenting both sides of a story, he should feel an obligation to report also that it's a lie?

CRONKITE: I think you're probably obligated to report it—but you're also obligated to check the records first.

PLAYBOY: Can you think of a story in which a man who's been quoted has been shown by independent checking to be untruthful?

CRONKITE: Yes, that happens quite frequently. For example, there's a Pentagon announcement about the purchase of a new weapons system that's going to cost so much, and we point out that development costs have already run a lot more than that. This is a routine part of reporting.

PLAYBOY: The job of corroborating the facts in a story can be complicated by a newsman's closeness with his source. Jack Anderson and others say that most newsmen in Washington are so dependent on high-level sources, so impressed with being able to associate with the mighty, that they become their unwitting allies. Is this a fair appraisal of the Washington press corps?

CRONKITE: I think it's a serious problem, and not just for the Washington press corps. It's a serious problem for the county-court reporter, the police reporter in Sioux City or anywhere else. How close do you get to your sources? It's a hard decision. In order to protect your objectivity, you can turn your back on them socially; but by so doing, you can also cut yourself off from inside information.

PLAYBOY: Anderson insists that sources tell him things because they're afraid not to.

CRONKITE: Well, I think that's right. But I don't approve of everything Anderson does and everything he prints. He often has inadequate evidence. I think he takes the minor episodes and blows them into what appear to be major scandals. On the other hand, he's the one guy who's doing a consistent job of investigative journalism, at least on a daily basis in Washington. And I do agree with him that there are many reporters in Washington who deliberately seek social favors, to the considerable detriment of their reporting. But there are also a lot of lazy reporters who aren't high enough on the social scale, the impact scale, to get the big invitations. They simply find it's a lot easier to take the handouts and rewrite them than it is to do a day's work.

PLAYBOY: Another problem in Washington news coverage seems to handicap broadcast reporters more than the print press. The networks don't seem willing to spend the money for specialist reporters, and their general newsmen are shunted from story to story, never staying on one for a long time. Doesn't that handicap you?

CRONKITE: Yes, there's no question about it. It's part of our basic problem in network news, something the public should be aware of. The problem is lack of personnel. The reporters we have in the field are the best in the business, I think; most of them are graduates of newspapers and news services, and they are superb. But we don't have enough of them, and we're never going to—simply because we don't have the outlet for them. I mean, we may have room on the *Evening News* for maybe three or four reports oncamera and a total of 10, 12 or 15 other items that are going to run 15 to 20 seconds each. It's pretty hard in those circumstances to economically justify maintaining a staff equivalent to that of the A.P. or U.P.I.

In television, we can introduce the public to the people who make the news. We can introduce them to the places where the news is made. And we can give them a bulletin service. In those three particulars, we can beat any other news medium. But for the in-depth reporting that's required for an individual to have a reasonably complete knowledge of his world on any given day—of the city and county and state—we can't touch it.

PLAYBOY: There is a famous story that the CBS news director once pasted up your transcript of the *Evening News* onto a dummy of *The New York Times*, and it covered less than the eight columns of the front page.

CRONKITE: Yes. The number of words spoken in a half-hour evening-news broadcast—words spoken by interviewees, interviewers, me, everybody—came out to be the same number of words as occupy two thirds of the front page of the standard newspaper. We are a front-page service. We don't have time to deal with the back pages at all.

PLAYBOY: In recent years, the television press has been criticized not merely for the superficiality with which it reports the news but for actually creating or transforming news events—riots, for example. Do you think that's a valid criticism?

CRONKITE: There's a very serious problem with that. Demonstrations have always been staged for the purpose of attracting attention. There's no purpose for a demonstration except to get public attention and—it's hoped—sympathy. Certainly, the demonstrators are going to be where the cameras are. Certainly, they're going to let us know in advance that the demonstration will take place. Certainly, they're hoping for live coverage. Certainly, if you have live coverage, it's going to be a more lively demonstration than if you don't have live coverage. But I don't think that we're responsible for the events. We unquestionably have an influence on them; but so does a newspaper reporter's or a still photographer's presence.

PLAYBOY: But TV camera crews are very conspicuous, whereas a newspaperman can be lost in the crowd.

CRONKITE: Lights are the biggest problem. And I guess for that reason the Chicago convention may have been the end of lighted demonstration coverage, because lights attract demonstrators like moths to a flame.

PLAYBOY: Television has been assailed at least as much for its coverage of the Vietnam war as for that of demonstrations against it here at home. Do you think we found out from television—soon enough, at least—what was really going on in Vietnam? In the early war years, network news executives seemed to subscribe to the conventional assumption that American generals and politicians were simply doing what had to be done to preserve freedom, and the war was covered accordingly. It wasn't until long afterward—1968 and later—that TV newsmen such as yourself began to express doubts about the justness of America's involvement in Indochina. Wasn't this lag in critical reporting one of broadcast news's great failures?

CRONKITE: I'm not sure I can give an entirely satisfactory answer. The coverage changed. Yes. It changed. It went through several periods. Let's go back to when American troops were first committed over there in sizable, easily identified units, as opposed to two or three American advisors working with the Vietnamese troops. Up to '65, as our involvement deepened, we were increasing our coverage. We were doing stories on advisors out in the field, and the dangers to them, and the occasional death. But it wasn't a daily flow of combat film. For one thing, we weren't interested in endangering our correspondents to do that kind of thing. But in '65, when we began committing total U.S. units, it was another story. Here were American boys fighting in a war. The news story became these boys at war. If you're going to do that honestly, you're going to have to go up where the blood is flowing. That's where the story is; the story's not back in the base camp. We were taking the war into the homes of America—and that's where it belonged. In a war situation, every American ought to suffer as much as the guy on the front lines. We ought to see this. We ought to be *forced* to see it.

PLAYBOY: But Vietnam wasn't just a visual story. It was a complex story of ideas, of political assumptions, of men's attitudes. To convey an understanding of the war on this level necessitated sophisticated reporting. How high was the journalistic quality of the TV newsmen who went over there in the early years? How about those guys who hung around the press headquarters in Saigon for the so-called "five-o'clock follies"—those no-comment news conferences? How long did it take them to realize they had to stop taking handouts and find out what was really going on?

CRONKITE: I don't think there was any lag at all. As a matter of fact, I was surprised—and a little annoyed—at reporters during my '65 visit over there. I had gone over believing in what we were doing; I came back concerned because I saw a build-up of forces far greater than our leaders ever told us we were likely to commit. That's when my disillusion began. But at first, when I arrived, as I say, I was annoyed at the skepticism of the reporters at the press conferences in Saigon. They were accepting nothing at the five-o'clock follies. More than seeking information, they were indulging in what I considered self-centered bearbaiting, pleasing their own egos, showing how much they knew. And I was a little offended. I thought they shouldn't betray their extreme youthfulness. Maybe, I thought, they were a little wet behind the ears. I wondered why they didn't just do their jobs, ask the questions and then go on and get the story.

CRONKITE: Didn't the military have a strong hand over there in directing the flow of news, deciding where a man could go with his camera?

CRONKITE: Yes, they did, but they always do in a war situation. And I think that the press ended up getting the truth anyway—and telling it.

PLAYBOY: Well, it wasn't a reporter who uncovered My Lai but a disgruntled soldier, Ronald Ridenhour, who tried for months to peddle his story to the press before *The New York Times* accepted it. There was great resistance on the part of the press to accept his version.

CRONKITE: That could very well be, because this sort of story comes to us quite frequently. There are a lot of things that, if we had the manpower and the time and so forth, we could investigate: the letters that come to us about conditions at mental institutions, or in prisons, or the welfare situation, that undoubtedly are true. But as for My Lai, had it come to us first, I don't know precisely how we would have handled it, but I can see where we would have had considerable difficulty in handling it. Here was one soldier's charge; we couldn't have just gone on the air with it. We would have had to go out and spend a tremendous amount of effort to check the thing out. A really overwhelming amount of effort. And we just haven't got the resources to do it.

I think that the attitude of a managing editor, faced with that tip, might very well have been, "God, that sort of thing goes on in all wars. It's probably not as bad as this soldier says it was. It's probably somewhere between that and not having happened at all. As a matter of fact, we've already reported several like that—obviously not as bad as that, but charges that civilians had been shot, and so forth." And just dismissed this story for that reason. My Lai, fortunately, *was* finally uncovered, to the very great credit of Seymour Hersh.

PLAYBOY: You were quoted as saying that if Daniel Ellsberg had brought the Pentagon papers to CBS, you wouldn't have run that story either.

CRONKITE: I didn't say that. Somebody else said it, I think. But I'm not sure that it's quite true. I think if he had brought them here, we would have gone to a newspaper and said, "Let's work together on this. Let us summarize them and you present the full text." But the Pentagon papers are a tough one. I don't know that if I were the editor of a newspaper, I would assign a reporter to try to get hold of the secret reports of the Pentagon. In fact, I'm pretty confident I wouldn't.

PLAYBOY: Why not?

CRONKITE: Because I think that going in from the outside to get hold of secret papers is legally indefensible. I don't think the press has a right to steal papers.

PLAYBOY: Isn't it just as legally indefensible to print papers stolen by someone else?

CRONKITE: No. Once they've come out of the secret files and are in circulation in any way whatsoever, I'd say then that the public is entitled to know whatever anybody else knows. But I don't think an individual is entitled to know what is inside secret files while they're still secret. Please understand, however, that I'm for complete declassification of secret papers. Overclassification is one of the areas in which the Federal Government is terribly culpable. But I think we have to get at it through legal means.

I don't believe we have any right to violate the law. I'm a real old-fashioned guy in that sense: I believe in law and order. I don't like the fact that the phrase has become a code word for bigotry and suppression of civil rights and a lot of other things. I don't believe in that for one damned ever-loving minute. But if you take the words for what they really mean, I think law and order are the foundation of our society. And I just don't believe that anybody should take it unto himself to violate the law, no matter what good he thinks can be achieved, because you can extend that right up to lynching. Now, what Ellsberg did is for his conscience to work on. I admire tremendously his courage and bravery and his fortitude in doing what he did. But I would never assign a man to do that for CBS.

PLAYBOY: So a public good came from something you oppose in principle.

CRONKITE: It's not clear yet that Ellsberg violated the law. The trial is still on as we talk today. Ellsberg, after all, was the *author* of much of this material. He was a participant in it, you know.

PLAYBOY: Whether or not Ellsberg is guilty of a crime, is there never an instance, in your opinion, in which breaking the law could be justifiable? What about civil disobedience as practiced by Martin Luther King?

CRONKITE: Clearly, there may come a time when civil disobedience and protest against what is considered an unjust law might be considered proper. I'm inclined to believe, though, that if I had to stand on absolutes, I'd prefer to stand on the absolute of law and order, even in such a case as that. I think there are means in our society to correct injustice, and I don't think that civil disobedience or sticks and stones provide the way to do it.

I'm glad that things have worked out to speed integration in this country; certainly, for 100 years we damn well did far too little—didn't do anything, in fact. I'm glad we've finally gotten off our behinds and gotten going here in the last couple of decades. We have probably been spurred to some degree by the demonstrations that the great Martin Luther King directed. So you've got to say, well, it works on occasion. But I still think the better way would be to do it within the law.

PLAYBOY: The opinions you've just expressed are stronger than any you've ever delivered on the air about this issue—which seems to reflect your views about the importance of remaining an objective reporter. Yet you departed from that policy when you returned from a visit to Vietnam in 1968 and advocated an early negotiated peace in a series of editorials at the end of your nightly newscast. Are you glad you did it?

CRONKITE: Glad? I'm not sure. In a lot of people's minds, it put me on a side, categorized me in part of the political spectrum. And I think that's unfortunate. It's a question in my wind now, looking back, weighing the long-term disadvantages with the short-term benefits. When I went over there, I didn't know what I was going to report back, actually. I didn't go over to do a hatchet job. I didn't go over to be anti-Vietnam, to be against American policy. I was leaning that way; I had been very disturbed ever since the '65 build-up. I was particularly disturbed over the lack of candor of the Administration with the American public, about the constant misleading statements as to the prospect of victory—the light-at-the-end-of-the-tunnel stuff. I thought—and I still think—that was the most heinous part of the whole Vietnam adventure. I had also been disturbed about the vast overkill, about what we were doing to the people of Vietnam.

But even then, I was still living with my old feeling of sympathy for the original commitment, in line with Kennedy's promise that "we shall support any friend to assure the success of liberty." Nobody was kidding himself about the nature of the South Vietnamese regime, but we thought we were trying to create conditions that would promote the growth of democracy, give them a right to self-determination. So I went out in '68 still basically believing in our policy but increasingly disenchanted with what we had actually been doing over there ever since '65. Then, after the *Tet* offensive, Johnson and Westmoreland and McNamara were saying we had won a great victory—you know, "Now we've got them; this was their last great effort." And it was clearly untrue. That was what broke my back. That's why I felt I finally had to speak out and advocate a negotiated peace.

PLAYBOY: What do you think was the effect of your editorials?

CRONKITE: I think the effect was finally to solidify doubts in a lot of people's minds—to swing some people over to the side of opposition to our continued policy in Vietnam. I must be careful not to be immodest here, but I happen to think it may have had an effect on the Administration itself.

PLAYBOY: On President Johnson?

CRONKITE: Yes, although he denied that to me personally. Not just about my reporting but about everybody else's. In fact, in our last conversation, ten days before his death, he went over that ground again, as he did in almost every conversation. It weighed on him very much, apparently. He talked about the *Tet* offensive and he said a lot of people were sure it was *Tet* that really turned him off, and he said it wasn't so and that it wasn't my reports that did it, either.

PLAYBOY: Did Johnson ever confide in you about his feelings on the war? In the course of those last interviews you had with him, did he say anything that contradicted his public statements in office?

CRONKITE: No, never. It was one of the disappointments of the interviews we did. I thought, when he was out of office, that he would let his hair down and say, "Well, there were some points where I think we went wrong; there were some things I did that I wish, looking back on it, I hadn't done." But that never happened, either in personal conversation or in the interviews. And I think that's because he didn't entertain any such thoughts. Our private talks were reasonably personal. I'm sure he thought that they were confidential, and therefore there would have been no reason not to say it if he felt it. He was a loquacious man in person, and I believe these feelings would have flowed if he had felt them.

PLAYBOY: Another about-face for you in '68 occurred at the Democratic Convention in Chicago. It seemed almost a coming-out for you in a lot of human ways. It was as though you had gotten fed up with being above the battle. You saw Dan Rather get punched out on the convention floor and you made a reference to thugs. And then you said you felt bad about having said that.

CRONKITE: Yes, I did.

PLAYBOY: Do you still?

CRONKITE: Yes. I know that outburst kind of makes me more human in the eyes of the public and therefore, perhaps, improves the impression that people may have of me—that I'm not just an automaton sitting there gushing the news each night. But I think that each network ought to have someone who really *is* above the battle. CBS has 24 minutes of news time every evening. I know I could do 22 minutes of news just as objectively as I'm trying to do it now, and then I could put on another hat and for two minutes I could give a scathing editorial opinion, analysis, commentary, whatever you want to call it. It would be right out of the guts and depths of my soul each day, and it probably would be a pretty good piece, I'd like to think. What was revealed about me in those two minutes wouldn't affect the objectivity with which I conducted myself for the 22 other minutes of that program. But I can't for one minute expect anybody else—except, perhaps, another journalist—to believe that.

PLAYBOY: Some critics have discerned traces of editorializing in other facets of your coverage. During the space flights, for example, you were affectionately referred to as "the other astronaut," and your enthusiasm was obvious.

CRONKITE: Well, I can see why they would come to that conclusion. I don't fault them for coming to it. I was a space booster; I believed in that program. But I don't think that affected my criticizing the program, which I did on many occasions. I thought they should have gone with an extra Mercury flight, for instance. There were a lot of things in Mercury and Gemini and Apollo—in the matter of equipment and delays and some of the usual hardware problems—that I didn't think were handled right. And I talked about that during the space shots. I didn't ever pull those punches. But that in no way dimmed my excitement over man in space. I think it was the most exciting adventure of our time and probably of centuries; probably since the original explorations of the New World. I have no apologies to make for that.

Now, of course, it's fashionable to criticize all the money that was spent—"We should have used it here on earth" and all that sort of thing—but I still don't think that's right. If you could guarantee that the 24 billion dollars would have been spent on our cities instead of on space, then I would be inclined to agree that the money was perhaps not apportioned in the right fashion. But you know it *wouldn't* have gone to the cities. I think history is finally going to have to make some decisions on this matter. I think that those who are being critical are going to have to eat some words before the whole thing is over, because I think we're going to find that space is terribly valuable to us.

PLAYBOY: On news events such as these, you're not only a correspondent but part of management as well. In fact, your title is managing editor of CBS News. How much editorial responsibility do you have?

CRONKITE: It's about like being managing editor of a newspaper. When I assumed that title, some of my friends in the press were critical—not in their columns but they suggested it was some kind of show-business gimmick, a title that had been lifted from the ancient and honorable print media. But when I pointed out what I did, I think I pretty well convinced them it was a sensible title. I participate in making assignments, in the decisions about what will be covered, future programing plans—what we're going to go after and, ultimately, what goes into the program. And I edit the copy. Every word that's said goes through my hands and is usually touched by my hands in some way. I edit almost every piece, rewrite many of them and originally write some of them.

PLAYBOY: If you were to quit tomorrow——

CRONKITE: There's a great idea.

PLAYBOY: Would the public get a substantially different picture of the news from CBS?

CRONKITE: Not really. I'm not sure, though, that some of the things I eventually hope to accomplish around here would be quite as easily and quickly done by somebody else, because I think I've established a certain degree of credibility with the public and with my employers as to my honesty and integrity. There's a mutual trust there. On that particular score, I may have a value beyond that of the daily broadcaster.

PLAYBOY: Actually, you're not only a network newsman but a TV star. Does that status affect the way you're able to cover a story?

CRONKITE: It's a major handicap. There's an advantage to it, quite obviously, in that I can reach people more easily than a less-well-known newsman could. This works around the world, I find. I get in to see heads of state, usually through their American representatives, ambassadors or what not, just because they've seen television coverage. But, on the other hand, just like the camera that appears at the scene of a riot, when I appear I change the nature of the situation. I can't go to a bar and take in an average conversation, because it changes when I'm there: They're talking to the press.

And the same thing is true even when I meet important people. Yesterday a journalist who was doing an interview with a very important person in Washington told me he thought that his interview subject was arrogant and domineering. Well, I haven't seen either of these characteristics in this man, and I said so. My friend said, "Well, he probably *isn't* that way with you. With you, he probably feels he's dealing with an equal, or has some fear of your power, and therefore is much more courteous, much more willing to exchange ideas." And I suppose that's true. But I think if I have enough time, I can break down most barriers. I think if I went back to that hypothetical bar for two or three days in a row, I'd find that I was accepted as a fairly regular fellow and the façade would wither away.

PLAYBOY: How do you feel about the personal side of being a television star? Do you like to be recognized, sign autographs and all that?

CRONKITE: Well, the autograph thing is flattering, that's exactly the word for it. But it's exceedingly tiring. It'd be nicer if you could turn it on once every few months, as sort of an ego builder, and then turn it off again. It's not fun to be the center of attention all the time. You know that people's eyes are on you. My wife and I like to dance, and we don't do it very often, but just the other night we were at a big occasion, an opening in New York, and we were Joel Grey's guests. In the early stage of the evening, at the Waldorf, we were dancing; but we suddenly realized, heck, everybody's kind of watching us dance. And that's not fun. I'm not an exhibitionist—at least not quite in that sense. I'd like to be a song-and-dance man; that's my secret ambition, but——

PLAYBOY: Wait a minute. You've always wanted to be a song-and-dance man?

CRONKITE: I've always thought one of the great things in life would be to entertain people with songs and dances and funny sayings. But it's just a fantasy. Another Walter Mitty dream.

PLAYBOY: Has your wife enjoyed the celebrity life?

CRONKITE: I think so, to about the same extent I have. That is, I can't deny it's nice getting a good table in a crowded restaurant without a reservation—a few emoluments of that kind. But I think both of us would have liked a more quiet life.

PLAYBOY: How do you escape? What do you do for privacy and enjoyment?

CRONKITE: Well, I enjoy totally escapist reading: I duck into historical sea stories. I enjoy the C. S. Forester kind of stuff—and there are 10,000 imitators of Horatio Hornblower who kind of keep me going. It's about a simpler period, a romantic period—strong men doing daring deeds, and a rather simplified moral code—and that makes it rather easy to take. I really enjoy solitude and introspection. That's why I like sailing. I like sitting in the cockpit of my boat at dusk and on into the night, gazing at the stars, thinking of the enormity, the universality of it all. I can get lost in reveries in that regard, both in looking forward to a dreamworld and in looking back to the pleasant times of my own life.

PLAYBOY: Tell us about that dreamworld.

CRONKITE: Oh, my dreamworld personally is to just take off on that boat of mine and not have to worry anymore about the affairs of mankind, and about reporting them, and taking the slings and arrows from all sides as we do today, since we can't seem to satisfy anybody. After ten years of it here in this particular spot, it gets tiresome. I'd like to be loved, like everybody else.

PLAYBOY: Do you feel the slings and arrows personally?

CRONKITE: Yes, I do. Most of them aren't directed at me personally, but they disturb me deeply anyway. And the criticism comes from both sides. The conservative press picks up the Administration line and hammers that back at us; and the liberal press snaps at us all the time about the things you've been bringing up, quite justifiably: about space, about civil rights, about our coverage of the war. So my dreams are to not have to fight the battles anymore.

My dreams for the world are the same. I get fearful about what the world is coming to. You know, most people are good; there aren't very many really evil people. But there are an awful lot of selfish ones. And this selfishness permeates society. It keeps us from the beauty of where we could go, the road we could travel. Instead of being always on these detours and bumbling along side roads that take us nowhere, we could be on a smooth highway to such a great world if we could just put these self-interests aside for the greatest good of the greatest number. It applies to the industrialist who puts out a product into which he builds obsolescence, and to the guy up in Harlem who throws his garbage out the third-floor window. It's everybody's fault. I just find it hard to understand how man could come so far, how he can be so damn smart and at the same time be so damn stupid.

PLAYBOY: You're not alone in being discouraged with contemporary society; some writers are beginning to call the age we live in "postconstitutional America." They view with particular alarm such trends as the tendency toward unregulated, unlimited surveillance. What's your opinion?

CRONKITE: I can't decry it enough. I just don't see how we can live that way. It's not America, and it's not what we believe this country stands for. It's so terrible that I'm convinced there's going to be a great revulsion to it. I think we've come as close as we can to living in a kind of chaotic police state—and I say chaotic because it doesn't have any central headquarters; everybody's doing it. We're living in a state where no one can trust his telephone conversations, nor even his personal conversations in a room, in a bar or anywhere else.

PLAYBOY: Have you ever suspected that your phone was tapped?

CRONKITE: Oh, yes. My home phone and the one here at my office. I think anybody in the public eye—even in private business—who believes that his conversations are sacred today is living in a fool's paradise.

PLAYBOY: Would it be fair to describe your position on most issues as middle of the road?

CRONKITE: I think it probably would. I just don't understand hard-shell, doctrinaire, knee-jerk positions. I don't understand people not seeing both sides, not seeing the justice of other people's causes. I have a very difficult time penetrating what motivates such people. I'm speaking now of the particularly militant left as well as the particularly militant right. But I'm also speaking of people in that great center, whom I sometimes despair of when they accept so glibly the condemnation of other factions within our society—whether it's welfare people or the rich.

There are many people in this silent America who are bitter against the rich. We forget that. You know, from my Midwestern background, I know the Archie Bunkers of Kansas City; they're really basically my own family. I know exactly how they felt about all other walks of society, the lower classes as well as the upper. Unless you were a 32nd-degree Mason living on Benton Boulevard in Kansas City, Missouri, and a white Protestant, there was something a little wrong with you.

PLAYBOY: With that kind of background, where did you get your sense of fairness?

CRONKITE: From my parents. My father was a liberal when he was a young man. Though he's basically kind of set in his ways, as older people are inclined to be, he was terribly upset over the treatment of blacks when we moved to Texas. He went down to teach at the University of Texas Dental School in Houston, and also to practice. And the very first crack out of the box, the first social occasion we went to, we were sitting on the porch of this rich sponsor down there, in a fancy section of town—such a fancy section it didn't have alleys—and we ordered ice cream. In those days, nobody had a freezer, so you ordered it from the drugstore. A young black delivery boy brought it over.

There wasn't any alley, as I say, and he parked his motorcycle out in front of the place and walked up the front walk, across the lawn. And this fellow sat, with rage obviously building in him, and watched him come up the walk. When this young man set his foot on the first step of the porch, this fellow leaped out of his chair and dashed across the porch and smacked him right in the middle of the face. He said, "That'll teach you niggers to walk up to a white man's front door." And my father got up and said, "We're leaving." We almost went back to Kansas City. Growing up in the South, one's attitudes are affected quite seriously by such early experiences.

PLAYBOY: Do any other such experiences come to mind?

CRONKITE: Well, there was another one that also involved ice cream. This time *I* was the drugstore delivery boy; I did bicycle deliveries and we had a couple of blacks who used motorcycles for more distant orders. They were both great guys. One of them was a particularly close friend of mine—as close as you could be in the environment of Houston at that time. We weren't about to go out together anywhere, but we were good friends at the drugstore and sat out back and pitched pennies and shot crap and a few things like that.

As I say, he was a very nice guy, came from a nice family. His mother was a washerwoman, his father was a yardman, but they had great dignity. He had three or four brothers and sisters. Anyway, one night, as he parked his motorcycle and was walking between two houses to deliver some ice cream to the back door, he was *shot* by one of the occupants—the one who hadn't ordered the ice cream. He was listed as a Peeping Tom and the murder was considered justified. Incredible. I mean, this guy was no more a Peeping Tom than I was—maybe less so. Of course, if he'd gone to the front of the house, the guy who ordered the ice cream might have shot him. I almost never got over that case.

PLAYBOY: When did you decide to become a journalist?

CRONKITE: About the time I started junior high school, I became the happy victim of childhood Walter Mittyism, and it's never really gone away. *The American Boy* magazine ran a series of short stories on careers. They were fictionalized versions of what people did in life. And there were only two that really fascinated me at that point. One was mining engineering and the other was journalism. Anyway, I started working on the high school paper in Houston and I found that was what I wanted to do. In fact, that's really *all* I wanted to do. I didn't want to go to school anymore. But I did. I worked my way through the University of Texas in Austin as a newspaper reporter and did a little radio. Did a lot of other things, too, such as working in a bookie joint for a while.

PLAYBOY: What was your job there?

CRONKITE: Announcer.

PLAYBOY: In a bookie joint?

CRONKITE: On the public-address system. When they hired me, they said, "You sit back here in this room, and as the stuff comes over, you read it out over the P.A. system." Well, I'd never been in a bookie joint before, so I gave them the real Graham MacNamee approach on this, describing the running of the race. A mean character ran the place, a guy named Fox, and he looked like one. He came dashing into the room and said, "What the hell you think you're doing? We don't want entertainment, we just want the facts!"

PLAYBOY: Your first critic.

CRONKITE: Yeah!

PLAYBOY: When you got out of school, according to your bio, you joined United Press and later covered World War Two for them, and among the dispatches you filed was one from the belly of a Flying Fortress during a bombing raid over northern Germany. Under those circumstances, was it good copy?

CRONKITE: Well, it had a dramatic lead. Homer Bigart, who was then a correspondent for the *New York Herald Tribune,* and I were at the same base. We were heading for the bomber command headquarters, outside London, to be debriefed after a long day's raid over Germany. We were both tired and I said, "Homer, I think I've got my lead: 'I've just returned from an assignment to hell. A hell at 17,000 feet, a hell of bursting flak and screaming fighter planes.'" I just recited it. I don't know if you knew Homer Bigart, but he stuttered very badly in those days—and he turned to me and put his hand on my arm and said, "Y-y-y-y-y-y-you wouldn't."

PLAYBOY: Did the experience teach you anything about war?

CRONKITE: I didn't need to be taught anything about war. I had already learned about it. But I still didn't understand—and don't understand today—how men can go to war. It's irrational, it's unbelievable. How can people who call themselves civilized ever take up arms against each other? I don't even understand how civilized people can carry guns.

PLAYBOY: Were you under fire as a correspondent?

CRONKITE: Lots. People take a look at my record, you know, and it sounds great. I'm embarrassed when I'm introduced for speeches and somebody takes a CBS handout and reads that part of it, because it makes me sound like some sort of hero: the battle of the North Atlantic, the landing in Africa, the beachhead on D day, dropping with the 101st Airborne, the Battle of the Bulge. Personally, I feel I was an overweening coward in the war. Gee, I was scared to death all the time. I did everything possible to avoid getting into combat. Except the ultimate thing of not doing it. I did it.

But the truth is that I did everything only once. It didn't take any great courage to do it once. If you go back and do it a second time—knowing how bad it is—that's courage.

PLAYBOY: After the war, you stayed on in Europe with United Press, finally returning to this country in 1948. Two years later, you joined CBS News in Washington, as a correspondent. Since CBS is a large, competitive organization, how did you manage to rise to your present position there?

CRONKITE: I was just plain old lucky to be in the right place at the right time. But I think that to take advantage of luck, you've got to have some ability to do the job. As far as the ability to work oncamera is concerned, that part of it was an absolute accident. I never trained for it; I'm just lucky to have it. Whatever it is, it seems to work. I was also ambitious as a young man and pushed myself along, not to become president of United Press but because I wanted to be where the story was. So I pushed to get where I could go. And I guess the whole thing just built up into a store of experience, and with experience came a certain amount of knowledge.

PLAYBOY: In the years since you've been reporting the news at CBS, we've seen America's belief in its own rightness and invincibility crumble, its moral sense lost, or at least mislaid. Has it been shattering to you—as a man who believes in the system—to see all this happen?

CRONKITE: No, not shattering. I'm still sitting here and doing my work; I'm not in a mental institution—although maybe some think I should be. But it *has* eaten at me. Sometimes I think about early retirement, simply to get out of the daily flow of this miserable world we seem to live in. But shattering? I have to say no. I think at times, though, that maybe I'm not as sensitive as I ought to be, that I ought to have gone nuts by now, covering all of this and seeing it firsthand. I sometimes wonder if maybe I'm not really a very deep thinker or a deeply emotional individual.

PLAYBOY: Are you serious about early retirement?

CRONKITE: Oh, I don't suppose it'll happen, at least not in the foreseeable future. I've just negotiated a rather lengthy extension of my contract.

PLAYBOY: So you wouldn't have accepted that Democratic Vice-Presidential offer we heard about, had it been made by George McGovern.

CRONKITE: No, I don't think so. Well, I don't know. I don't know what I would do with a political opportunity if it actually came down the pike.

PLAYBOY: Would you really have considered it?

CRONKITE: Well, if it were seriously tendered—and this is all so hypothetical, because it never was, you know, let's be perfectly honest about it. As I reconstructed it, the McGovern people were sitting around in a meeting and somebody simply said, "Look, I just saw a poll that said Walter Cronkite was the most trusted man in America, what about him?" And I think that's just about as far as it went. Nobody said that there were loud guffaws, but it would have gotten back to me directly if they had gotten any more serious than that. If they *had* gone any further with it, though, they would have uncovered the fact that I'm not a registered Democrat. I'm not a registered anything. I'm a total independent.

PLAYBOY: Do you have any other skeletons in your closet?

CRONKITE: Well, I'm just not going to talk about them!

PLAYBOY: Have you ever seen yourself as a statesman?

CRONKITE: Well, I must admit I've seen myself as a Senator. I see it in a very romantic way, jousting for justice and that sort of thing, on the floor of the Senate. But I don't know how effective I'd be in the political in-fighting. And I think we forget how hard public servants work. When you see them in action in Washington, you appreciate that they work awfully hard, long and tough hours. It must also be the most frustrating job in the world, spinning wheels as they do so much of the time. I really wouldn't want to undertake all of that. Far less would I ever want to be President. Even if I were temperamentally suited for the job, which I'm not, I wouldn't regard myself as qualified—except perhaps by good intentions.

PLAYBOY: Do you think Nixon is qualified for the job—temperamentally or professionally?

CRONKITE: Well, whether or not I agree with some of the things he's done as President, there's no question that he's had plenty of experience to qualify him for the job. As for his temperament, I think it's regrettable, particularly for a man in his position. I guess I just don't understand a man like Nixon—the completely private man. To stand off and almost hold your hands up and say, "Don't come any closer"—that bothers me in anybody, whether it's President Nixon or my next-door neighbor. It must be terribly sad and lonely to be so aloof, to be unable to throw one's arms around one's fellow man and hug him to you. I think President Nixon would like not to be that way; I think he'd like to be an outgoing, lovable man. But he knows he's not; it's not in his make-up. Somewhere in his genes, he just didn't come out that way. I think it bothers him, and I think it may affect a lot of his thinking.

You understand that I'm doing this analysis from about as remote a position as one can have. As you well know, I'm not exactly one of the inner circle. As a matter of fact, I'm cut off from the White House today, presumably because of my outspokenness about the war and about Administration attacks on freedom of the press. I regret this very much. I'm very sad, at this stage in my professional life—where, rightfully or wrongly, I have acquired a large audience and some prestige—that people in high places aren't inclined to invite me into their groups.

On occasions when I've been with President Nixon—and they've been fairly rare, countable on the fingers of one hand—I've had a tremendous feeling of wanting to reach out to him. I wanted to kind of help him. I wanted to say, "Look, let's let our hair down and talk about these problems." I have no doubt that this man wants to do what's right. But, as I said, I think what he's trying to do in several cases is absolutely dead wrong. I think that the attack on the press is so antithetical to everything that this country stands for that I just can't understand it.

I would love to be able to shut up about all of this. I don't want to stand out here as a spokesman for the free press against the President of the United States and against his Administration. That's not a comfortable thing to have to do. The attacks haven't come from our side, though. We're like the troops in the trench during a cease-fire that's being violated by the other side. You know, if we could just lay down our arms and say, "Come on, the Constitution says we have free speech and a free press, and broadcasting ought to be a part of it; now let's just admit that and acknowledge that this is the way this country has always run, and let's run it that way." Gosh, that would be great.

I just don't understand why the Administration took this position in the first place. The press wasn't that anti-Nixon in '68 or '69. I think most of the liberals in this country would say the press was cozying up to him, if anything. And yet, whammo, this whole explosive attack on the press. It all gets back a little bit, I think, to the President's personality, to his remoteness. He has never been able to sit down with newsmen, put his feet up, get out the bourbon bottle and say, "Come on, gang, let's have a drink; you guys sure laid it into me today." That's the sort of thing that goes on all over Capitol Hill every afternoon. And I think that because President Nixon can't do that, his aloofness grew into coolness, into misunderstanding of the press, and then into antagonism toward the press and eventually into a campaign against it.

PLAYBOY: Why does so much of the public seem to acquiesce in this campaign? Is it something about the times we live in?

CRONKITE: I think you put your finger on it right there. It's a revolutionary time and people are never comfortable in a period of revolution. I think they try to regain some sense of security through the use or threat of force. But force isn't the mainstay of our democratic system. Dialog-debate is, and that's regarded with suspicion and indifference by most people at this particular moment in history. I suppose it's only human, when you're backed into a corner in debate, to get mad, to lash out with your fist or to leave the room as a last resort. I think that's what's happening today. Demands for law and order are translated into suppression. As I said before, I believe in law and order, not as a code word but as a keystone— along with freedom and justice—of the democratic process. We've got to stand for law and order. But when the effect of maintaining order is to chip away at the Bill of Rights, to suppress dissent and debate, then I think we're in very serious trouble.

I think these charges by the Administration fall on receptive ears in much of our country, among so many classes of people, because they feel so afraid, so unable to understand, let alone cope with, the tumultuous times we live in, so helpless to hang on to the values they were taught to believe in, so threatened by the revolutionary changes they see going on around them, that they're looking for scapegoats—and the press is a handy one. It's tragic that they can't see the press as the bulwark of their own freedom. I suppose the only reason I keep going, the only reason I haven't been shattered by all this, as I said earlier, is that basically I have hope that it's all going to turn around. In time, I think there'll be a new tolerance, and with it will come a strong resistance to all of these pressures against our liberty.

PLAYBOY: Where will this resistance come from?

CRONKITE: I think it'll come from the people. You know, we're shown amazing resilience all these years of the American experience. We go through these dark periods, but eventually we come back into the shining light of day. And I think we'll come back again.

Playboy Interview Interludes

What I'm looking for in this total picture is an answer to one great question: Does man have a function in the universe? The human mind may be part of the requirement of having a regenerative universe that never runs down.

Buckminster Fuller, February 1972

The importance that our society attaches to sports is incredible. After all, is football a game or a religion? The people of this country have allowed sports to get completely out of hand.

Howard Cosell, May 1972

Nixon may decide that since it's his last four years, this is the time to reward his friends and punish his enemies. He may decide this is the time to indict, to take revenge on all those who have abused him.

Jack Anderson, November 1972

What kind of society isn't structured on greed? The problem of social organization is how to set up an arrangement under which greed will do the least harm. Capitalism is that kind of system.

Milton Friedman, February 1973

Thinking doesn't seem to help very much. The human brain is too high-powered to have many practical uses in this particular universe. I'd like to live with alligators, think like an alligator.

Kurt Vonnegut, July 1973

JOSEPH HELLER

June 1975
Interviewer: Sam Merrill

Perhaps no contemporary "serious" novel, save *Catcher in the Rye*, affected more young men growing up in the Sixties and Seventies than *Catch-22*. Its author, Joseph Heller, foretold with bitter humor a world of Vietnams and Watergates, and gave the English language a new phrase. Sam Merrill, a young writer from New York City, interviewed Heller and turned in a piece that was a refreshing change from the oratory of many other interviewees. Merrill and Heller together produced a small gem of an interview: quiet, witty, and civilized.

Merrill says that even today, years after the publication of the interview, when he meets Heller at a social function, the author will always point to him and say, to Merrill's embarrassment, "There's the guy who made me famous." Heller explained that, to his astonishment, it was his PLAYBOY appearance, rather than his years on the lecture circuit, or even the phenomenal sales of his book, that made him celebrated—with his students, his barber, and even his admirers abroad.

In 1961, Joseph Heller, a 38-year-old advertising and promotion executive for McCall's *magazine, finally completed the novel he'd been tinkering with in his spare time for the better part of a decade. The book was called "Catch-18," a title that was later increased by four upon publication of Leon Uris's "Mila 18"—Heller's editors didn't think people would buy two novels with the same number.*

They needn't have worried.

"Catch-22's" readership started as a small cult—the hardcover edition never appeared on a best-seller list—and expanded geometrically throughout the Sixties. Today, with sales of over 8,000,000 and counting—it sold

over 100,000 copies last year alone—"Catch-22" is the biggest-selling "serious novel" in American publishing history.

From the beginning, "Catch-22's" cult included some of the world's most distinguished, and disparate, citizens. Art Buchwald called it a "masterpiece." Philip Toynbee, in The London Observer, *said "Catch-22" was "the greatest satirical work in English since 'Erewhon.'" And newscaster John Chancellor printed up bumper stickers that read,* BETTER YOSSARIAN THAN ROTARIAN, *referring, of course, to the book's protagonist, an Assyrian-American World War Two bombardier who wanted to "live forever or die in the attempt."*

But when Yossarian went crazy, or seemed to, and asked to be grounded, he found there was only one catch: Anyone who was crazy could get out of combat duty. All he had to do was ask. But anyone who asked to get out of combat duty wasn't really crazy and had to keep flying missions.

"Catch-22's" spiraling insanity, which began to seem more and more sane as the Vietnam war dragged on, confused and irritated some early critics. But as readers became accustomed to the book's radical, time-warp structure, the complaints melted away and "Catch-22" passed through the invisible barrier that separates contemporary fiction from literature. And its title, symbolic of all oppressive tautologies, has become a part of our language.

The youngest of three children, Heller was born in Brooklyn in 1923. His father, a truck driver for Messinger's Bakery, died when he was five years old. The Hellers lived in a racially mixed residential section of Coney Island and young Joe did odd jobs while attending Abraham Lincoln High School, where he excelled at writing—and little else. After graduation, he became a file clerk at a casualty-insurance company (a job that re-emerged in "Something Happened" as the scene of Slocum's most agonizing sexual disaster).

After Pearl Harbor, Heller worked briefly at the Norfolk Navy Yard. At 19, he enlisted in the Army Air Corps. While bombardier Heller was stationed in Corsica with the 488th Squadron, 340th Bombardment Group, he flew 60 combat missions in a B-25 over Italy and France. After his discharge, as a first lieutenant, he enrolled in college on the GI Bill. He was graduated Phi Beta Kappa from NYU, received a master's degree in American literature at Columbia and studied English literature on a Fulbright scholarship at Oxford. While he was still an undergraduate, the most prestigious magazines in the country were eagerly publishing his short stories. By his senior year, he was already considered one of America's most promising young writers.

Then he stopped writing.

He taught freshman composition at Penn State for a few frustrating semesters, then got a job as a "copy and promo" man at a New York advertising agency. For the next ten years, Heller moved both vertically and horizontally in the promotion business: He did one long stint at Time

Inc. and ended up at McCall's. *During this period, he began writing again. In 1954, he published in "New World Writing" a story called "The Texan," which later became the first chapter of "Catch-22."*

The promising Young Turk of 1949 had been forgotten by the time "Catch-22" came out. The book might have been lost in the welter of first novels by nobodies except for the fortuitous accident of an interview with S. J. Perelman, published in the New York Herald Tribune. *Perelman, asked if he'd read any good books lately, mentioned a title nobody had heard of: "Catch-22." A spate of critical attention—some passionately pro, some viciously con—followed.*

A $15,000,000 film version of "Catch-22," directed by Mike Nichols, was the financial disaster of 1970. Nichols' budget was virtually unlimited (during production, he assembled the world's 12th largest bomber force). But the film sacrificed most of the book's humor in a vain attempt to establish a "story line"—something the novel didn't have to begin with.

Meanwhile, Heller continued to pursue his muse at a leisurely pace. As one close friend put it, "Joe likes to keep the rest of his life open, in case anything comes up." The summer after "Catch-22's" publication, Heller had begun accumulating notes for a new book. Robert Gottlieb, his editor, took out a somewhat premature advertisement: "Joseph Heller is now working on his second novel, 'Something Happened.' Publication date not set yet, of course—but look for it sometime before we get to the moon." As matters turned out, Neil Armstrong took his one small step for mankind long before anything *happened for Heller's publisher. As Heller put it, he kept being "interrupted": Throughout the Sixties, he toured the country, speaking and demonstrating against the Vietnam war. He did several short stints as a Hollywood "script doctor" and in 1965 took a two-year sabbatical to write and produce a play, "We Bombed in New Haven." Despite extravagant reviews, it did.*

Thirteen years and six lunar landings after "Catch-22," "Something Happened" was published and became an immediate international best seller.

Joseph Heller and Shirley, his wife of almost 30 years, winter in an elegant old courtyard building on Manhattan's Upper West Side and summer on the beaches of Long Island. Their two children, Erica and Ted, are grown and scattered.

At 52, Heller seems finally to have achieved it all: critical acclaim, popular success, a shucking of the dreaded one-book-author syndrome. So we thought it an opportune time to discuss life, literature and "the Snowdens of yesteryear" with him, and assigned writer Sam Merrill (whose "Mason Hoffenberg Gets in a Few Licks" appeared in PLAYBOY's *November 1973 issue) to interview Heller.*

Merrill reports:

"My first meeting with Heller took place at his summer home in

Amagansett, Long Island, a quiet little seashore town about two and a half hours out of Manhattan. When I arrived, Heller was encased in a set of massive headphones, listening to Wagner's 'Götterdämmerung' and reading Dickens' 'Nicholas Nickleby.' While we chatted on the sun deck—eating Jarlsberg cheese and drinking French-roast coffee—Heller removed his shirt. His chest and legs were firm, tanned, supple. Only his neck looked 52 years old.

"Heller seemed leaner, more wolfish in person than on his dust jackets. And his speech was a curious but thoroughly engaging amalgam. The words —spare, epigrammatic, meticulously considered—were delivered in unreconstructed Brooklynese. While he spoke, a toothpick danced magically from one corner of his mouth to the other. He told me he'd learned that trick, employing the treacherous cupped-tongue technique, while giving up smoking in 1955.

"Chewing his nails and squirming around uncomfortably, Heller obviously had trouble sitting still for an interview. Yet he fielded each question patiently, his expression flickering between Stud Poker Gothic and Bittersweet Irony 'Catch-22' Book Jacket Grin. He was a frequent and infectious laugher.

"Pulling out of his driveway that first afternoon, I caught a glimpse of Heller in my rearview mirror. He had begun to jog his daily three miles in a chilly, offshore fog that clung so close to the ground he was visible only from the waist up. The image reminded me of Kid Sampson, the young pilot in 'Catch-22' who was sheared in half by McWatt's propeller.

"Subsequent meetings took place at the Central Park South office/ apartment in which Heller wrote 'Something Happened.' His work space was in farcical contrast with his two tasteful homes. A three-foot beer bottle, a broken stereo and a ruptured couch dominated a decor that could perhaps best be termed Flatbush Moderne. It soon became apparent that when Heller is writing, he simply does not see anything else!

"Our conversations started with his own involvement in the events described in 'Catch-22.' "

PLAYBOY: How much of *Catch-22* is based on your own wartime experiences?

HELLER: Well, like Yossarian, I volunteered for the Army Air Corps and became a bombardier. But I didn't try to avoid being sent overseas, as he did. I actually *hoped* I would get into combat. I was just 19 and there were a great many movies being made about the war; it all seemed so dramatic and heroic. I remember my mother weeping as the trolley car pulled away with me on it. I couldn't figure out why she was so unhappy. I felt like I was going to Hollywood.

PLAYBOY: So you viewed World War Two as a kind of glorious crusade?

HELLER: No, but I saw it as a war of necessity. Everybody did. Young people today don't know what it's like to fight in a war that makes sense to anybody. And neither did the people in my parents' generation. World War One and the earlier wars in Europe were as nonsensical as Vietnam. But Pearl Harbor united this country in a strong and wholesome and healthy way.

PLAYBOY: About his war experiences, Yossarian complains that people he's never met keep shooting at him every time he flies into the air to drop bombs on them. We gather that you didn't feel persecuted.

HELLER: At first, I was *sorry* when nobody shot at us. I wanted to see a sky full of flak and dogfights and billowing parachutes. War was like a movie to me until, on my 37th mission, we bombed Avignon and a guy in my plane was wounded. I suddenly realized, "Good God! They're trying to kill me, too!" War wasn't much fun after that.

PLAYBOY: That sounds like the Avignon mission in *Catch-22,* when Snowden, the gunner, is killed.

HELLER: It is, and it's described pretty accurately in the book. Our copilot went berserk at the controls and threw us into a dive. Then one of our gunners was hit by flak and the pilot kept yelling into the intercom, "Help him. Help the bombardier." And I was yelling back, "I'm the bombardier. I'm OK." The gunner's leg was blown open and I took care of him. After Avignon, all I wanted to do was go home.

PLAYBOY: Was that because, like Yossarian, you began to suspect you were being sent on missions only to make your superior officers look good?

HELLER: No, it was because I began to suspect I didn't want to die. But I was a good soldier and did as I was told.

PLAYBOY: Did doing what you were told entail anything about which you're particularly sorry now?

HELLER: No, but there was one low-level bombing-and-strafing mission I didn't happen to go on. They couldn't find any military targets, so they shot up everything that moved: women, children, animals. The men were in good spirits after that mission.

PLAYBOY: If you'd gone on that mission, would you have machine-gunned women, children and animals?

HELLER: I might have. There's something sexual about being in a *big* plane, with a *big* gun and having *big* bombs to drop.

PLAYBOY: Aside from Yossarian, some of the other characters in *Catch-22* have become cult figures in their own right. Are any of them based on people you knew?

HELLER: Just Hungry Joe. His real name is Joe Chrenko and he's now an insurance agent in New Jersey.

PLAYBOY: Hungry Joe is the one who has screaming nightmares in his tent. Did Chrenko also run around Rome claiming to be a *Life* photographer so he could take pictures of naked girls?

HELLER: Only once.

PLAYBOY: Did he complain about the way you portray him in the book?

HELLER: His only complaint is that I didn't use his last name. He feels it would have helped his insurance business.

PLAYBOY: How about the rest of the characters?

HELLER: They're not based on anyone I knew in the war. They're products of an imagination that drew on American life in the postwar period. The Cold War, really. I deliberately seeded the book with anachronisms like loyalty oaths, helicopters, IBM machines and agricultural subsidies to create the feeling of American society from the McCarthy period on. So when Milo Minderbinder says, "What's good for Milo Minderbinder is good for the country," he's paraphrasing Charles E. Wilson, the former head of General Motors, who told a Senate committee, "What is good for the country is good for General Motors, and vice versa."

But I resisted the temptation to make Milo a bloated plutocrat stereotype. And I moved away from the other kind of stereotype—William Holden or Tony Curtis as the con man who gets things done. Instead, I gave him a mental and moral simplicity that, to my mind, makes him a horrifyingly dangerous person because he lacks evil intent. Milo uses the credo of the National Association of Manufacturers and the chamber of commerce—but I gave him a sincerity those organizations don't have.

PLAYBOY: How about Major Major, the timid officer whom nobody can get *in* to see unless he's officially *out*?

HELLER: He's drawn from the McCarthy period as well. An Army dentist, Captain Peress, had been promoted to major, even though he refused to sign loyalty oaths. Toward the end of the Army-McCarthy hearings, when he had little else to do, Joe McCarthy kept asking who had promoted Major Peress. I took a paragraph straight out of the news reports and slipped it into the chapter about Major Major, who was promoted by an IBM machine. When he becomes suspect because he studied English history—wasn't American history good enough for him?—people start running around Washington, asking, "Who promoted Major Major?"

PLAYBOY: And ex-Pfc. Wintergreen, the enlisted man who really runs the Army?

HELLER: Wintergreen came out of both my military and my corporate experience. In a large corporation, the way to get ahead is often to get in with mail clerks and secretaries of important people. Careers can be made or broken simply by tearing up certain memos, and in the Army, although I was an officer, the only people I was afraid of were the enlisted men in the orderly room. They could process or not process my requests, take me on or off combat duty. In my dramatization of *Catch-22,* there's a line that doesn't appear in the book. Wintergreen says, "I was going to cancel the Normandy invasion, until Eisenhower committed more armor."

PLAYBOY: Getting back to Yossarian, are any other of his experiences like yours?

HELLER: His encounter with Luciana, the Roman whore, corresponds exactly with an experience I had. He sleeps with her, she refuses money and suggests that he keep her address on a slip of paper. When he agrees, she sneers, "Why? So you can tear it up?" He says of course he won't and tears it up the minute she's gone—then regrets it bitterly. That's just what happened to me in Rome. Luciana was Yossarian's vision of a perfect relationship. That's why he saw her only once, and perhaps that's why *I* saw her only once. If he examined perfection too closely, imperfections would show up.

PLAYBOY: Murray Kempton once wrote that, although *Catch-22* is often considered a radical book, the only aspect of Yossarian's behavior that deviates from traditional morality is his "appreciation of lechery." Do you consider yourself a lecher?

HELLER: No.

PLAYBOY: So much for that. Returning to the war for a moment——

HELLER: I assume you'll be returning to my sex life later on.

PLAYBOY: In detail, if you insist. But for now, you said World War Two seemed glamorous to you, like a movie. Don't you think young people during the Vietnam era were more sophisticated than that?

HELLER: Wars are still initiated by a certain type of professional soldier whose ambition it is to act out fantasy scenes from war movies, and they're still fought by very young people who have no more exciting life to lead. One very practical reason war seemed glamorous to me was that the standard of living was higher in the Army than in Coney Island. I ate better and had more money in my pocket than ever before. And when I got home, I went to college on the GI Bill. In the face of so many advantages, death seemed like a relatively minor drawback.

PLAYBOY: But the country was just coming out of the Depression then. America was prosperous when we entered Vietnam.

HELLER: Not *all* Americans were prosperous. The Vietnam war found many blacks and Latins in the same situation I was in after Pearl Harbor. They could see no future in the ghetto; the Army offered travel, education and money.

PLAYBOY: Is that why the antiwar movement was largely a middle-class affair?

HELLER: It's one of the reasons. Middle-class draftees in the Sixties suffered economic deprivation. They could travel all over the world anyway. They were going to college anyway. They had good jobs waiting for them. But, of course, the antiwar movement was ideologically based, also. The people who were aware of how we had stumbled into Vietnam were the ones who wanted us to get out.

PLAYBOY: What do you mean by "stumbled into Vietnam"? Don't you see our involvement in that war as based on *some* reason or idea?

HELLER: No, I saw—I *see* the Vietnam war as an extension of the Cold War that began in the late Forties and ended with the decline of the domino theory soon after John Kennedy's death.

PLAYBOY: But if the Cold War ended in the mid-Sixties, why did we remain in Vietnam until 1972?

HELLER: For *no reason at all*. That's the point! We often continue believing in things—and this is true of religions as well as ideologies—long after the circumstances that gave rise to the beliefs have disappeared. The belief in stopping communism wherever it threatens to advance simply carried over into another culture long after the *reason* for the belief disappeared. We weren't fighting communism in Vietnam. We were fighting culture lag.

PLAYBOY: Eventually, Yossarian deserts an Army that doesn't make sense to him. Do you feel at all responsible for the guys in Vietnam—and apparently there were a lot of them—who went over the hill after reading *Catch-22*?

HELLER: If anyone accused me of being the operative force in any specific desertion, I would deny it. I don't believe one book can shape an attitude or an action. But if I *was* responsible for people's running away from the war, then I evaded that responsibility consistently.

PLAYBOY: In what way?

HELLER: Often, while I was speaking publicly against the war, young men would ask me, "What would *you* do?" or "What should *I* do?" I always avoided those questions, because it would have been easy for me to give them the answer they wanted: that I *wouldn't*, and they *shouldn't*, serve. I, however, was not facing prison or exile.

PLAYBOY: But Yossarian *does* desert, and you approve of his action.

HELLER: Yes, and I would have gone further than Yossarian. I would have condoned *any* method of avoiding military service in Vietnam—including the one Yossarian rejects as being corrupt.

PLAYBOY: You mean publicly endorsing the war in order to be sent home a hero?

HELLER: Yes, and others Yossarian doesn't even consider, like using influence or buying a deferment. I don't think anybody should ever be compelled to fight in a war whose objectives he does not endorse.

PLAYBOY: But to paraphrase Major Major, what if everyone felt that way?

HELLER: Then, to paraphrase Yossarian, I'd be a damn fool to feel any other way.

PLAYBOY: Do you prefer an all-volunteer Army?

HELLER: I have no fear that a professional Army is going to be out of touch with civilization. Conscripts have never exerted a softening effect on the military.

PLAYBOY: Do you still feel, as you did when you were 19, that World War Two was a necessary war?

HELLER: The fact that the political and economic survival of this country was at stake is no longer as important to me as it was. But, yes, I still feel it was a necessary war. *Catch-22* was criticized because Yossarian justifies his participation in World War Two until the outcome is no longer in doubt. It offended some people, during the Vietnam war, that I had not written a truly pacifist book. But I am not a true pacifist. World War Two was necessary at least to the extent that we were fighting for the survival of millions of people.

PLAYBOY: You mean the Jews?

HELLER: Jews first, then blacks, then the whole sequence of extermination that was operating in Europe.

PLAYBOY: As a Jew, do you have any special feelings about Israel's survival?

HELLER: That's a difficult, confusing question. Emotionally, I have a strong attachment to Israel, even though I've never been there and have no desire to go. A year ago, I was certain Israel would be sold out.

PLAYBOY: Now you're not so sure?

HELLER: Strategically, I'm beginning to understand why this country has stood by Israel for so long. In case any type of mischief becomes necessary, Israel would be the only reliable ally America would have in that part of the world.

PLAYBOY: When you say mischief, are you talking about a possible oil war?

HELLER: If the flow of oil is seriously interrupted, or the price raised again, Western civilization will be out of business. There'll be no alternative but to go in and take the oil—that is, if we still can. But Italy hasn't the navy or air force to take even Libya. France can't do it. Germany certainly can't. England can't. So it would be up to us. And Israel, which was disposable a year ago, would become useful again. We'd need a friendly place to land our airplanes, tie up our boats and see that our soldiers get laid.

PLAYBOY: Do you suppose an oil war would unite America?

HELLER: If you mean the way World War Two did, no. That war presented a unique set of conditions and I don't think we'll have another war like it— so we might as well give up hoping and resign ourselves to peace. Even in the Revolutionary War, there were huge sections of the population that didn't want to separate from England. I have a feeling they were right, that we'd be better off if we were part of England.

PLAYBOY: Why?

HELLER: We'd have a better form of government. The parliamentary system would be a vast improvement over what we have now. Our Constitution looks good on paper and probably worked quite well with 13 colonies and about 72 registered voters. But now there's too much distance between the citizen-voter and his elected representative. He doesn't know *I* exist, and I wish *he* didn't. And with over 200,000,000 people, the Presidency has become a kind of public-relations enterprise for the party in power.

PLAYBOY: But do you really *care* about politics? In 1972, you said you hadn't voted for a President in 12 years.

HELLER: Then I voted for McGovern.

PLAYBOY: Why?

HELLER: Nixon made me do it.

PLAYBOY: Has that experience changed you?

HELLER: Yes. Now I'm *never* going to vote again—for anybody. The smartest people in Washington are the political reporters. They write about their inferiors.

PLAYBOY: So, generally, you'd say American politics attracts a low class of people?

HELLER: Yes, with one exception. There is a type of person who is occasionally attracted to politics for idealistic reasons and, once elected, does a creditable job. This is the gentleman who already has as much money as he wants and aspires to public office for reasons that have little to do with personal ambition. I may be naïve, but I felt Averell Harriman was in that class.

PLAYBOY: Would you include Nelson Rockefeller?

HELLER: I would exclude Nelson Rockefeller. There's a vicious, emotional quality to *his* ambition. But I would include Elliot Richardson and Archibald Cox. These are people who aspire to high position out of boredom.

PLAYBOY: So you prefer a sated dilettante to a dedicated reformer?

HELLER: Yes, and I feel safer with someone who inherited his money than with a self-made man. I think people like Roosevelt and Harriman and Stevenson are better suited to public office than the "sun-belt" millionaires who surrounded Nixon. The self-made man scares me. He attaches too much importance to his own personal accomplishments and yet is never really secure with people who are born into the highest order of society. Truman was an exception. He wasn't a social climber. Eisenhower was.

PLAYBOY: Essentially, then, your ideal public official would be someone like Rockefeller or Kennedy.

HELLER: But *not* Rockefeller. Or Kennedy. The Kennedy Administration was like a bunch of spoiled fraternity brats celebrating after having bought a campus election. They cavorted around, pushing each other into swimming pools. I think Johnson was more entertaining than Kennedy—until the Vietnam war escalated and his Administration collapsed. I've been delighted to see how dismally Kennedy's people have fared politically since his death. They were a disagreeable bunch. Even John Kenneth Galbraith seems to be a man without principles—or, if he *has* any, they are of only joking importance. Otherwise, he wouldn't be so friendly with William Buckley. You get the impression that although the two may disagree over a minor concern like the world's economy, when they get down to important matters like yachting, they are still in the same club.

PLAYBOY: What have you got against Buckley?

HELLER: I feel sorry for anybody who has to tangle with Buckley. Even though his reasoning is defective, he carries off a debate with so much *élan* that he makes the argument itself almost superfluous.

PLAYBOY: Is there anyone you'd care to see elected President in 1976?

HELLER: No.

PLAYBOY: How about yourself?

HELLER: Oh, no! I believe the Government exists to serve the people, not the other way around. Hence, the term public servant. I wouldn't want to be President, because I wouldn't want to put myself in a menial position.

PLAYBOY: So you like the notion of a benevolent aristocrat in politics. What about a hard-nosed reformer?

HELLER: I don't like the way reformers react to our political process. They have a difficult time realizing they must compromise or remain outsiders.

PLAYBOY: In other words, they don't become corrupt quickly enough?

HELLER: Exactly. A member of a legislative body who does not prostitute his integrity at the earliest possible moment is doing a grave disservice to his constituents. Unless he cooperates with the "inner circle," he'll never get his bills passed and the people who elected him will suffer.

PLAYBOY: Do you think there is a better system of government in the world than the one we broadly call Western democracy?

HELLER: No system offers greater personal liberty; the citizens of the totalitarian countries of the left and right enjoy less freedom than we do. But Johnson and Nixon were frightening because they demonstrated that an American President—even in a democracy, without Government censorship—is capable of waging a one-man war. That would not be possible in Russia, which is a dictatorship run by committee, or in China, where there are several powerful men.

PLAYBOY: Is that power inherent in the Presidency, or did we just happen to elect a pair of megalomaniacs?

HELLER: The power to exercise dictatorial control over the military is manifest in the office. A President can make war in a moment of personal panic or insecurity and no one in Congress will stop him.

PLAYBOY: But Congress claims to have learned its lesson from Vietnam. Wouldn't it now be tougher on a President who asked for war powers?

HELLER: If another President faked another Gulf of Tonkin incident, there would still be only about two Senators voting against the resolution, and they'd be tossed out in the next election.

PLAYBOY: Shortly before his resignation, some people close to Nixon worried that he *would* push the panic button, try to mobilize the military in his defense. Others described his mental state as "serene." Do *you* think he was insane?

HELLER: I would say no. Nixon had a very powerful sense of his own weakness. He doubted his abilities to an extent that could be called neurotic. Some people who repress their self-doubts overcompensate with a form of egotism. It is interesting that Nixon was never able to do that. His mechanism of repression never functioned well enough, so his self-doubts were always on his mind. He could never convince himself he was a superior person, and consequently was afraid people would observe how weak he felt. At the end, as you say, people in Washington were frightened. There was a *suspicion* that Nixon was insane. And certainly during his farewell speech, he took leave of what is customarily called sanity. He was not in touch with the situation or with himself. But I believe that was a temporary abberation. The real Nixon was a pathetic, fearful man who spent his life prophesying his own failures and living up to his own prophecies.

PLAYBOY: You've been on the college lecture circuit twice—during the Sixties, as the author of *Catch-22* and one of America's leading antiwar spokesmen, and again recently, since the publication of your new book, *Something Happened*. Do you find that students have changed much since the war?

HELLER: For the record, the Vietnam war is still being fought. But if you're asking if college students have changed much since the draft was abolished and most American forces pulled out of Indochina, I'd say there has been a decline in political action and interest.

PLAYBOY: Why?

HELLER: There are two conditions that must exist simultaneously to excite political activity in *any* population. First, the issues must be important and, second, one must know *exactly* how one feels about them. For college students in the Sixties, the war and the draft met those conditions. Today, though the questions are important, there is no clear-cut sense of what to do about them. So we are back to a normal state of political interest— practically none.

PLAYBOY: We haven't talked about your own college experience. After you completed your wartime tour of duty and were shipped home—

HELLER: Shipped is right. I was so terrified on my last few missions, I made a vow that if I got out of the war alive, I would never go up in an airplane again. The guys who were in a hurry to get home flew back across the Atlantic. I waited for a boat.

PLAYBOY: How long did your antiflying vow last?

HELLER: Until 1960, when I got stuck on a train for 24 hours. Suddenly, falling out of the sky didn't seem like such an objectionable alternative.

PLAYBOY: What happened next, after you were literally shipped home?

HELLER: I met my wife, got married, entered college on the GI Bill, did graduate work at Columbia and Oxford and began writing seriously. And reading.

PLAYBOY: After reading something you liked, did you find yourself saying, "I wish I'd written that"?

HELLER: No, but with some authors I found myself saying, "I could have written that if I'd thought of it."

PLAYBOY: For instance?

HELLER: I felt I could have written the plays of Clifford Odets. Unfortunately, Odets had already written those plays.

PLAYBOY: Odets? That's not your style!

HELLER: I didn't have my style then.

PLAYBOY: But you *were* being published. Even as an undergraduate, your *Esquire* and *Atlantic* stories made you one of the country's most promising young writers.

HELLER: Those stories were written while I was taking a creative-writing course at NYU in 1946. After the war, everyone who could write dialog was copying Ernest Hemingway and John O'Hara, and everyone who couldn't was copying Irwin Shaw. It took more talent to copy Shaw, because he used language better. My stories were as imitative as the rest.

PLAYBOY: Imitative of whom?

HELLER: I was writing *New Yorker*-type stories, stories by Jewish writers about Jewish life in Brooklyn. By the time I was a senior in college, I'd done a little more reading and I began to suspect that literature was more serious, more interesting than analyzing an endless string of Jewish families in the Depression. I could see that type of writing was going to go out of style. I wanted to write something that was very good and I had nothing good to write. So I wrote nothing.

PLAYBOY: Did you formally "give up writing," or was it a day-to-day thing?

HELLER: I formally gave up writing those trivial stories. In fact, I haven't written a single short story since. But I formally *began* looking for a novel that I could consider important.

PLAYBOY: You mean you didn't come home from World War Two with *Catch-22* rattling around in your head?

HELLER: As I've said, *Catch-22* wasn't really *about* World War Two. It was about American society during the Cold War, during the Korean War, and about the possibility of a Vietnam. I didn't get the idea for *Catch-22* until I had read many more writers. Louis-Ferdinand Céline's *Journey to the End of the Night* was the book that touched it off. Céline did things with time and structure and colloquial speech I'd never experienced before, and I found those new experiences pleasurable. It was unlike reading Joyce, who did things I'd never seen but that weren't pleasurable.

PLAYBOY: How did Céline's book touch off *Catch-22*?

HELLER: I was lying in bed, thinking about Céline, when suddenly the opening lines of *Catch-22* came to me: "It was love at first sight. The first time he saw the chaplain, Blank fell madly in love with him." I didn't come up with the name Yossarian until later, and the chaplain wasn't necessarily an *Army* chaplain. He could have been a *prison* chaplain. Ideas of plot, pace, character, style and tone all tumbled out that night, pretty much the way way they finally appeared in the book. The next morning, at work, I wrote out the whole first chapter and sent it to my agent, Candida Donadio, who sold it to *New World Writing*. I was so excited I couldn't wait to begin chapter two.

One year later, I did.

PLAYBOY: You're not one of the world's fastest writers, are you?

HELLER: By the time I began *Catch-22*, I'd become *so* slow I suspected that might well be the only book I'd ever write.

PLAYBOY: Is one of the reasons for your breath-taking lack of speed the fact that you insist on doing all your own editing?

HELLER: If it weren't for the fact that I do practically *none* of my own editing, I'd never finish *anything at all*. As I submit sections of a manuscript to my editor, Bob Gottlieb, I indicate areas that might be cut. Then we discuss them and a decision is reached. That's the ideal situation for me, because without an editor I could trust, I'd still be in the middle of *Something Happened*, cutting out a section one week, putting it back the next, getting nowhere. I'm a chronic fiddler.

PLAYBOY: Have you a new book in mind?

HELLER: Several prospective openings have come to me. But I've been too busy to develop them.

PLAYBOY: Would you be willing to try out some possible openings on us?

HELLER: All right. People have always asked me what happened to Dunbar, a character who disappeared in *Catch-22*. That question intrigues me, so I considered writing a novel that would begin: "Dunbar woke up with his name on the door and a Bigelow on the floor and wondered how he had got there." It was going to be a novel about amnesia. It went nowhere.

PLAYBOY: Any others?

HELLER: "The kid, they say, was born in a manger, but frankly, I have my doubts." I liked that line for a while, but nothing came of it, either.

PLAYBOY: Can you produce these on command?

HELLER: I have to be bored. I'm going to Mexico for a couple of weeks with the hope of achieving perfect boredom. New York is distracting. I suffer from a nervous impulse that makes me find excuses to call my publisher.

PLAYBOY: Since *Something Happened* is one of the biggest money-makers Knopf has ever had, they must always be glad to hear from you. Why would you need an excuse to call them?

HELLER: I always need an excuse, because I can never bring myself to reveal the true nature of the call.

PLAYBOY: Which is?

HELLER: To prevent them from forgetting about me.

PLAYBOY: Don't you think that's a somewhat unrealistic fear?

HELLER: *I* don't think so. I also fear that a day will go by in which nobody in the whole country buys a copy of the book. I once mentioned this to the people at Knopf and they laughed, as though such a thing were totally out of the question. But I need constant reassurance that my publisher remembers me and that Americans are still buying books.

PLAYBOY: Besides striving to achieve perfect boredom, you're teaching. Why? Presumably, you don't need the money.

HELLER: I teach fiction writing at City College in New York to students who are either very interested or drop the course. I believe I'm known as a hard marker. Money is no longer a primary consideration, but I enjoy the feedback I get from the better students.

PLAYBOY: For some reason, we have difficulty relating to the idea that Joseph Heller still grades papers.

HELLER: That strikes me as a little fishy, too.

PLAYBOY: Have you considered giving up teaching so you could spend more time on your writing?

HELLER: If I gave up teaching, I would have no time at all for writing. When I was working on *Catch-22*, I had a demanding job during the day. I was too tired to go out at night, so I wrote *Catch-22*.

PLAYBOY: You wrote *Catch-22* in the evenings?

HELLER: I spent two or three hours a night on it for eight years. I gave up once and started watching television with my wife. Television drove me back to *Catch-22*. I couldn't imagine what Americans did at night when they weren't writing novels.

PLAYBOY: You're not into TV, then.

HELLER: There's nothing I like on television. I used to watch ball games.

PLAYBOY: Are you a sports fan?

HELLER: Not anymore. My wife and I went through a period of going to hockey games. We haven't done that for a while.

PLAYBOY: When was the last time?

HELLER: Nineteen fifty-four.

PLAYBOY: How about football, baseball, basketball?

HELLER: I'm not a football fan, but I *was* a fan of the football strike last year.

PLAYBOY: Were you sympathetic with the players' demands?

HELLER: I never found out what their demands were. I just like it when things erupt. That's why I was sorry to see Nixon resign. Impeachment, like the football strike, was a pleasant change in the news. Otherwise, it's just laws and wars, winning and losing, elections and touchdowns. I like it better when something happens.

PLAYBOY: What would you do with your time now if you weren't teaching?

HELLER: I'd probably run amuck in Rome. When a writer is between books, he needs responsibility to keep him from making a fool of himself. Authors go through a period of craziness between books. Some invest in uranium stock, others change wives and agents. Some commit suicide. It's worse when you're young. Luckily, I was 38 and pretty well set in my ways when *Catch-22* came out. I had a good job and a nice apartment. If I'd been, say, 27, and living in a cold-water flat, my marriage would have broken up, I would have bought an estate in East Hampton I couldn't afford and, to pay for it, I would have started a second novel too soon.

PLAYBOY: Do you think success is more damaging to a writer than failure?
HELLER: Both are difficult to endure. Along with success come drugs, divorce, fornication, bullying, travel, meditation, medication, depression, neurosis and suicide. With failure comes failure.
PLAYBOY: In balance, which is more beneficial to one's spiritual health?
HELLER: Failure.
PLAYBOY: Which do you prefer personally?
HELLER: Success.
PLAYBOY: Do you have any unfulfilled ambitions?
HELLER: Most of the things I've wanted in life I've either gotten or stopped wanting. *Catch-22* fulfilled all my fantasies but two: It didn't make me rich and it wasn't on the *New York Times* best-seller list. But in critical and popular esteem, it exceeded my wildest dreams.
PLAYBOY: Do you ever tire of reading and rereading your own work?
HELLER: No, I learn a lot from reading my work aloud, as I do on college campuses. I read sections of *Something Happened* at the University of Michigan recently and learned that for it to have remained a best seller as long as it has, it must be reaching a wider, older audience than *Catch-22*. I got a great response from the students with those passages dealing with Slocum's children. But during parts about his office, about fearing old age, there was silence. The attention was there, but the magic was gone.
PLAYBOY: During the 12 years it took to write *Something Happened,* you were no longer working as an adman, so presumably you wrote during the day. What was your schedule like?
HELLER: I wrote for two or three hours in the morning, then went to a gym to work out. I'd have lunch alone at a counter, go back to the apartment and work some more. Sometimes I'd lie down and just *think* about the book all afternoon—daydream, if you will. In the evenings, I'd often go to dinner with friends.
PLAYBOY: We've heard that you and your friends invented a game called Scapegoat and you played it fanatically while you were writing *Catch-22*.
HELLER: I and a few friends—George Mandel, Mario Puzo and some others—redesigned a board game played with a deck of cards. It's a good gambling game.
PLAYBOY: Did you, in fact, play fanatically?
HELLER: I don't know what you'd call fanatic. We'd stay up all night three or four times a week——
PLAYBOY: That's what we'd call fanatic.
HELLER: We were all writing novels at the time. It was a good release.
PLAYBOY: Would you tell us how it's played?
HELLER: No.
PLAYBOY: Most writers will do anything for money before they become successful; but you rewrote the screenplay for *Sex and the Single Girl* after *Catch-22* came out. Why?

HELLER: For the money. They paid me $5000 a week. I wish somebody would offer me $5000 a week to work on something right now. I'd take it.

PLAYBOY: Did you work on any other films?

HELLER: *Dirty Dingus Magee* and *Casino Royale.* Charley Feldman, a nice but very nervous man, was producing *Casino Royale* and he traveled all over the country, hiring writers to do various scenes. He wanted to make sure he had enough material. Woody Allen later told me that he and I both did versions of the same scene.

PLAYBOY: Few film makers have the luxury of choosing the Woody Allen or the Joseph Heller version of a scene. Which one ended up in the movie?

HELLER: Neither. Feldman threw them both out.

PLAYBOY: What was it like working on *Sex and the Single Girl*?

HELLER: It was an enriching experience. Natalie Wood didn't want to do the picture, but she owed it to Warner Bros. on a three-film deal. And Tony Curtis needed the money to settle a divorce. That's what I like best about the movie industry: the art and idealism.

PLAYBOY: Did you participate in the film version of *Catch-22*?

HELLER: No, because I was experienced enough in film making to have virtually no hope that *Catch-22* would become a good film. And if I had participated in making it, I would have been compelled to care how it turned out. So I refused generous screenplay offers.

PLAYBOY: Did you like the film?

HELLER: It was OK, but I can never get the image of Buck Henry, who did the screenplay, out of my mind. I imagine him tearing through a dog-eared copy of the book while moaning, "Oy, vay, there's no *plot* here!" But when they were getting ready to shoot, I became friendly with Alan Arkin and Mike Nichols. They were so concerned about doing "justice" to the book—which is, of course, impossible in *any* film—that I found myself rooting for them.

PLAYBOY: But the picture bombed. Do you think it deserved its bad reviews?

HELLER: I think if the same film had been foreign, in black and white, without stars and based on an unknown novel, it would have been a major critical success. This is not a comment on the quality of the film but on the consistency of film reviews.

PLAYBOY: Do you find that there is an exceptional thrill in seeing your work performed?

HELLER: It's intoxicating, misleading. It appeals to the basest parts of one's mental anatomy. I love it.

PLAYBOY: Your play, *We Bombed in New Haven,* opened to worshipful reviews. Several critics called it the most important play of the Sixties——

HELLER: And the Seventies.

PLAYBOY: But it was not a commercial success. Why?

HELLER: Because it made people feel guilty, made them accessories to murder. People like to walk out of a theater feeling virtuous.

PLAYBOY: Do you admire the work of any writers in particular?

HELLER: Hawkes, Barth, Céline, Beckett, Pynchon, Faulkner, Shakespeare. . . .

PLAYBOY: You have a pile of Dickens novels lying around.

HELLER: This year I'm alternating between one Dickens novel, or biography of Dickens, and one contemporary book. Last year I did that with Jane Austen. The year before that, Henry James.

PLAYBOY: Sounds as if you're catching up on your schoolwork.

HELLER: When I was in school, I had neither taste nor patience. Now at least I have patience.

PLAYBOY: How, in your view, does contemporary American fiction stack up against that of other countries, other periods?

HELLER: The health of American literature is excellent. Unlike the movie business, which cannot make money with serious works, there is enough of a market for good literature in this country to support many novelists who are not commercially minded. I would put Updike, Cheever, Vonnegut, Bellow, Mailer, Baldwin, Roth, Styron, Malamud, Barth, Pynchon and Hawkes in that category. And there are perhaps 15 or 20 more I haven't mentioned, who will never speak to me again. There is a reading public in America that wants good, challenging books. That public is one of our national treasures.

PLAYBOY: What about the rest of the reading public and the "popular" authors they support?

HELLER: There are two kinds of people doing what we'll call popular fiction. One kind is the hack, the producer of quick pornography, quick mysteries— opportunistic books. The hack knows he is writing junk. The other kind may not be an "intellectual" writer but believes that he or she is producing works that are as good as anything that has ever been written. This type of writer puts as much effort into the work as Beckett or Mann or any conscientious writer does. The readers of that type of book are not to be looked down upon, either. They're reading what, to them, is good literature.

PLAYBOY: What authors would you put into this category?

HELLER: I'd rather not mention names.

PLAYBOY: Oh, go ahead.

HELLER: Jackie Susann, Erich Segal, Irving Wallace.

PLAYBOY: Do you—or did you—know any of them personally?

HELLER: I know Irving Wallace. He may not write the type of book I enjoy reading, but he starts work at six in the morning and puts as much effort and energy into *his* type of book as I put into mine. Anyone who wants to usurp Wallace's position with his particular readers is, literally, going to have to get up pretty early in the morning.

PLAYBOY: Have you read *Love Story* or *Valley of the Dolls*?

HELLER: No, but I know people who read *Love Story* and were moved by it. They might have been embarrassed afterward, but there apparently was something in that book—a legitimate reading experience—that I can almost guarantee was quite difficult for Segal to achieve. The proof is that it is not as easy to imitate these people as it looks. Even Segal himself can't seem to do it. I know a woman who was envious of Susann's success, felt she was brighter, more talented, and tried to write a *Valley of the Dolls* type of novel. In spite of a lavish advertising campaign, the book did not succeed. The more intellectual writer is likely to have a hack attitude toward that type of story and not spend enough time with characterization and detail.

PLAYBOY: What about your old friend Mario Puzo? Where does he fit in?

HELLER: After two intellectual novels that did not sell, Mario did attempt to write a popular book and succeeded. But *The Godfather* was not an imitation of any particular author or style, and I don't believe he approached the work with a condescending attitude. Perhaps he *is* an exception.

PLAYBOY: Have you ever attempted any hackwork?

HELLER: When I was an undergraduate publishing in the *Atlantic* for $200, I figured I might as well publish in *Good Housekeeping* for $1500. So I tried to write what were then called women's stories and never came close. I'd send off first drafts with the feeling I was doing hackwork, whereas the people who were writing *good Good Housekeeping* stories were rewriting them eight, ten, 12 times.

PLAYBOY: Could you select one theme that you think connects all your writing?

HELLER: The two novels are so different. I put everything I knew about the external world into *Catch-22* and everything I knew about the interior world into *Something Happened*. But in both books I am concerned with the closeness of the rational to the irrational mind, the location of reality.

PLAYBOY: Reality is particularly difficult to locate in *Something Happened*. For example, in the scene in which Slocum discusses his problems with a psychiatrist. Afterward, the reader discovers that there is no psychiatrist.

HELLER: Slocum tells the psychiatrist he never has hallucinations. The psychiatrist replies, "What would you call this?"

PLAYBOY: In mapping that boundary between rational and irrational, you often employ humor. Why?

HELLER: I'm inclined to be serious about most matters, yet jokes keep coming to mind. That disturbs me.

PLAYBOY: Why?

HELLER: Because humor comes too easily and I'm suspicious of things that come easily.

PLAYBOY: Your conversation seems similar to your writing, in the sense that it careens between the serious and the farcical. Could this be "the Heller style"?

HELLER: Perhaps. . . . Perhaps there is more truth in that than I realize. I wasn't aware that *Catch-22* was a *funny* book until I heard someone laugh while reading it. The experience was pleasant but also unsettling. As I said, I'm suspicious of comedy.

PLAYBOY: Do you consider comedy trivial?

HELLER: Yes. I can spend an evening with the best comedian and love every second, have a very *good* evening, but it's not going to affect me or change my life.

PLAYBOY: And that's your definition of triviality—whether or not something changes your life?

HELLER: A good novel will permanently alter the way I think. Nothing else does that for me.

PLAYBOY: Earlier, while disclaiming responsibility for soldiers in Vietnam who deserted after reading *Catch-22,* you said one book couldn't shape an attitude or an action. Now you seem to be contradicting yourself.

HELLER: I don't believe one book could convince a "good soldier" to go over the hill. Perhaps one book could convince a soldier who was thinking of it anyway, and perhaps a group of books could, over a period of time, completely change someone's way of thinking to an extent that would be impossible after reading only one book. But one book *can* change or expand my way of perceiving the world. A comedy routine cannot.

PLAYBOY: When you say one book, do you mean only fiction, or do you read nonfiction, too?

HELLER: I'll read a nonfiction piece about something I'm interested in. I read the newspaper.

PLAYBOY: Are you interested in New Journalism as an art form? What's your opinion of Tom Wolfe's style?

HELLER: I used to read Tom Wolfe in the *New York Herald Tribune* and wasn't even aware he *had* a style. He writes about interesting subjects, so his work is interesting. But for me, reading nonfiction is like going to the movies. Trivial.

PLAYBOY: How much did you and Gottlieb cut out of *Something Happened*?

HELLER: About 150 pages.

PLAYBOY: And from *Catch-22*?

HELLER: Nearly 100.

PLAYBOY: What kind of material was it?

HELLER: Adjectives and adverbs.

PLAYBOY: *Catch-22* is a big, third-person novel in which you had 60 very different characters to play around with. But in *Something Happened*, everything is related through Bob Slocum, a psychic cripple. Didn't you feel cramped working through such a limited persona?

HELLER: T. S. Eliot said that when one is forced to write within a certain framework, the imagination is taxed to its utmost and will produce its richest ideas. Given total freedom, the work is likely to sprawl.

PLAYBOY: You spent eight years working on a book you *thought* was going to be called *Catch-18,* then just before publication, you were told to find another number. Did you take it hard?

HELLER: I was heartbroken. I thought 18 was the *only* number. It took two weeks to select 22. I don't like to rush into things.

PLAYBOY: When did you know that you'd "made it"?

HELLER: Made what?

PLAYBOY: Status.

HELLER: I knew I'd achieved *something* the first time someone I'd heard of but never met invited me to a party by naming all the famous people who were going to be there and indicated that those famous people were being invited at least partly on the basis that *I* would be there.

PLAYBOY: Any other times?

HELLER: Yes, when I bought a car recently. I didn't haggle, but if I had, I felt I could have gotten a sizable discount.

PLAYBOY: Just because you're Joseph Heller?

HELLER: No, because I'm a friend of Mario Puzo. I had to go around shaking hands with all the Italian salesmen. Status isn't all gay parties and caviar.

PLAYBOY: The title of *Catch-22* has passed into the language as a slogan, a concept. How do you feel when you see and hear it in everyday life?

HELLER: Good, proud. Again, that is something that appeals to one's basest instincts—an appeal I, for one, find irresistible. But I don't always like the people who use *Catch-22* or the way it is used. James St. Clair, Nixon's attorney, tried to get away with it before the Supreme Court. He made the argument that you can impeach a President only if you have evidence that he committed a crime, but you can't collect criminal evidence against a President. One of the Justices had to play Yossarian and say, "Wait a minute. You lose me there."

PLAYBOY: Do you think *Catch-22* is a radical book?

HELLER: Its structure is more radical than the content. The morality is rather orthodox—almost medieval. With the exception of the aforementioned "appreciation of lechery," the seven basic virtues and seven deadly sins are all in their proper place.

PLAYBOY: How about *Something Happened*? Would you consider *that* radical?

HELLER: Yes, but again, only in structure. The first and third person are fused in a way I've never seen before, and time is compressed into almost a solid substance.

PLAYBOY: Most of the reviews of *Something Happened* were quite good. But some were terrible.

HELLER: Apparently, I don't write books people like a *little.*

PLAYBOY: Were the reviews better or worse than you expected?

HELLER: Three out of four were favorable—better than I expected. I think most of the negative reviews and most of the positive reviews were good.

PLAYBOY: How can a bad review be good?

HELLER: Most negative reviewers either found the book repetitious or found Slocum not a sufficiently interesting character to warrant such a detailed examination. Those are valid opinions. The reviewers analyzed the book carefully. That's all any author can ask and far more than most authors receive. PLAYBOY published the only review I think of as being snotty. It wasn't really a review, just a paragraph that dismissed the book in an insulting way.

PLAYBOY: *The New York Review of Books* accused you of overweening ambition. It said *Something Happened* was a failed sequel to *Catch-22*, a sort of Everyman in war and peace.

HELLER: That review, along with some others, couldn't resist the temptation to compare the two works, taken together, to *War and Peace*. They said *Catch-22* was perhaps the definitive book about war, but that *Something Happened* was *not* the definitive book about peace. But it wasn't *my* hypothesis that Slocum is the Everyman of his generation. In fact, I'd *never* write a book in which the leading character was not a very distinct personality. I've said many times that I thought Slocum was perhaps the most contemptible character in all literature. Yet people have found him pathetic, even sympathetic. This surprises me. All these reviewers now claim to have loved *Catch-22*. Where were they when *that* book came out?

PLAYBOY: At least *The New Yorker* was consistent. Its reviewer hated both books.

HELLER: Consistency may be overrated as a virtue.

PLAYBOY: There's never much physical description in your writing. Is it that you don't want to distract the reader or that you think descriptive writing is trivial?

HELLER: Neither. I admire writers like Updike and Nabokov and Vidal, who have great powers of observation. I just don't seem to respond to visual stimulus. I once told my editor I couldn't write a good descriptive metaphor if my life depended on it. Every once in a while, I figure I'd better put in some visual description, but a flushed face and white shingles are usually as far as I get. Recently, someone told me my nephew has blue eyes. I said I'd never noticed. The boy is 28 years old.

PLAYBOY: There is a minor character in *Catch-22* named Scheisskopf. At one point, someone refers to him as a Shithead, with a capital S. Since *Scheisskopf* is German for shithead, it works like a pun, though it looks as if the capital letter were a typographical error. Was that intentional?

HELLER: Yes, and you're the first one to comment on it. I've waited 14 years for someone to pick that up. I've blabbed it to a couple of people *myself*, but nobody's *asked* about it.

PLAYBOY: Are there any other so-far-undetected jokes in *Catch-22*?

HELLER: There is one more.

PLAYBOY: Any chance you'll tell us what it is?

HELLER: No chance at all.

PLAYBOY: *Catch-22* has been translated into all the Western and many Eastern languages. Is there a special pleasure in knowing you are read worldwide?

HELLER: Yes, but there's a certain queasiness that goes with it. I can never be sure about what's *in* those foreign editions. They *look* like *Catch-22*, but who knows? I got a rather unsettling letter soon after the book came out. It said: "I am translating your novel *Catch-22* into Finnish. Would you please explain me one thing: What means *Catch-22*? I didn't find it in any vocabulary. Even assistant air attaché of the U.S.A. here in Helsinki could not explain exactly." I suspect the book lost a great deal in its Finnish translation.

PLAYBOY: You've been married to your first and only wife for nearly 30 years. To what do you attribute this unusually successful marriage?

HELLER: I didn't say it was successful. Maybe we just don't quit easily. I know many people whose marriages have ended for reasons that I don't think are serious enough. If everyone were to end a marriage because of disappointments or dissatisfactions or moods or temporary attractions, almost *no* marriage would survive.

PLAYBOY: Slocum says he would leave his wife if she had an affair. Would you?

HELLER: That falls into the realm of imagined experience.

PLAYBOY: Can you imagine leaving her?

HELLER: I think you may now be slipping into the tendency to assume that a novel is a personal statement rather than a work of literature. *Something Happened* seems to invite this sort of thing. While my agent, Candida Donadio, who knows me as well as I know myself, was reading *Something Happened*, she found herself continually saying, "Joe wouldn't do *that!*" I had to keep reminding her it was fiction. Now that we're back on the topic of sex, I'll have to remind you to ask another question.

PLAYBOY: OK. In *Something Happened*, Slocum says he can't run off with a 19-year-old girl because after two hours he won't have anything to say to her. He claims he is unable to fall in love and that is what keeps his marriage together. Is that your feeling, too?

HELLER: I would generalize and say that my imagination, like Slocum's, keeps me from making foolish mistakes.

PLAYBOY: Slocum says his fantasies are worthwhile only as long as he remains inert. Do you have any cherished fantasies you feel would be ruined if you acted upon them?

HELLER: Shirley and I often discuss moving to the south of France. But then I start thinking about getting a new driver's license, and what will happen when it gets cold and we have no one to talk to? And what are we going to do if we want a good piece of salami? I end up realizing that I like to live in a city that I know pretty well, among people I know pretty well, and the only place on earth that fits that description is Manhattan. But the south of France continues to be an appealing fantasy for us as long as we do nothing about it.

PLAYBOY: Have you any fantasies that are closer to home?

HELLER: Well, sometimes I think about moving out of the city, but it always takes the form of going to New Hampshire and living next door to J. D. Salinger. But, of course, if that happened, Salinger would immediately move to Montana. There I'd be, stuck out in the country with nobody to talk to.

PLAYBOY: You claim you're fond of young people, yet you once locked your daughter out of the apartment. Why?

HELLER: That was during my Pizza Period, when I didn't let *any* people in unless they were bringing me a pizza.

PLAYBOY: We've heard that you have an insatiable appetite. Is it true that some of your closest friends, members of the famous Gourmet Club, call you The Animal?

HELLER: It's not a club and we are not members. But, yes, the nonmembers do call me that.

PLAYBOY: You are apparently quite an expert on food. In the February *Playboy Interview*, Mel Brooks, a fellow Gourmet Club nonmember, quotes you as saying that 1000 years ago, there may have been egg in egg creams.

HELLER: I belong to the catastrophist school of egg-cream history, whereas Mel is a steady-state theorist. When Mel is in New York, we spend a lot of time together searching for egg creams.

PLAYBOY: Yossarian was orally fixated and, in *Something Happened,* Slocum sees the deterioration of American life in terms of food. Nothing tastes as good as it used to. He remembers the day he found out about a former girlfriend's suicide by recalling not his sorrow but the taste of the sandwich he ate afterward. Do you share the oral fixations of your two protagonists?

HELLER: Possibly. But I also believe that young people today will never know the taste of a good seeded roll or a mellow roll. They will never know good ice cream, good butter, good whipped cream—the stuff they spray out of cans isn't whipped and isn't cream. This is a legitimate measure of the deterioration of our standard of living.

PLAYBOY: How did the Gourmet Club start?

HELLER: Thirteen years ago, Ngoot Lee, the famous Chinese advertising man, began cooking dinner for a group of us once a week. Then Ngoot became successful and decided cooking put him in a subservient position, so we began going to Chinese restaurants instead.

PLAYBOY: We didn't know there were any famous Chinese admen.

HELLER: Ngoot cunningly hides his nationality by speaking Yiddish.

PLAYBOY: We've talked about your devotion to food. Are you a drinker?

HELLER: Yes, but never alone. If I'm at a party, I'll drink all night. I'm known as a nice drunk. I get very funny.

PLAYBOY: Do you think most writers like to drink?

HELLER: I can't speak for most writers. But most people I know who *are* writers don't like to drink as much as I do.

PLAYBOY: Are you into any other drugs?

HELLER: No, and I don't think drugs are valuable to a writer. They might distort your perceptions in a way that enables you to *see* more, but the ability to coordinate what you're experiencing with the very acute discipline of writing will be absent.

PLAYBOY: Do you have vivid dreams?

HELLER: Sometimes.

PLAYBOY: In color?

HELLER: No, black and white.

PLAYBOY: Have you used your dreams in your work?

HELLER: Almost all of Slocum's dreams are my own: ones in which he must get from one place to another and can't; he's in school and has to take a test, but he can't find the classroom. Freud himself had a recurring dream about not being able to pass an exam. When I was teaching at Penn State, I used to dream I was in the classroom with 15 minutes left and I couldn't think of a single thing to say. It was terrifying.

PLAYBOY: What else terrifies you? Do you believe in hell—or God?

HELLER: I don't care if there's a God or not.

PLAYBOY: What if Ralph Nader came up with a scientific study that *proved* there was a God and a heaven and a hell? Would that alter your behavior?

HELLER: No. The experience of life is more important than the experience of eternity. Life is short. Eternity never runs out.

PLAYBOY: Is there any special way you'd like to be . . . remembered?

HELLER: Remembered? In order to understand that question, am I to assume you have euphemistically deleted the word death?

PLAYBOY: We were hoping you wouldn't notice.

HELLER: It is impossible to predict or control how you will be remembered after your death. In that way, dying is like having children: You never know what will come out. In Beckett's *Endgame*, he asks his parents, in effect, "Why did you have me?" and the father replies, "We didn't know it would be you."

PLAYBOY: Yossarian wants to "live forever or die in the attempt," and Slocum wants to "outlive the Rockies." Do you fear death?

HELLER: I fear death, nursing homes and vaccinations.

PLAYBOY: Snowden's secret, which Yossarian learned when the young gunner's guts slithered out through a flak wound over Avignon, was that "the spirit gone, man is garbage. . . . Ripeness was all." Can you bring yourself to contemplate that inevitable transition from spirit to garbage?

HELLER: I've come to look upon death the same way I look upon root-canal work. Everyone else seems to get through it all right, so it couldn't be too difficult for me.

JIMMY HOFFA

December 1975

Interviewer: Jerry Stanecki

When interviewed the first time by PLAYBOY in 1963, Jimmy Hoffa responded to the last question about what he considered "Hoffa's most important accomplishment" with the remark, "Possibly that he's still alive despite lots of people." This same feisty cockiness was to pervade his second interview in the magazine—the last one he would give to anyone.

The second interview is reprinted here because it holds up best. Conducted by Jerry Stanecki—himself a rather feisty investigative reporter on WXYZ radio in Detroit—the interview took place just a month before Hoffa disappeared, presumably kidnaped and killed. Stanecki, on his own, had already begun a series of adversary conversations with Hoffa when he called PLAYBOY editor Barry Golson, Fisher's successor at supervising the interviews. Golson was dubious, since Hoffa had already been interviewed, but told Stanecki to proceed. (Hoffa had apparently forgotten about his first interview in the magazine, because before agreeing to continue with Stanecki, he protested that he didn't want to be in a magazine "with tits on the back of my picture.")

Hoffa seemed to enjoy mixing it up with Stanecki, and although he issued his usual denials about pension fraud or even the very existence of organized crime, he owned up to his violent past, spat out his contempt for the Kennedys, and implicated Teamsters boss Frank Fitzsimmons and President Nixon in a deal to keep him out of union politics. What seemed to be most on his mind, however, was the subject of death. Though arrogant about his own chances for a long life, he speculated about the deaths of the Kennedys, the deaths of other union officials, fictional deaths on television cop shows. It is easy to dramatize in hindsight, but one can hardly read this interview without feeling that he was fighting a premonition of his own.

Because of the timing of publication, PLAYBOY had a tremendous scoop on its hands. Hoffa disappeared on July 30, 1975, just five weeks after his final conversation with Stanecki. No other reporter had spoken with him in that period, so when the magazine became available in late October, speculation about Hoffa's killers was at its height. Hoffa's musings about attempts on his life thus made for fascinating reading. Because he was presumed to be dead, PLAYBOY agreed to release a portion of the tape to the CBS "Evening News." As the nation listened, it could hear the crackling voice of Jimmy Hoffa saying, "I don't cheat nobody. I don't lie about nobody. I don't frame nobody. . . . So what the hell's people gonna try and kill *me* for?"

The bumper sticker read: WHERE'S JIMMY HOFFA? CALL 313-962-7297. *It was on an old flatbed truck on the John C. Lodge Freeway in Detroit. Thousands of similar bumper stickers on cars and trucks across the country asked the question: What happened to the "little guy" who wheeled and dealt with money, words and clubs from the streets of Detroit to the huge white monument of a building known as Teamster International Head-quarters in Washington?*

Hoffa has been missing since July 30, 1975. His family last saw him when he reportedly left his home to attend a meeting with alleged mobster Anthony "Tony Jack" Giacalone, former Teamster vice-president Anthony "Tony Pro" Provenzano—a New Jersey man with alleged Mafia ties—and Leonard Schultz, a labor consultant and reputedly a key associate of Giacalone's. Supposedly, the meeting was arranged to mend fences after Hoffa and Tony Pro had a falling out while both were serving time at the Federal penitentiary in Lewisburg, Pennsylvania.

At 2:30 P.M., *Jimmy called his wife, Josephine, and asked, "Has Tony Giacalone called?"*

At 3:30 P.M., *Hoffa called longtime friend Louis Linteau, who runs an airline-limousine service in Pontiac: "Tony Jack didn't show, goddamn it. I'm coming out there."*

Two witnesses placed Hoffa in front of the Machus Red Fox restaurant in Bloomfield Township, Michigan, around the time of the call to Linteau.

Hoffa has not been heard from since.

Interviewer Jerry Stanecki, an investigative journalist for WXYZ Radio in Detroit, reports:

"I first met Jimmy about two years ago. His wife and son had been tossed out of their Teamster jobs—Jimmy, Jr., a lawyer, as counsel, Jo as head of the women's political-action group. Newspapers were filled with

speculation about a deepening Hoffa-Fitzsimmons rift. Most of the reports suggested that Hoffa himself had planted the speculation in the press. It was only after I called the manager of the condominium Jimmy owns in Florida and asked her to knock on his door with a request that he call me that I learned Hoffa hadn't talked with any reporters. 'I said no such a goddamn thing,' he told me.

"Apparently, he was impressed with the idea that I had gone to the trouble of finding him and getting his side of the story. From then on, Jimmy was available to me. He checked me out to see if I could be trusted, of course. And apparently I could be trusted. Often during the past two years I have gotten calls from Teamster officials, saying, 'Jimmy says you're OK. Here's what's going on.'

"I saw him many times and talked with him on the phone literally hundreds of times. Hoffa, a man who hated the press, seemed to consider me a friend.

"Jimmy lived in a modest lake-front home in Lake Orion, about 40 miles from Detroit. It sits on four acres of land that is neatly trimmed and decorated with statues of deer. He installed a teeter-totter and a merry-go-round for his grandchildren, to whom he was obviously devoted.

"When I arrived at his home to begin the 'Playboy Interview,' Hoffa was dressed in work pants, blue shirt and chukka boots. He was feeling good. It was a warm, sunny May day. We walked first to the lake in front of his house, where he had been raking leaves and sticks from the swimming area. Back at the house, he offered me some coffee and we walked to his new kitchen. There we sat down and began to talk."

PLAYBOY: You're 62 this year. Have you mellowed any?

HOFFA: Oh, I wouldn't say mellowed. I'd just say I got more common sense now than I had before. I used to take anybody on. Now I select who I take on.

PLAYBOY: How wealthy are you?

HOFFA: I think I'll be able to eat and live comfortable for the rest of my life. But so far as what I have . . . let it speak for itself. It's been in the press.

PLAYBOY: Are you a millionaire?

HOFFA: I would say.

PLAYBOY: We heard that you and Jimmy, Jr., got into a discussion on money and you commented, "How many men can come up with two million cash immediately?"

HOFFA: I would say, exactly right. I'll put it to you this way: I just read an article the other day where the estimate that there's less than one half of one percent of people who can lay their hands on $50,000 liquid cash overnight.

PLAYBOY: So you're comfortable. What else are you living for?

HOFFA: For the sake of living. I enjoy every minute of it, good, bad or indifferent. I enjoy life every day—and I'm looking forward to spending that life as part of the labor movement.

PLAYBOY: OK, let's get into that. By the terms of your release from prison, you've been banned from participating in the labor movement until 1980, and you're appealing that in the courts. If the courts ruled in your favor and you got your position back as president of the Teamsters, what would be your first priority?

HOFFA: Restructure the union back the way it was when I was there and reinstitute the trade divisions. Likewise, I'd reinstitute some additional organizers for the purpose of having master contracts. There's no other way unions can survive, except with master contracts—whether it's the building trades, retail clerks, meatcutters or anybody else. We need a common expiration date for the contracts of *all* unions.

PLAYBOY: That would virtually give you the power to bring the entire economy to a halt.

HOFFA: Well, corporations have it. The oil cartel, the lumber cartel, the steel cartel—they're all exactly the same.

PLAYBOY: But they're not united, the way you want the unions to be.

HOFFA: Of course they're united. There isn't a damned thing that happens in one of those industries that doesn't conform to what industry leaders decide together. The only thing they don't discuss collectively—at least openly—is prices. But as far as everything else goes, you'll find they have a master organization, a master contract. Put it to you this way: So far as power is concerned, does anybody believe the premiums of insurance companies are almost all uniform by accident? Is it an accident that if the price of gasoline goes up in one company, all the other prices go up the same rate in a matter of weeks?

PLAYBOY: Still, giving one man control over union contracts with a common expiration date isn't something the Congress would look upon very favorably.

HOFFA: The Congress of the United States wants to be judge, jury and prosecutor over what's good for the American people. And they think anyone who has a bloc of votes is dangerous. Truth is, everything the Congress has touched has been a failure. Can't show me one progressive thing they've did that didn't turn out a failure.

PLAYBOY: Have the Teamsters gone to hell since you were forced out?

HOFFA: Well, they haven't advanced. There are no master contracts, other than the ones I left them. The organizing campaigns and the joint councils of the local unions have deteriorated. And the morale of the local officers, the organizers, is at an all-time low, from what I hear. Even the members feel uncomfortable they don't have someone steerin' the ship. The leaders are too busy on the golf course, flyin' around in seven jet airplanes they own. Why the hell do they own *seven*? Most corporations don't own that many.

PLAYBOY: Do you blame the present head of the Teamsters, Frank Fitzsimmons?

HOFFA: Fitzsimmons has failed. He has failed in every promise he made to the union convention. He can't show one single thing that he said he would do that he did. Can't show one thing. Not one.

PLAYBOY: How did you and Fitzsimmons split?

HOFFA: Well, as far as I'm concerned, when I found out that Fitzsimmons, uh, lied when he said he'd been talking confidentially to John Mitchell about getting me out of prison.

PLAYBOY: Let's backtrack a bit. At first you thought Fitzsimmons was doing everything he could to get you out of prison?

HOFFA: During the whole time I was in prison, Fitzsimmons kept tellin' everybody—my son, my lawyers, all the union representatives—"Now, don't do anything, you'll rock the boat. I'm taking care of it with Mitchell." Well, when Mitchell later gave his deposition, he said the first time Fitzsimmons ever talked to him about me was in June 1971. I'd been in jail five years. It was when I'd already resigned and given Fitzsimmons the green light to become president. Then I found out that he'd fired Edward Bennett Williams as Teamsters' counsel and replaced him with Charles Colson. And when I found out there was a restriction on my parole until 1980, it didn't take a ton of bricks to fall on me to put two and two together—that he'd been lyin' all along.

PLAYBOY: You said Fitzsimmons kept saying he was going to work on Mitchell. Meaning what?

HOFFA: He claimed to all and any that he was responsible for getting me a rehearing on my parole and that Mitchell was going to take executive action to get me out of prison. As I said, when Mitchell gave his deposition later on, he said, "I talked to Fitzsimmons about Hoffa, among other things, in June 1971." Well, what a flat lie Fitzsimmons had been tellin' everyone in the union—for a period of almost five years!

PLAYBOY: How was Fitzsimmons going to persuade Mitchell?

HOFFA: I suppose by using his alleged influence with Nixon and by using his, uh, political arm to support the Republican Party.

PLAYBOY: With campaign contributions?

HOFFA: I don't know about that. I suppose he said he'd give him $14,000 [a publicly disclosed campaign contribution], which is a lot of nonsense. But the truth of the matter is he never did anything. I also found out from Dean that he didn't even *know* Fitzsimmons and he was sitting right outside Nixon's door.

PLAYBOY: John Dean?

HOFFA: Yeah. And it'd be damned funny that anyone could go in and out of the White House without knowing John Dean. In any case, what Colson did was wait until the President was coming in or out of his office, then introduce him: "Mr. President, this is Frank Fitzsimmons." "Hello, how are ya?" Then Colson would take him up to have dinner in the Senate Building.

Well, that's a hell of a big deal. Anybody must be out of their mind if they're head of the Teamsters Union and can be brushed off that way. In any case, John Dean testified that he and Colson had discussed the 1980 restriction and what with Colson already having the offer from the Teamsters to become general counsel, it all adds up to . . . it *leads* me to believe that Fitzsimmons deliberately double-crossed, uh, the membership, the convention, my lawyers and myself. And that's it. So I don't wanna do business with a double-crosser . . . or a liar.

PLAYBOY: If Fitzsimmons, Colson and Dean were working against you, how *did* you finally get a parole?

HOFFA: It came about because over 1,500,000 signatures were sent to the President of the United States. It came about by hundreds of thousands of letters going to the Attorney General and the President. Since Nixon was facing an election, in my opinion he didn't want to have to face all those people. So he met with Mitchell, according to Mitchell's affidavit, and they discussed the release of one James R. Hoffa. And it was agreed I would be released before Christmas 1971.

Immediately after that, when the recommendation was sent out, Dean intercepted it. Dean testified, or implied, that he and Mitchell talked about inserting the 1980 restriction into the recommendation at that time. Mitchell denies this.

PLAYBOY: So the original recommendation made by Mitchell and President Nixon did not have the 1980 restriction.

HOFFA: It did not. Furthermore, Dean called in Colson and [Presidential aide] Clark Mollenhoff and they decided on the restriction without talking to the Attorney General or the President and rewrote the recommendation, keeping it confidential even from everyone else at the White House— until 14 minutes after I was out of jail. They were convinced that if I knew the 1980 restriction was there, I wouldn't have accepted.

PLAYBOY: But the President *did* sign the order, didn't he?

HOFFA: Aw, sure. Along with 212 other ones. But I'm sure the President didn't think Mitchell had changed what they'd agreed upon. And I'm sure he didn't read through 212 commutations and pardons.

PLAYBOY: How about you? You read it, didn't you?

HOFFA: I *couldn't* read it! I wasn't there. Wasn't anything I signed.

PLAYBOY: And your attorneys?

HOFFA: *Nobody* knew! Fourteen minutes after I'd gotten out of jail, they announced the restriction to the warden, to my attorneys, to the public. I found out about it hours later on the news. When I went to see the head of the parole board after the holidays, *he* didn't know about it. Nobody had informed him. He had to call Washington to find out what they were talking about and it wasn't until January 14, 1972, that I received notification of the restriction in the mail. And I refused to sign it.

PLAYBOY: There was no hint, no suggestion before you left prison?

HOFFA: I had asked the warden specifically, was there any restriction other than the one banning me from union activity until March 1973 [when Hoffa would have been released anyway]? He called Washington and said, "No."

PLAYBOY: But you signed *something* to get out of Lewisburg, didn't you?

HOFFA: Commutation. Read every word of it. Being suspicious-minded as I am concerning public people. I asked the warden to call Washington and find out if that's all there was. He came back and said that was all there was to it.

PLAYBOY: And you blame whom?

HOFFA: In my opinion, Dean, Mollenhoff, Colson and Fitzsimmons.

PLAYBOY: So there was a conspiracy to keep Hoffa out of the union?

HOFFA: I would say, uh, there certainly was an understanding of, uh, everyone of 'em getting a piece of the pie they wanted. And they used Dean to get the pie.

PLAYBOY: Straight question: Was there any *financial* deal made with Nixon to get you out of prison?

HOFFA: Fitzsimmons says no. He says he only gave him $14,000.

PLAYBOY: So there was no offer of what might be called a bribe?

HOFFA: Absolutely not. Positively not. I did not.

[At this point, there was an interruption and Hoffa walked over to the window of his kitchen. The tape recorder was turned off, but, by mutual agreement, the conversation remained on the record. The interviewer asked: "Come on, Jimmy, was *any* money paid to Richard Nixon to get you out of prison?"

Hoffa turned from the window and said, "Yaaaaa."

The interviewer asked, "How much?"

The reply, deadly serious, came after a long pause: "You don't *wanna* know."

A week later, with the tape recorder turned on, the interviewer reminded Hoffa of this exchange. Hoffa denied saying "any such goddamned thing."]

PLAYBOY: But you had no one approach Nixon and say, "Look, $100,000 goes into your campaign . . ."?

HOFFA: I had nobody go there. If anybody went there, it was without my knowledge—even though there *is* a statement floating around that Allen Dorfman [a special consultant to the Teamsters' largest health-and-welfare fund] said at his trial in New York that he had a receipt signed by Mitchell for a large sum of money—as a contribution.

PLAYBOY: How large was the sum supposed to be?

HOFFA: Now, that's never been proven. Mitchell denied it under oath. What the hell's the name of the other guy—Stans? Yeah, Stans. He denied it, too.

PLAYBOY: Is this Dorfman a friend of yours?

HOFFA: A hundred percent.

PLAYBOY: Isn't he the man you set up in business through your Chicago contacts back in the Fifties?

HOFFA: No. Nobody set him up in business at all. Allen Dorfman submitted a sealed bid for the insurance. And by unanimous vote of the trustees, he became the agent for the insurance company.

PLAYBOY: But didn't you control the trustees at the time?

HOFFA: I spoke my piece in favor of Dorfman. Of course I did.

PLAYBOY: All right. Besides Fitzsimmons, it seems as if Colson were the one person who stood to gain most by the 1980 restriction. When did he go on the Teamsters' payroll?

HOFFA: Within months of the time I got out of prison. He certainly didn't command, by reputation, the retainer he got. Certainly didn't do that.

PLAYBOY: How much did he get from the Teamsters?

HOFFA: All told, probably in the neighborhood of $300,000 a year.

PLAYBOY: What qualifications did Colson have to be a Teamsters lawyer?

HOFFA: Well, he had a shingle.

PLAYBOY: So it was a deal?

HOFFA: In my opinion.

PLAYBOY: Jimmy, what *about* Frank Fitzsimmons?

HOFFA: Well, what the hell about him? I already said he's a double-crosser. And that's all there is to it.

PLAYBOY: You said——

HOFFA: A man I took off the truck! Made him an officer in the union, saw that he had more than one suit for the first time in his life, that he lived in a decent home, had an expense account! Kept raising him through the ranks of labor! And when I went to jail, he took over the presidency and then he became power hungry. He accepted the belief that he was a great labor leader and came about doing what he did in the 1980 restriction. In my opinion.

PLAYBOY: Why did he come to believe he was a great labor leader?

HOFFA: How the hell do I know? Look at some of the Congressmen and Senators we got. They couldn't spell rat backward, they couldn't make a living! They get elected and, for Chrissakes, they're on TV, yakking around, telling you how to run the world, and they can't even run their own life! Same thing with him. People look in the mirror too often. They grow by inches—sideways and down—but they don't grow. Their heads get fatter, but they don't get any more sense than they had before. I just think Fitzsimmons has gone completely power nuts, that's all. Someone took him up to the top of the mountain. Showed him the valley, and he bought the valley. But he forgot the membership and he forgot the officers and forgot his responsibility to the oath he took for office.

PLAYBOY: Will Fitzsimmons be in office through 1980?

HOFFA: I don't think Fitzsimmons will run in 1976.

PLAYBOY: Why?

HOFFA: Well, the best evidence is he's building a home at La Costa. With his golfing and parading around all over the country in his jet, I don't think he'll be a candidate.

PLAYBOY: You were the one who extended the first loan to develop La Costa, somewhere around $10,000,000, isn't that right?

HOFFA: Somewhere around there, yeah. Been a long time ago.

PLAYBOY: How did it start?

HOFFA: Well, Moe Dalitz was the major owner of the Desert Inn. We loaned him money, he paid it back. When he wanted to go into the La Costa enterprise, real estate was booming at the time. And it couldn't go wrong. *That* real estate's a good buy today!

PLAYBOY: Was Meyer Lansky part of that?

HOFFA: Meyer Lansky had no more to do with Moe Dalitz than you had, in my opinion.

PLAYBOY: Aren't you and Lansky good friends?

HOFFA: I know him.

PLAYBOY: Ever do business with him?

HOFFA: Nope. Never asked me to. My opinion, he's *another* victim of harassment!

PLAYBOY: Then you don't think he's a member of organized crime?

HOFFA: I don't believe there is any organized crime, period. Don't believe it. Never believed it. I've said it for the last 40 years. *Hoover* said it! Supposed to be the greatest law-enforcement man in America, with the means to find out. He said there was no Mafia, no so-called organized crime.

PLAYBOY: No Mafia?

HOFFA: That's what *he* said. That's what Hoover said.

PLAYBOY: But in 1958, during the McClellan hearings, it was said that you knew more dangerous criminals than Dave Beck.

HOFFA: Ah-ha! That's a different question! I don't deny the fact that I know, I think, what's going on in most of the big cities of the United States. And that means knowing the people, uh, who are in the big cities. I'm no different than the banks, no different than insurance companies, no different than the politicians. You're a damned fool not to be informed what makes a city run when you're tryin' to do business in the city.

PLAYBOY: What about people like Lansky and Frank Costello?

HOFFA: What about 'em?

PLAYBOY: The McClellan Committee said that they were organized-crime members, members of the Mafia.

HOFFA: Yeah, yeah, sure. They said I was associated with the Mafia. They said Dorfman was part of the Mafia. And it's a complete, 100 percent lie. They know it. Everybody else knows it. So it's easy to say, "Well, he's a Mafia member, 'cause he got an Italian name." Once in a while they say, for a man like Lansky, who's a Jew, "Oh, well, he was accepted."

PLAYBOY: How about Paul "The Waiter" Ricca?

HOFFA: What about him? Jesus Christ Almighty! He was in Chicago for 99 years and a day and if they thought he was so much involved in organized crime, why the hell didn't they arrest him? Hell of a note that the FBI, and the Congress, and the newspapers and everybody else says So-and-So's part of the Mafia; So-and-So's doing this. . . . Why don't they arrest him? Why the hell don't they put him on trial? What the hell they doing? Keeping him alive, like a mummy, so they can keep writing about him?

PLAYBOY: So where is Ricca now?

HOFFA: Dead! [Pause] Dead! Why the hell—— What are you talking about all these people?

PLAYBOY: What about Johnny Dio?

HOFFA: Friend of mine. No question about that.

PLAYBOY: Member of organized crime?

HOFFA: Like *you* are.

PLAYBOY: Member of the Mafia?

HOFFA: Like *you* are.

PLAYBOY: Wasn't he convicted of extortion?

HOFFA: Ah-ha! That's a different question. I know Johnny's case. I know what Johnny's in jail for. Don't agree with it. Trying to help him get out. Should be out. Our association's trying to help him get out. And he's a victim of newspaper publicity, just like I was. [Pause] Damned funny, though! All these people are supposed to have millions and millions of dollars. Can't afford to hire lawyers. [Pause] Damned funny. I saw some of the biggest ones that there was supposed to be, in prison. And their wives were on welfare and they didn't have enough money to come down and visit 'em. And yet they keep talking about the millions they got.

PLAYBOY: Like who?

HOFFA: Well, I don't care to mention their names and embarrass them. But I seen 'em. They're there. [Pause] Damned funny. I know people in town *here*, right in Detroit, say they're part of the Mafia! Well, Christ! They ain't making a living! How come, if they're part of the Mafia, they're not making a living?

PLAYBOY: Care to be specific?

HOFFA: No, I don't want to . . . everybody knows who they are . . . the police department knows, the prosecutor's office knows, the media knows. . . .

PLAYBOY: What about Tony Giacalone?

HOFFA: Giacalone! Giacalone! Giacalone's a businessman!

PLAYBOY: Didn't he have dealings with La Costa?

HOFFA: La Costa! What the hell's *he* got to do with La Costa?

PLAYBOY: You mean he had no involvement at all?

HOFFA: Record speaks for itself. Got nothin' more to do with La Costa than *you* have. May have *visited* it—went to the spa or to one of the golf tournaments down there, 'cause he's a golfer. Why, he's got as much to do with La Costa as *you* have!

PLAYBOY: But Giacalone was named as a member of organized crime by a Senate committee back in——

HOFFA: What the hell has that got to do with it? I appeared in front of the same committee and they lied about me! They lied about Giacalone! They never proved it! And if they *had* such a charge, why in the hell didn't they charge everybody with conspiracy and go to court?

PLAYBOY: Conspiracy's hard to prove; it's almost *impossible* to prove.

HOFFA: Like *hell*! The easiest crime in the world to prove. Anybody indicted for a conspiracy, a lawyer will tell you it's the easiest crime the Government can prove. And that's why they put it on the books as conspiracy. The mere fact that you meet with somebody, or the fact that circumstantial evidence is involved. . . . What the hell're you talking about? It's the easiest crime in the book to prove. That's why they use conspiracy.

PLAYBOY: As far as conspiracies go, you've always believed that the Government was out to "get Hoffa," haven't you?

HOFFA: Of course. First, Bobby Kennedy wanted to use the Teamsters as a vehicle to get the Kennedy name out front with something that was probably the greatest thriller that ever appeared on TV [the televised McClellan hearings]. And when he couldn't bull me, when he couldn't take over the Teamsters, why, it became a vendetta between he and I. And he used $12,000,000 in Government money to convict me. Who the hell ever heard of the Kennedys before the McClellan Committee? They were nobody. A bootlegger, the old man. Common, ordinary bootlegger.

PLAYBOY: Have you ever wire-tapped anybody?

HOFFA: I've hired people to secure information for me where they could possibly secure it.

PLAYBOY: Did they secure it by wire tapping?

HOFFA: I didn't ask them. Not interested.

PLAYBOY: Did you ever tap Bobby Kennedy?

HOFFA: If they did, I don't know. But I *received* information on Kennedy. How they got it, none of my business. Wouldn't wanna know it.

PLAYBOY: Did you tap any FBI agents?

HOFFA: No. *I* didn't tap 'em. Somebody else . . . uh, Bernie Spindel [a freelance electronics expert] set up a monitoring system in Chattanooga and took information outta the air from three of the FBI radio channels. We found out the FBI was violating the law; they were surveilling my lawyers and my witnesses. We also proved they were attempting to get information which was tantamount to interfering with justice. And then we submitted the transcripts to the judge, Frank Wilson. He opened the envelope, then charged we had tricked him and he had a fit. The next batch we handed him, Wilson wouldn't open; I think it's because among the transcripts was one of him making a telephone communication to Bobby Kennedy—and that was in the middle of the trial.

PLAYBOY: So then you had issued orders to tap Wilson's phone?

HOFFA: No. It's not a question of tapping Wilson's phone.

PLAYBOY: Kennedy's phone, then?

HOFFA: No. Taken out of the air.

PLAYBOY: Bullshit! You can't just take phone conversations "out of the air."

HOFFA: Don't tell *me* it's bullshit! Don't tell me what they can do. I have the proof! Frank Wilson finally admitted he *did* talk to Bobby Kennedy during the trial, although he said he was talking about hiring clerks for overtime typing. But it took *45* minutes to do it! [Judge Wilson says that at no time did he communicate with Kennedy.]

As to taking out of the air, Bernie did it with about a ton of equipment he brought down with him. We gave him a suite and set it all up and, being the best expert in the United States, he just reached out with his communication system and took it out of the air. Right outta the air, everything that was going on. They knew it could be done. They do it every day in the week.

PLAYBOY: There's a story that you ordered Marilyn Monroe's phone tapped——

HOFFA: That's the silliest thing I ever read in my life.

PLAYBOY: And that the tapes are still supposed to be in existence.

HOFFA: Aw, that's a lotta crap! I never said no such thing. I read that stupid statement in that stupid book. And, uh, the "Mailer" who wrote that book, I think his name was——

PLAYBOY: Norman Mailer.

HOFFA: The stupidest thing I ever read in my life. He admitted he hardly interviewed anybody, that all he did was gather information other people had wrote and did a book on it. [It was not Mailer's *Marilyn* that contained the allegation Hoffa referred to, but *The Life and Curious Death of Marilyn Monroe,* by Robert F. Slatzer.] And I understand right now he's in the process of writing a book on me. When he does, I'm gonna sue him. Very simple.

PLAYBOY: What if Mailer called and asked to interview you?

HOFFA: Wouldn't talk to him, under no circumstances. I think he must be some kind of nut.

PLAYBOY: All right, what about the allegations about the Marilyn Monroe tapes?

HOFFA: Marilyn Monroe? I never knew she *existed* with Bobby Kennedy.

If I did, I would've told him about it in open hearing. I already *had* a tape on Bobby Kennedy and Jack Kennedy, which was so filthy and so nasty—given to me by a girl—that even though my people encouraged me to do it, I wouldn't do it. I put it away and said the hell with it. Forget about it.

PLAYBOY: What was on the tape?

HOFFA: Oh, their association with this young lady and what they had did, and so forth. I got rid of the tape. I wouldn't put up with it. [Pause] Pure nonsense.

PLAYBOY: You didn't feel you had a way to get back at Bobby?

HOFFA: I would not embarrass his wife and family.

PLAYBOY: Well, you've mentioned it now.

HOFFA: Let it be at that. Let it stay that way. I'm not talkin' about what's dirty and nasty. Maybe some people wouldn't think it. I did.

PLAYBOY: Who was the girl?

HOFFA: I'm not sayin' that. [Pause] *I* know.

PLAYBOY: All right. Did you ever threaten to kill Bobby Kennedy?

HOFFA: Nope. Another lie.

PLAYBOY: What about killing people?

HOFFA: Self-preservation's a big word.

PLAYBOY: Have you ever exercised your need for self-preservation?

HOFFA: Never had to.

PLAYBOY: You've never killed anybody?

HOFFA: Never had to exercise the self-preservation. But I'm certainly not going to let someone kill *me*.

PLAYBOY: Have you ever *ordered* anybody to be killed?

HOFFA: [Pause] Mmm, nope.

PLAYBOY: Killing isn't the way to solve a problem?

HOFFA: No, I don't think it solves anything. It just creates a few more problems—the FBI, the local police, newspapers. [Pause] Kill 'em by propaganda. Kill 'em by votes. But not *physically* kill 'em.

PLAYBOY: How about busting heads?

HOFFA: Nothin' wrong with that, if they're in your way, uh, tryin' to break a strike or tryin' to destroy the union. Nothin' wrong with that, in my opinion.

PLAYBOY: You *do* have a reputation for busting heads that goes way back.

HOFFA: Survival of the fittest, my friend. What do you think industry does? What do you think the police do? Police broke our heads every day of the week in 1932. Ford Motors? They cracked heads all *over* the lot. Unless you were able to take care of yourself, they'd crack your head where it'd kill you. I survived.

PLAYBOY: Have you ever hired any bodyguards?

HOFFA: Never. Don't need 'em. Don't need 'em. They're in your way.

PLAYBOY: But not everybody loves Jimmy Hoffa.

HOFFA: I'm not interested in what everybody does. You got a bodyguard, you become careless, and if you look at all the gangsters that were *killed* with bodyguards, you'll know they went to sleep. I don't *care* to go to *sleep*.

PLAYBOY: What do you mean, gangsters?

HOFFA: People who allegedly were, uh, involved in bank robberies and other kind of illegal enterprises individually. They had bodyguards. How about the question of Roosevelt? He had all *kind* of bodyguards down in Florida, didn't he? Little guy pops up nobody ever heard of. He starts shooting. He killed the mayor [Anton Cermak of Chicago], didn't he? Well, what do you want? What do you want? Bodyguards make you go to sleep and I don't care to go to sleep. The only guy who needs a bodyguard is a liar, a cheat, a guy who betrays friendship. I don't do any of them. What the hell do you need a bodyguard for?

PLAYBOY: So you're not afraid of anything?

HOFFA: What the hell am I gonna be afraid of? I'm 62 years old. I should've been dead maybe 25 years ago. Lived three lives. Well, what am I gonna be afraid of? Never was afraid in my life and don't intend to start tomorrow. Who's gonna bother me? *They* do? Well, then I'll do somethin' about *that*.

PLAYBOY: You'll do what, exactly?

HOFFA: Whatever I have to do.

PLAYBOY: What do you mean?

HOFFA: Just whatever I have to do to eliminate somebody bothers me. . . . I'll do whatever I *have* to do.

PLAYBOY: Such as killing them?

HOFFA: Well, if they try to kill *me* and I'm in the position to take away their gun, or whatever the hell they're using against me. If they get shot, that's their trouble. It ain't mine. Hell, if I had people try to kill me, I survived it. Didn't have no bodyguard, but I survived the . . . the *threat* of being killed, the *attempt* to be killed. I'm still here. 'Cause I keep my eyes open—drive my own car, go where I wanna go, never need no bodyguard. I don't cheat nobody. I don't lie about nobody. I don't frame nobody. I don't talk bad about people. If I do, I tell 'em. So what the hell's people gonna try to kill *me* for?

PLAYBOY: OK. How's your private life? Do you get out much, to restaurants, that sort of thing?

HOFFA: Eh. Once in a while. Very seldom. Now, when we go out, arm and a leg. What the hell're you gonna do? Number one, I don't like the crowds. Number two, I don't like the prices. Number three, I don't like the service. So what the hell am I gonna go out for? Why should Josephine get dressed up for two hours? The hell with it. It's getting to the point where a guy with four kids, his old lady and himself has got to spend $70 a week for groceries.

PLAYBOY: What's the most important thing in your life right now?

HOFFA: Oh, my family. No question about *that*.

PLAYBOY: For years you feuded with the Kennedys, one of the most powerful families in the country. What did you think, personally, of Bobby Kennedy?

HOFFA: He was a creep!

PLAYBOY: And John Kennedy?

HOFFA: Creep!

PLAYBOY: How about Teddy?

HOFFA: Well, I've known a hell of a lot of brothers in my life. Two, three, four to a family, the majority of 'em no good. And maybe one of 'em outta the lot, you couldn't *find* a better guy. Who the hell knows? Just because you're brothers, it doesn't mean you're the same type. Don't mean that. Don't mean that at all.

Ted Kennedy I hardly know. But I know people who've known him since the day he was born. Our people in Boston've known him. And they say he's different from all two of the others. They say he likes a good time and that he would be the kind of guy who would gather around him a lot of people who wouldn't go to work for any other Administration. I suppose they mean professors and what have you—I have no faith in 'em. So that's all I know about the guy. He never made any statement concerning me that I know of—even when it was fashionable. Of course, he can get in . . . any time he wants it, he's got it.

PLAYBOY: You mean the Presidency? You think he's going to run?

HOFFA: Oh, just as sure as you and I are here. Just as sure as you and I are here. It'll be a draft at the convention.

PLAYBOY: How much do you think Chappaquiddick will hurt him?

HOFFA: Aw, Christ! Fifty percent of the marriages are in divorces. And when you talk about morality, it went out the window. How the hell's that gonna hurt him? He's sure as hell gonna get the old people, the welfare people, the Puerto Ricans, blacks, Mexicans. He'll get the majority of those. No question of that in *my* mind. How the hell could be lose?

Unless—there's only one thing that could kill him and very well kill *all* Democrats. They got the House and the Senate now. If they keep fiddlin' around and not doing anything except quarreling with each other, very well, the American people could say, "Now, the hell with ya," and vote Republican. That's the way *I* see it. I don't see it no other way.

PLAYBOY: Why did Kennedy say he wouldn't run?

HOFFA: Get the heat off Chappaquiddick for 18 months. What the hell, they were banging him on the head with every kind of article, TV report, what have you. But you notice the very minute he said, "I'm not gonna run," it stopped. So he was smart.

PLAYBOY: Don't you think Chappaquiddick will have to be resolved at some point?

HOFFA: Phhht! He wasn't found guilty of no crime. What's he supposed to do? They didn't find him *guilty*!

PLAYBOY: If Teddy runs and gets elected, do you think he'll be killed?

HOFFA: Naw. I don't think— You just don't kill— What the hell! I don't think anybody's so cold-blooded that he'd shoot a guy because he's a Kennedy.

PLAYBOY: There was at least one publicized attempt on *your* life, wasn't there? In 1962, during your trial on charges of illegal kickbacks, a man walked into the courtroom and shot you from behind.

HOFFA: Yeah, don't know his goddamned name. I forgot it now. It's a matter of record. [It was Warren Swanson, a deranged drifter.] But everyone was searched that went in and out of the courtroom. How the hell did he get in with a gun? . . . I'm sure the marshal didn't overlook *him*. And he walked in with a gun, after everybody'd been searched! Like Martin Luther King. You're suspicious but you can't prove it.

PLAYBOY: The man had a pellet gun, right?

HOFFA: Which would go through a two-by-four. Kill you just as sure as a .22.

PLAYBOY: What's your version of what happened?

HOFFA: Well, I looked and I *seen* him. I ducked down, come up, broke his jaw, took his gun away from him. The marshals were behind the file cabincts, same as the Government lawyers, my lawyers, same as the judge. They all came pouncing out after it was all over. I got the guy knocked out and this marshal comes out with a blackjack and hits the poor bastard! I said, "Ya dumb bastard! Get outta here! The guy's knocked out already!"

PLAYBOY: How about the attempt on George Wallace?

HOFFA: Who the hell *knows*? They got a file on every kook there is.

PLAYBOY: And John Kennedy? Why do you think he was killed?

HOFFA: Who the hell knows what deals he had? That he didn't keep? Who knows?

PLAYBOY: Do you think Oswald did it?

HOFFA: Aw, who the hell knows? I saw that simulation of the assassination on TV, which made more sense to me than the Warren Report did. I'll be goddamned. You tell me a guy can figure out how to be there at the right moment, the right time, with a rifle—and hit a guy, you're a good man. I don't see how you do it. I see guys shooting at deer and I see *crack shots* shooting the deer. By God, *they* miss 'em. And a deer's about like a moving car. Ain't much difference.

PLAYBOY: Why did Jack Ruby kill Oswald, in your opinion?

HOFFA: That's the $64 question. Nobody'll ever figure that out. A fanatic, maybe. Who the hell knows?

PLAYBOY: What do you think of the conspiracy theories of that former district attorney in New Orleans, Jim Garrison? Is he just a kook?

HOFFA: No, sirree! Jim Garrison's a smart man. . . . Goddamned smart attorney. . . . Anybody thinks *he's* a kook is a kook themselves.

PLAYBOY: All right, back to the Bobby Kennedy assassination. You don't think Nixon had anything to do with it, do you?

HOFFA: Hell, no. Hell, no. He ain't that kind of guy.

PLAYBOY: So it was Sirhan acting alone?

HOFFA: Well, I handle guns all my life. Here's a kid that went out and got a gun. Not much practice with the damned gun. And I would question whether he was cold-blooded enough to be able to pop up and shoot the guy without someone . . . helping him. I just read about another guy, a ballistics guy, who said there was another type of bullet. Who the hell knows? *Who the hell knows?*

PLAYBOY: Do you think we'll ever know about all these killings?

HOFFA: Well, I watched the damned TV the other night, that *Police Story* and *S.W.A.T.* They killed more goddamned people than you got hair on your *head*! [Pause] Goddamned movies, TV! Kills 49 guys a night, for Chrissake—on Monday and Tuesday night! Forty-nine guys they kill! So who the hell knows what you can do? There was a nut on TV last night, just started *killing* people. Nobody knew why the goddamned fool killed people. Then they finally catch him . . . kill *him*. So he's dead. *He* can't tell why he killed 'em. People go off their rocker. Who can tell?

JERRY BROWN

April 1976

Interviewer: Robert Scheer

In the fall of 1975, there hadn't been much national publicity about California's young new governor. What there was seemed preposterous: a thirty-seven-year-old bachelor, a former Catholic seminarian with a penchant for Oriental mysticism, who preferred a bare mattress in a small apartment to the Governor's Mansion in Sacramento. PLAYBOY editor Golson had requested an interview, but was placed at the end of a long waiting list.

One afternoon in Chicago, Golson was having drinks with Robert Scheer, the former editor of *Ramparts* and a veteran of leftist politics in Berkeley. "I wish I knew how to cut through the red tape in Sacramento," Golson said. "No problem," said Scheer. "I dated the same woman Jerry did." Within a week Scheer was taping the first of over twenty hours with the governor of California.

It was the beginning of a memorable association between Scheer and the Playboy Interview. (He had already published several highly regarded articles in the magazine, including an acid profile of Nelson Rockefeller.) Scheer delivered a draft of the Jerry Brown interview six weeks later, advising Golson that he had also sent Brown a copy—for an accuracy check, he stressed.

A week afterward, the governor sent Scheer a "checked" version of the interview—a wholly rewritten, dull, sanitized piece of copy, far less interesting than the man himself was. It was then that Scheer and Golson decided to join forces. They flew to Sacramento together and confronted Brown in his office. The situation was unfair to both sides, they told Brown, so why didn't they just begin again?

The tape recorders were switched on, the conversation resumed, and the three men spoke for three consecutive nights. The interview was obviously going to be a good one, but it was not at all clear that Brown had abandoned his intention to rewrite his words. Although the conversation was lively and friendly, Brown was not above his own brand of politicking. Late one night, for example, as they were about to repair to a Japanese restaurant, Brown managed to separate Scheer and Golson, insisting that the PLAYBOY editor ride with him in his car while Scheer rode with an aide. Once inside the car, Brown suggested to Golson that they continue the interview alone—an offer that did not astonish the editor, since he had played the diplomatic Mutt to Scheer's more abrasive Jeff. Golson declined.

On the last night, as the interview drew to a close, Brown suggested once again that he keep the original transcripts, as well as copies of the new tapes—just to check facts and figures, he said. The interview ended shortly thereafter, and Brown and his aide took a break. The two journalists, alone in the governor's office, took one look at each other and immediately stuffed every tape cassette and every scrap of paper in the room into their briefcases. It was two o'clock in the morning and everyone was staggering from fatigue, which is probably why, when Brown and his aide returned, they didn't notice that the office was appreciably neater.

The following morning, Scheer and Golson caught the first flight back to Chicago, where they put together the interview, and where Scheer wrote an incisive article to accompany it. They did not hear from Brown again regarding the transcripts, and Scheer, discreetly, did not mention the rewriting incident in his introduction. He did, however, manage to include a private message to the governor, writing tongue-in-cheek that Brown "impressed me by not attempting to cut off the dialogue and by resisting the temptation to use the trappings of his office to get his way."

Notwithstanding the squabbles behind the scenes, the Brown who emerged from his unsanitized interview was a fresh voice in American politics. He elaborated on his philosophy of lowered expectations, confronted for the first time the rumors of his homosexuality, discussed the intellectual and religious influences in his life, and proclaimed his politics a new force on the American scene. The interview was to have far-reaching effects.

There are several impressive facts about Edmund Gerald Brown, Jr., and chief among them is that after only one year as governor of California, he is considered, at the age of 37, to be the most exciting potential candidate for the Presidency since John F. Kennedy. Time called him "the most inter-

esting politician in America" and, at a time when most American politicians are held in only slightly higher esteem than used-car salesmen, his approval rating by California voters is an astounding 85 percent. A product of a Catholic education and three and a half years of study to become a priest at a Jesuit seminary, Brown flirted with the Berkeley life-style of the early Sixties, then veered off to Yale Law School, from which he graduated in 1964. As the son of a popular two-term California governor, he found his family name was potent and his law practice in Los Angeles dull; so when his feelings of opposition to the Vietnam war intensified, he helped organize the state's peace slate, which became Eugene McCarthy's delegation to the Democratic Convention in 1968. He ran for a school-board post the next year, then for secretary of state in 1970. His crazy-quilt background resulted in the spectacle of a state governor who did things differently: He slipped away from fund raisers and disdained ceremonial functions; he slept on a bare mattress in a spare apartment, leaving Ronald Reagan's huge new governor's mansion empty; he used a Plymouth instead of the official chauffeured limousine. And Californians loved it.

Then there is the matter of his politics—elusive, wriggly and difficult to categorize. He manages to convince young and old, conservative and liberal, rich and poor that he is, each in turn, on their side.

Finally, there is the mystique—not Kennedy brand of charisma but mystique in the true sense of the word. Brown is not a flesh presser and does not arouse fierce emotions in crowds. Indeed, what he arouses is intense curiosity. He is variously reported in the press to be a lonely, misanthropic figure, given to Oriental mysticism and Jesuitical debating techniques. There have been references to his Zen meditational retreats, gurus presiding over cabinet meetings and dark hints that he disdains food and sex.

To probe below the surface of this complicated man, PLAYBOY *assigned Robert Scheer, a journalist with strong radical credentials whose last piece in this magazine was "Nelson Rockefeller Takes Care of Everybody," to conduct the interview. Scheer and Brown had crossed each other's path in Berkeley and, as Scheer's report attests, each seemed to find the other man a challenge:*

" 'Don't worry, Bob. I'll get that biographical material to you on the plane tonight. You can trust me. Hell, I'm the governor.'

"When Jerry Brown says he's the governor, I often feel a sense of disbelief. This antipolitician, whose style stresses deep suspicion of the ability of government to produce on a grand scale, is clearly the most popular high official in the country. He's also an unpretentious guy I've hung out with, drinking beer and club hopping on Sunset Strip and talking about everything under the sun.

"As to the interview itself, the governor hung in there for the long, sometimes grueling process without the protection of PR people and made his own decisions on what to say. He impressed me by not attempting to

cut off the dialog and by resisting the temptation to use the trappings of his office to get his way. The last session was the most exhausting. My PLAYBOY *editor, Barry Golson, had joined me for the final couple of sessions and Brown had to field questions from two sides, with both of us pinning him down on some contradictions. He hung tough and later commented, 'You know . . . I've spent more time with you than on anything this month. And it's made me ask myself whether or not I'd ever want to be President. There are just too many issues on which you have to have positions.' "*

PLAYBOY: As the chief executive of the nation's most populous state at the age of 37, do you ever ask yourself, "God, what am I doing here?"

BROWN: Yeah, the realization of the responsibility, of where I am in this country and what I'm supposed to be doing, sometimes is rather heavy. Yeah, sometimes. Especially in the morning after I've stayed out late at night, it all seems rather absurd.

PLAYBOY: Could it have happened if you hadn't been the son of a popular governor of California?

BROWN: Obviously, the fact that my father was governor had an impact. If my name had been Smith, I probably wouldn't have been nominated for governor or even elected secretary of state. His administration and constituency were very helpful to me and I received a lot of pluses—and some minuses. It made liberals tend to vote for me and conservatives vote against me.

PLAYBOY: On the night of your close victory as governor, you were quoted as telling your father, "I almost lost because of you."

BROWN: I was kidding him because he seemed to be taking so long at the microphone and I was getting restless. It was just my sense of humor, which for some is too dry.

PLAYBOY: Since taking office, however, you've surprised both your father's liberal constituency and the conservatives with your frugal spending policies.

BROWN: I've never been a big spender. Certainly not in my personal life— as my friends will attest—and not in the public offices I have held. I am not a fiscal conservative. I'm just cheap.

PLAYBOY: Would it be unfair to say that your administration and style are partly a revolt against your father?

BROWN: It has some truth to it. Every son emerging from his family has attractions and repulsions. And if some sons try to emulate their father, others may try to replace him. That's the stock analysis, but I think these kinds of relationships are far more complicated. I mean, some would say that carrying on the family business is a high form of admiration.

PLAYBOY: But before following your father into politics, you spent three and a half years in a Jesuit seminary. Wasn't that a pretty extreme response to growing up in politics?

BROWN: Well, I guess. Politics as a way of life didn't seem to me full enough or complete enough, so originally I didn't seek it out. But I don't see anything unusual in the fact that while my father was in public life I should be attracted to a seminary. He was more interested in action, programs and accomplishments and I was always drawn to ideas and philosophy. The seminary was obviously something I would consider, because it dealt with underlying questions and fundamental realities.

PLAYBOY: Didn't your father find your decision to study for the priesthood unusual?

BROWN: There's nothing strange about a young person who is a Catholic thinking about becoming a priest or a nun—at least there wasn't when I was growing up. But my father is a practical person and the idea of going off to a seminary for 15 years to study and pray and maintain virtual silence seemed impractical. It didn't *do* anything. It didn't seem to have a programmatic payoff in the way that becoming a lawyer or a politician might.

Yet, in my own mind, the life in a seminary still has a justification of its own. It's a life of service and I found it very good, at least until the time I decided to leave. The idea that the life of the mind or the spirit has a purpose that transcends mere financial or material considerations is still something I believe in. In other words, I think some of the most important things in an average person's life have nothing to do with government or politics. You can see that reflected not only in people's conversations but in the place that politics has in their everyday lives. Politics is a reasonably serious business and ought to be treated as such. But I don't think you should oversell what politics means, what government can do. I've always felt I could see its limitations because I was brought up in it.

PLAYBOY: A good part of your political style today seems to involve a rejection of an older political form your father typified: promises, programs, glad-handing, ceremonial activities.

BROWN: What can I say? Times are changing. We are coming out of an era of easy growth and up against new limits. Politicians talk of more G.N.P., but it doesn't come so easily and people are worried about the quality of life, not just the quantity of things they accumulate. Television, changing life-styles, the ruthless questioning, disillusion after Vietnam and Watergate—all these things make for different political forms today from those of 20 years ago.

PLAYBOY: What's an example of a political form from your father's era that has changed?

BROWN: I can remember listening to various speeches by politicians from that time and the audience not being very impressed—especially younger kids. College students in the audience were turned off. And I think that's had an impact on my feeling about speeches and rhetoric. I've tried to avoid a lot of that, which is one reason I gave a seven-minute inaugural speech. Of course, another reason is that I didn't start writing it until the night before.

PLAYBOY: What else turned you off traditional politics? Do you remember any incidents from your father's terms as governor?

BROWN: Well, I remember once going with him to a bomb-shelter conference in a New York hotel called by Governor Rockefeller. A number of governors and their military attachés were there. As I recall, so were Arthur Schlesinger and Roswell Gilpatric and Adam Yarmolinsky. All the people there just seemed to assume that the country should embark on a big bomb-shelter program. The discussion revolved around technical questions such as how to notify people when to get into their bomb shelters—by telephone, by electrical hookup or by radio? It is hard for me to remember the details, but that was the drift of the conversation. And so I asked my father to raise the basic question: Did such a bomb-shelter program make any sense? He leaned over to Schlesinger and asked him. Schlesinger turned and said, "Pat, we've got to have them." That was it. No fundamental questions for *that* group.

That meeting has always typified for me a central problem in government: Conventional wisdom and group thinking almost conspire to prevent serious challenge to widely shared assumptions. I take it as a very important thing in government that assumptions in the inner circles be challenged again and again. So I try to read a lot and meet people and encourage a diversity of ideas. Otherwise, you just become the prisoner of your perceptions or of those who provide you with the briefing papers.

PLAYBOY: Weren't you something of a prisoner of narrow perceptions while you were at the seminary?

BROWN: Perhaps. There was no radio, no TV, no newspapers, you didn't read *The New York Times*, much less PLAYBOY. I heard about Sputnik being launched two weeks after it occurred. There were no visitors—except for parents once a month. We were permitted to speak for brief periods after lunch and dinner and for an extended time one day each week.

Life was very simple. A bell would ring at five in the morning and we would get up and then, until nine in the evening, follow a strict schedule that was basically the same each day—meditation, Mass, Latin, waiting on tables, sweeping floors, working in the fields, reading spiritual books: Thomas a Kempis, the history of the Jesuit order and a three-volume work on ascetic virtues.

PLAYBOY: You never felt you'd go nuts, bang your head against the wall and say, "I've got to get out of this prison"?

BROWN: No. It was engrossing and it was where I wanted to be. It was very disciplined, all right, but for a purpose. Every hour of every day was part of the over-all training program to become a Jesuit priest and from the inside it was a very full life. I certainly have no regrets about it.

PLAYBOY: But at some point, obviously, you began to feel differently.

BROWN: Not at first. But after a few years, it seemed too limited and authoritarian for me. I began to feel I was missing something. I thought about it for a long time and then decided to leave and go to Berkeley.

PLAYBOY: Which must have been a remarkable contrast. Why did you decide on Berkeley?

BROWN: I thought it would be good to balance years of traditional education with a more open and skeptical process.

PLAYBOY: What were your first days in Berkeley like?

BROWN: I remember a certain exhilaration at being in a world where you could do anything you wanted—go anywhere, talk to anybody, read anything. It had a certain liberating effect.

But it was also depressing at times. There was a wasteland quality about experiencing the Berkeley campus in 1960—the thousands of people, the impersonal rules and bureaucracy, the lack of direction, the drift, the fragmentation, the void.

PLAYBOY: Were you shocked at any of the permissiveness—sex, drugs, music?

BROWN: In those days, such things didn't jump out at you unless you went looking for them. Whatever people did, they weren't as open about it as they are today.

PLAYBOY: Do you feel your moral outlook and your approach to politics were more influenced by the seminary than by Berkeley?

BROWN: I hope so. Everyone needs enough space and time to be himself. But we also need a life of service and common purpose. The contemporary search to satisfy every impulse that floats through your consciousness is doomed to failure. I don't think that's what people want, anyway.

PLAYBOY: What do you mean by the search to satisfy impulses?

BROWN: Even a superficial reading of history indicates there has rarely been a period of self-indulgence on such a mass scale as there is in America in 1976—the idea that the sum total of life is the accumulation of more and more creature comforts and status symbols that are expensive to maintain. Some of it is normal and good, but it certainly has limits, and I don't support the materialism you find in so many magazines and other media today.

PLAYBOY: Such as in PLAYBOY, for instance?

BROWN: Yes. I had some reservations about this interview because of the values the magazine projects to people, values I don't really agree with. It tends to create an image of self-indulgence that is becoming increasingly inappropriate and ultimately inconsistent with the survival of this country.

I see a need for a more austere and leaner style of life. Certainly, PLAYBOY has had an impact on breaking down some taboos, but it's not clear what the ultimate upshot of that will be. Some might look on it as a liberating philosophy, but on the other hand, it might be very limiting, too.

PLAYBOY: Given your reservations, why *did* you agree to do this interview?

BROWN: Because you were so persistent. And it's a way to communicate with a lot of people.

PLAYBOY: Is there a puritanical streak in you? Your speeches since you took office often emphasize the need to return to hard work and discipline.

BROWN: I wouldn't use the word puritanical, but, sure, I was taught in grammar school by the good nuns that idleness is the Devil's workshop. If you have a totally idle society, you're going to have a decadent society. I think there needs to be a greater sense of service to country and a commitment to resolving some of the issues that are tearing us apart.

PLAYBOY: Is that why you've shunned the perquisites of power—such as the governor's mansion and an official limousine?

BROWN: Yes. I don't see where politicians in this society should act like big shots. I can remember a time when I was going to a Giants game in my father's limousine, driven by a highway patrolman. At one point as we drove through the crowd, people started pounding on the windows. It made me disinclined to have a limousine, let alone drive around in one.

People have a a sense of equality. There is a demand for egalitarianism and institutions today lack credibility—and I mean labor and business just as much as government. Unless leaders become more austere and more closely attuned to what people want, I think many institutions are going to be in for tough times. People are not going to stand for it.

PLAYBOY: But when you give a television speech advocating that people stop consuming so much, your appearance is followed by a stream of commercials selling cars and other products, right?

BROWN: That's the way the system works.

PLAYBOY: But can you really regulate excessive materialism without also regulating advertising and the corporate system behind it?

BROWN: I recognize that we are going through certain economic and environmental changes. Our system worked well when the country was less developed and the air was cleaner and fuel cheaper. But until people begin to recognize the extent of our present dilemma, there is not much we can do about it. So much of what I am doing is attempting to enhance awareness of the fact that the country is changing. Until we are sufficiently awake, there is no point in talking about what we can do about it.

I don't see leadership as just passing laws. The fascination with legislation as the big solution to everything is overplayed. A person in a significant position of power can lead by the questions he raises and the example he sets. A lot of political energy comes from a certain vision, a faith that communicates itself to other people—as with Martin Luther King and other leaders, whose ideas and the way they presented them had a great influence on government. People who stand for an idea that has energy connected with it, that's power.

PLAYBOY: What do you mean by that, precisely?

BROWN: Just that sometimes even powerlessness has a power of its own. Who is it who took India? Some guy in his underwear. Gandhi seemed a pretty strange, powerless character. And yet because of the idea and the moment, he was able to galvanize millions of people. Power may be an idea, a style, things we haven't thought of before. Look at Vietnam. We thought we had the power, but events proved we didn't. The Viet Cong and the North Vietnamese had an idea and a collective purpose.

PLAYBOY: Who do you think has power today?

BROWN: Cesar Chavez has power. George Meany. Perhaps Ivan Illich. The women's movement. The *Whole Earth Catalog*. Bob Dylan is a person with power.

PLAYBOY: Dylan and the *Whole Earth Catalog*—would that imply you have at least some roots in the antimaterialist beatnik movement in the Fifties or that of the hippies in the Sixties?

BROWN: The only time I heard about the beatniks was when one of the priests at the seminary read us an article about them. No, I learned about their antimaterialistic philosophy after I came out and went to Berkeley. I'd go over to Robbie's for chop suey and rice and think, "This is where Allen Ginsberg used to hang out when he wrote *Howl*." A lot of ideas would go around and I used to listen and I learned a lot. I learned as much there as I learned sitting in class. I remember going to Greenwich Village to hear Dylan before anyone knew him.

PLAYBOY: So the governor's an early Dylan fan. What other music do you like? What record would you put on if you were depressed?

BROWN: *Adagio for Strings* by Albinoni or *Sketches of Spain* by Miles Davis.

PLAYBOY: What do you do to relax besides listen to music?

BROWN: I read a lot.

PLAYBOY: What kind of reading—fiction, poetry?

BROWN: Doris Lessing, Hermann Hesse, Robinson Jeffers, Yeats, Frost, Conrad, Joyce, Kafka, Henry Miller.

PLAYBOY: Can you ever really get away from it all?

BROWN: I go out for dinner or to a movie; I spend evenings with friends. A couple of times I've spent a few days at the Trappist monastery in Northern California. I've also gone to Tassajara, a Zen monastery in the mountains near Big Sur. They're two places where I can get away from photographers and tape recorders and let the accumulated images and problems of being governor recede from my mind.

PLAYBOY: Has the job ever gotten to you?

BROWN: There's an inescapable quality about being governor. I have to show up every day and answer to what I've been thinking and where I've been. This is a reality that has at times become oppressive. But as for the responsibility, it hasn't gotten to me yet.

PLAYBOY: When you say oppressive, do you mean it's impinged on your private life?

BROWN: Well, not exactly. I've met a lot of interesting people and certainly one of the best parts of the job is the new people with interesting ideas you run across. Maybe I wouldn't be having this conversation if I weren't governor, and this is interesting.

PLAYBOY: But people in the public eye have their private lives under constant scrutiny. How do you feel about discussing your off-duty hours?

BROWN: Well, about six hours a night I'm unconscious.

PLAYBOY: That still leaves some waking hours when you're not working. Do you really hate talking about your personal life?

BROWN: I don't hate it. But I mean, the personal aspects, why should one discuss them?

PLAYBOY: For one thing, it would be interesting to know if it's possible to lead a normal social life as a young bachelor governor.

BROWN: I think it is. But not if you talk about it all the time.

PLAYBOY: Good point. Say, why do some press reports describe you as humorless?

BROWN: Well, I think I have a good sense of humor. But a lot of the jokes people tell may not be the ones I happen to be telling or listening to. I don't watch the football games on weekends, so perhaps I lose some of the folklore.

PLAYBOY: You don't follow football? That may be the most controversial statement you've made as a politician. But getting back to the issue of privacy, wasn't there a lot of publicity because you started dating some Hollywood people?

BROWN: There wasn't that much publicity. I took out Liv Ullman for several months and no one knew about it. It took the press several months to get on to it.

PLAYBOY: How did you manage that?

BROWN: I wasn't that well known. I took her to a fund-raising dinner and no one recognized her. We sat in the back and listened. Then we went over to the Figaro for dinner.

PLAYBOY: Are you recognized now when you try to slip away from ceremonial occasions?

BROWN: Now, yes. I wasn't a couple of years ago.

PLAYBOY: Does it bother you?

BROWN: No. That's just the way it is.

PLAYBOY: Most people don't experience the transformation from obscurity to fame in a matter of a couple of years. How do you respond to the experience?

BROWN: My response is that it just is.

PLAYBOY: But some of it must be exciting.

BROWN: Obviously, it's exciting. There's a certain vanity in all this. That's presumably why people seek office—for some reason, they're attracted to it. I'd say I have mixed feelings.

PLAYBOY: Did you have trouble campaigning for the governorship as a single person? *The New York Times Magazine* said that you had compiled information on your opponents because you feared they were going to accuse you of being a homosexual—is that true?

BROWN: You never know what to expect in a political campaign. Primary contests among candidates of the same political party often degenerate into name-calling and groundless charges because of the lack of ideological differences. My staff did research the public records and statements of my opponents, but by any standard, the whole campaign was clean and very fair. As to what my opponents might accuse me of, I suppose in a campaign you can expect to be called anything from Communist to crook.

PLAYBOY: But why *that* particular name?

BROWN: Homosexual innuendo is a cheap shot that could be used against any single politician. It's like Red-baiting in the Fifties. Now I'm accused of running around the state with too many women. You're damned if you do and damned if you don't.

PLAYBOY: If you were to run for national office, do you think being single would be a political liability?

BROWN: No. It wasn't for Pierre Trudeau or Edward Heath. Sometimes it may even be an asset.

PLAYBOY: Do you intend to have a family?

BROWN: I have always assumed I would.

PLAYBOY: Do you think marriage can work when you have a career as consuming as yours?

BROWN: That's obviously a problem. I don't have an answer for that. Perhaps there are periods in one's life that require a commitment that isn't compatible with a family.

PLAYBOY: But some politicians manage to do it.

BROWN: Do they? I don't know, maybe some do. But if you look at the number of political divorces, maybe a lot of them don't manage in reality. The role of a leader takes tremendous emotional, spiritual and intellectual effort. And how many masters can you serve? I like the idea of the dream, but I don't quite see how you put it all together.

PLAYBOY: Do you feel the values of the traditional nuclear family are outdated?

BROWN: For most people, these are still very strong values.

PLAYBOY: But do you agree with them?

BROWN: I respect them. I'm not ready to offer any theory on how people should get along with one another. But I have no doubt the family has lasted a long time and will survive its latest critics.

PLAYBOY: One tradition that may not last is that of the man as dominant figure in the family. How do you feel about women's liberation?

BROWN: I have mixed feelings. It's liberating, but it's also creating new instabilities. Things had to change, but it's an emancipation from a traditional family structure that's served us very well. The family's being brought under pressure like it's never been before and relationships are hard enough.

PLAYBOY: If you have a family, won't you eventually have to use them as political props, as most public officials do?

BROWN: I have reservations about using my personal life for politics. After a while, it's possible to see your personal relationships as part of an over-all political equation. After that, it's not too difficult to become just another political commodity to be distributed through the media. But when it's over, after you've left office, you might not have much to show for it. Politics, like most of life, is transitory, and the scrapbooks and headlines that you accumulate won't be much comfort in your old age.

PLAYBOY: Is that why some people have described you as a loner?

BROWN: Perhaps I haven't kissed as many babies as my predecessors did.

PLAYBOY: But there's more to it than that. There's an impression that the private Jerry Brown is some kind of mystic who may be off meditating on a mountaintop at any given moment.

BROWN: Well, in some people's minds, politics is like a club. There are certain restaurants and gatherings where journalists, inside dopesters and hangers-on get together and form a type of inbred political establishment. Maybe I don't spend as much time as I should with these people. And I don't attempt to broadcast how I spend all my waking moments, especially when I have time off. So it's possible for some to conclude that I am off on a mountaintop, whereas I may be just sitting in a restaurant or going to a movie with a friend. I just don't see the point in always surrounding myself with political types.

PLAYBOY: But you go to fund raisers and other functions for politicians. You seem to get along fine with them.

BROWN: I hope so. Although I have removed some of the trappings and ceremonial aspects of this job, I am trying to work with those who make the political world function. The process needs to be opened up, but those who are an essential part of it can't be underestimated or ignored.

PLAYBOY: So this image of you as an ascetic is also exaggerated—you and those who work for you live fairly comfortable lives, don't you?

BROWN: That's true; I make $49,000 a year and have a nice home in Los Angeles and to a lot of people in this country, that's hardly ascetic. But I *have* cut back compared with my predecessor. Salaries of my staff were reduced seven percent. I've sold the limousines, cut out the inaugural ball, moved into my own apartment.

PLAYBOY: What do you have against the new governor's mansion?

BROWN: It's a huge place with nine bedrooms and six bathrooms—I'd feel like Casper the Ghost wandering through it. Besides, I don't think it's appropriate for a governor to live like that when so many people are being asked to sacrifice. That empty Taj Mahal that Reagan built could be one of the key symbols of 1976.

PLAYBOY: Are your politics a definite break with traditional Democratic politics as we've known them up to now?

BROWN: I'm a critic of centralization of power in Washington and of basing a political philosophy on the assumption of unlimited resources and the ability to draw on the resources of Third and Fourth World countries at a ridiculously low price.

PLAYBOY: All this sounds rather vague. How would people who think they agree with what you're saying be guided as to which Presidential candidate to vote for—say in the case of Humphrey versus Ford?

BROWN: Even if Ford and Humphrey campaign on their traditional positions, there's no doubt in my mind people should vote for Humphrey. He's concerned about taking care of people who can't take care of themselves and Democratic Party programs *have* worked. I do say this: The social programs we're embarked on now cost much more than we thought ten years ago and we have to recognize this.

PLAYBOY: Yet you want to decentralize power.

BROWN: That's been a traditional conservative idea, yes. I'm a governor of a state and I run up against rules from Washington that require staples, not paper clips, on food stamps—any number of things that make me feel that power ought to be returned to the state and local levels.

PLAYBOY: It's hard to see where you would stand on the issues. Is there a deliberate vagueness to your political approach?

BROWN: It is true that I don't often put forth a laundry list of six-point programs or appoint blue-ribbon commissions to come up with well-publicized solutions that don't do anything. I find that approach to have just about run its course.

Politicians are supposed to have all the answers, the grand solution. When I get questioned and say I don't know or turn the question back with another question, journalists get very upset. Politicians and the press often just go through a ritual. People think a question and an answer have been exchanged in a traditional interview, but in reality they haven't.

PLAYBOY: Obviously, voters have liked the fact that you say, "I don't know." But isn't that just a clever political technique? If you can't be pinned down on critical issues, how can your success or failure be measured?

BROWN: I am not holding out a poster with a ten-point agenda on it saying,

"Here it is, folks, do you like it?" But I do think you can judge me by whatever criteria you wish. You might start with how other governors are doing today or how my predecessors did. I don't really think that things can be as well programed in this particular period as they have been in the past. This is a time of transition and often we have to just let things emerge. Sometimes asking a question or exposing a contradiction is more valuable than a superficial program that purports to do more than it really can.

PLAYBOY: We come back to it again: Since you don't state your programs, it will be very difficult to judge their progress or failure.

BROWN: They emerge. I think they emerge through the dialectical process. They come out; things happen. I really don't think there's a problem in judging the progress or failure of my programs. There's no end to analyses of my administration. I meet often with people. I presented a 1000-page budget to the legislature. Last year I signed 1183 bills and vetoed 148. I have made dozens of appointments. All this gives a clear indication of my political philosophy and what I'm trying to accomplish. If you're interested in agendas, you might read the inaugural speeches of the last five governors. They say much the same thing: Down with crime, unemployment and taxes.

PLAYBOY: But there must be many conservatives who misread you because they believe you offer their brand of fiscal conservatism.

BROWN: Maybe they like what I am doing because I express some of the basic values they share.

PLAYBOY: Then why, in fact, do you call yourself a Democrat?

BROWN: I've run a Democratic administration, but to try to pigeonhole me within a framework that may have been more appropriate ten or twenty years ago is pointless. It's sloganeering to say that's Democratic, that's Republican. There are elements of both.

PLAYBOY: But if you fail to criticize Democratic candidates for supporting big-spending programs you obviously don't believe in, don't you sound like a basic party man, keeping your differences inside the club? What makes you in any sense a "new" politician?

BROWN: I'm trying to carve out a political program that responds to the needs of California. I've focused on the fact that a lot of the social programs aren't working the way we thought they would. The Democratic Party has stood for helping people, minimizing inequalities, being in the forefront, being experimental, and Humphrey, Jackson and Ted Kennedy all stand for those things. On specific issues, OK. Did I support the Vietnam war? No. Humphrey had a position on that which I opposed. Very simple, not much to talk about. So I think it's a complex reality that you have to take issue by issue. I'm trying to be open about what government can and should do. More than that I don't know. I hope it's new. I come from a new generation. And yes, politics isn't a question of trotting out your six or seven issues. It's a matter of experience, of development, and everyone's ready to develop at a particular moment.

PLAYBOY: Well, let's try a number of specific issues, anyway. Where do you stand on welfare?

BROWN: Reagan wrote a welfare-reform plan. Reagan solved the welfare problem, so how can that be an issue?

PLAYBOY: You're being facetious, of course.

BROWN: Well, he *said* he reformed it. He wrote a law and said it was a reform, so why is that a problem? It's there, it's still the law, nobody's changed it. Welfare hasn't gone up very much since I've been governor.

PLAYBOY: But what's *your* philosophy, *your* program?

BROWN: We have a welfare program in California. We have food stamps. We have Medi-Cal. We put hundreds of thousands of people to work through direct and indirect investment. But I would prefer to see stable neighborhoods and communities where people have jobs and a future and are part of the mainstream of society.

PLAYBOY: But certainly most people on welfare are unemployable, aren't they?

BROWN: Many are. But many could make important contributions to society. I believe most of them would much prefer to be a part of the mainstream and contribute their energy and be compensated accordingly. How we arrange that, given the economic and political rules of the road, I can't answer. But I know that societies don't long endure with so much energy unfocused and so many people with no self-respecting role. Matching people to the work—that's the political challenge of the next ten years.

PLAYBOY: On the national level, Ford's employment policies seem to be pretty much like yours: leaving it to the private sector.

BROWN: No. I wouldn't agree with that. I don't see much leadership or public investment or imaginative reordering of our priorities.

PLAYBOY: How can any of these things be accomplished without raising taxes?

BROWN: Taxes fund government programs, but most economists say that if we stimulate the private economy, we will generate adequate employment.

PLAYBOY: If you stimulate the economy in that fashion, you generate inflation, don't you?

BROWN: It is a complex equation. If I had a specific program, I would put it forth right now. I have suggested work sharing and flat pay raises as alternatives.

PLAYBOY: Are you for less government or more government?

BROWN: It depends upon the situation. I am very concerned about the increasing centralization of social services. Too often the intended beneficiaries get only what is trickled down through the increasingly powerful bureaucracies. I see a new class growing in political power. Instead of trickling the wealth down through the corporations, you trickle it down through the public bureaucracies, but the people at the bottom are still getting drops.

PLAYBOY: You have attacked Big Government; what about Big Business? Are you for cutting back on Government regulations of the large corporations?

BROWN: No. I would like to make the regulators more independent of corporate influence and I would question how big corporations really have to be in order to serve the economy.

Certainly, large corporations have their problems, but my experience with government suggests that the problems are just as great in this area. I preside over the biggest state government in the country and to get things done is not easy—not because people lack good will; it is just difficult to make large-scale institutions respond in the way that you might like. So even though you may not like multinational corporations, I am not sure turning them over to the state would make things much better. Maybe we need a combination, some new political or economic forms that we haven't formulated as yet.

PLAYBOY: You appear to share a large number of views with your conservative predecessor. As Reagan's successor, do you have any special insight into what kind of President he would be?

BROWN: I think he would continue the stalemate that exists between the Congress and the President. He is not one to question assumptions. He prefers inertia with a conservative cast. He would be slow to intervene in economic problems and not too aggressive with respect to protecting the environment.

I assume he would put more money into defense and attempt to cut the Federal bureaucracy. He would emphasize Big Business and the private sector. But given the reality of a Democratic Congress, I would expect drift and stalemate.

But I wouldn't overemphasize the impact of a Reagan Presidency. After all, we have had the best and the brightest in Washington and with them we got into one of the worst wars in our history. So I would be modest about predicting who will get us where this year.

PLAYBOY: Speaking of who will do what this year, what if the Democratic Party were to be deadlocked? Would you be willing to accept the Presidential nomination?

BROWN: I think it's a little presumptuous.

PLAYBOY: The question or the idea?

BROWN: The whole subject. It's an eventuality that seems rather remote to me, but I'm not making any Shermanlike statements. I'm living each day as it comes.

PLAYBOY: Does it surprise you that you should be considered for national office after such a brief time as governor?

BROWN: In one sense it surprises me, but what I'm saying has obviously

caught on with people. It's true there hasn't been time for much programmatic action, but there's a certain identification voters get about political
leaders. I'm not sure people care about all the issues raised. They get a certain feel for a person and that intuition probably decides most elections.

PLAYBOY: Does the eventuality—however remote—awe you?

BROWN: The responsibility, yes; it's an awesome one. And the requirement
to have solutions to so many problems, the demands to respond—"What
should we do? Lead us! Tell us!"—it's quite a burden, an awesome one and
a surprising one.

PLAYBOY: Do you think the governorship might be a better form of training for the Presidency than a seat in the Senate?

BROWN: Certainly, running a state enterprise has within it the same kinds
of challenges as those of a Federal office.

PLAYBOY: Even though you say you're not a candidate, there's been
speculation in the press that you might be a contender, so we'd like to
ask you about some national issues. Is that legitimate?

BROWN: It's legitimate.

PLAYBOY: How do you feel about military spending?

BROWN: I'd be surprised if there were dramatic savings to be made.

PLAYBOY: So you don't go along with liberal thinking on cutting the
defense budget?

BROWN: Military costs have gone up and I don't realistically think the
budget will be cut.

PLAYBOY: What about Kissinger's *détente* policy?

BROWN: I'd have to give that one a lot of thought. I don't think you can
be naïve about the world. It's a competitive place and the strong survive
and the weak don't. We're still a few generations away from the time
when swords will be turned into plowshares, and until then, we ought to be
ready.

PLAYBOY: Ready against whom?

BROWN: Well, Russia's obviously the strongest military power. We're all
becoming more interdependent, but we ought to realize that without substantial military strength, we're obviously jeopardizing our security. I
wonder what exactly will be the consequences of some of the agreements
that Kissinger is apparently bringing about. I've got some doubts.

PLAYBOY: Then on *détente* you're less optimistic than some Republican
spokesmen about the prospect of peaceful coexistence.

BROWN: Well, I get the impression that we're being pushed around a lot
and that America has become a big sap for the rest of the countries. And
I don't like it. We have a lot of strength, so I don't see why we should have
guilt feelings and act like we're always the fall guy.

PLAYBOY: The rest of the countries? Which countries are pushing us
around?

BROWN: Well, look at the vote in the UN on the Zionist resolution. And when the OPEC nations want to raise the price of oil, they get to do it.

PLAYBOY: You mean we should have prevented them from raising their prices?

BROWN: They've got that oil and they don't have much else, so they better get the price they can while the getting's good. But I think it indicates a certain weakness in our country.

PLAYBOY: So if our strength were credible, we should be able to set world prices in a way that would benefit us?

BROWN: I would rather we be in that position than not, and then be given the discretion to make that decision.

PLAYBOY: But should any country have the right to dominate other countries that way?

BROWN: Look, America's not perfect, but it's been a country of freedom, of a certain brand of liberty, and it's my country. I'm going to do my best to see it prosper, and I'm not making any apologies to *anybody*. It's easy to criticize, but other countries have done far worse. A lot of people have a death instinct about America that I don't share.

PLAYBOY: But you've said that you're against a policy that draws on the resources of the Third and Fourth World countries at a "ridiculously low price." Aren't these the same nations that are making a "big sap" of us?

BROWN: I would like to see those countries grow and prosper; I would like to share the fruits of this planet with everybody. But at the same time, the U.S. has a certain historical momentum that *will* be maintained. We have a certain pride of national character and you flout it at your peril. Right now, no country has done so well at attacking itself as the United States of America. The problems are how do we put it back together and how do we inspire people with confidence and pride in country and family and the things that normally hold people together? Today, it's very easy to find out what's wrong, the pessimistic side. Mere criticism won't build this unity.

PLAYBOY: But isn't that what you're doing? You've said throughout this interview that you're questioning assumptions about the way our institutions work. Aren't you one of the doubting Thomases, too?

BROWN: I'm raising questions, yes, but I'm providing answers. I'm engaged in the process of running a government.

PLAYBOY: From which you say people shouldn't expect much.

BROWN: I'm trying not to kid them about what government can and can't do.

PLAYBOY: And that doesn't raise people's hopes or restore their confidence.

BROWN: I guess the sum total of all this is that America faces some serious problems, and I'm not asking critics to refrain from their activities, nor am I refraining from asking questions myself. I think we have the ability and resources and spirit, but we need a greater awareness of how difficult things are.

PLAYBOY: When you say critics, you obviously include the press. Do you think the press has brought about these difficulties?

BROWN: Every institution in society has come under increasing scrutiny. Obviously, things have to be brought out, exposed. But if you stand back and look at it, there's been a tremendous volume of negative energy moving in this country. And there should be ideals, a common purpose. That common purpose is not being enhanced by all the attacks on our institutions.

PLAYBOY: Is it the press that's responsible for the loss of American ideals?

BROWN: I wouldn't leave it at just the press. But the press is looking at what's going on and it sees things, then it wants to see more and report more. And what seems to sell most on television and in newspapers are the things that are wrong with the country and things that are wrong with people. That has a momentum and a logic of its own, and it's gathering speed. Where it all goes, I just wonder.

PLAYBOY: Do you mean the press shouldn't have reported the abuses of such agencies as the CIA and the FBI?

BROWN: I have very mixed feelings. There've been abuses; these agencies have gotten out of control and have to be brought back into control. But in the process, we may end up throwing out the baby with the bath water. A vigorous free press is essential, but the constant harping on things that have gone on in this Government—I really wonder if they're that different from what's gone on in other governments.

PLAYBOY: That seems far from a liberal view of the press. You learned the truth about the Vietnam war—which you opposed—through the "constant harping" of the press, didn't you?

BROWN: As things come out, we have to know about them, but all I'm saying is that the country may be weaker, that's all. I'm glad the Pentagon papers were released and—

PLAYBOY: So you think Ellsberg did the correct thing in Xeroxing the Pentagon papers and turning them over to the public?

BROWN: In that instance, I'm glad he did. As a matter of fact, I was in the courthouse when he was acquitted. In any case, these things had to come out and the same can be said about the CIA and the FBI. But as a person in government, I have to wonder how we restore confidence in our institutions.

PLAYBOY: But you seem to be deploring *both* the abuses of government *and* their exposure by the press.

BROWN: The press is just a vehicle. And I suppose if we ever get to the final chapter of wrongdoing, the book can be closed. But I really wonder, given human nature and human history, whether we'll ever reach that point. And if that's the case, then the amount of criticism will keep increasing, and that's a rather foreboding possibility.

PLAYBOY: Again, you don't seem to be addressing the question. Was it Woodward and Bernstein who were responsible for Watergate or was it Richard Nixon? Was it Johnson and Kennedy who gave us Vietnam or was it David Halberstam? Very simply, toward which view do you lean?

BROWN: Well, I lean toward the view that the level of official corruption is intolerable. What I don't know is, are there any human beings so pure, any government so beyond reproach by the existing standards that we'll ever be satisfied? I wonder, since these things went on in former times, why they didn't seem to bother anyone then. Where do we finally hit bottom? Where do we finally purify the Government?

PLAYBOY: Shouldn't the press expose the fact that the CIA, for instance, tried to kill the heads of foreign governments? Shouldn't such exposure continue?

BROWN: I'm not sure that governments down through history were much different. And I would say that we haven't *begun* to go through major scandals. After we finish with government, we'll go to business and other institutions, and there'll be no less human frailty and malevolence uncovered.

PLAYBOY: Weren't you shocked by some of the revelations?

BROWN: No doubt about it. I never dreamed the FBI would be fomenting discord between one radical group and another or that corporations would be handing out millions of dollars in bribes and campaign contributions. I've been around government all my life and I was shocked.

PLAYBOY: When you say our standards of purity may be too high, are you proposing that we lower them?

BROWN: I don't think we can go back. Once these things happen, it's like a Greek tragedy. If something's done wrong at some point in time, it tends to persist like a curse, as in the house of Atreus, from one generation to another. And that may be where we are. We can't unring the bell.

PLAYBOY: You pose the problem, but if you agree that abuses must be exposed and at the same time regret the effects of the exposure, what do you propose we *do*? Is the press supposed to be more tolerant?

BROWN: A little bit of tolerance might go a long way.

PLAYBOY: Which may not be a practical remedy. Do you have something concrete to suggest?

BROWN: I'm certainly taking drastic measures to assure the integrity of this administration. I've pushed California's political-reform initiative for this reason. Viewed by traditional standards, it's absurd: No one may take more than ten dollars from a lobbyist. Every gift over ten dollars, relatives excepted, must be reported. This, in effect, makes parolees out of politicians. It needed to be done, but I just can't help wondering how difficult it will be to hold to these standards.

PLAYBOY: So you're inclined to be pessimistic?

BROWN: This is where we are in 1976. The press is playing its role, the politicians are playing their role and the Greek chorus is out there watching it all. That's just the way it is. I don't think I can do anything about it, but it doesn't stop me from wishing it were better.

Playboy Interview Interludes

Every article about me recently has been spouting the same bullshit about my politics. The only reason I was for the Nixon administration was because I knew that's who would end the war. None of those jerks walking around with those signs was ever going to end the war.

Bob Hope, December 1973

There are two things going on in PLAYBOY. On the one hand, it has some of the most important interviews that are being published. On the other hand, I think the magazine is bought, essentially, for the centerfold. It's the purchase of naked women.

Jane Fonda, May 1974

Let's assume it's 1980 and present Soviet strategic building programs—and our own limited programs—have continued at their present levels. That means the Soviets will probably have strategic superiority. . . . With half our oil still coming from the Middle East, it's clear the Soviets would have a great temptation to tighten their hold on that jugular.

Admiral Elmo Zumwalt, June 1974

I've never believed in that guru trip about drugs. You know, God, nirvana, that bullshit. I just like to gobble the stuff right out on the street and see what happens, just stomp on my own accelerator.

Hunter Thompson, November 1974

JIMMY CARTER

November 1976

Interviewer: Robert Scheer

The interview that nearly overwhelmed a presidential campaign began inauspiciously enough. While the issue carrying Jerry Brown's interview was still in production, Robert Scheer was assigned to cover the campaign of a Georgia governor who was showing surprising results in the first few primaries. Scheer's assignment was merely to write about the candidate, but he and his editor, Barry Golson, had discussd the possibility of getting Jimmy Carter to agree to a full-length interview. Getting that much time from an active candidate seemed a long shot at best, but, with the approval of editorial director Arthur Kretchmer, the magazine funded Scheer's travels through the primary states.

When the Playboy Interview with Brown hit the newsstands in April, Powell and Jordan were impressed. Brown announced his candidacy the week the issue appeared and promptly beat Carter in the first few primaries he entered—too late, as it turned out, to affect the final outcome. But Carter's aides had done an informal survey of voters in Maryland, the first state in which Brown defeated Carter, and found that many of the voters had been exposed to Brown's unorthodox views from two sources: in profile on "60 Minutes," and in his Play Interview.

The journalist found that he was one among many requesting time alone with the candidate. Carter aides Jody Powell and Hamilton Jordan were familiar with Scheer's work, and, in the interest of documenting the "article" Scheer was preparing for PLAYBOY, finally arranged for a fifteen-minute session with Carter during a flight from San Francisco. At a press conference that morning, Carter had said that though he held nothing against homosexuals, he considered their behavior a "sin." This provided an opening topic for Scheer: What *was* the candidate's idea of "sinful" behavior, and how did that square with his supposedly liberal politics? It was the sort of discussion Carter was not used to having with other members of the traveling press, and the conversation became lively and animated. From that point on, Scheer continued to inveigle more and more time with Carter from his aides, often in ten-minute snatches, sometimes for as long as an hour.

Although there was never a moment when it was decided that Carter was in fact doing *the* Playboy Interview, from then on Scheer was included in the schedule of exclusive interview sessions with Carter. (Scheer also recalls that Powell and Jordan had another motive for making further interview appointments: "Every time I got resistance from Powell when I asked for another session, I reminded him that I'd *already* asked Carter all that stuff about homosexuality and life-styles, so did Jody want an entire interview composed of *that*?") Within six weeks, Scheer had amassed about five hours on tape, and the topics ranged from their opening discussion to Carter's stands on most domestic and foreign policy issues.

Several times a week Scheer would call Golson in Chicago to report on how it was coming. The two of them became more strongly convinced than ever that Carter's religion was a topic worth pursuing, since he had already become impatient when Scheer had pressed him on it. At the time, Carter was wearing his religion on his sleeve, telling reporters that he prayed up to twenty-five times a day, lacing his speeches with references to God and Sunday School, and making a point of being photographed going in and out of his Baptist church. What interested Scheer was how Carter's pious image related to what the reporter knew already about the man's family and aides—many of them hard-drinking, Commandment-breaking types. Would Carter surround himself with religious zealots? Would he appoint judges on their moral stands? Would he support or oppose birth control, abortion, drug laws? Scheer already had some of this on tape, but more time was clearly needed with the candidate.

As the Democratic convention drew near, it became apparent that Carter had the nomination sewn up, so Scheer asked Powell for a final, long session after the convention. Powell agreed. Scheer then suggestd that Golson join him for the final interview, as he had with Governor Brown six months earlier.

Scheer and Golson arrived in Atlanta Tuesday afternoon, July 20. They met Powell for dinner and discussed the campaign. Scheer said that they planned to ask Carter to explain his religious beliefs as clearly as possible, once and for all. Powell urged him to do so; he had tried to get the message out himself many times, Powell said, and felt it was important that the public know that Carter was *not* holier-than-thou, as his image suggested. "How could he possibly have guys like Hamilton and me around if that were true?" Powell said.

When dinner was over, Powell wished them luck on their interview the next morning. It occurred to the journalists, many months later, that Powell may have conveyed the theme of their discussion by telephone to Carter that evening.

The next day the men flew to Plains. On September 30, after the uproar had begun, Golson wrote an article for *The New York Times* recalling that afternoon:

> When we arrived at Carter's home we said hello to Rosalynn, and, instead of walking back to his study, Carter suggested we sit around less formally in armchairs in his living room. For the next hour, we spoke of Vietnam, of tax reform, of multinational corporations, of European communism. I was a little awed by the occasion, and Scheer, a former editor of *Ramparts,* was persistent and serious. I stress this to say that Carter was responding to us as journalists. He had come to know Scheer as a well-informed interviewer, and the fact is I didn't show up wearing Bunny ears, either.
>
> I don't say he was unaware that we represented PLAYBOY, but as an editor who doesn't find journalism and nude pictures incompatible, I can tell you that sex—or even slang—wasn't part of the atmosphere that afternoon.
>
> When our time was up . . . I remember making one remark, ironic in hindsight: "We'll be publishing shortly before the election, so credit us—or blame us," and we all had a good laugh about that. As press aide Rex Granum stood holding the door open, we said to Carter, more as a parting comment than anything else, that the topic most of our friends were uneasy about was their perception of the Baptist faith. Carter responded by asking if we'd attended any of his Sunday School lessons at the Plains church, and went on to say it was a good way to learn something about the Baptist religion. I think Scheer and I both felt he was speaking to us personally in those opening moments, but as we continued it struck us that we were hearing a fresh, impromptu declaration of what his religion meant to him.
>
> A minute or two into it, we interrupted and got his agreement to keep taping the conversation, and he went on for another eight or nine minutes to speak about small-town religion, people's frailties and human temptation. Perhaps the biblical example he chose to illustrate temptation shouldn't have been lust, but in context it just didn't seem that illogical or unnatural. . . .

When Scheer and Golson drove away from Carter's home, they were elated—but not because Carter had used words like "screw" or "shack up." Not even because he had chosen an example of open-mindedness he thought two reporters from PLAYBOY would find appropriate and understandable. (Incidentally, although it has become known as the Carter lust-in-my-heart interview, he did not say precisely that. The quote was, "I've looked on a lot of women with lust. I've committed adultery in my heart many times." An important distinction, and especially so to Carter: According to Christ's "impossible standards," lusting is the same as committing adultery—in one's heart—although *every* normal man lusts and is forgiven for it.) What was journalistically interesting was that they had broken through a very guarded politician's reserve.

When they discussed it months later, the two men disagreed on Carter's motives during the doorway scene. Golson attributed the moment to naïveté on Carter's part, traceable to the candidate's soft-spoken words just seconds earlier: "I never knew anything except going to church. My wife and I grew up in innocent times." It seemed to Golson that Carter, frustrated after months of trying to tell Scheer that his deep religious faith didn't necessarily mean he would be intolerant, decided one last time to try to put the thought into language his listeners would understand. Golson felt he and Scheer must have seemed like a couple of wayward sons to Carter at that moment, and that he had used a couple of overly colloquial phrases to make his point as one of "the guys." Scheer, on the other hand, took a harder view, arguing that Carter knew precisely what he was doing—and that was playing to what he thought of as a PLAYBOY constituency. Carter, in Scheer's view, was being as cynical about his religious views as he was about other issues, playing to different audiences with deliberate forethought, and it was the unmasking of this cynicism that made it worthwhile journalism, and not merely the sensationalism of a few "vulgarisms," to use the term coined by The New York Times.

"The life-style questions we asked *were* more important than the political issues," Scheer said four years later. "It was the line of inquiry that ought to have been pursued by other journalists as well, because it showed—as his neatly packaged homilies on political issues didn't—how much Carter would shift with the breeze." It also foreshadowed another election campaign—that of 1980—in which religion and politics became irrevocably intermixed.

In any case, if the "vulgarisms" didn't seem that sensational in themselves to the two journalists, something else Carter had said *did* seem newsworthy. At the end of his monologue, with his fist clenched, he had said, "I don't think I would ever take on the same frame of mind that Nixon or Johnson did—lying, cheating, and distorting the truth. I think my religious beliefs alone would prevent that from happening." This was a slam at Lyndon Johnson at a time when the Texas vote was up for grabs, and *that* seemed to be the scoop to Scheer and Golson. (In fact, it was this remark that Golson placed beneath Carter's picture on the interview page, and not the lust quote.)

After editing the final portion of the interview, Scheer returned to California to write his article that would accompany the interview: "Jimmy, We Hardly Know Y'All." In this piece, Scheer, who had spent nearly three months interviewing Carter's friends and family, first introduced many readers to the next president's complicated Georgia roots. Some critics were to say later that the article was superior to the interview in assessing Carter's character. And it provided yet another newsbreak once the press stumbled on it: Hamilton Jordan's vow that "if, after the inauguration, you find a Cy Vance as secretary of state and Zbigniew Brzezinski as head of National Security, then I would say we failed. And I'd quit."

Back in Chicago, Golson and Kretchmer were preparing for what they knew was going to be a sellout issue: Certainly the remarks about lust would get attention, but Carter had also impugned LBJ, sworn never to intervene in a foreign war, explained his friendship with Hunter Thompson and Bob Dylan, discussed the possibility of assassination, and taken a relatively hard line against the Soviets and the SALT agreements. In a tired, vulnerable moment, he had also taken an uncharacteristically ferocious swipe at the press corps: "The national news media have absolutely no interest in issues *at all*. . . . There's nobody on the press plane who would ask an issue question unless he thought he could trick me into some crazy statement."

It was as sweeping a look as anyone had been given at Jimmy Carter. The editors were proud of Scheer's work, and, though it may be hard to believe in retrospect, maximizing the sensational publicity was not their major concern. Seeing that the interview was handled fairly was in fact a more urgent topic. Any number of statements, plucked out of context, could have made headlines, and it became clear to Scheer, Kretchmer, and Golson that just one month before the election they were handling something explosive.

It takes about three weeks to print six million copies of PLAYBOY. Once the first copies were being handled by printers and production people in early September, Kretchmer made the decision to release the entire text ahead of schedule—precisely because the editors were worried about the number of incendiary remarks that could have leaked to the press. A number of PLAYBOY executives were furious that the text of an interview should be released gratis three weeks before the magazine was available for purchasing on the newsstands. They were overruled.

The editors decided to mail over one thousand preprints of the interview to nearly every media outlet in the nation. Scheer and Golson conferred about the best, most "respectable" way to break the news the night before the preprints were mailed out. Golson tried *The New York Times,* telling a senior editor there that the paper could have it if they agreed to treat certain remarks circumspectly, and kept them in context. *The Times* declined the exclusive.

Golson then called the local AP writer in Chicago, told *him* that AP could have a print exclusive, but only if AP agred to lead with a general summary of the interview, and not the "lust" or LBJ quotes. AP agreed.

He then called Tom Brokaw and made the same arrangement with the "Today" show, agreeing that he and Scheer would appear on the show to describe the background of the interview. Brokaw accepted the ground rules. (Neither the AP story nor Brokaw's report mentioned Carter's lust comments until well into their accounts.) Scheer and Golson flew into New York, appeared on the show, waited for the morning newspapers to pick up the story, and then stepped back from the blast.

By midafternoon of September 20, there were headlines in every newspaper in the country. By the next day, they were in virtually every newspaper in the world: "SEX, SIN, TEMPTATION!" "I'VE COMMITTED ADULTERY IN MY HEART!" At the journalists' New York hotel, extra lines were put in to handle calls from reporters wanting to interview the interviewers. Carter's whistle-stop train ride, which had begun that morning, nearly ground to a halt. People in the press compartment were lined up, sharing hastily Xeroxed copies of the interview. The journalists told other reporters the same thing over and over again: "Yes, it was a sincere statement of his religious beliefs." "No, we did not bring up the subject of his sex life."

Days later, there was still no letup. "Is Carter Screwing Up Campaign?" blared the headlines. Columnists couldn't churn out copy quickly enough, ministers couldn't find words to express their shock, and Republicans couldn't reach reporters fast enough to file their denunciations. Cartoonists around the world lunged for their drawing boards.

As for Carter, at first he held firm. Asked initially about the interview, he said he hadn't had a chance to read it all, that he usually looked at other parts of the magazine first. Asked later, he called it a good, thorough interview about which he had no regrets. Powell also took the offensive: "This is the message we've been trying to get out all along."

Scheer, still on assignment, stayed on the campaign trail with Carter. On September 25, when Carter's schedule had him in Texas, the press, apparently sated for the moment with reportage on the sexual comments, finally discovered the LBJ quotes. At the Austin airport, reporters pressed Carter on his remarks. He said: "The unfortunate thing about the magazine interview was the postinterview statement about President Johnson, which completely distorts my feeling about him." Carter explained that, after the interview had ended, "there was a summary made" that "unfortunately equated" what had been said about Nixon with Johnson.

The implication was that the PLAYBOY editors had made the summary, not Carter. As Carter began to walk away, a number of reporters rushed off to file their stories. Scheer, meanwhile, was astonished at Carter's denial and rushed back to the press plane to pick up his tape recorder containing the original tape of the talk in Plains. He returned carrying the recorder. The reporters were still milling around and several of them turned to Scheer for a response to Carter's denial. No, said Scheer, the summary was Carter's own words, as the tapes would show; it was all very clearly on the record. He pointed to the tape recorder and caught the eye of Carter, who was starting to walk away. The reporters rushed up to Carter and stopped him.

Yes, Carter finally admitted, they *were* his words; he had made a mistake and he apologized for it. "But," he added, "I thought the interview was over. The PLAYBOY folks were leaving the house."

Under continuing pressure, Carter told a TV interviewer that PLAYBOY had not sent him the raw transcripts, as Scheer had said he would. The implication was that if the editors had kept their word, he would have been able to delete the troublesome remarks. It was, of course, wishful thinking: The policy of the magazine was to provide transcripts to a subject when asked, but only for purposes of checking accuracy, not for retraction. And in fact Golson had made an attempt to reach Powell in early September to deliver the transcripts confidentially to him, but, in the frenzy of the campaign, Powell had not managed to return his calls. In any case, the point was moot: PLAYBOY would not have acceded to any deletions.

Then came a flap over a series of Republican ads that had been placed in more than three hundred and fifty southern newspapers, showing a *Newsweek* cover of Gerald Ford and the PLAYBOY cover and suggesting voters make a choice based on the respectability of the two publications. While PLAYBOY's legal counsel considered what steps to take to halt the ads, Hefner got a call from the Ford White House. It was not about the ads: Ford's legal counsel, Benton Becker, wanted to confirm what he said was a "solid rumor" that Carter had been paid for the interview. Hefner denied it curtly.

In early October, Ford volunteered at a press conference that he, too, had been asked to do a Playboy Interview, but had "refused emphatically" on the grounds that it was unpresidential to associate with a magazine with "that format." The only problem was that it wasn't true. The editors had made a specific decision *not* to ask Ford for an interview. "We felt Carter was the one to go after because he was largely unknown," Kretchmer remembers. "Ford was a known quantity."

Hefner, Kretchmer, and Golson talked about whether or not to repudiate the president's claim. The men felt nervous about getting PLAYBOY any more involved with the election than it already was. They decided not to issue any statement for the time being.

During the third presidential debate, Carter was finally asked about the interview. He pointed out that many prominent people had been subjects, including even a member of Ford's cabinet (Treasury Secretary William Simon), but that if he had it to do over again, he wouldn't grant it. As Ford looked on, Carter finally disposed of the question.

But there were still questions about Ford. Journalists contacted PLAYBOY's editors to ask, since Ford had brought up the subject, when and how the president had turned PLAYBOY down. Hefner decided to release a statement to the press on the subject of the Republicans ads, condemning Ford's election committee for making political use of Carter's interview. In the same release, Golson denied that PLAYBOY had ever asked Ford for a Playboy Interview; furthermore, he said, the White House had *cooperated* in two earlier efforts by PLAYBOY to do articles about Ford.

More headlines and controversy. Ford's press secretary, Ron Nessen, released a letter from a PLAYBOY editor asking for about twenty minutes in the Oval Office so a writer could describe the scene; Nessen claimed that a White House response to that request constituted the turndown President Ford had referred to. There were more charges and countercharges, until, finally, and perhaps thankfully, time ran out. On November 4, the Man Who Spoke with PLAYBOY was elected president.

Despite a widespread certainty that the PLAYBOY interview damaged Carter, the magazine's own readership survey showed an overwhelmingly positive response to him—and over twenty-five million readers saw the magazine that month. As Andrew Young (whose own interview caused some controversy when he called Nixon and Ford "racists") said later, "I was always a believer that Jimmy's PLAYBOY interview was one of the things that helped him win the election. You know, I think every American has some pious relative who's a kind of moralistic godfather. I don't think we wanted a president who seemed to be a self-righteous judge of other people's actions. Jimmy Carter's problem before the election, especially in the big cities, was his religion. The PLAYBOY interview balanced that out very nicely."

No two people will agree, even today, on precisely how the Carter interview affected the 1976 election. But it just may be worth rereading in a changed political climate. Carter's high expectations of himself and his administration are there, along with a touch of cynicism, an uneasy vagueness, his awkward, hyperbolic attempts at sincerity, his gentleness, his testy responses to pressure. Read in its entirety, it is more than a period piece.

The biographical details are all too familiar by now and, indeed, may seem a little pointless this month. If Jimmy Carter is elected President of the United States a few weeks from now, the facts about where he spent his youth, how he was educated and the way he came out of nowhere to capture the Democratic nomination will soon enough be available in history books and on cereal boxes.

What will be less available and less familiar is what kind of person Carter is. To many Americans, the old charge that he was "fuzzy" on issues may be less accurate than the persistent feeling that he is fuzzy as a personality. Even this late in the campaign, Carter remains for many an unknown quantity.

When Carter agreed to do a "Playboy Interview," we decided we'd try our best not to add to all the hype that always gushes forth during a Presidential campaign. We wanted to pit him against an interviewer who would prod him and challenge him and not be afraid to ask irreverent questions. Our choice of interviewer was natural: Robert Scheer, the Bronx-born, Berkeley-based journalist who in the past year has done interviews with California governor Jerry Brown for PLAYBOY (which was widely regarded as the earliest and most thorough exposure of Brown's curious politics and beliefs) and both William and Emily Harris for New Times *(which provided crucial evidence in the trial of Patty Hearst.)*

For three months, Scheer dogged the footsteps of the peanut farmer who would be President, scrambling aboard press planes, sleeping in motels, hanging out with the pack of journalists that grew in size as the campaign gathered momentum. With the support of Carter's young aides—notably, press secretary Jody Powell and campaign manager Hamilton Jordan—Scheer and PLAYBOY managed to log more hours of recorded conversations with the candidate than any other publication or news medium—a fact Carter joked about at the final session. After writing an accompanying article about his experiences and about Carter ("Jimmy, We Hardly Know Y'All"), a very exhausted Scheer filed this report:

"It was the day after the Democratic Convention in New York City. Jody Powell was harried.

" 'Listen, Scheer, I'm not going to kid you. Now that he's the nominee, I've got over 700 requests from all over the world for interviews. He's told me to cut back, but I've got a prior commitment to you guys and I'm going

to honor it. So hop a plane down to his place in Plains. We'll just cut out an appointment with some future Secretary of State.'

"Jody keeps his sense of humor even when he's harried. I had already logged hours of tape with Carter under conditions that were never less than chaotic. Our conversations had started when his chances were shakier and his time slightly more available. But, as Jody had said, once he became the nominee, it was going to be even tougher.

"Some of our sessions were as short as half an hour on board the campaign plane, with the roar of engines and the pilot's announcements adding to the frenzy. PLAYBOY *and I both hung in there through the months, taking (and paying for) flights halfway across the country on the tentative promise of yet one more hurried chat. After all the baggage searches by the Secret Service and the many times I'd had to lurch up an airplane aisle, fumbling with my tape recorder, I was looking forward to a leisurely conversation with Carter at his home after the nomination.*

"Earlier this year, when I was working on the interview with Governor Jerry Brown, my PLAYBOY *editor, Barry Golson, had joined me for the final sessions at the governor's office in Sacramento. It had produced interesting results—I, the aggressive Berkeley radical, Golson, the Eastern diplomatic Yalie. We felt the Mutt and Jeff technique would be valuable with Carter as well, so Golson and I traveled to Plains for the final session.*

"Down in Plains, everything was normal. Brother Billy Carter was in his blue overalls, leaning against a storefront, drawling about this and that to one of the locals who hadn't been up to New York City for the big show. We drove past the Secret Service barricades, past daughter Amy's lemonade stand, and parked in front of the Carter home. As we entered the front door, the candidate, dressed in rumpled work clothes and dusty clodhoppers, was ushering out an impeccably dressed six-man contingent from Reader's Digest.

"As we said hello and sat down in his living room to adjust our tape recorders, I remarked to Carter that he must be in a puckish mood, talking to both the Digest *and* PLAYBOY *on the same afternoon. A week earlier, during the Democratic Convention, Golson had bumped into Jordan at a party in New York. Neither of them was entirely sober, and they discussed the interview. Golson said something about all the time Carter had spent with me. Jordan replied, 'We wouldn't do it if it weren't in our interest. It's your readers who are probably predisposed toward Jimmy—but they may not vote at all if they feel uneasy about him.'*

"For me, the purpose of the questioning was not to get people to vote for or against the man but to push Carter on some of the vagueness he's wrapped himself in. We tried to get beyond the campaigner to some of the personal doubts and confusions—as well as the strengths—of the man himself. Throughout my months on the campaign trail, I found Carter impatient with social chitchat and eager for challenging questions. He is

thin-skinned, as others have reported, and he'll glare at you if he doesn't like something you've asked. But he can take it as well as dish it out and, unlike many other politicians I've interviewed, he'll eventually respond directly to a question if you press him hard enough. The best evidence of this is contained in the final portion of the interview, an open and revealing monolog that occurred because we happened to ask him one last question on a topic about which he'd become impatient and frustrated.

"Oh, just incidentally, there's one bit of folklore about Jimmy Carter whose authenticity I can vouch for. When I've had a rough day, I've been known to toss down a drink or four, and I wondered what Carter did when he needed replenishment. I got my answer during one short session as I slipped into the plane seat next to him after he'd had a miserable day on the hustings. Between answers, he would gobble down handfuls of peanuts at about the same rate at which I drink. Different strokes, I thought."

PLAYBOY: After nearly two years on the campaign trial, don't you feel a little numbed by the routine—for instance, having to give the same speech over and over?

CARTER: Sometimes. Once, when I was campaigning in the Florida primary, I made 12 speeches in one day. It was the worst day I ever had. But I generally have tried to change the order of the speech and emphasize different things. Sometimes I abbreviate and sometimes I elaborate. Of 20 different parts in a speech, I might take seven or eight and change them around. It depends on the audience—black people, Jewish people, *chicanos*—and that gives me the ability to make speeches that aren't boring to myself.

PLAYBOY: Every politician probably emphasizes different things to different audiences, but in your case, there's been a common criticism that you seem to have several faces, that you try to be all things to all people. How do you respond to that?

CARTER: I can't make myself believe these are contrivances and subterfuges I've adopted to get votes. It may be, and I can't get myself to admit it, but what I want to do is to let people know how I stand on the issues as honestly as I can.

PLAYBOY: If you feel you've been fully honest, why has the charge persisted that you're "fuzzy" on the issues?

CARTER: It started during the primaries, when most of my opponents were members of Congress. When any question on an issue came up, they would say, "I'm for the Kennedy-Corman bill on health care, period, no matter what's in it." If the question was on employment, they would say, "I'm for the Humphrey-Hawkins bill, no matter what's in it." But those bills were constantly being amended!

I'm just not able to do that. I have to understand what I'm talking about, and simplistic answers identifying my position with such-and-such a House bill are something I can't put forward. That's one reason I've been seen as fuzzy.

Another is that I'm not an ideolog and my positions are not predictable. Without any criticism of McGovern, if the question had ever come up on abortion, you could pretty well anticipate what he was going to say. If it were amnesty, you could predict what McGovern was going to say about that. But I've tried to analyze each question individually; I've taken positions that to me are fair and rational, and sometimes my answers are complicated.

The third reason is that I wasn't a very vulnerable opponent for those who ran against me. Fuzziness was the only issue Congressman Udall, Senator Church—and others that are hard to remember now—could adopt in their campaigns against me. I think the drumming of that factor into the consciousness of the American voter obviously had some impact.

PLAYBOY: Still, not everybody's sure whether you're a conservative in liberal clothing or vice versa. F.D.R., for instance, turned out to be something of a surprise to people who'd voted for him, because he hadn't seemed as progressive before he was elected as he turned out to be. Could you be a surprise that way?

CARTER: I don't believe that's going to be the case. If you analyze the Democratic Party platform, you'll see that it's a very progressive, very liberal, very socially motivated platform. What sometimes surprises people is that I carry out my promises. People ask how a peanut farmer from the South who believes in balanced budgets and tough management of Government can possibly give the country tax and welfare reform, or a national health program, or insist on equal rights for blacks and women. Well, I'm going to *do* those things. I've promised them during the campaign, so I don't think there will be many people disappointed—or surprised—when I carry out those commitments as President.

PLAYBOY: But isn't it true that you turned out to be more liberal as governor of Georgia than people who voted for you had any reason to suspect?

CARTER: I don't really think so. No. *The Atlanta Constitution*, which was the source of all information about me, categorized me during the gubernatorial campaign as an ignorant, racist, backward, ultraconservative, red-necked South Georgia peanut farmer. Its candidate, Carl Sanders, the former governor, was characterized as an enlightened, progressive, well-educated, urbane, forceful, competent public official. I never agreed with the categorization that was made of me during the campaign. I was the same person before and after I became governor. I remember keeping a check list and every time I made a promise during the campaign, I wrote it down in a notebook. I believe I carried out every promise I made. I told several people during the campaign that one of the phrases that I was going to use in my inaugural speech was that the time for racial discrimination was over. I wrote and made that speech.

PLAYBOY: Considering what you've just said about *The Atlanta Constitution*, how do you feel about the media in general and about the job they do in covering the election issues?

CARTER: There's still a tendency on the part of some members of the press to treat the South, you know, as a suspect nation. There are a few who think that since I am a Southern governor, I must be a secret racist or there's something in a closet somewhere that's going to be revealed to show my true colors. There's been a constant probing back ten, twelve years in my background, even as early as the first primaries. Nobody probed like that into the backgound of Udall or Bayh or other people. But I don't object to it particularly, I just recognize it.

(The answer was broken off and, at a later session, Carter returned to the question of the press and its coverage of issues. This time he was tired, his head sunk far back into his airplane seat. The exchange occurred during one of the late primaries.)

Issues? The local media are interested, all right, but the national news media have absolutely no interest in issues *at all*. Sometimes we freeze out the national media so we can open up press conferences to local people. At least we get questions from them—on timber management, on health care, on education. But the traveling press have zero interest in any issue unless it's a matter of making a mistake. What they're looking for is a 47-second argument between me and another candidate or something like that. There's nobody in the back of this plane who would ask an issue question unless he thought he could trick me into some crazy statement.

PLAYBOY: One crazy statement you were supposed to have made was reported by Robert Shrum after he quit as your speechwriter earlier this year. He said he'd been in conversations with you when you made some slighting references to Jewish voters. What's your version of what hapened?

CARTER: Shrum dreamed up eight or ten conversations that never took place and nobody in the press ever asked me if they had occurred. The press just assumed that they had. I never talked to Shrum in private except for maybe a couple of minutes. If he had told the truth, if I had said all the things he claimed I had said, I wouldn't vote for *myself*.

When a poll came out early in the primaries that said I had a small proportion of the Jewish vote, I said, "Well, this is really a disappointment to me—we've worked so hard with the Jewish voters. But my pro-Israel stand won't change, even if I don't get a single Jewish vote; I guess we'll have to depend on non-Jews to put me in office." But Shrum treated it as if it were some kind of racist disavowal of Jews. Well, that's a kind of sleazy twisting of a conversation.

PLAYBOY: While we're on the subject of the press, how do you feel about an issue that concerns the press itself—the right of journalists to keep their sources secret?

CARTER: I would do everything I could to protect the secrecy of sources for the news media.

PLAYBOY: Both the press *and* the public seem to have made an issue out of your Baptist beliefs. Why do you think this has happened?

CARTER: I'm not unique. There are a lot of people in this country who have the same religious faith. It's not a mysterious or mystical or magical thing. But for those who don't know the feeling of someone who believes in Christ, who is aware of the presence of God, there is, I presume, a quizzical attitude toward it. But it's always been something I've discussed very frankly throughout my adult life.

PLAYBOY: We've heard that you pray 25 times a day. Is that true?

CARTER: I've never counted. I've forgotten who asked me that, but I'd say that on an eventful day, you know, it's something like that.

PLAYBOY: When you say an eventful day, do you mean you pray as a kind of pause, to control your blood pressure and relax?

CARTER: Well, yes. If something happens to me that is a little disconcerting, if I feel a trepidation, if a thought comes into my head of animosity or hatred toward someone, then I just kind of say a brief silent prayer. I don't ask for myself but just to let me understand what another's feelings might be. Going through a crowd, quite often people bring me a problem, and I pray that their needs might be met. A lot of times, I'll be in the back seat of a car and not know what kind of audience I'm going to face. I don't mean I'm terror-stricken, just that I don't know what to expect next. I'll pray then, but it's not something that's conscious or formal. It's just a part of my life.

PLAYBOY: One reason some people might be quizzical is that you have a sister, Ruth, who is a faith healer. The association of politics with faith healing is an idea many find disconcerting.

CARTER: I don't even know what political ideas Ruth has had, and for people to suggest I'm under the hold of a sister—or any other person—is a complete distortion of fact. I don't have any idea whether Ruth has supported Democrats or not, whereas the political views of my other sister, Gloria, are remarkably harmonious with mine.

PLAYBOY: So you're closer to Gloria, who has described herself as a McGovern Democrat and rides motorcycles as a hobby?

CARTER: I like them both. But in the past 20 or 25 years, I've been much closer to Gloria, because she lives next door to me and Ruth lives in North Carolina. We hardly saw Ruth more than once a year at family get-togethers. What political attitudes Ruth has had, I have not the slightest idea. But my mother and Gloria and I have been very compatible. We supported Lyndon Johnson openly during the 1964 campaign and my mother worked at the Johnson county headquarters, which was courageous, not an easy thing to do politically. She would come out of the Johnson headquarters and find her car smeared with soap and the antenna tied in a knot and ugly messages left on the front seat. When my young boys went to school, they were beaten. So Mother and Gloria and I, along with my Rosalynn, have had the same attitudes even when we were in a minority in Plains. But Ruth lives in a different world in North Carolina.

PLAYBOY: Granting that you're not as close to your religious sister as is assumed, we still wonder how *your* religious beliefs would translate into political action. For instance, would you appoint judges who would be harsh or lenient toward victimless crimes—offenses such as drug use, adultery, sodomy and homosexuality?

CARTER: Committing adultery, according to the Bible—which I believe in—is a sin. For us to hate one another, for us to have sexual intercourse outside marriage, for us to engage in homosexual activities, for us to steal, for us to lie—all these are sins. But Jesus teaches us not to judge other people. We don't assume the role of judge and say to another human being, "You're condemned because you commit sins." All Christians, all of us, acknowledge that we are sinful and the judgment comes from God, not from another human being.

As governor of Georgia, I tried to shift the emphasis of law enforcement away from victimless crimes. We lessened the penalties on the use of marijuana. We removed alcoholism as a crime, and so forth. Victimless crimes, in my opinion, should have a very low priority in terms of enforcing the laws on the books. But as to appointing judges, that would not be the basis on which I'd appoint them. I would choose people who were competent, whose judgment and integrity were sound. I think it would be inappropriate to ask them how they were going to rule on a particular question before I appointed them.

PLAYBOY: What *about* those laws on the books that govern personal behavior? Should they be enforced?

CARTER: Almost every state in the Union has laws against adultery and many of them have laws against homosexuality and sodomy. But they're often considered by police officers as not worthy of enforcing to the extent of disturbing consenting adults or breaking into a person's private home.

PLAYBOY: But, of course, that gives the police a lot of leeway to enforce them selectively. Do you think such laws should be on the books at all?

CARTER: That's a judgment for the individual states to make. I think the laws are on the books quite often because of their relationship to the Bible. Early in the nation's development, the Judaeo-Christian moral standards were accepted as a basis for civil law. But I don't think it hurts to have this kind of standard maintained as a goal. I also think it's an area that's been interpreted by the Supreme Court as one that can rightfully be retained by the individual states.

PLAYBOY: Do you think liberalization of the laws over the past decade by factors as diverse as the pill and PLAYBOY—an effect some people would term permissiveness—has been a harmful development?

CARTER: Liberalization of some of the laws has been good. You can't legislate morality. We tried to outlaw consumption of alcoholic beverages. We found that violation of the law led to bigger crimes and bred disrespect for the law.

PLAYBOY: We're confused. You say morality can't be legislated, yet you support certain laws because they preserve old moral standards. How do you reconcile the two positions?

CARTER: I believe people should honor civil laws. If there is a conflict between God's law and civil law, we should honor God's law. But we should be willing to accept civil punishment. Most of Christ's original followers were killed because of their belief in Christ; they violated the civil law in following God's law. Reinhold Niebuhr, a theologian who has dealt with this problem at length, says that the framework of law is a balancing of forces in a society; the law itself tends to alleviate tensions brought about by these forces. But the laws on the books are not a measure of this balance nearly as much as the degree to which the laws are enforced. So when a law is anachronistic and is carried over from a previous age, it's just not observed.

PLAYBOY: What we're getting at is how much you'd tolerate behavior that your religion considers wrong. For instance, in San Francisco, you said you considered homosexuality a sin. What does that mean in political terms?

CARTER: The issue of homosexuality always makes me nervous. It's obviously one of the major issues in San Francisco. I don't have any, you know, personal knowledge about homosexuality and I guess being a Baptist, that would contribute to a sense of being uneasy.

PLAYBOY: Does it make you uneasy to discuss it simply as a political question?

CARTER: No, it's more complicated than that. It's political, it's moral and it's strange territory for me. At home in Plains, we've had homosexuals in our community, our church. There's never been any sort of discrimination—some embarrassment but no animosity, no harassment. But to inject it into a public discussion on politics and how it conflicts with morality is a new experience for me. I've thought about it a lot, but I don't see how to handle it differently from the way I look on other sexual acts outside marriage.

PLAYBOY: We'd like to ask you a blunt question: Isn't it just these views about what's "sinful" and what's "immoral" that contribute to the feeling that you might get a call from God, or get inspired and push the wrong button? More realistically, wouldn't we expect a puritanical tone to be set in the White House if you were elected?

CARTER: Harry Truman was a Baptist. Some people get very abusive about the Baptist faith. If people want to know about it, they can read the New Testament. The main thing is that we don't think we're better than anyone else. We are taught not to judge other people. But as to some of the behavior you've mentioned, I can't change the teachings of Christ. I can't change the teachings of Christ! I believe in them, and a lot of people in this country do as well. Jews believe in the Bible. They have the same commandments.

PLAYBOY: Then you as President, in appointing Supreme Court Justices—

CARTER: I think we've pursued this conversation long enough—if you have another question. . . . Look, I'll try to express my views. It's not a matter of condemnation, it's not a matter of persecution. I've been a governor for four years. Anybody can come and look at my record. I didn't run around breaking down people's doors to see if they were fornicating. This is something that's ridiculous.

PLAYBOY: We know you didn't, but we're being so persistent because of this matter of self-righteousness, because of the moral certainty of so many of your statements. People wonder if Jimmy Carter ever is unsure. Has he ever been wrong, has he ever had a failure of moral nerve?

CARTER: Well, there are a lot of things I could have done differently had I known during my early life what I now know. I would certainly have spoken out more clearly and loudly on the civil rights issue. I would have demanded that our nation never get involved initially in the Vietnam war. I would have told the country in 1972 that Watergate was a much more horrible crime than we thought at the time. It's easy to say in hindsight what you would have done if you had had information you now have.

PLAYBOY: We were asking not so much about hindsight as about being fallible. Aren't there any examples of things you did that weren't absolutely right?

CARTER: I don't mind repeating myself. There are a lot of those in my life. Not speaking out for the cessation of the war in Vietnam. The fact that I didn't crusade at a very early stage for civil rights in the South, for the one-man, one-vote ruling. It might be that now I should drop my campaign for President and start a crusade for black-majority rule in South Africa or Rhodesia. It might be that later on, we'll discover there were opportunities in our lives to do wonderful things and we didn't take advantage of them.

The fact that in 1954 I sat back and required the Warren Court to make this ruling without having crusaded myself—that was obviously a mistake on my part. But these are things you have to judge under the circumstances that prevailed when the decisions were being made. Back then, the Congress, the President, the newspaper editors, the civil libertarians all said that separate-but-equal facilities were adequate. These are opportunities overlooked, or maybe they could be characterized as absence of courage.

PLAYBOY: Since you still seem to be saying you'd have done the right thing if you'd known what you know now, is it realistic to conclude that a person running for the highest office in the land *can't* admit many mistakes or moments of self-doubt?

CARTER: I think that's a human circumstance. But if there are issues I'm avoiding because of a lack of courage, either I don't recognize them or I can't make myself recognize them.

PLAYBOY: You mentioned Vietnam. Do you feel you spoke out at an early enough stage against the war?

CARTER: No, I did not. I never spoke out publicly about withdrawing completely from Vietnam until March of 1971.

PLAYBOY: Why?

CARTER: It was the first time anybody had asked me about it. I was a farmer before then and wasn't asked about the war until I took office. There was a general feeling in this country that we ought not to be in Vietnam to start with. The American people were tremendously misled about the immediate prospects for victory, about the level of our involvement, about the relative cost in American lives. If I had known in the Sixties what I knew in the early Seventies, I think I would have spoken out more strongly. I was not in public office. When I took office as governor in 1970, I began to speak out about complete withdrawal. It was late compared with what many others had done, but I think it's accurate to say that Congress and the people—with the exception of very small numbers of people—shared the belief that we were protecting our democratic allies.

PLAYBOY: Even without holding office you must have had some feelings about the war. When do you recall first feeling it was wrong?

CARTER: There was an accepted feeling by me and everybody else that we ought not to be there, that we should never have gotten involved, we ought to get out.

PLAYBOY: You felt that way all through the Sixties?

CARTER: Yeah, that's right, and I might hasten to say that it was the same feeling expressed by Senators Russell and Talmadge—very conservative Southern political figures. They thought it was a serious mistake to be in Vietnam.

PLAYBOY: Your son Jack fought in that war. Did you have any qualms about it at the time?

CARTER: Well, yes, I had problems about my son fighting in the war, period. But I never make my sons' decisions for them. Jack went to war feeling it was foolish, a waste of time, much more deeply than I did. He also felt it would have been grossly unfair for him not to go when other, poorer kids had to.

PLAYBOY: You were in favor of allocating funds for the South Vietnamese in 1975 as the war was coming to a close, weren't you?

CARTER: That was when we were getting ready to evacuate our troops. The purpose of the money was to get our people out and maintain harmony between us and our Vietnamese allies, who had fought with us for 25 years. And I said yes, I would do that. But it was not a permanent thing, not to continue the war but to let us get our troops out in an orderly fashion.

PLAYBOY: How do you respond to the argument that it was the Democrats, not the Republicans, who got us into the Vietnam war?

CARTER: I think it started originally, maybe, with Eisenhower, then Kennedy, Johnson and then Nixon. It's not a partisan matter. I think Eisenhower probably first got us in there thinking that since France had failed, our country might slip in there and succeed. Kennedy thought he could escalate involvement by going beyond the mere advisory role. I guess if there was one President who made the most determined effort, conceivably, to end the war by massive force, it was certainly Johnson. And Nixon went into Cambodia and bombed it, and so forth.

It's not partisan—it's just a matter that evolved as a habit over several administrations. There was a governmental consciousness to deal in secrecy, to exclude the American people, to mislead them with false statements and sometimes outright lies. Had the American people been told the facts from the beginning by Eisenhower, Kennedy, MacNamara, Johnson, Kissinger and Nixon, I think there would have been different decisions made in our Government.

PLAYBOY: At the Democratic Convention, you praised Johnson as a President who had vastly extended human rights. Were you simply omitting any mention of Vietnam?

CARTER: It was obviously the factor that destroyed his political career and damaged his whole life. But as far as what I said at the convention, there hasn't been another President in our history—with the possible exception of Abraham Lincoln—who did so much to advance the cause of human rights.

PLAYBOY: Except for the human rights of the Vietnamese and the Americans who fought there.

CARTER: Well, I really believe that Johnson's motives were good. I think he tried to end the war even while the fighting was going on, and he was speaking about massive rehabilitation efforts, financed by our Government, to help people. I don't think he ever had any desire for permanent entrenchment of our forces in Vietnam. I think he had a mistaken notion that he was defending democracy and that what he was doing was compatible with the desires of the South Vietnamese.

PLAYBOY: Then what about the administration that *ended* the war? Don't you have to give credit to Kissinger, the Secretary of State of a Republican President, for ending a war that a Democratic President escalated?

CARTER: I think the statistics show that more bombs were dropped in Vietnam and Cambodia under Nixon and Kissinger than under Johnson. Both administrations were at fault; but I don't think the end came about as a result of Kissinger's superior diplomacy. It was the result of several factors that built up in an inexorable way: the demonstrated strength of the Viet Cong, the tremendous pressure to withdraw that came from the American people and an aroused Congress. I think Nixon and Kissinger did the proper thing in starting a phased withdrawal, but I don't consider that to be a notable diplomatic achievement by Kissinger. As we've now learned, he promised the Vietnamese things that cannot be delivered—reparations, payments, economic advantages, and so forth. Getting out of Vietnam was very good, but whether Kissinger deserved substantial diplomatic credit for it is something I doubt.

PLAYBOY: You've said you'll pardon men who refused military service because of the Vietnam war but not necessarily those who deserted while they were in the Armed Forces. Is that right?

CARTER: That's right. I would not include them. Deserters ought to be handled on a separate-case basis. There's a difference to me. I was in the Navy for a long time. Somebody who goes into the military joins a kind of mutual partnership arrangement, you know what I mean? Your life depends on other people, their lives depend on you. So I don't intend to pardon the deserters. As far as the other categories of war resisters go, to me the ones who stayed in this country and let their opposition to the war be known publicly are more heroic than those who went and hid in Sweden. But I'm not capable of judging motives, so I'm just going to declare a blanket pardon.

PLAYBOY: When?

CARTER: The first week I'm in office.

PLAYBOY: You've avoided the word amnesty and chosen to use the word pardon, but there doesn't seem to be much difference between the two in the dictionary. Could it be because amnesty is more emotionally charged and pardon a word more people will accept?

CARTER: You know I can't deny that. But my reason for distinguishing between the two is that I think that all of those poor, and often black, young men who went to Vietnam are more worthy of recognition than those who defected, and the word pardon includes those who simply avoided the war completely. But I just want to bring the defectors back to this country without punishment and, in doing so, I would like to have the support of the American people. I haven't been able to devise for private or public presentation a better way to do it.

PLAYBOY: In preparing for this interview, we spoke with your mother, your son Chip and your sister Gloria. We asked them what single action would most disappoint them in a Carter Presidency. They all replied that it would be if you ever sent troops to intervene in a foreign war. In fact, Miss Lillian said she would picket the White House.

CARTER: They share my views completely.

PLAYBOY: What about more limited military action? Would you have handled the Mayaguez incident the same way President Ford did?

CARTER: Let me assess that in retrospect. It's obvious we didn't have adequate intelligence: we attacked an island when the Mayaguez crew was no longer there. There was a desire, I think, on the part of President Ford to extract maximum publicity from our effort, so that about 23 minutes after our crew was released, we went ahead and bombed the island airport. I hope I would have been capable of getting adequate intelligence, surrounded the island more quickly and isolated the crew so we wouldn't have had to attack the airport after the crew was released. These are some of the differences in the way I would have done it.

PLAYBOY: So it's a matter of degree; you would have intervened militarily, too.

CARTER: I would have done everything necessary to keep the crew from being taken to the mainland, yes.

PLAYBOY: Then would you summarize your position on foreign intervention?

CARTER: I would never intervene for the purpose of overthrowing a government. If enough were at stake for our national interest, I would use prestige, legitimate diplomatic leverage, trade mechanisms. But it would be the sort of effort that would not be embarrassing to this nation if revealed completely. I don't ever want to do anything as President that would be a contravention of the moral and ethical standards that I would exemplify in my own life as an individual or that would violate the principles or character of the American people.

PLAYBOY: Do you feel it's fair criticism that you seem to be going back to some familiar faces—such as Paul Warnke and Cyrus Vance—for foreign-policy advice? Isn't there a danger of history's repeating itself when you seek out those who were involvd in our Vietnam decisions?

CARTER: I haven't heard that criticism. If you're raising it, then I respond to the new critic. These people contribute to foreign-affairs journals, they individually explore different concepts of foreign policy. I have 15 or 20 people who work with me very closely on foreign affairs. Their views are quite divergent. The fact that they may or may not have been involved in foreign-policy decisions in the past is certainly no detriment to their ability to help me now.

PLAYBOY: In some respects, your foreign policy seems similar to that established by Kissinger, Nixon and Ford. In fact, Kissinger stated that he didn't think your differences were substantial. How, precisely, does your view differ from theirs?

CARTER: As I've said in my speeches, I feel the policy of *détente* has given up too much to the Russians and gotten too little in return. I also feel Kissinger has equated his own popularity with the so-called advantages of *détente*. As I've traveled and spoken with world leaders—Helmut Schmidt of West Germany, Yitzhak Rabin of Israel, various leaders in Japan—I've discerned a deep concern on their part that the United States has abandoned a long-standing principle: to consult mutually, to share responsibility for problems. This has been a damaging thing. In addition, I believe we should have stronger bilateral relations with developing nations.

PLAYBOY: What do you mean when you say we've given up too much to the Russians?

CARTER: One example I've mentioned often is the Helsinki agreement. I never saw any reason we should be involved in the Helsinki meetings at all. We added the stature of our presence and signature to an agreement that, in effect, ratified the take-over of eastern Europe by the Soviet Union. We got very little, if anything, in return. The Russians promised they would honor democratic principles and permit the free movement of their citizens, including those who want to emigrate. The Soviet Union has not lived up to those promises and Mr. Brezhnev was able to celebrate the major achievement of his diplomatic life.

PLAYBOY: Are you charging that Kissinger was too soft on the Russians?

CARTER: Kissinger has been in the position of being almost uniquely a spokesman for our nation. I think that is a legitimate role and a proper responsibility of the President himself. Kissinger has had a kind of Lone Ranger, secret foreign-policy attitude, which almost ensures that there cannot be adequate consultation with our allies; there cannot be a long-range commitment to unchanging principles; there cannot be a coherent evolution on foreign policy; there cannot be a bipartisan approach with support and advice from Congress. This is what I would avoid as President and is one of the major defects in the Nixon-Ford foreign policy as expressed by Kissinger.

PLAYBOY: Say, do you always do your own sewing? *(This portion of the interview also took place aboard a plane. As he answered the interviewer's questions, Carter had been sewing up a rip in his jacket with a needle and thread he carried with him.)*

CARTER: Uh-huh. *(He bit off the thread with his teeth.)*

PLAYBOY: Anyway, you said earlier that your foreign policy would exemplify your moral and ethical standards. Isn't there as much danger in an overly moralistic policy as in the kind that is too pragmatic?

CARTER: I've said I don't think we should intervene militarily, but I see no reason not to express our approval, at least verbally, with those nations that develop democratically. When Kissinger says, as he did recently in a speech, that Brazil is the sort of government that is most compatible with ours— well, that's the kind of thing we want to change. Brazil is not a democratic government; it's a military dictatorship. In many instances, it's highly repressive to political prisoners. Our Government should justify the character and moral principles of the American people, and our foreign policy should not short-circuit that for temporary advantage. I think in every instance we've done that it's been counterproductive. When the CIA undertakes covert activities that might be justified if they were peaceful, we always suffer when they're revealed—it always seems as if we're trying to tell other people how to act. When Kissinger and Ford warned Italy she would be excluded from NATO if the Communists assumed power, that was the best way to make sure Communists *were* elected. The Italian voters resent it. A proper posture for our country in this sort of situation is to show, through demonstration, that our own Government works properly, that democracy is advantageous, and let the Italian people make their own decisions.

PLAYBOY: And what if the Communists in Italy had been elected in greater numbers than they were? What if they had actually become a key part of the Italian government?

CARTER: I think it would be a mechanism for subversion of the strength of NATO and the cohesiveness that ought to bind European countries together. The proper posture was the one taken by Helmut Schmidt, who said that German aid to Italy would be endangered.

PLAYBOY: Don't you think that constitutes a form of intervention in the democratic processes of another nation?

CARTER: No, I don't. I think that when the democratic nations of the world express themselves frankly and forcefully and openly, that's a proper exertion of influence. We did the same thing in Portugal. Instead of going in through surreptitious means and trying to overthrow the government when it looked like the minority Communist Party was going to assume power, the NATO countries as a group made it clear to Portugal what it would lose in the way of friendship, trade opportunities, and so forth. And the Portuguese people, recognizing that possibility, decided that the Communists should not lead their government. Well, that was legitimate exertion of influence, in my opinion. It was done openly and it was a mere statement of fact.

PLAYBOY: You used the word subversion referring to communism. Hasn't the world changed since we used to throw words like that around? Aren't the west European Communist parties more independent of Moscow and more willing to respect democracy?

CARTER: Yes, the world's changed. In my speeches, I've made it clear that as far as Communist leaders in such countries as Italy, France and Portugal are concerned, I would not want to close the doors of communication, consultation and friendship to them. That would be an almost automatic forcing of the Communist leaders into the Soviet sphere of influence. I also think we should keep open our opportunities for the east European nations—even those that are completely Communist—to trade with us, understand us, have tourist exchange and give them an option from complete domination by the Soviet Union.

But again, I don't think you could expect West Germany to lend Poland two billion dollars—which was the figure in the case of Italy—when Poland is part of the Soviet government's satellite and supportive-nation group. So I think the best way to minimize totalitarian influence within the governments of Europe is to make sure the democratic forces perform properly. The major shift toward the Communists in Italy was in the local elections, when the Christian Democrats destroyed their reputation by graft and corruption. If we can make our own Government work, if we can avoid future Watergates and avoid the activities of the CIA that have been revealed, if we can minimize joblessness and inflation, this will be a good way to lessen the inclination of people in other countries to turn away from our form of government.

PLAYBOY: What about Chile? Would you agree that that was a case of the United States', through the CIA, intervening improperly?

CARTER: Yes. There's no doubt about it. Sure.

PLAYBOY: And you would stop that sort of thing?

CARTER: Absolutely. Yes, sir.

PLAYBOY: What about economic sanctions? Do you feel we should have punished the Allende government the way we did?

CARTER: That's a complicated question, because we don't know what caused the fall of the Allende government, the murder of perhaps thousands of people, the incarceration of many others. I don't have any facts as to how deeply involved we were, but my impression is that we were involved quite deeply. As I said, I wouldn't have done that if I were President. But as to whether or not we ought to have an option on the terms of our loans, repayment schedules, interest charges, the kinds of materials we sell to them—those are options I would retain depending upon the compatibility of a foreign government with our own.

PLAYBOY: To what do you attribute all those deceptions and secret maneuverings through the years? Why were they allowed to happen?

CARTER: It was a matter of people's just saying, Well, that's politics; we don't have a right to know what our Government is doing; secrecy is OK; accepting gifts is OK; excluding the American people is OK. These are the kinds of things I want to change.

PLAYBOY: It sounds as if you're saying Americans accepted indecency and lies in their Government all too easily. Doesn't that make your constant campaign theme, invoking the decency and honesty of the American people, somewhat naïve and ingenuous?

CARTER: I say that the American people are basically decent and honest and want a truthful Government. Obviously, I know there are people in this country, out of 214,000,000, who are murderers. There are people, maybe, who don't want a decent Government. Maybe there are people who prefer lies to truth. But I don't think it's simplistic to say that our Government hasn't measured up to the ethical and moral standards of the people of this country. We've had better governments in the past and I think our people, as I've said many times, are just as strong, courageous and intelligent as they were 200 years ago. I think we still have the same inner strength they had then.

PLAYBOY: Even though a lot of people support that feeling, many others think it makes you sound like an evangelist. And that makes it all the more confusing when they read about your hanging out with people so different from you in lifestyle and beliefs. Your publicized friendship with journalist Hunter Thompson, who makes no secret of his affinity for drugs and other craziness, is a good example.

CARTER: Well, in the first place, I'm a human being. I'm not a packaged article that you can put in a little box and say, "Here's a Southern Baptist, an ignorant Georgia peanut farmer who doesn't have the right to enjoy music, who has no flexibility in his mind, who can't understand the sensitivities of an interpersonal relationship. He's gotta be predictable. He's gotta be for Calley and for the war. He's gotta be a liar. He's gotta be a racist."

You know, that's the sort of stereotype people tend to assume, and I hope it doesn't apply to me. And I don't see any mystery about having a friendship with Hunter Thompson. I guess it's something that's part of my character and it becomes a curiosity for those who see some mystery about someone of my background being elected President. I'm just a human being like everybody else. I have different interests, different understandings of the world around me, different relationships with different kinds of people. I have a broad range of friends: sometimes very serious, sometimes very formal, sometimes lighthearted, sometimes intense, sometimes casual.

PLAYBOY: So when you find yourself at a rock concert or in some other situation that seems at odds with your rural, religious background, you never feel a sense of estrangement?

CARTER: None. No. I feel at home with 'em.

PLAYBOY: How did you get to feel this way without going through culture shock?

CARTER: I have three sons, who now range from 23 to 29, and the oldest of them were very influenced by Bob Dylan in their attitudes toward civil rights, criminal justice and the Vietnam war. This was about the period of time I was entering politics. I've been fairly close to my sons and their taste in music influenced my taste, and I was able to see the impact of Bob Dylan's attitudes on young people. And I was both gratified by and involved emotionally in those changes of attitudes.

Later, when I became governor, I was acquainted with some of the people at Capricorn Records in Macon—Otis Redding and others. It was they who began to meld the white and black music industries, and that was quite a sociological change for our region. So as I began to travel around Georgia, I made contact a few days every month or two with Capricorn Records, just to stay in touch with people in the state, and got to know all the Allman Brothers, Dicky Betts and others. Later on, I met Charlie Daniels and the Marshall Tucker Band.

Then I decided to run for President. I didn't have any money and didn't have any political base, so I had to depend substantially on the friends I already had. One of my potential sources for fund raising and for recruiting young volunteers was the group of recording stars I already knew. So we began to have concerts and I got to know them even better.

Of course, I've also been close to the country-music folks in Georgia, as well as the Atlanta Symphony Orchestra. The first large contribution I got—$1000—was from Robert Shaw, the music director of the orchestra. We've been over at the Grand Ole Opry a few times and gotten to know people like Chubby Jackson and Tom T. Hall.

PLAYBOY: There's been a lot of publicity about your relationship with Dylan, whom you quoted in your acceptance speech at the Democratic Convention. How did that come about?

CARTER: A number of years ago, my second son, Chip, who was working full time in our farming business, took a week off during Christmas. He and a couple of his friends drove all the way to New York—just to see Bob Dylan. There had been a heavy snowstorm and the boys had to park several miles from Dylan's home. It was after Dylan was injured, when he was in seclusion. Apparently, Dylan came to the door with two of his kids and shook hands with Chip. By the time Chip got to the nearest phone, a couple of miles away, and called us at home, he was nearly incoherent. Rosalynn couldn't understand what Chip was talking about, so she screamed, "Jimmy, come here quick! Something's happened to Chip!"

We finally deciphered that he had shaken Dylan's hand and was just, you know, very carried away with it. So when I read that Dylan was going on tour again, I wrote him a little personal note and asked him to come visit me at the governor's mansion. I think he checked with Phil Walden of Capricorn Records and Bill Graham to find out what kind of guy *is* this, and he was assured I didn't want to use him, I was just interested in his music.

The night he came, we had a chance to talk about his music and about changing times and pent-up emotions in young people. He said he didn't have any inclination to change the world, that he wasn't crusading and that his personal feelings were apparently compatible with the yearnings of an entire generation. We also discussed Israel, which he had a strong interest in. But that's my only contact with Bob Dylan, that night.

PLAYBOY: That brings us back to the reason so many people find it hard to get a handle on you: On the one hand, your association with youth culture, civil rights and other liberal movements; and on the other, your apparent conservatism on many issues. Would you care to put it in a nutshell for us?

CARTER: I'll try. On human rights, civil rights, environmental quality, I consider myself to be very liberal. On the management of government, on openness of government, on strengthening individual liberties and local levels of government, I consider myself a conservative. And I don't see that the two attitudes are incompatible.

PLAYBOY: Then let's explore a few more issues. Not everyone is sure, for instance, what you mean by your call for tax reform. Does it mean that the burden will shift to corporations and upper-income groups and away from the middle- and lower-income groups, or are you talking merely about a simplified tax code?

CARTER: It would involve both. One change I'm calling for is simplification, and the other involves shifting the income-tax burden away from the lower-income families. But what I'm really talking about is total, comprehensive tax reform for the first time since the income tax was approved back in 1913, I think it was.

It's not possible to give you a definitive statement on tax reform any time soon. It's going to take at least a year before we can come up with a new tax structure. But there are some general provisions that would be instituted that aren't there now. The income-tax code, which now comprises 40,000 pages, will be greatly simplified. Income should be taxed only once. We should have a true progressive income tax, so that the higher the income, the higher the percentage of taxation. I see no reason why capital gains should be taxed at half the rate of income from manual labor. I would be committed to a great reduction in tax incentives, loopholes or whatever you want to call them, which are used as mechanisms to solve transient economic problems; they ought to be on a basis of annual appropriation or a time limit, rather than be built into the tax structure.

In any case, these are five or six things that would be dramatic departures from what we presently have and they should tell you what side of the issue I stand on.

PLAYBOY: Would one of those be increasing taxes for corporations, especially the overseas and domestic profits of multinational corporations?

CARTER: No, I don't think so. Obviously, there have been provisions written into the law that favor certain corporations, including those that have overseas investments; I would remove those incentives. Tax laws also benefit those who have the best lobbying efforts, those who have the most influence in Washington, and the larger the corporations are, on the average, the smaller proportion they pay in taxes. Small businesses quite often pay the flat maximum rate, 48 percent, while some larger corporations pay as little as five or six percent. That ought to be changed.

But as far as increasing over-all corporate taxes above the 50 percent level, I wouldn't favor that. We also have the circumstance of multinational corporations' depending on bribery as a mechanism for determining the outcome of a sale. I think bribery in international affairs ought to be considered a crime and punishable by imprisonment.

PLAYBOY: Would you sympathize with the anticorporate attitude that many voters feel?

CARTER: Well, I'm not particularly anticorporate, but I'd say I'm more oriented to consumer protection. One of the things I've established throughout the campaign is the need to break up the sweetheart arrangement between regulatory agencies and the industries they regulate. Another is the need for rigid and enthusiastic enforcement of the antitrust laws.

PLAYBOY: To take another issue, you favor a comprehensive Federal health-care system. Why don't you just support the Kennedy-Corman bill, which provides for precisely that?

CARTER: As a general philosophy, wherever the private sector can perform a function as effectively and efficiently as the Government, I would prefer to keep it within the private sector. So I would like the insurance aspect of the health program to be carried out by employer/employee contribution. There would be contributions from the general fund for those who are indigent. I would also have a very heavy emphasis on preventive health care, since I believe most of the major afflictions that beset people can be prevented or minimized. And I favor the use to a greater degree of non-physicians, such as nurses, physicians' assistants, and so forth. Some of these things are in conflict with the provisions of the Kennedy-Corman bill.

PLAYBOY: Let me ask you about one last stand: abortion.

CARTER: I think abortion is wrong and I will do everything I can as President to minimize the need for abortions—within the framework of the decision of the Supreme Court, which I can't change. Georgia had a more conservative approach to abortion, which I personally favored, but the Supreme Court ruling suits me all right. I signed a Georgia law as governor that was compatible with the Supreme Court decision.

PLAYBOY: You think it's wrong, but the ruling suits you? What would we tell a woman who said her vote would depend on how you stood on abortion?

CARTER: If a woman's major purpose in life is to have unrestricted abortions, then she ought *not* to vote for me. But she wouldn't have anyone to vote for.

PLAYBOY: There seem to have been relatively few women in important staff positions in your campaign. Is that accurate?

CARTER: Women have been in charge of our entire campaign effort in

Georgia and in New York State outside New York City. Also in Nebraska, Kansas, a third of the state of Florida and other areas.

PLAYBOY: But whenever we hear about a meeting of top staff members, they almost always seem to be white males. Is that a failing in your organization.

CARTER: I don't know about a failing. The three people with whom I consult regularly—in addition to my wife—are white males: Hamilton Jordan, Jody Powell and Charles Kirbo. But we *do* have a lot of women involved in the campaign. We are now setting up a policy committee to run a nationwide effort to coordinate Democratic races and 50 percent of the members of this committee will be women. But Jody has been my press secretary since 1970, and Hamilton and Kirbo were my major advisors in 1966. It's such an extremely stable staff that there's been no turnover at all in the past five or six years. But we've made a lot of progress, I think, in including women, and I think you'll see more.

PLAYBOY: You mention very frequently how much you count on your wife's advice. Isn't there a strain during the campaign, with the two of you separated so much of the time?

CARTER: Well, when I was in the Navy, I was at sea most of the time and I'd see her maybe one or two nights a week. Now, when I'm home in Plains, I see her almost every night. And if I'm elected President, I'll see her *every* night. So there is obviously a time to be together and a time to be separated. If you're apart three or four days and then meet again, it's almost—for me, it's a very exciting reunion. I'll have been away from Rosalynn for a few days and if I see her across an airport lobby, or across a street, I get just as excited as I did when I was, you know, 30 years younger.

We have a very close, very intimate sharing of our lives and we've had a tremendous magnification of our life's purposes in politics. Before 1966, she and I were both very shy. It was almost a painful thing to approach a stranger or make a speech. It's been a mutual change we've gone through, because we both felt it was worthwhile; so no matter what the outcome of the election, the relationship between Rosalynn and me will be very precious.

PLAYBOY: Did you both have the usual share of troubles adjusting to marriage?

CARTER: We did at first. We've come to understand each other much better. I was by far the dominant person in the marriage at the beginning, but not anymore. She's just as strong, if not stronger, than I am. She's fully equal to me in every way in our relationship, in making business decisions, and she makes most of the decisions about family affairs. And I think it was a struggle for her to achieve this degree of independence and equality in our personal relationship. So, to summarize, years ago we had a lot of quarrels—none serious, particularly—but now we don't.

PLAYBOY: A lot of marriages are foundering these days. Why is yours so successful?

CARTER: Well, I really love Rosalynn more now than I did when I married her. And I have loved no other women except her. I had gone out with all kinds of girls, sometimes fairly steadily, but I just never cared about them. Rosalynn had been a friend of my sister's and was three years younger than I, which is a tremendous chasm in the high school years. She was just one of those insignificant little girls around the house. Then, when I was 21 and home from the Navy on leave, I took her out to a movie. Nothing extraordinary happened, but the next morning I told my mother, "That's the girl I want to marry." It's the best thing that ever happened to me.

We also share a religious faith, and the two or three times in our married life when we've had a serious crisis, I think that's what sustained our marriage and helped us overcome our difficulty. Our children, too, have been a factor binding Rosalynn and me together. After the boys, Amy came along late and it's been especially delightful for me, maybe because she's a little girl.

PLAYBOY: This is a tough question to ask, but because it's been such a factor in American political life, we wonder if you've ever discussed with Rosalynn the possibility of being assassinated. And, assuming you have, how do you deal with it in your own mind?

CARTER: Well, in the first place, I'm not afraid of death. In the second place, it's the same commitment I made when I volunteered to go into the submarine force. I accepted a certain degree of danger when I made the original decision, then I didn't worry about it anymore. It wasn't something that preyed on my mind; it wasn't something I had to reassess every five minutes. There is a certain element of danger in running for President, borne out by statistics on the number of Presidents who have been attacked, but I have to say frankly that it's something I never worry about.

PLAYBOY: Your first answer was that you don't fear death. Why not?

CARTER: It's part of my religious belief. I just look at death as not a threat. It's inevitable, and I have an assurance of eternal life. There is no feeling on my part that I *have* to be President, or that I *have* to live, or that I'm immune to danger. It's just that the termination of my physical life is relatively insignificant in my concept of over-all existence. I don't say that in a mysterious way; I recognize the possibility of assassination. But I guess everybody recognizes the possibility of other forms of death—automobile accidents, airplane accidents, cancer. I just don't worry.

PLAYBOY: There's been some evidence that Johnson and Nixon both seemed to have gone a bit crazy while they were in the White House. Do you ever wonder if the pressures of the office might make *anyone* mentally unstable?

CARTER: I really don't have the feeling that being in the White House is what caused Nixon's or Johnson's problems. Other Presidents have served without developing mental problems—Roosevelt, Truman, Eisenhower, Kennedy, for instance. As far as I've been able to discern, President Ford approaches—or avoids—the duties of the White House with equanimity and self-assurance.

I think the ability to accept oneself and to feel secure and confident, to avoid any degree of paranoia, to face reality, these factors are fairly independent of whether or not one is President. The same factors would be important if someone were chief of police, or a schoolteacher, or a magazine editor. The pressure is greater on a President, obviously, than some of the jobs I've described, but I think the ability to accommodate pressure is a personal thing.

PLAYBOY: We noticed your crack about President Ford's avoiding the duties of the White House. Do you agree with Senator Mondale's assessment, when he said shortly after the nomination that Ford isn't intelligent enough to be a good President?

CARTER: Well, if you leave Mondale out of it, I personally think that President Ford is adequately intelligent to be President.

PLAYBOY: And what about your Presidency, if you're elected—will you have a dramatic first 1000 days?

CARTER: I would hope that my Administration wouldn't be terminated at the end of 1000 days, as was the case with one administration. I'm beginning to meet with key leaders of Congress to evolve specific legislation to implement the Democratic platform commitment. If I'm elected, there will be no delay in moving aggressively on a broad front to carry out the promises I've made to the American people. I intend to stick to everything I've promised.

PLAYBOY: Thanks for all the time you've given us. Incidentally, do you have any problems with appearing in PLAYBOY? Do you think you'll be criticized?

CARTER: I don't object to that at all. I don't believe I'll be criticized.

(At the final session, which took place in the living room of Carter's home in Plains, the allotted time was up. A press aide indicated that there were other appointments for which Carter was already late, and the aide opened the front door while amenities were exchanged. As the interviewer and the PLAYBOY *editor stood at the door, recording equipment in their arms, a final, seemingly casual question was tossed off. Carter then delivered a long, softly spoken monolog that grew in intensity as he made his final points. One of the journalists signaled to Carter that they were still taping, to which Carter nodded his assent.)*

PLAYBOY: Do you feel you've reassured people with this interview, people who are uneasy about your religious beliefs, who wonder if you're going to make a rigid, unbending President?

CARTER: I don't know if you've been to Sunday school here yet; some of the press has attended. I teach there about every three or four weeks. It's getting to be a real problem because we don't have room to put everybody now when I teach. I don't know if we're going to have to issue passes or what. It almost destroys the worship aspect of it. But we had a good class last Sunday. It's a good way to learn what I believe and what the Baptists believe.

One thing the Baptists believe in is complete autonomy. I don't accept any domination of my life by the Baptist Church, none. Every Baptist church is individual and autonomous. We don't accept domination of our church from the Southern Baptist Convention. The reason the Baptist Church was formed in this country was because of our belief in absolute and total separation of church and state. These basic tenets make us almost unique. We don't believe in any hierarchy in church. We don't have bishops. Any officers chosen by the church are defined as servants, not bosses. They're supposed to do the dirty work, make sure the church is clean and painted and that sort of thing. So it's a very good, democratic structure.

When my sons were small, we went to church and they went, too. But when they got old enough to make their own decisions, they decided when to go and they varied in their devoutness. Amy really looks forward to going to church, because she gets to see all her cousins at Sunday school. I never knew anything except going to church. My wife and I were born and raised in innocent times. The normal thing to do was to go to church.

What Christ taught about most was pride, that one person should never think he was any better than anybody else. One of the most vivid stories Christ told in one of his parables was about two people who went into a church. One was an official of the church, a Pharisee, and he said, "Lord, I thank you that I'm not like all those other people. I keep all your commandments, I give a tenth of everything I own. I'm here to give thanks for making me more acceptable in your sight." The other guy was despised by the nation, and he went in, prostrated himself on the floor and said, "Lord, have mercy on me, a sinner. I'm not worthy to lift my eyes to heaven." Christ asked the disciples which of the two had justified his life. The answer was obviously the one who was humble.

The thing that's drummed into us all the time is not to be proud, not to be better than anyone else, not to look down on people but to make ourselves acceptable in God's eyes through our own actions and recognize the simple truth that we're saved by grace. It's just a free gift through faith in Christ. This gives us a mechanism by which we can relate permanently to God. I'm not speaking for other people, but it gives me a sense of peace and equanimity and assurance.

I try not to commit a deliberate sin. I recognize that I'm going to do it anyhow, because I'm human and I'm tempted. And Christ set some almost impossible standards for us. Christ said, "I tell you that anyone who looks on a woman with lust has in his heart already committed adultery."

I've looked on a lot of women with lust. I've committed adultery in my heart many times. This is something that God recognizes I will do—and I have done it—and God forgives me for it. But that doesn't mean that I condemn someone who not only looks on a woman with lust but who leaves his wife and shacks up with somebody out of wedlock.

Christ says, Don't consider yourself better than someone else because one guy screws a whole bunch of women while the other guy is loyal to his wife. The guy who's loyal to his wife ought not to be condescending or proud because of the relative degree of sinfulness. One thing that Paul Tillich said was that religion is a search for the truth about man's existence and his relationship with God and his fellow man; and that once you stop searching and think you've got it made—at that point, you lose your religion. Constant reassessment, searching in one's heart—it gives me a feeling of confidence.

I don't inject these beliefs in my answers to your secular questions.

(Carter clenched his fist and gestured sharply.)

But I don't think I would *ever* take on the same frame of mind that Nixon or Johnson did—lying, cheating and distorting the truth. Not taking into consideration my hope for my strength of character, I think that my religious beliefs alone would prevent that from happening to me. I have that confidence. I hope it's justified.

PAT MOYNIHAN

March 1977

Interviewer: Richard Meryman

After Daniel Patrick Moynihan announced his candidacy for the U.S. Senate in the spring of 1976, the editors decided to approach him for an interview. There was only one other political assignment out— Scheer on Carter—and that was still a long shot. But more important, Moynihan, unlike most other politicians, was a colorful, erudite man with unparalleled experience under four presidential administrations. Whether he won or not, he would be able to sketch in for readers his impressions of the past two decades of political history and add a little dash to what seemed like a lackluster campaign year. The editors were also curious to see how an intellectual from Harvard, whose policies straddled right and left, had survived such a range of people and politics.

Richard Meryman, a journalist and author, was given the assignment. Because he had been a personal friend of Moynihan's during their navy and postgraduate years, the editors felt Moynihan would speak more freely with him. The conversations, which ranged from stories about the Kennedy White House to theories on the decline of American power, continued into September 1976—at which point Moynihan cut off the talks. Momentarily surprised, Meryman suddenly realized what was going on: The furor over the Carter interview was breaking, and Moynihan was clearly concerned about the political implications of *his* interview-in-progress.

Early in October, as the controversy over Carter's interview refused to die down, Golson received a telephone call from Moynihan at the magazine's Chicago offices. They exchanged amenities and Moynihan came to the point: Was PLAYBOY going to publicize the fact that a Moynihan interview was in the works? Well, Golson said, there was certainly no intention to leak it; in fact, the editors could tighten security until after the November elections, if that was what Moynihan was getting at. It seemed to Golson that there was a sigh of relief at the other end of the line. Of course, Golson continued, it would be appropriate if Moynihan reciprocated by agreeing to continue the conversation with Meryman after the elections—there were a couple of topics that hadn't quite been addressed. In the spirit of a traditional political deal, Moynihan agreed. No word leaked out, Moynihan won his race and sat down with Meryman several days after the elections to speak freely.

Columnist George Will remarked in a 1977 piece that the Playboy Interview had become "the preferred place for a peculiar kind of political musing." The reference was picked up by Thomas Weyr in summarizing the effect of Moynihan's interview in *Reaching for Paradise*:

> Senator Moynihan, who is used to musing, mused his way through a PLAYBOY interview without a slip, and without winning any attention. That's a pity because nowhere else has Moynihan mused at quite such a length, or with as much grace and subtlety. It is as splendid a look at one of the more interesting social and political minds around the United States in the last quarter of the twentieth century as one is likely to find.

Weyr was not altogether correct about Moynihan's not slipping or winning attention. His comments about India exporting only "communicable disease" caused a major flap at the Indian Embassy in Washington and at the United Nations.

A brilliant, retentive intellect, an Irish gift of gab and wit, a 24-carat ego, a quick sense of outrage and a habit of telling the truth don't always lead a person to the U.S. Senate. And the fact is, they didn't lead Daniel Patrick Moynihan there, either—at least not directly. The stops that Moynihan made along the way make him a human touchstone of Government service throughout the Sixties and Seventies: Assistant Secretary of Labor under John F. Kennedy and Lyndon Johnson, an urban-affairs Cabinet member and Ambassador to India under Richard Nixon, Ambassador to the United Nations under Gerald Ford.

Moynihan was also a professor of government at Harvard University; and while some of his academic colleagues dismissed him as a papier-mâché scholar, some politicians sneered at him as a double-domed intellectual. His liberal positions infuriate the right wing and his conservative ideas incense the left. One liberal critic asked during Moynihan's campaign against in-

cumbent Senator James Buckley, "Why would the voters of New York State want an Irish hawk who apes the manners of the English gentry—when they already have one?" Today, no less than in the past, the press continues to find him an inviting target.

Moynihan, who was born in Tulsa, Oklahoma, in 1927, considers himself an activist intellectual who, right or wrong, feels obliged to work for his convictions in the real and dangerous world of Government. Admittedly, Moynihan always advanced under the aegis of admiring and ever more powerful patrons—Averell Harriman, Arthur Goldberg, Jack Kennedy, Richard Nixon. But his "Moynihan Report," written in 1965, raised a national furor. It still inflames black leaders with its thesis that Negro problems are rooted in unstable family life, which he described with such nettling phrases as "tangle of pathology." Nevertheless, he stayed on at Labor to help draft Johnson's antipoverty program, and he was appointed by Nixon to direct the Urban Affairs Council. He achieved Cabinet rank and in 1970 another uproar, when somebody leaked his famous "benign neglect" memo to Nixon on racial tension. But from 1969 to 1970, Moynihan designed and very nearly engineered passage of the Family Assistance Plan, a guaranteed-income program that would have been a first attack on the nation's welfare mess.

After two low-profile years as Ambassador to India, Moynihan exploded into the public consciousness again as a one-man tempest. Appointed Ambassador to the United Nations by Gerald Ford, Moynihan quickly dubbed it the "theater of the absurd" and began following his own dictum—"The U.S. spokesman should be feared for the truths he might tell." With fists pounding and voice angry, he publicly dished up unvarnished truths to Third World nations who denounced America while taking generous U.S. aid. Such unconventionally rip-roaring diplomacy enraged foreign delegates, journalists and the Department of State; everybody that is, except American taxpayers, who thought it was high time somebody told off suppliant nations who acted like enemies. Moynihan became something of a national hero. In the last seven months before he finally quit, irretrievably undermined by Henry Kissinger, Moynihan received 26,000 letters. Only 190 were hostile.

While Moynihan, back at Harvard, was considering whether or not he should give in to pressure to run for the Senate, PLAYBOY asked writer Richard Meryman to explore Ambassador Moynihan's remarkable range of experience. Meryman's report:

"I met Pat Moynihan in 1945 in the Naval Reserve Officers Training Corps at Tufts College and soon regarded him as one of my best friends. Pat was the ultimate companion, radiating energy and interest and a sense of the ironies of life. There was always a gala air about Pat, as though he were on his way to a circus.

"When we were commissioned—two callow ensigns—Pat and I were assigned to sister repair ships near Norfolk, Virginia. After the Navy, Pat *was back on the Tufts campus in the Fletcher School and I was in graduate school at Harvard. Then, as always before in our friendship, we made trips to New York and stayed with Pat's mother, brother and sister over the saloon they owned. I helped him clean the place, dragging the wooden flooring from behind the bar to hose it down on the sidewalk in the sun. And in the family, there was the unspoken information that by right of class and culture, they were better than their Hell's Kitchen life.*

"Hearing rumors of inflated wages in Alaska, four of us, including Pat, decided to work there in the summer of 1949. With the cheerful insensitivity of youth, we bought for our expedition a 1935 Packard hearse, which we outfitted with a bed where the casket usually rested. It seemed like a good joke. The trip was a succession of mechanical disasters; we ran low on money and detoured to Hungry Horse, Montana, where jobs were reportedly available on the dam then under construction.

"Pat lasted one day.

"I myself was fired the same week when I blew a fuse that idled the entire night shift at work building a cement-mixing tower. Pat and I decided to ride the freights back to Chicago. We rattled through dusty towns and caught rides in boxcars filthy with empty coalbags and luxuriated in the air-conditioned comfort of empty refrigerator cars. We half starved. We were kicked off cars by trainmen and chased by yard cops.

"In Chicago, we separated, pretty much for good. Pat went on to higher education and areas of interest we did not share. That year, I went to work as a reporter for Life. *The irresponsible part of our youth was finished.*

"I accepted the PLAYBOY *assignment in part because of the extraordinary, full-circle symmetry. When I arrived at Pat's house in Cambridge, Massachusetts, he carried my bag indoors. Our hair was gray. The leanness in our faces was gone. His hearty flow of ironic commetary was still there— but heavier, like our waistlines.*

"During our talks, many of them on airplanes as Pat flew to lecture dates, I began to see a special gift, one reason for his value to all those Presidents. He could jab through bewildering complexities to the core and pull out a single insight, surprising in its simplicity, that illuminated an entire problem."

PLAYBOY: Let's start with this burning issue: You are often referred to in the press as flamboyant. Is there any truth to those rumors of flamboyance?

MOYNIHAN: None. Oh, I raised a lot of hell when I was Ambassador to the United Nations, dealing with people I felt were adversaries of ours or enemies of ours. But it depends on what you're doing. As Ambassador to India, I kept a very low profile. And now that I'll be in the Senate, I have to say I don't regard anyone in Washington as an enemy of ours. Them's us. Besides, there's no more certain way of failing in your objectives than to come storming in and announce that anything that happens you're going to take credit for. No need for that. No desire for it.

PLAYBOY: Still, you've used what people see as a certain flair in your personality to become politically prominent. Couldn't that have an effectiveness for you in the Senate?

MOYNIHAN: Perhaps, if it puts enough people on notice that there really are things we have to do, claims we have to make. As a newspaper editorial put it, New York has some due bills it has to present to Washington. No concern about unpleasantness or controversy will deter me from making those claims. The only thing that could make me controversial—aside from a major foreign-policy issue—would be that there were no other way to get attention to New York's economic needs *except* by becoming that.

PLAYBOY: After all your years in Government service, how does it feel to be a freshman Senator, a new boy?

MOYNIHAN: Well, I've begun thinking of myself as a man who has been around a long time, which is new to me. Being a freshman Senator suggests a certain deference to people who have been around longer—but not where the interests of New York State are concerned. There's no one else in the Senate who knows more about them than you and your colleague, so in that sense, there is no deference. When I first went to talk with retiring Majority Leader Mike Mansfield a few days after the election, I was deferential as hell. But as he walked me down the hall to a meeting, he said, "Just remember, Pat, we're all equal here."

And in that sense, I have the same power any other Senator has—a vote. I've talked to Senators in the past and, without exception, they will tell you that what moves the Senate is the genuine judgment of the individual Senators. It's not to say that they're beyond helping one another out or trying to make sense of one another's interests, and so forth, but in the end, the system is just what it was meant to be: In the end, Senators stand up and vote as they think.

PLAYBOY: You sound almost lyrical about the U.S. Senate. What are your general thoughts about it, as an institution?

MOYNIHAN: Then Senate is, has always been, the alternative authority in Government to the Presidency. The House is too large and diffuse. The Senate has always been able to produce persons, symbols of the institution, who can embody a necessary alternative to the authority of the President. That's the constitutional role of the Senate, and it has worked extraordinarily. It has never failed to generate the tension it was intended to.

PLAYBOY: Tension? What do you mean?

MOYNIHAN: The constitutional idea is that concentration of power is a danger in a society. Therefore, you separate it and build tensions into the different branches. Freedom lives in the interstices of these arrangements.

On the other hand, when there is too much conflict in the system, you get the imperial Presidency—which tries to avoid the system altogether. Which is what I think happened in that sequence of Presidents who found the Congress so frustrating they just wished it weren't there. The real art of the Constitution is to use the tensions but make them cooperative enough so that no one branch tries to escape. And the Senate has a special place in this dynamic. It's just—it's the highest honor you can get in this republic other than the Presidency. It has a quality of class of persons about it and it imposes that condition on your behavior. The Presidency is something singular and in no way something people can calculate; nobody can think in terms of what it means to be in that office. But there are 100 Senators, and you can ask and get close to what it means to be a Senator. It means that you must be just absolutely fearless and try to be intelligent. I expect to be a good Senator.

PLAYBOY: Why did you decide to run for the Senate, especially after vowing when you quit as UN Ambassador not to do so?

MOYNIHAN: I got up one spring morning and they had closed the City University of New York. I was seething. There was always one unique thing about New York: It was the first city to establish a free college for the children of working people. Through ups and downs, for a century and a quarter, the college endured. I went to City College myself. It was opened again, but the closing of it was sacrilegious—it meant symbolically, My God, what have we come to? Have we handled our affairs so badly?

PLAYBOY: Surely, your reasons were more complicated than that.

MOYNIHAN: Well, yes. I had said I wouldn't run. I knew quite a bit about politics. Politics gets so personal and harsh. It seemed too much to impose on one's family—or on oneself. And I like to teach. Even now, I feel very bad about leaving Harvard. That's a life now that will not be lived, one I really expected to live . . . a path not taken . . . or a path taken and then abandoned. But, quite simply, I hated to feel, late in life, that I had a chance to be a U.S. Senator and passed it up.

PLAYBOY: Late in life? You're 49.

MOYNIHAN: Yes, and I suppose, in a way, that's an advantage, a consolation, considering the nature of campaigning. If I had run 15 years ago, it would have been a great shock to the system to find out how much can be alleged about your character. And there's not much I haven't been accused of, either. But what is that line from A. E. Housman—"Mithridates, he died old." You can take poisons in small doses.

PLAYBOY: First you sounded lyrical; now you're sounding old and cynical.

MOYNIHAN: About the campaign process, not the office. But to the degree that we all go through it, yes. There's a certain insensitivity to untruth that politicians acquire. Even to genuinely villainous distortion. They start saying, "Well, it's part of the game," and it should *never* be part of the game. You shouldn't become, as some do, amiable about it. It's wrong, because your capacity for indignation atrophies. If you become tolerant of distortion when it is done by other people, you become tolerant about doing it yourself. I really do think that happens.

PLAYBOY: Were you the object of villainous distortion during your campaign?

MOYNIHAN: Oh, it went on, but I don't want to talk about it. But I can say this: My opponent, Jim Buckley, was personally an altogether decent and genuinely conservative person. But he was talked into making some snarling accusations during the campaign. And if you're going to vote for a person, it's not because he makes snarling accusations. I have a very strong feeling that the public becomes quite punishing to politicians who are vicious in campaigns. They vote against them.

But the press *can get to you.* For example, *Women's Wear Daily* reported that I stormed into a meeting with a torn shirt and terrorized secretaries and staff for not catering to my whims—which included, the newspaper reported, bloody marys "early and often." There you are. That's what public life is all about. That particular incident happened while you were interviewing me for PLAYBOY. Would you care to give your version?

PLAYBOY: Glad to. It was we who ordered the bloody marys; you had a beer. We witnessed no terror tactics. But we do have to point out, in the interest of journalistic accuracy, that you did, indeed, have a hole in your shirt. Now, about your victory over Buckley—how, briefly, do you account for it?

MOYNIHAN: The debates we had opened up quite a gap between our views. I was running, for instance, against a man who had virtually never voted a penny for health, education or welfare. The question was clear: What kind of role did each of us want the national Government to play in the state of New York? His answer was, "As little as possible." Mine was, "As much as we can get that will help."

PLAYBOY: Aside from the name-calling, was the campaign an unpleasant, exhausting chore?

MOYNIHAN: To the contrary. Campaigning is Antaeuslike. You take strength from the American citizens. They may absolutely intend to vote against you, but they always say, "Good luck," and smile at you. In eight months of campaigning—beginning with my work for Senator Henry Jackson—I don't think I had three unpleasant words. The only bad moment I can remember was talking with a fellow about Northern Ireland. I couldn't satisfy him about my views. And I said, "What is your name, sir?" And he said, "My name is Dooley." And I said, "I've got a dog named Mr. Dooley." And he said, "You really know how to get to a fellow, don't you?"—and stormed away.

It is the fund raising in a campaign that is agony. There were times when I was sort of let out onto the streets as if, "You've earned it, now that you've raised $6000 today. For that you can go out and campaign." But there's no way of avoiding the fact that the real campaign takes place on television; you can't talk to 15,000,000 people on the streets.

PLAYBOY: What do you think your effect was on the national campaign? Some people say if you hadn't carried New York by as large a margin as you did, Carter might have lost the state.

MOYNIHAN: Well, there came a time when we definitely needed at least a 600,000-vote lead. And it's probable that if I hadn't made that target, Carter would have gone down. We might have had a great constitutional crisis, a theoretical case. Carter would have lost 41 electoral votes here, lost the election, but would have had a slight plurality of the popular vote.

PLAYBOY: Speaking of the national campaign, there's something interesting about the fact that Carter's *Playboy Interview* became a national issue, and here you are, the first political figure since then to appear in the same format. Do you have any thoughts about that?

MOYNIHAN: I think what happened with Jimmy Carter's *Playboy Interview* is that it produced a dissonance between the image he'd projected up to then and the one that came out in all that publicity. He probably failed to observe certain political conventions regarding personal expressions—though, to anticipate your next question, that is the politician's responsibility, not the publication's. But, obviously, a lot of people who voted for him weren't as upset as the press made out in the heat of the campaign. As far as I'm concerned, the interview helped those who read it with open minds see that Carter was a man of more complexity than the one who'd been presented before.

PLAYBOY: What made you decide to agree to do the interview?

MOYNIHAN: Last spring, I was meeting with some very bright young people around a table at Harvard. I was asking about Presidential preferences, and several of the best-informed people said they were for Jerry Brown. When I asked why, they said, "Because of the *Playboy Interview*." So I've thought of this as a perfectly good way to get your ideas across to people. The personalities featured in this format are presented in a complex, often absorbing way.

PLAYBOY: You've known a number of complex personalities in your political life, among them five Presidents. You served four of them in very high positions, which is a remarkable, if not unique, record. Would you tell us your opinions of the five men?

MOYNIHAN: Well, Eisenhower was a great politician. In a long and successful life, when things went wrong, some one of his subordinates was always to blame. He never exposed the Presidency, never exposed his military leadership to damage it couldn't sustain. This is not a question of being devious; it's a question of knowing how to maintain an effective power position.

He was an immensely intuitive man. I used to try to get the Nixon Administration to follow his lead on things. I wanted to get up a memorial to him—establish an institute for the study of the military-industrial complex . . . that was very shocking. All the vast analysis that McNamara's people put into Vietnam never equaled the import of Eisenhower's two-sentence forecast in his farewell address. Eisenhower also said, "When Lee was down in Virginia, nobody could touch him; the minute he got up into Pennsylvania, he was in trouble." And that's the essence of the Vietnam war.

PLAYBOY: Yes, but what made him such a good politician?

MOYNIHAN: His devastating capacity to make his enemies underestimate him. The popular view of Eisenhower among educated Eastern people was that he was a boob. He talked in convoluted, involuted sentences that didn't parse when transcribed, unlike the rest of us, who like to think we come out in lapidary prose. It was very agreeable to think, He's not as smart as I am; that's what's the matter with him. It was probably a very agreeable thought to Eisenhower. That's the way people got their balls cut off.

Eisenhower—he was born in Texas—and Kennedy illustrate a South/North distinction between politicians. The Southerner is that kind of good ole boy who will just sit there and scratch his bottom and pick his ears and say, "My golly, you shore must be smart. You say you're from New York City? Well, I hear there are some awful smart people up there and you tell me you're one of them and I guess you must be, because you talk so good."

PLAYBOY: Is that a description of Jimmy Carter?

MOYNIHAN: No. President Carter is more of a transition Southerner. He was introduced to audiences correctly as a nuclear physicist and a peanut farmer—and obviously more of a nuclear physicist. You have to have known the Congress that John F. Kennedy dealt with, dominated by Southerners before the advent of a standard accent, before everybody watched the *Today* show, before people got John Chancellor's nice, Mid-western voice. There were committee chairmen in Congress whose manners and accents were absolutely removed from metropolitan America. What's that line from *My Fair Lady*? "There even are places where English completely disappears."

PLAYBOY: We were talking about the Southern-style politician who allows you to underestimate him. What about the Northern, the Kennedy style?

MOYNIHAN: Kennedy was confident. Eisenhower had left the Presidency intact and, at the start, anybody could look good. Kennedy's style was to tell you how smart he was, how many degrees he had. If you didn't know that the Southerners were, in fact, concealing and that the Northerners maybe weren't as smart as they pretended, you made great miscalculations. Then you thought the village-pacification campaign in the Mekong Delta could be programed to where any Deputy Secretary could simply punch out the number of pacified villages each week.

PLAYBOY: Did Kennedy fall into Eisenhower's trap?

MOYNIHAN: I think maybe. His estimate of Eisenhower perhaps made him and his people feel their abilities were worth more than they were. We forget that the confidence was running out of the Kennedy Administration by the third year. Our program was dead in the water. The Southerners could still block everything. Congress felt no sense of urgency. Dick Donahue, his legislative liaison man with Congress, described Kennedy's relationship with Congress as "a mutuality of contempt." When Kennedy died, the only measure of any consequence that had passed the Congress was a four-year extension of the draft—which was debated for only ten minutes in the Senate.

And maybe your luck is running out when . . . you see, the Cuban Missile Crisis was actually a *defeat*. It left the Russians permanently in-stalled in a regime 90 miles off the coast of the United States and we agreed to do nothing to interfere with that regime. That's what they wanted. They agreed to take their missiles out, OK. But when anybody puts missiles into a situation like that, he should expect to have a lot of trouble with the United States, and real trouble—and all that happened was the agreement: "OK, you can have your man down there—permanently."

PLAYBOY: What was your impression of Kennedy the first time you met him?

MOYNIHAN: Oh, magic. Charisma *is* the word, but often less than satis-factory in its actual . . . The first time we met, he was arriving at the 1960 convention. I had been arguing with Averell Harriman to be for Kennedy. Harriman couldn't forgive the old man, the Ambassador. He kept going on about Joe Kennedy. And Kennedy said hello to the governor and then the governor introduced me and said I was at Syracuse University. Kennedy said, "Oh, I have an honorary degree from Syracuse University."

A perfectly sensible thing to say but rather disappointing to me. I wanted him to say something brilliant, never to be forgotten. An exchange of in-comparable lucidity and prophetic clairvoyance, instead of "Guy from Syracuse, I'll stick him with this, press the flesh and get on with it." So there was a disparity between the aura of the man and what he could produce at any given moment.

PLAYBOY: When you looked into his eyes, what did you see?

MOYNIHAN: You saw devilment. And behind it was: "It's a ball." He was watching it all. And enjoying it.

At the first meeting I ever had with Kennedy in the Cabinet room, we came over with a proposed program that I had helped put together under the direction of then–Labor Secretary Arthur Goldberg. It was to provide for union recognition in the Federal service. And in the history of labor and industrial relations, it was an important event.

We went in and presented this thing. And obviously the President hadn't been waiting six months, as we had assumed, for us to get this work done. And he really scarcely remembered that he had made this agreement. So before we were quite able to tell him about all the wonderful parts of this perpetual-motion machine we had put together, he said, "Well, great." And out he went.

Suddenly, he reappeared. You go right through the door to the little secretarial room and then the Oval Office, and suddenly he came ripping out and at the end of the Cabinet table, he put down this open paper and it was *The Dallas Morning News*. Ted Dealey had written: "We need a man on horseback to lead this nation and many people in Texas and the Southwest think that they are riding Caroline's tricycle." And there on the editorial page of the first edition was a poem. President Kennedy said, "Listen to this." And he read the poem and we all said, "Uh-huh." And he said, "Don't you get it? The first letter of every line: S-H-I-T-O-N-T-E-D. Shit on Ted." And he turned to me and he said, "You know, it's a . . ." He wanted the word. And all I could say was, "Yeah, it's a . . ." I still block on the word.

PLAYBOY: Acrostic.

MOYNIHAN: Yes, if I had only said, "Mr. President, it's an acrostic," he'd have said, "You're right. Henceforth, you're Assistant Secretary of State for Cultural Affairs." On the spot. Field promotion. "Rise, Sir Patrick, you are Assistant Secretary of State for Cultural Affairs." But all I could say was, "Ah. . . ."

He was so pleased. "Shit on Ted." That was his idea of a good joke. And, of course, Dealey Plaza in Dallas was where he was murdered several months later.

PLAYBOY: Where were you when Kennedy was assassinated?

MOYNIHAN: I was in the White House at the moment the word came that he was dead. We were just a small group down in the southwest corner office, which had been Sherman Adams' and became Bob Haldeman's— just three doors from the Oval Office. That day, they were changing the rug in the Oval Office. All the furniture was piled out in the hallway and on top of the furniture was Kennedy's rocking chair—as if the President were leaving.

PLAYBOY: What was your reaction to the assassination?

MOYNIHAN: Shock, of course. Grief. But there was something else not usually mentioned. People found that, in a particular way, it enlarged their lives. They felt relations with other people they didn't normally feel. It was an event that people do not remember as a terrible event. They remember it as a sad one, a rich, emotional one.

That was a very good moment for me in terms of my wits. I was driving in the afternoon and I remember hearing on the radio that the police had arrested a man and he had been involved in Fair Play for Cuba. And it flashed to me that the Dallas police would kill that man, that we had to get physical custody of that man. And I went out to meet the Cabinet plane, which arrived around midnight at Andrews, and I went up and down the line of people who came off, saying we had to get custody of Oswald. No-body could hear me. For two days, I went to everybody in Washington. There was almost nobody of importance I did not have access to. Bobby Kennedy was just zonked, some were stunned, some were already maneuver-ing. None of them had ever been in a police station in unfriendly circum-stances. If you were raised in the streets, you have a sense of this.

PLAYBOY: Do you think the murder of Jack Kennedy was the result of a plot?

MOYNIHAN: No. I thought it was purely a random act. But after Oswald was killed, I went around Washington saying, "Look, we have to investigate the murder of Kennedy as if it were, in fact, a plot. Because if we don't, if the Warren Commission doesn't do its job, if it doesn't look into the jaws of hell on this thing, we will be living with a conspiracy plot for the rest of our political lives." There was a book I used to carry around that showed that the Jesuits had assassinated Lincoln. And all I got for my troubles, I'm afraid, was that Lyndon Johnson thought I was saying there was a conspiracy. And Johnson never forgave me.

PLAYBOY: Didn't the Warren Commission look into "the jaws of hell"?

MOYNIHAN: It did not. My friend Ed Epstein was up in Cornell, doing a master's thesis for the government department, and he wanted to do a study on how a Presidential commission works. He went down to study the Warren Commission, and the first thing he saw was how it did *not* work. The commissioners never went to the meetings. They started sending deputies and deputies started sending deputies. And Warren, at that point, had become a man of vast self-importance and rather small competence. So around Harvard today, you see kids with stickers on their notebooks that say, WHO KILLED J.F.K.?

It's what Thorstein Veblen called trained incapacity. When I was stand-ing with the Cabinet at Andrews Air Force Base, saying we had to get custody of Oswald, I was talking to overeducated people who had learned the word paranoid and who had been taught that people who go around being suspicious are crazy. Because awful things don't happen. As a matter of fact, awful things *do* happen. And ordinary people know that. And right now, in this country, for example, it's perfectly clear that sophisticated people know there's no danger from the Soviet Union. Because the notion of being threatened has acquired an almost class connotation. If you're not very educated, you're easily frightened. And not ever being frightened can be a formula for self-destruction.

PLAYBOY: You remained in the Johnson Administration for 20 months. How was it different from Kennedy's reign?

MOYNIHAN: The Johnson people were in a kind of tension with Ken-nedy's people—which was not bad. Everybody was trying to show, "We are as good as they were." Standards of achievement were being asserted by everybody. And Johnson knew more about the Federal Government than any President in history. He knew it because he had mastered it. The war spoiled all that. Johnson got more and more beleaguered, more and more conscious of the Presidency under siege—that people were trying to hurt, not help, that people betrayed him and nobody could be trusted. Lyndon Johnson ended up giving speeches on the flight decks of aircraft carriers off the coast of Southern California—the only way he could get a safe audience.

PLAYBOY: In private, he talked like a human blast furnace, didn't he?

MOYNIHAN: Yes, but remember that Lyndon Johnson was a schoolteacher, really the only job he ever had outside Government. But you can't get elected in Texas, or couldn't in those days, by being a schoolteacher. You had to be a cowboy, so, naturally, L.B.J. made a great thing of all that colorful, earthy cowboy talk. But actually, my hunch is that deep down, he was not a cowboy except in language. He wasn't *macho*. He didn't want to go to war; he tried everything he could to keep the war from getting bigger, but once he was locked into it, he accepted McNamara's strategy of slowly increasing the pressure by little increments, which meant that the North Vietnamese and Viet Cong never had to expect anything but a little bit more of what they were getting. They sensed that Johnson was not a destructive man; and this was his undoing with them, I think.

This was a very different message than Nixon sent to people. He, I think, communicated the possibility that he could, in fact, go crazy and do something incredible, if he just got mad enough. And that you had to treat him very carefully. And you'd better not risk finding out whether it was so or wasn't so. In a sense, it was Nixon who played the cowboy and Johnson who played the Quaker.

PLAYBOY: We'll get to Nixon in a moment, but wasn't L.B.J., whom you describe as a gentle man, pretty ruthless toward a lot of people?

MOYNIHAN: He could be absolutely, devastatingly indifferent. Sargent Shriver, Adam Yarmolinsky and I went over to present the poverty program to the Cabinet. And none of us had been to a Cabinet meeting. We were all pretty full of beans about this program. We wanted to pay for a big employment program by raising cigarette taxes. But Johnson was cutting taxes that year and he must have known ahead of time what we were going to say.

Anyway, we got to the Cabinet meeting. This would be spring of '64. And Johnson came in and sat down. Carl Rowan had just become director of the U.S. Information Agency and didn't sit with the rest. Johnson said to Carl, "Come on up here and sit at the table, Carl. What's the matter with you?" Rowan, of course, was acting correctly. He was not a member of the Cabinet.

Then Johnson got everybody started. "The first thing we're going to do is we're going to hear a report from the Secretary of State on the conditions in the Far East, South Asia and Vietnam." So Rusk starts talking. And I'm thinking, My God, we're really going to see how the Government works. And Rusk had got into his fourth sentence when Johnson reached down, picked up a telephone and said, "Get me So-and-so." And then he turned around and spent the rest of the Cabinet meeting talking on the telephone!

Every so often, he'd realize there was silence and he'd turn around and say, "You, Sarge, you go right ahead and tell us about this poverty program." And people would pretend they were talking to the President. Well, who are you talking to in that setting? You are talking to yourself. And when it was all over and we were walking out, Shriver said, "You know, I wish now I'd never been to a Cabinet meeting. He had every guy in the room in his pocket and he was working on some guy he didn't have."

PLAYBOY: When did you first meet Lyndon Johnson?

MOYNIHAN: He was Vice-President then. I remember looking into his eyes and thinking, This is a bull castrated very late in life. But he didn't make a great impression on me one way or the other. I shared the Kennedy attitude of who in the hell is this guy, anyway? It just seemed to me that everything for him was all over. We had beaten Lyndon Johnson. Now who were we going to beat next? Well, we found out different, didn't we?

PLAYBOY: Getting back to Nixon, whom you mentioned earlier, what were your first impressions of *him*?

MOYNIHAN: There was one thing I had always resented about Lyndon Johnson—that shortly after he took over in the White House, he ordered the floodlights that illuminate it turned off. He said it was an economy measure. And everybody thought this was very clever. Half the fathers in the country go around telling the children, "Will you turn out the goddamn lights in the closet?" I resented it bitterly. I took it as a sort of symbolic action of the lights going out. And I don't like governments where the lights are off. So when Nixon asked me to go to work for him, I'd never met him before and I said, "All right, but there's one condition, a very mild one, but I'd like to ask that you turn the lights on in the White House." "Done," he said. The lights were turned on again. But the next morning, I read that Nixon had announced it was done as an anticrime measure. Damn. Right away, I felt, No class.

PLAYBOY: Did you ever hear Kennedy venture an opinion about Nixon?

MOYNIHAN: Sure, the expression I just used myself: His great remark made after their first debate was, "No class." But those two guys *did* have a relationship. They had been through so many things together. Kennedy went to see Nixon down in Key Biscayne just after the election and there was a great opening line that Bob Finch told me about. Kennedy walked in and said, "How the hell did you carry Ohio?" Couple of friends. Win some, lose some.

PLAYBOY: Why did you, a Democrat, go to work for Nixon?

MOYNIHAN: Because he asked me. I was director of the Joint Center of Urban Studies of MIT and Harvard and had been running around saying that this country was in an awful, awful fix—that the rioting was threatening the stability of liberal institutions in this country. I felt I knew more about it than most of the people who were then advising Nixon. And I did. I was willing to take the bet that we could turn this around, because we had to.

Since then, I've heard a lot of complaining that I worked for a Republican, but nobody ever says that there never was another riot. By God, if a dozen cities had exploded the next summer, you'd have heard how I screwed up.

PLAYBOY: Did you have any qualms about working for Nixon?

MOYNIHAN: No, I felt there was one thing he had done that *did* have class. Whatever the facts are, Nixon thought the 1960 election had been stolen from him. And certainly at the level at which we write history, you can make that case. I'm not saying it's true in the least. But Nixon was urged to contest it and he didn't. Because all he could have done was to diminish the Presidency. He couldn't have *gotten* in. Eisenhower wasn't going to call out the troops and disallow the election.

PLAYBOY: When you worked for Nixon, did you admire him?

MOYNIHAN: Yes. Yes. But not unreservedly, by any means. I resigned at the time of Cambodia. I thought there was probably a strong military case but no political case of any kind. I went in to the President and said, "Look, I just have to leave." And he was very nice. He said, "I know what you're going through, and I know you have to leave. But would you stick around and get Family Assistance through Congress?" And I agreed to stay a few more months. But I stayed six.

PLAYBOY: Shouldn't you have publicly expressed moral outrage against the Cambodian invasion instead of staying on?

MOYNIHAN: That is the hardest question a person in Government faces. None of us faces it very well. Remember, when you leave, you lose your influence. And point one: I *had* resigned. And the war was not my area.

Point two: I really did believe the Administration when it said it was going to get in and get out of Cambodia. And within three weeks of my staying on, they had gotten out and there was only the record left.

And I had a certain relationship with Nixon. He had trusted me. Kissinger had told me Nixon expected me to leave early and denounce him, and I kind of didn't want to do that. It would have been easier to denounce somebody from your own party than someone who kind of expected you to.

PLAYBOY: But, at that time, Nixon was also bombing the hell out of South Vietnam and, some people think, actually destroying the country we were trying to save.

MOYNIHAN: I guess I didn't think that. I was working on domestic things. I was appalled by the war in Vietnam. Everybody knew my views. In the first memorandum I ever sent to Nixon—in January 1969—I said, "The war is lost. Don't identify yourself with it or you will be crushed."

I was national cochairman of Negotiation Now. And I guess my feelings were with Bob Kennedy. The war was over and we were abandoning the Vietnamese. They would be taken over by the Communists. Regardless of who was President in 1969, 1970, we'd made that decision. The disproportion of the American effort had been outrageous. But the effort itself was not. That's my view. And I dare to suggest that had the war been won, it would not be regarded now as having been so evil.

PLAYBOY: But the war dragged on for four more years.

MOYNIHAN: I guess I think Nixon never could admit that we had lost the war. Anyway, I stayed and worked through the summer on school desegregation in the South, and then in the fall—he had already asked me and I had said no—I finally agreed to become Ambassador to the UN. And one evening in December, I went out to dinner and asked Steve Hess to be my deputy. I went home and between the time I got into the elevator on the first floor and got out on the fifth floor, I decided, I don't want to be around this Administration anymore. And I called up my wife, Liz, who was miserable about the prospect of the UN, and I said, "I'm not going to stay. I'm going."

PLAYBOY: Still, you're doing something most politicians—especially Democrats—wouldn't do: You're defending Richard Nixon, to an extent.

MOYNIHAN: During those first few years of Nixon, there was some damn good government. But Nixon couldn't get any credit for it. The press and others just kept denying it, denying it, and he gave up. He gave up trying.

For example, when Nixon took office, 68 percent of black children in the old South were in all-black schools. By 1970, the figure had gone down to 14 percent. The public schools in the South ended up more integrated than the public schools in Michigan. And they still are. But at the time, nobody would say Nixon had done it. And, of course, he wouldn't say he had done it.

PLAYBOY: Why not? Modesty is not a politician's trait.

MOYNIHAN: He didn't want credit for it. He wanted to carry South Carolina. He wanted Strom Thurmond to say this is a good ole boy. And Strom Thurmond had trouble saying he was a good ole boy.

PLAYBOY: In *The Final Days,* the authors say Patrick Moynihan was shocked when he read the White House tapes, that this was a Nixon he never knew or heard.

MOYNIHAN: Yes, Arthur Burns and George Schultz and I all had this reaction. Nixon obviously had two personae. If you knew one, you didn't know the other. I used to titillate the President, if you will, by my foul language. Early in my two years there, we had a meeting of big-city mayors to talk about urban things. It was a successful meeting and the President, having used up his hour, said, "Now, look, everything's going well and Vice-President Agnew will carry on this discussion with you." But Agnew then began to get into useless arguments and everything was getting heated and the meeting broke up. Later, the President asked me, "How did that go?" And, describing what Agnew had done to the meeting, I used a good old Anglo-Saxon verb. Well, they all laughed and giggled—this terrible word had been used. This fellow uses naughty words. But then you find out that an hour later he's in there. . . .

PLAYBOY: Why did Nixon make the tapes in the first place?

MOYNIHAN: I'd heard in the White House that he bugged the Oval Office because he wanted to have a better Presidential library than Lyndon Johnson. You know: This will really grab them when they come through generations from now and hear President Nixon say to Secretary Kissinger, "Very well, Henry, I want you to go to Peking."

PLAYBOY: Why didn't he destroy the tapes?

MOYNIHAN: You have to start from the fact that the Watergate break-in itself was a small event. A crime, but not a massive one. Nobody was hurt. Unimportant. Nixon was a man who had put up with much more serious things. For example, his assumption that the 1960 election had been stolen. This time, he had been elected—49 states.

I can just imagine him not believing that anybody could take the Presidency away from him now, because three horse's asses he'd never met had broken into Larry O'Brien's files to get a copy of the letters to the creditors of the Democratic National Committee. "Didn't you receive our check? Well, we're very surprised. We sent that check out last week. If that check doesn't clear, you'll get a check in the next mail. We promise. Don't you worry. As always. Faithfully yours, Larry."

PLAYBOY: Yes, but why didn't Nixon destroy the tapes?

MOYNIHAN: You can't understand Nixon if you don't understand that he could not destroy the tapes. It was a combination of, one, being—at that level—an honest man. And, two, being a self-destructive one. He did not destroy the tapes and he did not blow up the world. He went peacefully from office. And I thought he left well.

And a case could be made—which I would not make—that Nixon was the victim of a coup. In which he collaborated. At first, all he had had to say was, "Look here, I didn't know anything about it at the time, and later I thought it better not to rock the Presidency; but, in point of fact, there was a break-in at Watergate, and I did use bad judgment, and that certainly isn't going to happen again." There would have been a furor, but it would have passed. But he didn't do that. Nixon did not see it develop into a question of character. But it did. And, in the end, it was not the crime of Watergate but the crime of concealment that destroyed him.

Actually, I have the theory that *I* am responsible for Watergate.

PLAYBOY: Please elaborate. You're thickening the plot.

MOYNIHAN: I got President Nixon involved in the idea that we *had* to do something about the international heroin traffic. When I left, John Ehrlichman took over the drug program and he passed it on to his assistant, Egil

Krogh, who took it up with a passion, and he looked for aides who would really believe in this case.

Now, G. Gordon Liddy had been brought into the Treasury Department for the same sort of thing. But Treasury realized that he was crazy and was getting rid of him. So he was hired at the White House because he was a shoot-'em-up, mow-'em-down, get-those-monsters-who-are-pouring-poison-into-the-veins-of-American-youth type. In the name of fighting the heroin traffic, a vicious criminal activity, a lot of things might be justified. But then they moved those methods over into politics. And it was Liddy who began telling those rather simple Christian Science lawyers, "I'll show 'em. I'll get those *mafiosi*, those sons of bitches. I'll get Larry O'Brien."

He was the loose cannon on the gun deck. Absent Liddy and what would there have been? The enemies list? Well, what the hell was that? A list of who *not* to ask to dinner at the White House. The enemies list was one thing; taping Martin Luther King, Jr., in bed with other women and revealing the details to reporters, which was done under a previous Administration, was surely of a greater order.

Actually, the violations by the Federal Government of civil liberties were much greater in magnitude under Johnson than under Nixon. The Church Committee has chapter after chapter on this. In a sense, Nixon paid for Johnson's transgressions as well as his own. God help the man who has done small things at the end of a long sequence of big things—when the people are finally sick of it.

PLAYBOY: Didn't you lose all your previous respect for Nixon after Watergate?

MOYNIHAN: Not really, if you accept the idea of tragic flaws in people, if you accept the idea of sin, if you accept a tragic view of life. He chose not to tell just one truth, in a dramatic context. It was a struggle of character and morality. Read William Shakespeare. That's what it's all about. The event of Nixon's destruction was, in some ways, no less a tragedy of character than was Lyndon Johnson's.

PLAYBOY: What was Johnson's flaw?

MOYNIHAN: Johnson had spent his whole life learning to manipulate adversaries. His entire life had been spent making people who didn't like or trust him do so. One dazzling triumph after another. And then, at the pinnacle of his career, he lost this ability. Events led up to a point where he had no option but to resign. In 30 years in Washington, Lyndon Johnson never got himself into that situation; he got *other* people into that situation. But probably he felt he *had* to lose his ability to manipulate at this time. Finally, something ultimately honorable was at stake—the American obligation, as he saw it, to struggle against communism.

PLAYBOY: And Nixon's flaw?

MOYNIHAN: A conviction that the people who were opposed to him were opposed for dishonorable purposes. And that they had no claim on him in consequence of their own failings. Which was not so. They had every claim in the world on him. They had the claim that everybody had. He was the President; they weren't. And it was required and expected of him that he be truthful. He wasn't.

PLAYBOY: Did you see Nixon during Watergate? You were in India then.

MOYNIHAN: Well, I knew that the settlement of India's rupee debt to the U.S. was going to be the biggest thing I would do in India. And I just had to get to the President to do so. But first I would have to see Kissinger. He was going to go out to see Nixon at San Clemente and said I could see him there. I knew if I hung around there long enough, I would eventually see Nixon. And, as it turned out, I just happened to spot him coming in on a golf cart and I rushed out and ran after him into his office. Nobody shot me. People certainly saw this guy chasing in the door after him. And I said, "I'd like to see you." "Oh, how are you?" "I'd like to talk with you a moment, if I could." "Fine, come in at 11 o'clock."

So I went in at 11 o'clock with Kissinger and there was talk about Brezhnev's visit that week. It was also the week in which young John Dean was testifying.

We did our business and all that and I said to the President, "Will you do me one favor?" "Yes, what is that?" "Will you turn that goddamn flag right side up?" His flag was upside down on his lapel, and that's a naval distress signal. He said, "Oh, goodness, yes, you're a Navy man, too, aren't you?" His cuff links were upside down, too. There were signs of internal disorder.

PLAYBOY: What was your perception of Ehrlichman and Haldeman?

MOYNIHAN: Pretty good men. Very representative of the men who come to the White House with any President. People who had been working with the man in other situations, acquired his trust before he acquired his power. But they didn't *know* a great deal. They got caught up in things they could not handle.

PLAYBOY: You once wrote that the Nixon men began to think of themselves as better than they were.

MOYNIHAN: Well, they found themselves so excoriated for things they knew they hadn't done that they began to think they were doing more, indeed, than they were. I mean, there was such an antinomian atmosphere in Washington.

PLAYBOY: Meaning what?

MOYNIHAN: It means the celebration of wrongdoing, the discrediting of institutions and people. It is the idea that if you believe the law is bad, then you can do anything. Many people who had been Cold Warriors and had been delivered from all that, then said none of their previous vows, obligations, standards had any claim on them. The more precious the secret, the more important it was to give it out. It's a very powerful recurrent aspect of culture.

PLAYBOY: Relate that to Ehrlichman and Haldeman.

MOYNIHAN: When they did something that their critics, in fact, thought was the right thing to do, they wouldn't get credit for it—it was claimed that they had done the opposite. Every time they increased the food-stamp allowance, the press would say they had cut it. I began to get nervous and I talked to friends in the press, saying, "You're disorienting those fellows. They know that what you say is not so. They're going to think nothing you say matters." And that is what happened. They were released from any feeling that any criticism was valid.

PLAYBOY: Weren't Ehrlichman and Haldeman just reflecting Nixon's hate relationship with the press?

MOYNIHAN: When they stopped being new boys from the Coast, yes. For Nixon, the press was just one protracted, nonnegotiable stalemate, an enmity of a permanent kind never, never to be misread for signs of change. I remember once sending him a complimentary column that *New York Times* columnist James Reston had written, and I said, "Isn't this very impressive?" And the answer came back from Nixon through Haldeman: "Look, if you ever let yourself take any satisfaction, any pleasure in what Reston writes, on that day you just open yourself to pain about what he writes the next day. So you don't have any reaction except record the information."

PLAYBOY: Since you haven't been shy about defending what you saw as Nixon's good points, what does a good Democrat like you have to say about Gerald Ford's Administration?

MOYNIHAN: I think Gerald Ford will be remembered as the President who bumped his head, had a wonderful wife and left Americans more at peace with themselves and the rest of the world than at any time since the United States became a world power. He got us out of the Watergate nightmare and got us back some pride and self-reliance.

Ford's Cabinet table talk was perhaps the best I've ever heard in Washington. When you had Ed Levi and John Dunlop and Bill Coleman triangulating a complex constitutional issue—"What does the Federalist Paper number 59 have to say about this?"—and you had Jim Schlesinger participating and Henry Kissinger listening—when he was there, which wasn't often—well, you had pretty high-quality conversation. And Ford was very good, presiding but not interfering. Not a bad Administration.

PLAYBOY: Let's turn to the subject of India, since you spent a term as Ambassador to that country. What is your view of Mrs. Gandhi?

MOYNIHAN: The culture of India is so extraordinarily complex that wrong notions can be as plausible as right notions. In the Thirties, at Oxford, Mrs. Gandhi acquired a very, very vague left view of the world in which the United States was seen as an ominous power acting out of capitalist, imperialist, racist motives. A caricature. And she just trundled all that junk home with her and nothing much was added later.

But she combined that with an intense and tactical knowledge of how individuals can be manipulated, frightened, enticed, intimidated. And she has the great sense that she gets from her father of her right to rule India. She is the spokesman of the masses. They are hers and she is theirs. You have to be born with that.

PLAYBOY: What was her effect on how the U.S. sees India today?

MOYNIHAN: While the second most populous nation in the world was a democracy, the United States had an enormous ideological interest in the prosperity and the success of that country. We want the world to know that democracies do well. So they've given up the one claim they had on us. When India ceased to be a democracy, our actual interest there just plummeted. I mean, what does it export but communicable disease?

PLAYBOY: After your two tours of duty as an Ambassador, what is your primary criticism of the U.S. State Department?

MOYNIHAN: In the past 30 years, there has been a high politics and a low politics in the Department of State. High politics was security politics. Those were the guys who were on the fast track, who got the important jobs. They were Ambassadors by 50 or moved up to Assistant Secretary rank. You knew they were moving from the minute they got started. Hard-nosed, tough, they dealt with real things—guns, bullets, bombs, tanks, planes.

Then there was low politics—what Averell Harriman would call drip. And drips would be people who deal with drip: all that ideological talk about freedom and liberty and totalitarianism, the free world and other worlds, capitalism, socialism.

Well, we've found out those ideological issues are *not* drip. They are *profoundly* serious. And when you get on the losing side of them—when the symbols of progress are captured by the other side—well, you are in trouble. And you're likely to stay that way.

PLAYBOY: Did Kissinger involve himself in ideological issues—in what you call drip—and did he share your view that the U.S. got on the wrong side of those issues?

MOYNIHAN: He did not himself encourage other people to concern themselves with drip, but he himself was very concerned. And you will not understand him at all if you do not know that he really felt—and this we share—that the decline of the West was a reality. And he felt the United States' behavior in recent years was accelerating that.

PLAYBOY: Are you saying that both you and Kissinger feel that American democracy is the wave of the past?

MOYNIHAN: I have said that democracy is beginning to look like monarchy in the 19th Century. It is the place where the world was, not where it is going. This is the one thing I've been trying to say to this country. There are about three dozen democracies left. Since 1946, there have been 78 new nations formed out of former colonial possessions; 70 of them began as full-blown constitutional democracies. Of the 70, there are only 11 left. And of those 11, seven are small islands—Granada, the Bahamas, Barbados, Mauritius, Fiji. I mean, I'm glad they're democracies, but it wouldn't make much difference if Fiji should become a small despotism. The land masses of Asia wouldn't shake!

So America is not what countries are going to be like. The chaos of Lebanon may be more of a model. Now, for the rest of our natural lives, we will be in a world in which there are very few of us and a great many of them.

PLAYBOY: Is that behind your advocacy of Israel?

MOYNIHAN: Israel is the democracy under attack just now. We don't know when it will be Canada, the United States or whoever. There aren't too many of us in the world and we've got to hang together.

Schlesinger came out and said what I've been saying privately—that Kissinger, probably without even knowing it, treated the Israelis like the South Vietnamese. The more you weaken their reputation, the more they'll give in and let you run things for them. He let the Israelis be discredited in the world.

PLAYBOY: What do you see as the main danger of that?

MOYNIHAN: We are not military allies of Israel. We *are* political allies. But a threat to any constitutional democracy is a threat to our national interests. And I think the chances of something really awful happening in Israel are high, including using an atomic bomb if they have one or develop one.

PLAYBOY: Why, in your view, is democracy eroding around the world?

MOYNIHAN: It's a hard discipline. It's easy to persuade yourself, as Mrs. Gandhi did, that your political opponents are a conspiracy of your enemies and democracy is not in the country's best interests. Mrs. Gandhi was told she had to leave office and she didn't. President Nixon was told the same thing and he did. How would you like to sit out in San Clemente and read all the books about yourself and hear about the movies?

The American Revolution didn't happen in 1776. It happened in 1801, when John Adams got the returns from South Carolina and said, "Well, that's it; the Republicans have won." And he turned over the Army and the Treasury and the Great Seal to Thomas Jefferson, went back to Quincy and felt a failure the rest of his life. But he had ensured that America would be a democracy. He did not shoot Jefferson; he did not arrest him. That's the event.

And if you corrupt and suborn a democracy, it is usually done in the name of totalitarian virtue. When you say we are going to have a higher, purer, more demanding discipline, in a funny way, that will be excused. That will earn you more credit in this country than admitting you don't want to deal with your opposition or saying you want to put more money in your Swiss bank account. So the language of totalitarianism appears very quickly in all these countries. And the world is turning against us pretty rapidly.

PLAYBOY: Do you think the Communist nations make America the scapegoat?

MOYNIHAN: Yes, propagating the idea that America is what is wrong with the world. But, of course, the underdeveloped nations are more and more a source of their own sorrows. And nobody dares say this. The government leaders have assumed all the entrepreneurship and profits—and ride around in Mercedeses, while the people in the bush walk around in bare feet. They call their government socialism, but it's not. It's not at all distributive. It's state capitalism, and the least efficient kind of capitalism.

PLAYBOY: Wasn't there a great deal of generalized animosity against you in the hallways of the UN?

MOYNIHAN: You're damn right there was—from those people who had been having a free ride. They'd vote against the United States 100 percent and nobody ever said a word to them, and suddenly I was saying, "You're sitting here, asking us for bread; you're sitting here, asking us for food; you're sitting here, asking us to help you against your traditional and mortal enemies, the mugwumps on the other side of the border; and there's your guy back there voting against us. How can we help you if you're not going to help us out?"

And suddenly, these ambassadors were getting cables from home, saying, "What in the hell are you doing? We need help against those mugwumps." Damn right they were standing around the bar in the diplomatic lounge, asking, "What the hell is this guy doing?" That is exactly what I intended them to be asking.

New York City has a tremendous sort of industry that is a social world built around the ambience of the UN. And they give you dinners and you give them dinners, and then they give you dinners and you go to receptions. And for anybody involved in that ambience to face up to those countries—

PLAYBOY: What *is* the State Department's attitude toward Third World countries?

MOYNIHAN: It has a fall-back position that goes: "They're not really quite grown up and you have to deal with them the way you deal with adolescent children." You know, like juvenile delinquents whose names must not be released to the public. I felt that was a shocking condescension. I was holding them accountable as mature, independent countries. They'd say they'd voted against us without really wishing to. I said no, you vote the way you desire to vote. That wonderful English line, "You may have the right to dissemble your love, but why did you kick me downstairs?"

PLAYBOY: Did you and Kissinger fight as much while you were at the UN as has been reported?

MOYNIHAN: As a matter of fact, though we had fierce arguments while I was in India, we had none in the UN. Not one. The fact is that Moynihan,

Kissinger and Schlesinger all shared the same view—that the balance of forces in the world is shifting against us and we are in mortal peril. My judgment of Henry Kissinger's view of the world was one of profound respect. Our disagreement was over what to do. Kissinger believed that America no longer had any fight left. Schlesinger and I thought we did. Our disagreements could be very bitter, but, you might say, they partook of that quality that Sigmund Freud described as the narcissism of small differences.

PLAYBOY: Your resignation from the UN, however, involved some pretty rough infighting with Kissinger, didn't it?

MOYNIHAN: Here's what happened: When my leave of absence was up at Harvard, I told President Ford I was willing to give up my tenure at Harvard and stay on at least through the end of the primaries. Then there would be no way that Reagan could assault him for my departure. I had told Kissinger this earlier. And the President said, "Fine. Good of you."

Two days later, Reston comes out with this column saying that the President and the Secretary of State deplore my conduct in private but have to support it in public. Someone had gone *right* at my belly the minute it was clear I would give up Harvard.

If you are the UN Ambassador, people have to be pretty sure that when you say such and such, that's what the Secretary of State *and* the President think, or that the President will back you up. So when dealing with me, one is dealing with the President of the United States. I'm his policy. Take on me, take on the President. Now, once the senior political correspondent of the U.S. has said, "You don't, in fact, speak for his private views, and he's stuck with you," you're naked. I read Reston in the midnight edition. I carried it into the bedroom and told my wife, "Back to Harvard." Because, as it happened, my tenure did not expire for five more days.

PLAYBOY: Did Kissinger ever speak to you about it?

MOYNIHAN: No, we never talked. But he put out nice statements, wrote me a nice letter, and was a little nervous, a little scared. About two months earlier, I went through a strange week. On Monday morning, I met Kissinger at the airport, as one does, and drove into town with him. A news magazine had an item that he had taken me to the woodshed the previous week over something. There had been a meeting, but, in point of fact, no woodshed. And he was saying to me, "Did you see that magazine piece? God*damn* those people. How *dare* they say things like that?" Kissinger was wondering who had *leaked* the story. Well, I hadn't and there were only two of us in the room.

So, the next day, there's another attack on me, and this one from the mouth of Britain's UN ambassador, Ivor Richard, who compared me to a trigger-happy Wyatt Earp, a vengeful Savonarola and a demented King Lear "raging amidst the storm on the blasted heath." Never in history has a British ambassador denounced an American Ambassador. I'm asked about it by the press and I say, "Look, I know these are the views of Ambassador Richard and I feel he has every right to express them. We're the best of friends." That's Wednesday. On Thursday, at lunchtime, at the Russian Embassy, Ivor comes up to me and says, "Say, you know, people are interpreting your statement to mean you think these are my personal views and not the views of the British government." I said, "Ho, ho, people will think anything, huh, Ivor?" And then I walked off. And about two minutes later, being the brilliant man I am, I say, "What the hell did he say? You mean they aren't his personal . . . ?" That night, I asked him point-blank if they were the official views of the British government. And he said, "Quite right."

PLAYBOY: You're saying that Kissinger was out to get you and arranged this with the British foreign secretary?

MOYNIHAN: Well, unless you choose to think that the British government for reasons of its own decided for the first time in history to publicly demolish a United States Ambassador.

PLAYBOY: You were just saying that you and Kissinger had no real disagreement. So why was he trying to torpedo you?

MOYNIHAN: Well, that will remain forever a mystery. Kissinger couldn't help himself. He couldn't help himself. It's a kind of nervousness in his character that will do this one day and say "My God, that was absurd" the next day. You don't let it bother you until it gets into a situation where you can't recoup. It could just as easily not have happened. There were all sorts of personal problems.

PLAYBOY: What were they?

MOYNIHAN: No. No. That's not fair.

PLAYBOY: What impression does Kissinger give personally?

MOYNIHAN: Oh, a man of enormous energy and power—and a larger command of the facts than you have.

PLAYBOY: What's his wit like?

MOYNIHAN: Aggressive. It diminishes somebody, usually you.

PLAYBOY: When you mentioned the Reston column about you and the UN, you were talking about the use of leaks to influence government. Would you discuss that?

MOYNIHAN: I think it's one of the big problems the press has today. The great fundamental principle of the press is to report what's going on. There was a big story last spring about the purported intent of Attorney General Levi to put before the Supreme Court an *amicus curiae* brief against busing. That was clearly a leak to kill it by revealing it. And if one side of the Justice Department is in a fierce fight with the other side of the Justice Department, that's one of the things that's going on. But if you can't say that because you are, in fact, printing something given to you by one side, well, then, the primal purpose of the press is being faulted. But I see progress. During this past campaign, Leslie Gelb in a news story about the

Carter camp noted, "This document was given to *The New York Times* by a person in the State Department who is interested in advancing the cause of Governor Carter." That's what I've been asking for—let the press identify whose ox is being gored and for what purpose.

PLAYBOY: Is there another such example from your own experience?

MOYNIHAN: Oh, sure. That "benign neglect" memorandum of mine. Here I am, in the middle of a Republican Administration, the advisor on urban affairs; we have got through one summer without the resumption of the riots of the Sixties, which had reached epidemic proportions by '69; we'd had one summer without any at all and I'm worried about the next summer. Wallace was getting stronger and stronger. You had the Black Panthers and people like that getting more strident. And you had people at the Justice Department goading the FBI to get involved and to get the Panthers to start fighting one another and fighting the FBI. We were polarizing.

I sent a long memorandum to the President that was basically about an argument I was having with Attorney General John Mitchell: "Stay away from that business of getting into confrontations with the Panthers." The United States Army, at one point, had surrounded New Haven. And the whole war room at the Pentagon was covered with maps of New Haven streets. All these initiatives came out of the FBI. I was trying to say "Cool it," and I wrote this memorandum. I said the time had come for a period when Negro progress continued and racial rhetoric faded—a time when the *issue of race* could do with the theory of benign neglect. That's a phrase from Canadian constitutional history. And about three months after I wrote that thing, out the memorandum came, and it was presented as a proposal to neglect blacks.

PLAYBOY: Who leaked it?

MOYNIHAN: Who knows?

PLAYBOY: Somebody trying to do you in?

MOYNIHAN: Probably, but not necessarily. But there you find yourself represented as saying the very opposite of what you said. And the desire to think the worst is usually very powerful in public things. So there you are.

PLAYBOY: How did that affect you and your career?

MOYNIHAN: It vastly affected the credence with which I could talk about those issues. But in a very subtle but pervasive way, it warned people away from this whole area. Because everybody in Washington knew that I was someone who absolutely believed in racial equality and was desperately trying to figure out how to get a guaranteed income. Maybe it was not a good idea, but certainly it was problack. They saw what happened to me and, boy, I think in Washington you could just feel them saying, "I see, just stay away from that subject. Nothing but loss."

PLAYBOY: Your election to the Senate must have measured, once and for all, your relationship with blacks.

MOYNIHAN: I carried the black vote by a five-to-one margin.

PLAYBOY: Getting back to the political game of selective leaking, don't you think President Carter will face the same sort of problem within his Administration—especially when he tries to reorganize Government bureaucracy?

MOYNIHAN: Absolutely. The bureaucracy will reveal the President's iniquitous intentions to the press constantly, constantly, constantly. . . . Actually, it's inevitable. The Civil Service has a vested interest in someone who wants to make the Civil Service more powerful. What happens to an Administration that wants to make it smaller, less powerful? Can it be done? I am telling you there is a lot of evidence that the answer is no.

PLAYBOY: So you think President Carter will be frustrated?

MOYNIHAN: President Carter is absolutely right that there is confusion in the bureaucracy, but it's confusion rising out of confused public policy. Congressional directives are often conflicting; national concerns are often ambivalent. The President will soon direct himself to where the problem is.

To my mind, the biggest of our problems in the period ahead is that nobody is confidently—much less passionately—bringing new ideas to Government. President Carter has undertaken to do a lot of very reasonable things. But no one should suppose there is any doctrine on how to go about it.

PLAYBOY: How about you? Will you, as Senator, be passionately advocating new ideas?

MOYNIHAN: I think so. I'm part of a movement in American history to assert the needs of the Northeast with respect to the national economy, which is a new idea. The needs have been there for a quarter of a century, but we haven't seen them. What has always been the richest part of the country, with obligations to the rest of the country, is no longer that; but because of what it still provides to the general health of the country, a decline in this region becomes a decline for everyone. Imagine this country without New York City—or imagine New York City becoming just a large Philadelphia.

I have an idea that this subject is related to the separation of power; it has a nice kind of constitutional quality to it. It originates with the struggle between Hamilton and Jefferson. Remember that when the Constitution was drafted, the capital was New York City, which is where Washington was inaugurated. This troubled Jefferson enormously. He'd lived in Europe and had this great dread of nations that had one capital for everything— government, finance, industry, the intellectual and cultural life. That was Paris, that was London, that was Europe. So it was important to him that the capital be moved out of New York City.

Hamilton felt differently and wanted the capital to be an important, central city. But there was something he needed from Jefferson: his support in getting the Federal Government to assume the Revolutionary War debt.

So he and Jefferson struck this bargain in a tavern in Broad Street, whereby Jefferson agreed to support Hamilton's position on the war debt in return for getting the capital moved to a malarial, miasmal swamp by the Potomac—that's where the term Foggy Bottom, for the State Department, later came from.

That produced a separation of power that was visible, only no one noticed it: The political capital went to Washington, while the capital in every other respect stayed in New York. So you never had that tremendous focusing of total power in one city that so many other countries have had.

PLAYBOY: But why should New York City feel it has the right to be the only alternative to power concentration in Washington?

MOYNIHAN: It doesn't. As time went on, you had the railroads meeting in Chicago, the river trade in St. Louis, the auto industry in Detroit. But the point is to think of it as a basic constitutional idea—to prevent all the power from gravitating to Washington. If we lose New York as the main capital of all those other things it represents, you'll be surprised at how much we lose. You won't recognize this country a half century hence, when the most important newspaper is *The Washington Post* and all the broadcasting is done out of buildings along Connecticut Avenue, and *Time* and *Newsweek* are published in Washington. There will be so much power at the center.

And this is what's beginning to happen. Time-Life Books has moved down there. The major financial houses have their computers down there. The Kennedy Center for the Performing Arts will have all the money it needs, forever, while the Metropolitan Opera will have to fight its deficit every year. Same goes for the museums. And someday a President might sit down and figure it was his right to consider what kinds of paintings were good, politically, for the country. I'm telling you, it's a serious thing.

PLAYBOY: It's pretty well known that New York City owes at least part of its present financial crisis to the staggering costs of welfare. You want Federal help, of course, but what are your thoughts beyond that?

MOYNIHAN: That the present system is madness. And it's not just the cities anymore; the suburbs are hurting, too. Probably most counties in New York State pay over half their budgets for welfare. The more you learn about the subject, the more you realize how deeply embedded it is in our system.

In the fall of 1965, newly elected mayor John Lindsay asked me to join a task force on poverty. I told the task force that welfare, specifically, and not poverty, generally, was the problem. I told them the numbers of welfare clients were going to zoom astronomically. They rejected my assertions unanimously. The fundamental belief was—they said it over and over again in various guises—"No, that's all over. That was due to the Tammany Hall types who put all these people on welfare to get votes. But now we've got good men, Yale men. It won't happen anymore." Well, the number of people on welfare in New York City went from 345,000 to 1,165,000 under Lindsay.

PLAYBOY: You expect help from Carter. *Can* he solve the welfare problem?

MOYNIHAN: *Sure* he can. . . . There are two ways of solving it. Either you admit welfare is a national problem and get the Federal Government to pay for it or you try to change the existing system somehow. President Carter is committed to the latter. Obviously, there's a question as to whether Congress will go halfway or all the way. That's part of the politics of the next two years.

PLAYBOY: Considering your crack about Yale men, you're something of a Harvard elitist who doesn't believe in the moral certitude of solutions worked out by elitists.

MOYNIHAN: Right. The president of Yale, Kingman Brewster, a notably fatuous man, once asked a faculty group, "What has happened to American morality?" Alexander Bickel, the law professor, replied, "We are drowning in it." Our capacity for moral judgments is being overloaded by a certain kind of moralist who makes too many activities into issues of right and wrong.

Hell, I'm a good example. I'm sitting aboard a plane as I talk to you. I've just had a drink of the cheapest orange juice I've ever had—and been badly served. And I'm investing it with moral significance. There is a degree of dereliction of duty that attains to moral infraction. . . . My God, there's an epigram!

PLAYBOY: We're following you, Senator, but just barely. Didn't you once write that it is hard for Government to appear to have succeeded?

MOYNIHAN: It is in the nature of democracy to promise that things will keep changing for the better. These promises translate into the realization that what exists is not satisfactory. It's what economist Joseph Schumpeter called the creative destruction of capitalism. After 10,000 years of plowing in the sun, using your back, using your wife, using your ox, along comes a Model T and farmers are out of the mud. But within 20 short years, the Model T isn't enough and has become an adjective for something out of date. When, with great difficulty, Government pulls off something pretty good, the sensation doesn't last.

PLAYBOY: You mean people saying, "If we can land a man on the moon, why can't we cure the common cold?"

MOYNIHAN: You've got it. In India, that is the first and primal condition and fact of life: All water is poison. Well! If you live in a world where a man like me develops an atavistic attachment for Coca-Cola, well . . . Why is Coca-Cola the most indomitable, irresistible . . . ? Because you don't get dysentery from it.

But try to tell people who live in Manhattan, "You're successful. You've got pure water." They'll ask, "What else have we got? Can you cure the common cold?" Creative destruction is part of our discontent.

PLAYBOY: Is built-in obsolescence of success related to our loss of national morale?

MOYNIHAN: We have been on a great S curve of progress. Once we could only shout across the street. Now we have the dial telephone. The miracle has happened; you talk to anybody in the world. I mean, phonovision isn't really much to add. And that is what is happening in urban programs and things like that. We are on the flat curve at the top of the S. We can't budge. There's no place to go. And conditions of life are not going to improve so very much.

PLAYBOY: The social scientists aren't going to be happy to hear that news.

MOYNIHAN: Oh, they can do a lot of things. The most useful, maybe, is to tell us what we can't do. There is just one social program of which its sponsors have said, "That works." And that is castration, as a treatment of sexual offenders. And you know where they practice that? Denmark.

Greely and Rossi in 1964 did a great study on how well the Catholic parochial schools did what they purposed to do—influence the religious practices of the children who went there. And this was the rather depressing conclusion: They don't.

The first results came in on Head Start and, "My God, it's marvelous! These four-year-olds from Head Start know twice as much as these four-year-olds who haven't been." But by the time they were all six, everybody knew about the same amount. Our assumption about how much you can influence behavior through manipulating this institution or that institution—more money here, less there or whatever—turns out to be *wrong*. The Safe Streets Act was a disaster. You spend four billion dollars and you don't get anything. Because you don't know anything about that. You've got to face up to what you haven't been able to do.

PLAYBOY: Where does that leave us?

MOYNIHAN: No happier, but with fewer illusions—and illusions produce expectations. And when illusions are not delivered on, that is easily interpreted as bad faith. You said you could do such and such, but you didn't. Therefore, it meant you didn't intend to. That's not good for anybody. You set out to win the hearts and minds of the Vietnamese and you don't know how to do that. And the next thing you know, you're calling one another names in the most awful way.

PLAYBOY: Earlier, you sounded optimistic, even excited about the possibilities of shaping Government in the Senate. Now you're sounding a bit more realistic about what can be changed. What *do* you think you'll affect in the Senate?

MOYNIHAN: Let me give you an example. I had a family-assistance plan before the Senate for three years. It was essentially a negative-income-tax plan, but at the end of the three years, I doubt there were a dozen Senators who really understood the principle of a negative income tax any more than I understood nuclear fission. The question I have come to be preoccupied with is that of collective intelligence. There isn't a lot of it in Government, compounding the troubles we already have. The intelligence of a democracy is easily strained.

PLAYBOY: One last question on a topic we discussed earlier: Do you expect criticism for appearing in PLAYBOY?

MOYNIHAN: No, not at all. I expect that people will read this to see what I have to say, to agree or disagree. It should serve to get people to think a bit more seriously about our form of Government. Doing something like this in depth has gotten me to reflect a bit on the past few years and on the future. I look forward myself to seeing it in print—and to the photography as well.

JAMES EARL RAY

September 1977
Interviewer: James McKinley

The interview with the convicted killer of Martin Luther King, Jr., provides an example of drama, timeliness, coincidence, and the fact that a magazine with a three-month lead time can be a part of the breaking news.

When James Earl Ray, through his lawyer, agreed to tell PLAYBOY his version of the King assassination, Golson and Senior Editor Laurence Gonzales—who had edited a long-running series entitled "Playboy's History of Assassination in America"—decided to send the author of that series, James McKinley, to Ray's Tennessee prison. The Senate Select Committee on Assassinations was in the midst of its own investigation of Ray's story, and evidently Ray felt he could gain public support for an appeal by stating his case to the magazine. What happened next surprised the interviewer, the editors, and, probably, Ray himself.

Before the interview was half over, and after he had tantalized McKinley with remarks about escaping, Ray did precisely that—he jumped over the wall and wandered through the woods for two and a half days before being recaptured. Less than two days later, Ray was sitting with McKinley again (and with editor Gonzales, who had joined them after the escape), boasting about his escape and again denying that he had killed King.

McKinley and Gonzales, putting a hypothetical case to Ray, idly asked if he would take a lie-detector test to prove he did not kill King. Ray just as casually said he would. With the tape recorder off, the journalists made a deal with Ray: PLAYBOY would publish the results of the lie-detector test exactly as they came out, if Ray made no efforts to repress them if they turned out against him. Ray unaccountably agreed.

Gonzales called Golson in Chicago, who arranged for a respected polygraph-examination firm to send a representative to Tennessee to give Ray the test. There, in the visitors' room at Brushy Mountain Penitentiary, James Earl Ray did something official investigators had been trying to get him to do it for years: He took his first and only lie-detector test. He failed it decisively. Although the results are still not admissible in court, the polygraph experts told the magazine's editors there was no doubt as to their conclusion: that Ray killed King, and that he did so alone.

On the evening of April 4, 1968, the Reverend Dr. Martin Luther King, Jr., stepped from his room onto the balcony of the Lorraine Motel in Memphis. He leaned over the rail to joke with his friends and followers below, asking them to sing a favorite song, "Take My Hand, Precious Lord," that night. Just then, at 6:01 P.M., came the shot. The .30-'06 slug ripped into King's right jaw, careened to the spinal column, killing America's greatest civil rights leader almost instantly.

As Ralph Abernathy, Jesse Jackson and others rushed to King, as they pointed across Mulberry Street toward the derelict rooming house from which the shot seemed to have come, the shock waves of King's murder began to ripple across America. Within hours, Attorney General Ramsey Clark announced that the assassin had dropped a bundle of incriminating physical evidence at the scene, that he'd soon be caught, that the evidence indicated that a single, crazed assassin was responsible. Simultaneously, more than 100 American cities erupted with racial rioting. Several major cities were brought to their knees by the looting and fire-bombing. And, in time, the agony of black America would join the Tet offensive, L.B.J.'s abdication, the Chicago Democratic Convention riot and the assassination of Robert F. Kennedy in marking 1968 as the nadir in recent American history.

On June 8, 1968, two months after the murder, the suspected assassin was arrested at London's Heathrow airport and turned out to be a 40-year-old, pale, nervous escaped convict from St. Louis with a long record of smalltime, unsuccessful crime. His name was James Earl Ray and as far as the authorities were concerned, there was no doubt about it: He and he alone had killed King.

Except, of course, there was doubt, and it wasn't going to go away. Each bit of the puzzle deepened the mystery. From the beginning, some major complications emerged. To list a few:

• Ray claimed he had been working with an accomplice named Raoul, who had hired him as a "mule," smuggling unspecified commodities across borders while Ray was at large from Missouri State Penitentiary for Men.

• *Ray admitted buying the weapon found by the police. But, he said, he had bought it for Raoul as part of a gun-running scheme and had never fired it himself, even though his fingerprints were on it.*

• *During the 14 months he was out of the Missouri prison, Ray spent an estimated $10,000 in his 20,000 miles of travel. He has never come up with a satisfactory explanation of where he got the money, saying only that it came from Raoul.*

• *His pattern of crime was armed robbery. He had never—as far as the record showed—shot anyone. And he was a marked loser: a smalltime crook and little-league con artist. Could he, then, have turned into a deadly one-shot sniper? And one so elusive that he could travel in four foreign countries and more than a dozen states, obtaining passports under aliases and avoiding the finest man hunters in the world?*

• *Even the murder weapon came under some question. Ballistics tests failed to tie the murder slug conclusively to the rifle.*

• *The state's one eyewitness was alleged to be an alcoholic (and some darkly suggested that he had been paid by the police for his testimony).*

All in all, it presaged another nightmare of false leads and elaborate conspiracy theories. Some hoped that Ray's trial would answer those vexing questions. But there was no trial. Instead, nine months after his capture, a subdued Ray pleaded guilty and accepted a 99-year sentence, while his famous criminal lawyer, Percy Foreman, stood by as the State of Tennessee stipulated its evidence: the fingerprints, the eyewitness, the renting of a run-down room, Ray's white Mustang laden with physical evidence of his postassassination flight from Memphis to Atlanta. The sniper had even obligingly dropped in a doorway next to the rooming house a bundle containing the rifle, toilet articles, binoculars, cans of beer with Ray's fingerprints on them and even a radio with his prison number on it. The authorities could also trace Ray's movements.

He fled to Atlanta and then back to Canada, then to England and Portugal—from where he supposedly tried to travel to a white-supremacist country such as Rhodesia—and finally back to London to be captured. With all that against him, few wondered that he pleaded guilty.

But within a week, he applied for a new trial. And, following that, his long succession of attorneys took turns raising questions about his guilt, as the theories sprouted like thistles. Everyone from the Teamsters to the CIA, from the Cubans to militant blacks, from white racists to the FBI, was accused at one time or another. And yet, ultimately, nothing was known except that Ray looked like a reasonable candidate for America's gallery of assassins.

Ray agreed to talk with PLAYBOY *for the first in-depth interview since 1969. James McKinley, who wrote "Playboy's History of Assassination in America," was dispatched to Brushy Mountain Penitentiary in the wild, wooded country of east Tennessee. A surprise interviewee turned out to be Jerry Ray, who walked in on McKinley and Ray as they talked in the visitors' room. Ray's younger brother, who has also been jailed in the past for smalltime criminal activities, is alleged to have played a role in the King case, according to one theory propounded in* New Times *magazine, which suggested that he was the mysterious Raoul for whom Ray was covering up. Jerry, too, agreed to be questioned.*

But when the interview was half completed, another drama intervened. Ray went over the wall in a show of bravado worthy of the early days of Hollywood. Ray was caught and returned to the prison, filthy and hungry but unharmed. Not, however, before he had eluded hundreds of guards, police, FBI, National Guardsmen and bloodhounds for 54 and a half hours in some of the roughest mountain wilderness in this country.

Less than two days after he was returned to prison, Ray again sat down to complete the interview with McKinley, who was then joined by PLAYBOY *Senior Editor Laurence Gonzales, who had edited "Playboy's History of Assassination." They report on this, the fullest interview Ray has ever granted, and the exclusive story of his bold escape:*

"Ray looked fit after his mountain escapade, just as he had before— about six feet tall, tanned and strong-looking, with only a hint of the paunch a 49-year-old man might be expected to have, especially if he'd spent half of his adult life in prison. His handshake was tentative, a lifetime of wariness and shyness behind it. His slack-limbed shuffle was characteristic of people who move in small spaces, under constant, suspicious eyes. And what we first took for indolence turned out to be a keen patience, a brooding vigilance.

"There is no better proof of that than the fact that in pre-escape sessions, Ray seemed to be teasing us, even as we began the interview, with an oblique hint that he was planning to break out. What we thought was simply 'warm-up' small talk turned out to be quite telling a few days later."

April–June 1977

PLAYBOY: Do they treat you well here in the Brushy Mountain Penitentiary?

RAY: Yes; since August 1975, I've been part of the regular prison population.

PLAYBOY: What's an average day like for you here?

RAY: You may not believe it, but this place keeps you very busy. Seven hours of work and you've got to exercise. I work in the laundry five days a week. Usually go to the yard for exercise in the afternoon and evening.

PLAYBOY: Do you have any hobbies?

RAY: I've got too many legal problems to be making purses.

PLAYBOY: Do you encounter a lot of homosexuality?

RAY: My views on this are known. I don't associate with them and they keep to themselves. I'm in a poor position to be passing judgment on anyone else. They're nothing to get excited about, though. I wouldn't want Anita Bryant up here or anything like that.

PLAYBOY: You've been sentenced to 99 years. Does that make you eligible for parole at any time?

RAY: In Tennessee, the only way you can get any relief is if the governor commutes your sentence. I think on 99 years, you have to do 35 years to even be eligible for parole [*the actual length of time is 30 years*].

PLAYBOY: You escaped once from the Missouri State Penitentiary when you were doing time for armed robbery before the King killing. Then you attempted to escape from here. Will you try to escape again?

RAY: I would if a wall fell down or something.

PLAYBOY: You claim that you deserve a new trial. What do you think you would gain by that?

RAY: I think I'd be acquitted.

PLAYBOY: What would you do if you got out?

RAY: If I got out of the penitentiary, I think I'd go to some foreign country. Australia or somewhere. There's too much heat around here. I might go to Switzerland.

PLAYBOY: This country has an unfortunate gallery of political assassins. Do you belong in that gallery?

RAY: I don't believe so. I have serious doubts that people think I'm involved in these assassinations. I don't want to comment about Sirhan or Oswald. They've got their problems and I've got mine. Of course, Oswald don't have any. But most of these types are overzealous. They're trying to promote some political idea.

PLAYBOY: You've answered this question a hundred times. Did you kill Martin Luther King?

RAY: No.

PLAYBOY: Do you know who did?

RAY: No, I'm not positive. We've done a lot of investigation, but I don't know.

PLAYBOY: What's your best guess?

RAY: From what I've read and who I've talked to, the FBI made some kind of arrangements so that King wouldn't have any security or nothin' like that.

PLAYBOY: Who do you think pulled the trigger?

RAY: I couldn't say that. Until I got arrested, I never paid too much attention to how these intelligence agencies operate. Based on what I've read, it appears that no Government agency like the FBI or the CIA would shoot any one person. Their *modus operandi* in foreign countries seems to always be to have someone else do it. The Mafia or some foreign intelligence agency. I thought that, and I think the evidence would support it. But I don't think anyone will ever know until you get the FBI files on King declassified.

I told the House committee that I'd take a lie-detector test or anything they want if they would get the Government materials declassified. But it's going to have to be a *quid pro quo*. I'm not going to go through all these tests and then they're going to say, "Well, we're not going to come up with anything."

PLAYBOY: Will you take a lie-detector test for us?

RAY: I wouldn't have no objection to it.

[*The results of this polygraph test, taken June 22, 1977, appear just before the end of the interview*.]

PLAYBOY: What is the single most important fact that you think proves your innocence?

RAY: The single most important fact is the suppression of all the evidence by the Government.

PLAYBOY: Do you mean to say that the single most important point is not that you are simply innocent of the crime?

RAY: See, there's something about always playing on your innocence. Even something that I could prove as being impossible for me to commit—say, killing Jesus Christ—I don't like to keep saying I'm innocent of the charge, because even though I am, it's just some kind of psychological thing. It seems like you're crying.

PLAYBOY: Are you capable of standing up and saying, "I did not pull the trigger"?

RAY: Oh, there wouldn't be no question about that.

PLAYBOY: Say it.

RAY: Well, I did not pull the trigger, but I really don't see much significance [*in saying that*].

PLAYBOY: If you didn't pull the trigger, why did you plead guilty? Haven't you testified that your lawyer, Percy Foreman, made you do it?

RAY: I think maneuvered would be a better word. Now, I thought the state had a circumstantial case, but the FBI was making numerous threats against my family. Plus Foreman visited them in St. Louis, they said, to persuade them to get me to plead guilty, the gist being that if the plea were not forthcoming, the FBI might have one or both of my brothers indicted for complicity in the King homicide. The most vicious threat was that they'd arrest and rejail my father at Fort Madison, Iowa, where he'd escaped some 40 years earlier.

PLAYBOY: What were you trying to say when you stood up after your guilty plea and said you didn't agree with Foreman, Attorney General Ramsey Clark and FBI Director J. Edgar Hoover that there had been no conspiracy? Were you saying you thought there *was* one?

RAY: Well, yes, I was just telling them more or less just that.

PLAYBOY: Well, then, is it your guess that some Government agency is involved in such a conspiracy?

RAY: Possibly in collusion with some foreign intelligence agency. I've read articles about the CIA where they give these foreign intelligence agencies millions of dollars. I think they give some shah several million dollars every year. Well, they don't give money like that unless you get favors in return.

PLAYBOY: Which foreign government do you think was involved?

RAY: I wouldn't want to speculate on that. I think you have to develop that in some way with the House select committee on assassinations. I don't want to keep harping on this classification question, but everything's been classified on this case, so you really don't know nothing.

PLAYBOY: Do you consider yourself a dupe?

RAY: I think that I was just a worker and that I just happened to be on the scene. I was arrested for it. I don't know if dupe is the right word, though.

PLAYBOY: Are you claiming you were set up to take the fall?

RAY: I think that is very possible. I don't think that anyone had any malicious intent toward me personally. Naturally, in a case like this, someone had to go to jail for it. And I think I'm really kind of the ideal candidate for it, because certain classes in this country don't have no political influence. The working-class whites are one.

PLAYBOY: Do you consider yourself a member of that class?

RAY: Yes. Like the Black Muslims, there's someone always on their case. The Indians have been taken advantage of. Also the Cubans.

PLAYBOY: You mentioned the Black Muslims. How do you feel about black people?

RAY: Well, they're just here and I'm here. I don't really have no really strong feelings one way or the other. I guess they're looking out for their interests as everyone else is. And, of course, I'm trying to look out for mine. But I don't see no conflict there.

PLAYBOY: That sounds like a very pat, rehearsed answer. Did you work it out in advance?

RAY: I'd thought about how you answer that. It's a question they keep asking you and it's a tricky question in certain ways. There is a certain prevailing attitude, in other words. You have to have one opinion.

PLAYBOY: It's a simple question: Are you racially prejudiced?

RAY: I don't think that people are prejudiced against a certain race. I think there are certain cultural differences—like music or something like that. I can't see Hirohito, the emperor of Japan, doing the watusi. They just don't mix. But I don't think that's grounds to shoot the emperor. There's just a difference.

PLAYBOY: Then to what cultural group do you find yourself least attracted?

RAY: My association with different groups has been somewhat limited except in prison. The one that I find myself mostly attracted to are the

Latins. They're easygoing. They're not too bothered by rules and regulations.

PLAYBOY: Didn't you refuse to live in an integrated dormitory when you were in Leavenworth for forging postal money orders?

RAY: I did refuse to be transferred to the farm and the supposedly integrated dormitories. But the overriding reason was a prison policy of handing out extra time for marijuana possession—possession being anything found in your immediate area in the dormitory.

PLAYBOY: You mean you felt the blacks smoked dope and that you would be punished for it?

RAY: Maybe.

PLAYBOY: When you attempted to run to South Africa or Rhodesia after the death of King, wasn't that because of the racial policies in those countries?

RAY: I tried to go to ten or twelve countries. Brazil, Colombia in South America, Australia, Canada—and I did try to go to Rhodesia once. I was in Puerto Vallarta, Mexico, once and saw an ad in the *U.S. News & World Report* wanting immigrants to Rhodesia. So I wrote them a letter. I never did get no answer. And after I got to Portugal in May 1968, before I was arrested in England, I did try to catch a ship. I wanted to get to any country in the southern part of Africa.

PLAYBOY: Why did those countries appeal to you?

RAY: They were close to Europe from where I was at. You can go to countries like Canada and South Africa, where they have large immigrant populations, and if you're English-speaking, you can just blend in with the population.

PLAYBOY: You still haven't answered the question: Are you a racist?

RAY: Well, there's a certain instinct that makes people want to associate with their own race. But the problem is answering these questions. People are all uptight about answering. A lot of middle-class people want to be on the right side of everything.

The difference is between committing violence on someone and maybe not wanting to associate with someone. Some newspapers might describe one person as a racist and another as a nationalist. It all depends on how they perceive you and if they think you're hostile toward them.

PLAYBOY: Let's try it another way: You're very careful to use the word black with us. Wasn't nigger a part of your vocabulary before you were arrested for killing King?

RAY: I don't use that term much. Of course, I probably have used it. But not usually. Well, in here, the blacks call one another that. But I didn't pay too much attention to these words before I got arrested.

PLAYBOY: Why do you pay attention to them now?

RAY: I wouldn't have, except that I was charged with killing King. I'm not as free to say anything as I was then because of how it will be interpreted and how it will be printed in the press. You can say something and it could be twisted around. So it's not so much what you say, it's what you're quoted as saying.

PLAYBOY: Most press accounts say there's ample evidence that you hated King. How do you answer that charge?

RAY: I really don't have any thoughts one way or the other about him. I felt about him the same way I feel about Gerald Ford or President Carter. It's necessary for these people to have a certain amount of hypocrisy—Carter talking about human rights or others talking about poor people. That gets on my nerves once in a while. I know it's difficult to believe, but I didn't really know too much about King before he was shot. When I was in Missouri, I was in virtual isolation. There's no television or radio. I was in solitary for two years, and in universal isolation, you're not even allowed a newspaper. You could be at war and not know it. [*According to prison officials, Ray had access to newspapers.*]

PLAYBOY: What do you think of Carter?

RAY: Well, I don't think much of him. He's just a carbon copy of Ford or past ones.

PLAYBOY: Your brother Jerry, whose role in the King assassination has been speculated upon, gave us a colorful description of Carter. He referred to him as "that smiling jackass in the White House."

RAY: See, that type of statement is foolish. My brother's never even voted. He's never been involved in politics. And so they [*Jeff Cohen and David S. Lifton in "New Times"*] wrote an article charging that he might have been involved with the King murder and now he starts making political statements. It's just foolish to do stuff like that. I wouldn't make any adverse comments against the President, because, in the first place, it would be foolish and, in the second place, it wouldn't be any need for it, because they're really all the same.

PLAYBOY: In maintaining that you did not kill King, you have consistently said that there was another individual—whom you call Raoul—and, in naming him, you imply that he was involved in the murder. You have said that the two of you had a rendezvous at a rooming house in Memphis and that you and he were involved in a gun-smuggling scheme. It was from that rooming house that the shot was fired that killed King. Do you think Raoul murdered King?

RAY: I don't know.

PLAYBOY: What is your alibi? Where were you at 6:01 P.M., when King was shot down?

RAY: Most likely, I was several blocks away, leaving or having just left a service station. I was asking about getting a tire fixed. I think I was there at between five minutes to six and six minutes after. Wouldn't be no way to get it down pat just what time it was. I left the rooming house at about

5:30 and went to a tavern about two and a half blocks north. I had a sandwich and a beer there, sat there probably 15 minutes and then returned to get the car and went to the filling station.

PLAYBOY: Did you then go back to the rooming house and see the police who had surrounded the area?

RAY: Yeah. That's when I circled the area and took off.

PLAYBOY: Did you contact anyone after you fled from Memphis?

RAY: After that, I didn't have no contact with anyone. That includes family members.

PLAYBOY: How did you manage to get the passports you used to fly from Canada to England and Portugal?

RAY: Well, I looked in back newspaper files for the names to apply for Canadian passports. I selected three persons whose age corresponded with mine. Since the population of Toronto is mostly of English extraction, a resemblance to me wouldn't seem unusual.

PLAYBOY: Going back to the scene of the crime, you've said you were fleeing the Memphis area in your white Mustang when you heard on the radio that King had been killed. What went through your mind at the time?

RAY: Nothing went through my mind too much right then. I was concerned when I heard they were looking for a Mustang. I think they mentioned a white man. And I thought when I first saw the police around the rooming house that possibly the police had raided the place and found a bunch of guns up there.

PLAYBOY: You mean the guns you claim were part of your gunrunning plan?

RAY: Yes. And I did intend to make a phone call and find out what was going on, because that's the standard procedure whenever you get an arrest. You call the police station or have someone else call up and find out if so-and-so has been in jail or something.

PLAYBOY: Whom were you going to call?

RAY: New Orleans.

PLAYBOY: *Who* in New Orleans?

RAY: I would just have called a number. 'Course, I wouldn't have asked for Raoul. I would have just told them that there's been a disturbance in the rooming house and I'd ask them if they could find out what it was or if they wanted me to call the police station or something.

PLAYBOY: Who would have answered the telephone?

RAY: They had an answering service. I don't know who he was. Just an individual.

PLAYBOY: Did you call?

RAY: No, I didn't call. I didn't know of any phone in the area. That was in between when I was leaving the area and I think after King had been reported shot, but before there was any report of a Mustang.

PLAYBOY: That's hard to believe—you couldn't find a phone booth, but if you had, you were going to call the police?

RAY: Well, either have the other party call the police—

PLAYBOY: What other party?

RAY: The one in New Orleans. That's the standard procedure you use when you get involved in situations like that.

PLAYBOY: You mean the standard procedure that criminals use?

RAY: Yes.

PLAYBOY: So you would call or have someone in New Orleans call the police. To find out what?

RAY: To try to find out what's going on. If anybody's going to jail. You can always palm yourself off as a lawyer or something. I'd find out what happened, whether the police had raided the place or whether this was an accident or what.

PLAYBOY: You mentioned that the police may have found guns at the rooming house. Of course, they found your Remington .30-'06 rifle, which the FBI says killed King. Do you still hold to your story that you gave that weapon to Raoul?

RAY: Yes.

PLAYBOY: And that you gave it to him in the rooming house just before the killing?

RAY: Yes.

PLAYBOY: How did you meet Raoul?

RAY: I first met him in 1967, after I escaped from Missouri. We met in The Neptune Tavern in Montreal. I was there trying to get merchant seaman's papers to get out of the country. Possibly roll a merchant seaman and take his papers.

PLAYBOY: What did Raoul look like?

RAY: Average height, looked like a Latin, sandy-colored hair.

PLAYBOY: Latins don't generally have light hair, do they?

RAY: He could've dyed it.

PLAYBOY: How did he dress?

RAY: Just a dark suit, shirt. I never saw him wear a tie.

PLAYBOY: R-A-O-U-L is the French spelling of that name and you met in Montreal. Yet you maintain he was Latin. Did your Raoul speak Spanish?

RAY: Yes, I think so.

PLAYBOY: Did you ever hear him speak Spanish?

RAY: No, but I could tell by his accent. One time I asked him about some Spanish word and he was noncommittal. But from my association with various Mexicans and having lived with them, I could tell a Spanish accent. His wasn't too strong. But once you get an accent from birth, it's hard to get rid of it.

PLAYBOY: What did you do for Raoul when you were working with him?

RAY: I'd take packages across the border, from Canada to here, later from the United States to Mexico.

PLAYBOY: We understand this picture looks like Raoul. Is that correct?

RAY: Oh, that would be this one here [*points*].

PLAYBOY: The one on the left?

RAY: Yeah. Percy Foreman showed me that the first time. It's a picture that I found out the Rockefeller Commission had classified.

PLAYBOY: This isn't classified.

RAY: It isn't?

PLAYBOY: It's been published often—this is a picture of some so-called tramps in Dealey Plaza just after John F. Kennedy was killed.

RAY: Well, the name's classified.

PLAYBOY: We don't think *anybody* knows his name. Who does that look like?

RAY: Well, I've seen all these pictures, I've looked at a hundred of them. That's the first one Percy Foreman showed me. See, Foreman at one time wanted to have this individual arrested. I'm pretty sure that was the individual. Then bring him to Memphis, then I was going to identify him and he was going to use that in the defense. I didn't want to do it, because I wasn't 100 percent sure of this picture. [*Foreman remembers showing photographs to Ray but denies wanting to arrest anyone. He said: "There was no Raoul. Ray told me he invented him to feed conspiracy theories."*]

PLAYBOY: What does a picture linked to John Kennedy's assassination have to do with your case?

RAY: All I said was he had a striking resemblance to this Raoul.

PLAYBOY: What is that supposed to mean?

RAY: Just that it has a striking resemblance. Of course, I never made a 100-percent-positive identification. I'd say there was a really strong resemblance. We'll still look at other pictures, but I'm not going to be no state witness against anyone.

PLAYBOY: You're the one who linked the two killings; here's a question out of the blue. Were you involved in the Kennedy assassination?

RAY: I was in jail at the time.

PLAYBOY: Back to Raoul. Are you certain you didn't make up the story about him?

RAY: Oh, no, I never made it up. Of course, these names like Eric Starvo Galt [*one of Ray's aliases*] don't mean anything. They're all aliases. See, that picture was shown to me a dozen times, it and about a hundred others. They always emphasize that one, though, because there was a composite drawing done right after King was shot and it had a striking resemblance to that picture. Of course, a person can change his features a little bit.

PLAYBOY: Richard Sprague, the investigator who recently resigned from the House select committee on assassinations, was quoted as saying, "There was no Raoul as previously claimed by Ray." How do you respond to that?

RAY: I think Sprague was probably misquoted. I didn't tell him that. I may have commented that a lot of these names were aliases.

PLAYBOY: Is there anything that might prove the existence of another person involved in this murder, whether or not he was called Raoul?

RAY: Well, a lot of it was mentioned in a PLAYBOY article in June 1976 [*Part VI of the "History of Assassination" series*]. One thing is part of a phone number, plus some address I came across when I crossed the border from Tijuana into the United States. I'll explain it to you. I shook down my car, which is my practice. I found a pack of cigarettes in a cigarette case dropped down between the bucket seats in the Mustang. There was a business card in there. I think on one side it had this person's name, crossed out, and what looked like the name of a city. Had two parts, like New Orleans. And it had LEAA on it, that Law Enforcement Assistance Administration. And on the other side, it had some name wrote down in longhand, I think it was Randolph Rosen-something. Anyway, years later, we had them investigated and come to find out, it wasn't really Rosen, it was Rosenson and he lived in Miami.

PLAYBOY: How might this Rosenson fit into the murder case?

RAY: We found out he had a criminal record, yes, for narcotics.

[PLAYBOY *located the criminal record of a Randolph Erwin Rosenson— in New Orleans. Rosenson has a long criminal record for narcotics and Customs violations. Unfortunately for Ray's story of finding the LEAA card, this agency was not created until August of 1968—almost a year after Ray crossed into Mexico.*]

PLAYBOY: Do you have any plausible ideas for a motive for the killing of King?

RAY: I suspect you'd have to depose some of King's associates—Andrew Young and people like that. From what I've read, King made a decision in March 1967 for radical changes in his organization. He was going to get off the integration thing and start making economic demands. He was against the Vietnam war. If he was going to make radical changes in his policy—emphasizing economics and foreign policy instead of civil rights— then that may have been a motive. But, again, I think that people within his organization can answer that a lot better than me—Young and people like that.

PLAYBOY: Do you believe the FBI is now involved in a cover-up?

RAY: Not necessarily. Rather, I believe it is the Department of Justice. Like the department's task force recommended in their recent reinvestigation that Congress pass a special law authorizing the destruction or sealing of big portions of the FBI investigation files.

PLAYBOY: That bill concerned King's personal life. They would seal it only to protect his memory.

RAY: I'm concerned that they'd put everything in there, rather than just King's personal life. This might just be a smoke screen to destroy things. I don't think we'll ever clear up this case until we get the FBI to declassify that material.

PLAYBOY: And how would that help clear things up?

RAY: I'd like to get this resolved one way or another. I'm not exactly interested in filing suits until I'm 90 years old. There has been considerable material filed with the courts. But I think PLAYBOY is the only place it got published. Right now, the Government's got more information than I have. Everybody thinks I know everything and that I'm holding back. I think it's the other way around.

PLAYBOY: Your case never went to trial, because you pleaded guilty. You agreed to 55 stipulations of guilt, but the question of how strong the government's case is has never been answered or tested in the adversary system of a public trial. How do you characterize its case against you?

RAY: Circumstantial and weak.

PLAYBOY: Let's run down a few of the major points that would have come up in a trial. Did you buy the .30-'06 Remington rifle in Birmingham less than a week before King was shot?

RAY: Yes.

PLAYBOY: For Raoul?

RAY: That's correct.

PLAYBOY: At first, you bought a .243-caliber rifle. Then you exchanged it for the .30-'06. Why?

RAY: I think what happened when I went back the second time is they give me a catalog and Raoul pointed out what kind to get. I don't recall that he mentioned .30-'06. There was a mention of a deer rifle. The first time I told the clerk the brand name and I wanted a deer rifle. I took it back to Raoul and it was the wrong kind. Then I came back the second time and we started talking about this deer rifle again. The salesman said, "Oh, I thought you were talking about an Alabama deer versus a Wisconsin deer."

PLAYBOY: It has been reported that it was the other way around, that you were the one talking about deer.

RAY: I don't recall.

PLAYBOY: Didn't you tell the clerk you were going deer hunting in Wisconsin with your brother?

RAY: Yes.

PLAYBOY: Do you see any significance in the fact that you mentioned your brother several times before King's murder?

RAY: No, I don't see any. You wouldn't go in and say, "My criminal accomplice," or something like that.

PLAYBOY: It's been alleged that your brother Jerry was involved with you in a plot to kill King. Was he?

RAY: I've never known Jerry's interest to be far removed from a six-pack. I know he's not involved in anything like this. That'd be too big a coincidence.

PLAYBOY: What would you say if someone told you it was Jerry in that rooming house with that rifle?

RAY: It would depend on who that anyone was. If it was a Government official, I would sue Jerry for false incarceration.

PLAYBOY: Did you ever fire the rifle you bought?

RAY: No.

PLAYBOY: Did you ever see anybody fire it?

RAY: No.

PLAYBOY: Have you ever used rifles, except for your stint in the Army?

RAY: No. Oh, .22s, but that was years ago.

PLAYBOY: Do you expect people to believe you didn't fire the gun when your fingerprints are all over it?

RAY: Well, the FBI found all my prints, and yet they didn't put my identification out over the wire right away. They didn't say whose they were until two weeks later. It seems to me that if they have your prints, they can identify you within a matter of hours.

PLAYBOY: Are you suggesting your prints *weren't* there?

RAY: I don't know. Possibly after they found out who I was, they transferred my prints to some objects so they could use that as evidence.

PLAYBOY: That seems like a paranoid fantasy. Do you consider yourself paranoid?

RAY: No. I think a lot of times you get that way, you get suspicious, especially being locked up. I call it cautious. You know, there's different degrees of paranoid.

PLAYBOY: To which objects do you think the FBI may have transferred prints?

RAY: The beer cans are the only thing I can think of. I believe my prints would have been on the gun. I seldom drink beer. I never buy it. I would have bought whiskey.

PLAYBOY: So the other pieces of evidence found in the doorway near the rooming house—beer cans and so on—should not have had your prints on them?

RAY: No.

PLAYBOY: We're told that the ballistics tests failed to prove that your rifle, to the exclusion of all others, killed King. Do you consider that a major point in your favor?

RAY: It wouldn't mean too much to me either way how the tests come out, even if they were negative.

PLAYBOY: Because you didn't fire the rifle?

RAY: Yes.

PLAYBOY: Another question that comes up often is where you got the roughly $9500 it would have taken to cover your expenses while you were at large. You traveled extensively, bought a $2000 Mustang, camera equipment, a rifle and new clothes and lived pretty well. Where did you get all that money?

RAY: I had worked in a restaurant in a suburb of Chicago for about two months immediately after escaping from the Missouri prison [*in 1967*]. I made about $800. I brought a small amount out of prison, too.

PLAYBOY: You claim the rest came from Raoul?

RAY: Yes. He was giving me money to take these packages across the border and he promised me a passport. He didn't come up with the passport, although I did get the money out of him. Gave me money in Birmingham for the car. The first time, I crossed the border from Canada, it was Detroit, it wasn't more than $1500. Another time he give me money in New Orleans. I met him in a bar called, I think, The Rabbit's Foot. He gave me $500.

PLAYBOY: It has been reported that you made a substantial amount of money from dope peddling in prison, that you sent that money out to your brother Jerry and then got it back from him after you escaped. Is that true?

RAY: Jerry never gave me any money. See, when you're in prison that long, there's a lot of letters from convict informers telling officials what kind of operations you're running. The Missouri Corrections Director examined my record thoroughly and there was nothing indicating that type of activity. I've never been any type of big operator in drugs in Missouri.

PLAYBOY: The FBI thinks you may have staged some robberies during 1967 to finance your escapades. Did you?

RAY: Except for holding up a whorehouse and a gambling establishment in Montreal in July 1967, I staged no robberies in Canada or England. [*According to Scotland Yard, Ray robbed a savings and loan bank in England during this period.*]

PLAYBOY: Another reason authorities claim you must have been preparing for some sort of major criminal act is that during your escape from Missouri, you did some unusual things, such as learning to be a locksmith and having plastic surgery done on your nose.

RAY: The plastic surgery was just to make my features more difficult to identify in pictures. I was gonna, in fact, get more surgery done on my ear. Locksmithing I was just interested in.

PLAYBOY: Moving ahead to the day of the King killing: Charles Stephens is an eyewitness who claims he saw you running down the hall of the rooming house just after King was shot. What would your defense have been against his testimony?

RAY: Right after the offense, CBS interviewed this Stephens and he said the man didn't look like me at all. They showed him a sketch.

PLAYBOY: He said it was a "sharp-nosed man." Isn't that you?

RAY: He said he identified me by a sharp pointed nose, but at that time, the FBI didn't know I'd had plastic surgery on my nose in Los Angeles. The FBI got to him.

PLAYBOY: Stephens' wife, Grace Walden, gave a different description of the running man, saying he was stocky, plaid-shirted, balding. Did Raoul look like that?

RAY: No.

PLAYBOY: Actually, doesn't the description fit your brother Jerry?

RAY: Uh—

[*Jerry Ray walked into the room at that point in the interview. Physically, he is shorter and stockier than his brother and is balding.*]

PLAYBOY: Well, speak of the devil. Here is Jerry Ray himself. We were just talking about you. Jerry, there has been a lot of speculation about your role in the King assassination. Why don't you take this opportunity to respond? For instance, is it true that just after your brother James got out of Missouri, he said, as has been reported, that he was going to kill the "big boy, King Coon"?

JERRY RAY: No, that's crazy.

PLAYBOY: Did James tell you that he wanted to establish residence in Birmingham, so that when he killed Martin Luther King he could get a pardon from Alabama governor George Wallace?

JERRY RAY: That's crazy. In the few times we met during that period, I think three or four times, King's name was never mentioned. Never brought up. I've taken an oath on this, a sworn statement.

PLAYBOY: Isn't it true that you met with James in Chicago shortly after the Missouri escape?

JERRY RAY: Yeah, in Northbrook, Illinois. We met, and we'd drink, and we'd go into Chicago sometimes together. Maybe three or four times.

PLAYBOY: Another allegation is that you, Jerry, were the money man for that murder; that you got money from J. B. Stoner's right-wing, racist National States Rights Party and then said, "OK, I've got a guy who will kill King for you—my brother James."

JERRY RAY: It's all crazy.

PLAYBOY: Isn't it true that Jerry contacted Stoner to act as your attorney, James?

JAMES RAY: After the guilty plea, I had Jerry contact two attorneys—Stoner was one—in an effort to rescind Foreman's plea.

PLAYBOY: Why Stoner?

JAMES RAY: First time I heard of him, well, an organization wrote me a letter in England and offered me free legal services. And said Stoner was their lawyer. Later on, when I got to Memphis, I recalled his name.

PLAYBOY: Was the organization that wrote to you Stoner's group?

JAMES RAY: I don't know. That was the extent of it.

PLAYBOY: Is it true that Jerry once worked for J. B. Stoner?

JAMES RAY: Fact is, I was the one that told Jerry to go down there, you see, because the FBI was harassing him.

PLAYBOY: You told your brother to join Stoner? Why?

JAMES RAY: Around a lawyer, with a witness around, it'd be hard for the FBI to frame or harass him.

PLAYBOY: But with Stoner's reputation as a racist, wouldn't it have looked pretty bad for you—especially if he gave Jerry money for you?

JAMES RAY: He never gave me a nickel; I believe he paid you, Jerry, when you worked down there doing postal work.

JERRY RAY: Yeah, I got a salary when I worked for him.

PLAYBOY: Was that before or after King's assassination?

JERRY RAY: I never even heard of Stoner before Martin Luther King's death.

PLAYBOY: So both of you maintain this killing was not a brother operation?

JAMES RAY: Yes.

JERRY RAY: Yes.

[*At that point, the interview was recessed. Arrangements were made for another meeting with Ray the following week, June 13. However, some days later, on Friday evening, June 10, the news broke: Ray had done the impossible—he had gone over the wall of an "escape-proof" prison. While national attention was focused on the woods around Petros, Tennessee, where the penitentiary is located, the interviewers traveled to Lake Zurich, Illinois. There, in a ramshackle structure just off the main highway, Jerry Ray agreed to continue his part of the conversation from a bar stool in a pizza parlor. Some highlights of the conversation follow.*]

June 11, 1977

PLAYBOY: How do you think James will get along on the loose?

JERRY RAY: Only thing that bothers me, it's just like Mark Lane said: The FBI keeps coming in on it. The FBI has no business in this. They came out here last night around three o'clock. I said, "You got an arrest warrant?" They said, "No," so I wouldn't talk to 'em. I said, "Why are you out here? He's on a state charge, a murder charge in Tennessee, not a Federal charge." They said, "Well, he might have crossed state lines." I said, "Well, if he can walk across that damn state line so fast, then he shouldn't be in prison at all."

PLAYBOY: Did you have any advance word that James might try to escape?

JERRY RAY: No. See, that's one reason nothin' comes out on him. Nobody knows what he's thinkin' or nothin', because he don't tell nobody nothin'.

PLAYBOY: What do you suppose James will do for money while he's out?

JERRY RAY: Well, he's been broken out before and he always managed to get some. He might even go look Hefner up and try to get some off him.

PLAYBOY: Do you think he'll survive? It's pretty wild in those mountains.

JERRY RAY: He can eat a few rattlesnakes.

PLAYBOY: Do you think he'll hold anyone up to get money?

JERRY RAY: Well, that's his livelihood. That's his trademark, robbing people. He ain't gonna go out and apply for welfare. He'd have to paint himself black to draw welfare.

PLAYBOY: The racist in you seems to be coming out. You are one, aren't you?

JERRY RAY: No. Hell . . . the people *I'd* get on are Mexicans, takin' jobs from Americans. I'd like to get on that nigger and spick station in Chicago, Channel 26, and tell 'em that. But, listen, I went on a promotion tour with Mark Lane and Dick Gregory for their book. Lane's a Jew and Gregory's black. That's proof I ain't a racist.

PLAYBOY: Did you have anything to do with your brother's escape?

JERRY RAY: The FBI'd have me outside punchin' on me for that.

PLAYBOY: One final point, because it was difficult to believe James's answer when we asked him: What do you think he felt about Martin Luther King?

JERRY RAY: James didn't like him or dislike him. Same as me. Even if James had disliked him, well, if you went out and shot everybody you disliked, you'd have one hell of a record.

[*At 4:30* A.M., *June 13, the interviewers were told that James Earl Ray had just been captured. They returned to Tennessee and word was sent to them that Ray would complete the interview. They met Ray in a small room stacked high with dirty foam-rubber mattresses. Ray ambled in with a characteristic half-smile, looking to the interviewers both sheepish and somewhat proud of himself. His hands and arms were scratched and he had a few days' growth of beard. His brief recess from prison life—the first in nine years—seemed to have raised his spirits.*]

PLAYBOY: How are you feeling?

RAY: All right. I've got poison ivy on my legs. It itches, but it's not very bad.

PLAYBOY: Were you trying to tell us something before you escaped? Were you thinking about the escape when you said you might go out if a wall fell down?

RAY: Yeah. Things like that go through your mind constantly, sometimes pretty strong and sometimes dormant. I suspect that everyone in here has it in the back of his mind. The only thing is whether they got the fortitude to go through with it. Some of them talk about it all the time. Of course, there's some who just want to stay and run the penitentiary.

PLAYBOY: You were out running for 54 and a half hours. Had you trained for the escape?

RAY: Not really. Most people in prison are fairly well conditioned. They run around the yard. That's about all there is to do.

PLAYBOY: What did you want to do after going over the wall?

RAY: Actually, my intention in escaping wasn't too much the *getting* away. The extreme difficulty is staying away permanently. I was thinking about possibly escaping and making some sort of arrangements to turn myself in in exchange for a trial. I know that don't work, but the only way that that would be successful is if the Attorney General entered into some type of friend-of-the-court arrangement with my lawyer. So I had it in the back of my mind to make some arrangements—public relations or something— to try to force the government to give me a trial. I figured I could possibly make a deal, then maybe I could get Griffin Bell to come in. He's indicated that he wants a full airing of the situation. You know, I don't think the state has that much of a case against me. I believe I'd have a good chance of getting acquitted.

PLAYBOY: But how would you have gotten word to Bell?

RAY: When I was arrested, they found two pieces of paper on me. One was a map of Tennessee and the other was the address of Nancy Becker [*a newscaster from ABC-TV in Chicago who had spoken to Ray once before*]. I would have made some kind of arrangement to contact Bell indirectly, through her.

PLAYBOY: Well, until you could get to her house, what would you have done if you had got through the dragnet and out of the area?

RAY: I would have done the same thing that I had done in Missouri. Go to one of these Goodwill places or a run-down place where you don't look too conspicuous going in there tattered up. Get some secondhand clothes and then go from there. I probably would have laid low for three or four days. Usually, the heat gets off after seven or eight days. Something else will happen and they can't concentrate on you. Then you can go ahead and get out.

PLAYBOY: How would you have lain low?

RAY: You would have to disguise your appearance and then go into some run-down neighborhood and rent a room. Lay under a bridge, if you have to. Try to blend into the neighborhood. If it's a run-down neighborhood, I'd have a run-down appearance, which is probably where I would have went.

PLAYBOY: When did you start planning the escape?

RAY: After various adverse court decisions on my case. I'd say I had it in mind two, three months.

PLAYBOY: Why did you pick that particular time to escape?

RAY: I just picked this weekend. I thought that would be best. Things are less organized on the weekends. People are on vacations.

PLAYBOY: Is there less security?

RAY: Yeah, I suppose.

PLAYBOY: When did you make the final decision to go?

RAY: Friday. The same day. I thought that that was the time. I'd been thinking about it and that was the opportune time. So I just picked that day. It ended up that I did it on my own, but of course there were other people involved. You can't do anything in here alone. I'm talking about when you actually start the escape. For instance, when I was on the yard, 15, 20 people come around and they see me putting the ladder against the wall, so some of them followed me.

PLAYBOY: It wasn't organized?

RAY: They didn't know anything about it. They just seen a ladder and just instinctively started going over. About seven went over.

PLAYBOY: We know you used a ladder constructed from plumbing pipe and lightning conduit. But how exactly did you do it?

RAY: I gave it a little thought. Then I got the various things together. It was kind of simple. I just carried the pipe out on the yard. Usually, they check when you come outdoors. I got behind another convict to carry the materials on the yard. And, coincidentally, two, three fights started on the yard. They do that almost every night, fighting over ball games and things.

PLAYBOY: Come on. Was the fight really just a coincidence?

RAY: Yes.

PLAYBOY: What materials did you use in the escape?

RAY: I used a one-and-a-half-inch black pipe I got from the laundry. They put a lot of new equipment in and there were excess pipes and things. I just used what I needed.

PLAYBOY: Did you design the ladder yourself?

RAY: Yeah.

PLAYBOY: And you got all the pieces from the prison laundry?

RAY: Most of them.

PLAYBOY: So you're going to stick to the story that this escape was yours from beginning to end?

RAY: Of course, my escape's mine. I mean, now all these other guys—the six or seven or whatever—who escaped, they were all on their own, I guess. Somebody told me a guard was reading a PLAYBOY magazine and that's why he didn't see them. [*After the interviewers' last session with Ray, prison authorities announced that a guard had been fired for reportedly "reading on duty or looking the other way."*]

PLAYBOY: Did you discuss the escape with anyone?

RAY: No. If I'd discussed it with a lot of guys, I'd probably have been shot going over the wall. I don't want to go too far in discussing this, but all those people ran off on their own. It was on the spur of the moment. There was no plotting with me or coercion or anything.

PLAYBOY: If there were, you wouldn't tell us anyway, right?

RAY: That'd probably be right. But it didn't happen that way. If I had entered into even the vaguest conspiracy, I couldn't tell the press. I think the evidence now indicates that every one of the escapees was on their own. Most of them I didn't know, and the rest of them I just knew casually. The only individual I knew was my cellmate, Earl Hill, and, of course, he was always close by. The others, they were all around. They knew what was going on. There's one guy that worked in the kitchen, a black guy. He was looking out the window and he saw what was going on. He runs all the time for exercise. So he got the guards to let him out of the kitchen and ran around the yard and went over the wall. So it couldn't have been any conspiracy, 'cause he didn't know what was going on. He just happened to look out the kitchen window. It could just as easily have been a guard looking out the window.

PLAYBOY: Aren't you lying to us when you say you didn't work with someone on this escape?

RAY: No. I wouldn't want to go into too many details, but I'm not lying. But I don't want to take total responsibility or anything.

PLAYBOY: Anyway, you know you're a liar.

RAY: Yes, I know that.

PLAYBOY: How long did it take you to put the ladder together once you were in the yard?

RAY: Oh, it didn't take long at all once I got started on it. Ten or fifteen minutes.

PLAYBOY: You mean you were out in the yard for 15 minutes putting the ladder together? And no guards noticed?

RAY: Yeah. Well, it was coincidental that a fight broke out. They were breaking the fights up. It wasn't a laxity of the guards or anything, the only thing was that this coincidence happened that we—that I—got a few breaks when the fight started. No one else was involved. In fact, I didn't know anything about the other guys until I got up on the hill and I heard somebody run up beside me, so I figured someone may have been following me. Then I heard a bunch of shots and I heard cheering.

PLAYBOY: Cheering?

RAY: Yeah. Later on, I found out what it was. They shot the last guy to escape and he fell down. When he got up, the prisoners watching started cheering. Then they shot him again.

PLAYBOY: They shot him a second time?

RAY: Shot him in the head the second time. It just grazed him and knocked him out.

PLAYBOY: Did you hear anything else as you went away?

RAY: No. I heard them talking once or twice; sound carries quite a way in the mountains. I just kept going. Finally, the talk died out and that's the last that I heard. That's wilderness out there. I must have been places up there that no person's ever been, way back up in some of those gullies. There's heavy brush up there and things like that.

PLAYBOY: What was it like out there?

RAY: The mountains are pretty good. You hear a lot of rumors that there's all these snakes. I didn't see no snakes. All I saw was two squirrels and a ground hog. He was about two feet high and about five foot long. He ran before I did.

PLAYBOY: Did you feel free?

RAY: Yes; I'd rather be out there than in here.

PLAYBOY: What were you thinking about?

RAY: Usually, a food problem is what you have out there.

PLAYBOY: Did you take any provisions?

RAY: Just wheat germ. Mostly, I thought about food, that's the problem when you get out there. This time of year, there's nothing up there except green berries.

PLAYBOY: It would seem that after nine years in prison, the fact that you were out in the woods on your own would make you absolutely ecstatic.

RAY: Well, effectively, I was glad. Of course, you feel better than in jail, but, like I said, you don't have any food or anything. There is physical discomfort. But I think that the mental makes up for the physical. I can't describe all this. I felt fairly well mentally. I've been through this before, you know. If I had got out of the area, it might have been different. But ecstatic? I think that might be exaggerating a little bit.

PLAYBOY: Do you have any memories of your 54 and a half hours of freedom that stand out—were there any high points for you?

RAY: I was on one particular mountain one time—that must have been the highest point out there. You could see various towns and you could see a long ways off. That's a nice sight from up there. Something like California, like looking over Los Angeles; I was there once. I understand that a lot of people go up into those mountains to get away from it all, to be up that high. It's kind of a solitary feeling up there. I never did hear any dogs. These mountains are a big range. . . . The planes were flying over and they'd come back every ten or fifteen minutes, so they really didn't know where I was.

PLAYBOY: How did you react when those dogs came sniffing around you?

RAY: Actually, I didn't know the dogs were around. I thought they would bark. They used to have a lead dog here that would bark all the time, but they got rid of him and they got these new ones that are silent. They get up on you before you know it. Well, I looked up and they wasn't more than 20 feet away from me. They had five or six police with them. I lay on my back and just threw a few leaves over me, but it didn't do any good, because the dogs had my scent. And I didn't think nothin'. They just got me. That was it. They told me to get up. I just thought if they had me, I couldn't have got away if they was that close. They just handcuffed me and that was that. They asked me if anyone else was around and I said no. Shook me down and brought me back in.

PLAYBOY: What was the first thing they said to you?

RAY: They said not to move or they'd shoot me. 'Course, that wasn't inappropriate.

PLAYBOY: How did you feel when you were caught? Like crying?

RAY: I wouldn't want to give them the satisfaction of crying. Of course, there's no point in crying, anyway. It's disappointing being caught, but it's not the end of the world. There's tomorrow.

PLAYBOY: You mean you might be going out again?

RAY: There's always something that comes along later on. Naturally, I wasn't happy about being run down. But the hunger really kind of dulls your emotions in some ways.

PLAYBOY: There were some people who wanted to go out and use bullhorns, asking you to give up. Your attorney, for example. What would you have done if you had heard your lawyer calling down at you from a helicopter?

RAY: Ask him to throw down his I.D.

PLAYBOY: Were you able to sleep out there?

RAY: Yes, an hour or two at a time. I slept in the daytime and traveled at night. I never saw any caves up there, but there are a lot of cliffs with ledges on them. You can sit under the ledges. There are coal mines up there, but it would be foolish getting into one of those things. That's usually what they shake down first.

PLAYBOY: What if you'd been shot? Have you ever felt that you'd rather be dead than spend the rest of your life in prison?

RAY: Well, I've never looked at this as a long-term thing. There's no way of knowing what's going to happen tomorrow, so I'll take it on that basis. As for being shot, I think I'd be doing something of a favor to the Government, or something. I'd rather be alive than dead.

PLAYBOY: You'd rather stay alive and take your chances that something will come along?

RAY: Well, yes, for something worthwhile.

PLAYBOY: Such as getting over the wall again?

RAY: Yeah, like getting over the wall. Ah, I didn't have to say that.

PLAYBOY: Let's go back to your early days and talk about how you got started. Why did you become a thief?

RAY: I don't know; that's very difficult to explain. I guess to supplement my income. It started in 1951, 1952. I held up a few liquor stores, small-time stuff. I recall one time I robbed one with a sawed-off shotgun. When I ran out of the door, through the back of the place, I tripped on a wire and shot myself in the foot.

PLAYBOY: Did you ever kill anyone?

RAY: No.

PLAYBOY: Did you ever shoot anyone?

RAY: No.

PLAYBOY: Stab anyone?

RAY: I can't remember ever stabbin' anyone. Of course, I've been in a few fights.

PLAYBOY: Would you have any qualms about killing someone?

RAY: Yes, sir.

PLAYBOY: Would you kill to escape?

RAY: I can't see myself killing anyone to get out of the penitentiary both for moral and for legal reasons.

PLAYBOY: Would you ever shoot your way out?

RAY: No, I'd get out in a surreptitious manner.

PLAYBOY: Ever think of any crimes besides robbery? There was a report recently that you and your brother John discussed kidnaping someone for ransom after you escaped from Missouri.

RAY: That's completely false. I can think of a long line of offenses, maybe even including homicide, but kidnaping would be the last thing I would ever enter into. Chances of success are just nil, you might say.

PLAYBOY: Do you feel there's much chance for success in liquor-store robberies?

RAY: That type of robbery is nonsense. You don't get any money, plus you get just as much time as if you rob something substantial.

PLAYBOY: What do you consider substantial?

RAY: Well, a supermarket. That's really a corporation's money and they're probably gougin' it out of somebody else, anyway. Better to rob them than an individual.

PLAYBOY: So you have a set of principles?

RAY: See, you have to understand that when I got out of the Missouri penitentiary in 1967, I was in my late 30s. Crime isn't worthwhile then. So I had no intention of committing a crime again. My intention was to escape, not to go back out and start a series of petty robberies. I just can't think of any crime you could commit and get away with—well, who's this guy who jumped out of the plane with $200,000—D. B. Cooper? Now, *then* you could quit and go about your business.

PLAYBOY: Did you consider that an ideal crime?

RAY: Tolerable.

PLAYBOY: Do you consider yourself a professional criminal?

RAY: I don't consider myself a professional criminal any longer, because I was retired—if that's the right word for it—in 1967. I'd done enough time. Let someone else take over from there on.

PLAYBOY: It sounds as if you're making a moral argument and you mentioned a moral argument against killing. Do you have your own set of rights and wrongs?

RAY: I think you have to live with some type of code—or right or wrong, or whatever it is—in order to succeed in what you're trying to do. I don't know about morals. That's just a personal feeling. I don't have any fixed ideas on what's right and wrong. If I did, I would probably be writing editorials in newspapers.

PLAYBOY: Is it wrong that you're in prison for killing King?

RAY: I believe that's wrong, but, on the other hand, I can't just sit here dwelling on the fact I'm innocent. I'm here, they got me framed. I look at it a different way. I had my opportunity when I escaped from Missouri. I should have stayed in Canada. It's difficult for me to explain all these things. I'm just looking at it this way: They've got me in here and it's up to me to get out. Guilt or innocence is inconsequential. Of course, from your point of view, that's the wrong way to look at it. But they got me in here, either rightly or wrongly, and it's up to me to get out—rightly or wrongly. I've read some of these philosophy books, like the *History of Philosophy,* and in one of them I read that a handful of might is a bagful of right. I go along with that. I may have the right, but that doesn't mean anything. See, there's something about always saying you're innocent; I don't like to keep saying I'm innocent. That seems like you're crying or something.

PLAYBOY: Are you religious? Do you believe in God?

RAY: I don't disbelieve in Him, but I really don't give too much thought to the other side. I was christened a Catholic. I went to church when I was living in Illinois. My grandmother was Irish and was hooked on the Catholic religion. My mother was Catholic.

RAY: What kind of a man was your father?

RAY: That's hard to describe: I don't like to be making judgments on others. I've always gotten along with him fine.

PLAYBOY: What was your dad in prison for?

RAY: It had something to do with money. I think it was for grand larceny, I believe.

PLAYBOY: Your father was a thief and both of your brothers have done time. In fact, one—John—is in prison now for bank robbery. It kind of runs in the family, doesn't it?

RAY: The relatives on my mother's side were immigrants from Ireland and none of them had any criminal records, except one. But on my father's side, there was this outlaw stuff. I think Jimmy Carter said one of his ancestors was a horse thief. It's no big deal.

PLAYBOY: How do you feel about your brother Jerry? He obviously feels a great deal for you?

RAY: Well, Jerry's all right. I like him and I assume he likes me, too. I just don't like to get too expressive, these terms love and all that stuff.

PLAYBOY: Why not?

RAY: There are just certain terms that I don't care about using, because they sound mushy or something. Your mother might use that term or something, but I don't think that a man sits around talking about love and so on. It sounds sort of odd to me.

PLAYBOY: Were your family ties close?

RAY: Yes, I think they always were. When I was ten or twelve years old, I used to spend most of my time in Quincy, Illinois. My grandfather used to run a tavern and I used to hang around there quite a bit.

PLAYBOY: Were you always a loner?

RAY: There are degrees between being an introvert and an extrovert. You can't just associate with everyone that comes along. But most people, whether they're man, woman or in between, don't want to get associated with me in any manner. I can understand that.

PLAYBOY: Do you have a girlfriend on the outside?

RAY: No, most of my associates are in jail.

PLAYBOY: You've expressed yourself very coldly throughout this interview. Do you have any strong emotions? Can you get angry or love someone?

RAY: No, I can't explain about the emotions. I understand certain types of individuals, say the Latins, are more expressive than others. But I can't compare myself to someone else, to how emotional they get. For instance, women—they'll break down and cry and all that stuff.

PLAYBOY: Have you ever cried?

RAY: Not for a long time, since I was 12 or 14.

PLAYBOY: Have you ever been in love with a woman?

RAY: I've never been married or anything like that. I lived with them a few times.

PLAYBOY: Did you love those women?

RAY: I doubt that very much, because I never had a long period of association. I mean, usually just two or three months with most of them. I respect them and think they're probably more of a higher human than the man is. They seem more independent than the man is. I'm not saying anything about women's lib. I don't agree with that.

PLAYBOY: Throughout this interview, you've claimed to be innocent of King's assassination. You've just escaped and been caught again. Your legal options seem almost exhausted. What chance do you think you have of ever getting out?

RAY: I don't think that I'll have too much of a chance getting out legally unless the FBI information is declassified. If all this material would be declassified in some kind of proceeding, I'd be willing to forget the whole thing.

PLAYBOY: You mean if everything were declassified and you saw that there was nothing that would clear you, you'd give up attempts for a new trial?

RAY: Yes.

PLAYBOY: Do you really think the FBI has material that would clear you?

RAY: I'm positive. I told the House committee the only thing I wanted was to get this material declassified in the Justice Department.

'Course, I'm not even sure the files would help me. I believe they would, because if they wouldn't, they wouldn't make such an effort to suppress them.

PLAYBOY: You sound indomitable, despite your situation. And you've spent more years in solitary than many inmates ever spend in prison. How do you survive?

RAY: In Nashville, I was in solitary for five years [*prison officials say it was four years*]. The only way solitary affected me is my concentration. For example, normally if I read a book, I just read it straight through. In segregation, though, you can only read 30 or 40 pages at a time and then you have to stop. Of course, it runs you down physically, but when you're out two or three months, you get recuperated.

PLAYBOY: That sort of isolation didn't affect you mentally?

RAY: I don't know if it did or not. I may have gotten funny in the head.

PLAYBOY: You've come off as a very tough character. Is anybody going to get the best of James Earl Ray?

RAY: I don't know. Legally they have, I know that.

PLAYBOY: As of this moment, the Tennessee governor is asking that you be put in Federal prison. How do you feel about that?

RAY: Oh, I'm gonna fight that. They're going to have to use physical force to get me out of here. See, the FBI has agents in residence in all these different prisons. An individual could kill you.

PLAYBOY: Do you mean that if you were in a Federal penitentiary, you think the FBI would have someone kill you?

RAY: Yeah, I think it might be similar to the King operation. They'd get the security off or they might put you on one of those drug projects or something. They tried to transfer me once to the Springfield, Missouri, behavior-modification program, a mental program where they give you drugs. This was at Nashville. The deputy warden called me down and said they was sending me there. I told him he had no such authority and he said he was going to do it anyway. So I sued. In the end, nothing happened.

PLAYBOY: Let's ask this once again: What would you say is the single most important fact that proves your innocence?

RAY: As I said, the suppression of all the evidence by the Government.

PLAYBOY: Not that you didn't pull the trigger to kill King?

RAY: Well, yes, but not from a legal point.

[*The prison guards entered the room to take Ray back to his cell. As Ray began to walk away, there was a final, hurried exchange.*]

PLAYBOY: You're sure, James, that you didn't kill Martin Luther King?

RAY: Well, I'm not sure until I get the evidence out of the Justice Department.

PLAYBOY: What? You have to *know* if you did it.

RAY: I'm really serious. I don't think anything will be resolved until we get that. I'll just be making denials and the Justice Department will be saying I'm guilty and that'll be it. This is an unusual case.

James Earl Ray's Lie-Detector Test

For the first time since the assassination of Martin Luther King, Jr., James Earl Ray agreed to take a lie-detector test, at PLAYBOY's request. The editors hired Douglas Wicklander, a polygraph expert with John E. Reid & Associates, to administer the test to Ray—with his lawyer's permission—at Brushy Mountain Penitentiary on June 22, 1977. Following are the significant questions and answers:

Q.: Did you kill Martin Luther King, Jr.?
RAY: No.
Q.: Did you fire the shot that killed Martin Luther King, Jr.?
RAY: No.
Q.: Do you know for sure who killed Martin Luther King, Jr.?
RAY: No.

Wicklander, Reid and director Joseph J. Buckley gave PLAYBOY the following opinion:

"It is the opinion of the examiner, based on this subject's polygraph records, that he is not telling the truth on the previously listed questions."

To explore the subject of a possible conspiracy, we asked the polygraph examiner to conduct a second test. Following are the questions and answers:

Q.: Did anyone ask you to kill Martin Luther King, Jr.?
RAY: No.
Q.: Did you arrange with anyone to kill Martin Luther King, Jr.?
RAY: No.
Q.: Did anyone give you any money to kill Martin Luther King, Jr.?
RAY: No.

The examiners gave PLAYBOY their opinion on those answers:

"It is the opinion of the examiner, based on this subject's polygraph records, that he is telling the truth on the above listed questions."

To summarize, the polygraph tests indicate that Ray did, in fact, kill Martin Luther King, Jr., and that he did so alone. (Ray's response to the news that the test results were negative appears on the next page.)

The tests were conducted with all the controls standard to such procedures. John E. Reid & Associates is among the oldest polygraph-examination firms in the country and one of the most respected. Wicklander has personally administered over 2500 tests and Reid is the author of a text used by polygraph trainees and the designer of the "control question" technique used throughout the field.

When PLAYBOY asked officials of the firm if there were any doubt whatsoever about their conclusions, the answer was, "None."

June 25, 1977

PLAYBOY: You've just heard that the results of the polygraph test you took at our request show you were not telling the truth. If the test is reliable, it means you did kill King and you did it alone. What's your reaction?

RAY: Well, I don't know if there's anything accurate about these lie-detector tests. Senator Sam Ervin, I think, called it a medieval contraption or something. See, when I took the test, I had a headache all day. I took a bunch of aspirin. I don't know if that would affect the test or not. They also asked me a series of [*control*] questions about other robberies—a lot of those questions can cause certain anxiety if you've been accused of them.

Another time, I was given a psychological-stress test that showed the opposite. [*The psychological-stress evaluation, or P.S.E., is a test in which a tape of the subject's voice is analyzed for stress. Although neither polygraph nor P.S.E. results are generally admissible in court, the P.S.E. is widely considered to be the more controversial.*] I think you could get someone to argue that this one's false and the P.S.E. is correct. It was done without me being there, so I wouldn't have worried one way or the other. I think it's best to answer questions when you're not hooked up and all that stuff—machines. But I'm still more concerned about the Justice Department files and this Rosenson business than I am with this test.

ANITA BRYANT

June 1978
Interviewer: Ken Kelley

Anita Bryant had been making news for over a year with her successful crusade against homosexual teachers and against the "disease" of homosexuality in general. The woman seemed both sincere and dangerously misinformed in some of her public pronouncements, and with the support she was picking up across the country (and a whopping political victory at home in Dade County, Florida), PLAYBOY's editors felt she would be an ideal subject for an extended interview.

Free-lancer Ken Kelley, a writer from San Francisco, offered to do the interview, and after a great deal of negotiation—and ingratiation—Kelley enlisted the cooperation of Bryant and her husband/manager, Bob Green. Kelley stuck by her side as Bryant and Green toured the Bible Belt preaching sermons against sexual decadence and holding press conferences—including one in which Bryant was splattered with a cherry pie in the face, and Kelley fought back in her behalf.

In a sidebar to the interview, Kelley described their time together and recalled some bizarre moments:

> For such a sexual naïf, Anita can with startling incongruity become quite the barroom flirt. "Just wait till you see my show, Ken," she bubbled as she made up her face before her Mississippi State Fair show. . . . She stood up and looked away from her mirror. "I have to dress now, so y'all shoo." I headed for the exit. "Oh, Kennnn . . ." Anita lifted her skirt to mid-thigh and winked. "You can stay if you want to. Hah hah." . . .
>
> Several months later, in her last phone call to me, Anita said, "Hiya, boyfriend," in her fetchingest corn pone. She was calling, she said, to wish me good luck for the new year and to tell me that

her whole family prayed for me every night. And, oh, yes . . . by the way—"Ken, I hope you realize that I have made myself tremendously vulnerable to you. I opened myself up to you in ways I've never done before. I've shared some things with you I'd never even shared with my husband." A beat. "Now that's a sacred obligation on your part." I mumbled something about doing my best. "Well, do a good job now, or I'll put the curse of God on ya, hear?" She laughed. I did not laugh.

This interview endures not so much as an examination of backlash against homosexuals or even of religious intolerance, but as a psychological profile—in the subject's own words—of a true believer.

Most, though not all, readers agreed that the interview did an equitable job of exposing the misinformation on which Bryant's crusade was based. But even some homosexuals wrote in to say they thought the interviewer was too rough on her. Thomas Weyr, who was himself critical of Kelley's own "naïveté" in the interview, nonetheless wrote in *Reaching for Paradise*: "No other interview captured quite as many contradictions, or made the point of PLAYBOY's endless diversity as well. . . . Bryant emerged as a troubled, honest, and bewildered woman—and as deadly as a striking cobra. She must have persuaded as many people of the justness of her cause, and of the evils of homosexuality, as she dissuaded and frightened. And much of her impact is due to the room PLAYBOY gives her ruminations about God, love, sex, childhood, ambitions and fears."

To say nothing of her ruminations on marriage, and her attitudes toward men, whom she admitted "hating" for many years, and her need for a solid home life because of the trauma of her parents' divorce. In one of the sadder ironies to occur as a postscript to this interview, Bryant announced in the spring of 1980 that she and Bob Green were divorcing.

For her first 36 years, Anita Bryant was the stereotypic embodiment of the American dream; hers was a rags-to-riches saga in the best Horatio Alger tradition. For almost two decades, she'd been reasonably happy with her life: She'd evolved a system that enabled her to pursue both a lucrative career as a popular entertainer and a satisfying private life as a devoted wife and mother. She had a loyal husband, wholesome kids and a cozy home overlooking Miami's Biscayne Bay. Her life was comfortable and distinctly uncontroversial.

Last year, all that suddenly and dramatically changed. When the

Metropolitan Dade County Commission passed an ordinance that would, in effect, mandate that qualified homosexuals be hired as teachers in private and parochial schools, Bryant stepped forward to spearhead a drive to repeal it. The ensuing campaign was drawn along classic good-versus-evil lines. Bryant recruited a slew of religious leaders and conservative politicos under the banner of her ad hoc *organization, Save Our Children. Her pitch was simple: Homosexuality is a sin, and if homosexuals were given carte blanche to glamorize their "deviate life-style" in Miami-area classrooms, the American family would be destroyed and the American way of life would disappear. Miami homosexual leaders, armed with a hefty war chest, issued an urgent national SOS to supporters of "human rights"—if Bryant were successful, they said, America would turn into Nazi Germany—and liberals from Midge Costanza to Rod McKuen dutifully trekked to Miami to campaign against her. The national media seized on the issue almost from the start and a local election was turned into a national spectacle. On election day last June, the ordinance was overwhelmingly defeated and Bryant was photographed dancing a jubilant jig. But the battle was far from over; Bryant had become a fixture on the American political scene.*

It was her husband and manager, Bob Green, along with her Baptist pastor, who convinced her to defend motherhood and Christian ideals by taking the stand against the homosexual community last year. She was shocked when most of her bookings evaporated—most booking agents were scared off by the threats of homosexuals to protest her appearances— and she appeared mostly in religious shows, always accompanied by a phalanx of angry gay pickets. She was universally reviled in the national media and by Hollywood and became cannon fodder for comedians everywhere. By her estimate, she lost half a million dollars in bookings. A national "gaycott" of Florida orange juice almost cost her her $100,000-a-year contract with the Florida Citrus Commission, though after a year's waffling, the commission renewed it. She did lose a contract with the Singer company to host her own television show, as well as her perennial job as narrator of the Orange Bowl parade.

Bryant insists that she took her stand based on her religious convictions, dollars be damned, and that she'd do it all over again in a minute.

PLAYBOY *sent free-lancer Ken Kelley on an eight-day Bible Belt tour with Bryant and Green. At first, she "prayed to God for guidance" and decided against doing the interview for* PLAYBOY, *feeling that the nudity that appears in the magazine violated her moral standards. (She regards fornication between unmarried heterosexuals as no less a violation of the Lord's commandments than homosexual conduct.) Kelley continued the interview under assignment to* Rolling Stone, *but editorial differences developed and, at the end, he was able to persuade Green and Bryant that her startling views could be aired in* PLAYBOY, *as originally planned.*

PLAYBOY: Have you always been obsessed with homosexuality?

BRYANT: Not at all. If I had been, would I have waited until 1977 to speak up? We could have gone on the offense long ago. We would have tried to shut down their publications, which anyone can pick up at a local hotel, and which show that they can do what they want with kids of whatever age they want, and even what kind of sex they can have. The homosexuals have their national directory and it lists Miami as the most open city in the nation. I got involved only because they were asking for special privileges that violated the state law of Florida, not to mention God's law. You know, when I was a child, you didn't even *mention* the word homosexual, much less find out what the act was about. You knew it was very bad, but you couldn't imagine what they tried to do, exactly, in terms of one taking a male role and the other taking a female role. I mean, it was too filthy to think about and you had other things to think about. So when I finally found out all the implications, it was a total revelation for me.

PLAYBOY: Then when you opposed the Dade County ordinance, at first you didn't even have a clear idea *what* you were opposing?

BRYANT: Well, I knew some things, because Bob had told me—he *is* nine years older and he has taught me a lot of things about sex. He was born in the Bronx and I was raised in the Bible Belt—what can I say? I mean, you have visions of, well, now, what can they do as two men in bed or two women in bed? But I didn't really know the nitty-gritty of the thing.

PLAYBOY: Until when?

BRYANT: I'm not going to tell you.

PLAYBOY: Wasn't it when you got a letter in January 1977 with an explicit picture enclosed?

BRYANT: OK, yeah. And, I mean, I was absolutely appalled. I just couldn't believe it. And then, afterward, a local police sergeant gave a presentation in our church basement with slides and all about child pornography and it shocked our whole congregation. We understood then just how debased the whole thing was. I mean, it's a sin under the laws of God. And sin is like leprosy—it starts with just a little speck and you don't even notice or care. You think, That's not going to hurt me, and all of a sudden it begins to spread and you still don't worry until the sores spread to the shoulder and the pus starts oozing, but by then it's too late. God says the wages of sin are death, and one little sin brings on another. The homosexual act is just the beginning of the depravity. It then leads to—what's the word?— sadomasochism. It just gets worse at it goes on. You go further and further down the drain and it just becomes so perverted and you get into alcohol and drugs and it's so rotten that many homosexuals end up committing suicide. The worst thing is that these days, so many married men with children who don't have a happy marriage are going into the homosexual bars for satisfaction—if they're not careful, they're going to get caught up in it totally.

PLAYBOY: You believe in a kind of sexual domino theory, then?

BRYANT: Lots of wives and former homosexuals have testified to me about these things.

PLAYBOY: Didn't your biggest shock about homosexuals come when you realized that male homosexuals eat each other's sperm? A Miami reporter briefly quoted you as saying the reason God calls homosexuality an abomination is that homosexuals eat spermatozoa, the building block of blood, so, therefore, homosexuals are swallowing, and presumably digesting, the essence of life?

BRYANT: I did not . . . um . . . I did not say that to any reporter. I'm not that stupid.

PLAYBOY: Did you say it to anybody?

BRYANT: I was overheard talking to a reformed homosexual on the phone and I had no idea our conversation would ever get printed. It was a very personal thing and I never dreamed it would get printed. The reporter deceived me. I was very naïve about the media then—since then, I've been trained. At that time, I was like a babe among the wolves.

PLAYBOY: But you *did* say it.

BRYANT: It was a personal thing. I don't want to talk about it.

PLAYBOY: Why not?

BRYANT: Because it's just too gory, too raw for most people to comprehend.

PLAYBOY: You could take this opportunity to explain yourself, rather than let it stand as an overheard conversation.

BRYANT: Well, I was witnessing to this guy, and I didn't let on that I knew he had been a homosexual, and I threw the question at him because I wasn't sure myself and I wanted to find out. I had read about this phenomenon, but I wasn't sure it was true. See, I was at my desk one night and I was reading and studying; it was about one in the morning and when I read about it—

PLAYBOY: You mean swallowing sperm?

BRYANT: Yeah, when I read about it, I about fell through my chair. I said, "Oh, God, this can't be true." That was the first time I really knew. I mean, I had seen in writing before what they did in bed, and so forth, but I never knew that they ate the male sperm. I just wanted to fall off the chair. So when this guy called, I wanted to really find out if what I'd read was true. So I said very casually, "Oh, by the way, do you know that homosexuals eat the male sperm?"

PLAYBOY: What did he say?

BRYANT: He said yes.

PLAYBOY: And?

BRYANT: And I still couldn't believe it.

PLAYBOY: Why not?

BRYANT: Well, throughout the Bible, particularly in the Old Testament, men are referred to as trees. Even in the Garden of Eden, when God referred to the tree of life, He was talking about the whole spiritual salvation of men, and so forth. And in the New Testament, it says Jesus was called the fruit of the womb—which is very interesting, because even the homosexuals know this. Did you know there is a group in Seattle that calls itself The Fruit Loops?

PLAYBOY: So?

BRYANT: Why do you think the homosexuals are called fruits? It's because they eat the forbidden fruit of the tree of life. God referred to men as trees, and because the homosexuals eat the forbidden fruit, which is male sperm . . . There is even a Jockey short called Forbidden Fruit. Very subtle. Did you know that?

PLAYBOY: No. We've heard only of Fruit of the Loom.

BRYANT: You see, I agree with the antiabortion people that the beginning of life is when the male sperm fertilizes the female egg. The Scriptures talk about John the Baptist jumping in the womb when he was in the presence of the Mother Mary when Jesus was still in the womb, and that Jesus was conceived of the Holy Spirit. That was the beginning of life and I believe that—I cannot deny what I know to be true. That's why homosexuality is an abomination of God, because life is so precious to God and it is such a sacred thing when man and woman come together in one flesh and the seed is fertilized—that's the sealing of life, that's the beginning of life. To interfere with that in any way—especially the eating of the forbidden fruit, the eating of the sperm—that's why it's such an abomination. I can't deny it. When I discuss this with Christians, it revolts them, especially when they don't know the Bible and cannot see sin in its most hideous forms. You really turn people off when you speak in these blunt terms, and they can't believe I'm saying it. But you have to tell them that it's true. It's there, it's logical and it makes the sin of homosexuality all the more hideous because it's antilife, degenerative.

PLAYBOY: Surely, you must know that the eating of sperm is not confined to homosexuals. In fact, it's quite popular in heterosexual relationships these days.

BRYANT: It's true. I agree with you. The abomination is spreading. Ideally, of course, the relationship between a man and a woman should embody oneness with God—the most natural thing is the reproducing of life and having the first fruits from that oneness together.

PLAYBOY: So sex is only for procreation?

BRYANT: Oh, no. But God created the family to be a picture of perfection. Nothing is perfect, of course, but a woman's giving herself to her husband should try to resemble perfection, just as the husband's protection of his wife should be a love like he loves his own body. How many men do that with their woman? If you could see that bliss as an expression of God's perfection, it would make you yearn to know God.

PLAYBOY: You're saying that sexual intercourse between man and wife is an acknowledgment of God?

BRYANT: Right—it's a picture of the Church, in a sense. It's a beautiful thing, ordained of God, meant to be enjoyed and to be pleasurable, not looked on as debased or ungodly or dirty, as so many Christians unfortunately see it. Sex was never meant to be that. God tells us it's like a mystery—He means a coming together that releases the joy you have in that moment of climax when there is a oneness with you and your husband and with God. It's physical, but it becomes spiritual. I've often thought that at that moment, you experience the release and the purity that God meant to be. . . . Well, it's like the way Christ loves the Church. When you come together, it's like when the Church is brought up to meet Christ in the air, when we will all take on immortality. There is a releasing of all the burdens of the mortal body and such sheer release of joy and oneness—it's almost like floating in the air and you know someday you will be able to meet Christ. I think the reason there's so much promiscuity and so much emphasis on sex these days is because people leave out the spiritual part.

PLAYBOY: Is birth control an abomination against the Lord? Is taking the pill a sin?

BRYANT: No, because the way it's done, you are not wasting the sperm. I've never really gone into this before. I've never had that question asked of me. I do think it's important to realize God's glory when you come together—if there's not the oneness of the spirit, soul and body, then there's an imperfection. This whole discussion is so delicate—that's why it's so important that the Government and the public schools should not take the responsibility to explain sex to our children—it is the province of the parents.

PLAYBOY: Some parents may be less qualified to explain it than educators are.

BRYANT: I don't care, the child should hear it from the parents.

PLAYBOY: Many parents refuse to accept the responsibility. What then?

BRYANT: I know. It's not easy. I don't have all the answers. I know what you're talking about, because my mother and her mother didn't know how to talk about sex.

PLAYBOY: OK, let's get back to deviant sexual practices, as you characterize homosexuality. Why did you decide to oppose the Dade County ordinance last year? You'd never taken a political stand before.

BRYANT: Right, I never had. The basic reason was because I am first and foremost a mother, and I was standing up for my rights as a mother to protect my children after I realized what the threat the homosexuals were posing meant. That's why we called our organization Save Our Children, though we've since been forced to change it to Protect America's Children, because the Save the Children Federation took us to court. The ordinance the homosexuals proposed would have made it mandatory that flaunting homosexuals be hired in both the public and the parochial schools. My children attend a religious school. Freedom of religion is guaranteed by the Constitution, and if you believe that adultery, homosexuality, drunkenness and things like that violate your religious standards, you then have a right to prevent a teacher from standing up in front of your children and promoting sin. We were fighting religious bigotry. What gives the homosexual any more right to stand up in front of children and talk about his sexual preferences than a man who has a great Dane as his lover?

PLAYBOY: Bestiality is just around the corner, then?

BRYANT: Under the proposed ordinance, every sexual deviation would have been legally acceptable among schoolteachers. Right behind the homosexual community in Dade County was a group of prostitutes who were going to initiate similar legislation permitting whores to stand up in front of kids in the classroom and proclaim their sexual deviation and then ply their trade. Ad infinitum. The issue had nothing to do with what people do in the privacy of their bedrooms. If two men or two women live together and don't flaunt their deviant life-style, fine. Let them do what they want. But when they try to interfere with my right as a mother to raise my children the way I see fit, then I draw the line, I mean, no one got very excited about the ordinance—no one knew it was an issue, really, it was so secretive. It had passed two readings at the Dade County Commission before we even became aware of it. On the third reading, it would have become law—we only had a week and a half to try to stop it. The ordinance sounded very simple—it said there should be no discrimination in the areas of housing, public accommodations and employment. Who wants to discriminate? It's a no-no. But the discrimination they were talking about was not based on race or religion. Homosexuals would have us believe they're born that way, because they're in total darkness and they've never been told any different. But if they're a legitimate minority group, then so are nail biters, dieters, fat people, short people and murderers. Who will be the next in line to ask for special privileges? When it came down to a courtroom hearing, the homosexuals in Dade County said it's not a matter of housing, public accommodations and employment—we're already there, they said. Which they definitely are. They said, "The point is that we want to come out of the closet, we want to tell you where we're at and we don't want to lose our jobs because of it." One of the homosexual leaders made a statement before the Community Relations Board. He said he became a homosexual when he was seven years old but that it bothered him that he never had a role model to look up to.

PLAYBOY: Aren't you just resorting to the same kind of argument that Joe McCarthy used in the Fifties against communism? He insisted that

Americans could not be exposed to it lest they immediately turn into raving Marxists. Do you think "flaunting homosexuals," as you put it, will automatically turn America's children into homosexuals?

BRYANT: Of course it's not just an overnight thing. What happens is that the door then opens onto a lot of other things. It may not have an immediate effect, but certainly down the line it will—on your kids and your grandchildren, for generations to come. We can't see the evils of sin right off. It looks so innocent at first, but I've seen too many lives ruined by that kind of thinking.

PLAYBOY: A moment ago, you lumped homosexuals into the same category as murderers.

BRYANT: But I'm not saying homosexuals are murderers.

PLAYBOY: You're saying they're just as bad.

BRYANT: No, I don't say they're as bad. God says it. It's in the Bible. *First Corinthians,* I think.

PLAYBOY: Since you've never been connected with political causes before, how did you feel when you found yourself embroiled in a controversial issue as its leader?

BRYANT: I was petrified. I was devastated by the fears within me that I would make a fool out of myself. I knew what I was up against—the homosexuals in Dade County had amassed support from homosexuals around the country and they had the active backing of a wide range of liberal politicians. I asked myself, what can I possibly do that will matter? But, thanks to the encouragement of my husband and my pastor, I became aware of the difference one person can make. Similar ordinances had been passed in 36 other cities around the country and Congressman Ed Koch [now New York City's mayor] had even proposed a Federal bill along the same lines. The homosexuals in Miami knew that Dade County was one of the most liberal counties in the country. They said if they won, it would be a barometer for all of America. I'd really done my homework before I stood up. I went through a lot of anguish.

PLAYBOY: Your pastor convinced you it was a sin not to stand up?

BRYANT: Yes. I was totally convinced of that. My eyes had been opened and I really had no choice. Still, I vacillated between being weak and being strong. Then I told myself, well, if God is before me, who can be against me?

PLAYBOY: You had God on your side?

BRYANT: Yes. I had given the Lord my total being—I mean, everything. So I had a confidence, a strength that everything I had always tried to attain in my own flesh, and never could, would be now possible. When you give yourself to God, God gives you everything. My pastor, Brother Bill, had a much bigger picture than I did. He told me, "I don't know anyone else in the nation who could take a stand like this." He saw that I was the one person who could make a difference. When I finally surrendered to God, I gained a confidence and I've not been afraid since.

PLAYBOY: You weren't afraid when you got the bomb threats?

BRYANT: No.

PLAYBOY: The death threats?

BRYANT: No.

PLAYBOY: How about your children?

BRYANT: They're not afraid because we're not afraid. I'm not afraid for myself, but I am afraid for my children.

PLAYBOY: You must know that the homosexual leaders, as much as they loathe you, nevertheless credit you with helping them publicize their cause. You're saying it was a *quid pro quo*—that they had the same effect on *your* cause.

BRYANT: I don't owe anything to them. I owe it all to God, because God pushed me into that corner. I will never give the homosexuals the credit. In fact, the more the homosexuals rant and rave, the more the committed Christians are going to come out of the closet. It's God's plan. I am only His humble servant. I never wanted to be the leader of anything. In fact, knowing what I know now, if I had the choice, I would definitely have chosen the role way back when of just a simple wife and mother.

PLAYBOY: You'd have given up your career?

BRYANT: Yes, definitely, knowing what I know now. It's so much easier to do that than to stand up and rant and rave for your human rights against militant homosexuals.

PLAYBOY: All right, back to Miami. What was your first step when you decided to take a stand?

BRYANT: I wrote a letter to the nine county commissioners, stating my convictions. After I wrote the letter, the homosexual leaders united against me. They called the Florida Citrus Commission and threatened a national boycott of Florida orange juice. The commission was very upset—they didn't understand why I was standing up. Then the homosexuals went further— they said they'd make me the laughingstock of the country. They said they'd sue my A-S-S off.

It was just a scare tactic—we didn't know if they could follow through with their threats, but it *was* scary—we had never been up against anything like that before. I remember walking around the house for several days, talking to myself, wondering what to do; I'd get real bold one minute and the next minute I'd burst into tears, crying out loud. I was so scared. Anyway, before all of this happened, I'd agreed to go on a local radio station—the disc jockey was a real Christian gal, so I felt pretty safe in her hands. But I was trembling still—I had hoped my letter to the county commission was enough. But I decided I had to do the show, to help our cause, and I did it. It was great. I'd brought my daughter Barbara with me, and when we started driving back after the show, there was a drizzly rain. Suddenly, in front of us, there was a car crash. It was a real bad accident. I swerved around it, and to this day, I don't know how we escaped death. We were real shook up. I pulled over to the side of the road and I said to Barbara, "Let's just pray. Let's thank Jesus for saving us from this accident." I took her hand and we prayed—Barbara is like me. I mean, when she was born, she was 42 years old. She looked up at me and said, "If God can help us like this, can't He help you win against the homosexuals?" I tell you, my tears started coming and I knew then we would win.

PLAYBOY: Did Barbara understand what homosexual meant? She's nine years old. Had you discussed the issue explicitly with your children?

BRYANT: Yes. We had to talk with them in very practical terms on their age level.

PLAYBOY: How do you explain homosexuality to a nine-year-old?

BRYANT: Well, now you've got me on the spot. Basically, we explained to our children that marriage is a sacred vow and that in *Genesis*, God said He knew man was incomplete and man needed a helpmate, so God made woman, and that man and woman were meant to come together and multiply the earth. I explained in simple terms to the little ones that some men try to do with other men what men and women do to produce babies; and that homosexuality is a perversion of a very natural thing that God said was good, and that it is a sin and very unnatural. I explained to the children that even barnyard animals don't do what homosexuals do.

PLAYBOY: That's simply untrue. There is a lot of evidence proving not only that barnyard animals do engage in homosexuality but that in many primitive human cultures around the world, homosexuality is and has been institutionalized as part of tribal culture.

BRYANT: Well, I've never heard of it. The point is that God says it's an abomination of nature and it's wrong.

PLAYBOY: That's a different point—we're saying that among various species, human and animal, it is a common occurrence.

BRYANT: That still doesn't make it right.

PLAYBOY: Were there particular problems with your children after you took your antihomosexual stance?

BRYANT: There was one point where our daughters, Gloria and Barbara, told me that they didn't want to hold hands with their little girlfriends anymore. They were afraid people would think they were homosexuals. I had to sit down and talk to them—I told them in very practical terms that that had nothing to do with homosexuality. And then I talked to our other kids, individually, to make sure their views in regard to their friends weren't warped. You know how kids are—they tease kids who have effeminate qualities. They harass them.

PLAYBOY: You told your children it was wrong to harass boys who were effeminate?

BRYANT: Absolutely. I've taken great pains with the children to educate them that that kind of thing is not Christian. But kids are influenced by their peers; all of a sudden, they get very brave when they're with other kids. My kids aren't perfect—they might resort to that. Kids have a tendency to call each other queer or weird. We've stopped our kids from saying that, I think, through careful explanation of how wrong it is to do that. I think our kids are much more careful about that kind of thing, because they know the harm they can cause, especially in that the accusations can be false accusations. The militant homosexuals in Miami accused us of printing a KILL A QUEER FOR CHRIST bumper sticker. I mean, never would we endorse that kind of thing. That would be disrespectful to homosexuals as human beings. We would never say "queer" or "faggot"—I mean, "homos" is not that bad, really, but we would never say it. And that's a much more honest position than the militant homosexuals take.

I have no respect for homosexuals who insist that their deviant life-style is normal. We pray for them, we try to lead them out of it—that's more honest than the stance of saying what they do is normal. I mean, you ask them, "What is your role in the sex act—is it male or female?" They say, "Well, sometimes it's male, sometimes it's female." Isn't that playacting? Is playacting normal? Let's clarify the issue of what constitutes a homosexual. I think a lot of parents pass down to their kids a misconception—if a boy doesn't have masculine muscles and he doesn't go out for sports, that doesn't make him a sissy or a queer. I don't think a homosexual is a homosexual until he commits the act. I mean, just because a child fantasizes about another man—lots of psychiatrists claim that it's the latent homosexuality expressing itself in the brain of a little one. That's garbage. It's not a physical problem, it's a spiritual one. Just because this kind of kid has certain characteristics that make him different when he's growing up, and he was laughed at or mocked by other kids, that doesn't make him a homosexual, any more than it makes me a grandmother.

PLAYBOY: So a homosexual is not a homosexual until he commits a physical homosexual act?

BRYANT: That's what I consider a homosexual to be. I don't think that if you have fantasies or dreams or whatever counts. No matter if your father or your mother rejected you, no matter what happened in your life, still, it's a matter of choice in a context.

PLAYBOY: As far back as 1948, Dr. Alfred Kinsey showed that, from his research, two out of every five American males had committed a homosexual act. You've heard of his research, we assume.

BRYANT: Not that much, no. But, of course, we know where *he* was coming from, personally.

PLAYBOY: What does that mean?

BRYANT: Well, I mean, he had no spiritual beliefs, no religious beliefs.

PLAYBOY: Nevertheless, as a social scientist, Kinsey claimed that 37 percent of the American male population—and this was in the late Forties— had committed at least one homosexual act.

BRYANT: But that doesn't mean they were homosexuals.

PLAYBOY: But wait, just a moment ago, you said that committing the homosexual act defined the homosexual being.

BRYANT: Well, one or two acts don't make you a practicing, full-fledged homosexual.

PLAYBOY: You said precisely that.

BRYANT: Yeah, I did say the sex act constitutes . . . Look, what I'm saying is that people experiment—they may do it a couple of times. It doesn't mean they are practicing homosexuals for life. Some people will try it out just for the kicks—out of curiosity. They can still be forgiven for that sin.

PLAYBOY: In your most recent book, *The Anita Bryant Story*, you say that you don't know what causes homosexuality. Don't you think you should have studied its causes?

BRYANT: You see, that's the whole thing—the militant homosexuals contend that they are born homosexual and that it's a natural thing. All I know is that God condemns it as unnatural. That's why I insist on saying "homosexual" and "so-called gay." The word gay totally belies the homosexual life-style. I don't even know how the word gay was attached to the homosexual life-style. The militant homosexuals took the word and with the power that they have, they programed it into our modern vocabulary.

PLAYBOY: Is the tide now turning on your behalf? Your contract was renewed, you were named Most Admired Woman by readers of *Good Housekeeping,* and liberal columnists such as Nat Hentoff have come out defending your right of free speech.

BRYANT: It's too early to say, and I don't know what the homosexuals still have up their sleeve. They are very desperate people who will stop at nothing.

PLAYBOY: Do you feel any responsibility for homosexual suicides? Or for the murder of homosexuals? There was a lawsuit filed against you in San Francisco last year, later dismissed, that charged you with creating a homophobic hysteria that resulted in the murder of a young homosexual.

BRYANT: Yes, that's true. But I had nothing to do with any murders. There is a homosexual murder every day in San Francisco. It made me sad and it shocked me that anyone would think I had anything to do with it, but my conscience is clear. I can't be responsible for how people react to what happened in Dade County. My stand was not taken out of homophobia but out of love for them. Look, I'm not as stupid as people make me out to be, especially concerning homosexuality. In Richmond, four of them came up to me. One of them gave me the record *Hurricane Anita* and looked at me like he was waiting for me to faint dead away or turn pale, and I said I was familiar with it, and I wrote down a Scripture and said, "I love you." And one other guy came on real strong and he said, "You've broken my heart and I cry all night and day because you hate us." I said, "I don't hate you, I love you." I took his hand and said, "I love you; can you say you love me?" This guy started shaking. He said, "I can't say that."

PLAYBOY: That record is just one of the satiric attacks made upon you. There have been more Anita Bryant jokes than Polish jokes in the past year. Rod McKuen said—

BRYANT: He's really a . . . nothing.

PLAYBOY: People like Johnny Carson and Bob Hope and Martha Raye have also made jokes about you.

BRYANT: Right, and I really was hurt by them. I mean, I could tell you stories from being on U.S.O. tours with Bob Hope and Martha Raye that would make your hair stand on end, but I won't. Yet they attack me. I asked my son Bobby one day about it and he said, "Well, they have a lot of jokes around school about you."

PLAYBOY: Dirty jokes?

BRYANT: No, funny ones. And he said, "They don't bug me."

PLAYBOY: What other kinds of repercussions did you suffer from the so-called gaycott of you?

BRYANT: Well, I couldn't get booked on virtually any of the talk shows, where I'd always been welcomed before. And I recorded a song called *There's Nothing Like the Love Between a Woman and a Man,* a real up-beat, down-home country tune. All the record companies agreed it was great, but none of them wanted to risk putting it out.

PLAYBOY: In some jurisdictions, homosexual behavior is now prosecuted as a misdemeanor. Are you in favor of returning it to a felony status?

BRYANT: Yes, I think so. Any time you water down the law, it just makes it easier for immorality to become tolerated.

PLAYBOY: Let's say two adult men are caught in bed, fornicating. Under felony provisions, they could be sent to jail for 20 years. Do you think 20 years in prison would rehabilitate them?

BRYANT: Why make it easy for them? I think it only helps to condone it and to make it easier for kids who wouldn't be so concerned if it were just a misdemeanor, whereas a felony might make them think twice, especially the younger ones.

PLAYBOY: What if it doesn't? Boys should spend 20 years in jail for one act?

BRYANT: If they're on good behavior and everything, and they really—

PLAYBOY: What are you saying—that someone will be rehabilitated and turned away from homosexuality in *prison*? Surely, you know that prisoners are gang-raped routinely. Someone jailed on a homosexual charge is particularly vulnerable. You must know that.

BRYANT: They'll have plenty of time to think. Just because prisons are corrupt and not doing the right job in rehabilitation because they don't have enough spiritual emphasis doesn't mean that there should not be a strong punishment for that.

PLAYBOY: Does punishment lead to redemption?

BRYANT: It's in the Bible.

PLAYBOY: Twenty years in jail?

BRYANT: Well, there's no easy answer and I'm sure we don't have all the answers.

PLAYBOY: You're avoiding the question, not just the answer. To stick a kid in jail for committing a homosexual act would seem to most people the greater crime—and sin. If anything were going to reinforce his homosexuality, it would be prison.

BRYANT: But, you see, if there are no consequences for any kind of sin, if there's no law and order, if there's no price to be paid for—

PLAYBOY: But you're advocating making homosexuality a felony. The price would certainly exceed the "crime," if you had your way.

BRYANT: Are you saying do away with the law totally? Look, I'm just thinking of a deterrent to keep young people from going into it. That's why you've got the ministry in the prisons. They're trying to find an answer there. Maybe the answer is to put the homosexuals in a different place in the prison.

PLAYBOY: That's already the case; do you think that would deter them from homosexuality? How familiar are you with prisons? Have you ever performed inside one?

BRYANT: Yes, I did the Huntsville Prison Rodeo. It was great—the audience was very captive. [*Laughs*]

PLAYBOY: Did you get a firsthand look at the prison conditions?

BRYANT: No, I've read about them and I have mixed feelings, because I've heard a lot of radical people who come out and say the prisons are terrible, but you know where they're coming from—they want to do away with law and order because they're rebellious against God. I know what the cause of the prisons is. The cause is sin.

PLAYBOY: So for one sin, the sin of one man making love to another man, you would send them to jail? That's the Christian approach?

BRYANT: As a Christian, I know the only answer is the Gospel.

PLAYBOY: And you would set it up so that the Gospel you advocate would be preached to imprisoned human beings surrounded by the very crime you accuse them of.

BRYANT: All right, you have a point. Especially when you put it in terms of kids; I would like to be working with them to save them from their sins.

PLAYBOY: Let's explore some of your theological beliefs. For instance, nowhere in the New Testament does Jesus make any statement about homosexuality.

BRYANT: Well, Jesus did. He spoke about adultery and fornication.

PLAYBOY: But you didn't conduct a campaign against heterosexual swingers' teaching your kids. The fact remains that Jesus never even mentioned homosexuality and virtually every reference to it is in the Old Testament.

BRYANT: But he talked about fornication and he said, "If you love me, you'll keep my commandments." He was very plain on it. Jesus never wavered from sin one iota. To say that Jesus wasn't against sin is ridiculous. A lot of people who want to interpret the Bible for their own ends, such as the so-called Metropolitan Community Church, ignore parts of it to condone their immoral life-style. They make a sham of everything Jesus stood for. If he was not truly the Son of God, then he's just . . . nothing. It sounds like it's contradicting itself, but when you read the whole Bible, all of it together, then you understand why at certain points it seems like it's contradicting, but yet it's not. God is simply trying to explain the truth.

PLAYBOY: When did you come to that realization? When did you first sit down and read the Bible from cover to cover?

BRYANT: I never have. I have tried.

PLAYBOY: That's surprising.

BRYANT: See, I never went to a Catholic or a Baptist school where they made us do that.

PLAYBOY: Why haven't you read it on your own?

BRYANT: I don't know. Why did you ask me that? I just learned to love the Bible and read it and I read it all the time. But I've never had the time to read it from cover to cover.

PLAYBOY: What is your interpretation of heaven?

BRYANT: The Bible describes heaven as a place where there'll be no sorrow, no tears nor sin. No day and no night; a continuous joy and peace. I've been so high with the Lord that I believe I've had a foretaste of glory divine, of what it's going to be like to not have to put up with pressure and hassles from the physical body. There will be no temptation from the Devil, no evil thoughts will enter your head. I won't have to worry about a schedule, I won't have to live by my little black book, I won't have to write everything down, I won't have to be interviewed. I won't have to sing unless I feel like it. God talks about heaven in a very literal way. He says the streets are paved with gold, a pure gold, and He talks about the pearly gates—it'll be pure pearl. I believe it will literally have those things that are described; that's why it was described that way. A lot of the Bible I take literally.

PLAYBOY: And hell?

BRYANT: That is a place God did not make for mankind—He made that as a place for the Devil, a place He could put him because he was the maestro of music in heaven, and he betrayed God. God created hell to pass Lucifer down into it. In the meantime, He let him become friends of this world, and that's why we have to suffer a spiritual warfare until He comes back for His own.

PLAYBOY: Do you believe in purgatory?

BRYANT: No.

PLAYBOY: All or nothing, then. How does the Devil tempt Anita Bryant?

BRYANT: Through my kids, my husband, just getting on my nerves; my family is where I'm most vulnerable. If I get really tired, I can put my garbage on Bob very easily. Not like before—we used to really fight.

PLAYBOY: But how does the Devil get to you?

BRYANT: Like he gets to anybody. I know the days when I am so beaten down I can see 12 demons around me with billy clubs on my head and I know they're there and I verbally cast them out. I say, "Satan, get thee behind me." I mean, you can't let down your guard for a moment. You simply have to remember that God is your best friend and know the peace God can give you when you're in the flow of the stream of His wisdom and love. It's like they call me Hurricane Anita—the Weather Service sent me a letter telling me the name had been picked out ten years ago, for the storm that hit last spring. It was so weird, the timing. I just thought it was another of God's jokes. He has such a sense of humor, He really does, you know. So some Weather Service people sent me a picture of the hurricane and in the middle of all this turmoil is a perfect eye of stillness. That's me, in the center.

PLAYBOY: You often quote *Leviticus* and *Deuteronomy*—the "lawbooks" of the Old Testament—to support your beliefs against homosexuality. But the Bible is so ambiguous that people on fundamentally different sides can quote it against each other to support their positions.

BRYANT: There were certain things in the Old Testament that you had to do in order to be clean and righteous. Yet when Jesus came, he fulfilled the law. In other words, it's not the Ten Commandments that save you, it's the fact that Jesus died on the cross that saves you. You are not bound by *all* the things that it says to do in the Old Testament.

PLAYBOY: So you pick the ones that suit you?

BRYANT: Jesus was the fulfillment. He told us we were not to be concerned by the things the Old Testament said—that kind of thing—again.

PLAYBOY: Yet you consistently quote the Old Testament as a justification for your positions, particularly regarding homosexuality. It reminds us of the Scopes trial in Tennessee in 1925, when William Jennings Bryan insisted on a literal interpretation of the creation.

BRYANT: Well, when you start nitpicking, when we try in our own feeble minds to understand God . . . God says, "My thoughts are not your thoughts." There's no way you can comprehend what creation is. You're trying to come to a logical conclusion as to how God did it and there's no way we can know how God did it. From man's point of view, miracles never happen. From God's point of view, they do.

PLAYBOY: Does there have to be a conflict between belief in evolution and belief in God?

BRYANT: Except that Darwin did not believe in God.

PLAYBOY: That doesn't answer the question.

BRYANT: Look, because of his atheistic influence, Darwin is taught in the public schools as fact. That's fine, if people want to believe that, but I say we must also put *Genesis* and the Bible in the school teachings as an alternate belief. And, look, really, there's no way I can answer your question, because I don't know *how* God did it. I just believe He did it. It's like when Moses parted the Red Sea. To man, that was an impossible feat, yet it was one of the great miracles of the Bible when Moses lifted his rod again and the sea closed. I mean, it boggles your mind to think of the majesty and supernatural power it took to do that. My pastor put it this way: He said, for God, it took only the flick of His pinkie to part the Red Sea.

PLAYBOY: God has a pinkie?

BRYANT: Oh, I don't know, it's just an illustration. Actually, the biggest miracle of all was the constraint God showed not to split the earth in half when He parted the Red Sea. What I'm saying is that God didn't have to do things man's way. He spoke the universe into existence.

PLAYBOY: But even from your point of view, is it not still a miracle to create the universe over a period of billions of years?

BRYANT: Why would He take that kind of time? He doesn't have to.

PLAYBOY: Why not? If He is eternal, time is nothing to Him.

BRYANT: Well, that's true . . . but the Bible says God just spoke the universe into existence.

PLAYBOY: Many Biblical scholars aren't nearly as fundamentalist as you are in believing such things.

BRYANT: I don't know! What do I know? We'll know those answers when we get to heaven, all right? And you can ask God yourself!

PLAYBOY: Do you think that people who either don't believe in Jesus as *God*—Jews, for example—or those who have never been exposed to Christian teaching are condemned to hell?

BRYANT: Well, I personally have to believe that, because I believe God's Word. I didn't write the Bible, and that's what the Bible says. But there are a lot of Jews today who are accepting Jesus as the Messiah.

PLAYBOY: What about those who are not—the vast majority, in other words?

BRYANT: You're putting me on the spot again. As much as I would like to say other people can be saved by some other means than Jesus, I cannot deny what I know from the Bible. It doesn't make me feel good or give me any gratification to think someone's going to hell. I have great respect for my Jewish brothers. But I am what I am, I believe what I believe and I can't stick my head in the ground and say, "Well, I believe if people are really good and if they live by other standards, they can get absolved"— God just didn't say that. This whole question is very hard for me, because I have come to love Rabbi Weberman and the other Jewish people I have worked with in Dade County very much. I have a great respect for them, so I don't think in terms of hell-fire and damnation.

PLAYBOY: Presumably, you feel the same way about other faiths—the Moslem faith, for instance.

BRYANT: God is using so many people all over the world to get the Gospel to the Moslems, to *everybody*. Whether a person will accept or reject the Gospel is between him and God. I'm not responsible for that. I mean, God could just have made us all into robots, but He took a chance. He wanted us to choose His way.

PLAYBOY: If you tried to tell a devout Moslem about Jesus as savior, he would be just as immune to hearing your message as you would be if he tried to tell you Mohammed was the Prophet.

BRYANT: I don't have the answer for that. I can't approach it from an intellectual point of view. There's a lot of things I don't understand about God.

PLAYBOY: Where is your sense of justice? If someone truly lives a good life, if he's sincere and moral, just because he doesn't believe in Jesus—

BRYANT: Even though he is sincere, he is sincerely wrong. Sincerity doesn't make you right. The homosexual community believes it's sincerely right, too.

PLAYBOY: But, according to your way of thinking, Jews, Moslems, Pygmies, Eskimos and atheists are going to hell.

BRYANT: According to God's Word, they do. I mean, if there's no heaven and no hell, what are we talking about? You know, your problem is that you have to have all the answers. It's impossible to have all the answers!

PLAYBOY: How do you feel about the inferior status conferred on women in the Bible? Would you agree, as some women do, that it's because the Bible was written by men in the context of the times?

BRYANT: Well, no, men didn't write it, the Holy Spirit did. Most of the preachers are men, though, and I think that's brought about an unhealthy balance. It's a thing where you hear so much about "women, submit yourselves to your husbands," and that is Biblical, where women must submit first but it also says, "submit yourselves one to another." It has to be a submission of both women to men and men to women.

PLAYBOY: But you've also said that women are weaker vessels than men.

BRYANT: Well, they are. I don't think that has a bad connotation.

PLAYBOY: Weak isn't exactly a complimentary term.

BRYANT: Well, it's a Biblical term, you see. . . . All I know is God did have a plan. I don't always want to agree with it and I don't always understand it, but it's like the clay trying to understand the potter. All I know is that He did set the man over the woman. When He said we were to become as one flesh, He meant it in all ways. So if I don't submit to Bob—

PLAYBOY: Why shouldn't he have to submit to *you* first?

BRYANT: I believe that it's easier for the woman to submit. That's Biblical.

PLAYBOY: Why?

BRYANT: I don't know, but I just think that a woman has the capability of submitting. I really thought in my younger days that I could do anything that Bob could do and probably better, and for a time, maybe I showed that I could. But I had a limit. I could take only so much, whereas God has equipped men to take much more responsibility—He made them to be the head and He gave them a certain ability. Women come at things with a much more emotional point of view.

PLAYBOY: What do you mean, emotional?

BRYANT: I can't explain it. I just think women have a softer approach. We're more vulnerable, just like in the Garden of Eden. Bob has an ability to see things from a totally different perspective than I. I am much more trusting. Women are vulnerable as far as people are concerned, whereas men can see through things. Of course, I'm talking about the perfect specimen—everybody's different. But I believe there is an innate ability that men have that's different from women's.

PLAYBOY: If Bob told you to do something right now that was against the grain of your thought, would you simply submit to him?

BRYANT: I might rebel against it—and I have many times—but, Biblically, I would submit, yes.

PLAYBOY: You've gone against your own better judgment?

BRYANT: Oh, yes. For me to learn to submit was one of the most difficult things in the world, because from the time I was a little child, I was a very hardheaded, independent human being. Yet God showed me my weaknesses, showed me where I was the weaker vessel in many respects, and I still didn't want to recognize that. It was in real submission, when I was able to let Bob take over, that I really realized I was usurping his authority by not allowing him to be the person God meant him to be. Submission really means to throw oneself under, so the decision an equal person has to make is to become the one underneath, and that's a matter of choice. Jesus Christ is a terrific example of one who submitted. And either he *was* who he said he was or he was the greatest liar ever on the face of this earth.

I am not intimidated by being called the weaker vessel, because I know that in many areas I am the stronger vessel. I mean, for a long time, I really would have been in agreement with the feminist movement, particularly for the anger I had toward my father that I transferred to Bob. I usurped Bob's authority in many ways for many years and our marriage was rocky, really rocky, until I recognized I was in rebellion against God, and I got right and submitted.

PLAYBOY: You mentioned your anger toward your father. Let's talk about your upbringing.

BRYANT: You have to remember that my parents were first divorced when I was two years old and a lot of my insecurities started then. Mother had to go to work and I had to live with my relatives, and that affects a child greatly. They had married very young and they really had no idea of the responsibilities of marriage. I had lots of nightmares after the divorce and I walked in my sleep. I was a very hyperactive kid and a very sickly child. I caught everything that came around.

PLAYBOY: What happened after your parents remarried?

BRYANT: We moved to Oklahoma City and I thought it was the end of the world. It was the biggest city I'd ever seen and the adjustment was real hard. Then my mom and dad started fighting again. They divorced again when I was 12. I didn't see my father for a long time afterward—he moved to another city, found another job, and we'd hear from him once in a while, but it was a long time between phone calls. A lot of that period I don't remember. I guess I really don't want to. It was real painful and it just about killed my mother.

PLAYBOY: So you resented your father?

BRYANT: I tried very hard to forgive him for what he had done to my mother—and to me. Because of him, I think I went through life for a long time hating all men, including my husband, Bob. It took me a long time to get over my resentment of Daddy. For many years, I thought I'd forgiven him, when I really hadn't. It wasn't until 1974 that I truly forgave him, when I realized that I couldn't blame him for his actions. But it took a long time, let me tell you. It's like the movies. I loved romantic movies like *Gone with the Wind,* but I realized the effect of that kind of thing—when your home life isn't ideal, you seek it somewhere else, so that your natural relationship with your husband becomes distorted. For a long time, that was a real problem with me and Bob, because I was preserving my own ideal—Hollywood's ideal—and ignoring the real problems that come up between a husband and a wife.

PLAYBOY: Let's back up a moment. What gave your career its biggest push?

BRYANT: Arthur Godfrey. One of his talent scouts came to Tulsa and held a competition. I won hands down, week after week. I was determined I would win. When I won, the decision to go to New York was automatic—I didn't even have to pray about it, until my pastor talked to me. I really didn't have peace in my heart about leaving for the big time. What if God says no? I thought. I was miserable until I prayed to God and He gave a yes right back to me. I can't explain it, but I just knew it would be OK.

PLAYBOY: But you were already a star, in terms of Oklahoma. How did that affect your teenage life? In terms of boy-girl social intercourse?

BRYANT: Well, it didn't help my self-image. I was kind of scrawny—I'd never get the captain of the football team, I knew, so it was surprising to me that I got to date a lot of neat guys. As a matter of fact, I dated my pastor's son for three years. We made plans to get married. Oh, we were *so perfect*—he had a beautiful voice and we sang together in the church choir. I just adored him. But one night we went out in his car and he pulled out a cigarette. "Look, you don't really know me," he said. I said, "Of course, I'm surprised that you smoke, but what does that have to do with us?" He told me he wanted to live it up and get his kicks. So we broke up and, immediately, he started going with a gal who had a bad reputation.

It just broke my heart. I wanted to die. I felt the world was coming to an end and I didn't even go to school for a week. I was just sick. I decided then that I wouldn't marry until I was 25.

PLAYBOY: But you were glamorous by small-town standards. Surely, Satan tempted you in numerous ways—such as sex. How did you resist? Or did you?

BRYANT: See, the kids today have a much harder time dealing with sex, because it's no longer "in" to be a virgin. In my time, when I went to Will Rogers High School, it was not the hip thing to do to go to bed with somebody, or even to let a boy fondle you—you just didn't do that. Some girls did it, sure, but their reputation was ruined all over town. And because I was such a hardworking girl, I didn't date that much. I concentrated on my career, my church activities and my grade-point average, and I was just too busy to be tempted by the Devil. If I dated some guy who tried to pet with me, I just told him, "Look, you can take me home right now, if you want—I'm not gonna go any further. If you don't enjoy being with me as a person, just take me home." I mean, I *loved* the kissing part and, I must say, I had some pretty passionate feelings, too, because I'm no prude, but I knew where to stop. My faith was so much a part of me that I knew my body was a temple of God and that God held it sacred. And I knew that my husband would know if I had been promiscuous and that if I didn't save myself for my marriage, if I wasn't pure, I would miss out. The consequences just weren't worth it to me. I think a lot of it had to do with the fact that I was saved when I was eight years old and my beliefs were reinforced in the public schools then through prayer—this was before that atheist Madalyn Murray O'Hair made the worship of God illegal, you see. Kids today don't even know God, unless their parents are religious.

PLAYBOY: What about other teenage temptations? Is rock 'n' roll today something you disapprove of?

BRYANT: Oh, yes. In my days, the lyrics were understandable and you didn't have to slow it down to hear the dirty cuss words and the jargon that parents today can't understand.

PLAYBOY: Come on. You admit in one of your books that when you added a hard, driving beat to *Till There Was You,* you achieved your first 1,000,000 seller. And even when you were coming of age in the Fifties, there were plenty of sexual *double-entendres* in the rock lyrics.

BRYANT: Yeah, but it's not like today, where there are a lot of rock dances and rock music that are brainwashing the kids, because it's all very promiscuous and it glorifies promiscuity and acid rock and a lot of those things. The kids get into the dirty lyrics and the beat is just very, very seductive.

PLAYBOY: What do you suppose the thrill *was* that Pat Boone found on Blueberry Hill?

BRYANT: All I know is that there are a lot of filthy words I've heard in listening to the radio these days that are just shameful and outright sinful. I think a lot of evil things are much more prevalent these days. I think kids growing up today have pressures that we never had in the Fifties. It's so discouraging.

PLAYBOY: When you got married to Bob Green, did you find he felt as you did?

BRYANT: He'd dated a lot of girls, but he didn't drink or smoke—

PLAYBOY: And you shared the same religious beliefs?

BRYANT: Bob wasn't born again until the night before we got married.

PLAYBOY: Was that a deal you made?

BRYANT: We had no conflict about it. But I was very scared of marriage and I almost backed out at the last minute.

PLAYBOY: Was marriage everything you'd dreamed it would be?

BRYANT: It depends on what you mean.

PLAYBOY: Well, sexually, for starters.

BRYANT: I have a fantastic sex life!

PLAYBOY: Emotionally, then.

BRYANT: Marriage is very hard. Lots of problems are involved with two people working out a loving relationship and adhering to God's laws. And it upset me when I was told I could not bear children. We adopted our first child, Bobby, Jr. Later, when it turned out I *could* bear children, I had twins who were born months prematurely—and they almost died. Plus Bob was making a lot more money than I was then. Finally, Bob became my manager and that solved a lot of problems. He's been a great manager, and until I started getting boycotted and black-listed by the militant homosexuals last year, I had all the work I could handle.

PLAYBOY: We'll get back to that. First tell us about what you have described as the most important turning point in your life, when you had a nervous breakdown in 1974.

BRYANT: It was *not* a nervous breakdown—it verged on it, certainly, but it really makes me mad that the militant homosexuals try to use it against me by saying, "She flipped out, she went crazy."

PLAYBOY: Well, what *did* happen?

BRYANT: I lost three people very dear to me in one year. I sang at all their funerals. Dan Topping [the former owner of the New York Yankees], my Grandpa Berry and a gal named Teddy who was like a big sister to me and who was about my age when she died. I couldn't understand why God would just nip her in the bud when she was in the prime of her life. There are few people I can share any heart with, and I could talk to Teddy about things I couldn't even talk with Bob or my pastor about. It was that deep. Then Bob developed a heart condition and almost died, and I had to think for the first time about raising four kids alone without Teddy to lean on anymore. It was after Grandpa Berry's funeral when the straw landed that broke the camel's back. It was like God wanted to put me flat on my back so the only way I could look was up. He knew I was holding out on Him and He wanted the whole of me, not just part of me. He knew I had a lot of rebellion and anger and bitterness in me. I thought I'd forgiven my daddy, but I hadn't—I still hated and resented him, and the pent-up hatred was poisoning my marriage and my relationship with people all around me. So I collapsed after Grandpa's funeral—I totally gave up. I lay down and I just . . .

I was so tired. I think had I been anyone else, I probably would have had a heart attack or a total nervous breakdown, but I just came to a point where I didn't want to do anything. I just sat in my office and looked at the stack of letters from people who were asking me for advice and counseling—and I just couldn't be responsible anymore. *I* needed advice and counseling, and the one person I could have talked to, Teddy, was gone. I said, "No more," and I would just sit in my office all day. I said, "I'm not going to do anything else, ever." It scared me to death. Bob was scared to death, too.

PLAYBOY: Did you consider seeing a psychiatrist?

BRYANT: No, it was so painful—it was like I felt I'd be committing a sin by going to a psychiatrist; can you imagine that? I thought it would be denying Jesus. And I knew that a lot of psychiatrists tell you things totally contrary to Biblical teaching, such as in order to get along with your husband, go out and have an affair, or something like that. But friends of ours told us about this Christian retreat in Rosemead, California—it's sort of a Christian counseling center, quite famous. Marabel Morgan and lots of famous Christian people have gone there. So I decided I had to do something, that God was sending me out there.

We arrived at night and I met the psychologist and I liked him very much. When we got to the hotel, I just could not sleep. I didn't want to wake Bob, so I went into this tiny bathroom and closed the door and got down on my hands and knees and just started praying. Something from way down deep inside of me was trying to come out. It was so strange. I took a legal pad and a pencil and I started writing down these things that were bugging me. I filled 17 whole pages.

PLAYBOY: What did you write?

BRYANT: Some things I wouldn't want printed because it does no good to bring them up, but . . . well, the hatred of my father and the resentment toward Bob, things that went way back into my childhood and other more recent things, such as little difficulties I was having with the kids that I'd kept pent up.

Anyway, I felt like a different person when I walked into the psychologist's office the next day and showed him the 17 pages. He said, "It looks like my work has already been done for me."

PLAYBOY: Has your marriage improved since Rosemead?

BRYANT: I never realized before then how I dominated Bob, but, fortunately, he was stronger than I and we were able to work these things out. The main problem we had in our marriage was that, because of my father, I basically had a hate for men. I mean, there were times when I literally *hated* my husband—I couldn't help it. But I was responsible because I allowed it to fester and didn't take it to the Lord. And divorce wasn't in my vocabulary, because I'd suffered the scars of divorce as a child and I knew what *my* children would suffer from it. But, above all, I knew it was against God's Word. Bob and I *still* have our ups and downs, because I'm not a goody two-shoes. I know now I'm a human being, just like anybody else. If it weren't for Jesus Christ in my heart and life, I probably would have married several times. I probably would have slept around with guys and whatever. I always say that I'm just a sinner saved by grace.

PLAYBOY: What *are* your sins?

BRYANT: Oh, I don't know . . . maybe the sin of intolerance. [*Laughs*]

PLAYBOY: That's exactly what those you call militant homosexuals say about you.

BRYANT: I just meant it as a pun.

PLAYBOY: A pun? What pun?

BRYANT: I try not to be intolerant. All I'm saying is I don't have anything to brag about. The reason I can relate to the homosexual is because I've had emotional scars in my own life. I really felt the rejection of my father, and that is one of the things that maybe lead someone going into homosexuality. Look, I don't hate homosexuals—that's the truth, no matter what they think of my motives. I've always said I love the sinner but I hate the sin.

PLAYBOY: You've been saying that America and her children are being destroyed. You've compared America to Sodom and Gomorrah; you say God destroys the kind of nation that America has become.

BRYANT: Absolutely. I believe that's what has been happening to America.

PLAYBOY: Do you think it still is?

BRYANT: I believe now that we have a greater hope than ever before— that God is allowing America one last space to repent. If the parents of American children had stood by God's Word, had they not had their head in the sand for so many years, the destruction of America's moral fiber wouldn't have happened. But it happened so fast no one knew it was happening. But now it seems people have a hunger. They've seen how so-called humanism works. They were told, "Well, one way to change the world is to educate the people. You educate them to a certain point, they're going to change." Well, has that been true? Has that happened? No. Our country was strong for so long because we claimed we were one nation under God and God blessed us. I believe that right now, God has removed Himself from America. If we'll look through history, we're in the same situation as were Greece and Rome, when homosexuality and other sins were so rampant they became the norm.

PLAYBOY: So this and your crusade are America's last chance?

BRYANT: Yes. I didn't even come to the realization that America was so far gone until the time of the referendum, when I got letters from groups all over the country describing the fights they were in and how they were righting some of the same things and it looked to me like a big octopus that had its tentacles around America and was squeezing our country to death. And it grieved me. I mourned for America for several days.

PLAYBOY: You cried for America?

BRYANT: Yes, I really saw for the first time in my life what was going on. I had been very idealistic about America all my life—I am still—because in reading the last book of the Bible, I know what the hope for the world is. And I think there's a revival beginning in America now. What happened in Dade County is happening all over the country. I know that's how God rewards prayer, and Dade County was the answer to a lot of prayers world-wide.

PLAYBOY: Let's talk about the media for a moment. Do you think you've gotten a raw deal from the press?

BRYANT: Let's face it—quite honestly, the press can make anybody look like anything it wants to. I mean, there are a lot of things in all of our lives that you don't want known—nobody's perfect—that could ruin you. The press has placed me in a stereotyped box. Like, I'm not a prude, but that's the image they want to portray, because they're after me. I think it's snobbery. You see, there are so many intellectuals in this nation and they've really become snobs as far as how they approach grass-roots things. It's really true. Like, when we started the opposition to the Dade County ordinance—all the press figured it was for one of two reasons: either to run for public office or for publicity for my career. They just couldn't accept my real motivation, because they don't know me. It took me a while to see that I was really under a microscope and had to watch what I said. I'm OK now—I think I could handle the *Good Morning America* show and Gore Vidal.

PLAYBOY: You mean the show on which Vidal mentioned you in the same breath with Hitler?

BRYANT: Yeah; I think I could handle that now. I must be doing something right. I taped the *Today* show last fall and did so well against Tom Brokaw—and he wasn't being his usual nice self, let me tell you—that they asked us to tape a second segment, where he was nicer. So we're OK now. We've been trained.

PLAYBOY: A baptism by fire?

BRYANT: Yeah, I guess you could say that. I mean, I learned. Let me give you an example. After Dade County, some people from the media asked me, "Would you go to San Francisco and Los Angeles?" And I said, "Sure, if I'm asked and if after I've prayed about it God says yes." Well, immediately, they put it on the wire that Anita Bryant plans on going on a crusade across the country. OK, to counteract that, I say to the press, I am not going out on a "crusade" across the country, to do in other cities what we did in Dade County.

PLAYBOY: There is no crusade in the works?

BRYANT: God is saying there's a different route to go. There's a part of me that is a Carry Nation, that would very much like to go across this country. We could fill up every auditorium in America. If we had done so after our victory in Dade County, we could have gotten such a momentum going that we could have wiped the homosexual out. That was a very real possibility. We realized that. We could have made a lot of money, too.

PLAYBOY: That sounds brutal. Do you mean you'd wipe them out personally?

BRYANT: Well, not quite. But I must admit, when you've known that kind of power, it is easy to succumb to it and use it for your own advantage and to wipe out a lot of things that need wiping out. But sometimes the Lord has a different way.

PLAYBOY: Although at one point you claimed to have some sympathy for feminists, you nevertheless refer more often to the feminist movement as if it were some kind of conspiracy against decency.

BRYANT: Well, look at that Houston convention last year. The Government gave the feminists $5,000,000 and Phyllis Schlafly not one penny. It was a closed shop. It's almost Communistic the way Phyllis Schlafly and the ones who truly represent the grass roots of American women cannot even get the forums to be represented in.

PLAYBOY: So the Communists are conspiring to keep the patriots out of the picture?

BRYANT: Well, it's very suspicious that in many of the state conventions before Houston, they did not even pledge allegiance to the flag and they did not sing *The Star-Spangled Banner*. It goes hand in hand, it seems to me. Whether they're all in big conspiracy together, I can't say. You can't really say that anymore, because people pooh-pooh it and they say, "Well, that's a very right-wing cop-out," so you don't even say that; but it seems very obvious that the Communist element is a part of all this, because a lot of these people have no reverence for their country. *I* still believe that America, with all her faults and trials and tribulations, is the greatest country on the face of this earth, and if women could get their eyes off of themselves and their own human life, if they could look at what they have and be grateful and thankful for it . . . I mean, where else but in America could someone like myself have made it? Where else could someone who was raised in poor surroundings attain what I have attained at the age of 38? Who needs the E.R.A.? The key to women's rights is to activate the laws that are already on the books. Most of them are too lazy to do that. I mean, women are even admitted into the Armed Forces now. What more do they want? I mean, don't talk to me about discrimination.

I've experienced it. I'm an eighth Cherokee. My dad was a roustabout, low man on the totem pole. We didn't even have a decent house to live in. I went to school in hand-me-downs. I just praise God that I live in a land of plenty where someone can come from the bottom and go up. If you want to make it, you can.

PLAYBOY: That sharply contradicts what you were saying about America as a decaying nation, but let's go on. Do you have any heroes?

BRYANT: Hmmm. I don't have many. I don't know if I have *any*. I think the reason I'm so disillusioned is because I really looked at Jimmy Carter as a hero, as one who had caught the eye and the heartbeat of the grass roots of America. I really had great expectations of him, and I found that in life, when you put different individuals on a pedestal, God very carefully takes them off the pedestal and shows us that we're to put *no one* there.

PLAYBOY: Why did you sour on Carter?

BRYANT: Well, how can a born-again Christian who's truly born again not take a stand against the sin of homosexuality? He himself stated in the *Playboy Interview,* which my husband bought for me to read, that he was against homosexuality, and yet he allows [aide] Midge Costanza to go down to Dade County on a local issue and campaign for homosexuality. She was paid by our opposition to come down. I won't say any further what I know about her, because that's not important, but the thing is that she has an open door to the President of the United States, who claims to be a born-again Christian, when homosexuality is at the very core of what God is against.

PLAYBOY: You mean the *Playboy Interview* helped convince you to go for Carter?

BRYANT: I felt overall that it was not bad, except for some of the choice words he used, and I even understood why he felt compelled to use them.

PLAYBOY: Would you ever consider running for political office?

BRYANT: It's totally contrary to me, and yet my eyes have been opened to the need for involvement. The day after we won in Miami, as I was on my way to the airport, I bet I had 15 people who said, you know, "Run for President!" I mean, I laughed at them. I could not believe it. I just won't even think about it, let alone entertain the idea. It makes me sick inside. It makes Bob sick.

PLAYBOY: What if God tells you you have to run for office?

BRYANT: Well, I can't answer that until it happens. I feel I can be much more effective as a mother coming from my own motivations.

PLAYBOY: But if God came to you next year and told you to run for office, you wouldn't refuse?

BRYANT: I can't refuse God anything.

DOLLY PARTON

October 1978

Interviewer: Lawrence Grobel

Anyone whose press had been as universally adoring as Dolly Parton's presented a challenge to an interviewer. In the summer of 1978, the Tennessee-born performer was on the verge of making what musicians call a crossover—entering the mainstream of popular music rather than being labeled in the country-and-western category—and journalists invariably came away impressed with her frankness, her good humor, and her lack of guile. It seemed to PLAYBOY's editors an appropriate time not only to see whether all those compliments were justified, but to explore the apparent contradictions of a woman who was at once traditional, humorously sexy, artistically versatile, and in firm control of both her professional career and her public image.

Larry Grobel, a Los Angeles free-lancer and now a PLAYBOY contributing editor, was tapped for the assignment. He had recently completed an interview with Barbra Streisand which had stretched over a year's time and had left him exhausted. He was by then chary of high-powered show-business stars, especially those who attempted to dictate everything that was written about them, with an almost maddening attention to detail—as had been the case with the obsessive Streisand. He was used to waiting for hours, to broken appointments, to the manipulations of power. To his surprise, when he arrived at a motel in a town in West Virginia where Parton was making an appearance, the singer herself called him to introduce herself and ask him if his trip had gone well. If it was manipulation, it was a different and rare kind—solicitous and thoughtful.

"On her tour bus," Grobel recalls, "we talked all the way from Virginia to North Carolina. At the hotel we ate dinner together, talked until an hour before her performance, and often she would invite me to her room after the show for more talk. On one such night we wound up talking until sunrise. It was that kind of interview: refreshing, open, and completely enjoyable."

For Grobel, the biggest professional dilemma was how to keep his distance. "Dolly is a naturally flirtatious woman," he says, "and I've interviewed enough female celebrities to know that sometimes the vibrations can get a little personal—and that can spell the death of a good interview. One evening we were in her hotel room and she ordered a bowl of fruit; she flopped down on her bed and gestured that I should join her. All it amounted to was an innocent invitation to sit on the bed and bite into a pear as we talked, but it unnerved me. It was her total lack of pretension that repeatedly disarmed me. We shared food, jokes, stories, revealing moments. I felt I really got to know her and that, in the end, there simply wasn't much of an act. She is just what she says she is—and what others have said as well."

Grobel's interview is a portrait of a genuine person. *Cosmopolitan* magazine, in a profile of Parton two years later, called the interview the most revealing ever published of any celebrity. That may be arguable, but one small footnote makes a telling point about Parton.

Grobel, like many other journalists and editors who deal with celebrities, had become used to people who professed friendship during the exhausting hours spent together doing in-depth interviews, only to find that after publication all contact between them ceased. Parton, however, continues to call Grobel and meet with him once every couple of months, not because he can do anything for her, but because that's what courtesy and friendship mean in the hills of Tennessee.

Dolly Parton has come a long way from her Tennessee mountain home; she was born in a Locust Ridge "holler" in Sevier County in the Smoky Mountain foothills on January 19, 1946. The fourth of 12 children, she was the first in her family to finish high school, the first to become famous. "I never had a doubt I would make it," she reasons, "because refusing to think I couldn't *make it is the reason I could."*

For Parton, making it meant getting out of the backwoods and into the limelight. Her rise was rapid: She began writing songs at seven, recording them and singing on the Cas Walker radio and television show at ten, making her first appearance at the Grand Ole Opry at 12.

The day after she graduated from high school, she left with her uncle, Bill Owens, for Nashville to become a star. That same day she met, and within two years married, an asphalt worker named Carl Dean. Dean is a publicity-shy, earthy man who is as independent as Dolly and the two seem to have a solid, often at-a-distance relationship. She's on the road most of the year and he's at home working their land.

When country singer Norma Jean, who sang with Porter Wagoner on the road and on his syndicated TV show, decided to quit and get married in 1967, Wagoner asked Dolly if she'd like to join his show. Overnight, her salary rose from next to nothing to $60,000 a year and, at 21, she had achieved one of her goals: a broad and popular audience.

Although she and Wagoner became hugely successful and their duo albums sold well, she became restless and made a decision to go out on the road with members of her family. It proved to be almost disastrous. She and her Travelin' Family Band went from state fair to rodeo to high school gymnasium amateurishly managed and poorly booked. Making her most painful decision to date, she told her family it wasn't working out and took time off to put together a more professional band. She also hired a Los Angeles–based manager and public-relations firm, who saw enormous potential in this energetic and prolific woman.

By then, she was ready to "cross over" into the pop/rock world. Her albums were popular in Japan, France, Australia and England (where she was twice named Female Vocalist of the Year) and she coproduced her own album, "New Harvest." She followed that with her "new sound": "Here You Come Again," which recently went platinum, more than quadrupled the sales of many of her earlier albums.

With 20th Century-Fox offering her a three-movie deal, publishers bidding for the novel she's writing, her autobiography in the works, TV network executives trying to line her up for specials and record albums starting to sell in the millions, PLAYBOY decided to send free-lance writer Lawrence Grobel to talk with Dolly and see how it all happened and how it has affected her.

"I've met busy people before, but in Dolly's case, her scheduling is extreme. Her energy matches her ambition, which is limitless. If she's not writing or recording her own songs, she's recording with Linda and Emmylou, rehearsing with her band, taping a TV show, throwing a wedding for her younger sister, giving a concert for ABC-radio executives in Las Vegas or touring.

"I managed to pin her down for five hours in an apartment she rents in Los Angeles. The first thing I noticed was how sparse it was; nothing plush or comfortable, no indication that a star lived there, obviously a place used for little more than sleeping. The only bit of eccentricity was a small, low, round trampoline, which she said she used after giving up on jumping rope, 'for a couple of good reasons.'

"Dolly wasn't born with a voice like Streisand's, but what she has is an enormously infectious personality. To meet her is to immediately like her. Although she appears larger than life, she is actually a compact woman— dazzling in appearance; but if you took away the wig and the Frederick's

of Hollywood five-inch heels, she'd stand just five feet tall. Of course, her height isn't the first thing one notices upon meeting her. As she herself kids onstage, 'I know that you-all brought your binoculars to see me; but what you didn't realize is you don't need binoculars.'

"The next time I saw Dolly was in Winchester, Virginia, where she was scheduled to appear at the Apple Blossom Festival. By then, it was as if we were old and trusting friends and I soon discovered that she was the least hung-up celebrity I've ever been with. She was open, honest and only rarely asked to go off the record; and even then, it was on matters such as being unsatisfied with a particular dress designer or not wanting to dwell too much on godly topics. When it came to her personal life, her dreams, her ambitions, she never hesitated.

"One little girl who had written to Dolly came to visit her after a show. Dolly was in a nightdress and greeted the child as her father took Polaroid pictures. But the picture I'll always remember was of the father telling his wife to take a shot of him behind Dolly. He had this crazy gleam in his eyes, his tongue popped out of his mouth and I was sure he was going to cop a feel. But he restrained himself, as most people do around her. Because she is so open and unparanoid, she manages to tame the wildest instincts of men.

"Our last night together stretched out until morning. We talked from ten P.M. until five A.M., exchanging stories and not in the least bit tired. By the time we hugged goodbye, I was saddened that we were talked out. Our talk is what follows . . . though it does take a while to get over Dolly's appearance."

PLAYBOY: Hello, Dolly.

PARTON: Hi. I'll save you the trouble of askin': Why do I choose to look so outrageous?

PLAYBOY: Is that the first question interviewers usually ask you?

PARTON: That's what we usually end up talkin' about.

PLAYBOY: Actually, that was going to be our *second* question. We were going to start with the PLAYBOY cover. It's pretty eye-catching. Was it fun?

PARTON: I was afraid at first, when we talked about it. I didn't want to be naked or something on the front of a magazine unless everybody knew it was a joke. I mean, I wouldn't want to be naked even then. It might not offend *me*, but I was afraid maybe a lot of my country fans and some of the people who love me who are of a religious nature might not understand.

People will make jokes and things, not because of my beauty but just because of that physical thing that's built around my boobs. I didn't know if I wanted to be put in a category of where I was flaunting something I had never flaunted before. Then I thought, It isn't something I should be ashamed of. PLAYBOY's a real classy magazine. And I mean, who *else* but Dolly Parton should be on the cover of PLAYBOY? If you wanted an outrageous person to be an outrageous magazine cover, who else? I just hope people will take it in the spirit in which I did it—you know, something cute and off-the-wall for me.

PLAYBOY: OK. Now, why *do* you choose to look so outrageous?

PARTON: People have thought I'd be a lot farther along in this business if I dressed more stylish and didn't wear all this gaudy getup. Record companies have tried to change me. I just refused. If I am going to look like this, I must have had a reason. It's this: If I can't make it on my talent, then I don't want to do it. I *have* to look the way I choose to look, and this is what I've chose. It makes me different a little bit, and ain't that what we all want to do: be a little different?

It's fun for me. It's like a little kid playing with her paints and colors. I like to sit and tease my hair. If there's something new on the market in make-up, I like to try it. You've got to have a gimmick. You've got to have something that will catch the eye and hold the attention of the public. But the funny thing is, no matter how much I try new stuff, I wind up looking just the same.

PLAYBOY: Do you think you'll become a fashion trend setter? Isn't there already a Dolly Parton look?

PARTON: [*Laughing*] Can you imagine anybody wanting to look this way for *real*? When people first get to know me, they say, "Why do you wear all of this?" Then, after a week of knowing me, they totally understand. They know it's just a bunch of baloney. But why not? Life's boring enough, it make you try to spice it up. I guess I just throw on a little too much spice.

PLAYBOY: Why are there so many Dolly Parton look-alike contests?

PARTON: Because they're fun. Who would be better to impersonate than Dolly Parton? All you gotta do is get a big blonde wig, make-up, and if you're pretty well proportioned . . . or you can even fake it. The best parts of Dolly Parton look-alike contests are guys dressed up like girls. It's so *easy* to do me.

PLAYBOY: Have you ever met any of the winners?

PARTON: I sure have. They were the biggest bunch of pigs I ever saw, most of them. I thought to myself, Is that how people think I look? I thought, Oh, Lord, some of them were in worse shape than I even thought I was. I've only seen two that would even be classified as a human being.

PLAYBOY: So you don't think they've ever been able to imitate the real, sexy you?

PARTON: Listen, I never thought of myself as being a sex symbol. It never crossed my mind that anybody might think I was sexy.

PLAYBOY: But surely, after all the media exposure you've received, you have to be conscious of what people say and think about you.

PARTON: I didn't say what *you*-all thought. I said it never once crossed *my* mind, even now. I still can't get it through my head that people think I'm supposed to be sexy or somethin'. I don't want that responsibility. I don't want to have to keep up an image like that. I don't want to have to be like a beautiful woman, like a Raquel Welch—which is no trouble, I never would anyway. I'm just sayin' I wouldn't want people to look at me and if I gained ten pounds, they'd say, "Oh, God, she's ruined her looks." I'm made up of many things. I'm very complex. I have much more depth than just my looks, which to me are not all that hot, anyway. I've always looked a certain way and had an image. I like the big hairdo, the gaudy clothes. There's not much sexy about that. Men are not usually turned on by artificial looks and I've always been like that.

PLAYBOY: If that's true, why do you suppose there's such a huge cosmetic industry in this country?

PARTON: I'm talking about *my* kind—the big wigs, the total artificial look. I don't try to dress in style or to be really classy. I've got my work to do and I *like* to look good, but I don't try to keep an image other than just this gimmick appearance that I have. If I was trying to really impress men or be totally sexy, then I would dress differently.

PLAYBOY: How would you look?

PARTON: I would wear low-cut things. Try to keep my weight down. Try to really work on my body. I would find a new, softer, sexier hairstyle—it would be my own hair, some way. But why bother? I'm already married and *he* don't mind how I look. He likes me gaudy or ungaudy.

PLAYBOY: When were you first attracted to gaudiness?

PARTON: I was always fascinated with make-up. We didn't have any when I grew up. We weren't allowed to wear it. But we used to have this medicine, what you call Merthiolate, that's what I would put on my lips as a little kid. I'd paint my lips and there was nothin' Daddy could do. He couldn't rub it off. He would say, "Get that lipstick off you!" And I'd say, "It won't come off, it's my natural coloring, Daddy." Then he'd say, "Bull." When we wanted eyebrows, we'd get burned matches and make little eyebrows. When I was a sophomore in high school, the teased hair came into style and I started doing that, and ever since, I've done it. And I wore my skirts so tight I could hardly wiggle in them. I liked tight sweaters. I just like tight clothes, I always did.

I just like to feel things next to me, I guess. Even before I had a figure, I liked my clothes snug and tight. People would always kid me in school about my little butt and my little blue jeans or whatever. Momma, she always understood stuff like that. She'd say, "Don't get them so tight you can't move in them, where they cut your wind off." But she'd seam them up and if they weren't quite tight enough, I'd say, "Won't you fix them a little right in here?" And she would. See, she was a daughter of a preacher and when she was a child, they wouldn't let *her* wear any make-up. They all had long hair then and she wanted her hair cut. The very day that her and Daddy got married, she cut her hair off and she kept it short ever since. She said, "I swore then that when I had kids, I would not make 'em do things that they were uneasy with."

PLAYBOY: What did your father think of your tight clothes?

PARTON: Daddy didn't like us to wear real tight clothes back at the start. He was more strict with us, he just didn't understand how to be a father. A father of girls, especially. He just didn't want us to date. He trusted us, but he didn't trust the guys we was goin' with.

PLAYBOY: You must have looked more mature than a lot of your classmates when you were a girl.

PARTON: Well, I looked more mature, I *was* more mature. I used my mind in different ways. I developed my mind by writing and thinking deep and planning and dreaming. I *thought* serious. I looked as old as the teachers. When I was in high school, I looked like I was 25 years old.

PLAYBOY: Was the fact that you were physically more developed than the other girls a problem for you? Were you teased much?

PARTON: It was always a problem, to a degree. But I had a real open personality. I don't think I was teased openly; it was more what people were sayin' behind my back: "No, they're not real, she's got Kleenex in there."

PLAYBOY: Did that bother you?

PARTON: It was kind of embarrassing, but it must not have bothered me too much. I'm a real obvious person; all the things you see are obvious. But my body is not really as extreme as people make it out to be. I am just a small, tiny, little person, five feet tall, with a small frame. I have plenty, but it's not like what people say: "Oh, gosh, she must be 45 inches." I'm not nowhere near it, you know.

PLAYBOY: Why have you always refused to disclose your measurements?

PARTON: There's just no point. I'm not sayin' it's not *there*. A lot of people claim, "I remember when you wasn't that big." And I say, "Yeah, but you remember when I wasn't this fat, too." I'm not *that* well endowed. I'm not as *huge* as people make me out as being. I really ain't. I mean, if you look real *good* . . . I've got plenty, but I know a lot of people that are so big it's unhealthy, it hurts their back. I am so extreme, if I didn't have some, I would sure have made some. But from the time I was just a young girl, they've been there.

Some book said I had my bust lifted at Vanderbilt Hospital. Well, I never even been doctored at Vanderbilt Hospital. People will always talk and make jokes about my bosoms. When somebody says that this doctor claims he did it, I always say that plastic surgeons are all alike, they're always making mountains out of molehills. But, no, I didn't go to Vanderbilt Hospital. And if I had had something done, it would be a very private thing to me and it would be one of my secrets. But a lot of people that know me would know the difference. We won't say which-a-way *that* goes. So we will just leave the people wondering. But why dwell on that? Why don't they look underneath the breasts, at the heart?

PLAYBOY: All right. How would you describe yourself to someone who had never seen or heard you?

PARTON: Well, I would start by saying that I pride myself on being a fair and honest person. I am free and open enough to be able to try new things. I'm outrageous. I feel like I have a lot of depth that only the people closest to me really see. I'm compulsive and very ambitious. I'm playful. I'm joyful. I'm mischievous. Serious when I mean to be serious. I can be strong when I need to be and weak when I want to be. I can tell you where to put it if I don't like where you got it. I'm not a very moody person. I don't fall into great states of depression. Very sentimental and highly emotional. I'm a baby when it comes to bein' a baby. I like to be spoiled and petted. I get touched real easy. I'm curious, I have to know everything that goes on. I'm not a brilliant person, but I have a lot of guts. I just don't have a fear of life. I love life, so why should I not reach out to the things that I know I can touch? I'm strong-willed. I can think like a workingman because I know what a workingman goes through. I'm a person you could sit down with even if you were a total stranger and tell me the thing you thought was the most horrible thing and I would understand it. And I wouldn't tell. I'm a good friend. I'm loyal and devoted to the things that I believe in. . . . I'm full of shit!

PLAYBOY: That's quite a description. Now, how would you assess your talent?

PARTON: I like to be appreciated as a writer and, if not a great singer, at least a stylist and an original, creative person.

PLAYBOY: You don't feel you're that good a singer?

PARTON: I don't think so. My manager just hates me to say that, because he says it's not true. I don't have a great voice. I have a *different* voice and I can do things with it that a lot of people can't. But it's so delicate in other ways, there's no way I can do some of the things other singers can.

I just love to sing. It is joyful, it's something I can scream, it's a release for me. I used to have a lot of vibrato in my voice. It could almost be real irritating to a lot of people's ears. It was a natural thing for me, but some people say, "You sound like you been eating billy goat." Bah, bah. I guess I overdone it, so I tried to learn at takin' some of the vibrato out. I would like to improve my voice to be able to hit better notes. My notes are not always true. But my heart is always true. And the emotion I put in is always true.

PLAYBOY: Do you listen to yourself often?

PARTON: No, never. Unless I'm in the studio tryin' to decide what goes in the album. I'm not necessarily a fan of my own. I'm not one of my favorite singers.

PLAYBOY: Is it true that your husband doesn't like your singing?

PARTON: He didn't used to, but he's become a real big fan of mine now. I played this new album, *Heartbreaker,* and he really liked it.

PLAYBOY: Does that mean a lot to you?

PARTON: It means more than anybody could ever know.

PLAYBOY: You and Carl have been married 12 years and no one's ever seen a picture of the two of you together. Why the mystery?

PARTON: He just don't have *any* desire to be in show business. He don't want to have his picture in the paper. He don't want to go out to the super-market and have people say, "That's Dolly Parton's husband." There's been a lot of distorted press about how I only see him six weeks a year, which is not true. It's true that last year I was only at home about six weeks, but he joined me on the road a lot.

PLAYBOY: Is he as shy and bashful as the press makes him out to be?

PARTON: No. He's just the funniest, wittiest guy in the world. He's really bright. He's not backward at all. I just really wish that people would let him be. He's a home-lovin' person. He works outside, he's got his tractor and his grader, he keeps our farm in order. He wouldn't have to work no more, because I'm making good money now, but he gets up every morning at day-light. If he ain't workin' on our place, he'll take a few jobs, like grading somebody's driveway or cleaning off somebody's property, to pick up a couple of hundred bucks. He likes his own money to horse-trade with.

PLAYBOY: Do people say anything to him about Dolly Parton's husband grading their driveway?

PARTON: Oh, sure; he don't give a shit. He don't go up and say, "Hey, I'm Dolly Parton's husband, can I grade your drive?" If somebody knows it, he don't make a big thing of it; he'll play it down, he'll say, "Well, I ain't in show business, I got to work, now what can I do for you?" Or he'll say, "Hell, *she* ain't makin' no money." He's a man with a lot of pride; even though my money is his money, his money is mine.

PLAYBOY: Is he a jealous person?

PARTON: Not a bit.

PLAYBOY: Are you?

PARTON: I'm not, either.

PLAYBOY: Would it matter if he were seeing someone else while you were away?

PARTON: He's not.

PLAYBOY: If he were, would you want to know?

PARTON: No, I wouldn't want to know and he wouldn't want to tell me. But if he did, it wouldn't be like the end of the world for me. I would just say it was as much my fault as his. I would probably cry and pout for a day for the attention of it, and then it would be over. To me, life is life and people is people. You cannot control every emotion that you have.

PLAYBOY: How would he feel if you had an affair?

PARTON: The same way. He wouldn't want to know. I think I would keep it from him. He would be more apt to tell than me. He knows I ain't goin' nowhere. No matter who I met or what kind of an affair I might ever have, ain't nobody in this world could take Carl's place. There ain't no way in this world I'd ever lose this man.

PLAYBOY: Someone on the road as much as you are could sleep around a lot—

PARTON: How do you know I don't?

PLAYBOY: Because you speak so freely and guiltlessly about your relationship with Carl. You'd have to really be a good actress to cover up a lot of affairs.

PARTON: Oh, I *am*. I guess men think they can get away with it or somethin'. That all depends on the person. I just feel what's fair for the goose is fair for the gander. Whether I do or whether I don't is my concern. If I was ever weak enough to do something like that, it would never involve him, he would never know it, he would never feel any effects from it. Those are very personal questions and I'm a very private person, but I'm just like you—you don't always tell everything, do you? Let's put it this way: If I wanted to do it, I would; if I should do it, it would affect nobody but me and the person involved. Maybe it would be somethin' that would even make me be a happier person.

PLAYBOY: But couldn't it also lead to complication in your life?

PARTON: Well, kiss me, we'll see.

PLAYBOY: This is what's known as an awkward pause.

PARTON: There are a few people that I have been attracted to real strong, but I avoid that. There is no way in heaven's name that I could ever leave Carl, so why should I put myself and another person through that kind of torment?

PLAYBOY: It sounds like marriage at a distance can be healthy.

PARTON: It is. We're so used to the life-style, if I'm home two or three weeks, I want to get to work and he wants to get back to work, so he's just as anxious to see me go as I am to leave. It probably don't make much sense, but it makes sense to us.

PLAYBOY: When you are home, do you entertain much?

PARTON: When I'm home, we don't like people at the house other than our family and our own friends. That's why we bought a piece of property where we could have the privacy to get out in the yard in shorts or looking tacky.

PLAYBOY: How tacky?

PARTON: Tacky-tacky . . . no make-up, looking like anybody.

PLAYBOY: Is privacy a problem?

PARTON: We do have fans that jump the fence. That's not a very polite thing to do, but I don't get bent out of shape over it. I just figure if it's that important to somebody, least you can do is try to be nice.

PLAYBOY: Have you had any difficulties getting your fans to accept your new image? Are there diehard country-music buffs who can't accept your crossing over into the pop/rock field?

PARTON: We had some of that when I started, when I first got the bigger band and started doin' more rocky things. Some people hollered, "Do your country, we don't need your rock 'n' roll." I don't *do* rock 'n' roll. I knew what I was tryin' to do and I didn't have time to try to explain it to them.

I have not changed because of success, and I never will. The only thing success does to you, it just don't allow you to be alone anymore. Everybody is tryin' to get to you. It just gets to the point where people demand so much from you you just can't give it and you have to take all kinds of hurts and insults. It bothers you. Of all things, for somebody to say that I've changed, that just burns me up.

PLAYBOY: But your music *has* changed to some degree. Didn't you say that your *Here You Come Again* album is slicker than you wanted it to sound?

PARTON: Well, you see, that was the first thing that I did after I made the change and it was not exactly what I had in mind. But it proved to be the smartest thing. I knew *Here You Come Again* would be a hit song, but I don't know if I should be identified with it, because it's so smooth and pop-sounding. That's such a good song a monkey could have made it a hit. Well, you're looking at a million-dollar monkey.

PLAYBOY: Do you feel that in order to reach a larger audience you have to sweeten or smooth out your sound?

PARTON: Yeah, here and there. I was kind of afraid that people would think, Boy, this is too drastic. I just didn't want the country people to think that I totally left them. That was *such* a polished pop sound! But it was the biggest country record I ever had, as well.

PLAYBOY: Are you close to most of your band members?

PARTON: I'm close to all the people in my band. I'm not above them just because I am the star. They are not sidemen to me. We are all musicians making a living for each other. The way we travel, I couldn't work with a bunch of loonies, a bunch of squirrels. I don't mind drugs, I don't mind drinkin' in my group as long as it don't interfere with my show. We're together 24 hours a day, but that one hour onstage is mine. That's what I pay for. I don't care what you do after the show, I don't care what you do until four or five hours before the show. As long as everybody is straight, so if I want communication when we're onstage, I have it.

PLAYBOY: And you feel you're close to that now?

PARTON: My group is pretty clean. See, I live with the band. I travel with 'em, I don't like to separate myself from my group. In summertime, we take our barbecue grill and travel by bus. We only fly when we have to. Rather than stopping at a truck stop or a restaurant, we get a volleyball net out, we stop along the side of the road and have a picnic. I cook, there's another girl in my group, we have a real good time. We have water fights, cake fights, food fights . . . like brats. It's like a family. When the day comes when I can't enjoy it or there's no fun doin' it, there's lots of things that I can find joy in, and I would.

PLAYBOY: You once toured with members of your own family. What happened to your Travelin' Family Band?

PARTON: There was a lot of hurt caused by some press. They made it sound like I had fired my family. I did not fire my family. I had brothers and sisters and cousins in my group and I was really havin' to go through things I shouldn't have—poor lighting, poor sound, poor management, poor everything. I just decided I was goin' to quit for a few days, just stop everything and do some thinkin'. Because I won't let somethin' run me to a psychiatrist or to a doctor; I can take care of my own things, me and the Lord can talk it over. I was brought up religious and even if I'm not a fanatic, I have a communication with God, which helps me like a psychiatrist might help somebody else.

PLAYBOY: Were either of your parents musically talented?

PARTON: All of my momma's people were singers, writers, musicians. And a lot of my daddy's people were really involved in music. But it was just around home and in church; nobody had ever done anything as far as making any money with it. I was the first one that ever became popular doin' it, but there's a lot of 'em a lot more talented than me. I just had this grit and all these dreams and plans.

My momma's people and my daddy's people grew up as good friends, that's how they met, so there's a lot of marriages between the Partons and the Owenses. In the mountains, there's not that many people, so most people are related on one side or the other, and then they marry in, which makes you all kinfolks. I have double first cousins, first second cousins, stuff like that.

PLAYBOY: What is a double first cousin?

PARTON: Let me see if I can explain it. My mother's mother's sister married my daddy's brother. So their kids are my first—second?—cousins. It sounds like I'm my own grandpa, don't it? Anyway, you can figure it out later. However it is, we got some double first cousins and first second cousins. That kind of thing. Who can tell about mountain people?

PLAYBOY: Did you go to school with all your relatives?

PARTON: We lived in the mountains and there were very few people lived where we did, way back in the holler; our closest neighbors were a long ways off. We walked a long way to school, a one-woman school that had the first through the eighth grade. Only like 10 or 15 people in the whole school and one teacher. The grades were in rows: There might be two kids in the first grade, three in the second, one in the third . . . and so the teacher would just take a chair and sit in the aisle and the other kids had to study. I was the first one in our family that went to high school. My daddy didn't particularly want me to go to school, my momma didn't care. In the mountains, schoolin' is not that important.

PLAYBOY: How did you know it *was* important?

PARTON: I wanted to finish high school just so I could say I did, because I knew I'd learn things there that I would probably need to know, because I had already decided I was going out into the world. I was the most popular girl in school but in the wrong way. I wore tight clothes and told dirty jokes.

I never failed a subject, but I was never a good student. I never studied, I just used my own common sense to get by. I wanted to take band so I could bring my grades up. I didn't want to play horn or anything I had to really learn, so I asked if I could play the drums. I never did learn to read a note of music. I got like 98 in band, which brought up my grades at the end of the semester. But I didn't play well. I didn't know what I was doin'.

PLAYBOY: Did you like school?

PARTON: I hated it. Even to this day, when I see a school bus, it's just depressing to me. I think, Those poor little kids having to sit there in the summer days, staring out the window. It's hot and sweaty in the schoolroom. It reminds me of every feelin' and every emotion that I had in school. I'd hate to have to make my own kids go to school. I know that sounds terrible. A lot of people will say, "What a dumb person." I hated school every day I went, but it was better than stayin' home every day. Momma was sick a lot; we had some real hard times.

PLAYBOY: What were those hard times like?

PARTON: Momma had kids all the time—she had one on her and one in her. She was always pregnant, and the time she wasn't pregnant, she was just really run-down sick, and back then, you didn't have doctors that much. Momma took spinal meningitis once. The doctor said there was no way she could live, only one person in a thousand did live, and if she did live, she'd be crippled up. He told Daddy and my grandma she wouldn't live through the night. So they had church that night and they prayed all night. They packed Momma in ice, her fever was way past where it would do brain damage, and the next mornin', when the doctor came in, Momma was sittin' up in bed, kickin' her foot—Momma always kicked her foot, like I do, it's a rhythm thing. The doctor came in and she said, "I've been healed." And he said, "You sure have been healed, there's been a miracle happened here." They never could explain it. The only thing it did to Momma, it left her deaf in one ear, which just made her talk louder.

PLAYBOY: How old were you at that time?

PARTON: Eleven, twelve.

PLAYBOY: Were there other illnesses at home?

PARTON: One time, Momma had a miscarriage. It was really scary. We were all little. She started having this miscarriage . . . and she would always read the Bible; she'd be in bed and sing sacred songs—that was real depressing. We always knew when Momma was bad sick, she would do that.

It was during school, my first year. The way we got to school was we walked to this green barn. The man who owned that property had some bulls and they were mean. We had to walk along the fence row to get to school, and if the bulls would start out for us, we'd just roll under the fence. Anyway, Momma was at home with the two younger kids, they were just, like, two and three years old. Momma knew she was gonna die if somebody didn't do somethin' for her. So she told my little brother and sister what they had to do: "Now, you get your stick and go to the schoolhouse and get the kids, because Momma's sick. You take the stick and walk along the fence and if the bulls start after you, just roll under the fence or just hit 'em with the stick." Here was these little kids, it was really sad. It was a long way, even for us. And these two little kids must have took forever. We were in the middle of class and these two little kids . . . it was just so sad, there's a lot of things that almost make you cry. My little brother stuttered a lot and he couldn't talk good. The other kid couldn't even talk at all yet. But my older sister, Willadene, knew what was up when she saw them there. She jumped up and grabbed the rest of us and said, "Let's go, Momma's sick." So we just all ran home. My two older brothers had to run and find somebody to help us. At the time, we had some neighbors that didn't like us. We'd had a feud—it was kinda like the Hatfields and the McCoys. But they were good that time; it was just God's will, I guess.

PLAYBOY: What was the feud about?

PARTON: These people that lived near us, they had big kids and they were just mean. In the country, you're just born mean. They would whip us every day as we walked to school, hit us with rocks. Daddy made us another path through the woods where we could go to school and avoid 'em. They got to where they would meet us on the trail and still beat us up. Well, Daddy just got tired of it. He just went to the people and told them, "I'm gonna kill somebody if your kids don't stop beatin' my kids up." It started from that and then it got all the older people involved. My daddy and brothers got in a fight with these people and Daddy whupped about five grown people in that one family. So it was a real bad thing, we couldn't go by their house—they had dogs and they'd let them loose on us if we had to walk that way. But when Momma was near dyin', we just had nowhere else to go, which goes to show you there is good in everybody. These two women came and they ran out to the main road, which was a long, long way, and they had to track Daddy down. Daddy was workin' at a sawmill somewhere.

PLAYBOY: And then what happened?

PARTON: There was only two funeral homes in Sevierville, which was the nearest town to us. The funeral home that we didn't even belong to, they come to get Momma. It was just a bloody mess. We didn't have sheets on our beds; Momma would always just sew up rags. I remember seeing these people coming in these white jackets and this stretcher with these snow-white sheets, and you could see it a mile away. We just ran behind the house, cryin' and prayin' that Momma wouldn't die.

PLAYBOY: Did you understand death then?

PARTON: We understood that it was final. When Momma had spinal meningitis, she was pregnant and all the effects went to the baby she was carrying. When it was born, it only lived nine hours. It was the first time I'd ever seen my daddy cry.

We always looked forward to the babies born. A lot of people thought we were crazy. Even our relatives. I remember when my little brother died, I heard somebody say at the funeral home, and it stuck with me forever, "It's a blessing the little thing died." As if we didn't need any more kids. I thought, What a cruel thing to say, because we waited for each baby. It was like a joy. And there were so many of us Momma would say, "Now, this one's gonna be yours." And we kinda took care of it; it was like a new baby doll. With Momma being at the hospital and Daddy having to be with her a lot, we were by ourselves and it was just a real hard, depressed time.

PLAYBOY: What kind of man is your father?

PARTON: Daddy never had an education, but he is the smartest man I ever knew. There was never a time when Daddy didn't know what to do. My daddy used to make moonshine when he and Momma were first married. He got out of it because Momma didn't like it, but that's just the way of life in the country. That's revenue money. If somebody's gonna drink it, somebody's got to sell it.

PLAYBOY: Did you ever drink it?

PARTON: No, I never did drink moonshine. I tasted it. It tasted terrible. It's not a really good drink. I mean, you'd have to want it real bad to drink that stuff.

PLAYBOY: Did your parents discipline you a lot?

PARTON: Momma was so lenient, she just practically grew up with us. He was strict, he kept us in line. If he was mad, he whipped us with his belt. He didn't beat us, but he'd whip us hard. We'd have to go get a switch and they were pretty good-sized ones. I don't remember ever getting whupped with a board; I remember getting whupped with a stick of stove wood once.

PLAYBOY: Did you have a lot of childhood fantasies?

PARTON: We didn't have television and we didn't have radio. We didn't have electricity. Every now and then, if we could afford the battery—we had a battery radio—we'd listen to *The Grand Ole Opry* and *The Lone Ranger* maybe once or twice a week.

But we'd see catalogs—the wishbook, Momma called it. Made you wish you had things you didn't have. I wanted fancy clothes, I wanted jewelry, I wanted to be pretty.

We related to the Bible a lot, lots of stories we played out were from the Bible. We were Disciples and we would paint on our feet these sandals, and then we found these staffs and we just roamed those hills as shepherds. We played out Jacob and Joseph and the coat of many colors. I wrote a song once . . . my favorite story was the coat of many colors.

So that was kind of a fantasy we lived in. We didn't have books to read, except at school, and we tried not to read those.

PLAYBOY: Did you see magazines or newspapers at all?

PARTON: We'd hear about war stories and about famous people, movie stars. Sometimes my aunt in Knoxville would bring newspapers up, which we used for toilet paper. But before we used it, we'd look at the pictures. And we'd hear about people who would get rich and you'd have all the food you wanted to eat and fancy clothes and houses. In our minds, there was so many of us, anybody that had a clean house was rich.

PLAYBOY: When did you first use a flush toilet?

PARTON: My aunt in Knoxville had a toilet in the bathroom and we were *so* fascinated. We were afraid to use it. I just thought it was goin' to suck us right down. She also had the first television we ever saw.

PLAYBOY: What about bathing?

PARTON: Funny, I was just thinkin' how nobody has ever asked me about how we bathed or how we . . . you know, because we didn't have . . .

PLAYBOY: Toilets and facilities?

PARTON: Yes. We made our own soap and in the summertime, we'd go to the river. That was like a big bath. And we'd all go in swimming and we'd wash our hair, wash each other's hair. Soap was just flowin' down the river and we were so dirty we left a ring around the Little Pigeon River.

PLAYBOY: What did you do in the winter?

PARTON: In the wintertime, we just had a pan of water and we'd wash *down* as far as possible, and we'd wash *up* as far as possible. Then, when somebody'd clear the room, we'd wash *possible*.

PLAYBOY: How often did you bathe in the winter?

PARTON: I had to take a bath every night to be clean, 'cause the kids peed on me every night and we all slept three or four in a bed. As soon as I'd go to bed, the kids would wet on me. That was the only warm thing we knew in the wintertime. That was our most pleasure—to get peed on. If you could just not fan the cover. If you kept the air out from under the cover, the pee didn't get so cold. When you started fanning that cover, then it got bad, cold. Lord, it was as cold in the room where we slept as it was outside. We'd bundle up to go to bed.

PLAYBOY: When you bathed in the river, was it in the nude?

PARTON: We were real modest as kids. The boys would go swimmin' naked and the girls, sometimes we would, but we didn't go naked swimmin' together. As soon as you started sproutin' at all, you put on a shirt and you didn't take it off. I never did see Momma and Daddy naked. I'm glad I didn't.

PLAYBOY: Did your parents teach you the facts of life or did you learn them in school?

PARTON: It's somethin' I learned in the *barn*. [*Laughs*] I probably shouldn't say this, but it's just the truth: We were always just findin' out things on our own. We had uncles and cousins that were maybe two or three years older than us that knew a lot of stuff. When they would come to visit us, they'd teach us all kinds of meanness or tell us about this or that. And soon as we got a chance, we'd try it.

PLAYBOY: Are we talking about sexual things?

PARTON: Now, what were *you* talkin' about?

PLAYBOY: Just making sure.

PARTON: We were real curious. A lot of people won't admit it, but I just always had an open mind about sex. We all did. It was not a vulgar thing. We didn't know what we were doin', we just knew we weren't supposed to let Momma and Daddy know it. You never imagine your parents ever—

PLAYBOY: With 12 kids, they obviously did.

PARTON: Yeah. A lot of people say, "Well, how in the world could you live in a house with 12 kids and never hear things?" I don't know how they did it or where, but we never did know nothin' about it. But they *must* have done it.

PLAYBOY: So your mother never explained where all you kids came from?

PARTON: Momma always told us early that God was responsible for people havin' babies. I don't even know how I learned it. I learned real early. I think I probably knew it before Momma did. [*Laughs*] She learned when she was about 15 and I don't think she knew what was goin' on until she done had four kids. I was just so open-minded that I found out. If somebody wouldn't tell me, I'd ask the first person I thought I could ask.

PLAYBOY: What were the kinds of things you were asking? Where it comes from? Does it feel good? Does it hurt?

PARTON: Yeah. We just never did have a bunch of hang-ups. Momma never said, "Oh, don't do this, you'll go to hell." She didn't say *do* it, either. She didn't *say*. Daddy would have probably blistered our rear ends if he'd caught us foolin' around. We would just play doctor and nurse, just explore and experiment.

PLAYBOY: What about those guys who used to beat you all up—your neighbors—did they ever sexually abuse any of you?

PARTON: No. That's why they beat us up—because we wouldn't do anything. [*Laughs*] We didn't want to do it with them. I mean, we *were* choosy! But we never got sexually jumped or anything by them.

PLAYBOY: What was your first sexual experience like?

PARTON: I always loved sex. I never had a bad experience with it. I was just very emotional. I felt that I could show my emotion just like I show my emotion with words. If I felt I wanted to share an emotion, then I did. To me, sex was not dirty. It was somethin' very intimate and very real. I don't ever remember bein' afraid of it. I wasn't afraid the first time I tried it.

PLAYBOY: How old were you the first time?

PARTON: Now, I can't tell you that, because that would probably be real perverted. As little kids, we were *always* experimenting.

PLAYBOY: Well, you seem to have had a healthy childhood. Did you share your dreams of being a star with your parents?

PARTON: Yeah. I started writing songs before I went to school. Momma always wrote down stuff that I'd make up. I just had a gift of writing. I'd hear my people talk about relatives' bein' killed and I would make up all these heartbreakin' songs about it. They'd forget they'd talked about it and they couldn't imagine where I would come up with all these ideas. I just knew how to put it into story form. And Momma would write them down.

PLAYBOY: When did you start singing on the radio?

PARTON: I had an uncle that told me there was this radio show in Knoxville and that sometime he might take me down there and I might get to be on it. I wanted to do that. So, when I was ten years old, I sung on the radio. And they all liked me real good, so they wanted me to work in the summer months. They said they'd pay me $20 a week. My aunt in Knoxville said she would take me up to the radio stations and the TV shows if Momma and Daddy would let me stay, and she did. I worked there in the summers until I was 18. I went from $20 a week to $60 when I left.

PLAYBOY: What kinds of songs were you singing?

PARTON: I sung country music, some songs I wrote. I was singing by myself and playing the guitar. But I guess it was because I was a little kid they were sayin' people liked it. I wasn't that good.

PLAYBOY: Were any of your songs recorded then?

PARTON: I made my first record when I was around 11.

PLAYBOY: And when did you make your first appearance at the Opry?

PARTON: I was just a kid, 12 or 13. My uncle told the man at *The Grand Ole Opry* that I wanted to be on. The man said, "You can't be on *The Grand Ole Opry,* you are not in the union." And I said, "What is a union?" I didn't know if it was a costume or a room to practice or what. I kept tellin' everybody. I said I'll just sing one song. Most of the artists at the Opry at that time had two spots. Nobody would let me sing and I walked up to Jimmy C. Newman, who was goin' to sing next, and told him I wanted to be on. He told Johnny Cash that I was goin' to sing. And so Johnny Cash brought me out and I sung and I just tore the house down. I had to sing it over and over and over. I thought I was a star. That was my first time.

PLAYBOY: How did you feel?

PARTON: I was kind of scared, but I was excited, because I knew Daddy and Momma were listenin' on the radio. I didn't grasp all what it meant, but I knew I had to be on *The Grand Ole Opry,* that is all there was.

PLAYBOY: Were you always encouraged to be whatever you wanted to be?

PARTON: Where I came from, people *never* dreamed of venturing out. They just lived and died there. Grew up with families and a few dozen of them went to Detroit and Ohio to work in the graveyards and the car factorics. But I'm talkin' about venturing out into areas that we didn't understand. To me, a little kid coming from where I did and having that ambition and sayin' I wanted to be a star, people would say, "Well, it's good to daydream, but don't get carried away." People would say you can't do this or you can't become this. Well, if you don't think you will do it, nobody else will think it.

I've got more confidence than I do talent, I think. I think confidence is the main achiever of success, I really do. Just believin' you can do it. You can imagine it to the point where it can become reality. When I made my change to do what I'm doin' now to appeal to a broader audience, people said, "You can't do that, because you are goin' to wreck your whole career; you are goin' to lose your country fans and you're not goin' to win the others, and then you're goin' to have nothin'. You just better *think* about that, girl." That didn't matter to me, because I knew I had to do it and I knew I *could* do it.

PLAYBOY: What other kinds of things could you do as an entertainer?

PARTON: I don't think there's anything I can't do. Under the right conditions, I could just about do anything. Even a Broadway play, if it was a mountain musical where I didn't have to be a Streisand-type singer or have a beautiful trained voice. If it was somethin' written just for me, I think I could do anything. Most people don't have that kind of confidence in themselves.

PLAYBOY: Have you seen many Broadway plays?

PARTON: I've never seen a Broadway play . . . I've never been to an opera . . . I've never seen a live stage performance. I guess I'm not very classy.

PLAYBOY: But you *have* been to the movies and you may be doing three films.

PARTON: I never wanted to be in the movies. I have never done any acting at all, never thought I'd be particularly good at it. But the people at 20th Century-Fox really feel like I can be, or that I am, a natural actress. When they approached me, all I said was, "I don't know if I can or can't, but if you think I can and you want to take that chance, I'll take it with you." It's as simple as that. Can you imagine me bein' an actress? But a lot of people are interested. Sandy Gallin, my manager, is making a hellacious deal, but no one knows if I can do it at all.

PLAYBOY: Do you have any favorite movies?

PARTON: My favorite movie of all times is *Doctor Zhivago*. I've always liked movies with lots of production in them, especially things that were true, like *The Ten Commandments*.

PLAYBOY: Have you ever seen a porno movie?

PARTON: Yes, I have. Once, this secretary that worked in one of our offices, her husband had a print of a real awful one. I'd never seen anything up until that time. I always wanted to, but I didn't want anybody to know I was doin' it. She brought it to work and she brought the projector. When everybody left for lunch, she said, "Why don't we all watch?" Because none of us had ever seen one. We got to watchin' that thing and we got so embarrassed with each other. It, of course, moved you, but it was real embarrassing. And it got real gross, too.

Another time, I saw one in a public place. My girlfriend and me went to New York. This was a long time ago, I was about 21, and I wasn't that recognized. We had always wanted to see a *real* one. We thought it would be somethin' dirty enough to enjoy. We tried to sneak in when nobody would see. There is somethin' real shameful about goin' there, but we dared each other to do it, so we went. It had an awful smell in that theater.

PLAYBOY: Where was it?

PARTON: I don't know; it was down in one of them slum areas. We just got a cab, it was a Friday night, and this terrible thing happened. We sat at the very back, in case there were some maniacs in there. It was mostly men, a couple of women alone, no couples. Me and my girlfriend was sittin' in the back, so we were goin' to make a quick exit if we needed to, and then this movie came on. It looked OK for a few minutes, and all of a sudden, it got into the most gross things. I didn't know how to react and she didn't either. We were embarrassed in front of each other, we didn't know whether to look or not. We were so curious we couldn't keep from lookin'. I didn't know how to react with her. If I had Carl there or somethin', we might have got down to business. So we ran out and we started runnin', so nobody would know where we came from. At that time, we didn't know that prostitutes ran in pairs in New York City for protection. And there is no way in the world that you can catch a cab on a Friday night in New York City. We didn't know that.

All of a sudden, these men started approachin' us on the street. They thought we were up for sale. You can imagine how ridiculous I looked. I would look like a streetwalker if you didn't know this was an image. I would look like a total whore, I suppose. I'm sure we looked just like what they thought we were. But I had a gun. I never traveled without a gun, still don't. I always carry a gun.

PLAYBOY: What kind?

PARTON: A .38 pistol. I have a permit for it in Nashville. I just carry it for protection. I feel safer when I've got it. I just don't like the idea of knowin' I'm totally helpless. I'm always scared in a big city and New York was totally foreign to us. Anyhow, these men would approach us and I'd say we're from out of town. We didn't understand why they were after us. I said we were waitin' on a cab and weren't interested, but thanks for the compliment. [*Laughing*]

I was doin' all the talkin', because my girlfriend always knew I'd get us out of any situation, and she started laughin' at me. That made me mad, because I was *so* scared! This one man came at me and he was really pullin' at me, he was tryin' to handle me, just maul me, the whole works. I told him, "Just get away and don't bother me anymore." He kept sayin', "Oh, come on, honey, I know you want it." He was offerin' us money and I said, "Look, I don't know what it is, we are *not* interested, we are *not* on the make, we are tryin' to get home, don't you understand that?" There I was with, my big Southern accent and my big wig. He just thought if he bargained long enough that I'd give in. He kept pullin' at me and I was getting furious and I was cussin' him, and I don't cuss that much. I was sayin', "You son of a bitch, you dirty bastard!" Just things like that is not like me at all, but I was *terrified*, and I was mad, too, because I can't stand people who pull at me unless I want to be pulled at. And my girlfriend was against the wall, dyin' laughing. We could have both been raped or killed, but she was gettin' such a kick, because she'd never seen this side of me before. I got furious at her and I told her, I said, "Boy, you just better stop laughing or I'm gonna beat the shit out of *you,* too!" And I got my gun out of my pocketbook. I told the man, "If you put your hands on me one more time, I swear to God that I will shoot you." And I *would* have. I wouldn't have shot him in the stomach or nothin', I would have shot his feet off or shot at the ground. My girlfriend was just hollerin', laughin', and, boy, I told her when we got rid of him, "If you ever do that to me again, I swear to you I may not whup your ass, but I'll be caught dead tryin'." [*Laughing*] She never did quit laughin', she just thought that was the funniest thing she'd ever seen. We headed out to a porno movie and it wound up bein' a comedy.

PLAYBOY: Was that your first time in New York?

PARTON: It was, and for years I thought I hated New York City for that very reason. Since then, it has become one of my very favorite cities; I go back all the time, there's great people there. It's just that then I didn't understand them and they *sure* didn't understand me.

PLAYBOY: Now that you've had your say about New York, let's try Los Angeles. You've been spending a lot of time out there lately. Do you like it there?

PARTON: It's beautiful and it's exciting. I really enjoy it for a week. After that, I go L.A. crazy. I just got to get out of there, it's so crazy and wild, especially the places I have to be and the people I have to be around when I'm out there; most of them are so spaced out or just involved in all sorts of weird things, even the people you work with, especially show people. I just have to get away from them. I get homesick. The country in me says, "What in the world are you doin' walkin' on concrete when you could be rollin' in the grass?"

PLAYBOY: Let's get to the country in you. Do you get insulted when people put down country music?

PARTON: Terribly insulted. Saying somethin' about country music is like saying somethin' about a brother or sister or my momma and daddy. Because it has made me a livin', it is somethin' I love and appreciate. I know what it stands for, I know what it is. It is a music to be respected.

PLAYBOY: What is it about country music that attracts people?

PARTON: It's the simplicity of it, it is everyday stories about everyday people. It deals with human emotions, human relationships; it is love and heartbreak and fun things and honky-tonk . . . the way that the truck drivers and the average middle-class American lives.

Then, too, country music through television and radio started getting broader. When country started gettin' on TV, people realized that we are not just hillbillies and hicks, toe jam and bare feet—we only go barefooted 'cause we want to, not 'cause we can't do no better. To me, it's the greatest music because it does deal with life, with people, and it deals with simple sounds. If it is done right, it is the best music there is.

PLAYBOY: What would you say is the difference between country singing and pop or rock singing?

PARTON: There is a certain quality, a certain purity in country voices. They sound plainer, countrier, more blunt. They don't do a lot of screams and squalls.

PLAYBOY: Are you more prolific as a songwriter than most?

PARTON: Yes. It's just a natural gift. I like to write and I write all the time. I've written less in the last year and a half, but even at that, I've written more than most writers do. It's just so easy. I've got hundreds and hundreds of songs, thousands, actually. I've had a few hundred published and recorded. The good thing about it is this: I've been writin' all these years, if I never wrote another song, I've got it made. People are going' back now and gettin' songs of mine and recordin' them, things I did on albums years ago. Of course, I still will write. It's like most people will sit down and smoke a pipe, I just sit down and pick up a piece of paper. . . .

PLAYBOY: What do you feel when you're performing your songs onstage?

PARTON: I just get *real* excited onstage, because I love to sing and perform. It takes me about three hours to come down. Your openin' tune is usually the one you get off on if you're goin' to get off. Sometimes I get so excited over a certain moment onstage, I could just swear that it's the same thing as sex. . . . Music is the closest thing to it to me.

PLAYBOY: Do you have any ideas about how you might change the kinds of shows you perform now?

PARTON: I would want to be more bizarre as time goes on. I would like to have a screen behind me onstage when I do the songs and tell the stories of the mountains.

I'm havin' some people even now begin to film things from the mountains, like the tobacca-spittin' contest, the greased-hog contest and the horse-turd-throwin' contest that they have in Kentucky every year. That's a real occasion, the Annual Kentucky Horse Turd Throwin' Contest. Can you imagine gettin' crowned Horse Turd Queen of the day? They probably make a crown out of horse turds. I'm not tryin' to be dirty, I swear that's what they call it. An audience would love to see that, because they've never seen it. I'd like to have that onstage, narrate the happenings, and then have the music. I just have a lot of crazy, wild ideas and some of these days I'm gonna get them all together and hope somebody don't steal them. And if you do, you're a sorry son of a bitch!

PLAYBOY: Where do you see your career at the moment?

PARTON: Most people say in this business the life-span of a career is five years from the time you really get hot to the time you start getting colder, like an Elton John. Maybe I shouldn't call names. That's just what I heard, that you don't expect to really be the hottest except for maybe five years, and with a TV show, it's usually a three-to-five-year thing, and then you cool off, people have seen what you do. I think maybe I am right now starting in my first year of from one to five. That's what I'd like to think.

PLAYBOY: Since we're on the subject of names, let's get your opinion of some of your contemporaries. We'll start with the woman you think is the true queen of country music, Kitty Wells.

PARTON: She was the first extremely popular female country singer. She was like a pioneer for all the rest of us. She sold all kinds of records to soldiers and jukeboxes and honky-tonks. She is such a natural, pure and authentic singer. She sings from the heart and she don't worry about what the noise is goin' to sound like.

PLAYBOY: Johnny Cash?

PARTON: Johnny is dramatic. I don't think Johnny is a good singer, but I think he is one of those people that is so believable that people can relate to it. He's got a way of deliverin'; you just know that it had to happen if Johnny said so.

PLAYBOY: Loretta Lynn?

PARTON: Sings with a lot of human emotion and country emotion, a lot of purity and honesty in her voice. Similar to Johnny Cash's—not the greatest voice I've ever heard, but it's believable.

PLAYBOY: Her sister, Crystal Gayle?

PARTON: A beautiful voice. Crystal clear, if you'll pardon the expression.

PLAYBOY: Tanya Tucker?

PARTON: If she ever gets with the right producer and the right label and gets the right manager, I think she can really be great, especially as a rock-'n'-roll singer. Her voice is so powerful, like a Janis Joplin or a Linda Ronstadt. . . . She could really be a huge artist, because she is great on the stage.

PLAYBOY: Janis Joplin?

PARTON: Her voice was like mine, you either liked it or you didn't. I never particularly cared for it. It was different. But I do appreciate what she left behind in the world of music.

PLAYBOY: Linda Ronstadt?

PARTON: She is one of the greatest female voices I ever heard.

PLAYBOY: Emmylou Harris?

PARTON: I love Emmy's voice, it's so delicate and so pure.

PLAYBOY: Did you ever meet Elvis?

PARTON: No, I never did. But I always felt that we were kin. I feel like I know exactly how he was. Every time he'd come in town, even if I was home, I just wouldn't go, somethin' always kept me from goin'. There were other people I liked to hear sing better, but there was nobody that I ever related to more.

PLAYBOY: What was it about him you related to?

PARTON: He was very loving, very emotional, very sensitive, very giving, very humble, thankful, grateful. I always felt that he was totally in awe of his own success and he didn't quite understand why he had been so chosen and why he was such an idol. How he felt about God and religion was always somethin' I related to a lot, because I know he was brought up with his mother in the Assembly of God. It was a real free-spirited, shoutin' church. I watched and heard how he reacted to Gospel music and how he loved that the best of all and how he almost seemed to feel he had a callin' to do somethin' different and maybe more spiritual than what he actually was doin', but you know, he never got a chance to try. He touched people's lives in a lot of ways. He was the sex symbol of the world and when he started gainin' weight and gettin' fat, he lost a lot of his glamour to a lot of people. I always thought his manager was brilliant, as well. They built that mystery up about him. When he started losin' his glamour and doin' those concerts, he became more ordinary. That's when they started publishing all the things about him. Then people realized that he was not a god of any sort, but he was just an extraordinary human bein'. I think if he hadn't died when he did, within the next five years he wouldn't have been a hero at all, because he was talked about too much . . . seen too much. That's how cruel the public can be.

PLAYBOY: Do you think that there will be another Elvis, or someone of his stature, to come along?

PARTON: I don't think it will be soon, I don't think it will be anythin' you and me will ever see.

PLAYBOY: What about a female Elvis?

PARTON: That is possible. I think there is due a person, a female, which there has never been. A person of that type, with that great magnetism and that great mysterious thing, that great love, that charisma and magic to draw people to her, that can help people in many ways just through her music. Yes, I think that a female is due, I do. And your next question: Do I think it is me?

PLAYBOY: You're the one smiling.

PARTON: Well, let me say, I would never be an Elvis, and I would never want to be an Elvis. But I would like to be a person truly loved enough to be able to have that much of an impact on people as far as bein' able to guide them or help them or let them see that you're caring.

PLAYBOY: Your mother has said that she always expected you to lead people to the Lord. Do you think that someday that might happen—besides just singing, you might start preaching?

PARTON: Yes, I think that is definitely possible. My mother and many people have always said that they saw the love of God in me. I expect that someday, in some way, before I die, I'll have done some good for God, who I think has done all the good in me that's ever been done. I think that people for years have passed God right up, looked right past Him, thinkin' that He was some great monster in the sky and that you had to live with these horrible guilt feelin's and you had to crawl under a bed if you'd done somethin' wrong. I have a totally different concept of God. I'm God-fearin', but I'm not afraid of God. The way I look at God is, I think He means somethin' different to everybody. We are all God's children, if we just clear a way for Him to work through us. You don't have to be standin' in a church house to reach people to change their lives to do good. I don't want to get so involved in this that people think, Oh, another country-music fanatic, because I'm not a fanatic, never was. If I need to make a decision or somethin', I just talk out loud to God. I joke with God. He don't ever say nothin' back.

PLAYBOY: Do you go to church?

PARTON: No, not anymore. Carl and I are probably afraid we'll become total Christians and then we'll . . . I don't know. I always want to go home when they're havin' a revival, though. Someday, when I can have some time off, I want to go back to the house and stay home for a couple of months, spend the summer, work the fields and go to the orchards, can apples and peaches—do stuff like I used to. And if they're havin' a revival, I'll go. I'll get up and sing, too.

PLAYBOY: You first became nationally prominent as part of a team with Porter Wagoner. Tell us about your relationship with him.

PARTON: Porter has been one of the greatest and most popular country artists of all times. I can never take the credit away from Porter for givin' me a big break. I learned a lot from him. He inspired me and I inspired him. We were good for each other in many ways and just a disaster for each other in a lot of ways. I'll always love him in my own way.

PLAYBOY: In what ways did your working together become a disaster?

PARTON: We just got to where we argued and quarreled about personal things. Things we had no business quarreling and arguing about. It was beginning to tarnish a really good relationship. We didn't get along very well, but no more his fault than mine. We were just a lot alike. Both ambitious. I wanted to do things my way and he wanted to do things his way.

PLAYBOY: He has said that for two years he devoted 95 percent of his time to you and then he didn't hear from you for a year. He sounds bitter.

PARTON: I'm sure he is bitter at this particular point. He is so strong-headed and bullheaded, he won't accept things sometimes the way they are. I won't either, sometimes. We're kind of involved in some legal things. I'm tryin' to buy my part of the catalog back, where I'll have all my songs back together. Someday I hope we can be friends. We are not enemies. We just don't ever see each other.

PLAYBOY: How much money was Porter paying you?

PARTON: The years I was with Porter, I worked for $300 a night, which is another reason I needed to get out on my own; I needed to make more money.

PLAYBOY: That was how much a year?

PARTON: Sixty thousand dollars a year. I started from no money at all and that sounded like a *lot* of money to me. And it was. But why should I work for hundreds and thousands when I can work for hundreds *of* thousands?

PLAYBOY: How much a night did you make when you worked on your own, after leaving Porter?

PARTON: When I went out on my own, I was working for $2500, then it got up to $3000, and now I have no idea. It is way up in the thousands.

PLAYBOY: Is it around $30,000?

PARTON: I don't know exactly how much I make; I would say anywhere from $15,000 up a night now. I know I got $30,000 for some shows I've done recently. And I was offered $50,000 to do a special show, but for some reason, I didn't do it. That's the most I've been offered at this point, I think.

PLAYBOY: How many businesses do you own?

PARTON: Quite a few. I own three publishing companies. I'm startin' a production company. I own quite a bit of property. I have the Dolly doll, for which we own the company. We have program books, colorin' books, souvenir things of that type. I have lots of investments, lots of tax shelters. I've got some good smart business people now. I have some really wild dreams and plans. I really love to hear crazy ideas. I'm goin' to have a line of wigs. I think that would be a perfect business for me.

PLAYBOY: We've been meaning to ask about your wigs. Are they real hair or synthetic?

PARTON: Synthetic. They never lose their curl.

PLAYBOY: Loretta Lynn has said that while most singers aren't particular in the dressing room, you always go behind a little curtain to dress. She says nobody has ever seen you without a wig on.

PARTON: Loretta has seen my own hair. I think she forgot or just wanted to make a bigger thing than it was. Maybe she just didn't recognize it as bein' my own hair. My own hair is blonde. I keep it blonde. I'll eventually wear my own hair again, once I become so successful that people know you can become successful by lookin' and bein' any way you want to if you've got enough ambition and talent. A lot of people have approached me in a way that sounded like I was supposed to dress and undress in front of other people. I happen to be a very modest person and I just won't dress in front of people. I don't know why they would want to look, anyway. Out of curiosity, I guess. What other people do does not bother me at all. I only wish that what I do wouldn't bother them.

PLAYBOY: Let's wind this up by asking you some random questions. If you coud go back in time and be someone else for a while, who would you like to be?

PARTON: That's not a random question, that's a *great* question! I've never thought about that in my life. . . . I think, maybe, Will Rogers. He reminds me of my own people and of myself.

PLAYBOY: What if you could invite any five people from history to a dinner party—whom would you choose?

PARTON: Will Rogers would be my main guest. Beethoven. Bob Hope. Strother Martin. Festus, from *Gunsmoke*.

PLAYBOY: What would you serve them?

PARTON: Fried potatoes and green beans, country-style creamed corn, corn bread and biscuits, pinto beans and turnip greens, meat loaf, I'd probably make up a vanilla pudding. I'd have to fix Beethoven a chef's salad. I don't think he'd want all that grease.

PLAYBOY: What's your favorite food?

PARTON: Potatoes. I'm a starch freak. I'm a junk-food person, too. I like pizza, potato chips, Fritos. My main weakness is overeating. Now it's beginning to dawn on me that I have a weight problem and I have to learn to control it some way. I am getting approached for so many things, for movies, for the PLAYBOY cover. So I'm on a diet.

PLAYBOY: Weren't you once on a liquid-protein diet, which lately has been proved to be dangerous?

PARTON: I did that and I lost 23 pounds. Fat persons don't care if they die tryin' to get it off. [*Laughs*]

PLAYBOY: Are you attracted to thin or to muscular men?

PARTON: I've always been more attracted to real slender men. My husband is skinny as a rail, and tall. They say that you usually will be attracted to the opposite of yourself.

PLAYBOY: Is it hard to design clothes for you?

PARTON: It's not hard, 'cause all you got to do is make up the gaudiest thing you can make. Just pile as much stuff that don't belong on it as you can and I'll like it.

PLAYBOY: How many rooms of clothing do you have?

PARTON: I've got clothes in the closets of every room in my house—23 rooms. One whole wing of my house is filled with costumes and casual clothes.

PLAYBOY: And you sometimes shop at Frederick's of Hollywood?

PARTON: I buy my shoes there; it's the only place I can find shoes high enough and sexy enough to suit me. I buy thousands of dollars of shoes every year. I can't wear their clothes, because I can't buy clothes off a rack.

PLAYBOY: Do you support the Equal Rights Amendment?

PARTON: Equal rights? I love everybody. . . .

PLAYBOY: We mean equal rights for women.

PARTON: I can't keep up with it.

PLAYBOY: Do you read any books on the women's movement?

PARTON: Never have. I know so little about it they'd probably be ashamed that I was a woman. Everybody should be free: If you don't want to stay home, get out and do somethin'; if you want to stay home, stay home and be happy.

PLAYBOY: Do you have favorite books or authors?

PARTON: I don't read that much. I probably should be ashamed to say that. I read mostly articles and things I'm interested in. I always liked Agatha Christie, but I never did read all that many of her things. I like books like *The Magic of Believing*. Positive-thinking books, self-improvement books. Long before I knew there were books aobut that stuff, that was my philosophy of life.

PLAYBOY: What about politics?

PARTON: I hate to say this and people probably think I'm real dumb to do it, but I am so involved in my work and my music I don't even know what's goin' on in the world. I don't even know who the Vice-President is. Well, I *do* know . . . but as far as gettin' politically involved, it's like bein' denominations. If you're a Democrat, the Republicans hate you; if you're a member of one church, then the other ones hate you. Every denomination thinks they're the only ones gettin' to heaven and they feel sorry for the other denominations. I think we can all get there if we work right.

PLAYBOY: Moving right along . . . has sex changed for you over the years?

PARTON: Sex? Yes, it gets better. The reason it gets better is because you get more mature, you're more relaxed, you experience more things until you become more comfortable with them, and then you feel also comfortable to experience new things, totally new and different things. It takes you a while to trust somebody enough to be able to tell your fantasies.

PLAYBOY: How strong are your fantasies?

PARTON: Pretty strong. But I think all creative people and highly emotional people have strong fantasies.

PLAYBOY: What are some of yours?

PARTON: I'm not tellin' you all that stuff. . . . Get over here and I'll show you. [*Laughs*] Are you perverted?

PLAYBOY: Why? Are you sexually aggressive?

PARTON: I'm very aggressive. I don't mind bein' the aggressor if it comes to somethin' I need or want.

PLAYBOY: Do you like dangerous sex?

PARTON: Nothin' better than sex when you think you have to sneak it.

PLAYBOY: Now for the big question: Do you sleep in the nude?

PARTON: It has just been the last couple of years that I've really started sleepin' naked. Sometimes I sleep naked with Carl and sometimes I don't. If I'm up writin' and I have on a robe, I'll write until I fall asleep and crawl into bed. If we go to bed together, I usually go naked. But I have to have a cover on me, summer or winter. I can't stand just a sheet.

PLAYBOY: How would someone who had written something get a song to you?

PARTON: Do you mean to tell me that we've spent all these days and hours and went through all this horseshit just so you could pitch me a song?

PLAYBOY: You're a funny lady. Is it true you used to flirt with local disc jockeys when you'd appear in various towns?

PARTON: Either my life is a total flirt or I'm not a flirt. I just go in with open arms and open heart. I'm just using my personality. But the only ones I ever flirted with were the ones I was attracted to. Can't say I never flirted with one, but I never flirted with one to get my record played.

PLAYBOY: And what about all the erotica you used to write as a teenager? You claimed you were very horny.

PARTON: All teenagers are horny, some just keep it hid better than others. I'm writin' a story even now; it's pretty hot and heavy. It's got a lot of sex and love and violence and religion, all the human elements.

PLAYBOY: Will you shock a lot of people?

PARTON: Yeah; that's why I ain't puttin' them out today or the day after tomorrow. When I decide to publish some of my books, I'm goin' to write in the front that those who think they might be offended, don't read them. Then, if you are offended, don't blame me, because now I'm not just a singer but also a writer; and as a writer, I have to have freedom of total expression.

PLAYBOY: Would you use a pseudonym?

PARTON: I want to do everythin' under my own name, 'cause when I go down in history, I want to go down good and solid.

PLAYBOY: They could put that on your tombstone: Good and solid.

PARTON: I don't want a tombstone. I want to live forever. They say a dreamer lives forever. . . . I want to be more than just an ordinary star. I want to be a famous writer, a famous singer, a famous entertainer; I want to be a movie writer; I want to do music movies, do children's stories; I want to be somebody important in time; I want to be somebody that left somethin' good behind for somebody else to enjoy.

Everybody wants to be successful at whatever their inner dream is. I'm not near with what I want to do, with what I want to accomplish. When I feel like I have accomplished the things that I want to accomplish, then maybe I will personally think of myself as a superstar. I want to be somebody that extremely shines. A star shines, of course, but I want to be really radiant.

Playboy Interview Interludes

My reaction to porn films is as follows: After the first ten minutes, I want to go home and screw. After the first *twenty* minutes, I never want to screw again as long as I live.

Erica Jong, September 1975

This country is far more hip and sophisticated than the networks think, but TV has psyched out such large segments of our society that many people have come to believe they *are* witless, corn-fed rubes.

Norman Lear, March 1976

Patty Hearst had me on the move more than anyone else—certainly more than the law. I'd think, "Oy, she's gotta come *here*! Who needs this? I got *enough* problems."

Abbie Hoffman, May 1976

I wish I had killed him. Oh, Ford is a nebbish. I have nothing against him personally. It was the office of the Presidency I was trying to attack . . . I was stunned that I missed. My aim was true, the shot was good—it was just that the .38 was a faulty gun.

Sara Jane Moore, June 1976

I probably shouldn't tell you this. I've never even told Howard—there's a bar down South where, during the football season, all the regulars put in a few bucks and on Monday night they buy an old TV set and a load of buckshot. Then they draw lots and, the first time Howard Cosell's picture comes on the screen, the winner gets to blast the TV set to smithereens.

Roone Arledge, October 1976

MARLON BRANDO

January 1979
Interviewer: Lawrence Grobel

Marlon Brando had long been up there with Greta Garbo and J. D. Salinger on the list of "impossible" interviews for PLAYBOY or any other publication, having confined himself for nearly twenty years to impassioned lectures on the plight of the American Indian and, on several occasions, to punches thrown at reporters or photographers. But in 1977, when Hugh Hefner personally provided bail funds for the imprisoned leader of the American Indian Movement, Russell Means, Brando got word to the magazine that he was grateful, and told the editors he would like to do something with PLAYBOY. The magazine immediately proposed an interview. Brando agreed in principle, but with the expectable hitch: He would only speak about American Indians. Well—at least the door was ajar.

Lawrence Grobel, fresh from his marathon with Dolly Parton, was given the assignment. His description of the *seventeen* months of negotiations sets the scene for this interview, which is remarkable for the interplay between Brando, denouncing any and all questions about acting or his personal life as trivial and unimportant, and Grobel, patiently circling, finding associations and ideas with which to slip in questions about the man and his work. It may be the most reluctant interview PLAYBOY ever published, and it also provides a study in the interview form itself. Brando knows journalism, has spent a lifetime dancing away from its traps, and so provides a running commentary on Grobel's efforts as the conversation proceeds. And what is clear is that Brando, despite himself, is thoroughly enjoying the game.

In his description of the months of fruitless telephone calls to Brando's office, Grobel does not mention that several times, when the telephone was not answered by Brando's longtime secretary, Alice Marchak, Grobel found himself talking to a male voice that seemed disguised. Sometimes with a heavy dialect, other times a raspy falsetto, the voice would claim to Grobel that neither Miss Marchak nor Mr. Brando was available. When Grobel finally made telephone contact with Brando several months later, there seemed to be something familiar about the unmistakable voice—apart from its familiarity in dozens of movies—but Grobel couldn't quite put his finger on it. He never asked Brando about it; it just didn't seem fair.

After the seventeen-month wait, and after ten days of interview sessions on Brando's private island near Tahiti, Grobel flew home, sending PLAYBOY editor Golson a postcard that read simply: "You've got an interview. I'm exhausted. Larry." But it wasn't over. Several weeks later, as Grobel worked on the six hundred pages of transcripts in his West Hollywood apartment, an unexpected visitor showed up. It was Brando, wanting to follow up on a couple of points he had made about the Indians. He couldn't remember, he told Grobel, if he'd mentioned a certain historical incident about the Blackfeet. Grobel said he had, but, while they were on the subject of Brando's memory, what about his reported lapses of memory on movie sets, which required that other actors sometimes paste cue cards on their foreheads?

Brando, off-guard, launched into a justification of his memory lapses, saying it made for more realistic dialogue—then stopped and shouted, "Oh, you got me! You got me right in the bush!" He began to laugh. "I'm talking about acting, aren't I?" Feeling puckish, he continued on the topic and, for the first time, gave the public his insights into a craft he affects to despise.

After publication, Brando also affected displeasure over the interview, but only because the magazine had not published every word he'd said about the Indians. (It would have meant an interview not merely sixteen thousand words long, as it was published, but perhaps one hundred thousand words long.) But the actor had some grudging praise for Grobel's work.

During the interview, off the record, Brando had asked Grobel and the editors for background research on a previous interview published in PLAYBOY. The editors didn't know it at the time, but Brando had accepted the role of George Lincoln Rockwell in the upcoming TV production of "Roots II." When the program was broadcast several months later, it was history at its most circular: There was Brando, in his first television role, his own PLAYBOY interview not long off the newsstands, portraying a man sitting for *his* PLAYBOY interview, telling the magazine's first interviewer that it was nothing personal, he just didn't like niggers—as the "Roots" saga moved toward its present-day conclusion. . . .

He is considered by many to be the world's greatest living actor, the man who changed the style of the movies, the most influential and widely imitated actor of his generation. He burst onto our consciousness wearing a torn T-shirt, mumbling, growling, scowling, screaming for "Stel-la!" as Stanley Kowalski in Tennessee Williams' "A Streetcar Named Desire," first on Broadway, then on film. It marked the beginning of a career that was to be as wild as many of the characters he so expertly portrayed.

An intensely private man, Marlon Brando stirs emotions and elicits reactions that go beyond his status as either actor or political activist. He's been called brilliant, a lout, considerate, arrogant, gentle, selfish, a chauvinist, generous, an egomaniac, selfless. He has passed into myth, become history. The highest-paid and most respected actor in America, he is one of the select artists who will doubtless be remembered into the next century.

There are those who saw him as the ruthless, sexy Stanley Kowalski during his year-and-a-half-long run on Broadway who can still describe the way he moved onstage. Critics quickly hailed him as the most gifted actor of his generation. But the role was demanding and led Brando into analysis, which lasted for a decade. It also led him into films, which he openly disdained but which offered him the opportunity to make more money, work fewer hours and reach a wider audience. Brando went to Hollywood and never returned to Broadway.

From 1950 to 1955, Brando starred in eight films, the first six of which, as actor Jon Voight recently said, "were absolutely enormous." Those films were "The Men," "A Streetcar Named Desire," "Viva Zapata!", "Julius Caesar," "The Wild One" and "On the Waterfront." Brando had established the Method as the acting force to contend with.

What Paul Muni called Brando's "magnificent, great gift" was recognized in 1955 when he won the Oscar for Best Actor for his role as Terry Malloy in "On the Waterfront," which he accepted. Eighteen years later, he won his second Oscar, for his role as Don Vito Corleone in "The Godfather," but by then, Brando's social consciousness had risen dramatically and he disdained awards, refusing to accept it and asking an American Indian woman to stand before the academy and the world to explain why.

Between "On the Waterfront" and "The Godfather," Brando made 19 pictures (he's made 30 in his 28-year career to date, including "Superman" and the yet-to-be-released "Apocalypse Now"). Some of them have been strong and sensitive, such as "The Young Lions," "Reflections in a Golden Eye," "Burn!" and "The Nightcomers"; and some have been embarrassing and trite, such as "A Countess from Hong Kong" (written and directed by Charles Chaplin) and "Candy." But whatever the role, his acting has consistently surprised and often confused his audience with its unpredictability.

Throughout his career, Brando has preferred to speak out on issues of social importance rather than on acting and the movies, involving himself in causes far removed from make-believe. He has actively participated in marches and spoken out on behalf of the Jews, the blacks, the American Indians, the downtrodden and the poor; and against capital punishment, bigotry, awards, most politicians, and policing organizations whenever they seem to infringe upon individual rights and freedoms. For UNESCO, he flew to India during a famine; in the state of Washington, he was arrested for participating in an Indian fish-in over river rights; in Gresham, Wisconsin, he ducked bullets along with radical Indians from the Menominee tribe demanding a return of disputed land.

Attacking critics who dubbed him insincere, Shana Alexander wrote in a Newsweek *column, "No American I can think of has taken his own initiative to reduce injustice in this world more often, and been knocked down for it more often, than Marlon Brando."*

His relationships with mostly foreign women have been mysterious and often stormy. He has been legally married and divorced twice: in 1957, to British actress Anna Kashfi, who had claimed to be of East Indian origin, and in 1960, to Mexican actress Movita. He had a child with each woman and, for a dozen years, he publicly battled through the courts with his first wife for custody of their son. In Tahiti for "Mutiny on the Bounty" in 1960, he met his co-star, Tarita, with whom he now has two children.

While in Tahiti, he discovered Tetiaroa, an atoll of 13 islands 40 miles north. When it came up for sale, he purchased it and he goes there as often as he can, usually about four months of each year. To find out more about this complex and intriguing man, who has refused until now to sit for any lengthy interview, PLAYBOY *sent free-lancer Lawrence Grobel (who also interviewed Barbra Streisand and Dolly Parton for us) to Tahiti at Brando's invitation. Grobel reports:*

"When I got this assignment—17 months ago—I was told that Brando was ready to talk and I should prepare for the interview immediately. Having waited nearly a year to see Barbra Streisand, I should have known better. One had only to do a little research to see that the man disliked talking about acting almost as much as he loathed discussing his private life.

"By October 1977, I was ready to see him, but he was far from ready to see me. Phone conversations with his secretary Alice Marchak, who has been with Brando for 23 years, indicated that she was as much in the dark about when we'd get together as I was. Then one day while I was talking with Alice, Brando picked up the phone. He apologized for the delay, wanted to know how old I was and warned me that the only thing

he was interested in talking about was Indians. I told him for an all-encompassing interview, Indians was not enough.

"After two more postponements, he asked if I'd like to do the interview in Tahiti. Naturally, I agreed and a date was set for April.

"By mid-June, I finally boarded a jet for Papeete. I landed at 4:30 A.M. and was met by Dick Johnson, an American who lives in Tahiti and works as Brando's accountant there. On the following day, I flew to Tetiaroa, where Brando, looking like a ragged version of an East Indian holy man, was waiting as I disembarked. For the next ten days, we ate our meals together, went for walks along the beach, went night sailing, played chess and managed to tape five sessions, lasting anywhere from two to six hours each. It seems only appropriate to begin the interview with a question about Tetiaroa."

PLAYBOY: This island you own is certainly a perfect place to talk—no phones, no unexpected visitors, no interruptions.

BRANDO: It's very elemental here. You have the sky, the sea, trees, the crabs, the fish, the sun . . . the basics. Once, I was the only person here, absolutely alone on this island. I really like being alone. I never run out of things to think about when I'm here.

PLAYBOY: As a kid growing up in Nebraska, did you ever imagine you'd end up as the caretaker of a South Sea island?

BRANDO: I knew that when I was 12. In school, I was flunking four out of five subjects and I'd be sent to study hall, where I'd read back issues of the *National Geographic*. I always felt an affinity toward these islands. Then, in 1960, I came down here and it just sort of confirmed what I'd always known.

PLAYBOY: For most of your career, you've avoided doing any long interviews. Why?

BRANDO: I've regretted most interviews, because they don't write what you say or they'll get you out of context or they'll juxtapose it in such a way that it's not reflective of what you've said. I've read so many interviews with people who are not qualified to give answers to questions asked—questions on economics, archaeological discoveries in Tuscany, the recent virulent form of gonorrhea. . . . I used to answer those questions and then I'd ask myself, What the fuck am I doing? It's absolutely preposterous I should be asked those questions and, equally preposterous, I found myself answering [*laughs*]. I don't know a fucking thing about economics, mathematics or anything else. And then you can say something in a certain spirit, with a smile, but when it appears in print, there's no smile.

PLAYBOY: We can always indicate that with brackets. But when you do make a rare public appearance, as you did with Dick Cavett a few years ago, you don't do much smiling. With Cavett, you stubbornly insisted on spending 90 minutes on one topic, Indians, which seemed to make him very nervous.

BRANDO: Yeah. He kept asking me questions, kept me uncomfortable. Dick was having trouble with his ratings at the time. He's a good interviewer: bright, witty, intelligent, he buzzes things along. But he blew it in my case, because I was intransigent and intractable and would not answer what I thought were silly questions. Which made his show dull.

I had another discouraging experience with the BBC. I went on a show that was something like *Tonight*. I was very nervous. All the host did was ask me questions about *Superman*—how much money I got and stuff like that. He said, "Were you able to get into your costume for *Superman*?" And I would say, "Well, in 1973, Wounded Knee took place." I just didn't want to hold still for any of the crap questions, but I wanted to be courteous at the same time. They edited the thing so I said nothing. I really looked like an idiot.

Then I went downstairs to talk to seven reporters from the London *Times,* from all the papers. I talked for three hours with them about the American Indian. They all ran pictures of me in my *Superman* costume and that's all they wrote about. Then, once in a while, on the back page, "And . . . blah blah blah blah blah the American Indian." I was appalled. I didn't believe the quality of journalism in England was such that they would have to go for the buck that way. It was revolting.

PLAYBOY: But not very surprising. Getting you to talk about Indians isn't much of a journalistic scoop, is it? Not to denigrate what you have to say about that subject, but the fact is, anyone who interviews you would like to get you to talk about other things as well—acting, for example.

BRANDO: Yeah, but what a paltry ambition. I know if you want to schlock it up a little, the chances are the interview is going to be more successful, because people are going to read it; it's going to be a little more provocative and down the line—get your finger under the *real* Marlon Brando, what he really thinks and all that. But I'm not going to lay myself at the feet of the American public and invite them into my soul. My soul is a private place. And I have some resentment of the fact that I live in a system where you have to do that. I find myself making concessions, because normally I wouldn't talk about any of this, it's just blabber. It's not absorbing or meaningful or significant, it doesn't have much to do with our lives. It's dog-food conversation. I think the issue of the Indian is interesting enough so that we don't have to talk about other things. But I have the vague feeling that you know where the essence of a commercial interview lies, and what would make a good commercial story wouldn't necessarily be one that would mention the American Indian at all. To me, it's the only part that matters.

PLAYBOY: But you just mentioned celebrities who talk about things that aren't relevant to their fields of endeavor. Your passion is with the Indians, but your expertise is as an actor.

BRANDO: I guess I have a burning resentment of the fact that when people meet you, they're meeting some asshole celebrity movie actor, instead of a person, someone who has another view, or another life, or is concerned about other things. This *idiot* part of life has to go in the forefront of things as if it's of major importance.

PLAYBOY: But an entire interview dealing with nothing but the problems of Indians would inevitably become boring.

BRANDO: I'd *like* to be able to bore people with the subject of Indians . . . since I'm beginning to think it's true, that everybody *is* bored by those issues. Nobody wants to think about social issues, social justice. And those are the main issues that confront us. That's one of the dilemmas of my life. People don't give a damn. Ask most kids about details about Auschwitz or about how the American Indians were assassinated as a people and they don't know anything about it. They don't *want* to know anything. Most people just want their beer or their soap opera or their lullaby.

PLAYBOY: Be that as it may, you can be sure that people *will* be interested in what you'll undoubtedly be saying about past and present social injustices. But why not also respond to topics that may not be serious but are just plain interesting—such as the fact that, to take a random example, Marilyn Monroe's one ambition was to play Lady Macbeth to your Macbeth?

BRANDO: Look, you're going to be the arbiter of what is important and what you think the particular *salade niçoise* ingredients of this interview ought to be—it's going to have a little shtick, a little charm, a little of Marlon's eccentricities, we're going to lift the lid here and pull the hem of the gown up there, then we're going to talk about Indians. But there are things that you full well know are *important.* Food is one of them, UNICEF is another, human aggression is another, social injustice in our own back yard is another, human injustice anywhere in the world. . . . Those are issues that we have to constantly confront ourselves and others with and deal with. Maybe what I'm going to say about them is meaningless or doesn't have any solutions, but the fact is, if we all start talking about them and look at them, instead of listening to my views on acting, which are totally irrelevant, maybe something can get done.

When I say irrelevant, it's certainly relevant to money. You have to have something as a sort of shill for the reader, so if he gets to page one and he reads about what I think about Marilyn Monroe's thoughts about me, King Lear to her Cordelia or something as absurd as that, or did she have a nice figure and what do you think about women using dumbbells to develop their busts?—I'm exaggerating to make the point—then people are going to read that, and then they may go on a little further and read something about Indians that they didn't know.

PLAYBOY: Well, we're finally coming to some agreement. You're absolutely right. So how do you respond to that little item about Marilyn?

BRANDO: I don't know how to answer the question. [*Mockingly*] "Oh, well, that's nice, my goodness, I didn't know Marilyn cared for me in that respect. . . . Hey, well, she's a remarkable actress, I certainly would have enjoyed—" I can't respond to that. It bores the shit out of me.

PLAYBOY: Can you respond to what happened to her?

BRANDO: No, I don't want to talk about that, that's just prattle, gossip, shitty . . . it's disemboweling a ghost. . . . Marlon Brando's view of Marilyn Monroe's death. That's horrifying. What she said about me and what I'm to say about her can lead to the consequence of nothing.

PLAYBOY: Not necessarily. What if the point of this were to lead to the subject of suicide? You don't know what directions these questions might take.

BRANDO: Now you're giving me your yeshiva bocher, you know what that is? That's two Jews under the Williamsburg Bridge. It's the equivalent of the Christians' arguing about how many angels dance on the head of a pin. I'm not casting aspersions on your efforts. All I'm saying is these are money-oriented questions. Those that have the best return are the most controversial, the most startling, the most arresting. The idea is to get a scintillating view that has not yet been seen by somebody, so that you have something unusual to offer, to sell. I just don't believe in washing my dirty underwear for all to see, and I'm not interested in the confessions of movie stars. Mike Wallace had a program, it was an astounding program, some years ago. He got people to come on and talk about themselves. And in conversation, they'd throw up all over the camera and on him, the desk, in their own laps, and tell us about their problems with B.O. or drinking or their inability to have a proper sexual relation with their pet kangaroo. I was floored. I was fascinated with that program. He was wonderful. He's a damn good investigative reporter. Anyway, what people are willing to do in front of a public is puzzling. I don't understand why they do it. I guess it makes them feel a little less lonely. I always found it distasteful and not something I cared to do. Did you ever read any of Lillian Ross's Hollywood profiles in *The New Yorker*? They were mostly quotes of what celebrities said. They just hung themselves by their own talk.

PLAYBOY: That's what many critics said about you when Truman Capote profiled you in *The New Yorker* during the making of *Sayonara,* 22 years ago. Was that the piece that turned you away from doing interviews?

BRANDO: No. What I was very slow in realizing was that money was the principal motivation in any interview. Not necessarily directly but indirectly. We're money-bound people and everything we do has to do with money, more or less. Our projects and activities have to do with the making of money and the movement of money. I am a commodity sitting here. Our union has to do with money. You're making money, PLAYBOY's making money and, I suppose, in some way, I'm making money. If money were not involved, you wouldn't be sitting here asking me questions, because you wouldn't be getting paid for it. I wouldn't be answering the questions if there weren't some monetary consideration involved. Not that I'm getting it directly, but I'm paying a debt, so to speak. When Hugh Hefner paid the bail for Russell Means [leader of the American Indian Movement] a couple of years ago, I was grateful. But people look for the money questions, the money answers, and they wait for a little flex of gelt in the conversation. You can tell when you're talking, they get very attentive on certain subjects.

PLAYBOY: Why don't we just proceed? You *know* people are interested in you for more complicated reasons than those.

BRANDO: No, they're not. You know you wouldn't interview out-of-work movie stars. I just happen to be lucky and have had a couple of hits and some controversial pictures lately, but I was down the tubes not long ago. I always made a living, but I wasn't . . . I wasn't . . . sought after. I suppose if I hadn't been successful in a couple of movies that I would have been playing different kinds of parts for different kinds of money, and you wouldn't be sitting here today.

PLAYBOY: No one wanted to interview you when your career took a dive?

BRANDO: You could see it on the faces of the air hostesses; you could see it when you rented a car; you could see it when you walked into a restaurant. If you've made a hit movie, then you get the full 32-teeth display in some places; and if you've sort of faded, they say, "Are you still making movies? I remember that picture, blah blah blah." And so it goes. The point of all this is, people are interested in people who are successful.

PLAYBOY: And in people who will be remembered. Which is why we're talking.

BRANDO: I don't know. I think movie stars are . . . about a decade. Ask young kids now who Humphrey Bogart or Clark Gable was. "Didn't he play for the Yankees?" "No, no, he was a tailback at Cincinnati."

PLAYBOY: So you think the fascination with someone like yourself is fleeting?

BRANDO: There's a tendency for people to mythologize everybody, evil or good. While history is happening, it's being mythologized. There are people who believe that Nixon is innocent, that he's a man of refinement, nobility, firmness of purpose, and he should be reinstated as President, he did no wrong. And there are people who can do no right. Bobby Seale, for some people, is a vicious, pernicious symbol of something that is destructive in our society that should be looked to with great caution and wariness, a man from whom no good can emanate. To other people, he's a poet, an aristocratic spirit.

People believe what they will believe, to a large degree. People will like you who never met you, they think you're absolutely wonderful; and then people also will hate you, for reasons that have nothing to do with any real experience with you. People don't want to lose their enemies. We have favorite enemies, people we love to hate and we hate to love. If they do something good, we don't like it. I found myself doing that with Ronald Reagan. He is anathema to me. If he does something that's reasonable, I find my mind trying to find some way to interpret it so that it's not reasonable, so that somewhere it's jingoist extremism.

Most people want those fantasies of those who are worthy of our hate— we get rid of a lot of anger that way; and of those who are worthy of our idolatry. Whether it's Farrah Fawcett or somebody else, it doesn't make a difference. They're easily replaceable units, pick 'em out like a card file. Johnnie Ray enjoyed that kind of hysterical popularity, celebration, and then suddenly he wasn't there anymore. The Beatles are now nobody in particular. Once they set screaming crowds running after them, they ran in fear of their lives, they had special tunnels for them. They can walk almost anyplace now. Because the fantasy is gone. Elvis Presley—bloated, over the hill, adolescent entertainer, suddenly drawing people into Las Vegas— had nothing to do with excellence, just myth. It's convenient for people to believe that something is wonderful, therefore they're wonderful.

Kafka and Kierkegaard are remarkable souls; they visited distant lands of the psyche that no other writers dared before—to some people, *they* were the heroes, not Elvis Presley.

PLAYBOY: Do you think all people have heroes?

BRANDO: They have to have. Even negative heroes. Richard the Third: "Can I do this and cannot get a crown? Were it further off, I'll pluck it down!" In other words, the fact that life was denied to him, then he would do his best at being bad, he would make a career of being bad. The worst kind of bad you could be: memorably bad, frighteningly bad, powerfully bad. Had he had the opportunity, he might have been powerfully creative, powerfully loving, powerfully noble. He didn't have the opportunity, because he was twisted and deformed and embittered by that experience. It's wonderfully stated, Shakespeare: "Now is the winter of our discontent/ Made glorious summer by this sun of York." People's energies—whether negative or positive—are here to be used and they will apply, somehow.

PLAYBOY: Bringing this back to you and your own energies, you once said that for most of your career, you were trying to figure out what you'd really like to do.

BRANDO: "You once said." There ought to be a handbook for interviewers and one of the don'ts should be: Don't say, "You once said," because 98.4 percent of the time, what you were quoted as having said once isn't true. The fact is, I *did* say that. For a long time, I had no idea really what it was that I wanted to do.

PLAYBOY: And you didn't feel that acting was worthwhile or fulfilling enough?

BRANDO: There's a big bugaboo about acting; it doesn't make sense to me. *Everybody* is an actor; you spend your whole day acting. Everybody has suffered through moments where you're thinking one thing and feeling one thing and not showing it. That's acting. Shaw said that thinking was the greatest of all human endeavors, but I would say that feeling was. Allowing yourself to feel things, to feel love or wrath, hatred, rage. . . . It's very difficult for people to have an extended confrontation with themselves. You're hiding what you're thinking, what you're feeling, you don't want to upset somebody or you *do* want to upset somebody; you don't want to show that you hate them; your pride would be injured if they knew you'd been affected by what they said about you. Or you hide a picayune aspect of yourself, the prideful or envious or vulnerable, and you pretend that everything's all right. "Hi, how are you?" People look at your face and it's presentable: "And I shall prepare a face to meet the faces that I meet."

So we all act. The only difference between an actor professionally and an actor in life is the professional knows a little bit more about it—some of them, anyway—and he gets paid for it. But actually, people in real life get paid for acting, too. You have a secretary who has a lot of sex appeal and a great deal of charm and she knows it, she's going to get paid for that, whether she delivers sexual favors or not. A very personable, attractive young man, who reflects what the boss says, is smart enough to know what the boss feels and likes and wants and he knows how to curry favor . . . he's acting. He goes in in the morning and he gives him a lot of chatter, tells him the right kind of jokes and it makes the boss feel good. One day the boss says, "Listen, Jim, why don't you go to Duluth and take over the department there? I think you'd do a bang-up job." And then Jim digs his toe under the rug and says, "Oh, gosh, I never thought, J.B. . . . Gee, I don't know what to say. . . . Sure, I'll go. When?" And he jumps into the plane and checks off what he's been trying to do for four years—get J.B. to give him the Duluth office. Well, that guy's acting for a living, singing for his supper, and he's getting paid for it.

The same thing is true in governmental promotion or of a member of a Presidential advisory committee, if he's playing the power game—'cause a lot of people don't want to get paid in money, they want to get paid in something else, paid in affection or esteem. Or in hard currency.

PLAYBOY: But there does seem to be a difference between the professional actor, who does what he does consciously, and the subconscious behavior of the nonprofessional.

BRANDO: Well, the idiot tome on acting was written by Dale Carnegie, called *How to Win Friends and Influence People.* It's a book on hustling. Acting is just hustling. Some people are hustling money, some power.

Those in Government during the Vietnam war were trying to hustle the

President all the time so their opinion would be taken over that of others and their recommended course of action would be implemented. That play was running constantly. I can't distinguish between one acting profession and another. They're all acting professions.

PLAYBOY: What about acting as an art form?

BRANDO: In your heart of hearts, you know perfectly well that movie stars aren't artists.

PLAYBOY: But there are times when you can capture moments in a film or a play that are memorable, that have meaning—

BRANDO: A prostitute can capture a moment! A prostitute can give you all kinds of wonderful excitement and inspiration and make you think that nirvana has arrived on the two-o'clock plane, and it ain't necessarily so.

PLAYBOY: Do you consider *any* people in your profession artists?

BRANDO: No.

PLAYBOY: None at all?

BRANDO: Not one.

PLAYBOY: Duse? Bernhardt? Olivier?

BRANDO: Shakespeare said . . . Poor guy, he gets hauled out of the closet every few minutes, but since there're so few people around, you always have to haul somebody out of the closet and say, "So-and-so said." That's like saying, "You once said." [*Laughs*] But we *know* what he said. "There's no art to find the mind's construction in the face." Which very plainly means that being able to discover the subtle qualities of the human mind by the expression of the face is an art, and there should be such an art. I don't think he meant it seriously, that it should be established among the seven lively arts, to become the eighth: the reading of physiognomy. But you can call anything art. You can call a short-order cook an artist, because he really does that—back flips, over and under his legs, around his head, caroms 'em off the wall and catches them. I don't know that you can exclude those things as art, except you know in your bones that they have nothing to do with art.

PLAYBOY: So you have never considered yourself an artist?

BRANDO: No, never, never. No. Kenneth Clark narrated a television program called *Civilization*. It was a remarkable series. It was erudite, communicative, polished, interesting to listen to. There was a man who knew who the artists of the world were. He didn't talk about any paltry people that you and I might mention. He doesn't know those people. He talked about *great* art. He certainly didn't refer to the art of film.

PLAYBOY: But film is reflective of our art and culture. Clark's *Civilization* covered a broad spectrum of history. Maybe in 50 or 100 years, the next Kenneth Clark will include the art of film.

BRANDO: Why don't you do an interview with Kenneth Clark and tell him that I want to know [*laughs*] if he considers Marlon Brando an artist?

PLAYBOY: Assume he would say yes.

BRANDO: If Kenneth Clark said that I was an artist, I would immediately get him to a neurosurgeon.

PLAYBOY: Now you're ignoring the authority you've cited. If actors can't be artists, could films be works of art? Would you consider *Citizen Kane* a work of art?

BRANDO: I don't think any movie is a work of art. I simply do not.

PLAYBOY: Would you go as far as saying that a collaborative effort can't be a work of art?

BRANDO: Well, the cathedral in Rouens or Chartres was a collective work, brought about over perhaps 100 years, where each generation did something. But there was an original plan. Michelangelo's Saint Peter was created by him, but thousands of people were involved in it. Bernini or Michelangelo would conceive a piece of sculpture and then have their students, artisans, knock the big chunks out.

PLAYBOY: Who is the artist in such cases?

BRANDO: The person who conceives it, and also executes it.

PLAYBOY: In *A Streetcar Named Desire* and *Hamlet,* Williams and Shakespeare are artists, right?

BRANDO: Yeah.

PLAYBOY: So couldn't there be artists who interpreted those works?

BRANDO: Sure. Heifetz certainly is an artist, for God's sake. He is a particular kind of artist; he's not a creative artist, he's an interpretive artist.

PLAYBOY: Can singers be artists?

BRANDO: [*Long pause*] No.

PLAYBOY: Lyricists? Cole Porter, Harold Arlen?

BRANDO: Shakespeare's a lyricist, he wrote many songs. Yeah, I suppose any creative writing. But you get so far down on the scale. You're not going to call The Rolling Stones artists. I heard somebody compare them—or The Beatles—to Bach. It was claimed they had created something as memorable and as important as Bach, Haydn, Mozart and Schubert. I *hate* rock 'n' roll. It's ugly. I liked it when the blacks had it in 1927.

PLAYBOY: When it was called jazz?

BRANDO: No, it was called *rock 'n' roll.*

PLAYBOY: We thought Alan Freed coined the term in the Fifties.

BRANDO: That's not a new phrase. Rock 'n' roll is as old as the beard of Moses.

PLAYBOY: What about someone like Bob Dylan, who both writes and performs his own work?

BRANDO: There are people who aspire to being artists, but I don't think they're worthy of the calling. I don't know of any movie actors, or any actors. . . . There are *no* people. . . . We can call them artists, give them the generic term if they're comfortable with that, but in terms of great art—magnificent art, art that changes history, art that's overwhelming—where are they? Where are the great artists today? Name one. When you look at Rembrandt or Baudelaire or listen to the *Discourses* of Epictetus, you know the quality of men is not the same. There are no giants today. Mao Tse-tung was the last giant.

PLAYBOY: If we limit the discussion to the world of film, there are plenty of actors today who bow to you as a giant. You may be repelled by that, but people such as Al Pacino, Barbra Streisand, Pauline Kael, Elia Kazan have given you that label.

BRANDO: I don't understand what relevance that has. Chubby Checker was the giant among twisters. I don't know what that illustrates. When you talked earlier about film being reflective of art and culture, the question went *flaming* through my mind: What culture? There's no culture in this country. The last great artist died maybe 100 years ago. In *any* field. "And we petty men peep about between his legs to find ourselves dishonorable graves."

PLAYBOY: Shakespeare?

BRANDO: Shakespeare. So we've somehow substituted craft for art and cleverness for craft. It's revolting! It's *disgusting* that people talk about art and they haven't got the right to use the word. It doesn't belong on anybody's tongue in this century. There are no artists. We are businessmen. We're merchants. There is no art. Picasso was the last one I would call an artist.

PLAYBOY: Picasso, you know, was also a very commercial property. If he signed a check for less than $75, it would be worth more if you sold the signature than if you cashed the check.

BRANDO: I think that's a wonderful joke. It's enormously clever. That he could draw the outlines of an outhouse and give it to somebody and it's worth $20,000. 'Cause it's making a commentary on the obscenity of our standards. He knew it was absolute trash, horseshit, but it's just like a Gucci label. Yeah, it's just a label, a Picasso label.

PLAYBOY: Well, the Brando label is also highly valued. Are you astounded by the money you get for a film?

BRANDO: I don't know how we *segued* into that.

PLAYBOY: A lot of artists, like Picasso, who received large sums of money also considered themselves worthy.

BRANDO: Are you making an association of worthiness with money? These are hustling questions. It's a disposition to get Brando to talk about these issues. You can always feel when something in the conversation is fertile and it's got a dollar sign on it.

PLAYBOY: What we're getting at is that the L.A. County Museum, for one, considers you enough of an artist to have recently sponsored a Marlon Brando Film Festival.

BRANDO: Oh, gee, I missed that. Shucks.

PLAYBOY: There aren't many film festivals of contemporary actors in museums. Isn't that at least . . . kind of nice?

BRANDO: Kind of nice, I guess that covers it. Better than a poke in the eye with a stick. How come you have to know about acting all the time? What else ya got?

PLAYBOY: All right. We'll work politics into our next question: Didn't the Italian-American Civil Rights Organization say that you defamed their community with your role as Don Corleone in *The Godfather*?

BRANDO: I don't know. If they said that about me, then they must have felt that was true.

PLAYBOY: Is it true that you vetoed Burt Reynolds for James Caan's part in *The Godfather*?

BRANDO: Francis would never hire Burt Reynolds.

PLAYBOY: But do you have that kind of control over who acts with you?

BRANDO: Well, you have to have rapport.

PLAYBOY: Have you been accused of ethnic slurs when you've played other nationalities in your films?

BRANDO: No. I played an Irishman who was a freak psychopath [*The Nightcomers*] and I didn't get any letters from any Irish-American organizations. It would have been difficult to make *The Godfather* with an eighth Chinese, a quarter Russian, a quarter Irish and an eighth Hispanic. Very difficult to take those people to Sicily and call them O'Houlihan.

PLAYBOY: Did you receive $100,000 from Paramount to talk to the press after making *The Godfather*?

BRANDO: I can't remember. When I hear something like that, I always remind myself of the Congressman with his hand in the till.

PLAYBOY: Another lapse of memory associated with you is your inability or your refusal to memorize lines. Do you have a bad memory or is it that you feel remembering lines affects the spontaneity of your performance?

BRANDO: If you know what you're going to say, if you watch people's faces when they're talking, they don't know what kind of expressions they're going to have. You can see people search for words, for ideas, reaching for a concept, a feeling, whatever. If the words are there in the actor's mind . . . *Oh, you got me!* [*Laughing*] *You got me right in the bush*. I'm talking about acting, aren't I?

Actually, it saves you an awful lot of time, because not learning lines . . . it's wonderful to do that.

PLAYBOY: Wonderful not to learn lines?

BRANDO: Yeah, you save all that time not learning the lines. You can't tell the difference. And it improves the spontaneity, because you really don't know. You have an idea of it and you're saying it and you can't remember what the hell it is you want to say. I think it's an aid. Except, of course, Shakespeare. I can quote you two hours of speeches of Shakespeare. Some things you can ad-lib, some things you have to commit to memory, like Shakespeare, Tennessee Williams—where the language has value. You can't ad-lib Tennessee Williams.

PLAYBOY: But how does it affect an actor who is working with you if he's got your lines written out on his forehead or wherever?

BRANDO: It doesn't make any difference. They're not going to see the signs. [*Names a book title.*] I just saw a title on the bookshelf. You didn't see me looking for it, you didn't know that I was even doing that. I can do the same thing if I have . . . Well, anyway, it's more spontaneous.

PLAYBOY: So it is true that you no longer memorize lines when you act. But you did during the early stages of your career, when you were doing Williams and Shakespeare.

BRANDO: That's quite a different thing, because you cannot . . . Well, you're getting me. [*Laughs*]

PLAYBOY: But not nearly enough. You can be very interesting when you talk about your profession, but you have an almost psychological reluctance to divulge experiential information that comes naturally to you. Why?

BRANDO: Some politicians will play full ball; that means they'd do anything to get their point across. Some people draw the line at various places.

PLAYBOY: It's interesting that you so easily interchange the words politician and actor. You obviously won't play full ball in an interview, but can't you go at least a few innings? A lot of readers will feel cheated if you simply refuse to discuss the roles you've played as well as your personal background.

BRANDO: That's an odd word to use.

PLAYBOY: Because we're playing, circling. When you said before, "You got me!" we thought you were quoting a line. It's like the minute you click on the word acting, you stop talking about it.

BRANDO: Because I know that your antenna's up.

PLAYBOY: All right, let us ask you about *Superman,* which is opening the same month this interview appears.

BRANDO: I don't want to talk about it.

PLAYBOY: Is there anything at all you can say about it?

BRANDO: I don't want to talk about *Superman.* That's not relevant.

PLAYBOY: For a man who likes to talk, it's a pity that you brake yourself.

BRANDO: I'm fascinated with everything. I'll talk for seven hours about splinters. What kind of splinters, how you get them out, what's the best technique, why you can get an infection. I'm interested in any fucking thing.

PLAYBOY: But will you talk for seven hours about your career?

BRANDO: Of course not. Not two seconds about it.

PLAYBOY: But you have, on occasion, talked with reporters about acting.

BRANDO: I was in error. I made a lot of errors and I don't want to repeat the errors. If we repeat our errors, then it makes this seem forlorn. There's nothing sadder or more depressing than to see yourself in a series of similar errors.

PLAYBOY: Why do you insist on putting down acting?

BRANDO: I don't put it down. But I resent people putting it up.

PLAYBOY: Where would you put acting, then?

BRANDO: It's a way of making a living. A very good way.

PLAYBOY: Do you *like* acting?

BRANDO: Listen, where can you get paid enough money to buy an island and sit on your ass and talk to you the way I'm doing? You can't *do* anything that's going to pay you money to do that.

PLAYBOY: You do take acting seriously, then?

BRANDO: Yeah; if you aren't good at what you do, you don't eat, you don't have the wherewithal to have liberties. I'm sitting down here on this island, enjoying my family, and I'm here primarily because I was able to make a living so I could afford it. I hate the idea of going nine to five. That would scare me.

PLAYBOY: Is that what bothered you about acting in the theater?

BRANDO: It's hard. You have to show up every day. People who go to the theater will perceive the same thing a different way. You have to be able to *give* something back in order to get something from it. I can give you a perfect example. A movie that I was in, called *On the Waterfront*; there was a scene in a taxicab, where I turn to my brother, who's come to turn me over to the gangsters, and I lament to him that he never looked after me, he never gave me a chance, that I could have been a contender, I coulda been somebody, instead of a bum. . . . "You should of looked out after me, Charley." It was very moving. And people often spoke about that, "Oh, my God, what a wonderful scene, Marlon, blah blah blah blah blah." It wasn't wonderful at all. The situation was wonderful. *Everybody* feels like he could have been a contender, he could have been somebody, everybody feels as though he's partly bum, some part of him. He is not fulfilled and he could have done better, he could have been better. Everybody feels a sense of loss about something. So *that* was what touched people. It wasn't the scene itself. There are other scenes where you'll find actors being expert, but since the audience can't clearly identify with them, they just pass unnoticed. Wonderful scenes never get mentioned, only those scenes that affect people.

PLAYBOY: Can you give an example?

BRANDO: Judy Garland singing *Over the Rainbow*. "Somewhere over the rainbow bluebirds fly, birds fly over the rainbow, why, oh, why can't I?" Insipid. But you have people just choking up when they hear her singing it. Everybody's got an over-the-rainbow story, everybody wants to get out from under and wants . . . [*laughing*] . . . wants bluebirds flying around. And that's why it's so touching.

PLAYBOY: Had another person sung that song, it might not have had the same effect. Similarly, if someone else had played that particular *Waterfront* scene with Rod Steiger—a scene considered by some critics among the great moments in the history of film—it could have passed unnoticed.

BRANDO: Yeah, but there are some scenes, some parts that are actor-proof. If you don't get in the way of a part, it plays by itself. And there are other parts you work like a Turk in to be effective.

PLAYBOY: Did you know that *Waterfront* scene was actor-proof when you were doing it?

BRANDO: No, at the time, I didn't know.

PLAYBOY: Was it a well-rehearsed scene or did Kazan just put the two of you there to act spontaneously?

BRANDO: We improvised a lot. Kazan is the best actor's director you could ever want, because he was an actor himself, but a special kind of actor. He understands things that other directors do not. He also inspired me. Most actors are expected to come with their parts in their pockets and their emotions spring-loaded; when the director says, "OK, hit it," they go into a time slip. But Kazan brought a lot of things to the actor and he invited you to argue with him. He's one of the few directors creative and understanding enough to know where the actor's trying to go. He'd let you play a scene almost any way you'd want.

As it was written, you had this guy pulling a gun on his brother. I said, "That's not believable; I don't believe one brother would shoot the other." The script never prepared you for it, it just wasn't believable; it was incredible. So I did it as if he *couldn't* believe it, and that was incorporated into the scene.

PLAYBOY: Many actors cite your performance in *Reflections in a Golden Eye* as an example of superb improvisational acting. Did any of that have to do with the direction of John Huston?

BRANDO: No. He leaves you alone.

PLAYBOY: What about Bernardo Bertolucci's direction of *Last Tango in Paris*? Did you feel it was a "violation," as you once said?

BRANDO: Did I say that once? To whom? [*Laughing*] "As you once said."

PLAYBOY: What you said was that no actor should be asked to give that much.

BRANDO: Who told you that?

PLAYBOY: I read it.

BRANDO: I don't know *what* that film's about. So much of it was improvised. He wanted to do this, to do that. I'd seen his other movie, *The Conformist,* and I thought he was a man of special talent. And he thought of all kinds of improvisations. He let me do anything. He told me the general area of what he wanted and I tried to produce the words or the action.

PLAYBOY: Do you know what it's about now?

BRANDO: Yeah, I think it's all about Bernardo Bertolucci's psychoanalysis. And of his not being able to achieve . . . I don't know, I'm being facetious. I think he was confused about it; *he* didn't know what it was about, either. He's very sensitive, but he's a little taken with success. He likes being in the front, on the cover. He enjoys that. He loves giving interviews, loves making audacious statements. He's one of the few really talented people around.

PLAYBOY: Pauline Kael made some pretty audacious statements when she reviewed *Last Tango,* saying it had altered the face of an art form. Did such critical reaction to the film surprise you?

BRANDO: An audience will not take something from a film or a book or from poetry if it does not give something to it. People talk about great writers, great painters, great thinkers, great creators, but you cannot fully understand what a great writer is writing about unless you have some corresponding depth, breadth of assimilation. To some people, Bob Dylan is a literary genius, as great as Dylan Thomas was. And Pauline Kael, unconsciously, gave much more to the film than was there. You learn an awful lot about reviewers by their reviews—a good reviewer, that is. From bad reviewers, you can't learn anything, they're just dummies. But Pauline Kael writes with passion, it's an important experience to her. No matter what they like or dislike, talented reviewers reveal themselves, like any artist.

PLAYBOY: For a moment there, we thought you said *artist*. Are there any directors you'd like to work with, such as Bergman, Fellini, Truffaut?

BRANDO: No.

PLAYBOY: What happens when you improvise and the actor you're working with wants to stick to the script?

BRANDO: If an actor can't improvise, then perhaps the producer's wife cast him in that part. You wouldn't be in the film with such a person. Some actors don't like it. Olivier doesn't like to improvise; everything is structured and his roles are all according to an almost architectural plan.

PLAYBOY: Critics often lean toward either you or Olivier as the greatest living actor. Since Olivier's done the classics, do you think that gives him the edge?

BRANDO: That's speculation. Speculation's a waste of time. I don't care what people think.

PLAYBOY: Do you care, though, when people say you don't always give 100 percent when you act?

BRANDO: Stella Adler, who was my teacher, a most remarkable woman, once told me a story about her father, Jacob P. Adler, a great Yiddish actor who brought the European tradition of theater to this country with him. He had said that if you come to the theater and you feel 100 percent inspiration, show 70. If you come to the theater another night and you feel maybe 50 percent, show 30. If you come to the theater feeling 30 percent, turn around and go home. Always show less than you have.

PLAYBOY: Have you ever just walked through a part?

BRANDO: Certainly. Yeah.

PLAYBOY: Often?

BRANDO: No.

PLAYBOY: What about *A Countess from Hong Kong,* directed by Charles Chaplin?

BRANDO: No, I *tried* on that, but I was a puppet, a marionette in that. I wasn't there to be anything else, because Chaplin was a man of sizable talent and I was not going to argue with him about what's funny and not funny. I must say we didn't start off very well. I went to London for the reading of the script and Chaplin read for us. I had jet lag and I went right to sleep during his reading. That was terrible. [*Laughs*] Sometimes sleep is more important than anything else. I was miscast in that. He shouldn't have tried to direct it. He was a mean man, Chaplin. Sadistic. I saw him torture his son.

PLAYBOY: In what way?

BRANDO: Humiliating him, insulting him, making him feel ridiculous, incompetent. He [Sydney Chaplin] played a small part in the movie and the things Chaplin would say to him . . . I said, "Why do you take that?" His hands were sweating. He said, "Well, the old man is old and nervous, it's all right." That's no excuse. Chaplin reminded me of what Churchill said about the Germans, either at your feet or at your throat.

PLAYBOY: Was he that way with you?

BRANDO: He tried to do some shit with me. I said, "Don't you *ever* speak to me in that tone of voice." God, he really made me mad. I was late one day, he started to make a big to-do about it. I told him he could take his film and stick it up his ass, frame by frame. That was after I realized it was a complete fiasco. He wasn't a man who could direct anybody. He probably could when he was young. With Chaplin's talent, you had to give him the benefit of the doubt. But you always have to separate the man from his talent. A remarkable talent but a monster of a man. I don't even like to think about it.

PLAYBOY: What about when you direct yourself, as you did in *One-Eyed Jacks*? That was a first and last experience for you; did it cure your desire to direct?

BRANDO: I didn't desire to direct that picture. Stanley Kubrick quit just before we were supposed to shoot and I owed $300,000 already on the picture, having paid Karl Malden from the time he started his contract and we weren't through writing the picture. Stanley, Calder Willingham and myself were at my house playing chess, throwing darts, playing poker. We never got around to getting it ready. Then, just before we were to start, Stanley said, "Marlon, I don't know what the picture's about." I said, "I'll tell you what it's about. It's about $300,000 that I've already paid Karl Malden." He said, "Well, if that's what it's about, I'm in the wrong picture." So that was the end of it. I ran around, asked Sidney Lumet, Gadge

[Kazan] and, I don't know, four or five people; nobody wanted to direct it. [*Laughs*] There wasn't anything for me to do except to direct it or go to the poorhouse. So I did.

PLAYBOY: Was it a new experience for you?

BRANDO: No, you direct yourself in most films, anyway.

PLAYBOY: Didn't the studio take the film away from you, finally?

BRANDO: I kept fiddling around and fiddling around with it, stalling, so they went and cut the film. Movies are made in the cutting room.

PLAYBOY: Looking back at your body of work, are there any of your films that you aren't at all happy with, that you would like to erase if you could?

BRANDO: No.

PLAYBOY: Would you change many of them if you had a chance to re-edit them now?

BRANDO: No, I wouldn't want to do that. Good God, one of the most awful places in the world to be is in the cutting room. You sit all day long in a dark place filled with cigarette smoke.

PLAYBOY: Do you always see the final results of what you do?

BRANDO: Sometimes you see it in the dubbing room. I've been in the screening room sometimes. Some films I haven't seen. You're bound to run into them on television someplace. One film I liked a lot—the only time I ever *really* enjoyed myself—it was called *Bedtime Story,* with David Niven. God, he made me laugh so hard. We got the giggles like two girls at a boarding school. He finally had to ask me to go to my trailer, I couldn't stop laughing. [*Laughing*] We both thought it was such a funny script, a funny story.

PLAYBOY: Would you have liked to do more comedy?

BRANDO: No, I can't do comedy.

PLAYBOY: Are there any recent films that have made you laugh?

BRANDO: I haven't gone to that many movies. I liked *High Anxiety*. Mel Brooks makes me laugh. They had a Laurel and Hardy festival on television; boy, I laughed at that. It went on all night long; I was up half the night laughing.

PLAYBOY: Was it anything special Laurel and Hardy did that cracked you up?

BRANDO: I suppose Hardy's exasperation with Laurel and doing dead takes into the camera and shaking his head. Exasperatedly patient. [*Laughing*] That's ridiculous.

PLAYBOY: What about Marx Brothers films?

BRANDO: No. When I was young, they were funny, but I look at them now and it's embarrassing.

PLAYBOY: Have you ever seen Lily Tomlin?

BRANDO: Yeah. Good God, is she angry. Whew! She gives me the impression of somebody incandescent with rage that comes out in this crinkle-eyed smiling face. Acid. She's funny, but all of her humor comes from anguish, rage and pain. Don Rickles, too. Most humor does.

PLAYBOY: Even Bob Hope's?

BRANDO: Bob Hope will go to the opening of a phone booth in a gas station in Anaheim, provided they have a camera and three people there. He'll go to the opening of a market and receive an award. Get an award from Thom McAn for wearing their shoes. It's pathetic. It's a bottomless pit. A barrel that has no floor. He must be a man who has an ever-crumbling estimation of himself. He's constantly filling himself up. He's like a junkie—an applause junkie, like Sammy Davis, Jr. Sammy desperately longs to be loved, approved of. He's very talented. What happens to those people when they can't get up and do their shtick, God only knows. Bob Hope, Christ, instead of growing old gracefully or doing something with his money, be helpful, all he does is he has an anniversary with the President looking on. It's sad. He gets on an airplane every two minutes, always going someplace. It didn't bother him at all to work the Vietnam war. Oh, he took that in his stride. He did his World War Two and Korean War act. "Our boys" and all that. He's a pathetic guy.

PLAYBOY: What about Woody Allen?

BRANDO: I don't know Woody Allen, but I like him very much. I saw *Annie Hall*—enjoyed it enormously. He's an important man. Wally Cox was important. Wally Cox was a lifelong friend of mine. I don't know why I put them together. They're similar to me. Woody Allen can't make any sense out of this world and he really tells wonderful jokes about it. Don't you think it was remarkable that his time came to get his door prize at the Academy Awards and he stayed home and played his clarinet? That was as witty and funny a thing as you could do.

PLAYBOY: Wit certainly wasn't your intention when you had an Indian woman turn down *your* Academy door prize for *The Godfather,* or was it?

BRANDO: No. I think it was important for an American Indian to address the people who sit by and do *nothing* while the Indians are expunged from the earth. It was the first time in history that an American Indian ever spoke to 60,000,000 people. It was a tremendous opportunity and I certainly didn't want to usurp that time. It wasn't appropriate that I should. It belonged much better in the mouth of an Indian. I thought an Indian woman would generate less hostility. But those people considered it an interference with their sanctified ritual of self-congratulations.

PLAYBOY: Do you feel all awards are ridiculous?

BRANDO: Of course they are. They're ridiculous. The optometrists are going to have awards for creating inventive, arresting, admirable, manufactured eyeglass frames—things that hook onto the nose, ones that go way around under the armpit for evening wear. Why shouldn't they? We have newscasters' awards, Globe awards . . . they should have an award for the fastest left-handed standby painter who's painted the sets with his left hand and who has dropped appreciably less paint on the floor while doing it. And then the carpenters' union should have an award for somebody who can take a three-pound hammer and nail two-by-fours together.

PLAYBOY: When you were given the NAACP's Humanitarian Award in 1976, you turned that down.

BRANDO: Yeah, I did. I don't believe in awards of any kind. I don't believe in the Nobel Peace Prize.

PLAYBOY: You did, however, accept the Academy Award in 1955.

BRANDO: I've done a lot of silly things in my day. That was one of them. At the time, I was confused about it and I made a judgment in error. An error in judgment.

PLAYBOY: Do you have a sense of guilt that perhaps—

BRANDO: No, I don't. [*Laughs*] I know some people do, but I've been fortunate in escaping that, I don't know why.

PLAYBOY: Not once in your life did it strike you—

BRANDO: No, and I've been amazed that most people are struck down with that. It hasn't *fazed* me!

PLAYBOY: Would you like to finish the question yourself?

BRANDO: Do I have guilt about . . . [*thinks, long pause, yawns*] . . . no, I cannot. OK, finish it.

PLAYBOY: Do you have any guilt about—

BRANDO: No, I don't. [*Laughing*] I answered that before; why do you keep asking me?

PLAYBOY: Well, you've effectively answered, so let's move on. There's a certain quote having to do with women that has been following you around for some time now.

BRANDO: That's a much better way of saying "You once said." You been rehearsing that?

PLAYBOY: It has to do with your saying, "With women, I've got a long bamboo pole with a leather loop on the end of it. I slip the loop around their necks so that they can't get away or come too close. Like catching snakes." Do you know that quote?

BRANDO: I don't know that quote. That's: When did you stop beating your wife? It's odious. It's unfair. And it's unimaginative to refer to quotes, because you know as well as I do, the press being what it is, it's going to write anything that sounds sensational. To take that as a frame of reference for a potentially volatile question or one that has color in it, it's not proper.

PLAYBOY: Why not think of it as clearing the record, especially if you didn't say it, or if you said it in sarcasm, in jest, and it came out in seriousness?

BRANDO: Who in the world cares? Who would want to dignify that claptrap and crap? We'd be all day doing that. It's a hopeless and useless task. I don't care what people write or what they think. Good Lord, I gave up caring about 20 years ago. Those are mostly conversational scavengers who sit around and wait for some slop to fall off the table. If there isn't any, then they invent some. It's of no consequence at all. Just like all questions about acting.

[*Later, lying on the beach late at night, Brando pointed at the sky.*]

BRANDO: That star next to the moon is always there. I remember I was in Marrakesh on a sparkling, crystalline desert night and I saw the same star. I'd been talking to this girl a long time—it was four in the morning—and the muezzin came out in his minaret and started chanting. It was an enchanted moment. It made me feel like I was in Baghdad in the 12th Century.

PLAYBOY: Was she a Moslem girl?

BRANDO: Nah. Airline hostess.

PLAYBOY: All right, let's stay with women but move away from your personal affairs. Have you had any involvement with the women's movement or with the passage of the E.R.A.?

BRANDO: No.

PLAYBOY: Any feeling about it?

BRANDO: Yeah, it's something that has to pass inevitably and I'm absolutely astounded that the business community has not seen the E.R.A. as an advantage to it, because the intellectual force women can bring to production standards would be very much to its interests. When you consider something like 75 percent of the doctors in Russia are women and 30 percent of the judges in Germany are women, we rank perhaps second only to Switzerland with an antiquated view that women belong in the kitchen doing menial chores.

PLAYBOY: Why do you think certain states won't ratify the amendment?

BRANDO: Why do people hate blacks? Why do people discriminate against Indians? Why is AIM referred to as Assholes in Moccasins in South Dakota rather than the American Indian Movement? People have unconscious fears and floating anxieties, maybe guilt, and they will attach themselves like a raindrop to a speck of matter. People have built-in prejudice, they've got hatred piled up in a very neat place and they don't want to have it scattered by logic.

PLAYBOY: What is it that men hate about women?

BRANDO: I think, essentially, men fear women. It comes from a sense of dependence on women. Because men are brought up by women, they're dependent on them. In all societies, they have organizations that exclude women; warrior societies are famous the world over for that. It comes from fear of women. History is full of references to women and how bad they are, how dangerous. There are deprecating references to women all through the Bible. The mere fact that a woman was made out of a man's rib, as a sort of afterthought. Men's egos are frightened by women. We all have made mistakes in that respect. We've all been guilty, most men, of viewing women through prejudice. I always thought of myself not as a prejudiced person, but I find, as I look over it, that I was.

PLAYBOY: So you *do* feel guilty about your feelings about women in your past?

BRANDO: Not at all. I don't feel the slightest bit of guilt. Guilt's a useless emotion; it doesn't do anybody any good. A healthy sense of conscience is useful.

PLAYBOY: What about gay rights?

BRANDO: The lack of rights that apply to *children* are the ones that appall me. That's head and shoulders above any other rights group. Down here in Tahiti, and in many places, children are treated with respect, like small adults without much of a frame of reference. But for some reason, we feel superior to children, and we also feel a sense of ownership. Mothers feel about their children the way husbands feel about women. It's *my* kid. Women who are in the women's movement, some of them say they are *not* their husband's possession, but then they'll unconsciously refer to their child as a possession. They use the same kind of language about their children as they would hate for their husbands to use about them.

PLAYBOY: A part of your life that's not widely known is your long involvement with UNICEF. How long has it been?

BRANDO: About 20 years.

PLAYBOY: What kind of work do you do for them?

BRANDO: We've put on shows in Paris, London, Japan, the United States, traveled around the world, done promos. This has been the Year of the Child. Mainly, my task has been trying to communicate what UNICEF has done, how much the world needs UNICEF, and what a valuable investment children are, and what an enormous deficit they can be if they're not raised properly. Bring a half-sick child into the world and it costs you a great deal more, because the child will never become independent, the child will constantly be needing attention. You can't bring him up educationally deprived, physically and morally deprived. By the Eighties, there will be some 700,000,000 children without enough to eat, with no jobs and no education. It will hit Southeast Asia first. The most rapidly increasing birth rate is in Mexico. But Bangladesh now has a runaway population growth.

PLAYBOY: Well, we've come this far without really getting into the issue of the Indians as much as you hoped for, so let's begin with—

BRANDO: Let me ask you why you *want* to talk about the Indians.

PLAYBOY: Well, as you know, it's a hell of a lot more interesting than discussing our views on sex or show business or—

BRANDO [*Cracking up, strong laughter. Finally*]: It's funny, I was laughing, seeing the words in the interview, and then your line. [*More laughter*] That's funny. I love those kinds of outrageous retorts.

PLAYBOY: Do Indians have the kind of sense of humor you do?

BRANDO: People never think of Indians' having a sense of humor, but they are the most hilarious people I ever met. They'll laugh at anything. They'll laugh at themselves. They're sarcastic, sardonic, they're funny on every single level. They simply could not have survived without their superb sense of humor.

PLAYBOY: How did you first become conscious of the Indians?

BRANDO: I read a book by D'Arcy McNickle, a Flathead Indian who had a degree in anthropology from the London School of Anthropology or something, and another book by John Collier, who was then head of the Bureau of Indian Affairs. Then I went to see D'Arcy McNickle in Tucson. I discussed with him Indian affairs and history. He recommended that I see a group called the National Indian Youth Council. So I attended many of its meetings and, through that, I became absorbed in American Indian affairs.

PLAYBOY: And through your absorption, what is it that is most shocking to you?

BRANDO: What is shocking to me is that we can consistently try to expunge an entire people from this planet and not have known to the world the silent execution that has taken place over a period of 200 years. And that this Government that we live under—which we all say is wonderful and fall to our knees and worship—has systematically deprived the Indian of life, liberty, the pursuit of happiness and, at the same time, has screamed around the world, like a whistling skank with rabies, that we believe in life, liberty and the pursuit of happiness. How in the world can we do that at the same time that we're strangling the life out of the only native culture that existed on this land? The American Government has shot them, murdered them, starved them, tried to break their spirit, stolen from them, kidnaped their children and reduced them to rubble. That is what shocks and angers me.

I am *ashamed* to be an American and to see fellow human beings who, if human rights mean anything at all, have every right to the land they live on, and more land than they have. There were 10,000,000 Indians, according to the *Encyclopaedia Britannica,* at the time of Columbus. There are now about 1,000,000. They owned all of the United States; they have precious little to call their own now. They were independent; they have nothing now. Any time a white man wanted a piece of land from an Indian, he was able to get it. So they took all the river valleys, they took all the fertile land, they took almost all the forests, they took everything and left the Indian *nothing*. Nothing but memories, and bitter ones at that.

When the Government didn't do it militarily, it did it with documents and promises. We lied, we chiseled, we swindled; swindle, swindle, swindle, nothing less than swindle. Swindled the Indian. And we now will say we did not swindle. We *did* swindle. We *did* kill. We *did* maim. We *did* starve. We *did* torture. We did the most heinous things that could be done to a people. We will not admit it, we do not recognize it, it is not contained in our history books, and I want to pull my hair out when I read high school textbooks that deal with the destruction of a people in two paragraphs.

Our relationship with the American Indian is unprecedented in history. There's no country in the world that has made as many solemn documents, agreements, treaties, statements of intention as the United States has and broken every one of them, and had every intention of breaking them when it made them. No group of people has ever so consistently and cruelly suppressed another group of people as the Americans have the Indians. There were some 400 treaties written—*not one* was kept. That's a terrific record. Not one treaty! It is outrageous, it's shocking and unfair and a *lot* more important than whether or not I like to get up in the morning, put my Equity card in my pocket, go to the studio and put on my make-up and do my tap dance, going through a day of let's pretend. There's something obscene about that.

PLAYBOY: With all that has been done to them, what is it the Indians now want from the Government?

BRANDO: What the Indians want is very plain: They want their own laws to apply in Indian land; they want an increase in the land base that was stolen from them; they want their treaties recognized. They want sovereignty, hunting and fishing rights, no taxation. They want to pursue their lives as they see fit. They want their economy reinstated.

They want nothing more and nothing less than what the Jews have in Israel. We have long, loud and often said people have a right to self-determination, and we stand behind any country in the world that so determines that it is going to be an entity unto itself. We went to Vietnam and killed millions of Vietnamese and thousands of Americans to prove that what we've said was true; we backed it up with force. But we are not willing to offer reinstatement to the American Indian, because there's no future in it. We reinstated the Japanese and the Germans because we wanted to be a presence in Asia and Germany. And a lot of Nazis got back into power so that the organization could be created to resist the Russians. But the American Government just hopes that the Indian will fade away into history and disappear.

PLAYBOY: Do you really think the American Government would willingly carve up American land and give it to the Indians, establishing a separate country within the United States?

BRANDO: Of course; why not? Drive through the Southwest and you're impressed with how little of the country is used. We probably have the fewest people per square mile in the United States than almost anyplace in the world. There's ample room for the Indian to be given back enough land to live on; future populations could be accommodated in that area. There are enough riches in this country so that the Indian could be properly re-established as a viable community. France gave all of its colonies back; for the most part, so have the Dutch, the Belgians, the British. Some of them gave up their colonies screaming, kicking, scratching, fighting; some did it because they read the handwriting on the wall. No Indian has the hope that the Niña, the Santa Maria and the Pinta are going to sail up the Hudson one day and we're all gonna get on them and go back to jails in England. But it's a very reasonable and logical expectation to assume that America is going to do what every other colonial power has done.

PLAYBOY: What do you think was the biggest mistake the Indians made?

BRANDO: If Indians had joined together and made a concerted effort to keep the white man from stealing their land and decimating their people, they could have wiped the people off the face of the earth as soon as they hit Plymouth Rock. But the Indians don't get along with one another. They never thought of themselves as a unified people.

But I'm on the horns of a dilemma, because I am not the spokesman for the American Indian. They have orators, poets, people who are giants, people who are able to talk better than most poets we know who write. Wonderfully articulate people. But they're never asked for an interview in PLAYBOY, they're never asked to go on *60 Minutes*. When there's an occasion, newsmen always stick the microphone in my face. I don't know how many times I've said, "Listen, there are perfectly eloquent gentlemen standing to my left and to my right, please ask them, they are Indians, I am not; they know far better than I do why they're here; don't ask me why I'm here." But their editors say, "Go out and get a recording of the fire coming out of Marlon's nose." It's so distasteful to me that nobody gives a *shit*. I've called up I don't know how many magazines, spoken to writers of international renown, to Senators who head the investigating committees—everybody's out to lunch.

PLAYBOY: Would you say that Indians have been more discriminated against than blacks were before the Civil Rights Act?

BRANDO: It's not an ouch contest.

PLAYBOY: What about missionaries? Have they done any good for the Indians?

BRANDO: The Church has a tremendous debt that it owes to the Indian. The Church was borrowed by the Government as a force to so-call civilize the Indian. It was simply designed to disenfranchise the Indian, which it did. The Church was in control; they sat in a room and they divided Indian reservations up like pies: Catholics here, Protestants here, you take this, we'll take that, go get 'em, boys. And they went in there in force and threw the Bible around with a will.

PLAYBOY: Had you been born an Indian, do you think, knowing what you know, that you'd be militant?

BRANDO: That's like saying if your aunt had balls, she'd be your uncle. I don't know what it's like to be an Indian. I can only imagine. And what I imagine is it's pretty horrible to be an Indian who cares about being an Indian, cares about maintaining himself as an Indian, cares about trying to establish an image of himself in front of his children. I suppose it would make me pretty goddamn mad.

PLAYBOY: Dennis Banks is the Indian activist who was recently granted political asylum in California by Governor Brown. Banks had fled South Dakota, where he faced sentencing on riot and assault convictions, and he was involved in a shooting with the Oregon highway patrol some time ago. His trailer was shot up and when the police traced the ownership, it was found that it belonged to you. Could you have been charged with aiding and abetting a fugitive?

BRANDO: I am not now nor have I ever been a Communist. [*Laughs*] Let me put it this way: I would certainly aid and abet any Indian if he came to me at this time. I had Dennis down here in Tahiti. I invited him to come down, because they were after him.

PLAYBOY: How long did he stay?

BRANDO: About two months.

PLAYBOY: Did the Government know Banks was here?

BRANDO: Yeah. Dennis Banks is a remarkable man, he's a man who's got finely honed instincts; lives by his wits, which are considerable. He's the kind of man young Indians can look to to be inspired by. Russell [Means] is the same.

PLAYBOY: Why didn't the FBI go after you?

BRANDO: The Justice Department didn't see a practical way of indicting me, because it would have inflamed the issues and gotten a lot of coverage. For Russell Means to be thrown in jail is one thing, but for me to be put under indictment for aiding and abetting an American Indian who was forced to go underground due to political pressure—the entire thing was fraught with a very special kind of concern that it did not get too large.

Had the people in Wounded Knee been black or white, they would have had them dead within 20 minutes. You would have seen something that would have made the S.L.A. shoot-out look like a strawberry festival. But they couldn't do it. The only reason they didn't do it was not for any humanitarian reason but because the silhouette of the American Indian around the world is so famous, thanks to Hollywood.

PLAYBOY: When did you come to feel that, second only to the Government, Hollywood has done more harm to the American Indian than any other institution?

BRANDO: I can't give you a date when the light bulb went off in my head. I became increasingly aware just recently of the power of film to influence people. I always enjoyed watching John Wayne, but it never occurred to me until I spoke with Indians how corrosive and damaging and destructive his movies were—most Hollywood movies were.

PLAYBOY: Have you ever discussed this with Wayne?

BRANDO: I saw John Wayne only once. He was at a restaurant. He came over, very pleasant, wished us all a good evening and a happy meal and walked away. First and last time I saw him.

PLAYBOY: In 1971, in his *Playboy Interview*, John Wayne said that he didn't feel we did wrong in taking America away from the Indians. He thought the Indians were "selfishly trying to keep it for themselves" and that what had happened in the past was so far back that he didn't feel we owed them anything. Care to comment?

BRANDO: That doesn't need a reply, it's self-evident. You can't even get mad at it; it's so insane that there's just nothing to say about it. He would be, according to his point of view, someone not disposed to returning any of the colonial possessions in Africa or Asia to their rightful owners. He would be sharing a perspective with Vorster if he were in South Africa. He would be on the side of Ian Smith. He would have shot down Gandhi, called him a rabble rouser. The only freedom fighters he would recognize would be those who were fighting Communists; if they were fighting to get out from under colonial rule, he'd call them terrorists. The Indians today he'd call agitators, terrorists, who knows? If John Wayne ran for President, he would get a great following.

PLAYBOY: Do you think his views are prevalent in Hollywood?

BRANDO: Oh, sure, I think he's been enormously instrumental in perpetuating this view of the Indian as a savage, ferocious, destructive force. He's made us believe things about the Indian that were never true and perpetuated the myth about how wonderful the frontiersmen were and how decent and honorable we all were.

PLAYBOY: Besides Wayne, you've been outspoken about the insensitivity of many of the Jewish heads of studios, who were in power during the heyday of the cowboy-and-Indian pictures. What made you so angry?

BRANDO: I was mad at the Jews in the business because they largely founded the industry. The non-Jewish executives you take for granted are going to exploit *any* race for a buck. But you'd think that the Jews would be so sensitized to that that they wouldn't have done it or allowed it. You've always seen the wily Filipino, the treacherous Chinese, the devilish Jap, the destructive, fierce, savage, blood-lusting, killing buck, and the squaw who loves the American marshal or soldier. You've seen every single race besmirched, but you never saw an image of the kike. Because the Jews were ever watchful for that—and rightly so. They never allowed it to be shown onscreen. The Jews have done so much for the world that, I suppose, you get extra disappointed because they didn't pay attention to that.

PLAYBOY: Has there been any Jewish reaction to what you've said about the Jews in the movie industry?

BRANDO: No. You have to be very careful about that issue, because the blacks are concerned about the blacks, the Indians are concerned about the Indians, the Jews are concerned about the Jews. In the United States, people are trying to look out for their own. The Puerto Ricans are not going to take up the Indian cause. The Indian cause is not going to be concerned about the injustice to the Japanese. Everybody looks to whatever's close at hand.

PLAYBOY: Your anger over Indian rights is well known; but so is your rage against people who impinge on your privacy—the press, photographers. In fact, you've reacted violently, haven't you?

BRANDO: Oh, I've punched photographers out. Any time it has to do with the kids, I just go berserk. I can't stand any kind of invasion of privacy like that. I can't go to Italy anymore, because I'll be in jail. Last time I was there, a bunch of *paparazzi* were out there. I was saying good night to some guests. I had my son in my arms and I was outside and they started taking pictures. I put the kid down and ran after this guy. [*Laughs*] I took a terrific fucking swing at this guy. I couldn't see, they had lights on me, hell. I missed him and fell on my ass. Then I ran in and got a bottle of champagne and came running out the front door looking for anybody I could get hold of. One guy jumped on the hood of a car and then on the sidewalk. I followed him, chased him two fucking blocks. He was more scared than I was mad. I reached out to catch him and he jumped onto this streetcar and took off. I went back, two o'clock in the morning, and there's this tough guy banging on the door. My kids are in there, my wife. So I got a knife and I was just going to have it out with him. Tarita was wrestling and fighting me for the knife. Then I got myself together and realized, What the fuck am I doing? Go out and stab somebody in Italy and it's goodbye, Rachel.

So I called the American Embassy and said, "Let me speak to the Ambassador." They said he was asleep. I said, "I don't care what the fuck he's doing, I didn't ask you that, I told you to get him on the phone!" I was just pissing mad. Poor guy was intimidated. He got the Ambassador out of bed. "Mr. Ambassador," I said, "I'm being intimidated here and I'm not going to stand for much more of this. You're going to have to make some arrangements." I went on and on.

The next morning, two *carabinieri* are out in front of my house in their fucking uniforms. And a photographer was out there, too. I had to go to work and the guy pointed his camera at me and the *carabiniere* put his hand right over the lens. He had no business doing that at all, it's completely against the law. But he did that, pushed the guy into a car, took him down to headquarters, said, "What have you got here, dope in this camera? Heroin? What is this stuff?" Opened the camera. "Oh, film. Sorry." They never bothered me after that.

PLAYBOY: What about Galella?

BRANDO: With Ron Galella, I really had to sit down and talk about that. I broke the guy's jaw. Sure, he was annoying me, but then, if it's so annoying to me, I should be in the lumber business. But the guy *wanted* to get hit. He was looking for some kind of incident like that. This guy was following me all day long. Taking pictures while I was on [Cavett's] show. And afterward, Dick and I went to Chinatown to get something to eat and the fucking guy comes around to take pictures. Finally, I started to get exasperated. I went over to the guy and said, "Would you please just take a few more pictures? You've had enough for today; give us a break." He was drawing crowds around us. So he said, "Well, if you'll give me some decent poses, take off your glasses, maybe I'll think about it." I didn't think. Just the attitude was overbearing. And that was it. He used me. Cost me $40,000. No, it cost me $20,000; the rest was taken off in taxes. The last time I saw him, he was wearing a football helmet with a feather coming out of the top.

PLAYBOY: You're known to have kept friends since childhood. Do any of them talk about you?

BRANDO: None of my friends, if they're my friends, talk.

PLAYBOY: What happens to friends who write books about you?

BRANDO: They're not friends to begin with. Friends don't write books, acquaintances do.

PLAYBOY: Have you ever read any of those books?

BRANDO: No. Life is not about that. Surely, life is about something other than sitting and reading books about yourself.

PLAYBOY: Are there many people in your profession for whom you have a lot of respect?

BRANDO: There are not many people in anybody's *life* that one can have a lot of respect for. No. How many people in your life do you have a lot of respect for?

PLAYBOY: A handful.

BRANDO: A handful? Well, same here.

PLAYBOY: What about Jane Fonda, Robert Redford?

BRANDO: I think Jane Fonda has done something. I could see her doing most anything. Redford's certainly been effective in pursuing his interests.

PLAYBOY: Tony Bennett.

BRANDO: Yeah, Tony Bennett. He's been extremely helpful all the way along. He's a very decent guy, a very kind man. But I've never met a movie actor yet who made me fall to my knees in awe and wonder.

PLAYBOY: Since we've got you talking about one actor, you'll understand it if we *segue* into opinions on other actors. Wasn't there a rivalry between you and Montgomery Clift in the old days?

BRANDO: I think that's beneath me. It's too silly.

PLAYBOY: We had to ask.

BRANDO: I know you had to ask me, but then I had to say it's too silly when you did ask me.

PLAYBOY: Another such rivalry, according to the press, is between you and Frank Sinatra, stemming from the fact that you got the better role—and better songs—in *Guys and Dolls*. Sinatra has apparently called you the most overrated actor in the world.

BRANDO: I don't think that's true. You didn't hear him say that. Vas ya dere, Charley? And you weren't. So, unless he says that to my face, it's not going to have any great significance. And even if he did say it, I don't know if it's going to break my stride.

PLAYBOY: The press does play up rivalries, obviously.

BRANDO: Of course they do. That's how they make their bread and butter. What else are they going to do, write serious stories about people?

PLAYBOY: What magazines do you read?

BRANDO: *Scientific American, Science Digest, The New York Review of Books, The Co Evolution Quarterly.*

PLAYBOY: Serious stuff. Do you ever lighten it with something like the *Reader's Digest,* to keep in touch with the common man?

BRANDO: The *Reader's Digest* is the most popular publication in America, outside of the Bible, as far as I know. It is also the worst piece of trash I've ever seen in my life. I shouldn't say that—maybe they'll do an article about Indians. [*Laughs*] But I think they know it is not *The New York Times Book Review*; it's not *Esquire*; it's not PLAYBOY; it's not *Scientific American.*

PLAYBOY: What about books?

BRANDO: I used to read an awful lot. Then I found that I had a lot of information and very little knowledge. I couldn't learn from reading. I was doing something else by reading, just filling up this hopper full of information, but it was undigested information. I used to think the more intelligence you had, the more knowledge you had, but it's not true. Look at Bill Buckley; he uses his intelligence to further his own prejudices.

Why one reads is important. If it's just for escape, that's all right, it's like taking junk, it's meaningless. It's kind of an insult to yourself. Like modern conversation—it's used to keep people away from one another, because people don't feel assaulted by conversation so much as silence. People have to make conversation in order to fill up this void. Void is terrifying to most people. We can't have a direct confrontation with somebody in silence—because what you're really having is a full and more meaningful confrontation.

PLAYBOY: It's a good thing you didn't express that in the beginning of this interview or it would have been a very short interview, indeed. Before we began taping, you told us of a recurrent nightmare you have about being sick, in the Korean War—

BRANDO: I didn't say the Korean War. I said that it just would be horrible . . . to be someplace in a war where you're freezing and sick, you have diarrhea, no way of getting back . . . it would be awful.

I always wondered why people went off to war, get themselves blown apart. The Korean War, the Vietnam war, why would they do it? Why not say, Christ, I'll go to jail for five years and that will be worth it, but I'm not going to get my head blown off, that's absurd, I'm not going. A lot of them did it. But the number who did not go was not so impressive as the number who went.

PLAYBOY: When you were of draft age, how did you avoid the Army?

BRANDO: I beat the Army by being declared psychoneurotic. They thought I was crazy. When I filled in their forms, under "Race," I wrote, "Human"; under "Color," I wrote, "It varies." Also, I got thrown out of military school, which helped.

PLAYBOY: You must have made your parents proud.

BRANDO: When I was kicked out of military school, my father thought I was a nogoodnik, I wasn't going to amount to anything. When I went into acting, that was the worst thing. When I started making money at it, he couldn't believe the kind of money I was making. It kind of blew his mind. He didn't know how to handle it.

PLAYBOY: How about yourself? How did you respond to the pressure? Did you ever become dependent on drugs or drink?

BRANDO: How individuals or society responds to pressure is the determination of their general state of mental health. There isn't a society in the world that has not invented some artificial means to change their minds, their mood, whether it's cacao or kola nut or alcohol. There are 5,000,000 or 10,000,000 alcoholics in the United States.

But all kinds of drugs have been with man forever and a day. If they're used as a means of escaping from problems, then the problems are only going to increase. Confrontation of problems is the only manner of solution of problems. Problems don't go away. Drugs are not a solution, they're a temporary relief.

PLAYBOY: A lot of people who can afford it go into analysis to get help with their problems, but those who can't often resort to drugs or alcohol.

BRANDO: It would be nice to say that poor people aren't happy, but rich people are snorting cocaine, that's the rich people's drug. When *all* the kids are smoking, dropping acid, taking cocaine, then you have to say there must be something wrong. In the main cities, when you can't walk out in the streets without getting mugged or being in fear of your life, something's wrong. All the rich people do is move farther and farther away from the areas of trouble.

PLAYBOY: Until you finally come to an island?

BRANDO: Until you finally come to an island.

PLAYBOY: Do you think the rich take cocaine as a means of escape or for pleasure, to enhance sexual activity, as a stimulation, whatever?

BRANDO: If it's a pleasure not to be yourself, not to have doubts about yourself, or to have an exaggerated sense of your own importance, then perhaps it is a pleasure. But it's a questionable one, because you're dealing with an unreal world and eventually you're going to have a rendezvous with a brick wall, and you'll have to return to whatever you are.

PLAYBOY: Well, we all know who you are, at least as an actor and an activist, but who would you have liked to be if you could choose any period in history in which to have lived?

BRANDO: I think I would have liked to be a cave man, a neolithic person. It would have been nice to see what the common denominator of human existence was before it started to be fiddled with.

PLAYBOY: Would you have wanted to be an extraordinary cave man?

BRANDO: I would have been Ralph Kramden. Just your average cave dweller.

PLAYBOY: We think we just spotted another *segue*—at least it makes us think of the mumbling cave man you portrayed in *Streetcar*, which made Method acting a household word. Does being labeled a Method actor mean anything to you?

BRANDO: No.

PLAYBOY: Does it bother you?

BRANDO: B-O-R-E. Bore.

PLAYBOY: Is that what a Method actor does—to bore through to the core of a character's being?

BRANDO: It bores through and goes beyond the frontiers of endurable anguish of interviews.

PLAYBOY: Well, this painful interview is almost over.

BRANDO: Oh, listen, it hasn't been painful at all. It's been delightful. Although I feel like I got in a rummage sale: Would you want this dress? No, that *shmatte*. How about this corset? Well, we could take the rubber out and make a slingshot out of it. I'm dizzy. We've gone from the shores of Marrakesh to the halls of William O. Douglas.

PLAYBOY: A couple of final questions: Do you believe in God?

BRANDO: I believe there must be some order in the universe. So far as there is order, there is some force in the universe. It's hard for me to conceive it's just happenstance or a confluence of disorder that makes the universe what it is.

PLAYBOY: And are you optimistic or pessimistic about the future of life on this planet?

BRANDO: You can't live a life saying, Well, this is the end, so we might as well get out the banjo and the rowboat and get it on, just go laughing and scratching along until Gabriel blows his horn. Whatever the circumstances are, one has to keep trying to find solutions. Even if it seems impossible. They have never invented a system that worked: Religion didn't do it, philosophy didn't do it, ethics didn't do it, economic systems won't do it. None of the systems that deal with man's problems have ever worked. But to live a life of hopelessness, it's not possible.

PLAYBOY: Are you afraid of death? Do you think about it?

BRANDO: "Of all the wonders I yet have heard, it seems to me most strange that men should fear; seeing that death, a necessary end, will come when it will come." Another wonderful speech on death.

PLAYBOY: Do you remember more of Shakespeare than of any other author?

BRANDO: He's *worth* remembering. "For God's sake, let us sit upon the ground/And tell sad stories of the death of kings." I can't remember it all. [*Thinks*] "That rounds the mortal temples of a king/Keeps Death his court and there the antic sits,/Scoffing his state, and grinning at his pomp." "And with a little pin/Bores through his castle wall, and farewell, king!"

PLAYBOY: It was announced in the papers that you had consented to play *King Lear* on Broadway and that Elia Kazan would direct. Yes or no?

BRANDO: No.

PLAYBOY: Here's an offbeat question for you: What are things that repulse you?

BRANDO: The most repulsive thing that you could *ever* imagine is the inside of a camel's mouth. It's so awful! That and watching a girl eat small octopus or squid. I mean, I'm not squeamish about anything, I could make an ocarina out of a petrified turd with no problem, but that . . . There's a certain frog that carries its eggs on its back and after they are fertilized, these froglings burst forth from the skin. . . . It just makes me sick. I don't like to look at somebody's sticky saliva. These people who laugh—ha, ha, ha—and there's a stringer of saliva from their upper tooth to the bottom lip and it bends every time they go *ha, ha,* it pulsates. Jesus, with one girl, you could take her saliva and walk across the street with it and lay it down on the sidewalk and still be connected. The viscosity of some people's saliva is remarkable.

PLAYBOY: What else offends you?

BRANDO: Bullfighting. I'd like to be the bull but have my brain. First, I'd get the picador. Then I'd chase the matador. No, I'd walk at him until he was shitting in his pants. Then I'd get a horn right up his ass and parade him around the ring. The Spaniards don't think anything more of picking an animal to pieces than the Tahitians do of cutting up a fish.

PLAYBOY: Which brings up, full circle, back to Tahiti. This island of yours is an unbelievably beautiful setting.

BRANDO: Yeah. I could open this up for tourism and make a million dollars, but why spoil it?

PLAYBOY: Do you find it impossible to leave this place once you're here?

BRANDO: It's very hard. But . . . "miles to go before I sleep, and miles to go before I sleep."

PLAYBOY: Didn't Marilyn Monroe write that?

BRANDO: I think Marilyn did, yeah. It was either her or Fatty Arbuckle, I can't remember.

EDWARD TELLER

August 1979
Interviewer: Gila Berkowitz

If by 1980 the Playboy Interview had become a tradition, and now and then that tradition required that it present unexpected and uncomfortable ideas to its readers, then the recent interview with Edward Teller rings some old bells. At a time when many young and liberal people were agitating against nuclear energy, the editors decided to feature as the interview subject the man who most vividly personified the pro-nuclear point of view. Among the no-nukes crowd, Dr. Teller was spoken of as a reactionary, mad scientist who had learned to love the H-bomb.

Gila Berkowitz, a journalist in Palo Alto, was assigned the interview and spent many weeks persuading the crusty scientist that he should preach to the unconverted. As she reported:

> The initial request was squelched by a growling, Hungarian-accented No! I parried with examples of preeminent men who had been the subjects of the Playboy Interview, men like Jimmy Carter and Jerry Brown. It was the worst possible argument. Edward Teller disdained the offer *because* liberals such as Carter and Brown had been interviewed.
>
> It is a measure of the man that, several weeks later, he changed his mind. Colleagues at the Hoover Institution, Stanford's repository for Nobel laureates, professors emeritus, and right-leaning thinkers, had persuaded him that PLAYBOY was, after all, an appropriate forum for his ideas. One colleague insisted: "More scientists read PLAYBOY than any of the professional journals."

If another tradition of the Playboy Interview is uncanny timing, then this interview lives up to it. Assigned merely as a way of exploring the other side of the nuclear debate, the interview had been agreed to by Teller before the failure at Three Mile Island occurred. Berkowitz was thus able to confront the scientist with a dramatic example, and record his changing attitudes as the news developed.

In October 1959, our very first editorial statement, "The Contaminators," warned against the dangers of radioactivity—in that case, from nuclear-bomb-test fallout. In the intervening years, we have provided a forum, through the "Playboy Interview" and elsewhere in the magazine, for proponents of soft-energy alternatives to nuclear power: environmentalist Barry Commoner, actor/solar-energy crusader Robert Redford, actress/activist Jane Fonda. Now, in the wake of "The China Syndrome," the near catastrophe at Three Mile Island and, in the biggest demonstration since Vietnam, the march of some 65,000 persons on Washington, demanding that nuclear power plants be shut down, it seems an appropriate time to probe the other side of the argument. We have chosen to present an interview with the man who is perhaps nuclear energy's most outspoken advocate, Edward Teller—the so-called father of the H-bomb. An almost Strangelovian figure to his detractors, Teller is a man of archconservative views who is now considering a race for the U.S. Senate.

Teller's twin passions are nuclear energy and nuclear defense. He is convinced that atomic energy is both needed and safe, and he is a leading proponent of new and more potent weapons for the U.S., including the proposed neutron bomb. Because of these stands, he has been castigated by his enemies as a mad scientist playing with dangerous toys.

His supporters, on the other hand, see him as the savior of American economic and military might, as a Cassandra warning the country of impending energy starvation and terrible defeat at the hands of a powerful Russia.

In this post-Vietnam, ecologically sensitive era, Teller's ideas are often unpopular. The pointed manner in which he expresses them causes even greater resentment. Yet his influence on national military and energy policies has been felt through eight administrations, and he retains close ties with many persons in political power. His unquestioned ability as a scientist lends considerable weight to his beliefs. In Washington, Teller is thought of as one of the last of the Cold Warriors, and somewhat eccentric, at that. But even those who oppose him ideologically respect his professional opinions.

Teller, a lawyer's son, was born in 1908 in Hungary. His early aptitude for mathematics and science was encouraged by a first-rate education, culminating in doctoral studies at Leipzig and postdoctoral studies at

Göttingen, Germany. Two notable things happened during his youth. In 1919, Hungary was briefly taken over by a Communist government. That harsh period incubated Teller's severe distaste for the left and his lifelong Russophobia. And while a student in Germany, Teller lost his right foot in an accident.

As World War Two approached, Teller fled to the United States. He was an academic, a purely theoretical physicist—until he was called upon to join in building the first atomic bomb. At Los Alamos, the country's first weapons laboratory, Teller played an important but not central role in the making of the A-bomb. That weapon was based on the principle of fission (splitting an atomic nucleus to release large amounts of energy), but during the war, Teller became intrigued with the idea of a potentially far more powerful explosive, a fusion bomb (in which atomic nuclei are united to form heavier nuclei, releasing huge amounts of energy), and set the theoretical groundwork for it.

After the war, Teller was left with the preliminary plans for his super-atomic weapon. In vain, he sought the support of the Government and of fellow scientists, but Hiroshima had spoiled the appetites of would-be bomb makers. Then, in 1949, the Soviets tested their first nuclear weapon. The West was frightened, the Cold War was on and Teller got the support he wanted. In 1951, the first thermonuclear bomb was tested. It remains the most powerful weapon ever devised.

About the same time, the Russians developed their own version of the hydrogen bomb. The creator of the Soviet weapon was Andrei Sakharov, whose public life is a curious counterpoint to Teller's. The Russian physicist has been the most visible of his country's political dissidents. His outspoken opposition to repressive Soviet policies won him the Nobel Peace Prize. But neither Sakharov nor Teller has won the Nobel for physics; the H-bomb seems too hot to handle, even for the committee that oversees the fortune of the inventor of dynamite.

In 1954, Teller became embroiled in a controversy that changed his life, as well as the nature of the relationship between scientists and the Government in the United States. J. Robert Oppenheimer, a brilliant physicist and a major contributor to the development of the atomic bomb, was denied continued security clearance on the basis of very casual acquaintances with leftists. The hearings on the Oppenheimer case were steeped in the spirit of McCarthyism. Teller was called upon to testify against him, because Oppenheimer had long been opposed to the H-bomb and other Teller projects. Teller denied that the accused was disloyal but testified that he would prefer seeing the reins of power in other hands. In the end, the charges of disloyalty were struck down, but Oppenheimer still lost his security clearance and his career was effectively ended.

The scientific community saw the affair as a vicious attack by political yahoos on a great scientist, with Teller as the hatchet man, a traitor to his

*own kind. Teller and Oppenheimer made personal peace after some years,
but Teller has still not been forgiven by many of his colleagues.*

*Despite those resentments, Teller has been a productive man in his field.
He has always enjoyed support from some politicians and industrialists—
most notably, the late Nelson Rockefeller—which has been vital in achieving his goals. He created the nation's second weapons laboratory, the
Lawrence Livermore in California, and developed numerous ideas for the
peaceful implementation of nuclear power.*

*Although he did not continue to concentrate on theoretical physics,
Teller was not a one-shot scientist. Even his political foes admit that his
intellect is superb; his friend, Nobel laureate Eugene Wigner, has called
Teller's mind the most imaginative one in modern physics—and he was not
forgetting Albert Einstein.*

*Outside of the Pentagon, Teller is America's most outspoken supporter of
increased weapons research. For decades, he has decried what he sees as the
regression of the United States as a world power. That view made him a
popular man in the Fifties, a villain to the youth of the Sixties and a subject
of renewed controversy in the Seventies.* PLAYBOY *sent writer Gila
Berkowitz to interview Teller. She reports:*

*"Teller is 71 years old, and looks it, but he does not look as if the years
have diminished his powers. Of course, the great drooping eyebrows, the
shock of hair are far less forbidding now that they are white. But the biting
wit is consistent; his brittle irony and stinging opinions do not mellow after
hours of interviewing.*

*"And yet, for so vigorous a personality, Teller is also remarkably de-
fensive. He clearly hates being branded a Dr. Strangelove, a reactionary,
even if it is by those for whom he has little respect. His place in the history
books is already sealed, but he cares about what his peers think now. In
the midst of describing his most controversial views, his most unyielding
positions, his face will suddenly melt into a poignant little smile, as if he's
asking for approval.*

*"Teller, of course, can also be imperious, stubborn and abrupt. He
dismisses his opponents with facile one-liners and glosses over the faults of
his favorites, whether they are people or ideas.*

*"By the time we concluded our last session, I regretted having to leave.
To know Edward Teller is not necessarily to be persuaded, but it is certainly
to be spellbound."*

[*This part of the interview was conducted within five days of the nuclear
accident at the Three Mile Island plant near Harrisburg, Pennsylvania.*]
PLAYBOY: What do you make of this catastrophe?

TELLER: I would not call it a catastrophe; I would not call it a disaster; I would not call it an accident. I would call it a malfunction.

If I undertake something really dangerous, such as driving a car, and the car stops and I can't make it work, but no one is hurt, that is called a malfunction. If someone is hurt, that is called an accident. In the Three Mile Island malfunction, no one was hurt.

PLAYBOY: But there is great fear that people will be hurt in the future.

TELLER: I am very confident that no one will be hurt. Should I be invited to visit there, I would do so, and I wouldn't feel like a hero, as I have every confidence that I would be all right.

In the functioning of many reactors, health-damaging accidents have been avoided. There is no exception. It just so happens that the antinuclear movement, lacking a real accident, has latched on to this one, promoting it into something that it isn't.

PLAYBOY: Nevertheless, it is the most serious malfunction—if that's what you want to call it—that has occurred so far.

TELLER: Indeed. I estimate that the financial damage will be even greater than it was in the Browns Ferry malfunction, which cost $120,000,000. My hunch is this will cost even more.

PLAYBOY: For which, of course, the utilities' customers will be paying.

TELLER: If we don't have nuclear reactors, the utilities' customers will be paying much more, because even counting in these costs for shutdowns, nuclear reactors are still cheaper than the next cheapest source of electricity, coal, and much cheaper than oil or gas.

A $500,000,000 loss, while it may hurt the customers in the long run, has an immediate and severe impact on the utility concerned; it will suffer loss, compared with other utilities. Therefore, the utility has the most direct financial interest in seeing that such a malfunction never occurs again. Right now, there are enormous numbers of responsible engineers who are carefully analyzing the questions: What has gone wrong and what other things may still go wrong? When the story is over, we will know how this kind of nuclear plant might malfunction, and therefore, we will know more about how to keep it safe. Utilities will be more careful in seeing that every component is safe, that instruments are employed in the reactor that will appropriately inform the operators, so that wrong judgments can be avoided. They will train operators to avoid mistakes that may have been made here. So, as a net result, we will have bought added safety for our money, without sacrificing human life or human health.

[*This portion of the interview was conducted several weeks after the Three Mile Island accident.*]

PLAYBOY: When we were speaking just after the Three Mile Island incident, you refused to call it a catastrophe or a disaster. You would concede only that it was a malfunction. What do you say now?

TELLER: It was an accident. People have cried wolf so often that when I heard about the catastrophe, I thought it was a false alarm. It turned out that this time it wasn't. The accident was quite a bit more serious than ever before. There's one very important point, however. Absolutely no one was hurt. Now this, of course, is exceedingly important in itself, because of the value of each human life and the health of each individual. But it is also important for another reason. Since no one was hurt, in the long run, I believe it will be possible to discuss this accident in a detached manner with some objectivity and without any exaggerated emotions—emotions that, of course, would be there if people had really suffered.

PLAYBOY: According to the information that you have now, isn't there a possibility that people could have suffered, or might in some future accident?

TELLER: From each accident, we learn how to avoid its repetition. This was an accident that, in a way, I expected. Many years ago, when I was chairman of the first Reactor Safeguard Committee—more than 30 years ago—I came to the conviction that nothing is foolproof. If you believe that it is, it will turn out in the end that the fool is bigger than the proof. The Pennsylvania reactor turned out to be even safer than we expected, but the operators seemed to be less prepared than we hoped.

PLAYBOY: Are you claiming that the problems were mostly of human error?

TELLER: There was, it seems to me, an accumulation of human errors— human errors that are completely understandable, because I don't want to use the word blame. These people worked under stress. The comparison that comes to my mind is that not very long ago, over Flint, Michigan, an airplane lost a wing flap and went into a spin. The pilot took over at once and, thinking very fast and very ingeniously, doing much more than working by the book, managed to bring the airplane under control and saved the plane and the passengers. Now some pilots, I guess, are being paid $100,000 a year. Reactor operators, I have inquired, are being paid $25,000 a year. We are not as careful in selecting and training reactor operators as we are in training pilots. We could, and should, have really excellent people at each plant. These people can be found and more can be educated. This is a situation where mistake after mistake is made simply because it seems the job is too hard for the people presently there. It is very clear that we need more competence and I'm sure we can get it.

PLAYBOY: We pay pilots well and accept the risks of air travel because the advantages are obvious. But are the advantages of nuclear reactors so obvious that we should take the risk of having something so susceptible to human error, in which the possibilities of disaster are so great?

TELLER: First of all, reactors are not so easily susceptible to human error. On Three Mile Island, insult after insult was suffered by the reactor; yet not a single person was hurt. The estimate of the damage now stands at approximately $500,000,000, but no human life was taken. Now, if we didn't have reactors and if we did not build more, what would we have? It has now been proposed, by Jane Fonda and other experts, that all our reactors be shut down. If they were, we would pay six billion dollars per year more for imported oil. The dollar would depreciate further. All of us would be even more dependent on the tender mercies of OPEC. If we continue to build reactors, there's a much greater chance to break the monopoly of OPEC—a monopoly that would never be tolerated in the United States, incidentally.

Now, you may ask, Why not coal? The answer is the health hazards of coal—in coal mines, by accidents, by black-lung disease, by air pollution to the general population—are almost 100 times greater than any accident associated with the reactor. In the operation of the reactors themselves, there have been no health hazards.

PLAYBOY: Secretary of Health, Education and Welfare Joseph Califano would dispute that. He testified in front of a Senate subcommittee that because twice as much radiation was emitted from Three Mile Island as originally estimated, at least one to ten cancer deaths could be expected among the 2,000,000 people living near the power plant.

TELLER: Secretary Califano wasn't speaking about real expectations but about the worst possible case. The procedures for making those estimates are difficult and are not based on direct statistics. The committee of the National Academy of Sciences that came up with the estimate was split when it rendered its opinion, and it may even now be reconsidering the latest estimate. But taking all that into account, remember that out of a population of 2,000,000, some 325,000 cancer cases are expected normally. In the worst possible case, ten people might contract cancer along with the 325,000. So, although even this cannot be verified statistically, Califano's statement will have the effect of making any of those 325,000 people think, Maybe I'm one of the ten. I believe this an improper use of scientific hypothesis and an improper way to inform the public.

PLAYBOY: It nonetheless suggests to us that the nuclear plant poses a greater health hazard than you were willing to admit. And you can't deny that radiation poses a danger to pregnant women and children, can you?

TELLER: Pregnant women, or, rather, their offspring, are in greater danger. Small children are in less danger, old people like myself are in least danger.

Airline hostesses regularly get excess amounts of radiation because cosmic radiation at the 30,000-foot altitude at which jets fly is much greater than it is at sea level. The airlines used to have a policy of grounding hostesses when they got married. The hostesses protested and took the matter to court, and the courts decided that they must be allowed to fly. Nobody bothered to enlighten the hostesses that if they should get pregnant, even in the period before their pregnancy is recognized, the excess radiation might be damaging to their children. They are exposed to amounts larger than those the protesters are protesting about. This kind of double standard makes me feel that the reasons that the protesters are protesting are a little more complex than they appear to be.

PLAYBOY: Governor Jerry Brown asked to shut down the California plant that is a replica of the T.M.I. plant. Don't you think that was a prudent, justified move?

TELLER: I am quite sure it is unjustified.

If Governor Brown succeeds in getting that plant shut down, there will be a need for another 30,000 barrels of oil a day. [*The Rancho Seco nuclear plant in California was shut down on April 28.*] We can't have that unless there is a good reason for it, and from everything I know, there is no such reason. There may be some real or imagined political advantage for Governor Brown, who is exceedingly nimble in jumping on any band wagon, of any description, going at any speed.

PLAYBOY: How did you react when you first heard about the T.M.I. incident? Didn't it strain your confidence in nuclear power plants?

TELLER: I thought: Nobody has been hurt so far, nobody will get hurt, we will learn something. It will cost something, but it's worth it.

But that mass hysteria should have reached this proportion, that it should have remained top news for as long as it has, that is unprecedented. And it is a thoroughly unhealthy sign; it shows that we have lost all sense of balance.

The very thing that makes reactors safe—that we worry in detail about possibilities—gives fuel to the antinuclear propagandists, who have exploited these worries literally to scare people stiff. For example, detailed calculations lead to the probably correct conclusion that in the Pennsylvania reactor there was a gas bubble. Its existence was not proved but, on circumstantial evidence, is highly likely. The newspapers were full of the term time bomb. They said maybe it would go off in two days, maybe three.

It was reasonable to say, "There appears to be a bubble; it might be hydrogen; it conceivably may lead to danger; let's get rid of it in the most cautious manner possible." All those statements are reasonable. That this should feed headlines, should give rise to petitions and marches, is not as reasonable. I wonder: The energy industry lost, say, $500,000,000, but did the newspaper industry make $500,000,000? Was that money siphoned off from the energy industry, which needs the money badly, and given over to the amusement industry, which served the public by amusing it in a somewhat perverse way with horror stories?

PLAYBOY: How do you assess the danger of living near a nuclear plant?

TELLER: According to my daughter, this is a male-chauvinist-pig story, but anyway, it is told that at the hearings about a certain Illinois reactor, Dresden III, one of the protesters, a Dr. T., was confronted by a young man from the Atomic Energy Commission. The man said, "Dr. T., what do you think you get more radiation from, leaning up against an atomic reactor or sleeping with your wife?" Dr. T. didn't know and was confused by the question. So the man from the Atomic Energy Commission said, "I don't want to alarm you, but all human beings have radioactive potassium in their blood—and that includes your wife. This reactor may have *more* radioactivity but much greater shielding. If you compare the two for radiation, you get just a bit more from Dresden III than from your wife."

That's why I do not advocate a law forcing married couples to sleep in twin beds, but from the point of view of radiation safety, I must warn against the practice of sleeping every night with *two* girls, because then you would get more radiation than from Dresden III.

The postscript to this story is that we had a very hard winter, a coal strike, oil barges stuck on the frozen Ohio River. Illinois did not get into trouble, thanks to Dresden III, which was able to supply the energy needs of neighboring states.

PLAYBOY: What about the Government's reaction to the Three Mile Island accident? Has it been to your satisfaction?

TELLER: The Nuclear Regulatory Commission made a great effort, an honest effort and a useful effort—but perhaps not a sufficient one. I think that agency should be strengthened. However, President Carter did one thing that I think—at least I hope—will have a healthy effect. He appointed an 11-person commission. On the commission, there's not a single person representing the utilities or the nuclear industry. There's also not a single person representing the antinukes. I don't see how one can do better than follow the old legal procedure of appointing people who have open minds.

PLAYBOY: Despite your assurances, the dangers of radiation are what people fear most from both nuclear energy and nuclear weapons. Does the need for nuclear energy justify the harm that it has done or may do?

TELLER: There has been one and only one test—on February 28, 1954, in the Pacific—that did hurt some people. That test was carried out by the Los Alamos Laboratories. I had nothing to do with it, since I was working at Livermore Laboratories at that time. Some of the islanders got overexposed and 100 of them were affected. They would have gotten no ill effects had they known to wash off the fallout. As it was, they were taken care of and all of them recovered. This unfortunate occurrence happened because the bomb was exploded when there was a change in wind direction. Not enough caution was taken—but the mistake has never been repeated.

During that same test, patrols were sent beforehand to see if there were any ships in the area, but they missed one ship. One member of the crew became very sick and shortly afterward he died. We don't have the records to prove the man died of radiation, but I believe it would be highly probable.

That death invoked terrible reaction, and rightly so. First of all, a single human life is important. But there is more to it. It was, in my mind, not justifiable that we should have bombed Hiroshima and Nagasaki before giving the Japanese warning. If there had been a warning, if there had been a demonstration, we might have been able to end a horrible war by showing the power of science without killing people. If that had happened, all of us now would have a different impression of science, of the atomic nucleus. We would all be safer and happier.

I don't want to criticize: There were strong reasons for the bombing, to end the war as soon as possible, a war in which many people had died. Those bombings may have prevented other events that would have been even worse. But I still regret that we did not try a warning explosion.

At that time, however, there was no protest. Here is a remarkable contrast: more than 100,000 people dead in Hiroshima and Nagasaki—incidentally, very few of them, comparatively, from radiation. They died from the shock, from fire—practically all of both cities burned. The immediate physical effects were much more devastating than the physiological effects of radiation. The fact is that very many people died and there were no widespread protests. Later, in contrast, one person died and there were all these protest marches. It was a remakable psychological situation: I believe it was a delayed reaction to Hiroshima.

PLAYBOY: You're talking about radiation from a bomb blast. What about the reports of harmful effects from lower levels of radiation?

TELLER: These low-level radiations have not proved to be harmful, and the scare stories are just that, scare stories. They are exaggerated, they are unproved. People are easily frightened by what they don't understand.

The fact is, the whole human race and the whole living world has been exposed, during all of its existence, to radiation. The low-level radiations that are permitted by Government regulations are no greater than those we get from natural sources of radiation.

We have much more, and much more thorough and systematic, information about the effects of radiation than we have about the harmful effects of practically any other harmful agent, chemical or otherwise. Furthermore, radiation can be detected in exceedingly small quantities, and that is cause for safety, because when you see one millionth as much as is dangerous, you are already warned. But remarkably enough, these warnings, instead of reassuring people, excite them. There seems to be nothing as frightening as a ticking Geiger counter.

PLAYBOY: You have been quoted as claiming that more people have been harmed by the fear of radiation than by radiation itself. Why do you say that?

TELLER: It is a very real problem. Radiation has extremely important medical applications, and people are now scared away from these treatments.

Things have gone so far that people refuse even medical chest X rays. I know of a case where a woman became pregnant and a chest X ray was recommended. It is right to say that embryos should not be exposed to radiation; they are more sensitive to it than adults. A chest X ray, however, properly shielded, separating the upper part of the body, would not have affected the embryo. She refused the X ray and thereby an early diagnosis of tuberculosis was missed. I don't know the end of the story, but I do know that she was affected for the worse because of the radiation scare.

PLAYBOY: But it's been shown that excessive irradiation for such things as skin conditions has produced cancer. Isn't it irresponsible to downplay the dangers of radiation?

TELLER: That too much radiation is bad is quite clear. What scares me more is that people will not dare use radiation where it is justified.

This normal radiation to which we are all exposed may have some adverse effects, or it may have some beneficial effects—we don't know. There are some experiments on rodents that have been exposed to 100 times the maximum permissible dose, and on the average, they lived longer! People have objected to these animal experiments because these colonies of animals tend to be infected by pneumonia. What we know is that the life expectancy of pneumonia-infected colonies has been improved by radiation. But whether or not radiation stimulates something in the body that counteracts pneumonia, or what the connection is, we don't understand.

That there is no harmful effect from very little radiation, I don't know. That there is no *beneficial* effect from very little radiation, I don't know. And, furthermore, others don't know, either.

PLAYBOY: What about the recent reports of leukemia incidence among children in St. George, Utah?

TELLER: There was a big population exposed to some low-level radiation many years ago in Nevada, near the Utah border. A study has been made of the civilians who were exposed, with a peculiar result. I said that embryos are more sensitive than people. It is also true that children are more sensitive than adults, and particular emphasis was placed on investigating those who were children at the time of this radiation. We know that strong irradiation does have delayed effects and therefore is difficult to find out. But we are beginning to find out.

Now, with regard to these Nevada results, something very remarkable has happened. Thousands of people, I think even tens of thousands of people, were exposed. Among these, there was an incidence in the exposed population, as there is in all populations. In regard to leukemia, the incidence seemed rather greater; in the case of the other cancers, it seemed rather less. If you added up all the cancer cases, the effect was zero, but the media's reporting of the study was selective. The fact that there were more lukemia cases was reported; the fact that there were fewer other cancer cases was not reported. Whether or not either of these observations is significant, whether or not either has anything to do with additional radiation, we don't know. But there is an enormous amount of guessing and an enormous amount of fear. I cannot tell you with absolute certainty that those experiments may not have caused a dozen additional leukemia cases; they might have. I don't believe it, but they might have. I *can* tell you that the radiation scare has hurt tens of thousands of people.

PLAYBOY: What about the case of Karen Silkwood, who, some suspect, was murdered to prevent her from telling what she knew about health hazards in the nuclear plant in which she worked?

TELLER: Karen Silkwood had a conflict with the establishment that ran the place in which she worked. It was claimed that she was murdered and this was covered up. If you want to believe, as in the movie *The China Syndrome—*

PLAYBOY: Did you see it?

TELLER: I didn't see it, but I know its plot. If you want to believe that our public companies are at least as bad as the Mafia, then this is a sad situation. I don't believe it. I doubt that many people seriously believe that, but this has nothing to do with nuclear energy. It has to do with common questions of decency and of law enforcement. We share a respect for decency and law enforcement in this country that not even the President can escape, much less a company executive.

PLAYBOY: Many people would consider that a naïve confidence on your part. Are you really as happy as you seem with the accumulation of power in the hands of those who run the utilities?

TELLER: I didn't say I'm happy about it. I am not. Utilities are, however, under rigorous control. One can argue as to whether they are under wise control or unwise control, but, at any rate, utilities, which provide many people with needed energy, have in their systems something of the checks and balances of the American way of life.

Power concentration in our society does occur. It is far greater in the automobile industry and in labor unions than in the utilities. Whenever and wherever these concentrations of power occur, they should be scrutinized.

PLAYBOY: Chinese nuclear testing has resulted in fallout over American urban areas. Do those incidents, this time executed by a Communist power, worry you?

TELLER: They don't worry me in the slightest. I do know that nothing terrible has happened from fallout apart from the one incident in the Pacific, when nearby islands were exposed. It never should have happened; originally, I wanted such tests to go on in Antarctica. But if you disregard this one case, the worst other case of fallout, at the time of much more frequent testing, was an increase in radiation to some parts of human bodies in some places by ten percent over the normal level. In 1958, a friend, Albert Latter, and I wrote a book, *Our Nuclear Future,* in which we analyzed these cases in great detail. I have not seen the figures on recent Chinese explosions. I am quite sure that the fallout will not have added significant amounts of radiation received by anybody. And by significant amounts I mean more than what he would get by means of one year's normal radiation, more than what he would get by a few round trips from California to the East Coast.

You cannot say with any certainty that nobody has been hurt by these small amounts of fallout. But I know that if somebody has been hurt, we can't find him. Furthermore, it is an honest statement that the effect of low-level radiation—adverse, beneficial or otherwise—is something we don't know. Probably, it's more adverse than anything else; that is at least a cautious assumption that I would be willing to make and most other people do make. But I don't worry about it more than I'd worry if I were more than two percent overweight. Unfortunately, I am more than two percent overweight, and I am absolutely certain that is a more significant health problem.

PLAYBOY: Since there are so few experts on this subject, perhaps we should ask you for your thumbnail explanation of the nature of radiation—and its effects on humans.

TELLER: In the case of radiation, the only thing that matters significantly is the total amount of energy delivered to a tissue. If we know that irradiation has occurred, or if a radioactive substance has been taken up by the body, has carried radiation into a specific tissue, like the thyroid gland or the bone marrow, then we know that the effect of this radiation is directly related to the *amount* of energy delivered to that tissue. The paths of these radioactive substances in the body can be easily studied and have been carefully studied; therefore, we know the amount of danger. We know the effect is similar to the effect we get from background radiation, but we don't know whether or not the effect is dangerous in small quantities.

What we are afraid of in fallout, what people talk most about, is radiation taken up by the bone marrow through a particular kind of an atom, strontium 90. When we say that there is no unusual danger, we say that the bone marrow, which is most exposed in this case, is still exposed to much less radiation than it is from cosmic rays.

Cosmic rays affect the whole body; so do some particles of radiation that drift over after an explosion. But important effects of nuclear radiation usually affect only a small part of the body. Our regulations say that no part of the body must be exposed to more than our whole body will get in the normal course of events.

I probably shouldn't say this, since it's a joke, and my intent might be misinterpreted, but you know people are worried about genetic effects, and there is no doubt that radiation increases the rate of genetic mutation. It is also true that without mutations, we would still be in the state of an amoeba. All changes in the living world have been due to mutations. And while most of them are harmful, without mutations there would be no adaptation and no development.

One view of very ancient history is that during the ice ages that occurred in the past million years or so, people were driven into caves. Radiation in those caves is known to be greater than in the open. That the human race developed faster and became human may be due to radiation. But now we are out of the caves, we have stopped developing and we are becoming, therefore, stodgy and stupid. Now, please don't take this seriously! This is not a good argument—but it is no worse than the arguments people use to try to scare you about radiation. That this argument is no worse than their arguments is no great claim.

PLAYBOY: The question of nuclear energy is critical because of the energy crunch. Since you're so adamant about the scare tactics used against radiation, do you find that the energy crisis has been similarly overstated?

TELLER: The energy shortage is very critical. It is due to a great extent almost exclusively to lack of foresight. Years ago, it was perfectly clear that the shortage was coming, and we did nothing about it. Today, we still do too little about it.

There is no single solution. What we need to do is use every possible available energy source that can be had at a reasonable price and without unreasonable pollution. That means fossil fuels, hydroelectric power, development of solar power in some forms, nuclear power, which has been developed and continues to be cleaner, safer and, very practically, less expensive than any other form of power; and that is still not the end of the list. My most recent book is titled *Energy from Heaven and Earth*. By that title, I mean that we need energy from wherever we can get it, as long as it is reasonable. People who capriciously and unreasonably object to a particular energy source, be it coal or nuclear or oil, really do the community a very serious disservice.

Incidentally, the people who will be hurt in the worst way by the energy crisis are the poor people in the Third World. Without energy, the developing countries cannot develop, and without energy, we can't produce the fertilizer that their increasing populations require.

PLAYBOY: What about waste products from the production of nuclear energy? There is great concern over nuclear end products that can't be disposed of safely.

TELLER: Waste disposal has been practiced in the nuclear-weapons program for decades without accident, even though during the war, disposal was not done nearly as carefully as we are doing it now.

The American Physical Society conducted an extremely careful study on waste disposal and it published the results in January 1978. Now, the American Physical Society is not especially favorable to any particular form of energy. Its findings were unanimous: Waste disposal is a completely solved problem. Its implementation in civilian reactors has been delayed by our bureaucracy, and this delay is just plain wrong. The best characterization of this issue has been given by a very wonderful lady, now the governor of Washington, Dixy Lee Ray, who was chairman of the Atomic Energy Commission. "Waste disposal," she said, "is the biggest contemporary *non*problem."

PLAYBOY: What *are* the problems involved with nuclear reactors, as you see them?

TELLER: The problems are called Ralph Nader.

As long as people who have no understanding spread their views successfully, an important component of our energy production will not make sufficient progress. Public understanding is inhibited by people who should know better. Those who are lacking in knowledge should at least talk a little less. Ralph Nader was right about safety belts; I doubt that he was right about many other things.

PLAYBOY: That's a bit glib of you, as a major proponent of nuclear energy, to say—

TELLER: Excuse me, I am *not* a big proponent of nuclear energy, no more than I am of oil or coal or solar energy or geothermal energy or wave energy or wind energy or you name it, as long as it is feasible. When you have real shortages, you don't throw away any important components without very good reason.

It so happens that nuclear energy is the cleanest, safest, cheapest source of electricity where electricity is required in large amounts. For small generating plants, nuclear energy is no good. Furthermore, electricity is only a part of our energy requirements. Therefore, nuclear energy is certainly not the whole of the answer.

PLAYBOY: Haven't the large oil companies blocked research in other areas of energy?

TELLER: Large companies don't suffer these days from too much popularity. And oil companies seem to be less popular than others.

Actually, oil companies have supported research in other fields and they have developed methods for finding and producing oil that are quite ingenious. About three years ago, in California, we had a referendum, Proposition 15, on nuclear reactors. I happen to know that the oil companies supported nuclear reactors and gave money for that purpose. But they did not stand up and say so. The result was that they wound up being accused by everybody. Opponents of nuclear reactors found out that they had given money; proponents of nuclear reactors noticed that the oil companies wouldn't speak up for their convictions. They became uncertain as to whose side the oil companies were really on. So proponents didn't like them, either. Now, to be so cautious as not to dare say what you believe in is not a lovely role and to that extent, I can fault the oil companies.

I don't think it holds for all of them. In general, I think that big and rich companies do have some responsibility for the common good, and a part of that responsibility, it seems to me, would be to take a stand that is, in their own eyes, the best. Their judgment is probably better than their courage. Corporate courage is usually no greater than personal courage.

PLAYBOY: You've written extensively about the use of unusual energy sources, such as wave energy. Can such forms as wave energy and solar energy fill major energy needs in advanced technological societies?

TELLER: We have to take them case by case. By solar energy, people often mean a lot of different things: growing plants and using the plants for fuel; collecting solar heat for heating and even cooling houses. Many of these are feasible. In my book, I try to visualize what might happen in the year 2000—I try to be fairly optimistic. I make guesses: By the year 2000, 20 percent of our energy may come from nuclear sources, 12 percent from solar sources.

PLAYBOY: You have argued that solar power is not yet developed enough for mass use. One expert has stated that if all the new houses built in the U.S. in the next 14 years were solar heated, we could save as much energy as we expect to recover from the North Slope oil system of Alaska.

TELLER: I have not made this special calculation, but I can tell you a few things about this statement. Today, we have the means of heating water with solar power, and in our Southern states, that certainly could be done. Heating in the South, where we hardly need it, might also be done in an economic manner by solar means. But what will you do in New England or in the Midwest or in practically half the United States, where there isn't enough sunshine? I heard Lovins say in Brussels that all the electricity for Belgium could be produced by solar heat and windmills. This is certainly not true.

The question is, can solar energy be turned into electricity? It can, but only at a price that today is at least five times as great as the price for nuclear electricity. These high costs are due to a lot of fabrication that goes into making the parts of the solar machine; unless we mass-produce, we won't be able to pay for it. So small no longer will be beautiful; small will be expensive. When we mass-produce, that production will give incomparably more pollution and more danger than nuclear reaction. I don't think that solar electricity is impossible forever. There are people who are coming up with new ideas and I am working with them. I want to get energy from every possible source. From nuclear, from solar, from oil and from gas— but, if possible, not from OPEC.

To summarize, the problems of nuclear and solar energies are very different. In the case of solar energy, we don't have the practical technology yet, but it is slowly approaching the stage where its cost will not be too great per unit of energy produced. In the case of nuclear energy, we know how to produce it, but we don't apply common reason to something that is technically well understood. Unfortunately, Jimmy Carter, the nuclear engineer in the White House, forgot what he learned, if, indeed, he ever learned it.

PLAYBOY: But people far less sophisticated than Carter feel that the enormity of nuclear power is simply beyond their grasp—

TELLER: Nuclear power is certainly beyond the grasp of anyone who doesn't want to hear about it. If you want to understand it, you can grasp it very easily.

PLAYBOY: Considering the reservations many people have about it, don't we have a right to be informed about what nuclear power can provide that we don't already have?

TELLER: Today, nuclear power can produce electricity wherever it is needed in large quantities. For any country that has a good electrical-distribution net, it is the cheapest, cleanest, safest source. For the horribly huge cities, the slums of the Third World—Cairo, Mexico City, Bombay, Calcutta, Djakarta, where you have 10,000,000 people living in a crowded area— nuclear power could be used to great advantage without adding pollution. Even so, nuclear power is most useful in the advanced countries, where the distribution net already exists.

By utilizing nuclear power, within ten years, the advanced countries could decrease their need for oil by 30 percent. This oil could then go to developing countries. What nuclear power could do, therefore, is not only stabilize the shaky economics of the advanced world but also help a lot of the development of the developing world, which will not develop without energy.

There are some very interesting statistics about this. The United Nations' records from 1950 to 1975 show that per-capita commercial energy consumption in the developing countries increased in that period threefold. In the developed countries, it increased twofold. It is not true that the rich are getting richer and the poor are getting poorer. It is true that energy is needed for a decent standard of living. And it is further true that the developing countries continue to have too little energy.

The great development in the third quarter of the 20th Century has been made possible by oil. These possibilities have not ended, but the limits are in sight. For the sake of the developing world, we need added energy sources: nuclear and solar and geothermal and wave energy and others. Among these, nuclear is already here; so is coal. Nuclear energy could comprise, by the year 2000, about one fifth of the energy of the world. Today, it produces only two to three percent of the world's energy. That 20 percent could make a difference in the world, in stability, in the accelerated fight against poverty.

PLAYBOY: The most spectacular of your scientific achievements has been the development of the H-bomb. How do you feel about being called "father of the hydrogen bomb"?

TELLER: Well, it never sent me a Father's Day card. [*Laughs*]

PLAYBOY: Do you feel any pride in that accomplishment?

TELLER: You work on something because you feel it is the right thing to do, and pride is just not the word.

PLAYBOY: Then, are you ashamed? Do you regret your work?

TELLER: Certainly not! I feel it was necessary to do.

PLAYBOY: Is that how you feel about the rest of your work, too? Or are there things you did because you really wanted to do them?

TELLER: When I first chose my work, I decided not to work on applying science but to work on understanding the meaning of the word. I did that for many years with great pleasure and even occasionally with some pride, not that I like the word in any sense. Then came World War Two and I became involved in working on weapons because of necessity, because it seemed that it had to be done.

After the war, it seemed to me that the job was left unfinished. When I heard declarations of Stalin that he "had the atomic bomb and will have much more"—that's literally what Stalin said—there was even more reason for me to be interested. Yet I went back to theroetical physics and did nothing about it. But when the Russians exploded an atomic bomb, I became uneasy. Moreover, several of my friends came to me and said that it was now absolutely necessary that we do something about the situation. Eventually, it became clear that the Russians and we had gotten at the solution of how to make thermonuclear explosions at nearly the same time. All this was connected with much more personal and professional controversy than I have ever experienced before or after.

When it became clear that we had to work on the hydrogen bomb, I went to see my friend Enrico Fermi and implored him to take over the job. I would have been glad to work for him. He said no. I went to another friend, Hans Bethe. He said yes; then, a day or two later, he reneged. It's not that I wanted to do it—it had to be done.

The idea that any person can accomplish a lot in a complicated field like this one is quite misleading. Afterward, I wrote an article about the development titled "The Work of Many People." That is exactly what it was. Perhaps I worked on the problem somewhat longer than other people; perhaps I worked more consistently when the going, in a psychological sense, became quite difficult. In a way, I'm glad that we didn't fail. But all this has nothing to do with "pride."

Those words—father of the hydrogen bomb—are silly. I object to them mostly because they are in poor taste. I have *children*.

PLAYBOY: Did you advocate the use of nuclear weapons in Vietnam?

TELLER: I participated in the discussions of nuclear weapons in Vietnam and I opposed their use as completely and as forcefully as I have ever opposed anything.

I had a very simple reason for doing so. Nuclear weapons are not appropriate against guerrillas. They can be used against a massive invading force, but that is not what we were dealing with in Vietnam. Our forces had extensive military bases that were vulnerable to nuclear weapons. The Viet Cong was not vulnerable. For us to have initiated nuclear warfare in Vietnam would have been not only inhuman but, in every sense of the word, complete madness.

PLAYBOY: Why do you urge the development of more weapons? Don't we already have the capacity to kill our enemies—indeed, the whole world—many times over?

TELLER: The reason we need more and different weapons is that this idea of overkill is, quite simply, not true.

Let me say—on this I must absolutely insist—that the one purpose that I have is to avoid the horrible event of a nuclear exchange with Russia. But if there should be one, the Russians have taken precautions, so that, in all probability, the damage to human life in Russia would be considerably less than it was in the Second World War. They probably would lose less than five percent of their population. Since we have done virtually nothing about our civil defense, we would lose more than 50 percent of our population, and the U.S. would no longer exist as a power, a political entity, even as an idea. Our way of life would have become nonexistent, just as the enemies of Stalin have become nonpersons.

PLAYBOY: Wait a minute. Less than five percent of the Soviet population would be affected? Most published figures show that an *80 percent* destruction of Russia is expected in case of such an attack by the U.S. Where do you get *your* figures?

TELLER: That 80 percent figure, to the best of my knowledge, is out of date. The trouble is that all these discussions are carried out in secret and I don't even know how much of it can be quoted. My figure, five percent or less, comes from non-Government sources. It is compatible with a high degree of *property* damage, but I wouldn't say as high as 80 percent. However, the Russian *people* would survive, and the Russians have a superiority in number of nuclear explosives that might easily become great enough so that after such an exchange, they still had a terrific striking force by which they could coerce any nation on earth to deliver to them whatever they wanted—food, machinery, labor—so their property losses could be replaced in an exceedingly short time. Remember the economic miracle in Germany and Japan. Remember that our total national assets equal approximately three years of the gross national product, so it shows that property can be replaced, and rapidly, even without outside help. Human beings cannot.

PLAYBOY: But, going back to your figures, what makes you sure that the Russian population is so much more secure than the American? Does their civil-defense program really make them more secure?

TELLER: Our information shows that the great numbers of truly well-constructed shelters exist for those workers who would have to stay behind after evacuation.

PLAYBOY: But wouldn't the radiation levels after nuclear attack make the shelter programs useless?

TELLER: In a nuclear war, the so-called maximum permissible dose of nuclear radiation would be exceeded, perhaps for everybody in the whole world, but a radiation dose even 1000 times the so-called maximum permissible dose would still produce only limited damage. Damage, yes, but still limited. The direct effects of nuclear explosion—the shock, the heat, the fires—these are terrible. Because we have been oversensitized to the effects of low-level radiation, we have lost all sense of proportion when discussing a situation as bad as war. Just as 100,000 people were killed at the end of World War Two by nuclear weapons, and then one person died by fallout and got the public reaction, so in other cases where people talk about overkill, they project a chance of something that is terrible, but could still be avoided, into a prediction of certainty.

PLAYBOY: Do the Russians, in fact, have an edge on us in military and scientific capability?

TELLER: They have a proved edge on us in the *quantity* of weapons. We like to claim that qualitatively we are ahead. Unfortunately, the statement about quantity can be proved, but that about quality is much less provable.

In this country, military efforts are attacked from all sides. Scientists are discouraged from pursuing military projects. In Russia, work on weapons is encouraged to the limit.

PLAYBOY: Doesn't the ingenuity of American scientists make up for that— especially since Soviet scientists don't have much of a choice in the projects they work on?

TELLER: It may. The proverb "You can lead a horse to water, but you can't make him drink" is true, but it has its limits. Sooner or later, all horses want to drink. In the end, all scientists want to work on some technical problem. Any scientist, under most conditions, will try to do his best.

Consider a man like Andrei Sakharov. I don't know in any detail what is going on behind the Iron Curtain, but it seems he has made great contributions to Russian military preparedness. He turned around politically and is now in the opposition. This took an incredible amount of courage. One person among thousands has that kind of courage. The great majority will justify to themselves what they are doing. If you grow up in a country where the only permitted or publicized words are those of the Communist Party, it takes a rare combination of courage and intelligence to speak differently.

There are matters on which I differ from my fellow scientists, but not from the whole society. Even that limited experience has taught me how difficult it is to take a different view from that of those who are around you. What a man like Sakharov has to suffer is really terrible, and I think I understand how rare that kind of behavior actually is.

From what we can find out, the Russian scientists are highly ingenious, just as ingenious as American scientists. I think it is highly likely that among these many ingenious people, a much greater fraction works willingly on weapons than in the United States. It is likely that the Russians today have not only a greater quantitative advantage but probably even a qualitative edge.

Our Secretary of Defense, Harold Brown, a truly ingenious man, made a public statement when he first took office. It contained the sentence, "I consider it my job that we should not fall too far behind the Russians." For a Secretary of Defense to be as open as that is, in itself, a remarkable thing.

PLAYBOY: Isn't your advice based on a rather extreme distrust of the Russians?

TELLER: I trust the Russians to pursue their ideals. I don't happen to agree with some of their ideals. For instance, I don't happen to believe that the world would be best off under Russian rule. They feel that their way of life is the best, but on that point, some refugees seem to differ. I tend to agree with Alexander Solzhenitsyn more than I agree with Leonid Brezhnev. I also trust Solzhenitsyn more than I trust Brezhnev.

PLAYBOY: Do you see any point to the SALT talks?

TELLER: It may make sense to negotiate with the Russians from a position of strength. But today we are negotiating from a position of weakness—and that makes less sense.

PLAYBOY: Are you really convinced that the Russians want to conquer additional territory?

TELLER: It is very hard to be convinced of that, but their influence has greatly increased recently: in Afghanistan, perhaps in Iran, in part of Yemen, where one of the richest sources of oil, Saudi Arabia, may well get involved. The Russian influence in Ethiopia, in Angola, in Somalia is a matter of record. You cannot avoid the feeling that there is an explanation for why Russia insists on having enough arms to defend itself against an "attack" by the whole world. Their standard of living is low, yet they pour much more money and talent into military preparedness than do we in the United States. I cannot exclude the possibility that the Russians, who are convinced that their Communist way of life is the only right one, are altruistic enough to want to make sure that the rest of the world participates in their excellent way of life—whether it wants to or not.

PLAYBOY: If the Russians are both stronger and more aggressive than we are, you must be pretty pessimistic about this nation's defense.

TELLER: I am not pessimistic. I define a pessimist as a person who is always right but does not get any enjoyment out of it. An optimist is a person who imagines that the future is uncertain. I consider it a duty to be an optimist, because if you imagine the future to be uncertain, you are apt to do something about it.

PLAYBOY: Optimistic or not, you're still claiming the Soviets are ahead of us quantitatively and probably qualitatively. That doesn't square with what we read about U.S. superiority in multiple-warhead missiles, in missile submarines and in the superior accuracy of our weapons systems in general.

Isn't it a fact, for instance, that Russia's missiles are bigger than ours because they are less accurate?

TELLER: You are asking about Russian secrets, and Russian secrets are not only unknown to us but, to the extent that they *are* known, we keep them more tightly than our own secrets. I cannot talk about that. But there is a dangerous effect that everybody should keep in mind. If you do something your way, and I do something my way, I am very easily led to jump to the conclusion that you do things your way because you are a fool. It may be that you have reasons to do them that way, and if I were fully aware of the circumstances in Russia, I could answer the questions better—if I were allowed to answer them.

PLAYBOY: We can deal only with what we know. Why should we assume that the Soviets are more powerful than we are, if we have no solid evidence to that effect?

TELLER: We have quite a bit of evidence. For instance, we have evidence of their number of ships, their number of explosives, the weight of their explosives, from which we can quantitatively conclude that they are ahead. In areas where we can only guess, we imagine that we are ahead.

PLAYBOY: Can't we draw some conclusions from their space program? That deals with much the same technology as defense, and ours is considered far superior to theirs.

TELLER: By whom?

PLAYBOY: You don't think so?

TELLER: I don't think so and I don't think the opposite, either. I don't *know*. The Americans' emphasis was on an effort to land on the moon. We did, and in that respect, our victory was obvious and I'm happy about it. The Russians don't talk about everything they are doing. We know that they have very good people working on their space program. We know that the best of the Russian scientists are deeply involved in their military effort, while ours are not. We know that their military-research expenditures are greater than ours. We have here, in regard to quality, a race between the hare and the turtle. The American hare could still outrun the Russian turtle if he would only *run*; but we are resting on the glories of past accomplishments and our scientists generally don't like to work on the making of weapons.

PLAYBOY: Is there an area in which you see the U.S. at a military advantage?

TELLER: Yes. We're ahead in electronics, particularly computers. And that brings us to one of my favorite hobbyhorses, secrecy. Let's contrast nuclear weapons and electronic computers. In nuclear weapons, we had secrecy— now the Russians are ahead of us. In electronics and computers, we had practically no secrecy and we are way ahead of the Russians. That is not due to chance. Computers and other electronics in general, such as television and those other remarkable things, are badly needed in a consumerist society. Therefore, we are motivated toward the development of these instruments.

What we have not done but what we could and should do is to apply our advanced electronics, particularly miniaturized electronics, to produce instruments of war, so that we can take people farther away from the scene of action. In other words, I want to see remotely piloted airplanes, remotely navigated ships, remotely steered tanks. All these instruments can have any number of sensors. They can see, they can hear, they can feel, they can communicate. And they can take orders as to how to act under any circumstances.

This is a field in which I would like nothing better than cooperation with Israel. Israel has something to contribute. In the United States, as I said, for a scientist to work on defense is not easy. If he does so, and I should know, he is subject to all kinds of criticism—not all of it truthful, not all of it agreeable. In Israel, defense has been recognized as an honorable and necessary business.

PLAYBOY: What measures of defense can you recommend, besides weapons?

TELLER: The thing we must do, first of all, is establish civil defense, to make sure that in case of any disaster, earthquake, hurricane or war, we can save people. This is neglected in this country.

Do you know what China, Russia, Sweden and Switzerland have in common? They all have strong civil defense. Yet you would not call Sweden and Switzerland militaristic. There are many things we ought to do, but among my priorities, the highest is civil defense.

PLAYBOY: Are you saying we should get back to building bomb shelters, as we did in the Fifties during the bomb-scare period?

TELLER: What we did was *talk* a lot about bomb shelters. The Russians today are *doing* a lot with bomb shelters. We know they have a plan to evacuate their cities in case they judge a conflict inevitable. We should take the easy first step of arranging evacuation. Other steps may come later.

PLAYBOY: Aren't civil-defense measures pathetically ineffective in the face of nuclear war and its awesome radiation?

TELLER: I remember what people were talking about before World War Two. They said that cities woud be bombed and there would be no defense. But there *was* defense. The bombings were dreadful. They were also relatively ineffective in determining the outcome of the war. Measures taken—evacuation and going into cellars—turned out to be, in most cases, really effective.

This feeling that you are now experiencing, that a war would be the end, is the feeling I encountered in 1937. One effect of it was that it softened up the democracies for the attack by Hitler—it did not deter Hitler. Today, it makes us disregard civil defense. The same is not the case in Russia. I don't like to think about a nuclear war, either. War is not unthinkable, but to think about it is very disagreeable. Yet the only way to avoid it is to think about it.

The Russians have evacuation procedures, and if they do, it seems to make sense that we should, too. Furthermore, they have a system of inexpensive shelters that reduce radiation a hundredfold. They are supplied for two weeks. In almost all cases, radiation will have dropped to a tolerable level in two weeks. In the remaining cases, there could probably be decontamination crews coming around.

The difference between nuclear reactors and nuclear bombs should be emphasized. In a nuclear reactor, material is produced that is radioactive, not indefinitely but for a long time. In a nuclear explosion, the radioactivity that is produced lasts a very short time.

PLAYBOY: It seems that all sorts of countries are acquiring nuclear materials. Sometimes, as in the case of Pakistan, nuclear materials are acquired for supposedly peaceful purposes but actually with the intent to make weapons. How can we halt nuclear proliferation?

TELLER: The ban on reprocessing is supposed to help limit the spread of nuclear arms, but it does not. A ban is, however, a real impediment to the development of nuclear energy and, as a result, the energy crisis will become worse. More people will suffer, there will be violent fights over short supplies. The instruments of war will not have been diminished; the reasons for war will have increased.

There is another proposal, one that our President has made, but he has not so far followed it up. Instead of banning reprocessing, we should bring reprocessing under international control. The sense of this is not only in having a strong hold over proliferation but in holding down the high costs of reprocessing for each single reactor. It makes sense for small countries to do their reprocessing with others.

If we could build an organization that serviced many countries and was under thorough supervision, that would create progress, not only toward more and cheaper energy but also toward more, and more peaceful, international cooperation.

PLAYBOY: What else can be done to increase our sense of security?

TELLER: Minimizing secrecy to the extent that it is possible—which is to a very great extent. One of our main dangers is that we don't inform our public. We keep Russian secrets, in many cases, more carefully than our own. Our people live in a fool's paradise. Perhaps a realistic information campaign is even more important than any physical act of defense.

A few years ago, I gave a talk to the American Physical Society and I was asked afterward if I realized what merits Daniel Ellsberg had in fighting secrecy. My answer to that was that Ellsberg is guilty of a crime and a misdemeanor. The crime was that he himself classified gossip as secret while he worked at the Rand Corporation. The misdemeanor was that after he had so classified it, he published it in *The New York Times.*

As long as we have passed laws concerning secrecy-—whether these laws are right or wrong—I believe we should obey them. What we should do, however, is to convince members of Congress that these laws do not serve their purpose, that they should be changed. What I would like to see is a situation in which anything could be classified—and we should respect the classification—but the duration of that classification should practically never exceed one year. Most cases in which we really have to keep secrets are operational matters—such as where a submarine has gone—and a year later, that can be known.

PLAYBOY: Despite your calls for openness, you told us at the outset of the interview that the one topic you would not discuss was the article on the H-bomb that a court prevented *The Progressive* magazine from publishing. Why not?

TELLER: I feel very certain that something that is being contested in the couts should not be discussed in an interview. [*Ironically, nuclear scientist Theodore Postol claims that the* Progressive *article, which he has read, contains no new information beyond a previous article on the H-bomb written by Teller for the 1977 edition of "Encyclopedia Americana."*]

PLAYBOY: How do you feel about being called a reactionary?

TELLER: I deny that I am a left-winger or a right-winger. I am a middle-of-the-roader. I am pretty sure that I used to be a liberal. I used to be anti-militarist. Before the Second World War, the greatest danger to freedom was Adolf Hitler. Today the greatest danger to freedom is the Soviet Union. I don't think that I have changed my mind about freedom. I cannot feel that I am less liberal than I used to be. But there are people in this country and abroad who have not noticed that there is something really dangerous in Communist imperialism. As a young man, I was a liberal; today I feel I am a conservative. But I haven't changed; the world around me has changed.

PLAYBOY: What is the nature of your work now?

TELLER: I'm feeling badly overworked now, after just finishing my book on energy. I think that intellectuals who end up in hell will have to read page proofs and check indexes there. I am now editing a technical book on controlled fusion for advanced students who might go into that field. It has become an immensely complicated technical subject, and there is much progress in the field. I am also writing about the history of technology. And I have been urged to write something rapidly on the influence of technology on modern warfare.

I lecture quite a bit. On top of that, I am trying to understand one or two phenomena of nature. With all of this work, I would probably be going crazy, except for the fact that, probably, I already *am* crazy!

PLAYBOY: You've worked with some of the most famous scientists of the 20th Century—in physics and in mathematics. Who left particularly strong impressions on you?

TELLER: All of them. Of course, I was closer personally to some of them. I would like to mention one to whom I was not close in the scientific field but very close to personally. This was the aerodynamicist Theodore von Karman.

He was a truly wonderful person, a Hungarian. Another very close friend is the nuclear physicist Eugene Wigner. I seem to talk only about Hungarians, I don't know why.

PLAYBOY: What about Albert Einstein?

TELLER: I had little opportunity to know Einstein. He, of course, did really fabulous things when he was young. Later, he got involved in what he called unified field theory. He did not get very far with it.

He made some moralistic statemens with which I am in complete disagreement. He said some terrible things, such as, "If I had known what would come out of it, I would rather have been a plumber than a physicist." Actually, his scientific work had very little to do with atomic energy. The job of a scientist is to do science, maybe to apply it, and then, if he is capable of doing so, to explain what he has found. To feel responsible for what is in nature, or to feel responsible for having increased the capability of people to accomplish something—such feelings are completely misplaced. In a democratic society, the people should decide, or their elected representatives to whom they have delegated their decisions should. To believe that a scientist has more responsibility than to discover, to apply and to explain is a remarkable and wrong kind of immodesty.

PLAYBOY: No fewer than 11 of your scientific co-authors have won the Nobel Prize. A great many people think you ought to get it, too. Do you regret not getting it? Do you want it?

TELLER: In 1975, I got the Harvey Prize from Israel's Technion. That prize means more to me than any honor, any other prize. I still have some ambitions. My greatest one is to contribute what I can, in a very disturbing situation, to a safer future. That other prize, which happens to be named after the inventor of high explosives, is not one of my particular ambitions.

PLAYBOY: Many scientists with whom we've spoken feel your work clearly deserves that prize—

TELLER: But I disagree.

PLAYBOY: Nevertheless, there is a feeling among them that you were not awarded the Nobel because of your political stance.

TELLER: What makes me tick, what my motivations are, I understand only partly. The motives of others I cannot know at all. As far as I'm concerned, I wouldn't have awarded the prize to myself, and that should suffice.

PLAYBOY: Few events have affected you personally as much as the Oppenheimer affair. How do you recall it?

TELLER: Oppenheimer was accused of security violations. The question was raised whether his clearance, his access to secret material, in his continuing contributions to the work of defense, should be continued or not. In the hearings, one of the questions that was brought up was the controversy of the H-bomb. I had been for it. Oppenheimer was against it. The difference was brought up, I was asked to testify and I got—very much to my regret—involved in the case.

Because I disagreed with a man who stood up at the time for practically no more arms for the United States—I took the opposite view—I was harshly criticized. But I doubt that all of that is of any real significance.

There is one thing about the Oppenheimer case that is extremely important. It crystallized and reinforced in the minds of scientists the opinion that we should no longer work on weapons. The fact that today America is in a weak position and Russia is the strongest military power, and getting stronger every year, is due to the Oppenheimer case and the events surrounding it.

The Oppenheimer hearings should never have occurred. They did because two very difficult people were stubborn. One of them was President Eisenhower. Oppenheimer was accused of being a Communist, and it was clear that if the case were brought up publicly, there would be a bitter fight. If Eisenhower did not trust Oppenheimer, he simply should not have asked for his advice. If he had taken that path, there would have been no controversy, no case.

The other stubborn man was Oppenheimer himself. The chairman of the Atomic Energy Commission, my friend Lewis Strauss, said to Oppenheimer, "The President insists that your clearance be terminated. We have only to terminate it, we do not need to explain why." Oppenheimer said no, he wanted a hearing.

The reasons why Eisenhower and Oppenheimer wanted that confrontation were very different. That the confrontation occurred was a tragedy. I, unfortunately, was caught up in that confrontation, and under oath I had to say what I thought about the questions asked, even though my answers were quite unpopular among my colleagues.

PLAYBOY: You were unpopular because you seemed to be supporting the accusations against Oppenheimer. Of *course* he wanted a hearing. If you were in his position, a loyal citizen whose clearance suddenly came into question, wouldn't *you* want a hearing?

TELLER: No, and I'll tell you why. If I were told that my advice on military matters was not required, I would be perfectly content not to have to do anything more about it. No one should be a judge in his own case.

PLAYBOY: Are you saying that if your loyalty were questioned—as Oppenheimer's was—and aspersions were cast on your character—

TELLER: Look, excuse me, the aspersions were not a public affair. Oppenheimer had taken the position that his main interest was thenceforth in pure science. He was given the opportunity to withdraw from those affairs in which he said he did not have a primary interest. If one person felt that Oppenheimer was not loyal, well, perhaps that required that the question be cleared up as completely as possible. But you asked how I would react. *I* think I am loyal. If somebody wanted to destroy my clearance for any reason, I would leave it to others to judge and would not want to contest it. You asked me how I would behave and that is what I would do.

PLAYBOY: Most people wouldn't consider that an adequate answer.

TELLER: Why?

PLAYBOY: Because most people would not react that way. To have one's loyalty questioned in public or in private is a serious matter that caused Oppenheimer considerable grief.

TELLER: Look, if in my own mind I have a fair idea of my motives, whether others like my motives or not doesn't particularly bother me.

PLAYBOY: Then, as to your motives, can you say definitely that there was no feeling of malice in your testimony against Oppenheimer?

TELLER: May I say that that testimony was delivered under oath? To speak under oath is a heavy responsibility, and I felt it to be so. Under those conditions, to say anything except what you're convinced of cannot be pardoned, shouldn't be pardoned and usually is not pardoned. Oppenheimer was a man whom I admired, whom in many ways I did not understand, whom a few years later I recommended for the Fermi award. To the extent that I know myself, there was not any more malice in my testimony about Oppenheimer than there was in my recommendation that he get that award.

PLAYBOY: Do you think that our society rewards scientists appropriately, financially speaking?

TELLER: I doubt that in the greatest days of music, which is my favorite kind of art, the giants of the period became particularly rich men. I don't think that Bach, Mozart or Beethoven got rich. I don't think that it is a real necessity that excellent scientists today should do better in a financial respect.

Perhaps with fewer cares and difficulties, Mozart would have lived longer. I don't want to underestimate the importance of material rewards. Scientists get some. Whether or not it is enough, I am not particularly concerned. The reason to work is the work itself. The nice part of living in an affluent society is that financial rewards are no longer quite as improbable as they were when the lot of the average person was much harder than it is today in the United States.

PLAYBOY: What is your opinion of the caliber of American science today?

TELLER: There are a lot of excellent American scientists, a lot of admirable achievements. To praise it is superfluous and, in a way, meaningless, because you can't do so without going into details.

It is necessary, however, to criticize it. It tends to be overspecialized. American scientists, unlike Israeli scientists, have lost touch with the people. Perhaps because of that, they have tended to lose touch with one another. More and more, I see that scientists split up into tiny groups and only the "in" group understands the language. In the end, I suspect that some scientists might find themselves in a position where only they understand what they are talking about. More clarity, more attention to expressing one's ideas, in a generally understandable fashion, and a very little dose of modesty would do all of us good.

PLAYBOY: Of your generation of scientists, many were educated abroad. What is your opinion of scientific education in the United States today?

TELLER: I got my Ph.D. degree when I was barely 22 years old. There were many of my generation who got it at a younger age. American education is strung out over too long a period. It is planned in too great detail. Academic freedom today means that the professors can do whatever they like. Academic freedom in Europe meant that the students could study whatever they liked. I had the best of both worlds, because I was a student in Europe and a professor here. I still believe that a greater freedom of choice in the subjects of education and an earlier completion of education would be helpful. I am greatly worried about what is now going on in our high schools. I do not mean only the distractions, such as violence, I also mean that scientific subjects are presented in a boring manner and few students get the impression that there is high excitement in understanding the laws of nature.

There is one subject that is taught to our young people in a really first-class manner. Please don't take this in a facetious way—our teaching of football is excellent. The indication of this is that children who want to be good football players don't complain that the work is too hard. If we can establish the spirit where the young people want more rather than less, that is a good sign. But that sign is absent in the science classes of our high schools.

PLAYBOY: Science has been the religion of our time. You have been present at some of its most spectacular moments. Is science the answer, or a major answer, to the world's problems?

TELLER: I have to say no. It was said about Gertrude Stein that she asked on her deathbed, "What is the answer?" and didn't get any answer. Then she asked, "What is the question?" and at that point she died. I believe that not only does science lack the answer, it even lacks the question.

Science, like the very best of art, is fascinating. You could have asked me with equal justification whether or not Mozart had the answer. Almost equal justification, because science also has another role. Science has become closely connected with technology. In my mind, technology is the greatest of all humanizing influences. Of course, many young people today say that science is dehumanizing. What they mean is that technology can be misused. I say technology is humanizing because it makes the difference between us humans and the rest of the living world ever greater. Therefore, it makes us more human. I have not said whether it is good or bad to be human. I believe, in fact, it is both. Now, we have some sort of question, but it is not a question that can be answered by any single portion of human activity.

PLAYBOY: Are there any particular discoveries you wish you had gotten to first?

TELLER: There are many—but absolutely none about which I feel any regret. Scientific insight is beautiful. That excludes, or at least diminishes, any feeling of jealousy and any overemphasis on competition. But all that holds only as long as scientists remain strictly scientists.

PLAYBOY: *You* may not remain strictly a scientist. There have been rumors you might enter politics, perhaps run for the Senate from California against Alan Cranston. Would you care to comment?

TELLER: Now, I am going to tell you something that sounds very improbable: that is that I am thinking—and you know, thinking is a very dangerous occupation and I don't do it very often, partly because I find it habit-forming, partly because it sometimes gives surprising results—I am thinking of the possibility that I might conceivably be running for the Senate seat from California. When one starts to think, one never knows what will happen next.

PLAYBOY: Your reputation as a scientist has been contentious. Could you learn the political arts of compromise?

TELLER: There are many people I like from both political parties. There might be a very few with whom, in the end, I could not work. But they are a minority. You know, it turned out that even among physicists, I managed to work with a great number at one time or another, and if there is a group of people crazier than politicians, it may well be physicists.

PLAYBOY: Well, that wraps it up, unless there is something you would like to add.

TELLER: Best regards to the centerfold.

Playboy Interview Interludes

I figure if a sucker don't wanna get hisself capital punished, he shouldn't get the death penalty put on him. I mean, any damn fool that's stupid enough to get sentenced to death, what the hell's he got to snivel about afterwards?

Gary Gilmore, April 1977

Kissinger, Nixon and Ford did not face racism in their lives and tended to rule it out. Nixon and Ford did not face it because they were, in fact, racists. . . . There's a sense in which every American, black or white, is affected by racism. We've got to start talking about racism without putting moral categories on it so we can understand it.

Andrew Young, July 1977

When it's five below in New York, it's 78 in Los Angeles, and when it's 110 in New York, it's 78 in Los Angeles. There are two million interesting people in New York—and only 78 in Los Angeles.

Neil Simon, February 1979

I found Christ while I was watching "Monday Night Football."

Terry Bradshaw, March 1980

In terms of my own capacities, my children represent a very significant regression. My first wife—their mother—had not as high an academic-achievement standing as I had.

William Shockley, August 1980

JOHN LENNON and YOKO ONO

January 1981

Interviewer: David Sheff

In the summer of 1980, David Sheff, a Los Angeles writer who had written some perceptive profiles of rock musicians for *People* magazine, was in Golson's New York PLAYBOY offices, hoping to get his first interview assignment from the magazine. Golson mentioned casually that it had been a long time since John Lennon had been heard from and asked Sheff if he would check out the possibility of an interview with his contacts in the music world. Several days later Sheff called to say that he'd received word that, by coincidence, the Lennons were about to emerge from five years of privacy to record a new album and that they might be willing to speak to someone from the press. There followed weeks of negotiations as Yoko Ono, who made the business decisions for the couple, discussed the ground rules of an exclusive interview. (She based her decisions at least partly on astrological portents, as Sheff describes below in the introduction.) At one point in the negotiations, as Sheff and Golson met with Ono while Lennon was recording, Ono remarked that she was unimpressed with the other notables who had been interviewed by PLAYBOY; she said that presidents and politicians represented only their country, while she and Lennon represented the world. The journalists decided to include that episode in the introduction as an example of Ono's tough-mindedness, without knowing, of course, that what appeared to be an exaggerated self-description would prove to be tragically accurate.

About midway through the interview sessions, *Newsweek* magazine carried a short interview of its own with Lennon. This prompted Sheff and Golson to visit the Lennons together at their office in the Dakota. When they arrived, Lennon, lounging in an armchair, greeted the journalists. Golson held up a copy of the current *Newsweek* and said in mock anger, "John, you blew our exclusive." Lennon grinned sheepishly and said, "Yeah, I guess I don't know when to shut up, do I?" He stood up and said, "Well, what can I do to make it up to you guys?"

It was an interesting moment. Here was one of the world's most accomplished and sought-after personalities, sympathizing with the disappointment of a couple of magazine journalists, and offering his time and energy as compensation to them. They looked at each other, and Golson said, "David and I were talking the other day about what it would have been like to ask one of the great composers of the past how he came to write his symphonies." Lennon laughed, and Golson went on, "Have you ever gone over your entire work, song by song, to recall who wrote what, and under what circumstances, and what memories the songs might inspire?"

Lennon thought for a moment. "Y'know," he said, "I tried to do something like that ten years ago, but ever since then all I've been asked about is Beatles reunions and rubbish like that. You're asking about my work, about my *life's* work. And I'm proud of it. Let's get it on the record."

That afternoon, as Golson returned to his office, Sheff and Lennon sat down to record the former Beatle's musical recollections, and, through skillful interrogation, Sheff prodded Lennon into remembering far more than the origins of his music. The result was a memorable and definitive interview that would run over 20,000 words in the magazine.

Two months later, after the magazine had been out for about a week, the world heard the terrible news: Lennon had been murdered by a deranged fan in front of the Dakota. After the weeks they had spent with the Lennons, and the long nights laboring over the tapes, the journalists had come to feel they knew the man; with others throughout the world, they felt the loss personally. It was some small consolation that the magazine had helped to provide a conduit through which Lennon expressed some of his final thoughts on a life richly lived.

To describe the turbulent history of the Beatles, or the musical and cultural mileposts charted by John Lennon, would be an exercise in the obvious. Much of the world knows that Lennon was the guiding spirit of the Beatles, who were themselves among the most popular and profound influences of the Sixties, before breaking up bitterly in 1970. Some fans blamed the breakup on Yoko Ono, Lennon's Japanese-born second wife, who was said to have wielded a disproportionate influence over Lennon, and with whom he has collaborated throughout the Seventies. In 1975, the Lennons became unavailable to the press, and though much speculation has been printed, they emerged to dispel the rumors—and to cut a new album—only a couple of months ago. The Lennons decided to speak with PLAYBOY *in the longest interview they have ever granted. Free-lance writer David Sheff was tapped for the assignment, and when he and a* PLAYBOY *editor met with Ono to discuss ground rules, she came on strong: Responding to a reference to other notables who had been interviewed in* PLAYBOY, *Ono said, "People like Carter represent only their country. John and I represent the world." But by the time the interview was concluded several weeks later, Ono had joined the project with enthusiasm. Here is Sheff's report:*

"There was an excellent chance this interview would never take place. When my contacts with the Lennon-Ono organization began, one of Ono's assistants called me, asking, seriously, 'What's your sign?' The interview apparently depended on Yoko's interpretation of my horoscope, just as many of the Lennons' business decisions are reportedly guided by the stars. I could imagine explaining to my PLAYBOY *editor, 'Sorry, but my moon is in Scorpio—the interview's off.' It was clearly out of my hands. I supplied the info: December 23, three* P.M., *Boston.*

"Thank my lucky stars. The call came in and the interview was tentatively on. And I soon found myself in New York, passing through the ominous gates and numerous security check points at the Lennons' headquarters, the famed Dakota apartment building on Central Park West, where the couple dwells and where Yoko Ono holds court beginning at eight o'clock every morning.

"Ono is one of the most misunderstood women in the public eye. Her mysterious image is based on some accurate and some warped accounts of her philosophies and her art statements, and on the fact that she never smiles. It is also based—perhaps unfairly—on resentment of her as the sorceress/Svengali who controls the very existence of John Lennon. That image has remained through the years since she and John met, primarily because she hasn't chosen to correct it—nor has she chosen to smile. So as I removed my shoes before treading on her fragile carpet—those were the instructions—I wondered what the next test might be.

"Between interruptions from her two male assistants busy screening the constant flow of phone calls, Yoko gave me the once-over. She finally explained that the stars had, indeed, said it was right—very right, in fact. Who was I to argue? So the next day, I found myself sitting across a couple of cups of cappuccino from John Lennon.

"Lennon, still bleary-eyed from lack of sleep and scruffy from lack of shave, waited for the coffee to take hold of a system otherwise used to

operating on sushi *and* sashimi—*'dead fish,' as he calls them—French cigarettes and Hershey bars with almonds.*

"Within the first hour of the interview, Lennon put every one of my preconceived ideas about him to rest. He was far more open and candid and witty than I had any right to expect. He was prepared, once Yoko had given the initial go-ahead, to frankly talk about everything. Explode was more like it. If his sessions in primal-scream therapy were his emotional and intellectual release ten years ago, this interview was his more recent vent. After a week of conversations with Lennon and Ono separately as well as together, we had apparently established some sort of rapport, which was confirmed early one morning.

" 'John wants to know how fast you can meet him at the apartment,' announced the by-then-familiar voice of a Lennon-Ono assistant. It was a short cab ride away and he briefed me quickly: 'A guy's trying to serve me a subpoena and I just don't want to deal with it today. Will you help me out?' We sneaked into his limousine and streaked toward the recording studio three hours before Lennon was to arrive. Lennon told his driver to slow to a crawl as we approached the studio and instructed me to lead the way inside, after making sure the path was safe. 'If anybody comes up with papers, knock them down,' he said. 'As long as they don't touch me, it's OK.' Before I left the car, Lennon pointed to a sleeping wino leaning against the studio wall. 'That could be him,' Lennon warned. 'They're masters *of disguise.' Lennon high-tailed it into the elevator, dragging me along with him. When the elevator doors finally closed, he let out a nervous sigh and somehow the ludicrousness of the morning dawned on him. He broke out laughing. 'I feel like I'm back in "Hard Day's Night" or "Help!" ' he said.*

"As the interview progressed, the complicated and misunderstood relationship between Lennon and Ono emerged as the primary factor in both of their lives. 'Why don't people believe us when we say we're simply in love?' John pleaded. The enigma called Yoko Ono became accessible as the hard exterior broke down—such as the morning when she let out a hiccup right in the middle of a heavy discourse on capitalism. Nonplused by her hiccup, Ono giggled. With that giggle, she became vulnerable and cute and shy—not at all the creature that came from the Orient to brainwash John Lennon.

"Ono was born in 1933 in Tokyo, where her parents were bankers and socialites. In 1951, her family moved to Scarsdale, New York. She attended Sarah Lawrence College. In 1957, Yoko was married for the first time, to Toshi Ichiyanagi, a musician. They were divorced in 1964 and later that year, she married Tony Cox, who fathered her daughter, Kyoko. She and Cox were divorced in 1967, two years before she married Lennon.

"The Lennon half of the couple was born in October 1940. His father left home before John was born to become a seaman and his mother, in-

capable of caring for the boy, turned John over to his aunt and uncle when he was four and a half. They lived several blocks away from his mother in Liverpool, England. Lennon, who attended Liverpool private schools, met a kid named Paul McCartney in 1956 at the Woolton Parish Church Festival in Liverpool. The following year, the two formed their first band, the Nurk Twins. In 1958, John formed the Quarrymen, named after his high school. He asked Paul to join the band and agreed to audition a friend of Paul's, George Harrison. In 1959, the Quarrymen disbanded but later regrouped as Johnny and the Moondogs and then the Silver Beatles. They played in clubs, backing strippers, and they got their foot in the door of Liverpool's showcase Cavern Club. Pete Best was signed on as drummer and the Silver Beatles left England for Hamburg, where they played eight hours a night at the Indra Club. The Silver Beatles became the Beatles and, by 1960, when they returned to England, the band had become the talk of Liverpool. In 1962, John married Cynthia Powell and they had a son, Julian. John and Cynthia were divorced in 1968. Later in 1962, Richard Starkey—or Ringo Starr—replaced Best as the Beatles' drummer and the rest—as Lennon often says sarcastically—is pop history."

PLAYBOY: The word is out: John Lennon and Yoko Ono are back in the studio, recording again for the first time since 1975, when they vanished from public view. Let's start with you, John. What have you been doing?

LENNON: I've been baking bread and looking after the baby.

PLAYBOY: With what secret projects going on in the basement?

LENNON: That's like what everyone else who has asked me that question over the last few years says. "But what *else* have you been doing?" To which I say, "Are you kidding?" Because bread and babies, as every housewife knows, is a full-time job. After I made the loaves, I felt like I had conquered something. But as I watched the bread being eaten, I thought, Well, Jesus, don't I get a gold record or knighted or nothing?

PLAYBOY: Why did you become a househusband?

LENNON: There were many reasons. I had been under obligation or contract from the time I was 22 until well into my 30s. After all those years, it was all I knew. I wasn't free. I was boxed in. My contract was the physical manifestation of being in prison. It was more important to face myself and face that reality than to continue a life of rock 'n' roll—and to go up and down with the whims of either your own performance or the public's opinion of you. Rock 'n' roll was not fun anymore. I chose not to take the standard options in my business—going to Vegas and singing your great hits, if you're lucky, or going to hell, which is where Elvis went.

ONO: John was like an artist who is very good at drawing circles. He sticks to that and it becomes his label. He has a gallery to promote that. And the next year, he will do triangles or something. It doesn't reflect his life at all. When you continue doing the same thing for ten years, you get a prize for having done it.

LENNON: You get the big prize when you get cancer and you have been drawing circles and triangles for ten years. I had become a craftsman and I could have continued being a craftsman. I respect craftsmen, but I am not interested in becoming one.

ONO: Just to prove that you can go on dishing out things.

PLAYBOY: You're talking about records, of course.

LENNON: Yeah, to churn them out because I was expected to, like so many people who put out an album every six months because they're supposed to.

PLAYBOY: Would you be referring to Paul McCartney?

LENNON: Not only Paul. But I had lost the initial freedom of the artist by becoming enslaved to the image of what the artist is *supposed* to do. A lot of artists kill themselves because of it, whether it is through drink, like Dylan Thomas, or through insanity, like Van Gogh, or through V.D., like Gauguin.

PLAYBOY: Most people would have continued to churn out the product. How were you able to see a way out?

LENNON: Most people don't live with Yoko Ono.

PLAYBOY: Which means?

LENNON: Most people don't have a companion who will tell the truth and refuse to live with a bullshit artist, which I am pretty good at. I can bullshit myself and everybody around. Yoko: That's my answer.

PLAYBOY: What did she do for you?

LENNON: She showed me the *possibility* of the alternative. "You don't *have* to do this." "I don't? Really? But—but—but—but—but. . . ." Of course, it wasn't that simple and it didn't sink in overnight. It took constant reinforcement. Walking away is much harder than carrying on. I've done both. On demand and on schedule, I had turned out records from 1962 to 1975. Walking away seemed like what the guys go through at 65, when suddenly they're supposed to not exist anymore and they're sent out of the office [*knocks on the desk three times*]: "Your life is over. Time for golf."

PLAYBOY: Yoko, how did you feel about John's becoming a househusband?

ONO: When John and I would go out, people would come up and say, "John, what are you doing?" but they never asked me, because, as a woman, I wasn't *supposed* to be doing anything.

LENNON: When I was cleaning the cat shit and feeding Sean, she was sitting in rooms full of smoke with men in three-piece suits that they couldn't button.

ONO: I handled the business: old business—Apple, Maclen [the Beatles' record company and publishing company, respectively]—and new investments.

LENNON: We had to face the business. It was either another case of asking some daddy to come solve our business or having one of us do it. Those lawyers were getting a quarter of a million dollars a year to sit around a table and eat salmon at the Plaza. Most of them didn't seem interested in solving the problems. Every lawyer had a lawyer. Each Beatle had four or five people working. So we felt we had to look after that side of the business and get rid of it and deal with it before we could start dealing with our own life. And the only one of us who has the talent or the ability to deal with it on that level is Yoko.

PLAYBOY: Did you have experience handling business matters of that proportion?

ONO: I learned. The law is not a mystery to me anymore. Politicians are not a mystery to me. I'm not scared of all that establishment anymore. At first, my own accountant and my own lawyer could not deal with the fact that I was telling them what to do.

LENNON: There was a bit of an attitude that this is John's wife, but surely she can't *really* be representing him.

ONO: A lawyer would send a letter to the directors, but instead of sending it to me, he would send it to John or send it to *my* lawyer. You'd be surprised how much insult I took from them initially. There was all this "But you don't know anything about law; I can't talk to you." I said, "All right, talk to me in the way I can understand it. I am a director, too."

LENNON: They can't stand it. But they have to stand it, because she is who represents us. [*Chuckles*] They're all male, you know, just big and fat, vodka lunch, shouting males, like trained dogs, trained to attack all the time. Recently, she made it possible for us to earn a large sum of money that benefited all of them and they fought and fought not to let her do it, because it was her idea and she was a woman and she was not a professional. But she did it, and then one of the guys said to her, "Well, Lennon does it again." But Lennon didn't have anything to do with it.

PLAYBOY: Why are you returning to the studio and public life?

LENNON: You breathe in and you breathe out. We feel like doing it and we have something to say. Also, Yoko and I attempted a few times to make music together, but that was a long time ago and people still had the idea that the Beatles were some kind of sacred thing that shouldn't step outside its circle. It was hard for us to work together then. We think either people have forgotten or they have grown up by now, so we can make a second foray into that place where she and I are together, making music—simply that. It's not like I'm some wondrous, mystic prince from the rock-'n'-roll world dabbling in strange music with this exotic, Oriental dragon lady, which was the picture projected by the press before.

PLAYBOY: Some people have accused you of playing to the media. First you become a recluse, then you talk selectively to the press because you have a new album coming out.

LENNON: That's ridiculous. People always said John and Yoko would do anything for the publicity. In the *Newsweek* article [September 29, 1980], it says the reporter asked us, "Why did you go underground?" Well, she never asked it that way and I *didn't* go underground. I just stopped talking to the press.

It got to be pretty funny. I was calling myself Greta Hughes or Howard Garbo through that period. But still the gossip items never stopped. We never stopped being *in* the press, but there seemed to be more written about us when we weren't talking to the press than when we were.

PLAYBOY: How do you feel about all the negative press that's been directed through the years at Yoko, your "dragon lady," as you put it?

LENNON: We are both sensitive people and we were hurt a lot by it. I mean, we couldn't understand it. When you're in love, when somebody says something like, "How can you be with that woman?" you say, "What do you mean? I am with this goddess of love, the fulfillment of my whole life. Why are you saying this? Why do you want to throw a rock at her or punish me for being in love with her?" Our love helped us survive it, but some of it was pretty violent. There were a few times when we nearly went under, but we managed to survive and here we are. [*Looks upward*] Thank you, thank you, thank you.

PLAYBOY: But what about the charge that John Lennon is under Yoko's spell, under her control?

LENNON: Well, that's rubbish, you know. Nobody controls me. I'm uncontrollable. The only one who controls me is me, and that's just barely possible.

PLAYBOY: Still, many people believe it.

LENNON: Listen, if somebody's gonna impress me, whether it be a Maharishi or a Yoko Ono, there comes a point when the emperor has no clothes. There comes a point when I will see. So for all you folks out there who think that I'm having the wool pulled over my eyes, well, that's an insult to me. Not that you think less of Yoko, because that's *your* problem. What I think of her is what counts! Because—fuck you, brother and sister—you don't know what's happening. I'm not here for you. I'm here for me and her and the baby!

ONO: Of course, it's a total insult to *me*—

LENNON: Well, you're always insulted, my dear wife. It's natural—

ONO: Why should I bother to control anybody?

LENNON: She doesn't need me.

ONO: I have my own life, you know.

LENNON: She doesn't need a Beatle. Who needs a Beatle?

ONO: Do people think I'm that much of a con? John lasted two months with the Maharishi. Two months. I must be the biggest con in the world, because I've been with him 13 years.

LENNON: But people do say that.

PLAYBOY: That's our point. Why?

LENNON: They want to hold on to something they never had in the first place. Anybody who claims to have some interest in me as an individual artist or even as part of the Beatles has absolutely misunderstood everything I ever said if they can't see why I'm with Yoko. And if they can't see that, they don't see anything. They're just jacking off to—it could be anybody. Mick Jagger or somebody else. Let them go jack off to Mick Jagger, OK? I don't need it.

PLAYBOY: He'll appreciate that.

LENNON: I absolutely don't need it. Let them chase Wings. Just forget about me. If that's what you want, go after Paul or Mick. I ain't here for that. If that's not apparent in my past, I'm saying it in black and green, next to all the tits and asses on page 196. Go play with the other boys. Don't bother me. Go play with the Rolling Wings.

PLAYBOY: Do you—

LENNON: No, wait a minute. Let's stay with this a second; sometimes I can't let go of it. [*He is on his feet, climbing up the refrigerator*] Nobody ever said *anything* about Paul's having a spell on me or my having one on Paul! They never thought *that* was abnormal in those days, two guys together, or four guys together! Why didn't they ever say, "How come those guys don't split up? I mean, what's going *on* backstage? *What is this Paul and John business?* How can they be together so long?" We spent more time together in the early days than John and Yoko: the four of us sleeping in the same room, practically in the same bed, in the same truck, living together night and day, eating, *shitting* and *pissing* together! All right? Doing *everything* together! Nobody said a damn thing about being under a spell. Maybe they said we were under the spell of Brian Epstein or George Martin [the Beatles' first manager and producer, respectively]. There's always somebody who has to be doing something to you.

You know, they're congratulating the Stones on being together 112 years. Whoooopee! At least Charlie and Bill still got their families. In the Eighties, they'll be asking, "Why are those guys still together? Can't they hack it on their own? Why do they have to be surrounded by a gang? Is the little leader scared somebody's gonna knife him in the back?" That's gonna be the question. That's-a-gonna be the question! They're gonna look back at the Beatles and the Stones and all those guys are relics. The days when those bands were just all men will be on the newsreels, you know. They will be showing pictures of the guy with lipstick wriggling his ass and the four guys with the evil black make-up on their eyes trying to look raunchy. That's gonna be the joke in the future, not a couple singing together or living and working together. It's all right when you're 16, 17, 18 to have male companions and idols, OK? It's tribal and it's gang and it's fine. But when it continues and you're still doing it when you're 40, that means you're still 16 in the head.

PLAYBOY: Let's start at the beginning. Tell us the story of how the wondrous mystic prince and the exotic Oriental dragon lady met.

LENNON: It was in 1966 in England. I'd been told about this "event"—this Japanese avant-garde artist coming from America.

I was looking around the gallery and I saw this ladder and climbed up and got a look in this spyglass on the top of the ladder—you feel like a fool—and it just said, YES. Now, at the time, all the avant-garde was smash the piano with a hammer and break the sculpture and anti-, anti-, anti-, anti-, anti-. It was all boring negative crap, you know. And just that YES made me stay in a gallery full of apples and nails.

There was a sign that said, HAMMER A NAIL IN, so I said, "Can I hammer a nail in?" But Yoko said no, because the show wasn't opening until the next day. But the owner came up and whispered to her, "Let him hammer a nail in. You know, he's a millionaire. He might buy it." And so there was this little conference, and finally she said, "OK, you can hammer a nail in for five shillings." So smartass says, "Well, I'll give you an imaginary five shillings and hammer an imaginary nail in." And that's when we really met. That's when we locked eyes and she got it and I got it and, as they say in all the interviews we do, the rest is history.

PLAYBOY: What happened next?

LENNON: Of course, I was a Beatle, but things had begun to change. In 1966, just before we met, I went to Almería, Spain, to make the movie *How I Won the War*. It did me a lot of good to get away. I was there six weeks. I wrote *Strawberry Fields Forever* there, by the way. It gave me time to think on my own, away from the others. From then on, I was looking for somewhere to go, but I didn't have the nerve to really step out on the boat by myself and push it off. But when I fell in love with Yoko, I knew, My God, this is different from anything I've ever known. This is something other. This is more than a hit record, more than gold, more than everything. It is indescribable.

PLAYBOY: Were falling in love with Yoko and wanting to leave the Beatles connected?

LENNON: As I said, I had already begun to want to leave, but when I met Yoko is like when you meet your first woman. You leave the guys at the bar. You don't go play football anymore. You don't go play snooker or billiards. Maybe some guys do it on Friday night or something, but once I found *the* woman, the boys became of no interest whatsoever other than being old school friends. "Those wedding bells are breaking up that old gang of mine." We got married three years later, in 1969. That was the end of the boys. And it just so happened that the boys were well known and weren't just local guys at the bar. Everybody got *so upset* over it. There was a lot of shit thrown at us. A lot of hateful stuff.

ONO: Even now, I just read that Paul said, "I understand that he wants to be with her, but why does he have to be with her all the time?"

LENNON: Yoko, do you still have to carry that cross? That was years ago.

ONO: No, no, no. He said it recently. I mean, what happened with John is like, I sort of went to bed with this guy that I liked and suddenly the next morning, I see these three in-laws, standing there.

LENNON: I've always thought there was this underlying thing in Paul's *Get Back*. When we were in the studio recording it, every time he sang the line "Get back to where you once belonged," he'd look at Yoko.

PLAYBOY: Are you kidding?

LENNON: No. But maybe he'll say I'm paranoid.

[*The next portion of the interview took place with Lennon alone.*]

PLAYBOY: This may be the time to talk about those "in-laws," as Yoko put it. John, you've been asked this a thousand times, but why is it so unthinkable that the Beatles might get back together to make some music?

LENNON: Do you want to go back to high school? Why should I go back ten years to provide an illusion for you that I know does not exist? It cannot exist.

PLAYBOY: Then forget the illusion. What about just to make some great music again? Do you acknowledge that the Beatles made great music?

LENNON: Why should the Beatles give more? Didn't they give everything on God's earth for ten years? Didn't they give *themselves*? You're like the typical sort of love-hate fan who says, "Thank you for everything you did for us in the Sixties—would you just give me another shot? Just one more miracle?"

PLAYBOY: We're not talking about miracles—just good music.

LENNON: When Rodgers worked with Hart and then worked with Hammerstein, do you think he should have stayed with one instead of working with the other? Should Dean Martin and Jerry Lewis have stayed together because *I* used to like them together? What is this game of doing things because other people want it? The whole Beatle idea was to do what *you* want, right? To take your own responsibility.

PLAYBOY: All right, but get back to the music itself: You don't agree that the Beatles created the best rock 'n' roll that's been produced?

LENNON: I don't. The Beatles, you see—I'm too involved in them artistically. I cannot see them objectively. I cannot listen to them objectively. I'm dissatisfied with every record the Beatles ever fucking made. There ain't *one* of them I wouldn't remake—including all the Beatles records and all my individual ones. So I cannot possibly give you an assessment of what the Beatles are.

When I was a Beatle, I thought we were the best fucking group in the goddamned world. And believing that is what made us what we were—whether we call it the best rock-'n'-roll group or the best pop group or whatever.

But you play me those tracks today and I want to remake every damn one of them. There's not a single one. . . . I heard *Lucy in the Sky with Diamonds* on the radio last night. It's *abysmal,* you know. The track is just *terrible.* I mean, it's great, but it wasn't made right, know what I mean? But that's the artistic trip, isn't it? That's why you keep going. But to get back to your original question about the Beatles and their music, the answer is that we did some good stuff and we did some bad stuff.

PLAYBOY: Many people feel that none of the songs Paul has done alone match the songs he did as a Beatle. Do you honestly feel that any of *your* songs—on the Plastic Ono Band records—will have the lasting imprint of *Eleanor Rigby* or *Strawberry Fields?*

LENNON: *Imagine, Love* and those Plastic Ono Band songs stand up to *any* song that was written when I was a Beatle. Now, it may take you 20 or 30 years to appreciate that, but the fact is, if you check those songs out, you will see that it is as good as any fucking stuff that was ever done.

PLAYBOY: It seems as if you're trying to say to the world, "We were just a good band making some good music," while a lot of the rest of the world is saying, "It wasn't just some good music, it was the *best.*"

LENNON: Well, if it was the best, so what?

PLAYBOY: So—

LENNON: *It can never be again!* Everyone always talks about a good thing coming to an end, as if life was over. But I'll be 40 when this interview comes out. Paul is 38. Elton John, Bob Dylan—we're all relatively young people. The game isn't over yet. Everyone talks in terms of the last record or the last Beatle concert—but, God willing, there are another 40 years of productivity to go. I'm not judging whether *I Am the Walrus* is better or worse than *Imagine.* It is for others to judge. I am *doing* it. I *do.* I don't stand back and judge—I do.

PLAYBOY: You keep saying you don't want to go back ten years, that too much has changed. Don't you ever feel it would be interesting—never mind cosmic, just *interesting*—to get together, with all your new experiences, and cross your talents?

LENNON: Wouldn't it be *interesting* to take Elvis back to his Sun Records period? I don't know. But I'm content to listen to his Sun Records. I don't want to dig him up out of the grave. The Beatles don't exist and can never exist again. John Lennon, Paul McCartney, George Harrison and Richard Starkey could put on a concert—but it can never be the Beatles singing *Strawberry Fields* or *I Am the Walrus* again, because we are not in our 20s. We cannot be that again, nor can the people who are listening.

PLAYBOY: But aren't you the one who is making it too important? What if it were just nostalgic fun? A high school reunion?

LENNON: I never went to high school reunions. My thing is, Out of sight, out of mind. That's my attitude toward life. So I don't have any romanticism about any part of my past. I think of it only inasmuch as it gave me pleasure or helped me grow psychologically. That is the only thing that interests me about yesterday. I don't believe in yesterday, by the way. You know *I don't believe in yesterday.* I am only interested in what I am doing now.

PLAYBOY: What about the people of your generation, the ones who feel a certain kind of music—and spirit—died when the Beatles broke up?

LENNON: If they didn't understand the Beatles and the Sixties then, what the fuck could we do for them now? Do we have to divide the fish and the loaves for the multitudes again? Do we have to get crucified again? Do we have to do the walking on water again because a whole pile of dummies didn't see it the first time, or didn't believe it when they saw it? You know, that's what they're asking: "Get off the cross. I didn't understand the first bit yet. Can you do that again?" No way. You can never go home. It doesn't exist.

PLAYBOY: Do you find that the clamor for a Beatles reunion has died down?

LENNON: Well, I heard some Beatles stuff on the radio the other day and I heard *Green Onion*—no, *Glass Onion,* I don't even know my own songs! I listened to it because it was a rare track—

PLAYBOY: That was the one that contributed to the "Paul McCartney is dead" uproar because of the lyric "The walrus is Paul."

LENNON: Yeah. That line was a joke, you know. That line was put in partly because I was feeling guilty because I was with Yoko, and I knew I was finally high and dry. In a perverse way, I was sort of saying to Paul, "Here, have this crumb, have this illusion, have this stroke—because I'm leaving you." Anyway, it's a song they don't usually play. When a radio station has a Beatles weekend, they usually play the same ten songs—*A Hard Day's Night, Help!, Yesterday, Something, Let It Be*—you know, there's all that wealth of material, but we hear only ten songs. So the deejay says, "I want to thank John, Paul, George and Ringo for *not* getting back together and spoiling a good thing." I thought it was a good sign. Maybe people are catching on.

PLAYBOY: Aside from the millions you've been offered for a reunion concert, how did you feel about producer Lorne Michaels' generous offer of $3200 for appearing together on *Saturday Night Live* a few years ago?

LENNON: Oh, yeah. Paul and I were together watching that show. He was visiting us at our place in the Dakota. We were watching it and almost went down to the studio, just as a gag. We nearly got into a cab, but we were actually too tired.

PLAYBOY: How did you and Paul happen to be watching TV together?

LENNON: That was a period when Paul just kept turning up at our door with a guitar. I would let him in, but finally I said to him, "Please call before you come over. It's not 1956 and turning up at the door isn't the same anymore. You know, just give me a ring." He was upset by that, but I didn't mean it badly. I just meant that I was taking care of a baby all day and some guy turns up at the door. . . . But, anyway, back on that night, he and Linda walked in and he and I were just sitting there, watching the show, and we went, "Ha-ha, woudn't it be funny if we went down?" but we didn't.

PLAYBOY: Was that the last time you saw Paul?

LENNON: Yes, but I didn't mean it like that.

PLAYBOY: We're asking because there's always a lot of speculation about whether the Fab Four are dreaded enemies or the best of friends.

LENNON: We're neither. I haven't seen *any* of the Beatles for I don't know how much time. Somebody asked me what I thought of Paul's last album and I made some remark like, I thought he was depressed and sad. But then I realized I hadn't listened to the whole damn thing. I heard one track—the hit *Coming Up,* which I thought was a good piece of work. Then I heard something else that sounded like he was depressed. But I don't follow their work. I don't follow Wings, you know. I don't give a shit what Wings is doing, or what George's new album is doing, or what Ringo is doing. I'm not interested, no more than I am in what Elton John or Bob Dyan is doing. It's not callousness, it's just that I'm too busy living my own life to be following what other people are doing, whether they're the Beatles or guys I went to college with or people I had intense relationships with before I met the Beatles.

PLAYBOY: Besides *Coming Up*, what do you think of Paul's work since he left the Beatles?

LENNON: I kind of admire the way Paul started back from scratch, forming a new band and playing in small dance halls, because that's what he wanted to do with the Beatles—he wanted us to go back to the dance halls and experience that again. But I didn't. . . . That was one of the problems, in a way, that he wanted to relive it all or something—I don't know what it was. . . . But I kind of admire the way he got off his pedestal—now he's back on it again, but I mean, he did what he wanted to do. That's fine, but it's just not what I wanted to do.

PLAYBOY: What about the music?

LENNON: *The Long and Winding Road* was the last gasp from him. Although I really haven't listened.

PLAYBOY: You say you haven't listened to Paul's work and haven't really talked to him since that night in your apartment—

LENNON: *Really* talked to him, no, that's the operative word. I haven't *really* talked to him in ten years. Because I haven't spent time with him. I've been doing other things and so has he. You know, he's got 25 kids and about 20,000,000 records out—how can he spend time talking? He's always working.

PLAYBOY: Then let's talk about the work you did together. Generally speaking, what did each of you contribute to the Lennon-McCartney songwriting team?

LENNON: Well, you could say that he provided a lightness, an optimism, while I would always go for the sadness, the discords, a certain bluesy edge.

There was a period when I thought I didn't write melodies, that Paul wrote those and I just wrote straight, shouting rock 'n' roll. But, of course, when I think of some of my own songs—*In My Life*—or some of the early stuff—*This Boy*—I was writing melody with the best of them. Paul had a lot of training, could play a lot of instruments. He'd say, "Well, why don't you change that there? You've done that note 50 times in the song." You know, I'll grab a note and ram it home. Then again, I'd be the one to figure out where to go with a song—a story that Paul would start. In a lot of the songs, my stuff is the "middle eight," the bridge.

PLAYBOY: For example?

LENNON: Take *Michelle*. Paul and I were staying somewhere, and he walked in and hummed the first few bars, with the words, you know [*sings verse of* Michelle], and he says, "Where do I go from here?" I'd been listening to blues singer Nina Simone, who did something like "I love *you*!" in one of her songs, and that made me think of the middle eight for *Michelle* [*sings*]: "I *love* you, I *love* you, I *l-o-ove* you. . . ."

PLAYBOY: What was the difference in terms of lyrics?

LENNON: I always had an easier time with lyrics, though Paul is quite a capable lyricist who doesn't think he is. So he doesn't go for it. Rather than face the problem, he would avoid it. *Hey Jude* is a damn good set of lyrics. I made no contribution to the lyrics there. And a couple of lines he has come up with show indications of a good lyricist. But he just hasn't taken it anywhere. Still, in the early days, we didn't care about lyrics as long as the song had some vague theme—she loves you, he loves him, they all love each other. It was the hook, line and sound we were going for. That's still my attitude, but I can't leave lyrics alone. I have to make them make sense apart from the songs.

PLAYBOY: What's an example of a lyric you and Paul worked on together?

LENNON: In *We Can Work It Out*, Paul did the first half, I did the middle eight. But you've got Paul writing, "We can work it out/We can work it out"—real optimistic, y' know, and me, impatient: "Life is very short and there's no time/For fussing and fighting, my friend. . . ."

PLAYBOY: Paul tells the story and John philosophizes.

LENNON: Sure. Well, I was always like that, you know. I was like that before the Beatles and after the Beatles. I always asked why people did things and why society was like it was. I didn't just accept it for what it was *apparently* doing. I always looked below the surface.

PLAYBOY: When you talk about working together on a single lyric like *We Can Work It Out,* it suggests that you and Paul worked a lot more closely than you've admitted in the past. Haven't you said that you wrote most of your songs separately, despite putting both of your names on them?

LENNON: Yeah, I was lying. [*Laughs*] It was when I felt resentful, so I felt that we did everything apart. But, actually, a lot of the songs we did eyeball to eyeball.

PLAYBOY: But many of them *were* done apart, weren't they?

LENNON: Yeah. *Sgt. Pepper* was Paul's idea, and I remember he worked on it a lot and suddenly called me to go into the studio, said it was time to write some songs. On *Pepper,* under the pressure of only ten days, I managed to come up with *Lucy in the Sky* and *Day in the Life.* We weren't communicating enough, you see. And later on, that's why I got resentful about all that stuff. But now I understand that it was just the same competitive game going on.

PLAYBOY: But the competitive game was good for you, wasn't it?

LENNON: In the early days. We'd make a record in 12 hours or something; they would want a single every three months and we'd have to write it in a hotel room or in a van. So the cooperation was functional as well as musical.

PLAYBOY: Don't you think that cooperation, that magic between you, is something you've missed in your work since?

LENNON: I never actually felt a loss. I don't want it to sound negative, like I didn't need Paul, because when he was there, obviously, it worked. But I can't—it's easier to say what I gave to him than what he gave to me. And he'd say the same.

PLAYBOY: Just a quick aside, but while we're on the subject of lyrics and your resentment of Paul, what made you write *How Do You Sleep?*, which contains lyrics such as "Those freaks was right when they said you was dead" and "The only thing you done was yesterday/And since you've gone, you're just another day"?

LENNON: [*Smiles*] You know, I wasn't really feeling that vicious at the time. But I was using my resentment toward Paul to create a song, let's put it that way. He saw that it pointedly refers to him, and people kept hounding him about it. But, you know, there were a few digs on *his* album before mine. He's so obscure other people didn't notice them, but I heard them. I thought, Well, I'm not obscure, I just get right down to the nitty-gritty. So he'd done it his way and I did it mine. But as to the line you quoted, yeah, I think Paul died creatively, in a way.

PLAYBOY: That's what we were getting at: You say that what *you've* done since the Beatles stands up well, but isn't it possible that with all of you, it's been a case of the creative whole being greater than the parts?

LENNON: I don't know whether this will gel for you: When the Beatles played in America for the first time, they played pure craftsmanship. Meaning they were already old hands. The jism had gone out of the performances a long time ago. In the same respect, the songwriting creativity had left Paul and me in the mid-Sixties. When we wrote together in the early days, it was like the beginning of a relationship. Lots of energy. In the *Sgt. Pepper–Abbey Road* period, the relationship had matured. Maybe had we gone on together, more interesting things would have come, but it couldn't have been the same.

PLAYBOY: Let's move on to Ringo. What's your opinion of him musically?

LENNON: Ringo was a star in his own right in Liverpool before we even met. He was a professional drummer who sang and performed and had Ringo Startime and he was in one of the top groups in Britain but especially in Liverpool before we even had a drummer. So Ringo's talent would have come out one way or the other as something or other. I don't know what he would have ended up as, but whatever that spark is in Ringo that we all know but can't put our finger on—whether it is acting, drumming or singing I don't know—there is something in him that is projectable and he would have surfaced with or without the Beatles. Ringo is a damn good drummer. He is not technically good, but I think Ringo's drumming is underrated the same way Paul's bass playing is underrated. Paul was one of the most innovative bass players ever. And half the stuff that is going on now is directly ripped off from his Beatles period. He is an egomaniac about everything else about himself, but his bass playing he was always a bit coy about. I think Paul and Ringo stand up with any of the rock musicians. Not technically great—none of us are technical musicians. None of us could read music. None of us can write it. But as pure musicians, as inspired humans to make the noise, they are as good as anybody.

PLAYBOY: How about George's solo music?

LENNON: I think *All Things Must Pass* was all right. It just went on too long.

PLAYBOY: How did you feel about the lawsuit George lost that claimed the music to *My Sweet Lord* is a rip-off of the Shirelles' hit *He's So Fine*?

LENNON: Well, he walked right into it. He knew what he was doing.

PLAYBOY: Are you saying he consciously plagiarized the song?

LENNON: He must have known, you know. He's smarter than that. It's irrelevant, actually—only on a monetary level does it matter. He could have changed a couple of bars in that song and nobody could ever have touched him, but he just let it go and paid the price. Maybe he thought God would just sort of let him off. [*At presstime, the court has found Harrison guilty of "subconscious" plagiarism but has not yet ruled on damages.*]

PLAYBOY: You actually haven't mentioned George much in this interview.

LENNON: Well, I was hurt by George's book, *I, Me, Mine*—so this message will go to him. He put a book out privately on his life that, by glaring omission, says that my influence on his life is absolutely zilch and nil. In his book, which is purportedly this clarity of vision of his influence on each song he wrote, he remembers every two-bit sax player or guitarist he met in subsequent years. I'm not in the book.

PLAYBOY: Why?

LENNON: Because George's relationship with me was one of young follower and older guy. He's three or four years younger than me. It's a love-hate relationship and I think George still bears resentment toward me for being a daddy who left home. He would not agree with this, but that's my feeling about it. I was just hurt. I was just left out, as if I didn't exist. I don't want to be that egomaniacal, but he was like a disciple of mine when we started. I was already an art student when Paul and George were still in grammar school [equivalent to high school in the U.S.]. There is a vast difference between being in high school and being in college and I was already in college and already had sexual relationships, already drank and did a lot of things like that. When George was a kid, he used to follow me and my first girlfriend, Cynthia—who became my wife—around. We'd come out of art school and he'd be hovering around like those kids at the gate of the Dakota now.

I remember the day he called to ask for help on *Taxman,* one of his bigger songs. I threw in a few one-liners to help the song along, because that's what he asked for. He came to me because he couldn't go to Paul, because Paul wouldn't have helped him at that period. I didn't want to do it. I thought, Oh, no, don't tell me I have to work on George's stuff. It's enough doing my own and Paul's. But because I loved him and I didn't want to hurt him when he called me that afternoon and said, "Will you help me with this song?" I just sort of bit my tongue and said OK. It had been John and Paul so long, he'd been left out because he hadn't been a songwriter up until then. As a singer, we allowed him only one track on each album. If you listen to the Beatles' first albums, the English versions, he gets a single track. The songs he and Ringo sang at first were the songs that used to be part of my repertoire in the dance halls. I used to pick songs for them from my repertoire—the easier ones to sing. So I am slightly resentful of George's book. But don't get me wrong. I still love those guys. The Beatles are over, but John, Paul, George and Ringo go on.

PLAYBOY: Didn't all four Beatles work on a song you wrote for Ringo in 1973?

LENNON: *I'm the Greatest.* It was the Muhammad Ali line, of course. It was perfect for Ringo to sing. If I said, "I'm the greatest," they'd all take it so seriously. No one would get upset with Ringo singing it.

PLAYBOY: Did you enjoy playing with George and Ringo again?

LENNON: Yeah, except when George and Billy Preston started saying, "Let's form a group. Let's form a group." I was embarrassed when George kept asking me. He was just enjoying the session and the spirit was very good, but I was with Yoko, you know. We took time out from what we were doing. The very fact that they would imagine I would form a male group without Yoko! It was still in their minds. . . .

PLAYBOY: Just to finish your favorite subject, what about the suggestion that the four of you put aside your personal feelings and regroup to give a mammoth concert for charity, some sort of giant benefit?

LENNON: I don't want to have anything to do with benefits. I have been benefited to death.

PLAYBOY: Why?

LENNON: Because they're always rip-offs. I haven't performed for personal gain since 1966, when the Beatles last performed. Every concert since then, Yoko and I did for specific charities, except for a Toronto thing that was a rock-'n'-roll revival. Every one of them was a mess or a rip-off. So now we give money to who we want. You've heard of tithing?

PLAYBOY: That's when you give away a fixed percentage of your income.

LENNON: Right. I am just going to do it privately. I am not going to get locked into that business of saving the world onstage. The show is always a mess and the artist always comes off badly.

PLAYBOY: What about the Bangladesh concert, in which George and other people such as Dylan performed?

LENNON: Bangladesh was caca.

PLAYBOY: You mean because of all the questions that were raised about where the money went?

LENNON: Yeah, right. I can't even talk about it, because it's still a problem. You'll have to check with Mother [Yoko], because she knows the ins and outs of it, I don't. But it's all a rip-off. So forget about it. All of you who are reading this, don't bother sending me all that garbage about, "Just come and save the Indians, come and save the blacks, come and save the war veterans." Anybody *I* want to save will be helped through our tithing, which is ten percent of whatever we earn.

PLAYBOY: But that doesn't compare with what one promoter, Sid Bernstein, said you could raise by giving a world-wide televised concert—playing separately, as individuals, or together, as the Beatles. He estimated you could raise over $200,000,000 in one day.

LENNON: That was a commercial for Sid Bernstein written with Jewish schmaltz and showbiz and tears, dropping on one knee. It was Al Jolson. OK. So I don't buy that. OK.

PLAYBOY: But the fact is, $200,000,000 to a poverty-stricken country in South America—

LENNON: Where do people get off saying the Beatles should give $200,000,-000 to South America? You know, America has poured billions into places like that. It doesn't mean a damn thing. After they've eaten that meal, then what? It lasts for only a day. After the $200,000,000 is gone, then what? It goes round and round in circles. You can pour money in forever. After Peru, then Harlem, then Britain. There is no one concert. We would have to dedicate the rest of our lives to one world concert tour, and I'm not ready for it. Not in this lifetime, anyway.

[Ono rejoins the conversation.]

PLAYBOY: On the subject of your own wealth, the *New York Post* recently said you admitted to being worth over $150,000,000 and—

LENNON: We never admitted anything.

PLAYBOY: The *Post* said you had.

LENNON: What the *Post* says—OK, so we are rich; so what?

PLAYBOY: The question is, How does that jibe with your political philosophies? You're supposed to be socialists, aren't you?

LENNON: In England, there are only two things to be, basically: You are either for the labor movement or for the capitalist movement. Either you become a right-wing Archie Bunker if you are in the class I am in, or you become an instinctive socialist, which I was. That meant I think people should get their false teeth and their health looked after, all the rest of it. But apart from that, I worked for money and I wanted to be rich. So what the hell—if that's a paradox, then I'm a socialist. But I am not *anything*. What I used to be is guilty about money. That's why I lost it, either by giving it away or by allowing myself to be screwed by so-called managers.

PLAYBOY: Whatever your politics, you've played the capitalist game very well, parlaying your Beatles royalties into real estate, livestock—

ONO: There is no denying that we are still living in the capitalist world. I think that in order to survive and to change the world, you have to take care of yourself first. You have to survive yourself. I used to say to myself, I am the only socialist living here. [*Laughs*] I don't have a penny. It is all John's, so I'm clean. But I was using his money and I had to face that hypocrisy. I used to think that money was obscene, that the artists didn't have to think about money. But to change society, there are two ways to go: through violence or the power of money within the system. A lot of people in the Sixties went underground and were involved in bombings and other violence. But that is not the way, definitely not for me. So to change the system—even if you are going to become a mayor or something—you need money.

PLAYBOY: To what extent do you play the game without getting caught up in it—money for the sake of money, in other words?

ONO: There is a limit. It would probably be parallel to our level of security. Do you know what I mean? I mean the emotional-security level as well.

PLAYBOY: Has it reached that level yet?

ONO: No, not yet. I don't know. It might have.

PLAYBOY: You mean with $150,000,000? Is that an accurate estimate?

ONO: I don't know what we have. It becomes so complex that you need to have ten accountants working for two years to find out what you have. But let's say that we feel more comfortable now.

PLAYBOY: How have you chosen to invest your money?

ONO: To make money, you have to spend money. But if you are going to make money, you have to make it with love. I love Egyptian art. I make sure to get all the Egyptian things, not for their value but for their magic power. Each piece has a certain magic power. Also with houses. I just buy ones we love, not the ones that people say are good investments.

PLAYBOY: The papers have made it sound like you are buying up the Atlantic Seaboard.

ONO: If you saw the houses, you would understand. They have become a good investment, but they are not an investment unless you sell them. We don't intend to sell. Each house is like a historic landmark and they're very beautiful.

PLAYBOY: Do you actually use all the properties?

ONO: Most people have the park to go to and run in—the park is a huge place—but John and I were never able to go to the park together. So we have to create our own parks, you know.

PLAYBOY: We heard that you own $60,000,000 worth of dairy cows. Can that be true?

ONO: I don't know. I'm not a calculator. I'm not going by figures. I'm going by excellence of things.

LENNON: Sean and I were away for a weekend and Yoko came over to sell this cow and I was joking about it. We hadn't seen her for days; she spent all her time on it. But then I read the paper that said she sold it for a quarter of a million dollars. Only Yoko could sell a cow for that much. [*Laughter.*]

PLAYBOY: For an artist, your business sense seems remarkable.

ONO: I was doing it just as a chess game. I love chess. I do everything like it's a chess game. Not on a Monopoly level—that's a bit more realistic. Chess is more conceptual.

PLAYBOY: John, do you really need all those houses around the country?

LENNON: They're good business.

PLAYBOY: Why does anyone need $150,000,000? Couldn't you be perfectly content with $100,000,000? Or $1,000,000?

LENNON: What would you suggest I do? Give everything away and walk the streets? The Buddhist says, "Get rid of the possessions of the mind." Walking away from all the money would not accomplish that. It's like the Beatles. I couldn't walk away from the Beatles. That's one possession that's still tagging along, right? If I walk away from one house or 400 houses, I'm not gonna escape it.

PLAYBOY: How *do* you escape it?

LENNON: It takes time to get rid of all this garbage that I've been carrying around that was influencing the way I thought and the way I lived. It had a lot to do with Yoko, showing me that I was still possessed. I left physically when I fell in love with Yoko, but mentally it took the last ten years of struggling. I learned everything from her.

PLAYBOY: You make it sound like a teacher-pupil relationship.

LENNON: It *is* a teacher-pupil relationship. That's what people don't understand. She's the teacher and I'm the pupil. I'm the famous one, the one who's supposed to know everything, but she's my teacher. She's taught me everything I fucking know. She was there when I was nowhere, when I was the nowhere man. She's my Don Juan [a reference to Carlos Castaneda's Yaqui Indian teacher]. That's what people don't understand. I'm married to fucking Don Juan, that's the hardship of it. Don Juan doesn't have to laugh; Don Juan doesn't have to be charming; Don Juan just *is*. And what goes on around Don Juan is irrelevant to Don Juan.

PLAYBOY: Yoko, how do you feel about being John's teacher?

ONO: Well, he had a lot of experience before he met me, the kind of experience I never had, so I learned a lot from him, too. It's both ways. Maybe it's that I have strength, a feminine strength. Because women develop it— in a relationship, I think women really have the inner wisdom and they're carrying that while men have sort of the wisdom to cope with society, since they created it. Men never developed the inner wisdom; they didn't have time. So most men do rely on women's inner wisdom, whether they express that or not.

PLAYBOY: Is Yoko John's guru?

LENNON: No, a Don Juan doesn't have a following. A Don Juan isn't in the newspaper and doesn't have disciples and doesn't proselytize.

PLAYBOY: How has she taught you?

LENNON: When Don Juan said—when Don Ono said, "Get out! Because you're not getting it," well, it was like being sent into the desert. And the reason she wouldn't let me back in was because I wasn't ready to come back in. I had to settle things within myself. When I was ready to come back in, she let me back in. And that's what I'm living with.

PLAYBOY: You're talking about your separation.

LENNON: Yes. We were separated in the early Seventies. She kicked me out. Suddenly, I was on a raft alone in the middle of the universe.

PLAYBOY: What happened?

LENNON: Well, at first, I thought, Whoopee, whoopee! You know, bachelor life! Whoopee! And then I woke up one day and I thought, What is this? I want to go home! But she wouldn't let me come home. That's why it was 18 months apart instead of six months. We were talking all the time on the phone and I would say, "I don't like this, I'm getting in trouble and I'd like to come home, please." And she would say, "You're not ready to come home." So what do you say? Ok, back to the bottle.

PLAYBOY: What did she mean, you weren't ready?

LENNON: She has her ways. Whether they be mystical or practical. When she said it's not ready, it ain't ready.

PLAYBOY: Back to the bottle?

LENNON: I was just trying to hide what I felt in the bottle. I was just insane. It was the lost weekend that lasted 18 months. I've never drunk so much in my life. I tried to drown myself in the bottle and I was with the heaviest drinkers in the business.

PLAYBOY: Such as?

LENNON: Such as Harry Nilsson, Bobby Keyes, Keith Moon. We couldn't pull ourselves out. We were trying to kill ourselves. I think Harry might still be trying, poor bugger—God bless you, Harry, wherever you are—but,

Jesus, you know, I had to get away from that, because somebody was going to die. Well, Keith did. It was like, who's going to die first? Unfortunately, Keith was the one.

PLAYBOY: Why the self-destruction?

LENNON: For me, it was because of being apart. I couldn't stand it. They had their own reasons, and it was, Let's all drown ourselves together. From where I was sitting, it looked like that. Let's kill ourselves but do it like Errol Flynn, you know, the *macho,* male way. It's embarrassing for me to think about that period, because I made a big fool of myself—but maybe it was a good lesson for me.

I wrote *Nobody Loves You When You're Down and Out* during that time. That's how I felt. It exactly expresses the whole period. For some reason, I always imagined Sinatra singing that one. I don't know why. It's kind of a Sinatraesque song, really. He would do a perfect job with it. Are you listening, Frank? You need a song that isn't a piece of nothing. Here's the one for you, the horn arrangement and everything's made for you. But don't ask me to produce it.

PLAYBOY: That must have been the time the papers came out with reports about Lennon running around town with a Tampax on his head.

LENNON: The stories were all so exaggerated, but. . . . We were all in a restaurant, drinking, not eating, as usual at those gatherings, and I happened to go take a pee and there was a brand-new fresh Kotex, not Tampax, on the toilet. You know the old trick where you put a penny on your forehead and it sticks? I was a little high and I just picked it up and slapped it on and it stayed, you see. I walked out of the bathroom and I had a Kotex on my head. Big deal.

Everybody went "Ha-ha-ha" and it fell off, but the press blew it up.

PLAYBOY: Why *did* you kick John out, Yoko?

ONO: There were many things. I'm what I call a "moving on" kind of girl; there's a song on our new album about it. Rather than deal with problems in relationships, I've always moved on. That's why I'm one of the very few survivors as a woman, you know. Women tend to be more into men usually, but I wasn't. . . .

LENNON: Yoko looks upon men as assistants. . . . Of varying degrees of intimacy, but basically assistants. And *this* one's going to take a pee. [*He exits*]

ONO: I have no comment on that. But when I met John, women to him were basically people around who were serving him. He had to open himself up and face me—and I had to see what he was going through. But . . . I thought I had to move on again, because I was suffering being with John.

PLAYBOY: Why?

ONO: The pressure from the public, being the one who broke up the Beatles and who made it impossible for them to get back together. My artwork suffered, too. I thought I wanted to be free from being Mrs. Lennon, so I thought it would be a good idea for him to go to L.A. and leave me alone for a while. I had put up with it for many years. Even early on, when John was a Beatle, we stayed in a room and John and I were in bed and the door was closed and all that, but we didn't lock the door and one of the Beatle assistants just walked in and talked to him as if I weren't there. It was mind-blowing. I was invisible. The people around John saw me as a terrible threat. I mean, I heard there were plans to *kill* me. Not the Beatles but the people around them.

PLAYBOY: How did that news affect you?

ONO: The society doesn't understand that the woman can be castrated, too. I felt castrated. Before, I was doing all right, thank you. My work might not have been selling much, I might have been poorer, but I had my pride. But the most humiliating thing is to be looked at as a parasite.

[*Lennon rejoins the conversation.*]

LENNON: When Yoko and I started doing stuff together, we would hold press conferences and announce our whatevers—we're going to wear bags or whatever. And before this one press conference, one Beatle assistant in the upper echelon of Beatle assistants leaned over to Yoko and said, "You know, you don't have to work. You've got enough money, now that you're Mrs. Lennon." And when she complained to me about it, I couldn't understand what she was talking about. "But this guy," I'd say. "He's just good old Charley, or whatever. He's been with us 20 years. . . ." The same kind of thing happened in the studio. She would say to an engineer, "I'd like a little more treble, a little more bass," or "There's too much of whatever you're putting on," and they'd look at me and say, "What did *you* say, John?" Those days I didn't even notice it myself. Now I know what she's talking about. In Japan, when I ask for a cup of tea in Japanese, they look at Yoko and ask, "He wants a cup of tea?" in Japanese.

ONO: So a good few years of that kind of thing emasculates you. I had always been more *macho* than most guys I was with, in a sense. I had always been the breadwinner, because I always wanted to have the freedom and the control. Suddenly, I'm with somebody I can't possibly compete with on a level of earnings. Finally, I couldn't take it—or I decided not to take it any longer. I would have had the same difficulty even if I hadn't gotten involved with, ah—

LENNON: John—John is the name.

ONO: With John. But John wasn't just John. He was also his group and the people around them. When I say John, it's not just John—

LENNON: That's John. J-O-H-N. From Johan, I believe.

PLAYBOY: So you made him leave?

ONO: Yes.

LENNON: She don't suffer fools gladly, even if she's married to him.

PLAYBOY: How did you finally get back together?

ONO: It slowly started to dawn on me that John was not the trouble at all. John was a fine person. It was society that had become too much. We laugh about it now, but we started dating again. I wanted to be sure. I'm thankful to John's intelligence—

LENNON: Now, get that, editors—you got that word?

ONO: That he was intelligent enough to know this was the only way we could save our marriage, not because we didn't love each other but because it was getting too much for me. Nothing would have changed if I had come back as Mrs. Lennon again.

PLAYBOY: What did change?

ONO: It was good for me to do the business and regain my public pride about what I could do. And it was good to know what he needed, the role reversal that was so good for him.

LENNON: And we learned that it's better for the family if we are both working for the family, she doing the business and me playing mother and wife. We reordered our priorities. The number-one priority is her and the family. Everything else revolves around that.

ONO: It's a hard realization. These days, the society prefers single people. The encouragements are to divorce or separate or be single or gay—whatever. Corporations want singles—they work harder if they don't have family ties. They don't have to worry about being home in the evenings or on the weekends. There's not much room for emotions about family or personal relationships. You know, the whole thing they say to women approaching 30 that if you don't have a baby in the next few years, you're going to be in trouble, you'll never be a mother, so you'll never be fulfilled in that way and—

LENNON: Only Yoko was 73 when she had Sean. [*Laughter*]

ONO: So instead of the society discouraging children, since they are important for society, it should encourage them. It's the responsibility of everybody. But it is hard. A woman has to deny what she has, her womb, if she wants to make it. It seems that only the privileged classes can have families. Nowadays, maybe it's only the McCartneys and the Lennons or something.

LENNON: Everybody else becomes a worker-consumer.

ONO: And then Big Brother will decide—I hate to use the term Big Brother. . . .

LENNON: Too late. They've got it on tape. [*Laughs*]

ONO: But, finally, the society—

LENNON: Big Sister—wait till *she* comes!

ONO: The society will do away with the roles of men and women. Babies will be born in test tubes and incubators. . . .

LENNON: Then it's Aldous Huxley.

ONO: But we don't have to go that way. We don't have to deny any of our organs, you know.

LENNON: Some of my best friends are organs—

ONO: The new album—

LENNON: Back to the album, very good—

ONO: The album fights these things. The messages are sort of old-fashioned—family, relationships, children.

PLAYBOY: The album obviously reflects your new priorities. How have things gone for you since you made that decision?

LENNON: We got back together, decided this was our life, that having a baby was important to us and that anything else was subsidiary to that. We worked hard for that child. We went through all hell trying to have a baby, through many miscarriages and other problems. He is what they call a love child in truth. Doctors told us we could never have a child. We almost gave up. "Well, that's it, then, we can't have one. . . ." We were told something was wrong with my sperm, that I abused myself so much in my youth that there was no chance. Yoko was 43, and so they said, no way. She has had too many miscarriages and when she was a young girl, there were no pills, so there were lots of abortions and miscarriages; her stomach must be like Kew Gardens in London. No way. But this Chinese acupuncturist in San Francisco said, "You behave yourself. No drugs, eat well, no drink. You have a child in 18 months." And we said, "But the English doctors said. . . ." He said, "Forget what they said. You have child." We had Sean and sent the acupuncturist a Polaroid of him just before he died, God rest his soul.

PLAYBOY: Were there any problems because of Yoko's age?

LENNON: Not because of her age but because of a screw-up in the hospital and the fucking price of fame. Somebody had made a transfusion of the wrong blood type into Yoko. I was there when it happened, and she starts to go rigid, and then shake, from the pain and the trauma. I run up to this nurse and say, "Go get the doctor!" I'm holding on tight to Yoko while this guy gets to the hospital room. He walks in, hardly notices that Yoko is going through fucking *convulsions,* goes straight for me, smiles, shakes my hand and says, "I've always wanted to meet you, Mr. Lennon, I always enjoyed your music." I start screaming: *"My wife's dying and you wanna talk about my music!"* Christ!

PLAYBOY: Now that Sean is almost five, is he conscious of the fact that his father was a Beatle or have you protected him from your fame?

LENNON: I haven't said anything. Beatles were never mentioned to him. There was no reason to mention it; we never played Beatle records around the house, unlike the story that went around that I was sitting in the kitchen for the past five years, playing Beatle records and reliving my past like some kind of Howard Hughes. He did see *Yellow Submarine* at a friend's, so I had to explain what a cartoon of me was doing in a movie.

PLAYBOY: Does he have an awareness of the Beatles?

LENNON: He doesn't differentiate between the Beatles and Daddy and Mommy. He thinks Yoko was a Beatle, too. I don't have Beatle records on the jukebox he listens to. He's more exposed to early rock 'n' roll. He's into *Hound Dog*. He thinks it's about hunting.

Sean's not going to public school, by the way. We feel he can learn the three Rs when he wants to—or when the law says he has to, I suppose. I'm not going to fight it. Otherwise, there's no reason for him to be learning to sit still. I can't see any reason for it. Sean now has plenty of child companionship, which everybody says is important, but he also is with adults a lot. He's adjusted to both.

The reason why kids are crazy is because nobody can face the responsibility of bringing them up. Everybody's too scared to deal with children all the time, so we reject them and send them away and torture them. The ones who survive are the conformists—their bodies are cut to the size of the suits—the ones we label good. The ones who don't fit the suits either are put in mental homes or become artists.

PLAYBOY: Your son, Julian, from your first marriage must be in his teens. Have you seen him over the years?

LENNON: Well, Cyn got possession, or whatever you call it. I got rights to see him on his holidays and all that business, and at least there's an open line still going. It's not the best relationship between father and son, but it is there. He's 17 now. Julian and I will have a relationship in the future. Over the years, he's been able to see through the Beatle image and to see through the image that his mother will have given him, subconsciously or consciously. He's interested in girls and autobikes now. I'm just sort of a figure in the sky, but he's obliged to communicate with me, even when he probably doesn't want to.

PLAYBOY: You're being very honest about your feelings toward him to the point of saying that Sean is your first child. Are you concerned about hurting him?

LENNON: I'm not going to lie to Julian. Ninety percent of the people on this planet, especially in the West, were born out of a bottle of whiskey on a Saturday night, and there was no intent to have children. So 90 percent of us—that includes everybody—were accidents. I don't know anybody who was a planned child. All of us were Saturday-night specials. Julian is in the majority, along with me and everybody else. Sean is a planned child, and therein lies the difference. I don't love Julian any less as a child. He's still my son, whether he came from a bottle of whiskey or because they didn't have pills in those days. He's here, he belongs to me and he always will.

PLAYBOY: Yoko, your relationship with your daughter has been much rockier.

ONO: I lost Kyoko when she was about five. I was sort of an offbeat mother, but we had very good communication. I wasn't particularly taking care of her, but she was always with me—onstage or at gallery shows, whatever. When she was not even a year old, I took her onstage as an instrument—an uncontrollable instrument, you know. My communication with her was on the level of sharing conversation and doing things. She was closer to my ex-husband because of that.

PLAYBOY: What happened when she was five?

ONO: John and I got together and I separated from my ex-husband [Tony Cox]. He took Kyoko away. It became a case of parent kidnaping and we tried to get her back.

LENNON: It was a classic case of men being *macho*. It turned into me and Allen Klein trying to dominate Tony Cox. Tony's attitude was, "You got my wife, but you won't get my child." In this battle, Yoko and the child were absolutely forgotten. I've always felt bad about it. It became a case of the shoot-out at the O.K. Corral: Cox fled to the hills and hid out and the sheriff and I tracked him down. First we won custody in court. Yoko didn't want to go to court, but the men, Klein and I, did it anyway.

ONO: Allen called up one day, saying I won the court case. He gave me a piece of paper. I said, "What is this piece of paper? Is this what I won? I don't have my child." I knew that taking them to court would frighten them and, of course, it did frighten them. So Tony vanished. He was very strong, thinking that the capitalists, with their money and lawyers and detectives, were pursuing him. It made him stronger.

LENNON: We chased him all over the world. God knows where he went. *So if you're reading this, Tony, let's grow up about it. It's gone. We don't want to chase you anymore, because we've done enough damage.*

ONO: We also had private detectives chasing Kyoko, which I thought was a bad trip, too. One guy came to report, "It was great! We almost had them. We were just behind them in a car, but they sped up and got away." I went hysterical. "What do you mean you almost *got* them? We are talking about *my child*!"

LENNON: It was like we were after an escaped convict.

PLAYBOY: Were you so persistent because you felt you were better for Kyoko?

LENNON: Yoko got steamed into a guilt thing that if she wasn't attacking them with detectives and police and the FBI, then she wasn't a good mother looking for her baby. She kept saying, "Leave them alone, leave them alone," but they said you can't do that.

ONO: For me, it was like they just disappeared from my life. Part of me left with them.

PLAYBOY: How old is she now?

ONO: Seventeen, the same as John's son.

PLAYBOY: Perhaps when she gets older, she'll seek you out.

ONO: She is totally frightened. There was a time in Spain when a lawyer and John thought that *we* should kidnap her.

LENNON: [*Sighing*] I was just going to commit hara-kiri first.

ONO: And we did kidnap her and went to court. The court did a very sensible thing—the judge took her into a room and asked her which one of us she wanted to go with. Of course, she said Tony. We had scared her to death. So now she must be afraid that if she comes to see me, she'll never see her father again.

LENNON: When she gets to be in her 20s, she'll understand that we were idiots and we *know* we were idiots. She might give us a chance.

ONO: I probably would have lost Kyoko even if it wasn't for John. If I had separated from Tony, there would have been some difficulty.

LENNON: I'll just *half*-kill myself.

ONO: [*To John*] Part of the reason things got so bad was because with Kyoko, it was you and Tony dealing. *Men.* With your son Julian, it was women—there was more understanding between me and Cyn.

PLAYBOY: Can you explain that?

ONO: For example, there was a birthday party that Kyoko had and we were both invited, but John felt very uptight about it and he didn't go. He wouldn't deal with Tony. But we were both invited to Julian's party and we both went.

LENNON: Oh, God, it's all coming out.

ONO: Or like when I was invited to Tony's place alone, I couldn't go; but when John was invited to Cyn's, he did go.

LENNON: One rule for the men, one for the women.

ONO: So it was easier for Julian, because I was allowing it to happen.

LENNON: But I've said a million Hail Marys. What the hell else can I do?

PLAYBOY: Yoko, after this experience, how do you feel about leaving Sean's rearing to John?

ONO: I am very clear about my emotions in that area. I don't feel guilty. I am doing it in my own way. It may not be the same as other mothers, but I'm doing it the way I can do it. In general, mothers have a very strong resentment toward their children, even though there's this whole adulation about motherhood and how mothers really think about their children and how they really love them. I mean, they do, but it is not humanly possible to retain emotion that mothers are supposed to have within this society. Women are just too stretched out in different directions to retain that emotion. Too much is required of them. So I say to John —

LENNON: I *am* her favorite husband—

ONO: "I am carrying the baby nine months and that is enough, so you take care of it afterward." It did sound like a crude remark, but I really believe that children belong to the society. If a mother carries the child and a father raises it, the responsibility is shared.

PLAYBOY: Did you resent having to take so much responsibility, John?

LENNON: Well, sometimes, you know, she'd come home and say, "I'm tired." I'd say, only partly tongue in cheek, "What the fuck do you think *I* am? *I'm* 24 hours with the baby! Do you think that's easy?" I'd say, "You're going to take some more interest in the child." I don't care whether it's a father or a mother. When I'm going on about pimples and bones and which TV shows to let him watch, I would say, "Listen, this is important. I don't want to hear about your $20,000,000 deal tonight!" [*To Yoko*] I would like both parents to take care of the children, but how is a different matter.

ONO: Society should be more supportive *and* understanding.

LENNON: It's true. The saying "You've come a long way, baby" applies more to me than to her. As Harry Nilsson says, "Everything is the opposite of what it is, isn't it?" It's men who've come a long way from even contemplating the idea of equality. But although there is this thing called the women's movement, society just took a laxative and they've just farted. They haven't really had a good shit yet. The seed was planted sometime in the late Sixties, right? But the real changes are coming. I am the one who has come a long way. I was the pig. And it is a relief not to be a pig. The pressures of being a pig were enormous.

I don't have any hankering to be looked upon as a sex object, a male, *macho* rock-'n'-roll singer. I got over that a long time ago. I'm not even interested in projecting that. So I like it to be known that, yes, I looked after the baby and I made bread and I was a househusband and I am proud of it. It's the wave of the future and I'm glad to be in on the forefront of that, too.

ONO: So maybe both of us learned a lot about how men and women suffer because of the social structure. And the only way to change it is to be aware of it. It sounds simple, but important things are simple.

PLAYBOY: John, does it take actually reversing roles with women to understand?

LENNON: It did for this man. But don't forget, I'm the one who benefited the most from doing it. Now I can step back and say Sean is going to be five years old and I was able to spend his first five years with him and I am very proud of that. And come to think of it, it looks like I'm going to be 40 and life begins at 40—so they promise. And I believe it, too. I feel fine and I'm very excited. It's like, you know, hitting 21, like, "Wow, what's going to happen next?" Only this time we're together.

ONO: If two are gathered together, there's nothing you can't do.

PLAYBOY: What does the title of your new album, *Double Fantasy,* mean?

LENNON: It's a flower, a type of freesia, but what it means to us is that if two people picture the same image at the same time, that is the secret. You can be together but projecting two different images and either whoever's the strongest at the time will get his or her fantasy fulfilled or you will get nothing but mishmash.

PLAYBOY: You saw the news item that said you were putting your sex fantasies out as an album.

LENNON: Oh, yeah. That is like when we did the bed-in in Toronto in 1969. They all came charging through the door, thinking we were going to be screwing in bed. Of course, we were just sitting there with peace signs.

PLAYBOY: What *was* that famous bed-in all about?

LENNON: Our life is our art. That's what the bed-ins were. When we got married, we knew our honeymoon was going to be public anyway, so we decided to use it to make a statement. We sat in bed and talked to reporters for seven days. It was hilarious. In effect, we were doing a commercial for peace on the front page of the papers instead of a commercial for war.

PLAYBOY: You stayed in bed and talked about peace?

LENNON: Yes. We answered questions. One guy kept going over the point about Hitler: "What do you do about Fascists? How can you have peace when you've got a Hitler?" Yoko said, "I would have gone to bed with him." She said she'd have needed only ten days with him. People loved that one.

ONO: I said it facetiously, of course. But the point is, you're not going to change the world by fighting. Maybe I was naïve about the ten days with Hitler. After all, it took 13 years with John Lennon. [*She giggles*]

PLAYBOY: What were the reports about your making love in a bag?

ONO: We never made love in a bag. People probably imagined that we were making love. It was just, all of us are in a bag, you know. The point was the outline of the bag, you know, the movement of the bag, how much we see of a person, you know. But, inside, there might be a lot going on. Or maybe nothing's going on.

PLAYBOY: Briefly, what about the statement on the new album?

LENNON: Very briefly, it's about very ordinary things between two people. The lyrics are direct. Simple and straight. I went through my Dylanesque period a long time ago with songs like *I Am the Walrus*: the trick of never saying what you mean but giving the impression of something more. Where more or less can be read into it. It's a good game.

PLAYBOY: What are your musical preferences these days?

LENNON: Well, I like all music, depending on what time of day it is. I don't like styles of music or people per se. I can't say I enjoy the Pretenders, but I like their hit record. I enjoy the B-52s, because I heard them doing Yoko. It's great. If Yoko ever goes back to her old sound, they'll be saying, "Yeah, she's copying the B-52s."

ONO: We were doing a lot of the punk stuff a long time ago.

PLAYBOY: Lennon and Ono, the original punks.

ONO: You're right.

PLAYBOY: John, what's your opinion of the newer waves?

LENNON: I love all this punky stuff. It's pure. I'm not, however, crazy about the people who destroy themselves.

PLAYBOY: You disagree with Neil Young's lyric in *Rust Never Sleeps*— "It's better to burn out than to fade away. . . ."

LENNON: I hate it. It's better to fade away like an old soldier than to burn out. I don't appreciate worship of dead Sid Vicious or of dead James Dean or of dead John Wayne. It's the same thing. Making Sid Vicious a hero, Jim Morrison—it's garbage to me. I worship the people who survive. Gloria Swanson, Greta Garbo. They're saying John Wayne conquered cancer—he whipped it like a man. You know, I'm sorry that he died and all that—I'm sorry for his family—but he didn't whip cancer. It whipped him. I don't want Sean worshiping John Wayne or Sid Vicious. What do they teach you? Nothing. Death. Sid Vicious died for what? So that we might rock? I mean, it's garbage, you know. If Neil Young admires that sentiment so much, why doesn't he do it? Because he sure as hell faded away and came back many times, like all of us. No, thank you. I'll take the living and the healthy.

PLAYBOY: Do you listen to the radio?

LENNON: Muzak or classical. I don't purchase records. I do enjoy listening to things like Japanese folk music or Indian music. My tastes are very broad. When I was a housewife, I just had Muzak on—background music—'cause it relaxes you.

PLAYBOY: Yoko?

ONO: No.

PLAYBOY: Do you go out and buy records?

ONO: Or read the newspaper or magazines or watch TV? No.

PLAYBOY: The inevitable question, John. Do you listen to your records?

LENNON: *Least* of all my own.

PLAYBOY: Even your classics?

LENNON: Are you kidding? For pleasure, I would never listen to them. When I hear them, I just think of the session—it's like an actor watching himself in an old movie. When I hear a song, I remember the Abbey Road studio, the session, who fought with whom, where I was sitting, banging the tambourine in the corner—

ONO: In fact, we really don't enjoy listening to other people's work much. We sort of analyze everything we hear.

PLAYBOY: Yoko, were you a Beatles fan?

ONO: No. Now I notice the songs, of course. In a restaurant, John will point out, "Ahh, they're playing George" or something.

PLAYBOY: John, do you ever go out to hear music?

LENNON: No, I'm not interested. I'm not a fan, you see. I might like Jerry Lee Lewis singing *A Whole Lot of Shakin'* on the record, but I'm not interested in seeing him perform it.

PLAYBOY: Your songs are performed more than most other songwriters'. How does that feel?

LENNON: I'm always proud and pleased when people do my songs. It gives me pleasure that they even attempt them, because a lot of my songs aren't that doable. I go to restaurants and the groups always play *Yesterday*. I even signed a guy's violin in Spain after he played us *Yesterday*. He couldn't understand that I didn't write the song. But I guess he couldn't have gone from table to table playing *I Am the Walrus*.

PLAYBOY: How does it feel to have influenced so many people?

LENNON: It wasn't really me or us. It was the times. It happened to me when I heard rock 'n' roll in the Fifties. I had no idea about doing music as a way of life until rock 'n' roll hit me.

PLAYBOY: Do you recall what specifically hit you?

LENNON: It was *Rock Around the Clock*, I think. I enjoyed Bill Haley, but I wasn't overwhelmed by him. It wasn't until *Heartbreak Hotel* that I really got into it.

ONO: I am sure there are people whose lives were affected because they heard Indian music or Mozart or Bach. More than anything, it was the time and the place when the Beatles came up. Something did happen there. It was a kind of chemical. It was as if several people gathered around a table and a ghost appeared. It was that kind of communication. So they were like mediums, in a way. It's not something you can force. It was the people, the time, their youth and enthusiasm.

PLAYBOY: For the sake of argument, we'll maintain that no other contemporary artist or group of artists moved as many people in such a profound way as the Beatles.

LENNON: *But what moved the Beatles?*

PLAYBOY: You tell us.

LENNON: All right. Whatever wind was blowing at the time moved the Beatles, too. I'm not saying we weren't flags on the top of a ship; but the whole boat was moving. Maybe the Beatles were in the crow's-nest, shouting, "Land ho," or something like that, but we were all in the same damn boat.

ONO: The Beatles themselves were a social phenomenon not that aware of what they were doing. In a way—

LENNON: [*Under his breath*] This Beatles talk bores me to death. Turn to page 196.

ONO: As I said, they were like mediums. They weren't conscious of all they were saying, but it was coming through them.

PLAYBOY: Why?

LENNON: We tuned in to the message. That's all. I don't mean to belittle the Beatles when I say they weren't this, they weren't that. I'm just trying not to overblow their importance as separate from society. And I don't think they were more important than Glenn Miller or Woody Herman or Bessie Smith. It was our generation, that's all. It was Sixties music.

PLAYBOY: What do you say to those who insist that all rock since the Beatles has been the Beatles redone?

LENNON: *All* music is rehash. There are only a few notes. Just variations on a theme. Try to tell the kids in the Seventies who were screaming to the Bee Gees that their music was just the Beatles redone. There is nothing wrong with the Bee Gees. They do a damn god job. There was nothing else going on then.

PLAYBOY: Wasn't a lot of the Beatles' music at least more intelligent?

LENNON: The Beatles were, more intellectual, so they appealed on that level, too. But the basic appeal of the Beatles was not their intelligence. It was their music. It was only after some guy in the London *Times* said there were Aeolian cadences in *It Won't Be Long* that the middle classes started listening to it—because somebody put a tag on it.

PLAYBOY: *Did* you put Aeolian cadences in *It Won't Be Long?*

LENNON: To this day, I don't have *any* idea what they are. They sound like exotic birds.

PLAYBOY: How did you react to the misinterpretations of your songs?

LENNON: For instance?

PLAYBOY: The most obvious is the "Paul is dead" fiasco. You already explained the line in *Glass Onion*. What about the line in *I Am the Walrus*—"I buried Paul"?

LENNON: I said "Cranberry sauce." That's all I said. Some people like ping-pong, other people like digging over graves. Some people will do anything rather than be here now.

PLAYBOY: What about the chant at the end of the song: "Smoke pot, smoke pot, everybody smoke pot"?

LENNON: No, no, no. I had this whole choir saying, "Everybody's got one, everybody's got one." But when you get 30 people, male and female, on top of 30 cellos and on top of the Beatles' rock-'n'-roll rhythm section, you can't hear what they're saying.

PLAYBOY: What *does* "everybody got"?

LENNON: Anything. You name it. One penis, one vagina, one asshole—you name it.

PLAYBOY: Did it trouble you when the interpretations of your songs were destructive, such as when Charles Manson claimed that your lyrics were messages to him?

LENNON: No. It has nothing to do with me. It's like that guy, Son of Sam, who was having these talks with the dog. Manson was just an extreme version of the people who came up with the "Paul is dead" thing or who figured out that the initials to *Lucy in the Sky with Diamonds* were LSD and concluded I was writing about acid.

PLAYBOY: Where *did Lucy in the Sky* come from?

LENNON: My son Julian came in one day with a picture he painted about a school friend of his named Lucy. He had sketched in some stars in the sky and called it *Lucy in the Sky with Diamonds*. Simple.

PLAYBOY: The other images in the song weren't drug-inspired?

LENNON: The images were from *Alice in Wonderland*. It was Alice in the boat. She is buying an egg and it turns into Humpty Dumpty. The woman serving in the shop turns into a sheep and the next minute they are rowing in a rowing boat somewhere and I was visualizing that. There was also the image of the female who would someday come save me—a "girl with kaleidoscope eyes" who would come out of the sky. It turned out to be Yoko, though I hadn't met Yoko yet. So maybe it should be *Yoko in the Sky with Diamonds*.

PLAYBOY: Do you have any interest in the pop historians analyzing the Beatles as a cultural phenomenon?

LENNON: It's all equally irrelevant. Mine is to do and other people's is to record, I suppose. Does it matter how many drugs were in Elvis' body? I mean, Brian Epstein's sex life will make a nice *Hollywood Babylon* someday, but it is irrelevant.

PLAYBOY: What started the rumors about you and Epstein?

LENNON: I went on holiday to Spain with Brian—which started all the rumors that he and I were having a love affair. Well, it was almost a love affair, but not quite. It was never consummated. But we did have a pretty intense relationship. And it was my first experience with someone I knew was a homosexual. He admitted it to me. We had this holiday together because Cyn was pregnant and we left her with the baby and went to Spain. Lots of funny stories, you know. We used to sit in cafés and Brian would look at all the boys and I would ask, "Do you like that one? Do you like this one?" It was just the combination of our closeness and the trip that started the rumors.

PLAYBOY: It's interesting to hear you talk about your old songs such as *Lucy in the Sky* and *Glass Onion*. Will you give some brief thoughts on some of our favorites?

LENNON: Right.

PLAYBOY: Let's start with *In My Life*.

LENNON: It was the first song I wrote that was consciously about my life. [*Sings*] "There are places I'll remember/all my life though some have changed. . . ." Before, we were just writing songs à la Everly Brothers, Buddy Holly—pop songs with no more thought to them than that. The words were almost irrelevant. *In My Life* started out as a bus journey from my house at 250 Menlove Avenue to town, mentioning all the places I could recall. I wrote it all down and it was *boring*. So I forgot about it and laid back and these lyrics started coming to me about friends and lovers of the past. Paul helped with the middle eight.

PLAYBOY: *Yesterday*.

LENNON: Well, we all know about *Yesterday*. I have had *so* much accolade for *Yesterday*. That is Paul's song, of course, and Paul's baby. Well done. Beautiful—and I never wished I had written it.

PLAYBOY: *With a Little Help from My Friends*.

LENNON: This is Paul, with a little help from me. "What do you see when you turn out the light/I can't tell you, but I know it's mine . . ." is mine.

PLAYBOY: *I Am the Walrus.*

LENNON: The first line was written on one acid trip one weekend. The second line was written on the next acid trip the next weekend, and it was filled in after I met Yoko. Part of it was putting down Hare Krishna. All these people were going on about Hare Krishna, Allen Ginsberg in particular. The reference to "Element'ry penguin" is the elementary, naïve attitude of going around chanting, "Hare Krishna," or putting all your faith in any one idol. I was writing obscurely, à la Dylan, in those days.

PLAYBOY: The song is very complicated, musically.

LENNON: It actually was fantastic in stereo, but you never hear it all. There was too much to get on. It was too messy a mix. One track was live BBC Radio—Shakespeare or something—I just fed in whatever lines came in.

PLAYBOY: What about the walrus itself?

LENNON: It's from *The Walrus and the Carpenter. Alice in Wonderland.* To me, it was a beautiful poem. It never dawned on me that Lewis Carroll was commenting on the capitalist and social system. I never went into that bit about what he really meant, like people are doing with the Beatles' work. Later, I went back and looked at it and realized that the walrus was the bad guy in the story and the carpenter was the good guy. I thought, Oh, shit, I picked the wrong guy. I should have said, "I am the carpenter." But that wouldn't have been the same, would it? [*Singing*] "I am the carpenter. . . ."

PLAYBOY: How about *She Came in Through the Bathroom Window*?

LENNON: That was written by Paul when we were in New York forming Apple, and he first met Linda. Maybe she's the one who came in the window. She must have. I don't know. *Somebody* came in the window.

PLAYBOY: *I Feel Fine.*

LENNON: That's me, including the guitar lick with the first feedback ever recorded. I defy anybody to find an earlier record—unless it is some old blues record from the Twenties—with feedback on it.

PLAYBOY: *When I'm Sixty-four.*

LENNON: Paul completely. I would never even dream of writing a song like that. There are some areas I never think about and that is one of them.

PLAYBOY: *A Day in the Life.*

LENNON: Just as it sounds: I was reading the paper one day and I noticed two stories. One was the Guinness heir who killed himself in a car. That was the main headline story. He died in London in a car crash. On the next page was a story about 4000 holes in Blackburn, Lancashire. In the streets, that is. They were going to fill them all. Paul's contribution was the beautiful little lick in the song "I'd love to turn you on." I had the bulk of the song and the words, but he contributed this little lick floating around in his head that he couldn't use for anything. I thought it was a damn good piece of work.

PLAYBOY: May we continue with some of the ones that seem more personal and see what reminiscences they inspire?

LENNON: Reminisce away.

PLAYBOY: For no reason whatsoever, let's start with *I Wanna Be Your Man*.

LENNON: Paul and I finished that one off for the Stones. We were taken down by Brian to meet them at the club where they were playing in Richmond. They wanted a song and we went to see what kind of stuff they did. Paul had this bit of a song and we played it roughly for them and they said, "Yeah, OK, that's our style." But it was only really a lick, so Paul and I went off in the corner of the room and finished the song off while they were sitting there, talking. We came back and Mick and Keith said, "Jesus, look at that. They just went over there and wrote it." You know, right in front of their eyes. We gave it to them. It was a throwaway. Ringo sang it for us and the Stones did their version. It shows how much importance we put on them. We weren't going to give them anything great, right? That was the Stones' first record. Anyway, Mick and Keith said, "If *they* can write a song so easily, *we* should try it." They say it inspired them to start writing together.

PLAYBOY: How about *Strawberry Fields Forever?*

LENNON: Strawberry Fields is a real place. After I stopped living at Penny Lane, I moved in with my auntie who lived in the suburbs in a nice semi-detached place with a small garden and doctors and lawyers and that ilk living around—not the poor slummy kind of image that was projected in all the Beatles stories. In the class system, it was about half a class higher than Paul, George and Ringo, who lived in government-subsidized housing. We owned our house and had a garden. They didn't have anything like that. Near that home was Strawberry Fields, a house near a boys' reformatory where I used to go to garden parties as a kid with my friends Nigel and Pete. We would go there and hang out and sell lemonade bottles for a penny. We always had fun at Strawberry Fields. So that's where I got the name. But I used it as an image. Strawberry Fields forever.

PLAYBOY: And the lyrics, for instance: "Living is easy—"

LENNON: [*Singing*] "With eyes closed. Misunderstanding all you see." It still goes, doesn't it? Aren't I saying exactly the same thing now? The awareness apparently trying to be expressed is—let's say in one way I was always hip. I was hip in kindergarten. I was different from the others. I was different all my life. The second verse goes, "No one I think is in my tree." Well, I was too shy and self-doubting. Nobody seems to be as hip as me is what I was saying. Therefore, I must be crazy or a genius—"I mean it must be high or low," the next line. There was something wrong with me, I thought, because I seemed to see things other people didn't see. I thought I was crazy or an egomaniac for claiming to see things other people didn't see. As a child, I would say, *"But this is going on!"* and everybody would look at me as if I was crazy. I always was so psychic or intuitive or poetic or whatever you want to call it, that I was always seeing things in a hallucinatory way.

It was scary as a child, because there was nobody to relate to. Neither my auntie nor my friends nor anybody could ever see what I did. It was very, very scary and the only contact I had was reading about an Oscar Wilde or a Dylan Thomas or a Vincent van Gogh—all those books that my auntie had that talked about their suffering because of their visions. Because of what they saw, they were tortured by society for trying to express what they were. I *saw* loneliness.

PLAYBOY: Were you able to find others to share your visions with?

LENNON: Only dead people in books. Lewis Carroll, certain paintings. Surrealism had a great effect on me, because then I realized that my imagery and my mind wasn't insanity; that if it was insane, I belong in an exclusive club that sees the world in those terms. Surrealism to me is reality. Psychic vision to me is reality. Even as a child. When I looked at myself in the mirror or when I was 12, 13, I used to literally trance out into alpha. I didn't know what it was called then. I found out years later there is a name for those conditions. But I would find myself seeing hallucinatory images of my face changing and becoming cosmic and complete. It caused me to always be a rebel. This thing gave me a chip on the shoulder; but, on the other hand, I wanted to be loved and accepted. Part of me would like to be accepted by all facets of society and not be this loudmouthed lunatic musician. But I cannot be what I am not.

Because of my attitude, all the other boys' parents, including Paul's father, would say, "Keep away from him." The parents instinctively recognized what I was, which was a troublemaker, meaning I did not conform and I would influence their kids, which I did. I did my best to disrupt every friend's home I had. Partly, maybe, it was out of envy that I didn't have this so-called home. But I really did. I had an auntie and an uncle and a nice suburban home, thank you very much. Hear this, Auntie. She was hurt by a remark Paul made recently that the reason I am staying home with Sean now is because I never had a family life. It's absolute rubbish. There were five women who were my family. Five strong, intelligent women. Five sisters. One happened to be my mother. My mother was the youngest. She just couldn't deal with life. She had a husband who ran away to sea and the war was on and she couldn't cope with me, and when I was four and a half, I ended up living with her elder sister. Now, those women were fantastic. One day I might do a kind of *Forsyte Saga* just about them. That was my first feminist education.

Anyway, that knowledge and the fact that I wasn't with my parents made me see that parents are not gods. I would infiltrate the other boys' minds. Paul's parents were terrified of me and my influence, simply because I was free from the parents' stranglehold. That was the gift I got for not having parents. I cried a lot about not having them and it was torture, but it also gave me an awareness early. I wasn't an orphan, though. My mother was alive and lived a 15-minute walk away from me all my life. I saw her off and on. I just didn't live with her.

PLAYBOY: Is she alive?

LENNON: No, she got killed by an off-duty cop who was drunk after visiting my auntie's house where I lived. I wasn't there at the time. She was just at a bus stop. I was 16. That was another big trauma for me. I lost her twice. When I was five and I moved in with my auntie, and then when she physically died. That made me more bitter; the chip on my shoulder I had as a youth got really big then. I was just really re-establishing the relationship with her and she was killed.

PLAYBOY: Her name was Julia, wasn't it? Is she the Julia of your song of that name on *The White Album*?

LENNON: The song is for her—and for Yoko.

PLAYBOY: What kind of relationship did you have with your father, who went away to sea? Did you ever see him again?

LENNON: I never saw him again until I made a lot of money and he came back.

PLAYBOY: How old were you?

LENNON: Twenty-four or 25. I opened the *Daily Express* and there he was, washing dishes in a small hotel or something very near where I was living in the Stockbroker belt outside London. He had been writing to me to try to get in contact. I didn't want to see him. I was too upset about what he'd done to me and to my mother and that he would turn up when I was rich and famous and not bother turning up before. So I wasn't going to see him at all, but he sort of blackmailed me in the press by saying all this about being a poor man washing dishes while I was living in luxury. I fell for it and saw him and we had some kind of relationship. He died a few years later of cancer. But at 65, he married a secretary who had been working for the Beatles, age 22, and they had a child, which I thought was hopeful for a man who had lived his life as a drunk and almost a Bowery bum.

PLAYBOY: We'll never listen to *Strawberry Fields Forever* the same way again. What memories are jogged by the song *Help!*?

LENNON: When *Help!* came out in '65, I was actually crying out for help. Most people think it's just a fast rock-'n'-roll song. I didn't realize it at the time; I just wrote the song because I was commissioned to write it for the movie. But later, I knew I really was crying out for help. It was my fat Elvis period. You see the movie: He—I—is very fat, very insecure, and he's completely lost himself. And I am singing about when I was so much younger and all the rest, looking back at how easy it was. Now I may be very positive—yes, yes—but I also go through deep depressions where I would like to jump out the window, you know. It becomes easier to deal with as I get older; I don't know whether you learn control or, when you grow up, you calm down a little. Anyway, I was fat and depressed and I *was* crying out for help.

In those days, when the Beatles were depressed, we had this little chant. I would yell out, "Where are we going, fellows?" They would say, "To the top, Johnny," in pseudo-American voices. And I would say, "Where is that, fellows?" And they would say, "To the toppermost of the poppermost." It was some dumb expression from a cheap movie—à la *Blackboard Jungle*—about Liverpool. Johnny was the leader of the gang.

PLAYBOY: What were you depressed about during the *Help!* period?

LENNON: The Beatles thing had just gone beyond comprehension. We were smoking marijuana for breakfast. We were well into marijuana and nobody could communicate with us, because we were just all glazed eyes, giggling all the time. In our own world. That was the song, *Help!* I think everything that comes out of a song—even Paul's songs now, which are apparently about nothing—shows something about yourself.

PLAYBOY: Was *I'm a Loser* a similarly personal statement?

LENNON: Part of me suspects that I'm a loser and the other part of me thinks I'm God Almighty.

PLAYBOY: How about *Cold Turkey*?

LENNON: The song is self-explanatory. The song got banned, even though it's antidrug. They're so stupid about drugs, you know. They're not looking at the cause of the drug problem: Why do people take drugs? To escape from what? Is life so terrible? Are we living in such a terrible situation that we can't do anything without reinforcement of alcohol, tobacco? Aspirins, sleeping pills, uppers, downers, never mind the heroin and cocaine—they're just the outer fringes of Librium and speed.

PLAYBOY: Do you use any drugs now?

LENNON: Not really. If somebody gives me a joint, I might smoke it, but I don't go after it.

PLAYBOY: Cocaine?

LENNON: I've had cocaine, but I don't like it. The Beatles had lots of it in their day, but it's a dumb drug, because you have to have another one 20 minutes later. Your whole concentration goes on getting the next fix. Really, I find caffeine is easier to deal with.

PLAYBOY: Acid?

LENNON: Not in years. A little mushroom or peyote is not beyond my scope, you know, maybe twice a year or something. You don't hear about it anymore, but people are still visiting the cosmos. We must always remember to thank the CIA and the Army for LSD. That's what people forget. Everything is the opposite of what it is, isn't it, Harry? So get out the bottle, boy—and relax. They invented LSD to control people and what they did was give us freedom. Sometimes it works in mysterious ways its wonders to perform. If you look in the Government reports on acid, the ones who jumped out the window or killed themselves because of it, I think even with Art Linkletter's daughter, it happened to her years later. So, let's face it, she wasn't really on acid when she jumped out the window. And I've never met anybody who's had a flashback on acid. I've never had a flashback in my life and I took millions of trips in the Sixties.

PLAYBOY: What does your diet include besides *sashimi* and *sushi,* Hershey bars and cappuccinos?

LENNON: We're mostly macrobiotic, but sometimes I take the family out for a pizza.

ONO: Intuition tells you what to eat. It's dangerous to try to unify things. Everybody has different needs. We went through vegetarianism and macrobiotic, but now, because we're in the studio, we do eat some junk food. We're trying to stick to macrobiotic: fish and rice, whole grains. You balance foods and eat foods indigenous to the area. Corn is the grain from this area.

PLAYBOY: And you both smoke up a storm.

LENNON: Macrobiotic people don't believe in the big C. Whether you take that as a rationalization or not, macrobiotics don't believe that smoking is bad for you. Of course, if we die, we're wrong.

PLAYBOY: Let's go back to jogging your memory with songs. How about Paul's song *Hey Jude*?

LENNON: He said it was written about Julian. He knew I was splitting with Cyn and leaving Julian then. He was driving to see Julian to say hello. He had been like an uncle. And he came up with *Hey Jude.* But I always heard it as a song to me. Now I'm sounding like one of those fans reading things into it. . . . Think about it: Yoko had just come into the picture. He is saying, "Hey, Jude"—"Hey, John." Subconsciously, he was saying, Go ahead, leave me. On a conscious level, he didn't want me to go ahead. The angel in him was saying, "Bless you." The Devil in him didn't like it at all, because he didn't want to lose his partner.

PLAYBOY: What about *Because*?

LENNON: I was lying on the sofa in our house, listening to Yoko play Beethoven's *Moonlight Sonata* on the piano. Suddenly, I said, "Can you play those chords backward?" She did, and I wrote *Because* around them. The song sounds like *Moonlight Sonata,* too. The lyrics are clear, no bull-shit, no imagery, no obscure references.

PLAYBOY: *Give Peace a Chance.*

LENNON: All we were saying was give peace a chance.

PLAYBOY: Was it really a Lennon-McCartney composition?

LENNON: No, I don't even know why his name was on it. It's there because I kind of felt guilty because I'd made the separate single—the first—and I was really breaking away from the Beatles.

PLAYBOY: Why were the compositions you and Paul did separately attributed to Lennon-McCartney?

LENNON: Paul and I made a deal when we were 15. There was never a legal deal between us, just a deal we made when we decided to write together that we put both our names on it, no matter what.

PLAYBOY: How about *Do You Want to Know a Secret?*

LENNON: The idea came from this thing my mother used to sing to me when I was one or two years old, when she was still living with me. It was from a Disney movie: "Do you want to know a secret?/Promise not to tell/You are standing by a wishing well." So, with that in my head, I wrote the song and just gave it to George to sing. I thought it would be a good vehicle for him, because it had only three notes and he wasn't the best singer in the world. He has improved a lot since then; but in those days, his ability was very poor. I gave it to him just to give him a piece of the action. That's another reason why I was hurt by his book. I even went to the trouble of making sure he got the B side of a Beatles single, because he hadn't had a B side of one until *Do You Want to Know a Secret? Something* was the first time he ever got an A side, because Paul and I always wrote both sides. That wasn't because we were keeping him out but simply because his material was not up to scratch. I made sure he got the B side of *Something,* too, so he got the cash. Those little things he doesn't remember.

I always felt bad that George and Ringo didn't get a piece of the publishing. When the opportunity came to give them five percent each of Maclen, it was because of me they got it. It was not because of Klein and not because of Paul but because of me. When I said they should get it, Paul couldn't say no. I don't get a piece of any of George's songs or Ringo's. I never asked for anything for the contributions I made to George's songs like *Taxman.* Not even the recognition. And that is why I might have sounded resentful about George and Ringo, because it was after all those things that the attitude of "John has forsaken us" and "John is tricking us" came out— which is not true.

PLAYBOY: *Happiness Is a Warm Gun.*

LENNON: No, it's not about heroin. A gun magazine was sitting there with a smoking gun on the cover and an article that I never read inside called *Happiness Is a Warm Gun.* I took it right from there. I took it as the terrible idea of just having shot some animal.

PLAYBOY: What about the sexual puns: "When you feel my finger on your trigger"?

LENNON: Well, it was at the beginning of my relationship with Yoko and I was very sexually oriented then. When we weren't in the studio, we were in bed.

PLAYBOY: What was the allusion to "Mother Superior jumps the gun"?

LENNON: I call Yoko Mother or Madam just in an offhand way. The rest doesn't mean anything. It's just images of her.

PLAYBOY: *Across the Universe.*

LENNON: The Beatles didn't make a good record of *Across the Universe.* I think subconsciously we—I thought Paul subconsciously tried to destroy my great songs. We would play experimental games with my great pieces, like *Strawberry Fields,* which I always felt was badly recorded. It worked, but it wasn't what it could have been. I allowed it, though. We would spend hours doing little, detailed cleaning up on Paul's songs, but when it came to mine—especially a great song like *Strawberry Fields* or *Across the Universe*—somehow an atmosphere of looseness and experimentation would come up.

PLAYBOY: Sabotage?

LENNON: Subconscious sabotage. I was too hurt. . . . Paul will deny it, because he has a bland face and will say this doesn't exist. This is the kind of thing I'm talking about where I was always seeing what was going on and began to think, Well, maybe I'm paranoid. But it is *not* paranoid. It is the absolute truth. The same thing happened to *Across the Universe.* The song was never done properly. The words stand, luckily.

PLAYBOY: *Getting Better.*

LENNON: It is a diary form of writing. All that "I used to be cruel to my woman, I beat her and kept her apart from the things that she loved" was me. I used to be cruel to my woman, and physically—any woman. I was a hitter. I couldn't express myself and I hit. I fought men and I hit women. That is why I am always on about peace, you see. It is the most violent people who go for love and peace. Everything's the opposite. But I sincerely believe in love and peace. I am a violent man who has learned not to be violent and regrets his violence. I will have to be a lot older before I can face in public how I treated women as a youngster.

PLAYBOY: *Revolution.*

LENNON: We recorded the song twice. The Beatles were getting really tense with one another. I did the slow version and I wanted it out as a single: as a statement of the Beatles' position on Vietnam and the Beatles' position on revolution. For years, on the Beatle tours, Epstein had stopped us from saying anything about Vietnam or the war. And he wouldn't allow questions about it. But on one tour, I said, "I am going to answer about the war. We can't ignore it." I absolutely wanted the Beatles to say something. The first take of *Revolution*—well, George and Paul were resentful and said it wasn't fast enough. Now, if you go into details of what a hit record is and isn't, maybe. But the Beatles could have afforded to put out the slow, understandable version of *Revolution* as a single. Whether it was a gold record or a wooden record. But because they were so upset about the Yoko period and the fact that I was again becoming as creative and dominating as I had been in the early days, after lying fallow for a couple of years, it upset the apple cart. I was awake again and they couldn't stand it.

PLAYBOY: Was it Yoko's inspiration?

LENNON: She inspired *all* this creation in me. It wasn't that she inspired the songs; she inspired *me*. The statement in *Revolution* was mine. The lyrics stand today. It's still my feeling about politics. I want to see the plan. That is what I used to say to Abbie Hoffman and Jerry Rubin. Count me out if it is for violence. Don't expect me to be on the barricades unless it is with flowers.

PLAYBOY: What do you think of Hoffman's turning himself in?

LENNON: Well, he got what he wanted. Which is to be sort of an underground hero for anybody who still worships any manifestation of the underground. I don't feel that much about it anymore. Nixon, Hoffman, it's the same. They are all from the same period. It was kind of surprising to see Abbie on TV, but it was also surprising to see Nixon on TV. Maybe people get the feeling when they see me or us. I feel, What are they doing there? Is this an old newsreel?

PLAYBOY: On the new album, you close with *Hard Times Are Over (For a While)*. Why?

LENNON: It's not a new message: *Give Peace a Chance*—we're not being unreasonable, just saying, "Give it a chance." With *Imagine,* we're saying, "Can you imagine a world without countries or religions?" It's the same message over and over. And it's positive.

PLAYBOY: How does it feel to have people anticipate your new record because they feel you are a prophet of sorts? When you returned to the studio to make *Double Fantasy*, some of your fans were saying things like, "Just as Lennon defined the Sixties and the Seventies, he'll be defining the Eighties."

LENNON: It's very sad. Anyway, we're not saying anything new. A, we have already said it and, B, 100,000,000 other people have said it, too.

PLAYBOY: But your songs *do* have messages.

LENNON: All we are saying is, "This is what is happening to us." We are sending postcards. I don't let it become "I am the awakened; you are sheep that will be shown the way." That is the danger of saying anything, you know.

PLAYBOY: Especially for you.

LENNON: Listen, there's nothing wrong with following examples. We can have figureheads and people we admire, but we don't need leaders. "Don't follow leaders, watch the parking meters."

PLAYBOY: You're quoting one of your peers, of sorts. Is it distressing to you that Dylan is a born-again Christian?

LENNON: I don't like to comment on it. For whatever reason he's doing it, it is personal for him and he needs to do it. But the whole religion business suffers from the *Onward, Christian Soldiers* bit. There's too much talk about soldiers and marching and converting. I'm not pushing Buddhism, because I'm no more a Buddhist than I am a Christian, but there's one thing I admire about the religion: There's no proselytizing.

PLAYBOY: Were you a Dylan fan?

LENNON: No, I stopped listening to Dylan with both ears after *Highway 64* [*sic*] and *Blonde on Blonde,* and even then it was because George would sit me down and make me listen.

PLAYBOY: Like Dylan, weren't you also looking for some kind of leader when you did primal-scream therapy with Arthur Janov?

ONO: I think Janov was a daddy for John. I think he has this father complex and he's always searching for a daddy.

LENNON: *Had,* dear. I *had* a father complex.

PLAYBOY: Would you explain?

ONO: I had a daddy, a real daddy, sort of a big and strong father like a Billy Graham, but growing up, I saw his weak side. I saw the hypocrisy. So whenever I see something that is supposed to be so big and wonderful— a guru or primal scream—I'm very cynical.

LENNON: She fought with Janov all the time. He couldn't deal with it.

ONO: I'm not searching for the big daddy. I look for something else in men—something that is tender and weak and I feel like I want to help.

LENNON: And I was the lucky cripple she chose!

ONO: I have this mother instinct, or whatever. But I was not hung up on finding a father, because I had one who disillusioned me. John never had a chance to get disillusioned about his father, since his father wasn't around, so he never thought of him as that big man.

PLAYBOY: Do you agree with that assessment, John?

LENNON: A lot of us are looking for fathers. Mine was physically not there. Most people's are not there *mentally* and physically, like always at the office or busy with other things. So all these leaders, parking meters, are all substitute fathers, whether they be religious or political. . . . All this bit about electing a President. We pick our own daddy out of a dog pound of daddies. This is the daddy that looks like the daddy in the commercials. He's got the nice gray hair and the right teeth and the parting's on the right side. OK? This is the daddy we choose. The dog pound of daddies, which is the political arena, gives us a President, then we put him on a platform and start punishing him and screaming at him because Daddy can't do miracles. Daddy doesn't heal us.

PLAYBOY: So Janov was a daddy for you. Who else?

ONO: Before, there was Maharishi.

LENNON: Maharishi was a father figure, Elvis Presley might have been a father figure. I don't know. Robert Mitchum. Any male image is a father figure. There's nothing wrong with it until you give them the right to give you sort of a recipe for your life. What happens is somebody comes along with a good piece of truth. Instead of the truth's being looked at, the person who brought it is looked at. The messenger is worshiped, instead of the message. So there would be Christianity, Mohammedanism, Buddhism, Confucianism, Marxism, Maoism—everything—it is always about a person and never about what he says.

ONO: All the isms are daddies. It's sad that society is structured in such a way that people cannot really open up to each other, and therefore they need a certain theater to go to to cry or something like that.

LENNON: Well, you went to est.

ONO: Yes, I wanted to check it out.

LENNON: We went to Janov for the same reason.

ONO: But est people are given a reminder—

LENNON: Yeah, but I wouldn't go and sit in a room and not pee.

ONO: Well, *you* did in primal scream.

LENNON: Oh, but I had you with me.

ONO: Anyway, when I went to est, I saw Werner Erhardt, the same thing. He's a nice showman and he's got a nice gig there. I felt the same thing when we went to Sai Baba in India. In India, you have to be a guru instead of a pop star. Guru is the pop star of India and pop star is the guru here.

LENNON: But nobody's perfect, etc., etc. Whether it's Janov or Erhardt or Maharishi or a Beatle. That doesn't take away from their message. It's like learning how to swim. The swimming is fine. But forget about the teacher. If the Beatles had a message, it was that. With the Beatles, the records are the point, not the Beatles as individuals. You don't *need* the package, just as you don't need the Christian package or the Marxist package to get the message. People always got the image I was an anti-Christ or antireligion. I'm not. I'm a most religious fellow. I was brought up a Christian and I only now understand some of the things that Christ was saying in those parables. Because people got hooked on the teacher and missed the message.

PLAYBOY: And the Beatles taught people how to swim?

LENNON: If the Beatles or the Sixties had a message, it was to learn to swim. Period. And once you learn to swim, swim. The people who are hung up on the Beatles' and the Sixties' dream missed the whole point when the Beatles' and the Sixties' dream *became* the point. Carrying the Beatles' or the Sixties' dream around all your life is like carrying the Second World War and Glenn Miller around. That's not to say you can't enjoy Glenn Miller or the Beatles, but to live in that dream is the twilight zone. It's not living now. It's an illusion.

PLAYBOY: Yoko, the single you and John released from your album seems to be looking toward the future.

ONO: Yes, *Starting Over* is a song that makes me feel like crying. John has talked about the Sixties and how it gave us a taste for freedom—sexual and otherwise. It was like an orgy. Then, after that big come that we had together, men and women somehow lost track of each other and a lot of families and relationships split apart. I really think that what happened in the Seventies can be compared to what happened under Nazism with Jewish families. Only the force that split them came from the inside, not from the outside. We tried to rationalize it as the price we were paying for our freedom. And John is saying in his song, OK, we had the energy in the Sixties, in the Seventies we separated, but let's start over in the Eighties. He's reaching out to me, the woman. Reaching out after all that's happened, over the battlefield of dead families, is more difficult this time around.

On the other side of the record is my song, *Kiss Kiss Kiss*, which is the other side of the same question. There is the sound of a woman coming to a climax on it, and she is crying out to be held, to be touched. It will be controversial, because people still feel it's less natural to hear the sounds of a woman's lovemaking than, say, the sound of a Concorde, killing the atmosphere and polluting nature. Altogether, both sides are a prayer to change the Eighties.

PLAYBOY: What is the Eighties' dream to you, John?

LENNON: Well, you make your own dream. That's the Beatles' story, isn't it? That's Yoko's story. That's what I'm saying now. Produce your own dream. If you want to save Peru, go save Peru. It's quite possible to do anything, but not to put it on the leaders and the parking meters. Don't expect Jimmy Carter or Ronald Reagan or John Lennon or Yoko Ono or Bob Dylan or Jesus Christ to come and do it for you. You have to do it yourself. That's what the great masters and mistresses have been saying ever since time began. They can point the way, leave signposts and little instructions in various books that are now called holy and worshiped for the cover of the book and not for what it says, but the instructions are all there for all to see, have always been and always will be. There's nothing new under the sun. All the roads lead to Rome. And people cannot provide it for you. I can't wake you up. *You* can wake you up. I can't cure you. *You* can cure you.

PLAYBOY: What is it that keeps people from accepting that message?

LENNON: It's fear of the unknown. The unknown is what it is. And to be frightened of it is what sends everybody scurrying around chasing dreams, illusions, wars, peace, love, hate, all that—it's all illusion. Unknown is what it is. Accept that it's unknown and it's plain sailing. Everything is unknown—then you're ahead of the game. That's what it is. Right?

AFTERWORD

The popularity of "personality journalism" and the proliferation of Q-and-A formats on television has made the interview a familiar staple. But PLAYBOY has been plying this particular trade for nearly two decades. And there is something special about a long, thorough interview, in print, with someone who has led an extraordinary life. It inevitably will be different from a broadcast interview, because the words can be allowed to accumulate, then be savored and reflected upon; they do not vanish as quickly. And it will also be different from the excerpted highlights found in most news and feature magazines, because it presents a rounded portrait. Complexity usually takes patience, time, and space, and we live in an era of short attention spans.

This is why the preceding self-portraits remain special. They can be seen as oral autobiographies of people who have had an effect on our lives these many years. Some put their best foot very firmly forward; others revealed themselves reluctant and sometimes unwittingly. But as journeys into the lives and times of interesting people, these interviews have, and should continue to have, a special kind of endurance.